BARCODE IN BACK

Development Ethics

The International Library of Essays in Public and Professional Ethics
Series Editors: Seumas Miller and Tom Campbell

Titles in the Series:

The Ethics of the Environment
Robin Attfield

Academic Ethics
Robin Barrow and Patrick Keeney

The Ethics of Teaching
Michael A. Boylan

Military Ethics
Anthony Coady and Igor Primoratz

Engineering Ethics
Michael Davis

Social Work Ethics
Eileen Gambrill

Development Ethics
Des Gasper and Asuncion Lera St Clair

Correctional Ethics
John Kleinig

Police Ethics
Seumas Miller

Bioethics
Justin Oakley

Research Ethics
Kenneth D. Pimple

Business Ethics and Strategy,
Volumes I and II
Alan E. Singer

Computer Ethics
John Weckert

Development Ethics

Edited by

Des Gasper

Institute of Social Studies (The Hague) of Erasmus University Rotterdam, The Netherlands

and

Asuncion Lera St. Clair

University of Bergen, Norway, and Comparative Research Programme on Poverty (CROP)

ASHGATE

Published by
Ashgate Publishing Limited
Wey Court East
Union Road
Farnham
Surrey GU9 7PT
England

Ashgate Publishing Company
Suite 420
101 Cherry Street
Burlington, VT 05401-4405
USA

Ashgate website: http://www.ashgate.com

British Library Cataloguing in Publication Data
Development ethics.
1. Economic assistance–Moral and ethical aspects.
2. Economic development–Moral and ethical aspects.
I. Gasper, D. II. St.Clair, Asuncion.
174-dc22

Library of Congress Control Number: 2009920587

ISBN: 978-0-7546-2838-5

Mixed Sources
Product group from well-managed forests and other controlled sources
www.fsc.org Cert no. SGS-COC-2482
© 1996 Forest Stewardship Council
FSC

Printed and bound in Great Britain by
TJ International Ltd, Padstow, Cornwall.

Contents

Acknowledgements

The editor and publishers wish to thank the following for permission to use copyright material.

Elsevier for the essays: Amartya Sen (1988), 'The Concept of Development', in H. Chenery and T.H. Srinivasan (eds), *Handbook of Development Economics*, Amsterdam: Elsevier Science, **1**, pp. 10–26. Copyright © 1988 Elsevier Science Publishers B.V.; Amartya Sen (1980), 'Famines', *World Development*, **8**, pp. 613–21. Copyright © 1980 Elsevier Science Ltd; Denis Goulet (1980), 'Development Experts: The One-Eyed Giants', *World Development*, **8**, pp. 481–9. Copyright © 1980 Pergamon Press Ltd; Des Gasper (2007), 'What is the Capability Approach? Its Core, Rationale, Partners and Dangers', *Journal of Socio-Economics*, **36**, pp. 335–59. Copyright © 2007 Published by Elsevier Inc.; Roland Hoksbergen (1986), 'Approaches to Evaluation of Development Interventions: The Importance of World and Life Views', *World Development*, **14**, pp. 283–300. Copyright © 1986 Pergamon Press Ltd; Robert Chambers (1997), 'Responsible Well-Being – A Personal Agenda for Development', *World Development*, **25**, pp. 1743–54. Copyright © 1997 Elsevier Science Ltd.

Emerald Group Publishing Ltd for the essay: John Cameron and Hemant Ojha (2007), 'A Deliberative Ethic for Development: A Nepalese journey from Bourdieu through Kant to Dewey and Habermas', *International Journal of Social Economics*, **34**, pp. 66–87. Copyright © 2007 Emerald Group Publishing Ltd.

International Monetary Fund and the World Bank for the essay: Deepa Narayan (2000), 'Poverty is Powerlessness and Voicelessness', in *Finance and Development*, **37**, pp. 18–21.

The Johns Hopkins University Press for the essay: Denis Goulet (2005), 'Global Governance, Dam Conflicts, and Participation', *Human Rights Quarterly*, **27**, pp. 881–907. Copyright © 2005 The Johns Hopkins University Press.

Pearson for the essay: David A. Crocker (1996), 'Hunger, Capability, and Development', in W. Aiken and H. LaFollette (eds), *World Hunger and Morality*, 2nd edition, pp. 211–30. Copyright © 1996 Pearson Education Inc., Upper Saddle River, NJ.

Springer for the essay: Denis Goulet (1976), 'On the Ethics of Development Planning', *Studies in Comparative International Development*, **11**, pp. 25–43. Copyright © 2002 EBSCO Publishing.

Joseph Stiglitz for the essay: Joseph E. Stiglitz (2005), 'Ethics, Economic Advice, and Economic Policy', in *Policy Innovations*, Journal of The Carnegie Council, New York.

Taylor and Francis for the essays: Michael Cowen and Robert Shenton (1995), 'The Invention of Development', in Jonathan Crush (ed.), *Power of Development*, London: Routledge,

Series Preface

'Ethics' is now a considerable part of all debates about the conduct of public life, in government, economics, law, business, the professions and indeed every area of social and political affairs. The ethical aspects of public life include questions of moral right and wrong in the performance of public and professional roles, the moral justification and critique of public institutions and the choices that confront citizens and professionals as they come to their own moral views about social, economic and political issues.

While there are no moral experts to whom we can delegate the determination of ethical questions, the traditional skills of moral philosophers have been increasingly applied to practical contexts that call for moral assessment. Moreover this is being done with a degree of specialist knowledge of the areas under scrutiny that previously has been lacking from much of the work undertaken by philosophers.

This series brings together essays that exhibit high quality work in philosophy and the social sciences, that is well informed on the relevant subject matter and provides novel insights into the problems that arise in resolving ethical questions in practical contexts.

The volumes are designed to assist those engaged in scholarly research by providing the core essays that all who are involved in research in that area will want to have to hand. Essays are reproduced in full with the original pagination for ease of reference and citation.

The editors are selected for their eminence in the particular area of public and professional ethics. Each volume represents the editor's selection of the most seminal essays of enduring interest in the field.

SEUMAS MILLER AND TOM CAMPBELL
Centre for Applied Philosophy and Public Ethics (CAPPE)
Australian National University
Charles Sturt University
University of Melbourne

The Field of Development Ethics – An Introduction*

Development ethics, according to a classic formulation, considers the 'ethical and value questions posed by development theory, planning and practice' (Goulet 1977: 5). Its mission in Goulet's view is 'to diagnose value conflicts, to assess policies (actual and possible), and to validate or refute valuations placed on development performance' (1997: 1168). This volume reflects the field of thought that became known under this label in the 1950s (especially in French literature) and 1960s (in English, Spanish and Portuguese literatures). It appeared in response to the emergence of self-conscious fields – that include organizations, policies and programmes, research, education and training – of 'economic development' and development economics, 'social development' and development sociology/anthropology, 'politics of development', and so on, and overall of 'international development' and 'development studies'.[1] Recent surveys of development ethics include Crocker (1991; 2008), Dower (2008), Gasper (2004), and Schwenke (2008).

Though sometimes under different names, the field has long had relevant antecedents and clear forerunners, as we will see. Indeed, the notions of societal and human development, in their current senses, and the associated questions about purposes and priorities, have been discussed intensively for at least two hundred years. In this volume we concentrate on work from the 1960s and onwards, to provide an introduction to the strongly growing attention to the role of ethical thinking in regard to national and international development and global North–South relations. This increased interest is seen for example in the strengthening of the international human rights system and the growth of 'rights-based approaches' to development, in the United Nations Millennium Declaration, in intensified concerns with sustainability and business corporations' responsibilities, and in the increasing numbers of relevant journals and of academic courses or modules on ethics and development. While providing context and cross references, we centre the volume on the tradition of interdisciplinary work that has explicitly called itself development ethics, as articulated and represented by authors such as Denis Goulet and David Crocker.

This introduction gives an integrative summary of the selected papers and sets them in the context of the scope and trajectory, methods and debates seen in the field as a whole.

* Our thanks go to Tom Campbell for the invitation to prepare this volume; to the International Development Ethics Association and its successive leaders for supporting the stream of work which the volume presents; and to David Crocker and Desmond McNeill for incisive and very helpful comments on an earlier draft of this introduction.

[1] Development studies is widely also called international development studies, especially in North America.

Focus and Structure

The collection is divided into five parts. Part I opens with two essays (Chapters 1 and 2) which place work on development ethics in the historical and intellectual context of the growth of human powers to transform the human condition, notably in the past three centuries, and the growth correspondingly of enormous differentials of power and good fortune between different persons and groups within countries and between countries and regions. Chapters 3 and 4 address the nature of development ethics as a field: a foundational statement by Goulet, is followed by a reflection twenty years later on the achievements, limitations and alternatives for his formulation of the field.

Part II presents important aspects of work in development ethics: consideration of meanings of 'development' – as used by power-holders, by academics, and by ordinary people – and of the distribution of the benefits and costs in fundamental transformations of societies. Two of the key themes in development ethics have been as follows. First, the gains of some groups have been directly conditional on planned suffering for others – a theme for which we can use Peter Berger's label 'pyramids of sacrifice' (Berger 1974): as in the suffering of slaves in the processes of generation of agricultural and mining wealth from the Americas, or of rural labourers displaced to become urban proletarians in the industrialization of Western Europe and Russia. More generally, long-term societal development involves enormous investment by preceding generations to benefit later generations and not themselves– for example, the terracing of the Chinese landscape. This has been induced in diverse ways: through forced labour, physical displacement, and capitalist wage-labour, or labour seen as loyalty, duty, honour, or self-fulfilment. Second, good fortune can generate unintended suffering for others, such as when booming incomes in some sections of society or some parts of the world pull food resources out of poorer areas and out of the affordable reach of the poorest people, leading even to famine and death. Besides this 'calculus of pain' (Berger's term), both between peoples and across generations, Part II introduces what he called the 'calculus of meaning': how far does the acquisition of material comforts and conveniences bring or jeopardize a fulfilling and meaningful life? Berger's own later work within the tradition of Weberian historical sociology, notably his *The Capitalist Revolution* (1987), was strongly influenced by developments in East Asia and argued that a guided capitalism does better than comprehensive socialism, and acceptably well in the terms of both calculi.

In Part III we present some ethical theories that are prominent in discussing, and attempting to guide and constrain, the calculi of pain and meaning: in particular we look at examples of theories of need, of capability and of human rights. In line with this volume's size and a pragmatic and policy-oriented perspective, we have largely selected theory essays that emphasize the link to practice. We adopt what Crocker (Chapter 21) calls a shift in primary emphasis 'From Moral Foundations to Interpretative and Strategic Concepts', partly because many urgently needed changes can be justified from more than one type of moral foundation. Part IV then places abstracted theorizing in a richer and more realistic setting by looking at the conversion of proposed principles and criteria into working methodologies for value-conscious investigation, evaluation and design which can help to guide action and policy.

Part V contains essays on specific areas and themes in development policy – hunger, debt and forced displacement – and in development practice, including on responsible advice and responsible life-styles. We have chosen essays that illustrate broad themes and methodological stances because each of the policy and practice areas selected, and many others, could have been the subject of an entire collection. For example, Chapter 27, by Ellerman, considers how international development assistance can respect and promote the autonomy of recipients but often fails to. Its ideas have relevance far beyond international cooperation.

This collection of essays (particularly Parts IV and V) reflect that development ethics is an inter-disciplinary field and meeting place for disciplines and professions, and for interactions between theories and practice, rather than a more inward looking academic sub-discipline. The collection thus combines attention to real-world problems, theories and practices – including policies, politics, programmes, methodologies and movements.

One may look at work in development ethics as comparable to other fields of public and professional ethics such as business ethics, medical ethics and environmental ethics. A difference, however, is its all-encompassing scope, which renders it less a particular, even if huge, specialist area and more a meta-area that aims to link and inform many others. 'Development' of human societies can touch almost any topic. To avoid superficiality we have not attempted in this collection to cover each of a myriad of topics ('the ethics of development-and-A through Z'). The collection gives core attention to discussions of

- the values proposed as constituting the meaning of human, societal and/or global development, and proposed as requiring respect, prioritization and incorporation into legal frameworks and/or public action; (Parts II and III)
- evaluation of experience and alternatives (Parts II and V);
- methods and methodologies for such discussion, analysis, evaluation, incorporation and action (Parts IV and V).

We thereby follow the agenda articulated by Goulet in Chapter 3: looking at debates about principles concerning what is the human good (and bad), how it is and should be distributed, and by what processes decisions are and should be made. This volume's structure is similar also to Crocker's picture of development ethics (2008) in covering principles (our Part III), evaluations (Parts II and V), and proposals (Part V). In addition, we have considered it important to highlight methods and the theorizing around methods (Part IV), and the situating of the field historically and intellectually (Part I).

The Field of Development Ethics: History and Agenda

The volume opens with an essay that challenges the common yet misleading perception that 'development' simply concerns the planning, funding and execution of processes of socio-economic transformation occurring in low-income, mainly newly decolonized, countries after World War II. In Chapter 1 Michael Cowen and Robert Shenton set the historical stage, showing the emergence to prominence in early and mid-nineteenth-century Western Europe of a language of 'development', which referred to dramatic social change, the perceived associated societal problems, and how to respond to these. Thinkers like Saint-Simon, Auguste Comte, Friedrich List and J.S. Mill proposed theories and action aiming to diagnose and counteract damaging, disruptive or threatened effects of unguided societal transformation, which was seen as a quasi-natural process of 'progress' that must now be steered.[2] Response to the radical changes that flowed from modernity was the raison d'être of much of the thought of the founders of sociology. Cowen and Shenton show us that critical evaluation and idealistic programmes have been core features of development thinking from the beginning in societies exposed to rapid socio-economic change. This essay provides a historical and conceptual enrichment of interpretations of 'development' and undermines the notion that development thinking is a post-1945 phenomenon, a product of Cold War competition. It provides an introduction to their book on pre-1945 thinking, *Doctrines of Development* (1996), and helps to frame our collection, clarifying why debates about development outcomes and choices have always been debates about choices of values.

Kitching (1989) and Lutz and Lux (1988) (see also Lutz 1992), amongst others, similarly draw out the shared structures of debate in the contemporary analyses of the costs and benefits of industrialization in early nineteenth-century Europe and in post-1945 discussions for Asia, Africa and Latin America. Lutz and Lux go further and identify a connecting trail of authors who called for the reorientation of 'progress' to give priority to human development, each author explicitly influenced by predecessors and in turn influencing their successors; including from Sismondi to Thomas Carlyle to John Ruskin to J.A. Hobson in the nineteenth century, on through R.H. Tawney and Gandhi in the early and mid twentieth century, to E.F. Schumacher, the author of *Small is Beautiful* (1973) and 'Buddhist Economics' (1975). Other authors highlight the parallelism of much of the post-1945 discussions with debates in Russia in the late nineteenth and early twentieth centuries. Common to these two bodies of experience was the fate of co-existence with already dramatically more economically powerful countries in Western Europe and North America. The Russian intelligentsia elaborated a range of theories. Some justified seeking to follow the West European path; some others argued that the very existence of advanced Western Europe made that path unnecessary or impossible, so that a nationally specific and/or revolutionary path must be found; while yet others held either that West European experience showed the undesirability and inhumanity of the path of capitalist industrialization, which should be rejected, or rejected industrialization as a whole. The same range of options structures the later discussions in and for other countries (Callinicos 2007).

In Chapter 2 Bhikhu Parekh, one of the leading present day theorists of multiculturalism, puts into global context the discussion opened by Cowen and Shenton on responses to societal transformation. He looks at the inter-national rather than intra-national power differentials opened up by European advances, and at the views of a series of European theorists – Christian evangelists such as Bartolomé de las Casas, liberals such as John Locke, Immanuel Kant, and John Stuart Mill, and socialists such as Karl Marx and Friedrich Engels – on the ethics of relations between more economically powerful and less economically powerful countries and peoples. All advocated European colonialism. It would save the souls of the colonized, or save them from sloth and inactivity and raise their productivity and happiness, or at least prepare them to achieve those goods after a social revolution. Parekh sees considerable continuities between the European Christians, liberals and socialists, which he traces to an underlying Christian worldview. Ter Haar and Ellis remark similarly that development thinking has incorporated a vision that is specifically Christian in origin, and that still bears the traces of its

---

[2]   For parallel discussions in the USA in the 1830s, see Miller (2002). We thank David Crocker for this reference.

genealogy. Briefly, Christians traditionally believe in the prospect of a new and perfect world that will come into existence with the return of Christ to Earth. Over several centuries, politics and states in Europe assimilated these originally Christian ideas of perfection (Burleigh, 2005; 2006: 354). Dreams of perfection have often been used to justify drastic manifest imperfections along what is alleged to be the unavoidable path to reach the perfect state.

It is also the case that some Christian thinkers saw the fundamental problems that resulted from a type of global capitalism that accumulated, in part, by dispossessing others. A reframed, more humane vision of an economic system was one of the key inspirations for development ethics, notably through the influence of the French social economist and theologian Louis Joseph Lebret (1897–1966). In 1941 Lebret founded the movement Économie et Humanisme. It promoted a forerunner of the present day idea of human development, generated in an open dialogue between economics, other social sciences, theology and philosophy. Lebret's school had an important impact on Latin American thinking, and on the formation of liberation theology. He was the ghostwriter of Pope Paul VI's encyclical *Populorum Progressio,* one of the most influential sources for liberation theology and its thesis of 'the option for the poor' (Novak 1984:134 in Hebblethwaite 1994: 484). Unfortunately, not much of his work on socio-economic development has been translated into English.

Lebret was the key inspiration for Denis Goulet (1931–2006), who became probably the most prominent single writer on development ethics through the 1970s and 80s and whose work continues to be influential. Goulet led the emergence in English-language literature of an area of thinking under the name 'development ethics'. He drew from the more longstanding French literature that included Lebret's school of thought, and he connected equally to literature in Spanish and Portuguese. Variants of Lebret's theme of humanization of the economy, and the liberation strand, both continue strongly in the writings of contemporary Latin American philosophers and social theorists such as Enrique Dussel (1978, 2007).

Goulet's essay 'Tasks and Methods in Development Ethics' (Chapter 3) was the keynote lecture at the founding conference, in Costa Rica in 1987, of the International Development Ethics Association. The essay examines the negative effects of dominant theories and practices which had marginalized ethical discourse, and outlines an agenda for development ethics which informs this volume. Development ethics considers the contents of worthwhile development, the acceptable distribution of its costs and risks as well as its benefits, and the ethical quality of its methods of analysis and practice, including the questions of who should decide and who should act. Goulet argued that ethical thinking that was to make any real difference must become 'the means of the means', 'a moral beacon illuminating the value questions buried inside instrumental means appealed to by decision-makers and problem-solvers of all kinds' (p. 56). Since the fate of general intentions depends upon the character of the concrete means which are assigned to fulfil them – the institutions, rules, persons and procedures – so ethical ideals must be well embodied in those concrete means, must pervade and guide their detailed operation. The agenda for development ethics includes then not just abstracted theorizing but detailed attention to its linkages to attitudes, public action and policy making, to the roles of national and global institutions and civil society, and to the nature of practice-related ethical thinking in these contexts.

Des Gasper (Chapter 4) reviews Goulet's ideas about the scope of development ethics, its methodology, spheres of influence, and organizational format and identity. He examines Goulet's legacy in relation to subsequent work, and suggests aspects that demand further attention whether by rediscovery, deepening or replacement. Goulet emerges as a profound exponent of the notion of 'human development', but whose work illustrated different theoretical and methodological emphases from what is now the mainstream view seen in and around the United Nations Development Programme (UNDP)'s Human Development Reports founded by Mahbub ul Haq in 1990. While Goulet's vision of the scope of development ethics and its lines for influence seems sound, his pictures of methodology and organizational format require reconsideration or supplementation. The type of existential immersion that he advocated brings vital insights but is neither the only relevant methodology nor compatible with his notion of development ethics as a separate new (sub-)discipline. Ethics as the 'means of the means' is effected situation by situation in particular professional, physical and social niches, rather than by a cadre of super-generalists. At the same time, a widely influential development ethics also requires robust general theories of – needs, human rights, capability and deliberative democracy, and how such frameworks connect – in order to motivate and guide action and to communicate across wide spans of professional and physical territory.

Overall, the papers in Part I position development ethics as an interdisciplinary space of reflection which has a particular substantive set of tasks.

Development and Underdevelopment: Experiences, Meanings and Evaluations

The idea of modernity has many aspects and is also, inevitably, multiply interpreted. As a general idea it refers to a society which has distanced itself from an inferior past and discovered the secret of unending advance. More specifically, it refers to a particular type of society – commercialized, industrialized, urbanized, individualized. Following Weber, many interpretations see rationality as the underlying common thread. The modern is seen as the result of rational action. But the modern can also lead to traps, to 'iron cages', and to disenchantment. And, lastly, modernity refers to the type of lived experience found in that type of society – 'in an environment that promises us adventure, power, joy, growth, transformation of ourselves and the world – and at the same time, that threatens to destroy everything we have, everything we know, everything we are' (Berman, 1983: 15 cited by Callinicos 2007: 301). This is the society of simultaneous high promise and high vulnerability.

Development ethics arises as reflection on aspects of this lived experience, including reflection on the poverties within modernities that may bring disenchantment, alienation and loss of meaning, and from concern for the vulnerable and those who suffer. 'Some get the gains, others get the pains', remarked Michael Cernea (2006), the first and leading sociologist in the history of the World Bank, after a lifetime of observation of forced displacement of low-income populations. The creation of national parks, for example, has typically been comprehensively at the expense of the previous residents. Development ethics reflects, then, on what development means and ought to mean; it critiques the narrow conceptions often found in development policy bureaucracies. McNeill and St. Clair (2009) argue that, as the colonized countries gained independence, much of what we call 'development' activity became a sort of business: a specialized arena dominated by professional development experts and by 'agencies' dealing with 'recipients'. These experts shared an arcane language in which fundamental ethical issues and self-reflection on the costs and risks of their planning were absent or, when present, stripped of any direct and painful human content.

'Development', like 'modernity', figures as a family of concepts: as a desirable endpoint, or the criteria for defining such desirability; as the pathway(s) towards such desired states; as the activities and investments required to proceed along the pathway; and so on. Chapter 5 is an introduction by Nobel Prize winner Amartya Sen to his normative conception of development, a general idea of improvement. Development is presented as meaning good quality of life (including longevity, the quantity of an individual life) – or at least, real opportunity for good quality of life – rather than high quantity of inputs or high volume of economic activity. Assessing quality of life is understood as an evaluative question, not merely a measurement question. It is complicated by value heterogeneity across people, though Sen expects a significant degree of homogeneity, and by value endogeneity across time, since values are affected by life experiences and they also change across generations. Specifically, Sen proposes a concept of development as increase in the 'doings and beings' that we have reason to value, and/or increased real access thereto. The concept has been widely adopted and worked with, including in the Human Development Reports at global, national and local levels. In India every district is now required to prepare its own Human Development Report.

Following up the theme that the quantity of a person's life is central to 'quality of life', Chapter 6, also by Sen, analyses a series of major famines: the Bengal famines of 1943–4 and 1974 and the Ethiopian famines of 1973 and 1974, with reference also to nineteenth-century famines in India and Ireland. Famines are examples of lives wasted, often due to dramatic differences in endowments and entitlements across groups and across nations. Sen presents a theory of famines as caused not necessarily by lack of food but by poor people's lack of market power to command food, which can occur partly as a side-effect of richer people's greater power to command resources (Sen 1981; Dreze and Sen 1990). Mike Davis's account of the late-nineteenth-century famines in India, China and Brazil which led to tens of millions of deaths takes this insight further.[3]

> At issue is not simply that tens of millions of poor rural people died appallingly, but that they died in a manner, and for reasons, that contradict much of the conventional understanding of the economic history of the nineteenth century. Millions died, not outside the 'modern world system,' but in the very process of being forcibly incorporated into its economic and political structures. They died in the golden age of Liberal Capitalism; indeed, many were murdered, as we shall see, by the theological application of sacred principles of Smith, Bentham, and Mill (Davis 2001: 8–9).

Davis recounts how the impacts of climatic shocks caused by el Niño currents in the Pacific Ocean were mediated by new systems of global trade connections and economic ideology. Comparable shocks in the eighteenth century in China and India had been managed with far less loss of life, by governments that did not believe that starvation reflected immutable economic laws. In the late nineteenth and early twentieth centuries, with markets left free to determine allocation, some groups in drought-hit areas ended with no enforceable claims over food. Food flowed instead between regions and social groups in response to demand from those with money, locally and internationally. This relational explanation is presented by Sen in Chapter 6; it is still not well enough known, in comparison to his related thesis, that major famines tend not to occur in democratic countries, thanks to more open information and to public pressure upon governments which need public support.

---

[3]   Davis's study won the World History Association Book Prize in 2002.

Who the poor are and how to respond to their situation has long been a subject of research for 'experts', often economists, both in rich and low-income countries. In the history of poverty and development studies the views of the poor themselves are largely missing. A leading exception is the remarkable *Voices of the Poor* research project, summarized by Deepa Narayan in Chapter 7. Narayan directed the project for the World Bank as background work for the World Development Report 2000/1, *Attacking Poverty* (World Bank 2001). The three volumes of *Voices of the Poor* (Narayan, Patel, et al. 2000; Narayan, Chambers et al. 2000; and Narayan and Petesch 2002) present poor people's ideas about well-being and ill-being, drawing from views expressed by over 60,000 respondents around the world. This gives vivid insights into their everyday constraints and periodic crises, and shows them as active agents who manage their lives, via diverse coping mechanisms and immense resilience. Many of the component studies used a participatory methodology derived from pioneering work led by Robert Chambers (for example, Chambers 1997). *Voices of the Poor* gives dignity back to those who have historically been treated as objects studied and assisted or acted on by the 'experts'.

A classic piece by Denis Goulet (Chapter 8) generalizes and applies the themes of the previous three essays. It sketches a theory of value criteria relevant for development outcomes and development processes, and examines the value-conflicts and costs in typical development processes, with special reference to technology transfer (see also Goulet 1977). Chapter 9 functions as an extension of Chapter 8. Goulet here adds attention to the importance of understanding religion, faith-based value systems, as held by perhaps most people around the world, especially in lower-income countries. Material means, important as they are for a life of dignity, are insufficient for a truly human life; further, the meanings and use of material things depend on people's own values. Goulet's essay conveys strongly voiced perspectives from the South, on liberation theology (for example, Leonardo Boff and Gustavo Gutierrez) and on Buddhist traditions (for example, Gunatilleke et al. 1983), and advises development 'experts' that it may be impossible to design and implement projects well without understanding the roles that faith-based values often have in people's own conceptions of quality of life. This essay helped to stimulate much subsequent work (from this genre see, for example, Marshall and Keough 2004; ter Haar and Ellis 2006; Hicks 2000) and has a force and energy that give it continuing value.

In Chapter 10, Alan Thomas, the founder of the UK Open University's global Development Management programme, identifies the issues and challenges of development beyond the agendas of government development agencies and aid agencies, which often remain within the perspectives of liberal capitalism. It is important to look at the whole range of 'developers', including those from civil society, such as human rights organizations, and to step outside the world of immediate practice and take time for theorizing and ethical reflection. Thomas applies Cowen and Shenton's dissection of concepts of development (Chapter 1). In his view, current ideas of development continue to be dominated by a focus on interventions led by large formal agencies, which fails to grasp the complexity and ambiguity of processes of social transformation, and must be deepened to become more ethically reflective and self-critical. To contest dominant forms of development requires revealing the historicity and the value basis of processes of development. The best preparation for action is to reflect on visions of development, with attention to issues of justice, sustainability and inclusiveness. Thomas's paper helps to set the stage for Parts IV and V below on methodologies and policy practice.

Ethical Principles

From the great range of ethical perspectives and criteria that are used and debated in development ethics analyses and development practice we select three perspectives which have received specific elaboration in development ethics: namely, needs, capabilities and human rights, and the issue of their mutual relations. In doing so we give attention to other perspectives, including variants of utilitarianism and libertarianism (discussed by Parekh (Chapter 2), Sen (Chapter 5), Hoksbergen (Chapter 17) and Crocker (Chapter 21)). (Collections such as those by Aiken and LaFollette 1996, Aman 1991, and Goodin and Pettit 2005 complement the essays presented here.)

The Chilean economist and politician Manfred Max-Neef, known for his work on 'Barefoot Economics', elaborated a form of needs theory that is influential in community development practice worldwide (Max-Neef et al., 1989, 1991). It grows from a stream of human development theorizing in Latin America (including, for example, the work of Paolo Freire), and provides a rich format for discussing life-situations and priorities in particular communities. In contrast to those needs theories which involve an expert specification of priorities, Max-Neef's approach (Chapter 11) is concerned not only 'to promote the transformation of an object-person into a subject-person' but 'to respect and encourage diversity rather than control it' (p. 170).

The distinction between needs and their satisfiers is central to Max-Neef's work. However, some types of needs theory prominent in development economics have treated the satisfiers as the needs; for example, a house of at least a certain size and quality. The emphasis then became on needs as a set of things, rather than on needing as a relationship between priority values and specific personal and local situations, within which diverse potential satisfiers exist. Insistence on the difference in significance of a particular good according to the nature and wishes and situation of the person who has or uses it, led Amartya Sen and others towards the idea of capabilities. (See, for example, Crocker 2008, pp. 129–40, for detailed exposition of these background arguments.)

Martha Nussbaum (1947–) is after Amartya Sen and Denis Goulet perhaps the best-known academic voice in the development ethics of the last generation, prominent as a theorist of 'human development' (for example, Nussbaum 2000). Chapter 12 is a statement of her capabilities approach, as revised substantially in the late 1990s. Nussbaum argues for a set of fundamental capabilities – as requirements for a human life with dignity – that provide the grounding for basic rights claims. The essay characteristically combines ethical theorizing with vivid accounts of lived experience, covers gender issues in detail, and discusses the links between capabilities theory and the human rights tradition.

Amartya Sen (1933–) has opened many bridges between ethical theory, normative economics and policy design, using evocative integrative concepts like 'capability' and 'entitlement' and innovative and subtle reasoning. Sen has elucidated many inherently ambiguous concepts without seeking to misleadingly expunge that inherent ambiguity. His innovativeness and use of everyday language in often non-everyday senses, however, sometimes leads to misinterpretation by others. Chapter 13 by Des Gasper attempts a clarification and evaluation of the 'capability approach' work of Sen and his school, and its relationships to the work by Nussbaum and other writers on human development and human security. While Sen provides an open-ended framework for use in policy design and evaluation, Nussbaum tries to build foundations of a just constitutional order. (For valuable works which expound, compare and extend their work in greater detail see Alkire (2002), Deneulin (2006), Alexander (2008) and Crocker (2008).)

Mozaffar Qizilbash (Chapter 14) analyses not the differences between but the aspects shared amongst several perspectives that have been widely employed and extended in development ethics – theories of needs, of prudential values, Sen's and Nussbaum's variants of a capabilities approach, and the theories of John Rawls on primary goods and John Finnis on basic goods. His essay is not a substitute for the preceding three expositional papers but adds to them through a focus on what the perspectives share. For example, Nussbaum's approach, while essaying more substantive content than Sen's, similarly provides much space for variation in choices of valuable beings and doings, through respect for situational and cultural differences.

This open-ended character matches the interest in several essays (Chapters 7, 11, 13, 19, 20, 25) in deliberative methodologies and multi-level societal deliberation about development choices, and in dialogue across diverse cultural contexts. In Chapter 15 John Cameron and Hemant Ojha assess and selectively link relevant ideas from Kant and Dewey, Habermas and Bourdieu, and apply them to the hard realities seen in community forestry policy and practice in Nepal. A diverse set of actors and social groups with unequal power interact with each other and with nature. Drawing from French sociologist Pierre Bourdieu, Cameron and Ojha argue that decision-making is often dominated by those who hold symbolic power. Deeply held beliefs and practices then reinforce existing inequalities in voice between local and international elites, technical specialists and ordinary people. Kant's principles help to identify the unethical aspects of this 'habitus'. Using a conception of ethical thinking as a process, Dewey's notion of ethics as relational, and Habermas's conception of communicative action, the authors discuss how to counteract the undermining of people's agency and to improve deliberation so that poor and marginalized groups can participate better in decision-making that affects their lives. (Crocker 2008 takes such themes further.)

One achievement of the 'human development' paradigm created by Mahbub ul Haq (1934–98), Sen, Nussbaum and others, has been to bring a convergence of development thought with the project of universal human rights (Murphy 2006, Gasper 2009a). Related to the growth of separate bureaucracies for development and for human rights that began in the mid-twentieth century, the understanding of these two concerns took separate paths for several decades. In the same years as the rise of the human development paradigm and the associated capabilities approach, human rights thinking has become more central, in part through the engagement of former UN Secretary-General Kofi Annan and former UN High Commissioner for Human Rights, Mary Robinson. Revived discussion on relations between so-called first generation human rights (that is, civil and political rights) and second generation rights (that is, economic, social and cultural rights) led on to revisiting the idea of the 'right to development'. Often viewed as an abstract and inflated set of good intentions, the right to development as formulated in the 1970s and 80s had little impact in the work of development bureaucracies (McNeill and St. Clair, 2009). In Chapter 16, David Beetham, a leading contemporary theorist of human rights and democracy (see, for example, Beetham 1999), seeks workability through specificity: restriction of the idea of the 'right to development' to 'a nation's or people's right to economic development, ... something distinct from the different individual rights of the international human rights covenants, but also intimately connected with them, both as a crucial means to, and as a product of, their progressive realization' (Chapter 16, p. 285). In this form the concept adds something, and we can see more clearly when it is infringed. It directs attention to the severe harm done to poor countries and poor people by features of the current world economic order, to which we will come in Part V.

Methodologies

The ethical principles propounded in the essays in Part III and in similar work are still distant from being full practical methodologies to guide analysis and action, even the more process-oriented formats described by Max-Neef and Cameron and Ojha. The essays in Part IV consider the next step, to build and use working systems of investigation and evaluation.

Roland Hoksbergen (Chapter 17) examines the approaches to policy and programme evaluation that are used in a set of different theoretical and political traditions: the managerial-type evaluation in the 'logical framework approach', methods based on mainstream neoclassical economics, a humanist tradition and a religious tradition, each as applied in international development activities. He draws out how these approaches are based, sometimes explicitly and sometimes tacitly, on particular world views – including particular conceptions of society, of human personhood, of how to obtain reliable knowledge, and ideas about the good and the right.

The mainstream economics methods reflect particular variants and combinations of utilitarian and libertarian values, and a profoundly individualistic world view, centred on markets seen as expressions of freedom and essential tools of progress. Many employ the utilitarian principle of maximizing net benefits – the sum of estimated benefits minus the sum of estimated costs – regardless of on whom the benefits or costs fall: Lenin's readiness to 'break eggs in order to make omelettes'. Along with the disputes over that formal principle comes the question of how it is applied in reality. Michael Cernea adds that 'we find much in evaluation work that is totally ethically unacceptable' (Cernea 2006); for example, studies that legitimated creating parks for rich tourists at the cost of removing the livelihoods of poor local residents, on the basis of projections of future numbers of tourists that were never plausible. We see here the combination of a methodology that allows poor people to be made poorer for the benefit of richer people, and a practice that exacerbates this feature by its openness to manipulation. Thus one criterion for assessment of evaluation methodologies is: how much room do they provide for hard-to-control-and-prevent manipulation?

Hoksbergen himself exemplifies a methodology for drawing out and assessing the ethical assumptions found in methods and exercises of planning and evaluation. After this work of identifying the world views and assumptions within given methods of development policy analysis, he illustrates also the reverse line of investigation by beginning with a specified world view and/or ethical perspective and then working out its possible implications for methods and procedures of policy analysis. The following chapters by Hansen and Sano (Chapter 18) and Jolly and Basu Ray (Chapter 19) also show this approach. (So do Crocker (Chapter 21) and Drèze (Chapter 22); given their attention in detail to particular policy areas, we have placed them in Part V.)

From the large recent literature on human rights-based approaches to development planning (for example, Alston and Robinson 2005; Gready and Ensor 2005), we select Jakob Kirkemann Hansen and Hans-Otto Sano's essay (Chapter 18) because they distinguish and compare different interpretations, identify both the strengths and limitations of a human rights-based approach, and do not claim that such approaches are a panacea that will have 'equal relevance in all spheres of development thinking' (p. 341). They reveal how attention now centres less on continued refinement of, for example, an ethical case for clean water for all, and rather on building a human rights culture, marked by principles of universality, accountability, non-discrimination and empowerment that helps to ensure that the ethical case is not marginalized by 'narrow economistic and political' concerns (p. 339).

The thinking about human development that Haq, Sen and others helped to consolidate into a policy movement has evolved to include a sister theme of 'human security'. In Chapter 19, Richard Jolly (a former head of UNDP's Human Development Reports and former deputy director of UNICEF) and Deepayan Basu Ray present this theme and show how it has been applied by a series of national Human Development Reports that have taken human security as their lead topic. They articulate the methodology that is implied in the set of reports: a case-specific focusing on the particular threats to the specific priority aspects of life that are felt to be at risk in the place and time concerned, followed by wide-ranging analysis of those factors' causes and effects. They argue that the reports demonstrate how such a wide-ranging value-led transdisciplinary approach, that shows for example how certain types of economic policy may generate major morbidity and mortality impacts amongst poorer groups, can yet have a manageable scope of attention.

Chapter 20, by Asunción Lera St Clair, is an attempt to learn from other fields in applied ethics and from the pragmatist tradition, to reduce the risk that ethical analysis has no policy impact. It matches a central theme in Goulet's thinking, the use of development ethics as not merely philosophical reflection. St. Clair draws on ideas from the sociology of science and sociology of policy-making, to help orient development ethics work to become better-embedded in development policy and public action. Whereas medical doctors and their institutions have become accustomed to have 'embedded ethicists' in their teams, the field of economic and social development concerns fundamental features of intra- and inter-national systems of power and remains riddled with resistance to ethical thinking and queries as to its legitimacy and value-added.[4] Development ethics is thus not just one more area of applied ethics. St. Clair suggests a rethinking of what is an optimal entry point for the ethical analyst, and investigation of the processes of knowledge production. Critically, this extends the scope of development ethics to connect to tools developed in the sociology of knowledge and social studies of science. Ethical thinking needs to be complemented with epistemological reflection, on how different cognitive and social values can guide attention and research choices, and are in turn constrained by them. Grasping this theme may be fundamental for bringing in insights from social sciences other than economics, and from local knowledge, and thus indirectly for advancing global justice. Boaventura de Sousa Santos argues that 'cognitive justice' – the democratization of expert knowledge and openness to alternative non-Western and non expert-based knowledge – is fundamental for construction of alternative globalizations (De Sousa Santos 2005, 2007). The theme of channels for influencing policy practice leads us into Part V.

---

[4]   McNeill and St. Clair (2009) identify further obstacles encountered by work to embed ethical and human rights perspectives in the work of development aid bureaucracies: it can challenge their power as institutions, it would force government representatives in their boards to rethink their countries' position in the global scene, and it challenges the established power balances within organizations by making explicit that economic analysis of poverty and development is seriously insufficient for understanding and decision-making on these issues.

Ethical Development Policy and Practice

Many important 'sectoral' topics in development ethics overlap with sister fields, for example business ethics, environmental ethics and human rights. (Good edited collections at these intersections include, amongst others: Alston and Robinson 2005; Brooks 2008; Claude and Weston 2006; Ekins and Max-Neef 1992; Engel and Engel 1992; Nussbaum and Glover 1995). We concentrate in Part V on a few substantive topics, including famine and forced resettlement, as foremost illustrations of the themes of fair and unfair distribution, and on international debt and international cooperation, to show the global context of development efforts and its enormous and distorting power differentials. The selected essays reflect these topics, but at the same time illustrate ideas of wide general relevance about styles of analysis and of management.

David Crocker (Chapter 21) argues, with reference to food policy, famine relief and famine prevention, how the capabilities approach and associated thinking have contributed to important reorientations in ethically-driven thinking about development. For US-based philosophers and development activists he sums up the shift in thinking as 'from an ethics of aid to an ethics for development' (p. 384), away from a focus only on crises and palliatives, to a concern with systems and causes. The essay conveys how Sen and Drèze's form of capabilities analysis can help to strategically redirect development policy analysis.[5] (For full-scale applications see for example Drèze and Sen's 1989 book on hunger and their 2002 book on India.)

Jean Drèze (Chapter 22), Sen's closest collaborator, goes a step further, showing how the campaign for the right to food tries to operationalize the claims arising from analyses of food needs and basic capabilities. Drèze summarizes ideas for applying a 'rights-based approach' within a real, often unfavourable, political and institutional context, that of India. He offers concrete arguments not just for the right to food, as a prerequisite for what he calls economic democracy, but for how to try to advance that right even where there is no single clear-cut duty holder.

Using human rights language to frame specific development issues has generated powerful work such as Paul Farmer's account of global health challenges (2004) and Thomas Pogge's analysis of current world poverty as a matter of human rights violation (2008). In Chapter 23, Joe Hanlon shows the application of ideas of basic needs, fair process and human rights to the global equity issue of international debts. Representing work that played an important role in the Jubilee 2000 campaign that led to lightening of the debt burdens of the poorest countries, his essay outlines the history of credit, debt, default and debt relief or forgiveness or repudiation, through the nineteenth and twentieth centuries. Periodic default or relief can be seen as a normal, occasional hazard inherent in the overall richly profitable history of lending. However, the same countries that had defaulted or repudiated debts in the nineteenth and early twentieth centuries were to the fore in the late twentieth century in enforcing repayment of external debts by low-income countries that were in economic crisis, driving them to cut their already low expenditures on basic services for water, health and education. The debtor and creditor countries are signatories to the Universal Declaration of Human Rights. The main victims of the cuts have been poorer people and children who bore no responsibility for the debts, which had sometimes been corruptly arranged. But financial power brings

---

[5] Crocker refines these arguments in chapter 8 of his 2008 book

influence on governments, both directly and indirectly; governments have feared to let the biggest irresponsible lenders collapse because of the knock-on effects, and have given priority to supporting them. (Joseph Stiglitz's essay (Chapter 26) shows how the IMF and its lead member, the US government, have repeatedly given priority to bailing out rich lenders while cutting or diverting resources from the poor.) Hanlon illustrates how critical analyses in terms of basic needs and the associated human rights generate demands for measures of debt relief for the poor that have had real impact.

Peter Penz's essay (Chapter 24) analyses the ethics of forced displacement – the relocation of people due to development projects. He comments on three methodologies of applied ethics for considering such cases: disputation between explicit ethical theories; at the other extreme, reliance on intuition or regnant community values; and, sometimes more fruitful, an intermediate approach that 'focuses on generalisable principles, but does not commit itself to a particular normative theory' (Penz, p. 442). Next, he identifies the traditional national framework assumed in ethical discussions, and its limitations in a world interconnected by powerful agencies and unforeseen causal chains and divided into state territories created through violent histories and now administered by sometimes negligent or predatory authorities. He constructs a case for moral cosmopolitanism and then, using his intermediate methodology, considers the responsibilities of foreign agents (distinguishing between businesses, foreign governments and development NGOs) in cases of actual or threatened forced displacement.[6] Taking Penz's line of argument further, Oxfam and other international development NGOs have consolidated and disseminated principles of the 'free, prior and informed consent' of local residents in disputes over new investments in their localities. While such codes of practice on displacement have gained some support from inter-governmental funding agencies, other tendencies are less favourable: shifts in funding from multilateral to private banks and to less socially-concerned foreign governments have partly sidelined the painstakingly achieved ethical codes for investments (Johnston and Garcia-Downing 2004).

The essential partners for the forms of analysis described in Chapters 21–24 are social movements that represent and/or support the claims of the weakest groups in national and global society. Denis Goulet's last major essay, presented here as Chapter 25, brings together older themes of the distribution of the costs and benefits from development activities such as dam construction, and the distribution of rights to be informed and be heard, with newer themes of the roles of global development organizations and global social movements. He argues that Brazilian experiences in popular participation in decision-making around dam construction and in participatory municipal budgeting show the possibility of fruitfully realizing old ideals – partly through the types of global social movement which had their main launching pad in Brazil. Fora of globalized resistance such as the World Social Forum (WSF) have given new dimensions as well as theoretical clarification to the oft-mentioned phrase that 'another globalization is possible'. Compared to the case of forestry management in Nepal

---

[6]   Penz, Drydyk and Bose (2009/forthcoming) have now constructed a fuller system of ethics for cases of threatened or actual displacement. It amends and extends the perspective advanced by the World Commission on Dams (2000). Penz et al. derive a series of ethical guidelines for local, national and international responsibilities, with special reference to dam projects, on the basis of a proposed synthesis of core values found in United Nations and other work, that they suggest constitutes a widely accepted 'human development ethic'.

(Chapter 15), Latin America's strong traditions of collective action have led to more optimism in participatory governance and more truly democratic deliberation (Van Cott 2008).

The final two chapters deal with international development cooperation and raise general themes of fundamental importance. After his years as Chair of the Council of Economic Advisers to the US Government under Bill Clinton, and as Chief Economist of the World Bank, Nobel Prize winner Joseph Stiglitz wrote on the crucial roles that ethics should play in the professional work of economists (Chapter 26). He adopts a pragmatic methodology, applying a set of widely accepted ethical precepts rather than seeking to prove them: honesty (including not withholding important information); fairness (treating similar cases similarly); social justice (fulfilling basic needs, including for dignity); and responsibility (including taking into account, and being accountable for, external effects that one causes). Honesty and responsibility imply that we should make clear the limits of the information and understanding on which we advise, or press, others to act. This has often not been done by the international financial institutions and rich country governments whose relations with developing countries he examines. Instead they have typically relied on power, financial muscle, to enforce their prescriptions, such as for full mobility of capital, leaving the risks to be borne by the weakest parties. They have also not treated like cases alike: the arguments about social dislocation which rich countries have used to block global free movement of labour have been waved aside when used by developing country governments to argue against global free movement of capital. Systematically and devastatingly, Stiglitz applies the precepts to 1990s international economic decision-making. His review leads him to a further precept: maintain rather than tear apart the existing fabric of social norms and cooperation. He considers this principle to have been grossly violated in the shock economic reforms that destroyed the value of ordinary people's pension rights in Russia while distributing enormous wealth to a new privilegentsia. Elsewhere he argues for more and deeper democracy at all levels (Stiglitz 2007).

David Ellerman's essay (Chapter 27) complements Stiglitz. It draws on his experience as special adviser in the World Bank and on a historical survey of thinking about the requirements of 'Helping People to Help Themselves' (Ellerman 2005). He uses theories of learning to look at processes of development cooperation that could promote recipient autonomy, and concludes that autonomy-promoting assistance turns out to be very close to rights-respecting assistance. Unhelpfully intrusive 'help', whether it is 'help' that replaces beneficiaries' own activity or 'help' that dictates their pattern of activity and hence replaces their decision-making, simultaneously offends their felt rights to be active makers of their own lives and leaves underutilized their capacities, knowledge and will. These two lines of counter-productive effect then reinforce each other in scenarios of indifference and resistance.

For the last essay we have chosen not a report on experiences with particular professional codes, but a discussion of the spirit without which such codes can remain dead letters. (On formal codes, see e.g. Gasper 1999, Inter-American Initiative 2007.) In Chapter 28 Robert Chambers summarises ideas from a lifetime as a leader in innovative, participatory and respectful development practice that has explored the sort of principles articulated by Ellerman (e.g., Chambers 1983, 2005, 2008). He has been an advocate and theorist of, for example, 'immersion visits' in which development professionals spend some days or weeks living with poor people. Development as good change relies, he argues, on individual persons and personal actions, in addition to and underlying the action of organizations and policies. The most fundamental 'means' that should be imbued by a development ethic – acting as 'the means of the means' – are professionals, at many levels. Chambers discusses elements of an informal professional ethic, an ethos of ethical development: sensitivity to the power of language and to who controls it, and a search for effective generative concepts; an openness to listening, which is found to be the most important element in the use of techniques of participatory research and planning, far more important than the technical details; and an openness to self-criticism, including about one's own lifestyle, and to learning how to be more while having less. These themes are taken further by, amongst others, Hamelink (1997), Giri (2002), Sharma (2006), and Crocker (2008).

Concluding Observations: A Pragmatic Ethics of Societal Transformations in a Global Context

To conclude this introduction we touch on possible future directions for development ethics. This collection introduces the reader to a field that inhabits an uneasy space of critique and reaction against unreflective, ahistorical and allegedly value-free conceptions of development planning and policy, and that also constructs alternatives for improving conceptualization of development and its practices, policy making and methodological tools. A single-volume compilation of previously published work inevitably has gaps, both in the areas of critique and reaction and in the construction of alternatives. Some discussion here of the future of the field will help to situate it within contemporary debates about the future of development itself, and in the context of increasing globalization and the concerns about what has been its neo-liberal mainstream. Fundamental challenges that have been repeatedly highlighted, such as widespread severe poverty and hunger, lack of access for all to clean water, basic health and education, violence against women, and the replacement of colonial and neo-colonial systems by well functioning democracies, all remain in large part unresolved. The 'aid industry' is under serious pressure to improve or change, from opposing forces on both the left and the right, North and South (Easterly 2008, Tandon 2008, Riddell 2007). As Thomas points out in Chapter 10, this may in part be because international development was left so much in the hands of a narrow group of agencies – the World Bank, FAO, USAID, DFID, and so on – and transformed into a professionalized field located within liberal capitalism, remote from ordinary people's lives (see also McNeill and St. Clair 2009). More broadly, global climate change and financial crisis raise fundamental question marks about contemporary systems of economic organization and governance.

How can development ethics thought be deepened and become better-embedded in the work of key actors in development and contribute to more efficient and fair activity, improved quality of life and less suffering? Providing answers requires an enrichment of development ethics along at least three key dimensions: forging a space for recognition and deliberation with ethical, faith-based and indigenous value systems across the globe; engaging more with the worlds of activism and practice of global justice; and seeking further influence in action and policy making through strategies and methodological tools that incorporate ethical thinking.

The essays in this volume do not offer full answers for those questions and tasks but give valuable pointers. Forerunners of development ethics include all those authors who have been critical of the nature of transitions to modernity, including the purely instrumental use of nature and human beings in industrialization and economic growth. The historical readings in this volume remind us that modernity has always exacted a price, paid largely by the weakest.

Social theorist Robert Pinker argues that poorly theorized and economistic descriptions of the causes and solutions to poverty in Britain during the nineteenth century, were amongst the main drivers of the stigma and exclusion that poor and vulnerable groups suffered (Pinker 1971). Millions of the poor in India paid with their lives for the lack of interest of their colonial rulers in balancing the forces that controlled their access to food in an increasingly market-dominated economic system (Davis 2001).

What we learn from even an incomplete excursion in development ethics is that moral arguments have usually had little force to change policy and action, for they have tended to remain 'external critiques' outside the scope of 'expert' knowledge for development, and the ethical critiques come from many diverse sources often with little recognition of or knowledge about each other. But we also learn that with an appropriate strategy, more reflection on the negative consequences of growing human powers is indeed possible and that some improvements in the practices of assessment, design and evaluation of development interventions have occurred. For example, the now widely accepted definition of development as centering on how people can live as judged by a range of human values (the human development conception) was clear in the work of Lebret in the 1950s or Goulet in the 1960s and 70s, yet only became much more visible and influential when taken up by a network led by a well-situated and charismatic policy entrepreneur (Mahbub ul Haq) in partnership with a prestigious economist (Amartya Sen), and thanks to a favourable combination of circumstances (Gasper 2009b; Haq and Ponzio 2008). Lessons for further work thus become clear.

Moving towards more fairness and less pain, more solidarity and self-reflection about how much is enough, and relational understandings of wealth and privilege requires more than sermons: it requires work on methodologies and methods that will be able to influence or effectively compete with dominant discourses. Parts IV and V in this volume present attempts along those lines. The role of economic experts in defining and framing development issues is particularly important, especially as they have central roles within powerful development bureaucracies and often reject ethical thinking as outside the scope of their planning and ideas (McNeill and St. Clair 2009). The essays by Penz and Stiglitz (Chapters 24 and 26) highlight for example that economists work on issues marked by major uncertainty and that it is fair to hold them responsible, like members of other professions, for, first, clarifying the degrees of uncertainty in their understanding and, second, protecting vulnerable poor people from the danger of unwanted effects resulting from their advice and decisions. George DeMartino takes the step of specifying more fully such a code (2005).

The voices of the poor rarely have access to the worlds of academic and policy publishing or to relevant forums of exchange and networking. The voices of non-English speakers are also much less heard. Several essays in this volume call for extensive and multilevel societal deliberation and one task for development ethics is to fashion spaces for such participation. This applies not just intra-nationally. One of the roles for development ethics, we suggest, is to be an enabler and provider for hearing ethical views (whether secular or religious or indigenous) from around the globe. It is important for the future of development ethics to acknowledge, relate to, and strengthen or revive dialogue with non-Western and non-English language sources of ethical thinking.

Development ethics overlaps to some extent with the concerns raised by the fields of global justice and global ethics that have emerged in the past twenty years in reaction to neo-liberal economic globalization (see for example Commers, Vandekerckhove and Verlinden 2008, Dower 2007, Pogge 2008, and St. Clair 2006). Growing concern with an unfair globalized world, in which pain and suffering are visible through global media and easy travel, and where many international systems have been manifestly and in major ways biased and hypocritical (as discussed here in the essays by Hanlon and Stiglitz (Chapters 23 and 26)), has led to intense thinking about social and global justice. The term global ethics was pioneered by Christian theologian Hans Küng (Küng 1991, 1998) and the 1993 Parliament of the World's Religions. The 1995 report of the World Commission on Culture and Development, organized by UNESCO, argued that the time had arrived for a global civic culture. Similar trends have occurred along the parallel track entitled global justice (Brooks 2008).

A deepened development ethics will be helpful to these sister fields, and vice versa. Clearly, as the 'global' impinges increasingly on every field of knowledge and practice, so too development, philosophy and ethics and the relations among fields of knowledge are affected. We doubt, though, that work on global ethics and global justice will absorb development ethics. Nor will it be absorbed, we think, into a particular influential strand like human development or human rights. We think it likely that a number of sister fields will continue and perhaps move in parallel directions. The distinctive scope of analysis shown by development ethics and sketched in this introduction is likely to remain, whether under this name or others.

References

Aiken, W. and LaFollette, H. (eds) (1996), *World Hunger and Morality* (2nd edn), New York: Prentice Hall.

Alexander, J.M. (2008), *Capabilities and Social Justice: The Political Philosophy of Amartya Sen and Martha Nussbaum*, Aldershot: Ashgate.

Alkire, S. (2002), *Valuing Freedoms: Sen's Capability Approach and Poverty Reduction*, Oxford: Oxford University Press.

Alston, P. and Robinson, M. (eds) (2005), *Human Rights and Development Towards Mutual Reinforcement*, New York: Oxford University Press.

Aman, K. (ed.) (1991), *Ethical Principles for Development: Needs, Capacities or Rights?*, Montclair, NJ: Institute for Critical Thinking at Montclair State University.

Beetham, D. (1999), *Democracy and Human Rights*, London: Polity Press.

Berger, P. (1974), *Pyramids of Sacrifice: Political Ethics and Social Change*, New York: Basic Books.

Berger, P. (1987), *The Capitalist Revolution*, Aldershot: Avebury.

Berman, M. (1983), *All That Is Solid Melts Into Air: The Experience of Modernity*, London: Verso.

Blaser, M., Feit, H., and McRae, G. (eds) (2004), *In the Way of Development – Indigenous Peoples, Life Projects and Globalization*, London: Zed.

Brooks, T. (2008), *The Global Justice Reader*, Oxford: Blackwell.

Burleigh, M. (2005), *Earthly Powers: The Clash of Religion and Politics in Europe from the Enlightenment to the Great War*, London: Harper and Collins

Callinicos, A. (2007), *Social Theory* (2nd edn), Cambridge: Polity.

Cernea, M. (2006), Remarks at symposium on the Global Environmental Facility; Institute of Social Studies, The Hague, 17 January.

Chambers, R. (1983), *Rural Development: Putting the Last First*, Harlow: Longman.

Chambers, R. (1997), *Whose Reality Counts? Putting the First Last*, London: Intermediate Technology Publications Ltd (ITP).

Chambers, R. (2005), *Ideas for Development*, London: Earthscan.

Chambers, R. (2008), *Revolutions in Development Inquiry*, London: Earthscan.

Claude, R.P. and Weston, B. (2006), *Human Rights in the World Community: Issues and Action* (3rd edn), Princeton: University of Pennsylvania Press.

Commers, R., Vandekerckhove, W. and Verlinden, A. (eds) (2008), *Ethics in an Era of Globalization* London: Ashgate.

Cowen, M.P. and Shenton, C.W. (1996), *Doctrines of Development*, London: Routledge.

Crocker, D.A. (1991), 'Towards Development Ethics', *World Development*, **19**, pp. 457–83.

Crocker, D.A. (2008), *Ethics of Global Development: Agency, Capability and Deliberative Democracy*, Cambridge: Cambridge University Press.

Davis, M. (2001), *Late Victorian Holocausts: El Niño Famines and the Making of the Third World*, London: Verso.

DeMartino, G. (2005), 'A Professional Ethics Code for Economists', *Challenge*, **48**, pp. 88–104.

Deneulin, S. (2006), *The Capability Approach and the Praxis of Development*, Basingstoke: Palgrave Macmillan.

De Sousa Santos, B. (ed.) (2005), *Democratizing Democracy: Beyond the Liberal Democratic Canon*, London: Verso.

De Sousa Santos, B. (ed.) (2007), *Cognitive Justice in a Global World: Prudent Knowledges for a Decent Life*, London: Lexington Books.

Dower, N. (2007), *World Ethics* (2nd edn), Edinburgh: Edinburgh University Press.

Dower, N. (2008), 'The Nature and Scope of Development Ethics', *Journal of Global Ethics*, **4**, pp. 183–93.

Drèze, J. and Sen, A. (1989), *Hunger and Public Action*, Oxford: Clarendon Press.

Drèze, J. and Sen, A. (eds) (1990), *The Political Economy of Hunger* (3 vols), Oxford: Clarendon.

Drèze, J., and Sen, A. (2002), *India: Development and Participation*, Delhi: Oxford University Press.

Dussel, E. (1978), *Ethics and the Theology of Liberation*, trans. B. McWilliams, New York: Orbis.

Dussel, E. (2007), *Política de la Liberación: Historia Mundial y Crítica*, Madrid: Editorial Trotta.

Easterly, W. (ed.) (2008), *Reinventing Foreign Aid*, Cambridge, MA: The MIT Press.

Ekins, P. and Max-Neef, M. (eds) (1992), *Real Life Economics: Understanding Wealth Creation*, London and New York: Routledge.

Ellerman, D. (2005), *Helping People to Help Themselves: From the World Bank to an Alternative Philosophy of Development Assistance*, Ann Arbor: University of Michigan Press

Engel, R. and Engel, J. (eds) (1992), *Ethics of Environment and Development: Global Challenge and International Response*, London: John Wiley and Sons Ltd

Farmer, P. (2004), *Pathologies of Power: Health, Human Rights and the New War on the Poor*, Berkeley: University of California Press.

Gasper, D. (1999), 'Ethics and the Conduct of International Development Aid: Charity and Obligation', *Forum for Development Studies*, 1999/1, 23–57.

Gasper, D. (2004), *The Ethics of Development*, Edinburgh: Edinburgh University Press.

Gasper, D. (2009a), 'Human Rights, Human Needs, Human Development, Human Security', in Patrick Hayden (ed.), *Ashgate Research Companion to Ethics and International Relations*, Ashgate: Aldershot.

Gasper, D. (2009b), 'Values, Vision, Proposals and Networks – the Approach of Mahbub ul Haq', in C.K. Wilber and A.K. Dutt (eds), *New Directions In Development Ethics, Essays In Honor Of Denis Goulet*, Notre Dame, IN: Univ. of Notre Dame Press.

Giri, A.K. (2002), *Conversations and Transformations: Toward a New Ethics of Self and Society*, Oxford: Lexington Books.

Goodin, R. and Pettit, P. (eds) (2005), *Contemporary Political Philosophy – An Anthology* (2nd edn), Oxford: Blackwell.

Goulet, D. (1977), *The Uncertain Promise: Value Conflicts in Technology Transfer*, New York: IDOC.

Goulet, D. (1997), 'Development Ethics: A New Discipline', *International Journal of Social Economics*, **24**, pp. 1160–71.

Gready, P. and Ensor, J. (eds) (2005), *Reinventing Development? Translating Rights-Based Approaches from Theory into Practice*, London: Zed Books.

Gunatilleke, G., Tiruchelvam, N. and Coomaraswamy, R. (1983), *Ethical Dilemmas of Development in Asia*, London: Lexington Books.

Hamelink, C. (1997), 'Making Moral Choices in Development Co-operation: The Agenda for Ethics', in C. Hamelink. (ed.), *Ethics and Development: on Making Moral Choices in Development Co-operation*, Kampen: Uitgeverij Kok, pp. 11–24.

Haq, K. and Ponzio, R. (eds) (2008), *Pioneering the Human Development Revolution: An Intellectual Biography of Mahbub ul Haq*, Delhi: Oxford University Press.

Hebblethwaite, P. (1994), *Paul VI: The First Modern Pope*, London: Fount Paperbacks.

Hicks, D. (2000), *Inequality and Christian Ethics*, Cambridge: Cambridge University Press.

Inter-American Initiative on Social Capital, Ethics and Development (2007), *Formulating and Implementing an Effective Code of Ethics – Comprehensive Guidance Manual for Public Institutions*, ATN/ED-9535-RG. Inter-American Development Bank, Washington, DC.

Johnston, B.R. and Garcia-Downing, C. (2004), 'Hydroelectric Development on the Bio-Bio River, Chile: Anthropology and Human Rights Advocacy', in Blaser et al. (eds), pp. 211–31.

Kitching, G. (1989), *Development and Underdevelopment in Historical Perspective* (2nd edn), London: Methuen.

Küng, H. (1991), *Global Responsibility: In Search of a New World Ethic*, trans. J. Bowden, London: SCM Press.

Küng, H. (1998), *A Global Ethic for Global Politics and Economics*, Oxford: Oxford University Press.

Lutz, M. (1992), 'Humanistic Economics: History and Basic Principles', in P. Ekins and M. Max-Neef (eds), *Real Life Economics*, London: Routledge, pp. 90–112.

Lutz, M.A and Lux, K. (1988), *Humanistic Economics – the New Challenge*, New York: The Bootstrap Press.

Marshall, K. and Keough, L. (2004), *Mind, Heart, and Soul in the Fight Against Poverty*, Washington, DC: World Bank.

Max-Neef, M. et al. (1989), 'Human-scale Development', *Development Dialogue*, **1**, pp. 5–81.

Max-Neef, M. et al. (1991), *Human Scale Development: Conception, Application and Further Reflections*, New York: Apex Press and London: Zed Books.

McNeill, D., and St. Clair, A.L. (2009), *Global Poverty, Ethics and Human Rights: The Role of Multilateral Organisations*, London and New York: Routledge.

Miller, W.L. (2002), *Lincoln's Virtues*, New York: Knopf.

Murphy, C. (2006), *The United Nations Development Programme: A Better Way?* Cambridge: Cambridge University Press.

Narayan, D., Chambers, R., Shah, M.K. and Petesch, P. (2000), *Voices of the Poor: Crying Out for Change*, New York: Oxford University Press.

Narayan, D. Patel, R., Schafft, K. and Rademacher, A. (2000), *Voices of the Poor: Can Anyone Hear Us?*, New York: Oxford University Press

Narayan, D. and Petesch, P. (2002), *Voices of the Poor from Many Lands*, New York: Oxford University Press.

Novak, M. (1984), *The Development of Catholic Social Thought*, New York: Harper and Row.

Nussbaum, M. (2000), *Women and Human Development: The Capabilities Approach*, Cambridge: Cambridge University Press.

Nussbaum, M and Glover, J. (eds) (1995), *Women, Culture, and Development: A Study of Human Capabilities*, Oxford: Oxford University Press.

Penz, P., Drydyk, J. and Bose, P. (2009), *Displacement and Development – Ethics and Responsibilities*, forthcoming from Cambridge University Press.

Pinker, R. (1971), *Social Theory and Social Policy*, London: Heinemann Educational Books.

Pogge, T. (2008), *World Poverty and Human Rights* (2nd edn), Cambridge: Polity Press.

Riddell, R.G. (2007), *Does Foreign Aid Really Work?*, Oxford: Oxford University Press.

St. Clair, A.L. (2006), 'Global Poverty: Development Ethics Meets Global Justice', *Globalizations*, **3**, pp. 139–57.

Schumacher, E.F. (1973), *Small is Beautiful: Economics as if People Matter*, New York: Harper & Row.

Schumacher, E.F. (1975), *Buddhist Economics: an Economics of Permanence*, Institute for the Study of Nonviolence.

Schwenke, C. (2008), *Reclaiming Value in International Development: The Moral Dimensions of Development Policy and Practice in Poor Countries*, Westport, CT: Greenwood Press.

Sen, A.K. (1981), *Poverty and Famines: An Essay on Entitlement and Deprivation*, Oxford: Clarendon Press.

Sharma, S. (2006), *Management in New Age: Western Windows, Eastern Doors* (2nd edn), Delhi: New Age Publishers.

Stiglitz, J. (2007), *Making Globalization Work* (expanded edition), New York: WW Norton.

Tandon, J. (2008), *Ending Aid Dependence*, London: Fahamu Books.

Ter Haar, G. and Ellis, S. (2006), 'The Role of Religion in Development: Towards a New Relation between the European Union and Africa', *European Journal of Development Research*, **18**, pp. 351–67.

Van Cott, D. (2008), *Radical Democracy in the Andes*, New York: Cambridge University Press.

World Bank (2001), *World Development Report 2000/1: Attacking Poverty*, New York and Oxford: Oxford University Press.

World Commission on Dams (2000), *Dams and Development – A New Framework for Decision-Making*, London: Earthscan, and www.dams.org.

Part I
The Field of Development Ethics: History and Agenda

[1]

THE INVENTION OF DEVELOPMENT

Michael Cowen and Robert Shenton[1]

A mankind which no longer knows want will begin to have an inkling
of the delusory, futile nature of all the arrangements hitherto made to
escape want, which used wealth to reproduce want on a larger scale.

(Adorno 1993 [1951]: 156–7)

INTRODUCTION

'Development' has been called the central organizing concept of our time.
The United Nations has its development agencies, and the World Bank takes
development as part of its official name – the International Bank for
Reconstruction and Development. Hundreds and thousands of people are in
development's employ and billions are spent each year in its pursuit. It
would be difficult to find a single nation-state in the North which does not
have its departments or ministries of local, regional and international development. Nor can any Third World nation expect to be taken seriously without
the development label prominently displayed on some part of its governmental anatomy.

What is development? This question is often posed in the initial stages of
books or courses on 'development studies,' but is rarely coherently answered.
Rather the reader or student is told that development means different things
to different people. The authors or lecturers then move rapidly on to a
discussion of 'the development debate.' As they proceed, the issue of what,
precisely, development is grows even murkier. While the student may initially
be informed that development is about the betterment of human kind through
the alleviation of poverty and the realization of human potential, he or she
quickly discovers that there also exists 'good' and 'bad' development, as well
as 'under' and 'over' development. Development can be 'autonomous,'
'appropriate,' 'gender-conscious,' 'sustainable,' or the opposite of all these

1 Robert Shenton wishes to acknowledge research support from the Canadian Social Science
   and Humanities Research Council. This is a much-truncated version of Chapter One of our
   Doctrines of Development, Routledge, forthcoming.

MICHAEL COWEN AND ROBERT SHENTON

and much else besides. Which words are used seems to depend upon the views and policies of those in positions of authority in universities, national governments and international agencies. Even critics of development policies affirm, in the very act of criticism, development's existence.

Development thus defies definition, although not for a want of definitions on offer. One recent development studies text, notably entitled *Managing Development* (Staudt 1991), advances 'seven of hundreds of definitions of development.' Development is construed as 'a process of enlarging people's choices'; of enhancing 'participatory democratic processes' and the 'ability of people to have a say in the decisions that shape their lives'; of providing 'human beings with the opportunity to develop their fullest potential' and of enabling the poor, women, and 'free independent peasants' to organize for themselves and work together. Simultaneously, development is defined as the means to 'carry out a nation's development goals' and to promote economic growth, equity and national self-reliance (Staudt 1991: 28–9).

Here, quite typically, the distinction between development as an action and development as a goal of action is conflated with another important distinction. When, for example, someone mentions the 'development of capitalism' we take development to be an immanent and objective process. But when the same person says that it is desirable that state policy should achieve 'sustainable development,' we are now told that there is a subjective course of action that can be undertaken in the name of development. This distinction, between development as an immanent process and an intentional practice, has been central to European theological and philosophical debate. In contemporary development texts it is often lost.

Staudt (1991) assumes that development can happen as the result of decision and choice. Yet, the question of how actions taken in the name of development relate to any preconceived end of development is unanswered. Furthermore, because development is both means and goal, the final outcome is routinely assumed to be present at the onset of the process of development. Thus, Staudt argues that the goal of development is to enlarge choice. Yet, for choice to be exercised, let alone enlarged, there must be desire and capacity to choose as well as knowledge of possible choices. Choice is as much a precondition for development as its result. Further confusion arises when Staudt ignores another distinction between, on the one hand, a state policy of development and, on the other, attempts to empower people through or indeed against the state in the name of development. Empowerment is merely another name for development and thus embodies all its difficulties.

During the nineteenth century, those who saw themselves as developed, believed that they could act to determine the process of development for others deemed less-developed. The development problem was thus resolved by the doctrine of 'trusteeship,' a doctrine which became central to the historical project of European empire. Now, in the late twentieth century, the 'entrusting' of the means of development to 'the developed' has no

THE INVENTION OF DEVELOPMENT

conviction. As a doctrine, trusteeship is condemned as Eurocentrism, a vestige of the post-1945 attempt to improve the living standards of poor colonies and nations through external state administration. Development as trustee-ship is taken to have no meaning for Third World countries. It has had its day and failed as an idea and a practice.

The period of development is now routinely assumed to be the span of imperial and post-colonial history since 1945. The subject of development is the imperial state (before and after political dismemberment); its object is colonial and Third World peoples. The recent *Development Dictionary* (Sachs 1992) informs us that 'underdevelopment began' on 20 January 1949, the day on which Truman called for a 'bold new program' for the improvement, growth and development of underdeveloped areas (Esteva 1992: 7). Five of the twenty essays in the *Dictionary* start with Truman's address and he is quoted at least ten times in the volume. Students are thus regularly instructed in the shallowness of development's history. A good deal of the confusion surrounding development arises from this sort of exercise in historical truncation. This essay argues, on the contrary, that development is a state practice rooted in the nineteenth century.

By truncating development's historical domain, we lose the crucial sense in which it emerged in the nineteenth century as a counterpoint to 'progress.' Development emerged to ameliorate the perceived chaos caused by progress. In many texts, the ideas of development and progress are seamlessly stitched together. There is little sense of a dynamic relationship between the two concepts (Harris 1989: 4–11; Thomas 1992: 7). In this chapter, we argue that the modern idea of development is necessarily Eurocentric because it was in Europe that development was first meant to create order out of the social disorder of rapid urbanization, poverty and unemployment. The story is of development's failure – a failure which occurred long before its supposed mid-twentieth-century birth.

THE EUROPEAN SETTING

The doctrine of development was already old before Truman's invocation. For example, Bourdillon, the British Governor of Nigeria, addressing the Royal Empire Society in London in 1937, stated that 'the exploitation theory ... is dead and the development theory has taken its place' (quoted in Cowen and Shenton 1991: 165). Nearly a century before, Robert Chambers (1969 [1844]: 360) wrote in his widely read anticipation of Darwin, *The Natural History of the Vestiges of Creation*, that 'the inorganic has one final comprehensive law, GRAVITATION. The organic, the other great de-partment of mundane things, rests in like manner on one law and that is, DEVELOPMENT.'

By the early twentieth century, the idea of development was already well established in British thought. So was that of underdevelopment. Responding

29

MICHAEL COWEN AND ROBERT SHENTON

to Joseph Chamberlain's injunction to develop Britain's imperial estates in Africa, the Liberal Prime Minister, Campbell-Bannerman, put forward a project of his own, 'to develop our underdeveloped estates in this country; to colonise to our own country' (quoted in Cowen and Shenton 1991: 147). Much earlier, John Henry (Cardinal) Newman, a contemporary of Robert Chambers, writing in a field totally remote from the concerns of late twentieth-century developers, had begun to define the modern idea of under-development. The concept emerged as part of a theory of development in Newman's 1845 'Essay on the Development of Christian Doctrine' (Newman, 1992[1845]), which, the historian Acton said, 'did more than any other book of the time to make the English "think historically," to watch the process as well as the result' (quoted in Chadwick 1957: ix). Although concerned with the development of Christian doctrine, Newman's book had a far wider influence. Pattison, a fellow cleric, wrote to Newman in 1878 that it was:

> A remarkable thing that you should have first state the idea – and the word – development, as the key to the history of church doctrine, and since then it has gradually become the dominant idea of all history, biology, physics, and in short has metamorphosed our view of every science, and of all knowledge.
>
> (quoted in Chadwick 1957: ix–x)

Newman's argument encompassed both development and underdevelopment. Emphasizing that history moved through 'true' developments, Newman believed that there were doctrines and practices which did not evolve in a manner that remained faithful to the originating concept. He called this 'corruption' and used it to distinguish between the true development and the perversion of religious doctrine. Newman's idea of corruption conveys much of the sense of decay and decomposition, of disarticulation and disintegration that is essential to the modern meaning of underdevelopment. In the history of Western thought, the idea of corruption as part of a theory of change long predates Newman. As Robert Nisbet (1969) has noted, it developed in classical times and was based on the life cycle of all living things. The growing and maturing organism deposits a seed to recreate life amidst its own decay and destruction. Applied to the history of the state, the metaphor predicted that periods of state building would lead to periods of 'disorder' and 'ruin' which were, in turn, the prerequisites for renewed political construction. Successful statecraft and the art of politics, as in the work of Machiavelli, aimed to prolong maturity and forestall degeneration. It could do no more. This older meaning of development expressed a dual character of change. Positive, constructive change emerged from negative moments of destruction and decay. Purposive human intervention could ameliorate and forestall but not prevent the destruction which was intrinsic to an ordered, determined and inevitable cyclical process.

The classical theory of cyclical change remained dominant until it was

THE INVENTION OF DEVELOPMENT

challenged by modern ideas of progress that began to emerge in work of thinkers from at least Fontenelle to Hegel more than a century later and that gradually but, not wholly, supplanted the concept of inevitable degeneration. The idea of progress also had Christian origins stemming from the doctrine of divine revelation in which Providence through history maps out a design in advance of human efforts (Brunner 1948; Baillie 1950; Wager 1967). Enlightenment thinkers constructed secular variants of this idea, giving autonomy to human purpose and proposing the prospect of unlimited improvement through unaided human effort.

It has become commonplace for those attempting to legitimize the supposed modern sub-discipline, development economics, to rummage through the writings of the Scottish Enlightenment, especially those of Adam Smith. These eighteenth-century writers are supposed to have come up with the first theory of development in their idea of human economic activity evolving through a series of stages, commencing with hunting and fishing, progressing through pastoralism and settled agriculture and culminating in commerce and manufacturing. As one commentator (Meek 1976: 255 quoted in Skinner 1982: 91) has suggested, 'the four stages, at any rate at the outset of its career, usually took the form of a theory of development embodying the idea of some 'natural' or 'normal' movement through a succession of different modes of subsistence.'

The attempt by modern would-be developers to find the origins of their development practice in the Scottish Enlightenment requires a very selective reading of texts. Smith, like Locke, was fundamentally concerned with the Hobbesian problem of how social and political order might be maintained. In addressing the old idea of the inevitable corruption of the 'body economic' Smith simultaneously, and perhaps unwittingly, held out the possibility of progress as a linear unfolding of the universal potential for human improvement which need not be recurrent, finite or reversible. In his *Inquiry into the Nature and Causes of the Wealth of Nations* (Smith 1937[1776]), commonly seen as an eighteenth-century precursor of the modern 'development debate,' Smith is credited with rejecting the classical view, that national wealth and power were subject to inevitable cycles of advance, decline and stagnation, replacing it with a 'new description of rich and poor countries interlocked in a system of free trade reflecting the realities of a changing world. He could see the possibilities of progress both for rich and poor countries offered by a system of natural liberty in foreign trade' (Hont 1983: 302). Yet, Smith's optimism was immediately challenged by contemporaries who observed the political disorder that followed the French Revolution and the social disorder that accompanied the birth of industrial capitalism. In these grim facts, they found reasons to question the idea of boundless human improvement.

Although Thomas Malthus' *Essay on the Principle of Population* (1986[1798]) is usually presented as an anodyne theory concerning the limits to the growth of population imposed by agriculture, his book, published in

MICHAEL COWEN AND ROBERT SHENTON

the wake of one of the first crises of industrial capitalism, presented primarily a moral argument. He used his theory of population growth to argue against the possibility of limitless social perfectibility. Malthus attacked Smith's optimistic views about the possibility of unlimited human improvement. In particular, he challenged the idea that increases in society's wealth would necessarily bring improvement or happiness to every part of it. He argued that Smith had 'not stopped to take notice of those instances where the wealth of a society may increase without having any tendency to increase the comforts of the labouring part of it.' For Malthus, an increase in society's wealth would only mean a consequent growth in population which was 'the great obstacle in the way of any extraordinary improvement in society and was 'of a nature that we can never hope to overcome' (Malthus 1986[1798]: 183–4, 198–9).

For those who lived through the early decades of the nineteenth century, Malthus' grim predictions seemed to be coming true. E.J. Hobsbawm (1968: 58–9) captures the spirit of the times when he observes that no period of British history was as tense, or as politically and socially disturbed, as the 1830s and early 1840s. According to Hobsbawm, much of the tension of the period was the result of the working class despairing that they had not enough to eat and manufacturers despairing because they genuinely believed that the prevailing political and fiscal arrangements were slowly throttling the economy. These 'troubled times' gave birth to Luddites, Radicals, trade unionists, utopian socialists, Democrats and Chartists (Hobsbawm 1988: 13; Hobsbawm 1968: 55). They also gave rise to development. In France in the 1840s, the same sense of imminent turmoil was apparent (Sewell 1980). The French economy was more backward than the British but it was plunged, by industrial capitalism, into even greater social and political turmoil. In 1848, the *Journal des travaillers* declared that 'unemployment is the most hideous sore of current social organisation' (quoted in Sewell 1980: 249). The modern meaning of development (imbued with an overt sense of design) emerged to confront this 'hideous sore.' This new meaning was in direct opposition to the idea of progress as a 'natural' process without intentionality.

THE DESIGN OF DEVELOPMENT

The Saint-Simonians, writing at the end of the 1820s, were the original positivists. Their ideas were nurtured during the rise of industrial capitalism and, like Adam Smith, they posed the problem of creating order in a society undergoing radical transformation. Their analysis and solutions differed markedly from Smith's. The Saint-Simonians argued that humanity was a collective entity that had grown from generation to generation according to its own law of 'progressive development' (Iggers 1972[1829]: 28). Progressive development demanded 'a progressive amelioration of the moral, physical, and intellectual condition of the human race.' By this process everyone would

THE INVENTION OF DEVELOPMENT

realize that individual prosperity was inseparable from the prosperity and growth of all (Iggers 1972: 79).

The Saint-Simonians divided human history into 'organic' and 'critical' epochs. Organic epochs were characterized by harmony, widerning associations and common goals. The Middle Ages was one such epoch. Religious ideas were paramount and the economy was regulated by feudal corporations. By contrast, 'critical' epochs of human history were 'filled with disorder; they destroyed former social relations, and everywhere tend(ed) towards egoism.' Although harmful, they were necessary and indispensable, destroying 'antiquated forms' and facilitating the emergence of 'better forms' (Iggers, 1972: 28).

The thinkers of the Enlightenment and the French Revolution had succeeded in destroying the basis of the old 'organic epoch' but were incapable of visualizing a new era. This was because they remained wedded to ideas which put a premium upon self-interested individual action. This prolonged the social agony and delayed the arrival of a new organic epoch in which men would once again be 'associated,' though on a new footing. The new basis of human association, would be industrialism, guided by intellect, and governed by 'sympathy.' Unlike many of their conservative contemporaries, the Saint-Simonians applauded industrialization but argued that egoism produced irrational and destructive industrial practices: 'The industrialist is little concerned with the interests of society,' they argued, 'his family, instruments of production, and the personal fortune he strives to attain, are his mankind, his universe, and his God' (Iggers 1972[1829]: 12).

According to the Saint-Simonians, '*laissez faire*' was the source of disorder. Amidst the 'throngs' who could testify to the disasters of this principle was the man 'who lives by his hands' who could never applaud the introduction of steam power to his trade. If, as the Saint-Simonians willingly acknowledged, steam was necessary and potentially beneficial for all, this was little consolation to the 'thousands of famished men' whose lives were dislocated by technological change. Moreover, *laissez faire* was continually threatened by overproduction as enterprise and capital rushed to profitable sectors of the economy. The outcome was 'overcrowding' and a 'death struggle' with a few triumphant and the majority completely ruined. 'Numberless catastrophes' and terrifying 'commercial crises' soon followed. Hard-working men were ruined and people began to believe that in order to succeed, 'more seems to be needed than honesty and hard work' (Iggers 1972[1829]: 13–15).

The Saint-Simonian critique of self-interest, the market and unregulated competition was echoed in England by movements of 'physiocratic anti-commercialism' and 'communitarian political economy.' These groups sought solace in a romanticized agrarian past or an unhinged millenarian future (Thompson 1988)

The Saint-Simonians, in contrast, tried to impose constructive order upon the industrial disorder of the present. Their designation as 'scientific socialists' indicates the extent to which they gave agency and purpose to the develop-

MICHAEL COWEN AND ROBERT SHENTON

ment process. No longer was development something that occurred during a period of history; it was the means whereby the present epoch might be transformed into another superior order through the actions of those who were *entrusted* with the future of society.

A THEORY OF TRUSTEESHIP

For the Saint-Simonians, the remedy for disorder lay with those who had the capacity to utilize land, labour and capital in the interests of society as a whole. Property was the major obstacle to this programme. 'Idle owners' entrusted the instruments of production to the 'hands of a skilful worker' and reaped the profits. The Saint-Simonians argued that this evil could only be overcome if property was placed in the hands of 'trustees' chosen on the basis of their ability to decide where and how society's resources should be invested. These trustees were none other than banks and bankers. The banks would be fitted for trusteeship through the creation of a 'general system of banks' headed by a central government bank. They would be the 'depository of all the riches, of the total fund of production, and all the instruments of work.' The destructive effects of progress would be tamed through reform of the banking system and the personal morality of the banker (Iggers 1972: 103–10).

Auguste Comte completed the invention of development which his Saint-Simonian colleagues had begun. Comte saw 'progress as the development of Order under the influence of Love' (Comte 1875[1851]: 264). Progress had to be made compatible with order. The two could be reconciled through the understanding and application of the science of history or 'sociology' which embodied the laws of 'social evolution' which, in turn, had two aspects: 'the *development*, which brings after it the *improvement*' (Lenzer 1983: 234).

Improvement had been stilted because of the failure to reconcile progress with order. To resolve this problem, Comtean positivism recast the problem of progress and social order. Comte argued that humanity was subject to laws of 'development' analogous to those pertaining in the natural world that could be discovered and understood. Humans, however, could comprehend the fact and possibility of order. To reconcile order with progress, humans needed to comprehend the applicability of these laws. Progress was relentless and inconstant but it had to be given the consistency and morality of order. Development was the means by which progress would be subsumed by order (Lenzer 1983: 329, 341–2).

Comtean positivism was to be the true path of developmental knowledge, a mature and altruistic mode of thought. In proclaiming altruism as the guiding force of the positivist age, Comte challenged the Scottish Enlightenment by arguing that 'No calculations of self-interest' could 'rival this social instinct' (Comte 1875[1851]: 12). Anticipating at least one stream of thought on 'women and development,' Comte argued that an essential precondition of the triumph of 'social sympathy' was the fulfilment of the 'social mission of woman.' Women had innate qualities, particularly 'the

34

THE INVENTION OF DEVELOPMENT

tendency to place social above personal feeling', which made them 'undoubtedly superior to man' (Lenzer 1983: 373). Only through this innate quality, itself rooted in maternity, could mankind's morality and 'progressive development' be assured. All of this could happen once those who had the knowledge of 'sociology' were in a position to guide development. The high priests of positivism would join the Saint-Simonian bankers as the trustees of collective development.

UNDERDEVELOPMENT

For Newman, true development was the counterpoint to corruption. Once Newman's understanding was extended from theology to political economy, corruption became synonymous with underdevelopment. The old idea of corruption as a distinct temporal stage in a cycle of birth, growth, maturity, and decay, was replaced by a view which saw underdevelopment as simultaneously part of development itself. Modern underdevelopment theories, as well as their critics, all derive from this view in one way or another.

Underdevelopment theorists argue that industrial progress and the emergence of a proletariat at the 'centre' is the only 'true' development. In contrast, capitalism is seen as incapable of true development in the 'periphery' (Frank 1983: 186).

As Gavin Kitching (1982: 143) has written, Friedrich List's *National System of Political Economy* (1991[1885][1856]) was the prototype for all subsequent defences of effective industrial protectionism. In 1825, List emigrated to the United States. There, he observed that the passage from 'the condition of the mere hunter to the rearing of cattle – from that to agriculture, and from the latter to manufacturers and commerce' that took untold centuries in Europe 'goes on' in North America 'before one's eyes' (List 1991[1885]: xxix). Progress was telescoped through the constructive, intentional intervention of the state. The state had to act because the unfolding of immanent progress (as promised by the Scottish Enlightenment) was impossible in a world of British commercial and industrial supremacy. Smith's focus on private enterprise was, for List, besotted by a disorganized individualism. Like the Saint-Simonians, who influenced him, List argued that the self-interested individual was feeble and destitute alone. But, unlike the early Saint-Simonians, he deflected development doctrine to the ends of the nation-state (List 1991[1885]: 136–7, 165, 171–2).

List distinguished between a subjective, technical division of labour in which individuals contribute to a single activity, such as the making of pins, and an objective division of labour in which an individual simultaneously contributes to a number of different activities, all toward 'one common object.' Since it possessed a common end, the nation was the proper organizing agency for individual work. List wanted to furnish the economical education of the nation. Movement from an agrarian to an industrial economy

35

MICHAEL COWEN AND ROBERT SHENTON

rested upon such economical education, something which could only be accomplished by state activism. List argued that the state needed to take up the task of constructive development. Nature intended that industry, cultivation, riches and power should not be the exclusive possession of any single nation. Only when all had elaborated their productive powers to their fullest extent *in the bosom of the nation* would it be possible to realize the Saint-Simonian dream of reconciling progress with order. This would occur through the harmonious universal association of nations. In the interim, the fact of war separated the agriculturalists of one nation from the manufacturers of another, while commercial revulsion by one nation prompted another to react to the selfish policy of the first. No spurious balance of trade could reconcile the disharmony between nations. For harmony, it was first necessary to reconcile humanity through national policies designed to augment their inhabitants' productive powers (List 1991[1885]: 119–308).

Without state-directed development, the future of agrarian nations would be bleak: 'A nation exchanging its agricultural products for articles of foreign manufacture is like an individual with but one arm who invokes the assistance of a foreign arm for his support.' A 'foreign arm' could never take the place of its own missing limb because its movements were 'subject to the caprice of a foreign head' (List 1856: 241). List described the loss of productive force of his native Germany in sentiments which would later be repeatedly echoed by dependency theorists:

> Germany would scarcely have more to supply this English world with than children's toys, wooden clocks, and philological writings, and, sometimes also an auxiliary corps, who might sacrifice themselves to pine away in the deserts of Asia or Africa, for the sake of extending the manufacturing and commercial supremacy, the literature and language of England.
>
> (List 1991[1885]: 160–2, 131)

Only through constructive development by the state could the loss of productive force, through idleness or emigration, be checked.

List argued that nations had unequal productive potential but that through the policy of 'economical development' all could activate their fullest potential. Then came the caveat: his precepts were not to be followed by that part of the human race existing in the 'savage states' of the 'torrid zone.' He argued that countries of the 'torrid zone' would make 'a very fatal mistake,' if they tried to become manufacturing countries. They would progress more rapidly 'in riches and civilization' if they continued to exchange their agricultural products for the manufactured goods of the temperate zone. List turned this caveat to an imperial advantage. It was a similar idea that, a century later, generated the controversy over the possibility of capitalist development in the Third World (List 1856: 75, 112).

While the tropical territories were naturally unsuited to manufacturing,

THE INVENTION OF DEVELOPMENT

they could still assist the process elsewhere. England had shown the way by augmenting the savings of its landlords and farmers with money profits from overseas colonization which were invested in manufacturing in Britain. Germany, too, must acquire colonies to break the English domination of the world. An imperial policy would, it was true, make tropical countries 'sink thus into *dependence* upon those of the temperate zone,' but dependency would be mitigated by the competition between temperate zone nations. Competition between industrialized imperial nations would 'ensure a full supply of manufactures at low prices' and thus 'prevent any one nation from taking advantages by its superiority over the weaker nations of the torrid zone.' A beneficial economic process would be complemented by a political mission within an imperial arena (List 1856: 75–8, 199).

Alongside the extension of trade would go 'the mission of political institutions to civilize barbarian nationalities, to enlarge those which are small, to strengthen those which are weak, and above all, to secure their existence and duration' (List 1856: 263). Agrarian countries of the empire would be 'civilized' by free trade:

> The economical education of a country of inferior intelligence and culture, or one thinly populated, relatively to the extent and fertility of its territory is effected more certainly by free trade, with more advanced, richer, and more industrious nations.
>
> (List 1856: 77–8)

If free trade proved insufficient to the civilizing mission then the surplus population of the temperate zone could be exported to assist in 'torrid zone' development (List 1856:199). In such circumstances, emigration would augment rather than sap the productive force of the industrialized nation. Ironically then, it was through the paleo-dependency theorist List that the positivist idea of constructive development (articulated by the Saint-Simonians as a remedy to surplus population created by progress in Europe) became a theory of imperial development. More ironic still is the contribution made by the British theorist of liberal democracy, John Stuart Mill.

POSITIVISM IN BRITAIN

Mill owed a great intellectual debt to the Saint-Simonians and especially Comte. In later years Mill tried to hide this debt but he did not change the ideas which he earlier acknowledged had been lifted from Comte. Reflecting on the Saint-Simonians, Mill wrote that they were 'writers by whom, more than any others, a new mode of political thinking was brought home to me.' Comte, in particular, 'seemed to give a scientific shape' to Mill's thought (Mill 1989[1873]: 131–2).

After he returned to England in 1831, Mill issued his *Spirit of the Age* (1942[1831]), which strikingly echoed Saint-Simonian thought in its analysis of the crisis of British society. Mill wrote that the affairs of mankind were always in one or the other of two states; the *natural* state and the *transitional* state. Again echoing the Saint-Simonians, Mill argued that in the natural state, the material interests of the community were managed by those with the greatest capacity for management. By contrast, the transitional state occurred when 'worldly power, and the greatest existing capacity for world affairs' are severed, when there were no established doctrines, and when the world of opinions was a 'mere chaos.' A transitional state would continue until a moral and social revolution replaced worldly power and moral influence in the hands of the most competent. Then society would be 'once more in its natural state' and able to 'resume its normal progress, at the point where it was stopped before by the social system which it has shivered' (Mill 1942[1831]: 35–7).

For Mill, as for the Saint-Simonians and Comte, the present age was one of transition: 'the old order of things, had become unsuited to the state of Society and of the human mind.' Referring to government, Mill cried out for 'not merely a new machine, but a machine constructed in another manner' (Mill 1942[1831]: 6–7). Yet if Mill agreed with the Saint-Simonians about the need for social transformation, he eschewed their solution for swiftly directed social change. Mill could not agree with a theory that made improvement conditional on individual genius. Generalized knowledge, not the genius of a secular priesthood, was the condition for development (Mill 1942[1831]: 8–10). The necessary preconditions were increased education and a radical extension of liberty. Education had played a central role in Comte's idea of 'development' but only in 'critical epochs' as a means of challenging and helping to destroy old ideas. There was no role for education in Mill's sense in the 'organic epoch.' Indeed, it was antagonistic to the epoch to be ushered in by Comtean positivism. However, Mill agreed with the positivist doctrine that progress and order needed to be reconciled. The problem preoccupies Book VI of Mill's *Logic* (1974[1843]), the publication of which marked his arrival as an influential intellectual figure.

To grasp the significance of Mill's reworking of positivism it is crucial to see what he believed education, in the widest sense, to be. Education encompassed issues as diverse as electoral and land reform, birth control and equality for women, as well as the rights of labour. All were simultaneously prerequisites for, and classrooms of, the education that would make 'the new machine' possible. The social machine could only be constructed through developing the minds of human beings. And minds could only be developed under the condition of liberty, a condition characterized by choice (Mill 1974[1843]: 833, 845, 861, 869, chs 3, 4, 5 *passim*).

Thus, the problem of choice in development was posed long before it became associated with colonial and Third World trusteeship. Mill, writing not as a late twentieth-century cultural anthropologist of Africa but as a mid-nineteenth-century commentator on England, observed that while:

customs be both good as customs and suitable . . . yet to conform to

THE INVENTION OF DEVELOPMENT

custom, merely *as* custom, does not educate or develop ... any of the qualities which are distinctive endowment of a human being. The human faculties of perception, judgement, discriminative feeling, mental activity, and even moral preference, are exercised only in making choice. The mental and moral, like the muscular powers, are improved only by being used.

And then continued:

He who lets the world, or his own portion of it, choose his plan of life for him, has no need of any other faculty than the ape-like one of imitation. He who chooses his plan for himself, employs all of his faculties. He must use observation to see, reasoning and judgement to foresee, activity to gather materials for decision, discrimination to decide, and when he has decided, firmness and self-control to hold to his deliberate decision. ... It is possible that he might be guided in some good path, and kept out of harm's way without any of these things. But what will be his comparative worth as a human being?

(Mill 1965[1859]: 307)[2]

Mill emphasizes the necessity of choice. Humans should 'use observation to see, reasoning and judgement to foresee, activity to gather materials for decision, discrimination to decide, and when (they have) decided, firmness and self-control to hold to (the) deliberate decision' (Mill 1965[1859]: 307). Choice implied the capacity to choose. Choice was a condition for development, and distinguished humans from apes. Individuality was the result of choice. In Mill's words it was 'the same thing with development,' the only thing that could produce well-developed human beings (Mill 1965[1859]: 312). Only 'well-developed human beings' were fit to enter the end-point of development – Mill's 'stationary state.'

A stationary state is often seen as the antithesis of progress. However, this confuses progress and development. For Mill, the stationary state was the condition where material progress (prompted by necessity in which minds were 'engrossed by the art of getting on') would cease to increase wealth and produce instead a legitimate effect – that of abridging labour. The 'Art of getting on' would be replaced by the 'Art of Living.' Development would do the work of education and make it possible to understand how the drive for material progress could be made consistent with an ordered life (Mill 1985[1848]: 115–17).

Progress not only needed to coexist with order but each was necessary for

---

2 It would be unfair to Mill not to reproduce the following footnote from his *Logic*: 'The pronoun *he* is the only one available to express all human beings, none having yet been invented to serve the purpose of designating them generally, without distinguishing them by a characteristic so little worthy of being made the main distinction as that of sex. This is more than a defect of language; tending greatly to prolong the almost universal habit, of thinking and speaking of one-half the human species as the whole' (Mill 1974[1843]: 837).

MICHAEL COWEN AND ROBERT SHENTON

the other. Development also required a political system consistent with this goal. In Mill's words:

> A party of order or stability, and a party of progress or reform, are both necessary elements of a healthy state of political life. Each of these modes of thinking derives its utility from the deficiencies of the other.
>
> (Mill 1965[1859]: 297)

The contradiction between progress and order – where what was negative for one gave positive purpose to the other – would continue until development had done its work. Then a single party would have so enlarged its 'mental grasp' that it could be a party equally of order and of progress. Only then might the stationary state prevail (Mill 1965[1859]: 297).

In Mill's vision of a stationary state, development successfully acts against the chaos of progress. This stationary state has a close kinship with what today's developers call 'sustainable development' though Mill's soaring rhetoric ought to make the prosaic modern day exponents of sustainable development blush:

> A world from which solitude is extirpated, is a very poor ideal. Solitude, in the sense of being often alone, is essential to any depth or meditation of character; and solitude in the presence of natural beauty and grandeur, is the cradle of thoughts and aspirations which are not only good for the individual, but which society can ill do without. Nor is there much satisfaction in contemplating a world with nothing left to the spontaneous activity of nature; with every rood of land brought into cultivation, which is capable of growing food for human beings; every flowery waste or natural pasture ploughed up, all quadrupeds or birds which are not domesticated for man's use exterminated as his rivals for food, every hedgerow or superfluous tree rooted out, and scarcely a place left where a wild shrub or flower could grow without being eradicated as a weed in the name of improved agriculture. . . . If the earth must lose that great portion of its pleasantness which it owes to things that the unlimited increase in wealth and population would extirpate from it, for the mere purpose of enabling it to support a large, but not a Better or Happier population, I sincerely hope, for the sake of posterity, that they will be content to be stationary, long before necessity compels them to it.
>
> (Mill, 1985[1848]: 115–16)

The development necessary to bring about the stationary state could only occur in societies not bound by 'custom' and where tolerance and rational discussion flourished. For Mill, as for unwitting modern development theorists, development could only occur where the conditions of development were already present. Societies in which they were not present had to be guided by the trustees from societies where they were.

40

THE INVENTION OF DEVELOPMENT

As an employee and theorist of the East India Company, Mill argued strenuously that India needed to be governed despotically by an incorruptible imperial cadre who exercised trusteeship in order to create the conditions under which education, choice, individuality – in a word development – might occur. Mill even opposed the transfer of administration from the East India Company to the British Crown after the 1857 mutiny on the grounds that the rule of India would be corrupted by British democracy. Although responsibility for Indian administration was transferred to the Crown, Mill counted it a personal victory that the principles of trusteeship would underpin the new administration (Mill 1990: 45, 50, 85).

CONCLUSION

Mill's direct involvement in the administration of India highlights one of the aims of our interpretation of the nineteenth-century origins of development. The words of the theorists discussed in this chapter are not instances of some disconnected, textualized 'developmental discourse.' Each theorist (alone and in combination with others) was a part of nineteenth-century developmental practice. The Saint-Simonians, for example, were the direct inspiration for the building of the Suez and Panama Canals. Comte's phrase 'Order and Progress' not only adorns the Brazilian flag but inspired a whole phase of nineteenth-century Latin American development policy. Australians and Indians alike came to see in the work of Friedrich List inspiration for the construction of their own national economies. Development was not simply thought or rhetoric; it was mid-century state practice.

For today's practitioners and students of development, the result of forgetting nineteenth-century development doctrine is all too evident. It is an attitude that Mill himself castigated, writing of it that:

> According to this doctrine we reject the sophisms and prejudices which misled the uncultivated minds of our ancestors, because we have learnt too much, and have become too wise ... We have now risen to the capacity of perceiving our true interests; and it is no longer in the power of impostors and charlatans to deceive us.
>
> (Mill 1942[1831]: 9–10)

Bjorn Hettne's *Development Theory and the Three Worlds* is one of a handful of development studies texts which pays some attention to the origins and ambiguities of development in earlier nineteenth-century European thought. After re-identifying the 'crises of development theory' in the East, West and South, Hettne proceeds quite reasonably to try and understand the 'development ideologies' in Western thought. For Hettne these ideologies and their progeny stand condemned as 'Eurocentric.' Yet, he never asks the obvious question: How could they be anything else? Hettne, like many others, has failed to grasp that the conditions which gave rise to

41

MICHAEL COWEN AND ROBERT SHENTON

intentional development as a redress to progress arose first in Europe (Hettne 1990: chs 1–2).

The dissemination of these Eurocentric theories to the Third World is condemned by Hettne as a form of 'academic imperialism' whose counterpoint is the rise of the dependency school's analysis of underdevelopment. But is dependency a *sui generis* response to Eurocentric thought? We have argued that the intellectual origins of what is now called underdevelopment are also fundamentally European. The problem is compounded when Hettne sets about proposing 'another development.' This will supposedly 'transcend the European model' and create a new kind of development thinking. This new model of development will be egalitarian, 'self-reliant,' 'eco-' and 'ethnodevelopmental.' Unfortunately for Hettne, when he introduces the precursors of the new thinking, we find ourselves face to face with the ghosts of Saint-Simon, Comte, Proudhon, and the Norodniks amongst others (Hettne 1990: ch. 6).

Hettne actually admits that the wellsprings of 'another development,' are to be found 'back where we started' in the developed world. He approvingly quotes Denis De Rougement who noted that:

> Europe is the continent that gave birth to the nation state, that was the first to suffer its destructive effects upon all sense of community and balance between men and nature . . . the continent which, therefore, has every reason to be first to produce the antibodies to the virus it itself generated.
>
> (Hettne 1990: 195)

Thus, in Hettne's words, development theory 'returns to Europe.' From a base in the 'new Europe,' the gospel of 'another development,' will be spread to the Third World (Hettne 1990: 195).

Hettne is certainly aware of some of the obvious questions raised by the idea of 'another development.' First, he asks why there is such interest in 'another development' in the West. The answer is that the 'collective consciousness of the industrially advanced countries is going through a transformation, against which spokesmen for the Mainstream will have a hard time finding a way out of the present impasse; a solution consistent with a worldview of automatic growth and eternal progress.' No Saint-Simonian ever said it better. Growth and progress are symptoms of De Rougement's 'virus.' Second, Hettne asks why the concepts of 'another development' (small-scale solutions, ecological concerns, popular participation, and the establishment of community) meet with greater enthusiasm in the rich countries than in the poor. The disinterest in the South is the product of corrupt Third World leadership. Small may be beautiful, but it does not mean power. Third World elites who aspire to Western standards of living 'do not intend to be fooled into some populist cul-de-sac' (Hettne 1990: 195–6, 154–5).

Given this impasse, how is another development to be brought to the

THE INVENTION OF DEVELOPMENT

masses in the Third World? The main vehicle will be an amalgam of official and non-governmental aid organizations whose task, in assuming the mantle of development, is to confront the destruction wrought by progress. In the face of a corrupt leadership, trusteeship (though none dare speak its name) will have to be exercised by the knowing and the moral on behalf of the ignorant and corrupt. The assembled ghosts of the Saint-Simonians, Comte, List, Mill and Newman would be much amused. So too would be the spirit of Marx seeing his own work consigned to the rubbish bin of history by those who scavenge through decidedly riper tips for choice intellectual morsels to be offered up as new fare. To the purveyors of an alternative and another development we may *either* reply with the words of Goethe's Mephisto,

> I am the spirit that negates all!
> And rightly so, for all that comes to be
> Deserves to perish wretchedly . . .
> (I am) part of the power that would
> Do nothing but evil
> And yet creates the good.
> (Goethe quoted in M. Berman 1982: 47)

or of Marx himself:

> Modern bourgeois society, a society that has conjured up such gigantic means of production and exchange, is like the sorcerer who is no longer able to control the powers of the subterranean world that he has called up by his spells.
>
> (Marx 1968[1848]: 66–7)

BIBLIOGRAPHY

Adorno, T. (1993) [1951] *Minima Moralia*, London: Verso.

Baillie, J. (1950) *The Belief in Progress*, London: Oxford University Press.

Berman, M. (1982) *All That is Solid Melts into Air: The Experience of Modernity*, New York: Simon and Schuster.

Brunner, E. (1948) *Christianity and Civilisation: Part One*, London: Nisbet.

Chadwick, O. (1957) *From Bossuet to Newman: The Idea of Doctrinal Development*, Cambridge: Cambridge University Press.

Chambers, R. (1969[1844]) *Vestiges of the Natural History of Creation*, New York: Humanities Press.

Comte, A. (1875[1851]) *System of Positive Polity*, vol.1, London: Longmans, Green, and Co.

Cowen, M. and Shenton, R. (1991) 'The origin and course of Fabian colonialism in Africa', *Journal of Historical Sociology* 4, 2: 143–174.

Esteva, G. (1992) 'Development', in W. Sachs (ed.) *The Development Dictionary: A Guide to Knowledge as Power*, London: Zed Books.

Frank, A.G. (1983) 'Introduction' and 'Crisis and transformation of dependency in the world system', in R.H. Chilcote and D.L. Johnson (eds.) *Theories of Development: Mode of Production or Dependency*, Beverly Hills: Sage.

Harris, G. (1989) *The Sociology of Development*, London: Longman.

Hettne, B. (1990) *Development Theory and the Three Worlds*, London: Methuen.

Hobsbawm, E.J. (1968) *Industry and Empire*, London: Weidenfeld and Nicolson.

—— (1988) *The Age of Revolution: Europe 1789–1848*, London: Cardinal.

Hont, I. (1983) 'The "rich country-poor country" debate', in I. Hont and M. Ignatieff, *Wealth and Virtue: the shaping of political economy in the Scottish Enlightenment*, Cambridge: Cambridge University Press.

Iggers, G. (trans.) (1972[1829]) *The Doctrine of Saint-Simon: An Exposition, First Year 1828–1829*, New York: Schocken Books.

Kitching, G. (1982) *Development and Underdevelopment in Historical Perspective: Petite Bourgeoisie*, New Haven, Connecticut: Yale University Press.

Lenzer, G. (ed.) (1983) *Auguste Comte and Positivism: The Essential Writings*, Chicago: University of Chicago Press.

List, F. (1856) *The National System of Political Economy*, Philadelphia: J.B. Lippincott.

—— (1991[1885]) (Sampson S. Lloyd, trans.) *The National System of Political Economy*, New York: Augustus M. Kelly.

Malthus, T. (1986[1798]) *An Essay on the Principle of Population*, Harmondsworth: Penguin.

Marx, K. (1968[1848]) *The Communist Manifesto*, New York: Washington Square Press.

BIBLIOGRAPHY

Meek, R.L. (1976) *Social Science and the Ignoble Savage*, Cambridge: Cambridge University Press.

Mill, J.S. (1942[1831]) *The Spirit of the Age*, Introductory Essay by Frederick von Hayek, Chicago: University of Chicago Press.

—— (1965[1859]) *On Liberty*, in Max Lerner (ed.) *Essential Works of John Stuart Mill*, New York: Bantam.

—— (1974[1843]) *A System of Logic, Ratiocinative and Inductive*, in J.M. Robson (ed.) *Collected Works of John Stuart Mill*, vol. VIII, Toronto: University of Toronto Press.

—— (1985[1848]) *Principles of Political Economy*, Harmondsworth: Penguin.

—— (1989[1873]) *Autobiography*, Harmondsworth: Penguin.

—— (1990) *Writings on India*, in John M. Robson, Martin Moir, and Zawahir Moir (eds.) *Collected Works of John Stuart Mill*, vol. XXX, Toronto: University of Toronto Press.

Newman, J. (1992[1845]) 'An essay on the development of Christian doctrine', in *Conscience, Consensus and the Development of Doctrine*, New York: Doubleday.

Nisbet, R. (1969) *Social Change and History: Aspects of the Western Theory of Development*, New York: Oxford University Press.

Sachs, W. (ed.) (1992) *The Development Dictionary: A Guide to Knowledge as Power*, London: Zed Books.

Sewell, W.H. (1980) *Work and Revolution in France*, Cambridge: Cambridge University Press.

Skinner, A. (1982) 'A Scottish contribution to Marxist sociology', in I. Bradley and M. Howard (eds.) *Classical and Marxian Political Economy: Essays in Honour of R.L. Meek*, London: Macmillan.

Smith, A. (1937[1776]) *Inquiry into the Nature and Causes of the Wealth of Nations*, New York: Modern Library.

Staudt, K. (1991) *Managing Development: State, Society, and International Contexts*, Newbury Park, California: Sage.

Thomas, A. (1992) 'Introduction', in T. Allen and A. Thomas (eds), *Poverty and Development in the 1990s*, Oxford: Oxford University Press.

Thompson, N. (1988) *The Market and Its Critics: Socialist Political Economy in Nineteenth Century Britain*, London: Routledge.

Wager, W. (1967) 'Modern views of the origins of the idea of progress', *Journal of the History of Ideas* 28 1: 22

[2]

THE WEST AND ITS OTHERS

Bhikhu Parekh

Thanks to the great geographical explorations from the sixteenth century onwards, Europeans came into close contact with non-European societies. They could have responded to the latter in a variety of ways, such as leaving them alone, quietly settling down among them as newly arrived immigrants, establishing regular trade relations and returning home, rejoicing in the diversity of human life, learning about the native ways of life and using that knowledge to acquire a better understanding of their own, killing the natives, conquering and ruling over them, and so forth. Without exception Europeans took over the countries they had 'discovered', and in some cases exterminated or uprooted those already settled there. They were largely motivated by the desire for wealth and domination, and took full advantage of their technological and material superiority.

Although the violence and the physical and moral suffering involved make painful reading, this is in no way peculiar to Europe. Within societies as well as between them, strong and powerful groups have always taken advantage of the weak and vulnerable, and found ways of justifying their actions to themselves and sometimes even to their victims. In this respect 'civilised' groups are no better than 'barbarians'. Their methods and aims might be more humane and restrained, but their pursuit of self-interest is just as, if not more, single-minded and ruthless.

During the period of colonial expansion Europe had at least three influential traditions of thought that were committed to the ideals of human unity, equality, freedom and the inviolability of the human person, and which were in principle hostile to the violence and exploitation inherent in the colonial enterprise. They were Christianity, liberalism from the early decades of the eighteenth century onwards, and Marxism from the last few decades of the nineteenth century onwards. It is striking that with only a few exceptions, the three bodies of thought approved

European colonialism. From time to time they did, no doubt, condemn its *excesses*, but rarely the colonial enterprise itself. In this paper I intend briefly to explore how they reconciled their basic moral commitments with their approval of colonialism, and were able to approve of colonialism yet condemn its excesses.

CHRISTIANITY

When Spaniards arrived in South America, they encountered long-established 'Indian' communities. The latter differed greatly among themselves, spoke different languages, practised different religions and followed different social practices. But these differences were inaccessible to the insensitive outsiders who saw them as a homogenous group. Spanish explorers were struck by two things. First, in some respects Indians were like them. They had a human shape, possessed the gift of speech, enjoyed music and dance, offered prayers, had families and a social structure, and so forth. Second, Indians also differed from them in several respects. They had no script, no system of exchange, wore scanty clothes, were sexually uninhibited and worshipped strange gods, and so forth. Spaniards were particularly struck by the fact that they made human sacrifices and in some cases ate human flesh.[1]

Spaniards, almost all of whom were devout Christians, had to decide how to treat the Indians, and that depended on how they conceptualised them. As Christians, they were committed to the view that since human beings were made in the image of God, they were all inviolable and entitled to equal treatment. What needed to be decided was whether Indians qualified as human beings. They were neither animals nor belonged to an intermediate species between animals and humans, an increasingly current description of Africans that informed much contemporary art and was frequently used to justify black slavery. Some Spaniards concluded that although Indians had a human 'shape', they had the 'nature' of beasts and were really 'savages', a term widely used at the time to refer to human beings displaying such an ambiguous identity. As Christians, Spaniards defined humanity in religio-moral rather than rationalist terms. They therefore concentrated on Indians' religious and moral practices, and concluded that since Indian made human sacrifices, ate human flesh, were 'mad', 'fierce', etc., they were children of Satan, governed by an evil spirit, and could not be said to have been made 'in the image of God'. They were not human beings in the full sense of the term, did not belong to the same species as the Spaniards and the rest of civilised mankind, and their lives, liberties and property lacked moral immunity.

Caines de Sepulveda put the difference starkly: 'There is a great difference between them [and us] as there is between *savagery* and forbearance, between violence and moderation almost - I am inclined to say - as between *monkeys* and men'.[2] Like others he was convinced that war against Indians was a holy duty:

> *The greatest philosophers declare that such wars may be undertaken by a very civilised nation against uncivilised people who are more* barbarous *than can be imagined, for they are absolutely lacking in any knowledge of letters, do not know the use of money, generally go about naked, even the women, and carry burdens on their shoulders and backs like* beasts *for great distances.*[3]

The view that Indians were not human beings proper, which was dominant during the early years of conquest, was effectively challenged by a large number of Christians both in Spain and in Mexico. Their style of reasoning was the same, but it stressed different aspects of Indian life. They started with the basic Christian premise that human beings were made in the image of God and necessarily had an intuitive knowledge of Him, which manifested itself in religious and moral life. If Indians could therefore be shown to possess religious and moral sensibilities, they could be proved to have been made in the image of God, and hence to be human. Accordingly several Christian theologians argued that although Indians worshipped strange and even evil gods, they did thereby display an awareness of the existence of a transcendental being, and that although they had many vices, they also possessed several virtues, thus demonstrating that they were endowed with a moral sense of 'natural light'. Indians therefore were human beings, flawed and grossly imperfect but nonetheless members of the human species, possessing not only a human shape but also human 'nature' or 'essence'.

An order of Charles V dated 1530 commanded the 'No one must dare to enslave any Indian, on the pretext of having acquired him through a just war, or repurchase, or purchase, or barter ... even if these Indians be considered as slaves by the natives.[4] In the papal bill of 1537, Paul III declared that Indians were 'true men', and commanded that they 'must not be deprived of their freedom and the ownership of their property'. For Bartolome de Las Casas, the Dominican Bishop of Chipas, Indians were just as human as Spaniards, and in some respects even better. As he wrote to Prince Philip in 1544, 'All the Indians to be found here are to be held as free, for in truth so they are, by the same right as I myself am free'. Las Casas was one of the most vigorous defenders of Indian dignity and rights, condemning the conquistadors in the strongest possible terms and even demanding their expulsion.

As a Christian, Las Casas believed that salvation was of absolute importance and that *extra ecclesian nulla salus*. Had Indians not been human beings, their salvation would not have mattered. But since they were, it mattered enormously, and could only be obtained by embracing Christianity. Since Indians were human, they *had to be* Christians, and must be converted by persuasion if possible, by coercion if necessary. Since Spanish colonisation was the necessary precondition of missionary activity, Las Casas was not opposed to colonisation but only to its inhumanity and excesses, and wanted it to be led by God-fearing persons of 'good conscience and great prudence' rather than by soldiers. As he grew old, he mellowed and urged that conversion should be the free choice of Indians. However he never relented on the importance of colonisation and conversion. For Las Casas's critics, Indians were not human beings and may be killed. Las Casas accepted their humanity and spared their bodies, but claimed their souls.

In Las Casas' view every man, being made in the image of God, had a natural propensity towards the true knowledge of God, and thus towards Christianity. Every man was therefore an actual or a potential Christian, and all good was ultimately

Christian in its nature and origin. Such Indian virtues as
obedience, humility, patience, gentleness and rejection of worldly
goods were basically Christian virtues. Since Indians already
lived as Christians, albeit unknowingly, their conversion was not
an external imposition but intimated by their own way of life
and a 'fulfilment' of their deepest aspirations. It was true that
Indians had several un-Christian vices and that their virtues
lacked discipline, but that only meant that their Christianity,
was 'wild' and unsophisticated. His conclusion was predictable.

> *At no other time and in no other people has there been such*
> *capacity, such predisposition, and such facility for*
> *conversion ... Nowhere in the world are there countries more*
> *docile and less restraint, or more apt and better disposed*
> *than these to receive the yoke of Our Lord.*[5]

Since Las Casas' deep and genuine concern for Indians arose
out of his commitment to Christianity, it suffered from obvious
structural limitations. He saw Indians through Christian eyes,
and lost sight of all that was distinctive about them. He only
saw their virtues and vices and ignored everything else about
their way of life. And he defined and judged their virtues and
vices in his terms and missed their specificity. It is striking that
his *Apologetica Historia* reduces Indians to characters in a
Christian morality-play and tells us little about their way of life.
Furthermore, since Indians mattered to him not as a distinct
people with their own virtues and limitations but as crypto-
Christians, he was convinced that he neither needed to
understand their way of life from within nor had anything to
learn from them. For him their importance lay in being symbols
of Christian virtues which the European Christians were in
danger of forgetting, and in preserving true Christianity. Since
Indians mattered to Las Casas not as human beings but as
unconscious Christians, his concern for them did not extend
either to Muslims whom he dismissed as 'the veritable barbarian
outcasts of nations', or even to blacks to whose slavery his
opposition was half-hearted.

Other missionaries rose above Las Casas' limitations. For
example, Diego Duran, a Dominican missionary, sought to

Said

understand the Indian way of life from within, gave a fairly faithful account of it, and paid generous tributes to it. However his efforts were deeply informed by a desire to highlight Indian analogues to Christian beliefs and practices, and to show not so much that Indians were crypto-Christians as that they had independently arrived at several Christian truths. While he generously acknowledged their originality, he defined and judged it in Christian terms and remained unable to respect their cultural integrity.

Some missionaries, such as Franciscan Bernardino de Sahagun, went yet further. He learned the local language, mastered the local culture, and explored the Indian way of life in its own terms. He respected its integrity and appreciated that it had grown out of and suited Indian 'aspirations and needs'. Although a devout Christian himself, he wondered if conversion was necessarily a good thing. Since it replaced their socially embedded gods with an alien and partially inassimilable Christian conception of God, it disorientated the Indians and sometimes led them to behave in a manner that was 'hateful to God'. Sahagun could not face the full implications of his argument, and ended by suggesting that while conversion should continue, the converted should be allowed to retain some of their religious and cultural practices. For advancing this view, his book was condemned by his superiors, and a royal edict by Philip II in 1577 forbade its discussion and circulation. Although both Duran and Sahagun showed some respect for the Indian way of life, neither saw any reason to disapprove of Spanish colonisation. For them Christianity was a superior religion and did much good to Indians. Since colonial rule had brought it to them and created the conditions of its spread, it was to be welcomed provided that it was humane and did not wantonly destroy the Indian way of life.

Spanish missionary attitudes to Indians then covered a wide range. Some refused to recognise their humanity, but this 'blasphemy' was vigorously challenged by others. Although the latter stood up for Indian rights and dignity, many of them were deeply hostile to the Indian way of life and attempted to dismantle it. Some saw its virtues, but translated them in Christian terms and undermined their integrity. Rare individuals resisted the temptation, respected the specificity of the Indian way of life, and even admired its unique features. However they did not know how to relate it to their Christian way of life and bring the two into fruitful interaction. By and large the vast majority of theologians and missionaries as well as the religious establishment found it difficult to respect the Indian way of life consistently with their belief that Christ was 'the way' to salvation. They already knew the truth and had nothing to gain from a sensitive exploration of and a sympathetic dialogue with other religions. Since Christian knowledge was in the ultimate interest of Indians, and since its dissemination was facilitated by colonisation, they all endorsed colonialism with varying degrees of enthusiasm.

Missionary attitudes in other parts of the world showed the same pattern, albeit with important difference. Take the case of India, the home of several well-developed religions. Initially European missionaries, be they British, French, Dutch or Portuguese, found Hinduism abominable and poured unmitigated scorn on it. Later they mellowed and adopted the Las Casas strategy. They argued that Hindus were 'unconsciously' groping towards Christianity, that Christ was their 'unknown God', that the commendable 'natural reason' of the Hindu sages was inadequate, and that Hindu fulfilment lay in embracing Christianity. This required the missionaries to study classical languages and texts, which they did with considerable skill. It also required them to study the vernaculars, and some of them did the excellent job of providing them with grammars, linguistic structures and scripts, sometimes even recreating the languages themselves. While their secular contribution was immense, their religiously motivated interpretations of classical and popular Hindu religious texts often left much to be desired.[6]

Some missionaries and theologians went further. They read Hinduism in its own terms, found some of its metaphysical and religious insight illuminating, and sought to integrate them into Christianity. By and large their approach to Hindu religious texts paralleled the traditional Christian attitude to the great Greek philosophers or to the Old Testament. The Hindu texts were good first drafts of the Bible, anticipatory of the final truth,

Said

incomplete in themselves but suggestive and stimulating. A genuinely open-minded and mutually exploratory dialogue with Indian religions was confined to very few, and never became part of mainstream Christian thinking in India.

Whatever their attitudes to Hinduism, the missionaries were convinced that it was inadequate in varying degrees, and had become particularly degenerate during the recent decades. As such it could not be the basis of a truly moral life, and it was in Indian interest to embrace Christianity. However since Indians were reluctant to convert, and since forcing them was politically unwise, the next best thing was to subject them to Christian values at the hands of politically sensitive Christian rulers. Since the British missionaries and religious leaders justified colonial rule in Christian terms, many of them were anxious that British rulers should behave as good Christians and set good examples of moral rectitude. When the colonial administrators failed to live up to these demands, they were criticised, sometimes in strongest terms, and reported to the government in London. While condemning the un-Christian excesses of colonial rule, the missionaries had no doubt about its 'civilising' value and importance. It was only after the anti-colonial struggle began in the 1920s in India that some of them showed any sympathy for it, and even then only a few actively supported it. The story in other parts of the European empires broadly followed the same pattern.

LIBERALISM

In many respects liberalism was secularised Christianity and reproduced many of the missionary attitudes to non-Europeans and colonialism. This is hardly surprising, for it grew up within a milieu suffused with fifteen hundred years of Christianity, and could hardly avoid imbibing its ethos and ways of looking at the world. Almost all early liberals were Christians. And even those liberals in the eighteenth and nineteenth centuries who were not largely rejected its theology, but neither its morality not its central categories. Although an atheist, Jeremy Bentham deeply admired Jesus' ethics and called him the 'first utilitarian'; the agnostic J.S. Mill thought that Jesus' teachings summed up the basic principles of his brand of altruistic utilitarianism; and while rejecting much of Christian theology, Tocqueville could not see how a liberal society could do without or be built on any other foundation than Christianity, the 'only religion of free men' as he called it. Since almost all liberals aimed to retain some aspects of Christianity, they reinterpreted it along liberal lines, of which Locke's suggestively entitled *The Reasonableness of Christianity* was an excellent early example. In liberalising Christianity, they Christianised liberalism, and took over such beliefs as that mankind constituted a unity and shared a common nature, that a single vision of life was valid for all, that those in the know had a duty to enlighten the ignorant, and that good had a duty to fight evil. The liberal civilising mission was embedded in these beliefs and represented a secularised version of its Christian original; which is why liberalism and Christianity were able to operate in tandem, and the expression 'spreading civilisation *and* Christianity' aroused no anxiety on either side.

When England began to colonise the 'new world' in the seventeenth century, its actions provoked muted criticism. The critics argued that since Indians had occupied and cultivated their land for centuries, it was their 'rightful inheritance' of which they should not be deprived. They also argued that since Indians had established stable societies, the latter were, like their European counterparts, entitled to non-interference by outsiders. Locke, one of the founding fathers of liberalism, took on the critics and advanced an articulate philosophical defence of English colonialism that bore considerable resemblance to that of the Christian missionaries.

For Locke, God created men and endowed them with several basic faculties, including, and especially, reason. They therefore enjoyed equal dignity and rights, and were entitled to the equal protection of their interests. Every man had a right to mix his labour with nature, and to use its fruits to satisfy his needs consistently with a due regard for others. Since God wanted men 'to be fruitful and multiply', every man had a duty to develop the earthly resources to the full and maximise the conveniences of life. As Locke put it, 'God gave the world to man in common, but ... it cannot be supposed he meant it should always remain common and uncultivated. He gave it to the use of the

Industrious and Rational'. Locke's equation of reason with industry is deeply suggestive.

Locke was well aware that some of his contemporaries did not consider blacks, Indians and others human. He knew how they had reached that conclusion.[7]

> *A Child having framed the* Idea *of a* Man, *it is probable,*
> *that his* Idea *is just like that picture, which the painter*
> *makes of his visible Appearances joined together; and such*
> *a Complication of Ideas together in his Understanding,*
> *makes up the single Complex Idea which he calls* Man,
> *where of White or Flesh Colour in England being one, the*
> *child can demonstrate to you, that a* Negro *is not a Man,*
> *because white-colour was one of the constant simple* Ideas *of*
> *the complex* Idea *he calls Man: And therefore he can*
> *demonstrate by the principle,* It is impossible for the same
> Thing to be, *and not to be ... that a* Negro *is not a Man.*

Locke rejected this reasoning. All human beings possessed shape, colour, size, etc, but none of these marked them out from animals. Furthermore, colour, etc, varied greatly, and no particular form of it could be considered a necessary feature of man. What distinguished man from the animal and needed to be added to the 'idea of man' was his capacity for 'rational discourse' or reason, which Locke defined as the capacity to perceive similarities and differences, to formulate general statements, to make logical deductions, and so on. All human beings, including Indians and blacks, possessed this capacity and were, as members of the same species, entitled to equal rights.

Since reason was the essence, the *differentia specifica*, of man and the basis of his dignity, he had a duty to lead a rational life. To be rational was to be industrious and energetic, to exploit the earth's resources to the full, to follow rules, to discipline one's passions, and so on. A rational way of life was distinguished by the institution of private property, without which human beings lacked both the incentive to develop the earth's resources and a sense of individuality and freedom. Since the religious duty to be fruitful and multiply 'contains in it the improvement too of arts and sciences', a truly rational society encouraged these as well. As for its political structure, it had a clearly defined territorial boundary, a cohesive, centralised and unified structure of authority, and a will to persist as an independent community.

In Locke's view the Indian way of life did not satisfy these conditions.[8] Indians were lazy, passive, unruly, undisciplined, wild, fierce, unpredictable. They roamed freely over the land, did not enclose it, and lacked the institution of private property. They had no arts, sciences and culture. And although they called themselves nations, they lacked the familiar features of the state. Since Indians had no sense of private property, 'their' land was really empty, free, vacant, and could be taken over without their consent. And since their society was not organised as a state, it enjoyed no immunity from others' interference. The English were not only at liberty to, but also had a duty to take over the 'surplus' Indian land and to interfere with their way of life. God had given man land on condition that he should exploit it to the full, and He had given him reason in the expectation that he would live a law-governed civil life. Since Indians did neither, they were in breach of God's commands and stood in need of discipline and education. English colonisation was indispensable to their transition to civilisation, and hence fully justified. Locke's argument bears a striking resemblance to that advanced by Las Casas a century and a half earlier.

Locke contrasted the English mode of colonisation with the Spanish. The latter was based on 'conquest by sword', violated the natural rights of Indians, and had failed to establish a civilised life among them. It was also contradictory because colonisation was motivated by a desire for economic gain, whereas the right of conquest extended 'only to the lives of the conquered' and not to their property. By contrast English colonisation was humane. It respected the basic natural rights of Indians, used force only when they refused to part with their vacant lands, and both morally uplifted them and drew them into an economically interdependent world. Locke had no doubt that English colonialism performed the moral miracle of serving God, mankind, Indians and, of course, the English themselves. He had no doubt either that when Indians rebelled against it, they forfeited their liberty in an 'unjust' war, and could be legitimately treated as slaves. In taking this view he fell far below the level of

183

the papal bull of 1537 and the anti-slavery arguments of the Spanish missionaries.

For Locke then, Indians were human beings and entitled to the protection of their basic rights and interests, which is why he condemned the early outrageous Spanish treatment of them in the strongest possible terms and took great pains to show that English colonisation was quite different. However, precisely because Indians were human beings, they were expected to live up to the rational and moral imperatives of their human nature. And since they were not doing so, the English were right to dismantle their way of life. For Locke only one way of life was truly rational, and those differing from it deserved no respect. His theory of man accepted Indians as equal *objects* of concern, but not as equal self-defining *subjects* entitled to choose their way of life themselves; that is, it protected them as *individuals* but not as a *community*, and respected their material interests but not their way of life and the moral and spiritual interests associated with it.

During the eighteenth and the early nineteenth centuries, European colonialism entered a new phase. Hitherto the 'empty spaces' of such countries as America, Australia and New Zealand had been subject to colonisation. Now it was the turn of the heavily populated countries of Asia and later of Africa. This new phase of colonialism, which did not involve colonial settlement, and is rightly called imperialism, needed a philosophical defence. Although Lockean arguments were not without value, they needed to be revised to suit the new circumstances. Among the many liberal writers who provided such a defence, John Stuart Mill was the most influential.

Like Locke, Mill divided human societies into two distinct groups, but his principle of classification was different.[9] In some societies, which he called civilised, human beings were in the 'maturity of their faculties' and had 'attained the capacity of being guided to their own improvement by conviction or persuasion'(pp117-8, 125). In his view most European societies had 'long since reached' that stage. By contrast non-European societies were all 'backward', and their members were in a state of 'nonage' or 'infancy'. Mill did not think much of Africa, a 'continent without a history'. And although he thought that

184

India, China and 'the whole East' had begun well, he was convinced that they had been 'stationary for thousands of years' (p118).

Since backward societies lacked the capacity for self-regeneration, Mill argued that they needed to be civilised by outsiders. He dismissed the likely objection that all societies including the backward had rights to territorial integrity and to develop at their own pace. Like Locke, he argued that the right to non-intervention only belonged to those capable of making a good use of it; as for the rest it was 'either a certain evil or at best a questionable good'. For Mill, as for Locke, backward *individuals* had equal *moral* claims to the protection of their rights and interests, but as *collectivities* they had no *political* claims to the inviolability of their way of life and territorial integrity.

The kind of argument advanced by the British liberals was also to be found in the writings of their French and even German counterparts. Writing to an English friend about the conquest of India, Tocqueville wrote, 'I have ... never for an instant doubted your triumph, which is that of Christianity and civilisation'.[10] He wrote to Nassar Senior after the Indian mutiny of 1857, 'your loss of India could have served no cause but that of barbarism'.[11] Like Sahagun Tocqueville admitted that French rule had unsettled and disorientated Algerian society, and made it 'much more wretched, more disorderly, more ignorant and more barbarian than it was before it knew us'. However he was convinced that colonial rule was in the interest of both France and Algeria: the former because it increased French self-confidence and influence in 'the general affairs of the world', the latter because it civilised the Algerians in the long run. Like Locke and Mill, Tocqueville was anxious that colonial subjects should not be 'exterminated', 'crushed' or 'enslaved', but he was convinced that they could neither be treated 'exactly as if they were our fellow-citizens and our equals', nor be educated except against a background of the 'unfortunate necessities' of violence and even terror. When the troops of M. le Marechal Bugeaud trapped and asphyxiated hundreds of Arabs in the Dahra caves, Tocqueville praised his 'great service to his country on the soil of Africa'.[12]

Said

When Herder challenged the current liberal distinction between civilised and uncivilised societies and attacked liberals for despising the latter, Kant wrote a scathing reply. Mocking Herder's admiration for the happy and carefree inhabitants of Tahiti, Kant asked: 'Why do they exist at all, and would it not have been just as well if this island had been populated with happy sheep and cattle as by human beings happy in mere sensual pleasure'?[13] For Kant, as for Locke and Mill, only the industrious, rational, energetic and purposive life was worthy of human beings. Since Tahitians failed to live up to it, they were little different from 'sheep and cattle' and had no claim to the respect of civilised societies. Kant's question, which goes to the very heart of the liberal view of non-liberal societies, had been asked by the Spanish colonisers. And since they concluded that 'primitive' people had no right to 'exist at all', they saw nothing wrong in following its murderous logic.

Although the general body of liberal thought approved of colonialism, some liberal writers such as Bentham, Voltaire and Diderot did not. They were a small group, and mostly marginal to mainstream liberal thought. Some of them attacked the colonial empires of other countries, but not their own. More importantly they disapproved of colonialism not on moral or cultural grounds, but because it was deemed to be expensive, unprofitable, inconsistent with the principle of free trade, or uneconomic in the long run. They never doubted that the European way of life, and in some cases the European *race*, were superior to the non-European, and thought that commerce and trade rather than colonial rule were the best means of civilising the latter. It was only when anti-colonial struggles gathered momentum, and made colonial rule impossible without considerable violence, that the main body of liberal thought swung against it.

Although liberalism has undergone important changes in recent years, its capacity to appreciate and accommodate cultural diversity remains too limited to restrain its propensity towards cultural colonialism. As post-war literature and government policies on the developing countries show, Western liberal experts cannot see why the latter should not bow to the 'logic of modernisation' and unreservedly adopt the liberal way of life.

186

They also feel deeply uneasy about the demands of native peoples, minority nationalities and nations, gypsies, tribals, immigrants and others to be allowed to lead their traditional ways of life with such changes as they freely wish to make. Even when liberals are sympathetic to these demands, they have considerable difficulty in making a convincing case on liberal grounds. Will Kymlicka, a sensitive liberal defender of the indigenous communities' right to their cultural integrity, is a good example of this.

Kymlicka advances two related arguments.[14] First, if members of an indigenous, ethnic or any other minority community are to make meaningful choices between their own and the modern ways of life, the former must exist as an option, and since it is under threat, it deserves special help and protection. Second, being culturally embedded, human beings need a secure cultural background to develop their capacity to make choices and appreciate the available range of options. To deprive them of their culture is to cripple this capacity. While Kymlicka's arguments are perceptive, they reveal the tension lying at the heart of liberalism.

Kymlicka sees culture not as an integral part of one's identity as some ethnic minorities do, nor as an ancestral inheritance to be cherished and transmitted as most indigenous communities do, but as a resource whose ultimate value consists in facilitating choices. This is a distinctly liberal view, which he uncritically universalises and imposes on communities who view their culture very differently. Furthermore, for Kymlicka a culture is an option, a contingent and detachable part of one's identity, a matter of conscious and deliberate choice. Accordingly he wants members of indigenous and ethnic communities to decide freely whether to retain or reject their way of life. It is not enough that they retain it out of habit or respect for their history and tradition, for this is presumably irrational; they must step out of it, locate it within a range of options, and choose it as a matter of conscious decision. For Kymlicka deliberate choice is the only proper way to relate to one's culture, and all alike must conform to it. He does not see that different communities might have different modes of conceiving and relating to their cultures, and that the liberal way is neither the only one nor the best. Kymlicka wants

Said

AmerIndians, Inuits and others to become liberals, that is, he liberalises the non-liberals , and is prepared to defend them only when, and to the extent that, they are prepared to behave as respectable liberals. Like the Christian missionaries and the liberal writers discussed earlier, he is unable to understand non-liberal modes of thought in their own terms and to respect their integrity. While genuinely appreciative of diversity at one level, he denies it at another and remains trapped within the parameters of liberal thinking developed by Las Casas, Locke and Mill.

MARXISM

Marxism is one of the most radical and emancipatory projects in Western thought. Few bodies of ideas match its commitment to the cause of the poor and the oppressed, and its concern for human freedom and wholeness. One would therefore expect it to be far more critical of colonialism than the liberals. In some respects it was, for it exposed the exploitative basis, racism and brutality of colonialism as well as the limitations of its familiar liberal defence. However it too found good historical reasons to justify colonialism.

For Marx man was a free and self-creating being whose nature and destiny consisted in creating a society free from non-human constraints. As he imagined it, a truly human or free society was one in which human beings were liberated from the 'tyranny' of God and other transcendental human projections, as well as from most of the constraints imposed by external and internal nature. Human beings enjoyed unmediated unity with their species, and were no longer imprisoned into narrow ethnic, cultural, national and other communities. Marx even thought that, since local languages stood between the individual and the species, they would and should eventually be replaced by a single universal language. The collective life of such a boundaryless society was based not on inherited customs and traditions but on self-consciously formulated rules and careful planning. Marx was also opposed to the division of labour on the ground that it imposed a specific occupational identity on its members and restricted the scope of self-creation, and imagined a society in which people would paint or write without becoming painters or writers.

Marx used this vision of human freedom to judge and classify societies and historical epochs. Since human self-creation was a protracted process and since, except in the communist society, it occurred without conscious human control, it entailed much suffering. Marx insisted that rather than condemn such suffering in abstractly moralist terms, once should judge it in terms of its contribution to the long-term interests of the species. Marx's theory of the nature and historical dialectic of human self-creation formed the basis of his theory of colonialism. Non-European societies were static, restrictive, technologically backward, mired in religious superstitions, lacked individuality, were slaves to nature, and cut off from the world history. Since they offered little freedom in Marx's radical sense of self-creation, they needed to be dismantled. And since they were unable to do so themselves, European colonialism was a historically necessary and progressive force. This was exactly the argument of almost all liberals from Locke onwards.

Marx agreed that the destruction of a long-established social order invariably caused 'terrible' suffering and was often 'sickening ... to human feeling', but insisted that it was in the long term interest of both the societies concerned and mankind as a whole. As he put it in relation to British rule in India:

> *Now sickening as it must be to human feeling to witness those myriads of industrious patriarchal and inoffensive social organizations disorganised and dissolved into their units ... we must not forget that the idyllic village communities, inoffensive though they may appear, had always been the solid foundation of Oriental despotism, that they restrained the human mind within the smallest possible compass, making it the unresisting tool of superstition, enslaving it beneath traditional rules, depriving it of all grandeur and historical energies ... We must not forget that the little communities were contaminated by distinctions of caste and by slavery, that they subjugated man to external circumstances, that they transformed a self-developing social state into never*

Said

> *changing natural destiny, and thus brought about a*
> *brutalizing worship of nature, exhibiting its degradation in*
> *the fact that man, the sovereign of nature, fell down on his*
> *knees in adoration of Hanuman, the monkey, and Sabbala,*
> *the cow.*
>
>   *England, it is true, in causing a social revolution in*
> *Hindostan, was actuated only by the vilest interests, and*
> *was stupid in her manner of enforcing them. But that is not*
> *the question. The question is, can mankind fulfil its destiny*
> *without a fundamental revolution in the social state of*
> *Asia? If not, whatever may have been the crimes of England*
> *she was the unconscious tool of history in bringing about*
> *that revolution.*[15]

Since most Indians did not see British colonialism in this way,
they often protested and even rebelled against it. Marx's
judgement on their actions was predictable. In so far as they
were reacting against the historically necessary suffering entailed
by colonialism, their protests, though understandable, were
unjustified. In so far as they were reacting against the gratuitous
or surplus suffering caused by the mindless brutality and
arrogance of the colonial rulers, their protests were both
understandable and justified. This is why Marx disapproved of
the Indian mutiny in 1857, but condoned some of the excesses
of the mutineers.

    Although Marx justified colonialism, he was too acutely aware
of its brutality and exploitative nature not to appreciate the need
for anti-colonial struggle. The point of the struggle was not to
end colonial rule 'prematurely', but to sustain the spirit of revolt,
to restrain colonial excesses, and to build up a movement until
such time as it was both possible and necessary to end colonial
rule. After the Russian Revolution in 1917, Lenin, Trotsky and
others supported the growing anti-colonial struggles first in India
and then in other parts of Asia and Africa. However their support
suffered from the limitations of the Marxist theory of colonialism.
Their primary concern was not so much to help the colonies
regain their freedom to fashion their self-chosen ways of life, as
to destabilise metropolitan capitalism by removing its sources
of profits and reducing its capacity to buy off internal discontent

and to pave the way for a world revolution.

Independence of colonies had largely an instrumental value, and it was hoped that after independence they would all follow the communist path of development. The thought that they might be left free, let alone encouraged to choose an alternative vision of life more consistent with their history and tradition, was dismissed out of hand. Not surprisingly communist anti-colonial struggles often had a colonial air about them, as later became evident in the Soviet attempts to control their post-independence destiny.

A CHALLENGE FOR OUR TIMES

The egalitarian potential of Christianity, liberalism and Marxism was emasculated by, among other things, their monistic vision of the good life. All human beings were endowed with dignity. But precisely because of that, they were expected to lead a truly human way of life. Those who did not were misguided, ignorant, moral and political infants, and stood in need of guidance from those who did. The basis on which the three traditions granted human equality thus contained an inegalitarian thrust. The equality was conditional and required inequality to actualise it. The three traditions could therefore both justify colonialism with a clear conscience, and criticise its excesses. *Qua* human beings, colonial subjects were entitled to a moral minimum. In order to enjoy *full* equality with 'civilised' mankind, they had to become like it under its tutelage.

In recent years all three traditions have begun to reconsider their commitments to their monistic visions of the good life. Many Christian writers and churches acknowledge that other religions are not all wrong and contain important spiritual insights from which Christianity can benefit. However the inter-faith dialogue, first initiated by the World Council of Churches and endorsed after some hesitation by the Vatican, has not proved easy. Many Christian leaders see it as a subtle attempt to deabsolutise Christianity, to 'reduce' it to one religion among many, and to undermine its doctrinal and historical identity. They welcome inter-faith dialogue so long as it aims to improve mutual understanding and to build alliances against the forces of

Said

secularism, but not if it involves accepting the equal legitimacy
of other religions, let alone opening up Christianity to their
influence, as the small group of Christian pluralists advocate.
Similar tensions are evident within the liberal and Marxist
traditions. Some liberals appreciate the need to enter into a
dialogue with and learn from non-liberal ways of life, including
the religious and the 'primitive'. Others see this as a cowardly
betrayal of the central liberal commitments. Marxism has long
remained too rigid to appreciate the need for a dialogue with its
'others', and it is difficult to foresee how it will respond in its
current mood of despondency.

In an increasingly interdependent and plural world in which
the belief in moral and cultural monism carries little conviction,
and is a source of much conflict, all major Western intellectual
traditions face an acute problem. Some form of moral and cultural
monism lies at their very basis, and several hundred years of
western hegemony have done much to reinforce their faith in it.
Not surprisingly, a radical reappraisal of their central
assumptions with a view to respecting the integrity of other ways
of thought and life, and creating the moral space required for an
open-minded dialogue with them, is proving extremely painful.
But the challenge of finding ways to reconcile equality with
difference and integrity with openness is one no major
intellectual tradition can any longer avoid.

*I am grateful to Judith Squires for her helpful comments on this
paper.*

Notes

1. Tzvetan Todorov, *The Conquest of America: The Question of the
Other*, Harper and Row, New York 1981. Spaniards were deeply offended
by the practice of human sacrifice, but apparently it did not occur to
them that their killing of the innocent in the name of civilisation and
Christianity was no different.

2. *Ibid*, p153.

3. *Ibid*, p156.

4. *Ibid*, p161.

5. *Ibid*, p163.

6. For a good discussion, see Wilhelm Halbfass, *India and Europe: An Essay in Philosophical Understanding, Motilal Banarsideas*, Delhi 1990, ch3.

7. Locke, *An Essay Concerning Human Understanding*, Bk11, ChXXIII.

8. See Locke, *Second Treatise*, §34, 38, 107 and 108.

9. *Utilitarianism, Liberty and Representative Government*, Dent, London 1912, p117.

10. Cited in Tzvetan Todorov, *On Human Diversity: Nationalism, Racism and Exoticism in French Thought*, Harvard University Press, Cambridge 1993, p194.

11. *Ibid*, p195.

12. *Ibid*, pp202f.

13. Robert T Clark Jr, *Herder, His Life and Thought*, California University Press, 1969, p325.

14. Will Kymlicka, *Liberalism, Community and Culture*, Clarendon Press, Oxford 1989, ch8.

15. Karl Marx, *Collected Works*, Lawrence and Wishart, London 1979, Vol12, p132. For the ambiguities of the Marxist and other views on colonialism, see Edward Said, *Culture and Imperialism*, Chatto and Windus, London 1993, pp288ff.

[3]

TASKS AND METHODS IN DEVELOPMENT ETHICS

DENIS GOULET

Nowadays development is increasingly denounced as a very bad thing. The noted French agronomist René Dumont sees the performance of the last forty years as a dangerous epidemic of misdevelopment.[1] In Africa, he argues, development has simply not occurred. Latin America, on the other hand, has witnessed the creation of great wealth, ranging from sophisticated nuclear and electronic industries to vast skyscraper cities. But this growth, Dumont laments, has been won at the price of massive pollution, urban congestion, and a monumental waste of resources. Moreover, the majority of the continent's population has not benefited. For Dumont,[2] misdevelopment is the mismanagement of resources in both the socialist and capitalist worlds; it is the main cause of world hunger and it afflicts "developed" countries as severely as it does Third World nations.

Other development writers strike the same theme: growth is often irresponsible, inequitable, destructive—and worsens the lot of poor people. The late Swiss anthropologist Roy Preiswerk and his colleagues judge that change processes have led to misdevelopment or maldevelopment, that is, a faulty orientation of development, in rich and poor countries alike.[3] In an earlier work, I termed much of what was called progress antidevelopment because it is the antithesis of authentic development, defined as qualitative improvement in any society's provision of life-sustaining goods, esteem, and freedom to all its citizens.[4]

Authors like the African Albert Tévoèdjré and the Haitian Georges Anglade reject the dehumanizing economic development which often prevails by recalling that the greatest wealth any nation possesses is its

---

[1]René Dumont and M. F. Mottin, *Le mal-développement en Amérique latine*, Paris: Les Editions du Seuil, 1981.
[2]See Bob Bergmann, "René Dumont on Misdevelopment in the Third World: A 42 Year Perspective," in *Camel Breeders News*, Ithaca, NY: Cornell University, Spring 1987, p. 19.
[3]See CETIM (Centre Europe-Tiers Monde), *Mal-Développement Suisse-Monde*, Genève: CETIM, 1975, p. 11.
[4]Denis Goulet, *The Cruel Choice*, New York: Atheneum Press, 1969, pp. 215–235.

DENIS GOULET is O'Neill Professor in Education for Justice at the University of Notre Dame, and author of *A New Moral Order* and *The Cruel Choice*. This essay was first presented at a symposium of the Kellogg Institute.

poor people themselves.[5] Their claim is that the poor, acting in concert, constitute a greater resource for developmental change than natural treasures, financial wealth, or technical assets. The most absolute attack on distorted development, however, comes from the pens of those who totally repudiate development, both as a concept and as a project. Prominent among these is the French economist Serge Latouche, who urges us to discard development because it is a tool used by advanced Western countries to destroy the cultures and the autonomy of nations throughout Africa, Asia, and Latin America.[6] Similarly, the Montreal-based Monchanin Intercultural Centre, through its quarterly review *Interculture*, tirelessly promotes the thesis that development must be rejected as the instrument which destroys native cultures, their political, juridical, economic, and symbolic meaning systems. The Cultural Survival movement, headquartered at Harvard University, has likewise struggled, since its creation in 1972, to prevent "development" from destroying indigenous peoples and their cultures. Its founder, anthropologist David Maybury-Lewis, writes that "violence done to indigenous peoples is largely based on prejudices and discrimination that must be exposed and combated. These prejudices are backed up by widely held misconceptions, which presume that traditional societies are inherently obstacles to development or that the recognition of their rights would subvert the nation state. Our research shows that this is untrue."[7]

Even those who seek to preserve the language and ideals of development while purging it of its failings, nonetheless insist that Third World nations should pursue an alternative to growth-focused change. They advocate instead meeting the basic needs of all, creating jobs in non-modern sectors, generating decentralized foci of autonomy, and nurturing cultural diversity.[8]

In the real policy-making world of national governments and international financing agencies, however, development is still operationally defined as maximum economic growth and a concerted drive toward industrialization and mass consumption. The national success stories praised worldwide are South Korea and Taiwan, twin paragons of high-capital and high-technology economic growth, allied to success in competitive international trading arenas.[9] Development reports remain discreetly si-

---

[5]See Albert Tévoèdjré, *La pauvreté, richesse des peuples*, Paris: Economie et Humanisme, 1978; and Georges Anglade, *Eloge de la pauvreté*, Montreal: ERCE, 1983.

[6]Serge Latouche, *Faut-il refuser le développement?*, Paris: Presses Universitaires de France, 1986.

[7]David Maybury-Lewis, Editorial letter "Dear Reader" in *Cultural Survival Quarterly*, Vol 11, No. 1, 1987, p. 1.

[8]On this see "What Now: Another Development," in *Development Dialogue*, No. 1/2, Uppsala, Sweden: Dag Hammarskjold Foundation, 1975; and Denis Goulet, "The Global Development Debate: The Case for Alternative Strategies," in *Development and Peace*, Volume 6, Autumn, 1985, pp. 5–16.

[9]Cf., *e.g.*, Lawrence J. Lau, ed., *Models of Development, A Comparative Study of Economic Growth in South Korea and Taiwan*, San Francisco: Institute for Contemporary Studies, 1986; Arnold

lent, however, about the costs in political repression attendant upon these economic successes.[10] The World Bank, the Organization for Economic Cooperation and Development, the International Monetary Fund, and most national planning agencies continue to promote strategies which treat maximum aggregate growth as synonymous with genuine development. What makes matters still worse is that many national planning ministries not only follow the old model of development, but simply "place on hold" or ignore those sound elements of policy contained in that old model. These elements called for investments in infrastructure, job-creation, and market expansion. National strategists are guided by a single imperative: to achieve "structural adjustment." Structural adjustment, however, is nothing but a euphemism for mere survival; it means, in fact, avoiding drowning or going under in a sea of debt, recession, or inflation. Under the banner of adjustment, policy recommendations ranging from tightened credit to budget discipline, wage freezes, and export expansion are urged upon one developing nation after another. The development efforts of poor countries are reduced to crisis management, to a race to generate revenues in order to pay off their paralyzing debts. Some observers, it is true, are concerned with the impact of macroeconomic policy on the lives of poor people and champion adjustment with a human face.[11] But in most cases even the "developmental" objectives of the earlier growth model (improved standards of living, job creation, better social services, and a diversified basket of available consumer goods) are forgotten or relegated to back burners. The rhetoric of development is still invoked, but in reality debt-servicing and avoidance of catastrophe now occupy center stage in arenas of development planning and policy-making.

Notwithstanding the residual but still dominant strength of growth models in policy arenas, however, a new development paradigm is now in gestation. One sign of its ascending legitimacy is that lip-service is now paid to its values even by those who pursue traditional growth strategies. These alternative values include the primacy of basic needs satisfaction and the elimination of absolute poverty over mere economic growth, the creation of jobs, the reduction of dependency, and the respect for local cultures. Although often perfunctory, such lip-service at least implicitly admits that development is essentially an ethical concern.

C. Harberger, ed., *World Economic Growth, Case Studies of Developed and Developing Nations*, San Francisco: Institute for Contemporary Studies, 1984.

[10]Selig S. Harrison, "Dateline South Korea: A Divided Seoul," *Foreign Policy*, No. 67 (Summer 1987), pp. 154–175. Yu-ming Shaw and Guo-cang Huan, "The Future of Taiwan," *Foreign Affairs*, Summer 1985 (Vol. 63, No. 5), pp. 1050–1080.

[11]See Richard E. Feinberg and Valeriana Kallab, eds., *Adjustment Crisis in the Third World*, New Brunswick, NJ: Transaction Books, 1984; and John P. Lewis and Valeriana Kallab, eds., *Development Strategies Reconsidered*, New Brunswick, NJ: Transaction Books, 1986. Also Giovanni Cornia et al., eds., *Adjustment with a Human Face*, New York: Oxford University Press, 1987.

Two recent formulations of this alternative paradigm reveal how thoroughly value-laden and ethical in nature is any serious talk about development. In September 1986, the Marga Institute held a week-long seminar in Colombo, Sri Lanka, on Ethical Issues in Development.[12] Theorists and practitioners gathered there reached a consensus that any adequate definition of development must include five dimensions
  —an economic component dealing with the creation of wealth and improved conditions of material life, equitably distributed;
  —a social ingredient measured as well-being in health, education, housing, and employment;
  —a political dimension including such values as human rights, political freedom, enfranchisement, and some form of democracy;
  —a cultural dimension in recognition of the fact that cultures confer identity and self-worth to people; and
  —a fifth dimension called the full-life paradigm, which refers to meaning systems, symbols, and beliefs concerning the ultimate meaning of life and of history.
Integral human development is all of these things.

Some years earlier a seminar on the essential components of Latin American development reached nearly identical conclusions. Its comprehensive definition of development centered on four pairs of words: economic growth, distributional equity, participation/vulnerability, and transcendental values.[13] The two final sets of words require some explanation. Participation is a decisive voice exercised by people directly affected by policy decisions. Vulnerability is the obverse side of the participation coin: poor people, regions, and nations must be rendered less vulnerable to decisions which produce external shocks upon them. The words "transcendental values" raise the vital question: "Do people live by GNP alone?" As David Pollock writes:

> Let us assume that a country's economic pie increases. Let us further assume that there is a heightened degree of equity in the way the fruits of that economic pie are distributed. Let us, finally, assume that decisions affecting production and consumption of the economic pie—nationally and internationally—involve the full participation of all affected parties. Is that the end of the matter? Does man live by GNP alone? Perhaps the latter has been the prevailing line of thought throughout the postwar period since, in the short-run, policy makers must focus primarily upon the pressing issue of increased incomes for the masses; particularly for those below the poverty line. But, despite the obvious importance of such short-run objectives, we should also be asking ourselves other, more uplifting questions. Should

---

[12]No documents have yet been issued from the seminar. The author participated in it and here reports from notes taken at the time.

[13]David H. Pollock, "A Latin American Strategy to the Year 2000: Can the Past Serve as a Guide to the Future?", *Latin American Prospects for the 80's: What Kinds of Development?*, Ottawa: Norman Patterson School of International Affairs, Carleton University, Conference Proceedings, Vol. I, November 1980, pp. 1–37.

we not take advantage of our longer-term vision and ask what kind of person Latin America may wish to evolve by the end of this century. What are the transcendental values—cultural, ethical, artistic, religious, moral—that extend beyond the current workings of the purely economic and social system? How to appeal to youth, who so often seek nourishment in dreams, as well as in bread? What, in short, should be the new face of the Latin American Society in the future, and what human values should lie behind the new countenance?[14]

Each of the five dimensions of development listed by Marga and the four dimensions listed by Pollock is value-laden. Indeed development choices pose anew, and in a new mode, ancient philosophical questions.

1

Development thrusts three basic moral questions to the surface:
What is the relation between the fullness of good and the abundance of goods?
—What are the foundations of justice in and among societies?
—What criteria govern the posture of societies toward the forces of nature and technology?

If providing satisfactory answers—normative and institutional—to these questions is what makes a country developed, it follows that not every nation with a high per capita income is truly developed.[15] One misses the "concrete dynamics of development"[16] if one fails to examine the ideals and institutions of the good life and the good society.[17]

What renders these ancient moral questions specifically developmental and the old answers obsolete is the unique cluster of modern conditions.

The first of these modern conditions is the vast scale of most human activities. In the size of our cities, bureaucracies, and factories, and in the sheer volume of images and fantasies which assault our senses, we have reached the point where, as Hegel put it, a quantitative difference produces a qualitative change.

The second modern feature is technical complexity and the specialized division of labor which ensues therefrom. No single set of skills—manual, intellectual, or artistic—can equip us to cope adequately with all our needs for unity, integration, and openness to change. We crave new facts but are crushed by information overload and can find no wisdom to match our science, no unifying threads through which to weave the countless strands of our expanding knowledge. In such a world it becomes almost impossible to answer such disarmingly simple questions as: what is the

---

[14]Pollock, *Ibidem*, p. 9.

[15]For an earlier statement of this point see Denis Goulet, "The United States: A Case of Anti-Development?", *Motive*, January 1970, pp. 6–13.

[16]Cf. L. J. Lebret, *Dynamique Concrète du Développement,* Paris: Les Editions Ouvrières, 1961.

[17]Cf. Anthony Arblaster and Steven Lukes, eds., *The Good Society: A Book of Readings,* New York: Harper Torchbooks, 1971.

good life? the relation between goods and good? the basis of justice and equity? the right stance toward nature and technology?

A third contextual condition of modern life is the web of interdependence which transforms local happenings into global events, and causes international conflicts to impinge on local destinies. The growing interdependence of nations, communities and individuals is a two-edged sword, simultaneously a good and a bad thing.[18] Starving pastoral populations in Ethiopia are rescued by food airlifted from Nebraska in the wake of a television report. But American weapons and mercenaries can also be used to kill innocent peasants in Nicaragua for reasons unrelated to their local decisions or those of their national leaders.

The fourth and most dramatic modern condition is the ever-shortening time lag between changes proposed or imposed on human communities of need, and the deadline these communities face for reacting to these changes in ways which protect their integrity. Mass media, modern medicine, and technology constantly affect the consciousness, values, and destinies of people, leaving them scant time to take counsel with themselves, their traditions, or their images of the future in order to shape a wise response.

Thanks to these four distinctively modern conditions, the moral questions all societies faced in the past have become contemporary developmental questions. By and large, however, these normative questions have been ignored or badly answered by development experts and ethicists alike. Galbraith chides fellow economists when he laments that "The final requirement of modern development planning is that it have a theory of consumption . . . a view of what the production is ultimately for—has been surprisingly little discussed and has been too little missed . . . *More important, what kind of consumption should be planned?*"[19] Should productive capacity be employed to produce a decent sufficiency of essential goods to meet the basic needs of all, or should it produce whatever goods will be bought by those who possess effective purchasing power? Most development experts flee value-laden questions, branding them unscientific or impressionistic. Ethicists, in turn, have rarely taken development processes and conflicts as the raw materials of their moral reflection. By remaining outside the dynamics of social change, however, ethicists risk imprisoning themselves within sterile forms of moralism which are useless or positively harmful. The answers to normative questions posed by development do not pre-exist in any doctrine, nor are they easy to supply. Neither ancient wisdoms interpreted in static fashion, nor uncritical modern scientific approaches suffice. Sound answers can issue only from new

---

[18]This ambiguity, as it affects international relations, is examined in Denis Goulet, "World Interdependence: Verbal Smokescreen or New Ethic?" in *Development Paper No. 21,* Washington, D.C.: Overseas Development Council, March 1976, pp. 1–36.

[19]John Kenneth Galbraith, *Economic Development in Perspective*, Cambridge, MA: Harvard University Press, 1962, p. 43.

dialogues between ancient wisdoms and modern visions in modes which avoid ethnocentrism, dogmatism, and ideological manipulation.[20]

The task is difficult because the very language of development conceals two ambiguities. An identical term designates both the goal of change processes, namely, some vision of a better life, and those very processes themselves seen as means to reach the goal. Moreover, the term "development" can be used either descriptively or normatively. One speaks descriptively when listing a country's GNP growth rates, trade balance, rate of savings or investment. But one may shift to normative language and condemn these very accomplishments by branding them modernization without development or by decrying the failure of quantitative growth to produce human development. These twin ambiguities are unavoidable, for development is simultaneously a goal and a means thereto, and a label of what is as well as a pointer to what ought to be.

Serious discourse on development is impossible except in ethical terms. According to the North American political scientist David Apter, "Perhaps the most important consequence of the study of modernization is that it brings us back to the search for first principles. By this I mean that it requires the unity of moral and analytical modes of thought."[21] Accordingly, development ethics needs to take its place alongside development economics, politics, anthropology, and planning to analyze and solve problems which are at once economic, social, political, cultural, technical, and ethical in nature. Ethicists are well-advised to display proper humility, however, as they enter policy arenas: their past performance there has, on the whole, been discouraging.

2

Although economic thought is resurrecting teleological questions long considered the special province of philosophy, nothing has equipped economics to answer its own questions. Consequently, more and more economists turn to ethics. Ever since the separation of economics from the study of morals, however, ethics itself has had a dismal career. Hence it too finds itself incapable of answering development's troubling normative questions.

Why is modern ethics so ill-prepared to answer normative questions posed by development economics? The emancipation of economics from moral philosophy wrought in the last two centuries is simply one mani-

---

[20]Cf. Robert Vachon, "Développement et Libération dans une Perspective Interculturelle et Cosmique," in *Bulletin Monchanin 8*, No. 2, Cahier 49, 1975, pp. 3–30. Cf. also Denis Goulet, "Development Experts: The One-eyed Giants," *World Development* 8 (7/8): 481–489 (July/August 1980).

[21]David Apter, *The Politics of Modernization*, Chicago: University of Chicago Press, 1965, pp. 5–6.

festation of a general trend toward specialization in knowledge. Major gains have been made since the Enlightenment by those branches of learning which made cumulative gains in knowledge by relying on empirical investigation derived from revisable inductive theories. Greatest methodological progress has come in the natural sciences. Such progress greatly facilitates observation and classification and has been the springboard for major breakthroughs in theory (evolution, relativity, astrophysics). Later, by borrowing freely from natural sciences, the "sciences of man" also reached impressive levels of theoretical generality (systems theory and general theory of action). But social sciences deal with life, and even recent gains have not dissipated the growing malaise of social scientists in the face of life's complexities.

Ethics, in turn, once stripped of its effective role as society's norm-setter, strayed along diverse paths. Very quickly all philosophies fell into disrepute. With each new success of the experimental method and the rising ascendancy of empirical science, philosophical speculation came to be regarded as an "armchair procedure" enjoying dubious value.[22] Many contemporary philosophers have taken highly subjective existentialist routes, a jungle maze replete with meandering byways. Others have embraced Marxist prescriptive doctrine and become exegetes of a new scripture, that of dialectical materialism. A third group, few in number and limited in influence, maintains allegiance to "natural law" morality. The majority of ethical theorists in "developed" countries, however, have chosen the road of positivism, which abandoned normative prescription on grounds that it is pretentious, unscientific, or both. Instead, ethics now seeks to derive guidelines for action from social preferences, positive law, psychological conditioning, or the demands of efficiency. By its own admission, positivist ethics regards teleology as meaningless. When, therefore, economists ask what consumption is for or what kinds of goods foster the good life, or what is the nature of welfare, positivistic ethics has nothing to tell them.

Marxist ethics does, it is true, supply one set of answers to these questions. But, as a growing number of its own contemporary champions acknowledge, Marxist ethics has long been under the spell of its own dogma and refused to examine a whole gamut of profoundly meaningful questions on the ground that such questions are vestiges of "bourgeois decadence."[23] In recent years, however, certain Marxist moralists have

---

[22]On this, cf. James K. Feibleman, *The Institutions of Society*, London: George Allen & Unwin, 1956, p. 61.

[23]Cf., *e.g.*, Adam Schaff, *A Philosophy of Man*, London: Lawrence & Wishart, 1963; the contributions of Roger Garaudy, Ernst Fischer, *et al.*, in *Dialogue*, an International Review published by Forum (Vienna), especially Vol. I, No. 1, Spring 1968, pp. 104ff. Also Peter Smollett-Smolka, "Revisionist International," *New Statesman*, April 28, 1967, p. 570; and David Crocker, *Praxis & Democratic Socialism*, UK: Harvester Press, 1983.

begun to view ethical inquiry as an essentially open-ended process without predetermined answers. In the words of Gilbert and Gugler, specialists in Third World urbanism, "Like any other theory, the closer neo-Marxian analysis approximates reality, the more complex it becomes and the less able it is to predict the future."[24] For their part, existentialists have either rejected social ethics as unimportant or engaged in tortuous, self-analyzing (and self-justifying) efforts to build dialectical bridges from their quasi-absolute commitment to personal freedom as the ultimate value to the demands of social philosophy. Such commitments to personal freedom necessarily render the formulation of a social ethic difficult. Camus and, in more explicitly critical terms, Sartre, have doubtless laid a foundation for bridging the gap between personal and societal ethics. But their language and style are so strongly conditioned by their particular historical experience of World War II and postwar France that their "social" morality has experienced difficulty in gaining wide acceptance in developing countries. As a result, many Latin American social philosophers find Marxism far more attractive than existentialism. For the Brazilian philosopher, Vieira Pinto, "The philosophy of existence, among all contemporary doctrines, is the one which most clearly exposes its followers to the danger of alienation." He believes the reason to be that "Existential philosophy is the philosophy of the centers of domination over underdeveloped regions."[25]

Thus, development economists do not receive much normative help from moral philosophers even when they seek it. On issues of importance to policymakers and development planners, available ethical systems provide little light. Existentialists are too individualistic and too complex, Marxists too deductively prescriptive and not sufficiently responsive to social and symbolic relativities. Natural-law ethicists are increasingly viewed as defenders of a particularistic confessional doctrine in a world become increasingly secular and pluralistic. Positivists suffer from an overdose of success in description and analysis, resulting in the atrophy of their ability to engage in normative and evaluative inquiry. To put it bluntly, the mainstream of moral philosophy has run dry.

Nevertheless, as the historian of philosophy Etienne Gilson remarks, "The first law to be inferred from philosophical experience is: Philosophy always buries its undertakers."[26] For over twenty-five centuries the death

---

[24]Alan Gilbert and Josef Gugler, *Cities, Poverty and Development*, Oxford: Oxford University Press, 1982, p. 12. (Cited in Mohammed A. Qadeer, "Understanding Third World Cities: Perceptions and Prescriptions," *Third World Affairs 1985*, London: Third World Foundation for Social and Economic Studies, 1985, p. 341.)

[25]Cf. Alvaro Vieira Pinto, *Consciência e Realidade Nacional*, Rio de Janeiro: Instituto Superior de Estudos Brasileiros, 1960, I, pp. 65–66. One should not be absolute, however, about Sartre's acceptance in "underdeveloped" countries. He did, after all, write the preface to Fanon's *Les Damnés de la Terre*, 1961. Cf. also A.A. Fatourous, "Sartre on Colonialism," *World Politics*, Vol. XVII, No. 4, July 1965, pp. 703–720.

[26]Etienne Gilson, *The Unity of Philosophical Experience*, New York: Scribner, 1937, p. 306.

of philosophy has been regularly attended by its revival. The present moribund state of moral philosophy is possibly the harbinger of a new spring. Among telltale signs of such a new spring are the ample debates generated by the publication of Rawls' study of justice in 1971 and a burgeoning normative literature on ecology and development. Few contemporary philosophical systems attempt to provide a total explanation of reality, in part because philosophers know how difficult it is to reach a synthesis of realities which are themselves fluid and complex. Permanent inquiry into meaning goes on, nonetheless, and new philosophies are in gestation whose hallmarks are non-dogmatism, a reaction against simplistic forms of relativism, and a genuinely self-critical spirit.

An "economic" law may be at work here: human societies cannot long endure unless their need for meaning is met by adequate philosophies. Technology and mass demonstration effects presently challenge the values of all societies. United Nations reports, development plans, and aid documents repeatedly invoke such normative terms as "better life," "greater equity in the distribution of wealth," the need to assure "social improvement" for all. Here is clear proof of the existence of a "demand" for development ethics. It is the "supply" side which is wanting. If moral philosophers prove incapable of supplying answers, or if they take refuge in concepts alien to the real experiences which alone can provide raw materials for their ethical reflection on development, others will try to formulate an ethics of development. Economists, anthropologists, sociologists, and psychologists will attempt it. They risk being reductionist. A more alarming possibility is that political demagogues, technological manipulators, or high priests of ideological thought-control will do it. There may still be time, however, for moral philosophers to stop "moralizing" and undertake serious analysis of ethical problems posed by development, underdevelopment, and planning. In order to succeed they must go to the marketplace, the factory, the planning board, and the irrigation project and create ethical strategies of social decision-making which enter into the dynamics and the constraint systems of major policy instruments: political, technical, and administrative.

Because development decisions pose value-laden questions, they call for ethical analysis which is no less systematic and rigorous than that supplied by economic planners or technical project designers. It thus becomes important to identify an approach to ethical strategizing which is capable of illuminating these choices.

3

Not every ethical approach or "way of doing ethics" is adequate to the task of integrating the diagnostic and policy domains of development with its value realms. It is easier to state what must *not* be done than to specify what is needed. Evidently, no abstract deductive ethics can serve. The discipline of development is an art, not a science: it deals with decisions and actions taken in domains of high uncertainty, not with orderly or perfect patterns of logic or design. Great practical wisdom is required in development affairs. Wisdom brings unity out of multiplicity only after facing contradiction and complexity. In this it is distinguished from naiveté whose unity of meaning is gained by fleeing from contradiction and is either ethnocentric or reductionist. On the contrary, development ethics must pay attention to political and economic imperatives, while recognizing that these operate in highly diverse settings marked by varied cultural antecedents, resource endowments, and explanatory meaning systems. The best way to characterize how development ethics must operate is to say that it must become a "means of the means." How can this enigmatic phrase be interpreted?

In a critical study of Nietzsche published in 1975 the French philosopher Gustave Thibon reinstates what he calls

> the Nietzschean ideal of the sanctification of power. Heretofore power and purity could coexist, one separate from the other. It was possible, without causing too much damage, for the first to remain spiritually impure and the second materially ineffectual simply because power had limited means at its disposal: The worst whims of caesars did not totally threaten the equilibrium and survival of humanity. But nowadays power disposes of almost infinite means of destruction; therefore, can we seek salvation elsewhere than in the union of force with wisdom?[27]

What Thibon seeks is not some new legitimation of political power, but some way of converting power to a higher ethic.

Ethicists no longer imagine that ethics can exorcise evil from realms of political power simply by preaching noble ideals. James Schall, S.J., argues that Christians "have no formal social and political doctrine and that they are free to take on whatever ideological or practical form they wish in order to achieve the goals of Christianity."[28] In short, the Gospel issues no warrant for *quo*. This view, however, is vigorously repudiated by a growing number of radical pacifists. Chief among these is John Howard Yoder who contends "that the ministry and the claims of Jesus are best understood as presenting to men not the avoidance of political options, but one particular social-political-ethical option."[29] Whatever one's theoretical position may be, however, there is no doubting the prophetic summons to liberation which inspires Latin American, African, and Asian theologians of liberation. Nevertheless, no theology of liberation or ethics

[27]Gustave Thibon, *Nietzche ou le déclin de l'Esprit*, Paris: Fayard, 1975, p. 75. (Translation mine.)

[28]James V. Schall, "The Nonexistence of Christian Political Philosophy," *Worldview*, 19 April 1976, p. 26.

[29]John Howard Yoder, *The Politics of Jesus*, Grand Rapids: Eerdmans, 1971, p. 23. Cf. Richard K. Taylor, *Economics and the Gospel*, Philadelphia: United Church Press, 1973. A useful attempt to evaluate the significance of disagreements in these domains is found in James W. Fowler, "Faith, Liberation and Human Development," in *The Thirkfield-Jones Lectures*, Gannon Theological Seminary, February 26–27, 1974, pp. 1–33.

of development wields prescriptive power unless it is able to take us beyond moralism. Ethics must somehow get inside the value dynamisms of the instruments utilized by development agents and become, as it were, a "means of the means."

Ethicists do not discharge themselves of their duty merely by posing morally acceptable values as goals or ends of economic or political action. Nor does it suffice for them to evaluate the economic and political instrumentalities employed to pursue those ends in the light of some extrinsic moral rule. Rather, ethicists must analyze and lay bare the value content of these instrumentalities from within their proper dynamism. For example, they must ask whether a policy of export promotion favors economic equity or not, whether it consolidates fragile local cultures or not, and so on. A kind of phenomenological "peeling away" of the value content—positive and negative—latently present in the means chosen by technicians of decision-making must take place. Any moral judgement must relate to the technical data pertinent to the problem under study in realistic terms. Moreover, such a judgement must utilize those data in ways which professional experts can recognize as faithful to the demands of their discipline. This is the sense in which ethics must serve as a "means of the means," that is, as a moral beacon illuminating the value questions buried inside instrumental means appealed to by decision-makers and problem-solvers of all kinds.

Too many ethicists who comment on social justice rest content with portraying ideal ends and passing adverse judgment on the means used by politicians, planners, or others to mobilize social energies. This approach fails because it remains outside the real criteria of decision invoked by those who, in plying their craft as decision-makers, make and unmake social values. One may legitimately postulate for ethics the role assigned to sociology by Ralf Dahrendorf in the following terms:

> It is the sociologist's business to consider what a modern civilized society might look like and what roads might lead to it. That is the domain of theory. It is also the sociologist's business once he is equipped with his theories to take part in the process of changing reality, in making what is reasonable real. This the domain of practice.[30]

Genuine ethics is a kind of praxis[31] which generates critical reflection on the value content and meaning of one's social action. Unlike the mere extrinsic treatment of means, ethical praxis conditions choices and priorities by assigning relative value allegiances to essential needs, basic power relationships, and criteria for determining tolerable levels of human suffering in promoting social change.[32] Alternative development strategies,

---

[30]Cited in David Walder, "Ralf Dahrendorf's Vision for the London School of Economics," *Change 8*, No. 5, June 1976, p. 24.

[31]See Richard J. Bernstein, *Praxis and Action*, Philadelphia: University of Pennsylvania Press, 1971.

[32]On human costs, see Peter L. Berger, *Pyramids of Sacrifice*, New York: Basic Books, 1974. For a critical review of Berger, see Denis Goulet, "Pyramids of Sacrifice: The High Price of Social Change," *Christianity and Crisis*, 34, 1975, pp. 231–237.

programs, and projects have varying impacts on populations victimized by poverty, class privilege, economic exploitation, or political domination. This is why an ethic of social justice and equity needs to harness concrete instruments in support of the struggle conducted by social classes at the bottom of the stratification ladder. It is a hollow, if not a hypocritical, exercise to speak rhetorically about human dignity unless one builds social structures which foster human dignity and eliminate what impedes it: endemic disease, chronic poverty, an unjust system of land tenure, or political powerlessness. A vital nexus links any society's basic value choices to its preferred development strategy and to the criteria it applies in all arenas of specific policy, be it employment, investment, taxes, or education.

Ethics is doubtless concerned with the means of human action, but as Morris Ginsberg writes: "It is concerned also with the relative worth of the different ends in relation to the costs involved in attaining them, and this task it cannot fulfill adequately without inquiry into the basic human needs and grounds of our preferences and choices."[33] Certain values stand as ends which are worthy for their own sakes. These ends guide and orient, even if they cannot fully command; the choice of appropriate means is crucial. As noted above, ethics must strive untiringly to become a "means of the means" by transmitting, from inside the very instrumentalities and constraints surrounding decisions and actions, selected value allegiances and value criteria. The greatest danger faced in this enterprise is that development ethicists will fall into the role played by plantation preachers in the days of slavery, namely, giving good conscience to the rich while providing spiritual, "other-worldly" solace to the victims of unjust structures. Thus development ethicists cannot discharge their function merely by harnessing human aspiration or values to such developmental imperatives as growth, modernization, or even structural change. This is to treat values instrumentally, as mere aids or obstacles to goals uncritically accepted as values. Ultimately, development itself must be critically subjected to the value tests of justice, human enhancement, spiritual liberation, and reciprocal relations. These values judge development, not vice versa. My point here is that values can only judge development choices by getting inside their concrete specificity. There is a sound epistemological reason for this, namely, that the closer any knowledge comes to human subjects—especially in their societal context—the more difficult it becomes to sustain any real difference between the observed connections among phenomena and the organization of ends of action. As one contemporary French philosopher, G. G. Granger, explains:

---

[33]Morris Ginsberg, *On Justice in Society*, New York: Penguin Books, 1965, p. 29.

What distinguishes epistemologically a "human" economics from traditional science is not that such an economics aspires to be normative, but
rather that it assigns a value and a role, in the pursuit of knowledge, to the
dialectic of the conscious intervention of the human agent over the products
of his own culture.[34]

4

Ethical discourse is conducted at four distinct levels: general ends, specific criteria which determine when these ends exist in concrete situations,
clusters of interrelated means or systems which constitute strategies congenial or uncongenial to the ends sought, and individual means taken
separately.[35]

The sharpest ethical disagreements in questions of social change arise
in the two middle realms—the criteria which specify when desired goals
are effectively reached and the system of means or strategies deployed to
obtain targeted objectives. Discussion over general ends, on the other
hand, rarely engenders debate for the simple reason that such ends are
universal and are easy to disguise behind verbal smokescreens. Thus even
tyrants profess to cherish freedom and warmongers peace. The fourth
level, that of individual means, breeds little discord because each means
usually can be put to a good or to a bad use and cannot be characterized
as ethically good or bad except by reference to diverse circumstances, motivations, constraints, and consequences. That most arguments should
rage at the two middle levels is not surprising once it is recalled that methodological differences usually mask ideological divergences. One's ethical
stance on ends is dramatically revealed in the means one adopts to pursue
them. Consequently, development ethics as "means of the means" requires not that moralists pose ideal goals and pass judgement on the
means used by others to pursue these or other goals, but rather that decision makers versed in the constraints surrounding vital choices promote
the values for which oppressed and underdeveloped groups struggle:
greater justice, a decent sufficiency of goods for all, and equitable access
to collective human gains realized in domains of technology, organization, and research. This stance differs qualitatively from an ethic of pure
efficiency in social problem- solving or the mere rationalization and defense of elite interests.[36] The difference lies between a view of politics as
the art of the possible (manipulating possibilities) or as the art of creating
new possibilities (altering the parameters themselves). A decisive choice
must be made between these two readings of political possibility. This is

---

[34]G. G. Granger, *Méthodologie économique*, cited in Hugues Puel, "Au fondement du développement: la problématique des besoins essentiels," in *Foi et Développement*, Paris: Centre
Lebret, No. 149/150, Avril-Mai 1987, p. 5.

[35]On this see Denis Goulet, *Etica del Desarrollo*, Barcelona/Montevideo: Estela/IEPAL, 1965,
pp. 77–80.

[36]On this see the interesting treatment of "mercenaries of the status quo" in Tibor Mende,
From Aid to Recolonization, New York: Pantheon, 1973, pp. 86-129.

so because development politics consists essentially in creating new possibilities, not merely in re-allocating resources of power, influence, and wealth within societies. In most cases structural changes are needed. Therefore, developers must be systems-transformers, not mere systems-maintainers. Indeed, development practitioners ought to adopt as their "moral imperative in development" those strategies which harness existing social forces to implementing the values to which they give their allegiance. In practice this means preferring strategies, programs, and projects (and even modes of reaching decisions) which assign more importance to ethical considerations than to mere technical criteria of efficiency.

In ideal circumstances, ethicists would share responsibility for the practical consequences of joint decisions taken by teams of development planners, economists, and technicians. Unless economists, planners, and technicians assess the ethical import of their decisional criteria from inside the dynamics of their respective specialties, however, they will fall prey to the determinisms of what Ellul calls "pure technique."[37] Conversely, ethicists need the critical input from problem-solvers if they are to avoid purely extrinsic moralism. Only dynamic interaction between the two categories of interlocutors can lead to the formulation of ethical strategies which are a "means of the means."

Development ethics has a clear mandate to adopt an intrinsicist methodology or procedure. Its need for a clear view of its tasks and functions is no less acute. The first task of development ethics is to raise high certain banners proclaiming such values as:

—the primacy of needs over wants (what economists call effective demand);

—obligations incumbent on favored nations and populations to practice effective solidarity with those less favored—obligations based in justice and not merely in optional charity;

—an insistence that the demands of justice are structural and institutional, not merely behavioral or reducible to policy changes; and

—an exegesis of politics as the art of the possible which defines the role of development politics as that of creating new frontiers of possibility and not merely manipulating resources (wealth, power, information, and influence) within given parameters of possibility previously defined in some static form.

It is futile to raise banners, however, without justifying and defending them. Development ethics has to make its intellectual case for the values just enunciated. It will have to argue persuasively the reasons why solidarity should be the norm and not some exclusionary "triage" or lifeboat

---

[37]See Jacques Ellul, *The Technological Society,* New York: Alfred A. Knopf, 1965. See also, J. Ellul, *The Technological System,* New York: Continuum, 1980. The danger of surrendering to the exigencies of "pure technique" is well illustrated in the realm of politics in Charles Frankel, "Mortality and U.S. Foreign Policy," *Worldview* 18, June 1975, pp. 13–23.

ethic. If Garrett Hardin is correct in posing limits to altruism,[38] development ethics must discover how these limits are to be transcended.

Its second essential function is to formulate ethical strategies for a multiplicity of sectoral problem-solving domains ranging from population policy to investment codes, from aid strategy to norms for technology transfers and criteria for evaluating human rights compliance.

Ethicists can strategize only by entering into the technical and political constraints of any problem domain and rendering explicit the value costs and benefits of competing diagnoses and proposed solutions to problems. They must also establish criteria and procedures by which technical, political, and managerial decision-makers may choose wisely and implement at the lowest cost possible what sociologist Peter Berger calls a calculus of pain and a calculus of meaning.[39]

Max Millikan, the late North American econometrician and development planner, as far back as 1962 wrote:

> The process of arriving at a national plan should be one in which the planners present to the community for discussion a variety of critical choices showing for each alternative the consequences for the society of pursuing that value choice consistently and efficiently. It is only by this process that the community can clarify its individual and social goals.[40]

The sad truth is that most development planning is not conducted in this mode; neither is most program or project design. One mission of development ethicists consists in discovering ways of rendering such an alternative planning process feasible.[41] This the ethicist may do by engaging, with others, in an innovative mode of decision-making.

Three distinct rationalities, or basic approaches to logic, converge in decision-making arenas: technological, political, and ethical rationality.[42] Each has a distinct goal and a peculiar animating spirit or basic procedure. Problems arise because each rationality approaches the other two in reductionist fashion, seeking to impose its view of goals and procedures on the decision-making process. The result is technically sound decisions which are politically unfeasible or morally unacceptable or, in other cases, ethically sound choices which are technically inefficient or politically impossible. From observing experimental innovations in negotiation, in are-

[38]Garrett Hardin, *The Limits of Altruism*, Bloomington, IN: Indiana University Press, 1977; also Garett Hardin, *Exploring New Ethics for Survival: The Voyage of the Spaceship Beagle*, New York: Penguin Books, 1971.

[39]Peter L. Berger, *Pyramids of Sacrifice*, New York Basic Books, 1974.

[40]Max F. Millikan, "The Planning Process and Planning Objectives in Developing for Economic Development," United States Papers prepared for the United Nations Conference n the Application of Science and Technology for the Benefit of the Less Developed Areas, Vol. VIII, Washington, D.C.: U.S. Government Printing Office, 1962, p. 35.

[41]For a detailed treatment of planning in consultation with the affected populace, see Denis Goulet, "Planificacion del Desarrollo en Forma de Diálogo," *Estudios Andinos*, Vol. 2, No. 2, 1971–72, pp. 67–86.

[42]Denis Goulet, "Three Rationalities in Development Decision-making," *World Development*, Vol. 14, No. 2, 1986, pp. 301–317.

nas as disparate as resettlement schemes in dam construction sites to the political empowerment of peasant associations seeking to redefine criteria of credit eligibility in large World Bank projects, I have concluded that the three rationalities must operate in a circular, not a vertical, pattern of interaction. This is the only way to avoid reductionism; it is the only way to avoid guaranteed bad decisions. Ethicists, no less than economic planners and other developmental problem-solvers, must earn their right to speak theoretically and normatively about development by engaging in action, or at least in consultation, with communities of struggle and of need. More consciously and intentionally than other specialists, development ethicists must undergo that "professional revolution" called for by Robert Chambers. This revolution of attitudes, or conversion, weans them away from elite values and allegiances to the values and allegiances of those left powerless and stripped of resources by the "normal" operations of resource transfers.[43] It is from within the constraint systems enveloping any development decision that ethicists must establish the phenomenology of values at play in those decisions and actions.

5

The essential task of development ethics is to render development decisions and actions humane. Stated differently, it is to assure that the painful changes launched under the banners of development and progress not result in antidevelopment which destroys cultures and individuals and exacts undue sacrifices in suffering and societal well-being—all in the name of profit, some absolutized ideology, or a supposed efficiency imperative. Development ethics as a discipline is the conceptual cement which binds together multiple diagnoses of problems with their policy implications, this through an explicit phenomenological study of values which lays bare the value costs of various courses of action.

More fundamentally, however, the primary mission of development ethics is to keep hope alive. By any purely rational calculus of future probabilities, the development enterprise of most countries is doomed to fail. The poor can never catch up with the rich—classes, nations, and individuals—as long as these continue to consume wastefully and to devise ideological justifications for not practicing solidarity with the less-developed. In all probability, technological and resource gaps will continue to widen and vast resources will continue to be devoted to destructive armaments. Catastrophes generated by environmental folly or demographic tunnel vision, to say nothing of nuclear or radiation poisoning, are likely scenarios of despair. Exacerbated feelings of national sovereignty will, in all likelihood, continue to co-exist alongside an ever more urgent need to institute new forms of global governance and

---

[43]Robert Chambers, "Putting 'last' thinking first: a professional revolution," *Third World Affairs*, London: Third World Foundation for Social and Economic Studies, 1985, pp. 78–94.

problem-solving. By any reasonable scenario projectable over the next fifty years, development will remain the privilege of a relative few, while underdevelopment will continue to be the lot of the vast majority. Only some trans-rational calculus of hope, situated beyond apparent realms of possibility, can elicit the creative energies and vision which authentic development for all requires. This calculus of hope must be ratified by ethics. Jacques Ellul writes eloquently of the need for hope in a time of abandonment.[44] He speaks in an openly theological vein, arguing that human beings cannot count on a *Deus ex machina* salvation from whatever gods they believe in. Only the human race can extricate itself from the human impasses—nuclear, ecological, economic, and political—it has itself created. yet human beings will despair of even attempting to create a wisdom to match their sciences, says Ellul, unless they have hope, and grounds for hope, in some God who has entrusted the making of history to them.

In analogous fashion, development ethics must summon human persons and societies to become their best selves, to create structures of justice and of what Ivan Illich calls conviviality[45] to replace exploitation and aggressive competition. There is hope for improvement, and the present dismal scenario is not ineluctable. The basis for hope is provided by René Dubos and other sociobiologists, who remind us that only a tiny fragment of human brain-power has been utilized up till the present.[46] This means that Africans, Asians, and Latin Americans are capable of inventing new and more authentic models of development. They need not become the consumers of a single pattern of modern civilization in order to become "developed." Robert Vacca,[47] in *The Coming Dark Age*, gloomily forecasts a world with no future. Development ethics offers a corrective view by reminding us that futures, like the past, are not foreordained. Indeed the most important banner development ethics must raise high is that of hope, hope in the possibility of creating new possibilities. Modern men and women have grown properly skeptical of facile Utopias; but they also understand that far more changes than were ever anticipated are possible.

Development ethics pleads normatively for a certain reading of history, one in which human agents are makers of history even as they bear witness to values of transcendence.[48] There is profound truth, even as there is literal exaggeration, in Marx's notion that till the present we have only witnessed pre-history. The beginning of authentic developmental human history comes indeed with the abolition of alienation. Develop-

(continued on page 172)

---

[44]Jacques Ellul, *Hope in a Time of Abandonment*, New York: Seabury Press, 1973.

[45]Ivan Illich, *Tools for Conviviality*, New York: Harper & Row, 1973.

[46]Réne Dubos, *Man Adapting* New Haven: Yale University Press, 1978.

[47]Robert Vacca, *The Coming Dark Age*, Garden City, NY: Doubleday & Co., n.d.

[48]Denis Goulet, "Makers of History and Witnesses to Transcendence," in *A New Moral Order*, Maryknoll, NY: Orbis Books, 1974, pp. 109–142.

GOULET *(continued from page 164)*

ment's true task is precisely this: to abolish all alienation—economic, social, political, and technological.

This long view of history and of development as a historical adventure is the only guarantee that development processes will ensure a future. Solidarity with the planet of which we human agents are the responsible stewards, and with future generations, is the ethical key to achieving a development which is at once human and sustainable. The late L. J. Lebret, a French pioneer in development ethics, defined development as a revolution leading to universal solidarity.[49] Here, in capsule form, we find a guide to the tasks and methods facing development ethics—to institute a universal revolution.

---

[49]L. J. Lebret, *Développement = Révolution Solidaire,* Paris: Les Editions Ouvrières, 1967.

[4]

Denis Goulet and the Project of Development Ethics: Choices in Methodology, Focus and Organization

DES GASPER

Des Gasper is an Associate Professor at the Institute of Social Studies, The Hague, the Netherlands

Abstract Denis Goulet (1931–2006) was a pioneer of human development theory and a founder of work on 'development ethics' as a self-conscious field that treats the ethical and value questions posed by development theory, planning, and practice. The present paper looks at aspects of Goulet's work in relation to four issues concerning this project of development ethics — scope, methodology, roles, and organizational format and identity. It compares his views with subsequent trends in the field and suggests lessons for work on human development. While his definition of the scope of development ethics remains serviceable, his methodology of intense immersion by a 'development ethicist' in each context under examination was rewarding but limited by the time and skills it requires and a relative disconnection from communicable theory. He wrote profoundly about ethics' possible lines of influence, including through incorporation in methods, movements and education, but his own ideas wait to be sufficiently incorporated. He proposed development ethics as a new (sub)discipline, yet the immersion in particular contexts and their routine practices that is required for understanding and influence must be by people who remain close to specific disciplinary and professional backgrounds. Development ethics has to be, he eventually came to accept, not a distinct (sub)discipline but an interdisciplinary field.

Key words: Development ethics, Denis Goulet, Human development, Interdisciplinarity

Career of Denis Goulet: lessons for human development and development ethics

"[W]hat kind of development can be considered 'human'?" asked the American philosopher, anthropologist and social planner Denis Goulet

D. Gasper

(1971a, p. 236). Already in 1960 he wrote, following his mentor Louis
Lebret, that 'development' means "changes which allow human beings,
both as individual persons and as members of groups, to move from one
condition of life to one which is more human in some meaningful way"
(Goulet, 1960, p. 14; 2006a, p. 7). Goulet's 1971 book *The Cruel Choice*
declared: "The aim of this work is to thrust debates over economic and
social development into the arena of ethical values. ... Is human
development something more than a systemic combination of modern
bureaucracy, efficient technology, and productive economy?" (1971a,
p. vii). Development's "ultimate goals are those of existence itself: to
provide all men with the opportunity to lead full human lives" (1971a,
p. x). He presented an ideal of "full, comprehensive human development"
(Goulet, 1979, p. 556), and praised the Sri Lankan Sarvodaya movement's
"concept of human development ... [based on] respect for all life and the
concept of the well-being of all" (1979, p. 559).

It is worth looking back at Goulet's career to identify questions and
possible lessons for the work on human development and capabilities
initiated by Sen, Haq and Nussbaum. Well before them, he advocated that
"authentic development aims toward the realization of human capabilities
in all spheres" (Goulet, 1971b, p. 205), and stressed that economic growth
and technological modernity must be treated as, at best, potential means
towards considered human values, not *vice versa*. At the same time he
insisted that principles of ethics and religion had to be confronted by, and
relate to, the full realities and complexities of modern economies (Goulet,
1960, p. 23).

Denis Goulet (1931–2006) brought the French-language project of
'the ethics of development' into the Spanish-language, Portuguese-
language, and English-language literatures and led this work for a
generation. In considering possible lessons for work on human development, the present paper does not attempt to cover all aspects of Goulet's
thought; for example, the particular ethical principles that he advocated.[1]
We shall look at four issues concerning the project of 'development
ethics': (1) its scope — does it, for example, cover too much, and thereby
nothing in depth?; (2) the methodology for such work; (3) its roles — has
it any realistic lines of influence, and on whom?; and (4) its choice of
organizational format and identity — is it to be seen as a (sub)discipline or
not? — which should reflect considered stances on scope, methodology
and roles.

Goulet's definition of the scope of development ethics combined a
broad view of it as social change ethics with an implied core audience
consisting of those who see themselves as working in development studies
or development policy. Does this allow development ethics to be a unified
field on a (sub)disciplinary model? Goulet did advocate it as a new
(sub)discipline, but will that format promote the required depth of
understanding and influence? Goulet thought hard about when and
how ethics can have influence, including through embodiment in

Denis Goulet and the Project of Development Ethics

methodologies, and envisaged a humane ethics as 'the means of the means'. Just as the means available for 'implementation' — the resources and organizations, persons and procedures — determine how declared purposes actually work out, so, he advised, ethics should help to structure those means so as to guide how they will operate in practice.

The term development ethics emerged in the mid-twentieth century in the work led by the French socio-economist Louis-Joseph Lebret (1897– 1966), founder in 1941 of the research centre *Économie et Humanisme*. Lebret worked extensively on a humanistic approach to national and international development. He "never tired of quoting with approval the phrase coined by Francois Perroux", his colleague, that development is for "every person and the whole person" (*"tous les hommes et tout l'homme"*) (Goulet, 2000, p. 34; 2006a, p. 58). Economic might must not be equated to societal right (Goulet, 2006a, p. 4).

Goulet became Lebret's student and protégé. After training in philosophy and theology he spent one and a half years in religious communities that lived amongst poor and marginal groups in France, Spain, and Algeria, during 1957–1958. He then studied and worked with the *Économie et Humanisme* group for three years in Paris and Lebanon. Lebret led him to "define my life's work to become a development ethicist operating in its several registers — theory, analysis, pedagogy, planning, and field practice" (Goulet, 2006a, p. xxxi).

In 1960 Goulet published "Pour une éthique moderne du développement", a manifesto for "a practical ethics of development" (Goulet, 1960, p. 12) that would transcend the rupture between utopian normative political theory that was not grounded in real life and predictive theory that had no interest in ethics. It should attend to the full development of persons (Goulet, 1960, p. 23) and not conflate the concepts of 'goods' and 'good', or 'having' and 'being' (a contrast stressed by Lebret among others); and should give balanced attention to the responsibilities of each of "governments, private investors, owners and labour unions" in relation to the development of all of a country and of all countries (Goulet, 1960, p. 12).

Goulet spent four years in Brazil in the early 1960s, undertaking doctoral research followed by technical cooperation work. His first book, *Etica Del Desarrollo* (Goulet, 1965), appeared in 1965 in Spanish and in 1966 in Portuguese (*Etica Do Desenvolvimento*; Goulet, 1966). Subsequently he performed field research also in southern Spain, Guinea-Bissau, Sri Lanka, Mexico, and again Brazil, and worked too in Poland (Goulet, 1992a). From 1979 to 2006 he was Professor of Education for Justice in the Department of Economics at the University of Notre Dame in Indiana, a charismatic voice who bridged disciplinary and theory–practice gaps. His most influential work, *The Cruel Choice* (Goulet, 1971a), prefigured much later development thinking, including current themes of human security. Its core concepts were 'existence rationality' and vulnerability (1971a, p. viii); Chapter Two was entitled "Vulnerability:

D. Gasper

the key to understanding and promoting development". Goulet concluded that: "Every person and society wants to be treated by others as a
being of worth, for its own sake and on its own terms, regardless of its
utility or attractiveness to others" (Goulet, 1975, p. 232). He proffered a
"general lesson": "every society must feel that its values are worthy of
respect if it is to embark on an uncertain future with confidence in its own
ability to control that future" (Goulet, 1971a, p. 49).

In a publishing career of half a century, Goulet did perhaps more than
anyone to promote a notion of development ethics as a distinctive and
required area in thought and practice: including 11 books, such as *The
Uncertain Promise* (Goulet, 1989a), and *Development Ethics* (Goulet,
1995), and over 160 papers, including work on methods of participation
and action research, technology transfer, and incentives and indicators. A
selection of his lifetime's writings has appeared as *Development Ethics at
Work: Explorations 1960–2002* (Goulet, 2006a). Many papers are available
online (http://www.nd.edu/~dgoulet).

Scope and character of development ethics

Development ethics as a body of work arose in the historical context of the
gradual emergence of capacities to ensure, for example, clean water and
essential drugs for everyone but the absence as yet of a working system of
rights and responsibilities that will fulfill those possibilities. Two aspects
deserve underlining: its global frame of reference and its focus on specific
local realities, thus with an expectation of difference as well as an interest
in commonality. Together these features make definition of a distinct field
more difficult.

Development ethics starts from the inequalities and relationships
within our world and within its parts. It deals explicitly with contexts in
which markedly, even dramatically, different ethics coexist, and examines
that coexistence. Mwanahewa, for example, proposes from a study of the
concepts and causes of corruption in Uganda that, while much of the
analysis internationally of corruption has had a generalized, universalist
character, "it remains evident that the aspect of context, namely the
meeting of the modern conventional and traditional, needs to be tackled";
"We can no longer afford to look at aspects of corruption and bribery as if
the human race was one homogeneous lot" (Mwanahewa, 2006, p. 17).
Goulet applied a similar principle, in an anthropological style that looks at
real cultural and historical settings not some supposedly timeless
'everywhere'. This context specificity and the resultant comparative
dimension are characteristic features in development ethics, even if not
universal in nor unique to it.

In outlining an aspirant or emergent field or subfield, one seeks to
specify a scope that has a good theoretical rationale and at the same time
finds a sufficient, interested audience. A field must be sufficiently
distinctive and rewarding that enough people will listen and engage with

Denis Goulet and the Project of Development Ethics

it and continue to engage despite their limited time and the many competitors for their attention. The rationale of development studies in general is that social, political, economic, medical and environmental change are fundamentally interconnected; and that the interconnections demand close attention for they bring enormous threats and opportunities for humankind. Correspondingly, development is intensely ethically laden — who benefits or loses, with respect to whose values; who decides, who is consulted, who is not? Development ethics is an untidily bounded subject about untidy and often unpleasant realities.

Goulet suggested therefore simply that development ethics considers the "ethical and value questions posed by development theory, planning and practice" (1977, p. 5). Its mission, he proposed, is "to diagnose value conflicts, to assess policies (actual and possible), and to validate or refute valuations placed on development performance" (Goulet, 1997b, p. 1168). These specifications had a number of implications.

First, as a field of practical ethics, development ethics should be grounded in intense observation of varied experience, not only the world-views of the powerful. Its normative discourses should be well related to empirical ones.

Second, the definition depends in turn on one's definition of development. This can be an advantage: it means the definition can accommodate different views. Alternative bounds for development ethics include (each to be qualified by the Goulet definition): (i) 'the South'; (ii) the South plus North–South relations; (iii) all nations (we then have 'social progress ethics'); and (iv) global relations and global issues, not only inter-national ones; and so forth. Over time, the case for broader bounds has steadily strengthened. Goulet always accepted it, as does current work on human development and capabilities. In a densely interconnected globe, where the quality and sustainability of the North's 'development' are also profoundly in question, there is a strong case for taking the scope of development ethics to be social progress ethics in all nations and their inter-relations, yet also some danger of losing a focus and an audience, and of losing a priority to the poorest.

However, thirdly, development ethics so conceived can at the same time still speak especially to relatively definite audiences that self-identify as development academics, funders, planners and practitioners, and their major clients, including students, rather than attempt to speak to everybody and as a result perhaps reach nobody. If development ethics tries to cover most of social ethics, that could result in duplication, lack of focus, and over-abstraction. Nigel Dower presents development ethics instead as the field that asks "How ought a society to exist and move into the future?", as partner to the traditional field of personal ethics that asks "How ought one to live as an individual?", and the emergent field of global ethics that asks the first question in terms of world society (Dower, 1988).

In sum, Goulet's flexible and pragmatic definition remains serviceable and allows us to combine a view of development ethics as social change

D. Gasper

ethics (and global change ethics) with yet a relatively specific primary audience — those who recognize themselves as within development studies or development policy — and an acceptance that within that audience there are multiple definitions of the bounds of "development theory, planning and practice". One can then have an audience, and a global orientation, and not lose a priority to poor people. This has been shown, and momentum achieved, in the stream within development ethics that centers on 'human development', as well as in some of the great river of human rights work. Goulet's own stream in development ethics remained small in comparison, for other reasons which we will come to.

On methodology: stages of observation, theory, advice, practice

Goulet came to his ideas through an ethnographic approach rather than centrally through reflection on welfare economics or western moral philosophy. He called for ethical investigation and debate that are driven by experience, not primarily based in academic philosophy and pre-set academic frameworks; and thus for field-based identification and reflection on values and value conflicts and on societal, corporate and global responsibilities. He espoused a process-oriented, practice-centered, locality-specific approach, not an elaborate generalized theoretical model.

Writing in 1971 just before Rawls's *A Theory of Justice* appeared, Goulet declared that philosophical ethics had become sterile, but also predicted the field's revival. Much of the revival, however, has failed his test that ethics must start from experience, from "the marketplace ... the factory ... the planning board and the irrigation project" (1971a, p. 11). Contrary to Rawls and the mainstream of philosophical ethics, he held that "Today's ethicians are forced by reality to renounce pretensions towards 'grand theory'" (Goulet, 1971a, p. 11). Life is too complex. Goulet emphatically advocated what others call 'practical ethics' rather than a theoretical ethics that would supposedly then be 'applied'. His vision of development ethics was as part of this other stream in the revival of ethics: a practical ethics that includes medical ethics, business ethics, bio-ethics and care ethics. Only a practice-based development ethics could have adequate "regard for constraints, for human desires and limitations, and for the unpredictable vagaries of local conditions" (Goulet, 2006a, p. 105) and avoid becoming entrapped in oversimple conceptual schemata (2006a, p. Ch.10).

Goulet's conception of development ethics, like that of Lebret or Peter Berger (1974), included strong attention to descriptive and explanatory ethics, to be done with more attention to dynamics than colonial ethnography had given. I will not attempt to summarize his views in descriptive ethics, but instead present and illustrate why he deemed such work central. Development ethics must start, he said, from study of how people in a given setting think and seek to make sense of the world and

Denis Goulet and the Project of Development Ethics

their lives and the forces and choices that face them. To grasp this "existence rationality" is essential if one is to offer relevant advice and not merely enunciate grand ideals.

> Any ethic — of development, of social practice, or of cultural reconstruction — is simultaneously an ethic of goals and a "means of the means." No extrinsic grafting of norms can truly work: norms must be drawn from the inner dynamisms of each arena in which they operate. At stake is the difference between hollow moralism and genuine ethical strategies. (Goulet, 1976, p. 40)

This descriptive and explanatory ethics, essential for serious ethically based strategy, requires a particular sort of research methodology, argued Goulet (1971a). He developed an approach from the French researcher Georges Allo for "integrating the living experience of ordinary people with philosophical investigation and empirical social science research" (Goulet, 1992b, p. 19).[2] For:

> in the case of values, the "object" studied has no intelligibility apart from its "subjective" resonances. ... [Further,] Values belong to realms of synthesis, not analysis: their proper domains are philosophy, poetry, meta-analytical symbolism. Only under stringent conditions ... is the study of values appropriate to social science. To reduce this synthesis of totality to that mere portion of reality which is measurable is to deprive life of its specificity and to falsify reality itself. (Goulet, 1971b, p. 208)

Ethnographic attention shows up the unrealism of narrowly defined forms of 'realism' found in some analyses in development economics, international relations and related policy studies. Let us take two examples, corruption in the South and consumption worldwide.

An ethnographically grounded descriptive development ethics takes us further than theories that look only at a grasping 'economic man' facing a set of opportunities for personal gain. Those have been applied with limited success in much contemporary analysis of corruption (for example, Klitgaard, 1988). Goulet held that exposure to the modernizing powers of Europe and North America had disrupted an 'equilibrium of desire' in pre-modern societies, of not wanting and craving what is not widely attainable. Demonstration effects "remove[d] curbs on desire before providing individuals with the means to expand resources" (Goulet, 1997a, p. 493). Aware of the malleability of effective desires, Goulet stressed the explosive danger of boosting desire in advance of productive capacity (1971a, ch. 11), a trap avoided in East Asia but perhaps not elsewhere.

This unleashing of desires would not by itself explain corruption. What must also have been removed are the constraints set by proscriptions concerning acceptable means and other inhibitions to the pursuit of maximum desire fulfillment. A second line of explanation therefore posits

D. Gasper

the felt strangeness of the public sphere in a new larger-scale society marked still by strong family and small-scale communal loyalties; the weakness as yet of new identities of professional and citizen; and weakly evolved corresponding peer groups, organizations and belief systems. Goulet argued that more complex societies operate a division between social spheres, a meta-principle that different principles apply in different spheres — for example, that 'something for something' is an exchange principle that must not be applied within the State. He suggested this division might not be easily adopted by simpler societies.

> Men learn to conduct their business life as though money were the supreme value, while continuing to abide by other values in their private lives. Such normative schizophrenia creates great personal stress, it is true. But it has at least protected modern societies from bearing the full consequences of the values to which they subscribe in the realm of productive activity. *Non-modern societies, on the other hand, are not psychologically prepared to dissociate economic values from more intimate value spheres.* If economic achievement is portrayed to them as important enough to warrant casting off all other concerns — including their most treasured family and religious practices — then why should their quest for more goods be moderated by considerations of the rights of others, prior claims of needier men, or the need for austerity in consumption so as to build up a solid production base in the nation? (Goulet, 1971a, pp. 223–224; original emphasis)

Societies not steeped in such dissociation could move to a value unitarism in which acquisitive and consumerist values become applied comprehensively, not only in restricted spheres.

Goulet's readiness to look at the empirics, not only formal analytics, of consumption led him on towards its normative assessment, and to issues central to the meaning of development. Like Sen, Goulet observed that people in general rank orders of desire, not merely intensities of desire — there are different orders of goods, and preferences about desires, not merely preferences about goods. He referred to ideas from Aristotle onwards about such ranking of types of good; for example, Aristotle's category of 'honorable goods'. People make these rankings for practical purposes, not only from love of distinction. Like Nussbaum later, Goulet stressed the need for a normative theory of consumption (for example, Goulet, 2006a, chs 3 and 4). "The plenitude of good is *not* proliferation of [economic] goods. ... The defense of freedom, in the face of the seductive flattery of the myth of happiness [through consumption], is the fundamental task of any development ethics which is realistic and effective" (Goulet, 2006a, p. 34; original emphasis — first published in 1976). He was impressed by the attitude of pity that the nomadic groups

Denis Goulet and the Project of Development Ethics

he had lived with in the 1950s and 1960s held toward people who are encumbered and dominated by things, by 'stuff'.

Goulet employed the same language of freedom as Sen, and likewise posited freedom as a universally held value, but he had more substantive theories of desire and of freedom. He distinguished "freedom from wants", obtained via the fulfillment of fundamental needs, and "freedom for wants", where one is autonomous, in charge of and not slave to the determinants of want generation (Goulet, 1971a, ch. 6). In Sen's system the danger of consumerism is a formal possibility not a central concern; in Goulet's system it is central. Often freedom from some constraints is achieved in ways that reduce human autonomy (Goulet, 1971a, p. 126). Restraint of material desires is an essential requirement for freedom (Goulet, 1971a, pp. 121–122), he argued, not only a prudent measure along a path of accumulation. "Genuine wealth, the [early Fathers of the Christian Church] contend, resides in the internal freedom which makes one use material goods instrumentally to meet needs, and as a springboard for cultivating those higher spiritual goods which alone bring deeper satisfactions: virtue, friendship, truth, and beauty" (Goulet, 2006a, p. 146). There is nothing specifically Christian in such claims, which are found in many traditions, and for example in the work of the nineteenth-century British economist Alfred Marshall, as well as in the accumulated results of modern research on well-being. Voicing such claims, in advance of and even now after these research findings, does not ensure popularity or attention; many writers prefer to pass by on the other side. The limited impact of Goulet's development ethics reflects, however, also some other factors besides voicing of unpopular ideas, as we will see.

His policy ethics, including emphases on participation and on being the agent of one's own development (see especially Goulet, 1989b), grew out of the descriptive ethics that he built through his methodology of investigation. His model of value systems and value change posited an existential core that must be respected and built from, and an outer zone of flexibility where adaptation is possible.

> ... to build development from tradition is the very opposite of reactionary. ... Since the will of most Third World communities is anchored in the cultural values from which they derive their identity, integrity and sense of life's meaning, there can be no justification for labeling a development strategy founded on the latent dynamisms in traditional, indigenous and local value orientations, as politically reactionary. On the contrary, the procedural commitment to respect values already in place constitutes a solid guarantee against falling in the twin traps of elitism and manipulation. To design and build development on tradition and indigenous values is to espouse a philosophy of change founded on a basic trust in the ability of people, no matter how oppressed or impoverished, to improve their lives, to understand the social forces that affect them, and eventually to

461

D. Gasper

harness these forces to processes of genuine human and societal development. (Goulet, 1987, p. 176)

Goulet's model for policy ethics is demanding: the examination in depth of a project, program, policy or even a national development strategy, identifying and reflecting on its multifarious value impacts; moving to an evaluation only through an in-depth description and attempt at understanding — as illustrated in his work on technology transfer, Mexico, Guinea-Bissau, Sri Lanka and Brazil. Some work by others is on similar lines, even maintained over several years (for example, Richards, 1985; Porter *et al.*, 1991; Uphoff, 1996). It requires exceptional inputs of sustained and wide-ranging attention, and is not readily funded. Mainstream work on value change, such as in the World Values Surveys, and even on the growth of consumerism or individualism, sometimes builds up sustained time series, but is done through large periodic sample surveys and has a very different character.

More work on development policy ethics has been directly normative, addressing urgent questions of choice, responsibility and priority, by application or extension of frameworks proposed as relevant from philosophical ethics. Compared with Goulet's call for an existentialist ethnography, human-rights based approaches, for example, contain ready-made frameworks for observation, monitoring and evaluation and for contributing in policy design. They seek to establish principles concerning rights and responsibilities, including with transnational application.

Limitations of Goulet's type of field ethics, deeply illuminating as it can be, concern not just the time and skills it requires, but its relative disconnection from communicable theory. Goulet himself inevitably could do less fieldwork as he grew older. His mistrust of analytical philosophy that lacked a rich experiential base meant that he did not deepen his thinking much further by that route. Instead, he increasingly restated his earlier insights rather than extend them. What we see in the most interesting development ethics work in the past 20 years (for example, Nussbaum and Glover, 1995; Pogge, 2002; Gready and Ensor, 2005), including more and more in work presented in the Human Development and Capability Association, the International Development Ethics Association, and so on, are attempts to combine case investigation and ethnographic insight with structured philosophical thinking. While in several respects Goulet had shown the way, we require also theoretical structures and systematic elaboration and ordering, in order to hold together and sustain practically oriented movements. Here Goulet seemed to lack patience. He did not undertake further conceptual refinement of notions of freedom. His incisive "embryonic theory of priority needs" (Goulet, 1971a, p. 248) remained embryonic, never fully elaborated in relation to ongoing work in psychology and philosophy.[3] Arguably he sought a different audience, more popular and less academic, and different lines of influence. He had indeed a conscious theory of the roles of ethics and of his own role. To these we now turn.

Denis Goulet and the Project of Development Ethics

On influence: teaching, research and advocacy in ethics

Ethics can play various roles, Goulet observed (1971a, Appendix 1). It has evaluative and critical roles in assessing and querying practices; a normative role in guiding the use of power and to constrain and coerce action; a role in grounding institutions, determining our view of what is normal, and our normal view, influencing where we look and how; a role to motivate action and "give exploiters a bad conscience"; and a pedagogical role, to teach critical awareness of the moral content of choices, including "as a pedagogy of the oppressed in case it is rejected as pedagogy by the oppressors" (Goulet, 1971a, p. 338).

Holding that "power without legitimacy must ultimately perish" (Goulet, 1971a, p. 341), he was aware that legitimacy and illegitimacy are not conveyed only through codes of ethics, but also through for example tradition and charisma. He had a clear vision then of the task facing development ethics, as more than "mere preachments addressed to the 'good will' and generosity of the powerful, and to the escapist sentiments of the powerless. It is ... in the interstices of power and in the structural relationships binding the weak to the strong that development ethics must unfold itself" (Goulet, 1971a, p. 19).

Following Danilo Dolci, Goulet stressed the primary power in successful revolutionary change of "moral rather than material considerations", including "a new sensitivity, a new capacity, a new culture, new instincts" (Dolci, cited by Goulet, 2006a, p. 25). At the same time Goulet urged that "mobilization strategies must protect the inner limits of old existence rationalities while expanding their outer boundaries" (1971a, p. 190), finding and using their "latent potential for change" (p. 192). His chosen example of such a combination — revolution based on traditional identity — was Meiji Japan. Change that does not threaten group survival, identity and solidarity may face little resistance (Goulet, 1971a, pp. 204–205).

Goulet was concerned thus not only with 'The Ethics of Power' — seeking to instruct and guide the Prince — but with 'the Power of Ethics', its force in constraining, motivating, inspiring, reconceiving. For him "politics as the art of the possible" covered also politics as the "art of redefining the possible" (Goulet, 1971a, p. 336). He declared that:

> Planners and other intellectuals find it so difficult to create a true professional ethic because they are crafters of words, ideas, and models. Consequently, they are timid about plunging into the heartland reality of ethics as existential power, and not as moral verbalism or conceptualism. Ethicists themselves constantly vacillate between ethical paralysis or compromise in the face of power, and energetic creativity newly released whenever they catch a faint glimpse of the power of ethics itself. ... the power of ethics to counter the power of wealth, of politics, of bureaucratic inertia, of defeatism, of social pathology. Such power can be won by a Gandhi, a Martin Luther King, a Danilo Dolci; it can never be

463

D. Gasper

institutionalized. But those others who lack ethical grandeur will inevitably lose hope in the face of larger powers, and accept compromises which strip their own ethics of its latent power. (Goulet, 1976, pp. 40–41)

Unfortunately, inspirational, charismatic leadership can as likely lead in bad directions as good. Further, leaders require a combination of a favorable conjuncture, capable supporters, strong networks, and relevant practicable proposals, in addition to an inspiring vision (Gasper, 2007). Influenced by and interacting with figures such as Dolci, Fanon, Paulo Freire, Ivan Illich and the movement of liberation theology, Goulet's emphasis on the possible prophetic roles of ethics, while valid, may not have provided the best guideline for his own work as a potential persuader through the crafting of words, ideas and models. He may have become dispirited in the era — one of charismatic leadership — of Reaganism, Islamism, born-again Protestantism, the suppression of liberation theology and the retreat from Vatican II, and of tragedies and disappointments in some countries he had engaged with closely, such as Algeria, Sri Lanka or Guinea-Bissau.

Goulet was clear, in Gramscian fashion, that much of what he said — like calling for voluntary austerity as the path to freedom — was in one sense utopian: "one can only be pessimistic" (1971a, p. 263). But he saw it also as the only realism. He took a long-run perspective, and was resigned to eras of conflict, violence and confusion, as inevitable in processes of major change (Goulet, 1971a, ch. 13 and Conclusion). In particular he held that "unless the ground rules of production and decision-making are profoundly altered within the United States, a world order of authentic development has no chance to be born" (Goulet, 2006a, p. 90 — originally published in 1970). By 1995 Goulet remarked that "Sustainable development, because it is found too difficult, may ... remain untried" (2006a, p. 155).

In such a historical setting we require not only recognition of the potential existential power of ethics, but careful theorization of influence and change.[4] Goulet constantly reiterated, through to perhaps his final published paragraph, that "the primary mission of development ethics ... is to keep hope alive" (Goulet, 2006b, p. 120). How? Three interconnected means are: incorporation of ideas in movements, incorporation in methods, and incorporation in education and training. Development ethics can seek in these ways to become, in Goulet's key phrase, 'the means of the means', embedded in and influencing the means of action: professionals and organizations, techniques and procedures, legislatures and courts. It must seek to not merely specify goals but to affect the processes and instruments through which the goals are, in practice, respecified and marginalized or given real weight.

Methods of policy analysis

Goulet's perspectives did not become sufficiently embodied in methods and methodologies. He was aware of the central importance of how

Denis Goulet and the Project of Development Ethics

routine operation is structured, as seen in his work on incentives and indicators (for example, Goulet, 1989c, 1992c), but was not fond of formalisms and formalized frameworks. He regretted "the excessive complexity and heaviness of [Lebret's] methodological instruments" (originally 1974, reprinted in Goulet, 2006a, p. 62). Yet incorporation into methods is a vital part of institutionalization, and formal methods are often key instruments for influence. Later he acknowledged that "Lebret's pre-planning studies offer a systematic way to engage in precisely such consultation" as is needed for a community to consider and clarify its value options and value choices (Goulet, 2000; reprinted in Goulet, 2006a, p. 180).

Various of Goulet's ideas have become embedded by other authors in relevant methodologies. His type of value-focused approach to local investigation and action has grown in the work led by Robert Chambers (1997) and others. His approach to policy ethics is close to the value-critical policy analysis of Martin Rein (1976), Frank Fischer (1995), Ronald Schmidt (2006) and others, which has been elaborated and applied quite extensively. His rethinking of development cooperation (Goulet, 1971a, ch. 8) has been greatly advanced by David Ellerman (2005) amongst others.

More broadly, the United Nations Development Programme (UNDP) human development approach and the attempts to devise and apply human rights-based approaches in development programming constitute important progress and suggest some lessons. Recent human rights-based approaches go beyond listing and affirming human rights criteria, to using them to steer each stage of planning and management (see, for example, Gready and Ensor, 2005). Similarly, the surprising degree of impact of the human development approach reflects more than a media strategy — the high-profile launches and accessible form of the *Human Development Reports*, the attention-catching use of summary indicators that reveal more than does Gross National Product per capita, and the evocative term 'human development' — significant though those are. It reflects the integrating force of a theoretical perspective — the thinking of Sen, Nussbaum and others about capability, and of Haq, Jolly, Stewart, Streeten *et al.* on human development — that brings a rationale and connection across a range of activities: the selection of focus, the language and measures for description, the choice of illustrative cases, the identification of alternatives, tracing of effects, and evaluation of processes and outcomes (Gasper, 2008). The human development indicators not only catch attention, but provide a route to surfacing and publicly discussing value choices.

Education and training

Goulet (1971a, ch. 8) espoused the educational model adopted by Lebret in his Paris institute: to train a corps of world developers, using a massive

D. Gasper

multidisciplinary syllabus and a professional code. He was not primarily interested in training apparatchiks or academics: "the aspiring generalist who does not gain his wisdom through the praxis of dialectical historical experience is doomed to fail" (Goulet, 1971a, p. 330). By 'generalist' Goulet appears to have meant those in his own mould, "the philosopher of development, the specialist of generality" (2006a, p. 26). This can hardly be the main target group.

The largest categories in development ethics education are general citizen education — including through popular media — and general school education. The United Kingdom and Ireland, for example, have taken steps in the space opened by national curriculum requirements for attention to international relations in general studies teaching. In the spaces of university and professional education, several important alternatives exist. First, the special short course, including summer schools; second, the dedicated course within an academic or professional training program; and third, incorporation into other courses and training. The first two alternatives have the advantage, if the courses are optional, of keen minority audiences. They give a place to work with potential future key resource persons, and to test and develop ideas that can be used to interact with bigger mainstream audiences. But the larger target is the third alternative, incorporation into existing courses of policy analysis and planning, economics, public policy, management, social policy, research methodology, and indeed any foundation course in sociology, politics, economics, human geography or development studies. Those audiences are far larger, and the danger otherwise exists — seen sometimes in gender and race studies — that consciousness-raising with small groups goes hand in hand with mistrust and increased resistance amongst majorities. Incorporation into existing 'regular' courses addresses also the central requirements for influence: to relate ethics ideas to other bodies of knowledge and to apply them in working procedures. Ethics teaching for not only a sympathetic self-selected minority is not easy to make effective and fruitful, however. Camacho (2006) illustrates a practical approach, of not trying to enforce any one doctrine, but providing a space for attention, heightened awareness and joint reflection.

Social movements and the dynamics of change

Incorporation of ideas into social movements is typically necessary for major social change (Murphy, 2005; Krznaric, 2007). Work in development ethics has to connect with significant movements, and eventually with agencies, if it is to be heard, tested, informed, upgraded, accepted and used; and it should study the instances of successful connection. Haq's induction of Sen into his UNDP work, for example, was part of the mobilization of a network of networks required for the coherence, credibility and communication of the human development paradigm. Haq brought together networks of several kinds, each necessary: from

Denis Goulet and the Project of Development Ethics

academe, not least from economics; from within United Nations organizations; from wider development organizations, such as the Society for International Development and the Third World Forum; plus intergovernment networks from his long service as official and Minister (Gasper, 2007). He further ensured that he could retain unimpeded access to them, by obtaining editorial independence for the Human Development Report Office.

While sympathetic to the UNDP-based movement of human development and to movements of participatory research and action, Goulet's active affiliation and quest for partners appears to have been especially within movements of progressive Christian thinking. Here the 1980s and 1990s were often times of retrogression instead. Compared with the 1970s Goulet's influence declined, in the absence of vehicles — organizations, journals, a clearly encapsulated methodology, related movements — that could extend, apply and adapt his approach. The model of an ethical grandee or Parisian prophet, dissemination of whose ideas looks after itself thanks to their power and elegance and the presence of a large waiting audience, did not fit. Two of the key audiences were too remote, physically or psychologically: movements of the poor who lived far away, and the northern rich, asked to reflect about their riches and about their relation to the distant poor.

Goulet was temperamentally close in some ways to the international human rights movement or movements, which has tried to institutionalize ideas of great existential power. He had doubts in the 1980s, however, about its generalizing and sometimes rather Eurocentric vision (Goulet, 1984). A decade later he felt that:

> The present intellectual climate and the political conjuncture are both favorable to a serious discussion of human rights and policies on their behalf. But a monumental problem arises: there are too many rights, too many competing claims. … Thus the very proliferation of rights and claims is itself an obstacle to the implementation of any of them. (Goulet, 1992d, p. 243)

Since then the human rights movement has continued to spread and gain influence, seen for example in campaigns for debt relief and for rights to food, water and basic drugs. There are lessons for the rest of development ethics, some perhaps sobering, some encouraging.

First, the rise of human rights thinking especially from the 1940s has not come primarily through ethics conferences or academic activities of any type. It represents a reaction to the experiences of totalitarianism in the mid-twentieth century, as well as a longer history of reactions to colonialism and imperialism (Crawford, 2002). Also of fundamental importance have been the rise of global communications, bringing a spread of images and life-stories that contribute to "an ethics of recognition" (Schaffer and Smith, 2004). The lesson would be familiar to Goulet: that much of any pressure behind development ethics will be

D. Gasper

from crises, national and global; and part will come from growing interconnection and communication. Development ethics then needs, in business language, a communications strategy not limited to waiting for leaders of ethical grandeur.

Second, the significance of human rights thinking is not solely dependent on its incorporation in legal systems. Human rights-based approaches now give attention to influencing all stages in public policy and management; to action in business, civil society, community groups, and everyday life; and to action on and through attitudes, and virtues, not only through attempted declaration and enforcement of duties. In such ways the approaches have important impact, despite the problem of many competing rights claims. The general lesson for development ethics matches Goulet's central theme: it must present ideas that function as "the means of the means", pervading and influencing actual uses of the means of action. How should we organize for that intention?

Organization of development ethics

I suggested that Goulet's distinctive strengths came through his ethnographic and sociological approach, rather than through a rethinking of welfare economics or application of western moral philosophy. His intense exposure in a series of small and marginal communities provided profound insights, but also perhaps a distancing from more abstracted and formal languages. Yet just as village ethics cannot suffice for more complex societies, so more elaborated, multi-part, dissociated and in some parts abstract, intellectual systems, methods and projects are needed in analytical and practical ethics (Gasper, 1996). We saw that Goulet's type of work requires partnership with the streams derived from economics and philosophical ethics. He sought, and often reached, a broad audience, but unless one also reaches relevant specialists then one's impact can be ephemeral. Reaching out to diverse important audiences requires diverse tools: sometimes eloquence and profundity, sometimes formalism and precision, sometimes standard working procedures, sometimes specific personal networks.

To take forward this work in building a field of development ethics that makes some difference, with systematic incorporation of ideas into methods, movements and education, what is an appropriate organizational format? Goulet argued that a disciplinary or (as an area within philosophical ethics) subdisciplinary format is appropriate. We criticized him for investing too little in theoretical system-building. If theoretical deepening and formalization are important, is not a separate (sub)disciplinary space essential? But the need is not for a specialist space within academic philosophy. The analyses required lie at the interfaces of different branches of philosophy, social sciences, management and humanities, and of academic work and practical action. It is important to reach the 'clerisy' of specialists, the 'religious orders' of the modern

Denis Goulet and the Project of Development Ethics

intellect, but not to create a new such order that will not communicate with nor be heard by the existing ones.

An intellectual area that calls itself development ethics needs instead to function like a nursery, cultivating ideas and persons that will be transplanted, even if they might remain in contact. The nursery is not the long-term destination. Such a self-conception would leave it as a minor ghetto. Influence on mainstreams is the objective. The characteristic development ethics perspective described earlier — comparative, inter-cultural, international, interdisciplinary, change-oriented and close to practice — implies that a disciplinary nest in which restricted and abstracted formulations of issues are pursued in great depth will not be ideal. It can form a permanent cocoon from which the fledgling does not graduate.

Goulet called for a form of philosophy that did graduate, into the world of action. We saw his advice:

> ... for moral philosophers to stop "moralizing" and undertake serious analysis of ethical problems posed by development, underdevelopment, and planning ... they must go to the marketplace, the factory, the planning board, and the irrigation project and create ethical strategies of social decision-making which enter into the dynamics and the constraint systems of major policy instruments: political, technical, and administrative. (Goulet, 1988, p. 155)

He never declared a moral position from on high, but based advice on *in situ* investigation, as well as a perspective of long-term change that had been informed by history, social science and local immersion. Goulet moved beyond only highlighting the normative significance and priority of goals and criteria besides economic growth. He showed the centrality of such goals in motivating and guiding people's behavior; and he sought to incorporate justified normative criteria into systems of decision-making. This moves development ethics' center of gravity from philosophy towards anthropology, psychology, sociology, economics and management.

Yet, paradoxically, he called consistently for development ethics to be a distinct discipline and specialism, a sort of secular priesthood (for example, Goulet, 1988, 1997b). 'The development ethicist' was the protagonist in many of his writings, which remained set in the mould of his 1960s and 1970s work. The envisaged development ethicist was a Goulet engaged in technical cooperation programs or employed as a specialist researcher and adviser, a worker philosopher. He considered it "inevitable that a new discipline, based on systematic examination — both instrumental and philosophical — of comparative values must someday join the ranks of ... comparative approaches to the study of development" (Goulet, 2006a, p. 26 — originally written in 1976). In reality there has been as much regress as progress in this direction. Goulet's own unusual career could not form a generalizable model.

D. Gasper

Goulet's insistence on evolution from tradition domestically in each country, and also on a separate specialism or subdiscipline of 'development ethicists', who should be added to decision-making in development policy and practice, form an uneasy combination. Where would a subdiscipline emerge except in North America where philosophical ethics is an enterprise of sufficient scale, in terms of numbers of courses and students and academics, for such a specialism to receive sustained attention? And what role would such implicitly expatriate or relatively distanced ethicists have in relation to domestic traditions? Goulet offered a parallel with specialist business-ethical and medical-ethical advisors (1988, pp. 160–162). But those in general live in the same cities as their clients. The paths of trying to influence methods, specialists and social movements are more relevant than trying to construct a new specialism or movement. To enrich and modify others' work is more feasible and more fruitful.

For those working in development ethics, 'discipline' is a central concept that requires extended examination, just like 'freedom' or 'need' (for one attempt, see Gasper, 2004). Goulet was aware of pitfalls in disciplinarity, and the vested interests of existing disciplinary redoubts that do not let new competitors readily emerge. Indeed he was based in a department of economics that was ultimately torn apart by conflict between a mono-disciplinary and an inter-disciplinary approach to economics. He himself never sought "to trespass on the proper autonomy of each discipline — which is something other than ... hermetic closure upon oneself" (1960, republished in Goulet, 2006a, p. 14) — nor did he seek "to win sectarian or partisan victories" (2006a, p. 15). In arguing for development ethics as a separate discipline, however, he perhaps misread the challenge. The demands *for* interdisciplinary communication in development ethics are so central, and the demands *of* interdisciplinary communication so considerable, that a disciplinary or subdisciplinary format does not fit well here.

Attempts to build a subdiscipline in academic philosophy have had slight impact. The difficulty to draw clear boundaries for development ethics contributes amongst other factors to the non-emergence of a sharply distinctive field. If we see development ethics in, for example, Dower's sense — as the field that asks 'How ought a society to exist and move into the future?' — then it cannot be a tidy subdiscipline. Rather, it is a concern that belongs in many choice arenas. The place for development ethics is as an inter-disciplinary field in which a variety of relevant disciplines exchange and enrich each other (Gasper, 1994). Development ethics authors in practice come from all backgrounds, not predominantly from philosophy.

Is such a framing of development ethics as an interdisciplinary meeting place, a looser academic and professional forum, truly fruitful as well as more feasible? If one is not a discipline — a self-enclosed, self-referential territory with one's own induction and indoctrination, system of rewards and punishments, loyalties and captive population, border controls and flag — can one achieve and maintain the focus, continuity,

Denis Goulet and the Project of Development Ethics

and critical mass needed for deep intellectual work? Truong and I suggest that in fact most of the areas of creativity and energy in development ethics lie at intersection points between a stream of practice — whether economic policy, human rights activism, emergency relief, business management or whatever — and a stream of ethically sensitive theorizing, whether from socio-economics, quality of life studies, religions, feminisms, jurisprudence, or so on (Gasper and Truong, 2005). There are multiple linked sites of such conversations. Development ethics includes and interconnects these sites. To do this it has various 'nursery' functions: in shared conceptualization, cross-fertilization, education and training. These need a long-term institutional base of professional groups and associations, textbooks, journals, even traditions. But since the primary task is one of reaching out, and of connecting diverse other streams of theory and practice, it is more realistic and accurate to describe the resulting field as one of interdisciplinary interaction rather than as a new discipline. We see this principle largely at work in the Human Development and Capability Association, and in the change of subtitle of the *Journal of Human Development* from 'Alternative Economics in Action' to 'A Multi-Disciplinary Journal for People-Centred Development'.

In his late work Goulet recognized "two different roads" for development ethics (1997b, p. 1166). The first was his own model, of "a new discipline with distinctive methods and research procedures" (*loc. cit.*). The second road was of development ethics as a type of work that overlaps with other types, with which it cooperates as partners in interdisciplinary activity. Goulet still saw prospects in the first road, and called his article 'Development Ethics: A New Discipline'. But he had become aware of the alternative model, of inter-disciplinary learning (Goulet, 1992b). This path has been followed much more. An important number of development practitioners and social scientists have become more self-consciously and systematically ethics oriented; for example, through the spread of rights-based approaches and human development perspectives. The required investigation in the marketplace, factory, planning board and irrigation project has been done not by philosophers, but by ethically aware anthropologists, economists, geographers, health specialists, journalists, planners, political scientists and others. In his final book Goulet continued to talk of using findings from "other disciplines" (2006a, p. xxxiii), as if development ethics was a comparable discipline. But he recognized development ethics "as an intrinsically interdisciplinary effort" (p. xxxii), and spoke of 'discipline' often now simply in the everyday sense, as a disciplined activity — "systematic, cumulative, communicable, and testable" (Goulet, 2006a, p. xxxiii).

Goulet was determined not "to pursue a vision of justice shrouded in a Utopian halo because it is not deeply imbedded in the world of real constraints" (2006a, p. 3). In the same spirit I have tried to draw lessons from his remarkable career, for ongoing work on human development and development ethics.

471

D. Gasper

Notes

1   On other aspects of Goulet's work, see his own overviews (for example, Goulet, 1976, 1995, 1997a, 2006b), before proceeding to, especially, *The Cruel Choice* (Goulet, 1971a). On the ethical principles he advocated — (1) self-determination, individual and collective; (2) 'decent sufficiency' of basic goods for all; (3) solidarity; and (4) non-elite participation and democratic decision-making — in ways that anticipate and can still enrich much of the later work on human development, Crocker (2006) and chapters 4, 5 and 8 in Goulet's (1995) *Development Ethics* provide introductions. Crocker makes comparisons with the later work and also suggests where it has advanced on Goulet.

2   Appendix 3 to *The Cruel Choice* outlined its four stages. The approach is similar to the 'Verbal Image' form of reporting presented by Howard Richards (1985), which aims to give a broad picture, a description and understanding of how a program works in its societal context, not a focus only on a few aspects taken out of their context. It thus tries to ensure coverage of non-measurable impacts, to grasp the human meanings in situations, and to make sense, to outsiders and insiders, of what has happened; and to have insiders systematically check the 'verbal image' that is constructed on the basis of their contributions. See Richards (1985, pp. 79–85; also Lee and Shute, 1991).

3   Thus the important 1976 presentations that form chapters 3 and 4 of his 2006 book *Development Ethics at Work* were not extended later to relate to the wealth of relevant material from contemporary social science and philosophy.

4   See Gasper (2006) for a complementary discussion of these themes.

References

Berger, P. (1974) *Pyramids of Sacrifice*, Basic Books, New York.

Camacho, L. (2006) 'Teaching ethics to employees of a public utilities company in a developing country', *Ethics and Economics*, 4(2), [http://ethics-economics.com//Volume-4-Numero-2.html], accessed 8 July 2008.

Chambers, R. (1997) *Whose Reality Counts?*, Intermediate Technology, London.

Crawford, N. (2002) *Argument and Change in World Politics*, Cambridge University Press, Cambridge, UK.

Crocker, D. (2006) 'Foreword', in D. Goulet (Ed.), *Development Ethics at Work: Explorations 1960–2002*, Routledge, New York, pp. xiv–xxix.

Dower, N. (1988) *What is Development? A Philosopher's Answer*, Centre for Development Studies, University of Glasgow, Glasgow.

Ellerman, D. (2005) *Helping People Help Themselves*, University of Michigan Press, Ann Arbor, Mich.

Fischer, F. (1995) *Evaluating Public Policy*, Nelson-Hall, Chicago.

Gasper, D. (1994) 'Development ethics — an emergent field?', in R. Prendergast and F. Stewart (Eds.), *Market Forces and World Development*, Macmillan, London, pp. 160–185.

Gasper, D. (1996) 'Culture and development ethics', *Development and Change*, 27(4), pp. 627–661.

Gasper, D. (2004) 'Interdisciplinarity', in A.K. Giri (Ed.), *Creative Social Research*, Lexington Books, Lanham, Md., and Sage, Delhi, pp. 308–344.

Gasper, D. (2006) 'What is the point of development ethics?', *Ethics and Economics*, 4(2), [http://ethics-economics.com/Volume-4-Numero-2.html], accessed 8 July 2008.

Gasper, D. (2007) *Values, Vision, Proposals and Networks — The Roles of Ideas in Leadership for Human Development: The Approach of Mahbub ul Haq*, GARNET Working Paper 24/07 [http://www.garnet-eu.org/fileadmin/documents/working_papers/2407.pdf], accessed 8 July 2008.

Gasper, D. (2008) 'From "Hume's law" to policy analysis for human development', *Review of Political Economy*, 20(2), pp. 233–256.

Denis Goulet and the Project of Development Ethics

Gasper, D. and Truong, T.-D. (2005) 'Deepening development ethics — from economism to human development to human security', *European Journal of Development Research*, 17(3), pp. 372–384.

Goulet, D. (1960) 'Pour une éthique moderne du développement', *Développement et Civilisations*, 3 September, pp. 10–23. [Translated into English in Goulet (2006a).].

Goulet, D. (1965) *Etica Del Desarrollo*, Editora Estela/IEPAL, Barcelona/Montevideo.

Goulet, D. (1966) *Etica Do Desenvolvimento*, Libraria Duas Cidades, São Paulo.

Goulet, D. (1971a) *The Cruel Choice*, Atheneum, New York.

Goulet, D. (1971b) 'An ethical model for the study of values', *Harvard Educational Review*, 41(2), pp. 205–227.

Goulet, D. (1975) 'The high price of social change — on Peter Berger's pyramids of sacrifice', *Christianity and Crisis*, 35(16), pp. 231–237.

Goulet, D. (1976) 'On the ethics of development planning', *Studies in Comparative International Development*, 11(1), pp. 25–43.

Goulet, D. (1979) 'Development as Liberation: Policy Lessons form Case Studies', *World Development*, 7, pp. 555–566.

Goulet, D. (1984) 'Some complementary remarks on Panikkar's "Human Rights, A Western Concept"', *Interculture*, XVII(83), pp. 63–67.

Goulet, D. (1987) 'Culture and traditional values in development', in S. Stratigos and P.J. Hughes (Eds.), *The Ethics of Development: The Pacific in the 21st Century*, University of Papua New Guinea Press, Port Moresby, pp. 165–179.

Goulet, D. (1988) 'Tasks and methods in development ethics', *Cross Currents*, 38(2), pp. 146–163.

Goulet, D. (1989a) *The Uncertain Promise: Value Conflicts in Technology Transfer*, New Horizons Press, New York.

Goulet, D. (1989b) 'Participation in development: new avenues', *World Development*, 17(2), pp. 165–178.

Goulet, D. (1989c) *Incentives for Development: The Key to Equity*, New Horizons Press, New York.

Goulet, D. (1992a) 'Ethics and development: a development ethicist at work', *National Geographic Research & Exploration*, 8(2), pp. 138–147.

Goulet, D. (1992b) 'Interdisciplinary learning in the United States: old problems, new approaches', *American Studies*, XII, pp. 7–20.

Goulet, D. (1992c) 'Development indicators: a research problem, a policy problem', *The Journal of Socio-Economics*, 21(3), pp. 245–260.

Goulet, D. (1992d) 'International ethics and human rights', *Alternatives*, 17, pp. 231–246.

Goulet, D. (1995) *Development Ethics: A Guide to Theory and Practice*, The Apex Press, New York and Zed, London.

Goulet, D. (1997a) 'Development: costs, alternatives', in W.K. Cummings and N. McGinn (Eds.), *International Handbook of Education and Development*, Pergamon, Oxford, pp. 489–499.

Goulet, D. (1997b) 'Development ethics: a new discipline', *International Journal of Social Economics*, 24(11), pp. 1160–1171.

Goulet, D. (2000) 'The evolving nature of development in the light of globalization', in L. Sabourin (Ed.), *The Social Dimensions of Globalisation*, Pontifical Academy of Social Sciences, Vatican City, pp. 26–46.

Goulet, D. (2006a) *Development Ethics at Work: Explorations 1960–2002*, Routledge, New York.

Goulet, D. (2006b) 'Development ethics', in D.A. Clark (Ed.), *The Elgar Companion to Development Studies*, Edward Elgar, Cheltenham, pp. 115–121.

Gready, P. and Ensor, J. (Eds.) (2005) *Reinventing Development — Translating Rights-Based Approaches from Theory into Practice*, Zed, London.

Klitgaard, R. (1988) *Controlling Corruption*, University of California Press, Berkeley.

Krznaric, R. (2007) *How Change Happens — Interdisciplinary Perspectives for Human Development*, Oxfam Research Report, Oxfam, Oxford, [www.oxfam.org.uk/publications], accessed 8 July 2008.

D. Gasper

Lee, R. and Shute, J. (1991) 'An approach to naturalistic evaluation', *Evaluation Review*, 15(2), pp. 254–265.

Murphy, C. (2005) *Globalization, Institutions and Development*, Routledge, London.

Mwanahewa, S.A. (2006) 'Bribery: an exploration of uganda perspectives', *Ethics and Economics*, 4(2), [http://ethics-economics.com/Volume-4-Numero-2.html], accessed 8 July 2008.

Nussbaum, M. and Glover, J. (Eds.) (1995) *Women, Culture, and Development — A Study of Human Capabilities*, Clarendon, Oxford.

Pogge, T. (2002) *World Poverty and Human Rights*, Polity, Cambridge.

Porter, D., et al. (1991) *Development in Practice*, Routledge, London.

Rein, M. (1976) *Social Science and Public Policy*, Penguin, Harmondsworth.

Richards, H. (1985) *The Evaluation of Cultural Action*, Macmillan, Basingstoke.

Schaffer, K. and Smith, S. (2004) *Human Rights and Narrated Lives: The Ethics of Recognition*, Palgrave, London.

Schmidt, Ronald, Sr. (2006) 'Value-critical policy analysis — the case of language policy in the United States', in D. Yanow and P. Schwartz-Shea (Eds.), *Interpretation and Method*, M. E. Sharpe, New York, pp. 300–315.

Uphoff, N. (1996) *Learning from Gal-Oya*, Intermediate Technology, London.

Part II
Development and Underdevelopment: Experiences, Meanings and Evaluations

[5]

THE CONCEPT OF DEVELOPMENT

AMARTYA SEN*

1. The background

"The French grow too fast", wrote Sir William Petty in 1676. Whether or not this was in fact the first recorded expression of what is clearly a traditional English obsession, it was certainly a part of one of the earliest discussions of development economics. Petty was concerned not merely with the growth of numbers and of incomes, but he also took a broad view of development problems, including concern with the exact content of the standard of living. Part of his statistical analysis was meant "to show" that "the King's subjects are not in so bad a condition as discontented Men would make them". While Petty had estimated national income by using both the "income method" and the "expenditure method", he had also gone on to judge the conditions of people in a broad enough way to include "the Common Safety" and "each Man's particular Happiness".[1]

Petty is regarded, with justice, as one of the founders of modern economics, and specifically a pioneer of quantitative economics.[2] He was certainly also a founder of development economics. Indeed, in the early contributions to economics, development economics can hardly be separated out from the rest of economics, since so much of economics was, in fact, concerned with problems of economic development. This applies not only to Petty's writings, but also to those of the other pioneers of modern economics, including Gregory King, Francois Quesnay, Antoine Lavoisier, Joseph Louis Lagrange, and even Adam Smith. *An Inquiry into the Nature and Causes of the Wealth of Nations* was, in fact, also an inquiry into the basic issues of development economics.

The fact that in the early writings in economics there was this noticeable congruence of development economics and economics in general is a matter of some interest, especially in the context of investigating the nature of "the concept of development". Interest in development problems has, traditionally, provided one of the deepest *motivations* for the pursuit of economics in general, and this broad basis of development economics has to be borne in mind when investigat-

---

*For helpful discussions and comments, I am most grateful to Hollis Chenery, T.N. Srinivasan and Paul Streeten.

[1]*Political Arithmetick*, in which these passages occur, was written by Petty around 1676 but it was published posthumously in 1691. The text could be found in Hull (1899, vol. I). The passages referred to can be found on pages 241–242, 311.

[2]It may be remembered that it was Petty, the anatomist and musicologist, turned economist, who had insisted at the Royal Society that in discussions in the society, "no word might be used but what marks either number, weight, or measure" [Hull (1899, vol. I, p. lxiv)]. Those who complain about the "recent craze" for mathematical economics might have to put up with the fact that the recent times began a long time ago.

ing the details of the concept of development. Having started off, rightly, with an ell, development economics can scarcely settle for an inch.

It is not hard to see why the concept of development is so essential to economics in general. Economic problems do, of course, involve logistic issues, and a lot of it is undoubtedly "engineering" of one kind or another. On the other hand, the success of all this has to be judged ultimately in terms of what it does to the lives of human beings. The enhancement of living conditions must clearly be an essential – if not *the* essential – object of the entire economic exercise and that enhancement is an integral part of the concept of development. Even though the logistic and engineering problems involved in enhancing living conditions in the poor, developing countries might well be very different from those in the rich, developed ones, there is much in common in the respective exercises on the two sides of the divide [on this see Bauer (1971)].

Sometimes development economists have been rather protective of their own domain, insisting on separating development economics from the rest of economics. While the underlying motivation behind this effort is easy to understand, it is important not to make too much of the divide, nor to confuse separateness with independence. Tools of standard economics may have much fruitful use in development economics as well, even when the exact problems addressed happen to be quite specialized. It is, however, arguable that for one reason or another, a good deal of standard economics has tended to move away from broad issues of poverty, misery and well-being, and from the fulfilment of basic needs and enhancing the quality of life. Development economists have felt it necessary to emphasize and justify their involvement with these – rather "old-fashioned" – problems, even though the relevance of these problems is by no means confined to development economics. There are also institutional differences that separate out the logistic issues in developing countries from those of developed ones, in the pursuit of economic development and the enhancement of living conditions.

Certainly, the systematic differences in institutional features is a matter of great moment in arriving at policies and deriving practical lessons regarding what is to be done. But the first issue – the emphasis on development objectives – is not a matter only for development economics as such, but of importance for economics in general [see Hirschman (1970)]. In this respect, too, insisting on a sharp division between development economics and other types of economics would be rather counter-productive. Development economics, it can be argued, has to be concerned not only with protecting its "own" territory, but also with keeping alive the foundational motivation of the subject of economics in general. The literature on the "concept of development" – whether explicitly put forward or discussed by implication – has to be examined in this broad perspective related to economics in general, rather than only in terms of "development economics" narrowly defined.

2. Production, growth, and development

The close link between economic development and economic growth is simultaneously a matter of importance as well as a source of considerable confusion. There can scarcely be any doubt that, given other things, an expansion of opulence must make a contribution to the living conditions of the people in question. It was, therefore, entirely natural that the early writings in development economics, when it emerged as a subject on its own after the Second World War, concentrated to a great extent on ways of achieving economic growth, and in particular increasing the gross national product (GNP) and total employment [see Rosenstein-Rodan (1943), Mandelbaum (1945), Dobb (1951), Datta (1952), Singer (1952), Nurkse (1953), Dasgupta (1954), Lewis (1955), Baran (1957), Hirschman (1958)]. The process of economic development cannot abstract from expanding the supply of food, clothing, housing, medical services, educational facilities, etc. and from transforming the productive structure of the economy, and these important and crucial changes are undoubtedly matters of economic growth.

The importance of "growth" must depend on the nature of the variable the expansion of which is considered and seen as "growth". The crucial issue, therefore, is not the time-dimensional focus of growth, but the salience and reach of GNP and related variables on which usual measures of growth concentrate. The relation between GNP and living conditions is far from simple.[3] To illustrate the problem, figures for GNP per head and life expectancy at birth in 1984 are given in Table 1.1 for five different countries, namely, China, Sri Lanka, Brazil, Mexico, and South Africa. South Africa, with about seven times the GNP per

Table 1.1
GNP and life expectancy

	GNP per head, 1984 (U.S. Dollars)	Life expectancy at at birth, 1984 (years)
China	310	69
Sri Lanka	360	70
Brazil	1,720	64
Mexico	2,040	66
South Africa	2,340	54

Source: World Bank (1986).

[3] For discussions on this, see Adelman and Morris (1973), Sen (1973), Adelman (1975), Grant (1978), Morris (1979), Kakwani (1981), Streeten (1981), Streeten et al. (1981), Stewart (1985), Anand and Harris (1986).

head of China and Sri Lanka, has a substantially lower expectation of life than the latter countries. Similarly, Brazil and Mexico also with many times the income of China and Sri Lanka have achieved considerably less in longevity than these two much poorer countries. To point to this contrast is not, of course, the same thing as drawing an immediate policy conclusion as to exactly what should be done, but the nature of the contrast has to be borne in mind in refusing to identify economic development with mere economic growth. Even though an expansion of GNP, *given other things*, should enhance the living conditions of people, and will typically expand the life expectancy figures of that country, there are many other variables that also influence the living conditions, and the concept of development cannot ignore the role of these other variables.

. Life expectancy is, of course, a very limited measure of what has been called "the quality of life". Indeed, in terms of what it directly measures, life expectancy is more an index of the "quantity" of life rather than of its quality. But the forces that lead to mortality, such as morbidity, ill health, hunger, etc. also tend to make the living conditions of the people more painful, precarious, and unfulfilling, so that life expectancy may, to some extent, serve as a proxy for other variables of importance as well. Furthermore, if we shift our attention from life expectancy to these other important variables, the relationship with GNP per head does not become any more immediate. Indeed, some of the variables related to living conditions, e.g. the prevalence of crime and violence, may sometimes have even a perverse relationship with average material prosperity.

This is a problem that applies not only to the poor, developing countries, but also to the richer ones. In fact, various studies of perception of welfare done in western Europe have suggested a rather limited role of real income in self-assessment of personal welfare [see van Praag (1978), Allardt (1981), van Herwaarden and Kapteyn (1981), Erikson, Hansen, Ringen and Uusitalo (1986)]. Reliance of self-assessment based on questionnaire information does, of course, have some problematic features also, but nevertheless there is enough evidence here to question the rather straightforward connection between material prosperity and welfare that is sometimes taken for granted in standard economic analysis.

In drawing a distinction between development and growth, a number of different sources of contrast have to be clearly distinguished from each other. First of all, insofar as economic growth is concerned only with GNP per head, it leaves out the question of the *distribution* of that GNP among the population. It is, of course, possible for a country to have an expansion of GNP per head, while its distribution becomes more unequal, possibly even the poorest groups going down absolutely in terms of their own real incomes. Noting this type of possibility does not question the relevance of income considerations as such, but argues against taking only an aggregated view of incomes. Undoubtedly, some of the cases in which achievements in living conditions fall far behind what might be expected on the basis of average per capita GNP (e.g. in South Africa, and to a lesser extent in Brazil and Mexico, as reflected in Table 1.1) relate closely to the distributional question. Indeed, the contrast can be brought out even more sharply by looking also at the distribution of life expectancy (and of mortality and morbidity rates) over the population (e.g. between the racial and class groups in South Africa, and class and regional categories in Brazil and Mexico).

A second source of difference between growth and development relates to the question of *externality* and *non-marketability*. The GNP captures only those means of well-being that happen to be transacted in the market, and this leaves out benefits and costs that do not have a price-tag attached to them. Even when non-marketed goods are included (e.g. peasant outputs consumed at home), the evaluation is usually restricted to those goods which have a market and for which market prices can be easily traced.[4] The importance of what is left out has become increasingly recognized, as awareness of the contribution of the environment and natural resources to our well-being has grown [see Dasgupta and Heal (1979), Dasgupta (1982)]. The argument can be applied to the social environment as well as to the physical one [see Hirschman (1958, 1970)].

Third, even when markets do exist, the valuation of commodities in the GNP will reflect the *biases* that the markets may have. There are important problems in dealing with different relative prices in different parts of the world. As has been shown by Usher (1968, 1976) and others, this can make quite a substantial quantitative difference. Even for a given economy, the relative importance that is attached to one commodity compared with another may be distorted vis-à-vis what might be achieved under perfectly competitive conditions if the market operations happen to be institutionally "imperfect", or if equilibrium outcomes do not prevail. There is an extensive welfare-economic literature on this, and the connection of that range of issues with the concept of development is obvious enough.

Fourth, the real income enjoyed by a person in a given year reflects at best the extent of well-being enjoyed by that person at that period of time. However, in assessing what kind of a life the person has succeeded in living, we have to take a more *integral* view of that person's life. The issues to be considered include interdependences over time [e.g. inter-period complementarities emphasized by Hicks (1965) among others], as well as the more elementary question of the *length* of that life. It is easy to construct two scenarios in which the time series of *per capita* GNP as well as *aggregate* GNP (and, of course, the population size) happen to be exactly the same in the two cases (period by period), but in one society people live twice as long as those in the other. There are difficult evaluative problems in judging what the "trade-off" should be between larger number, on the one hand, and longer life, on the other, but no matter in which

---

[4] Even when such market prices exist, reflecting the balance of actual demand and supply, the proper valuation of the non-traded units of tradeable variables may be far from easy. On the problem of including the value of leisure and leisure time expended at home, in the light of wage rates, see Nordhaus and Tobin (1972).

direction one argues, there is an issue here of great importance to the assessment of development that is completely obscured by the GNP information. Even if GNP did everything it is expected to do (and there are very strong reasons for doubting this possibility), even then the information provided by GNP must remain fundamentally inadequate for the concept of development.

Finally, it must be noted that GNP is, in fact, a measure of the amount of the *means* of well-being that people have, and it does not tell us what the people involved are succeeding in getting out of these means, given their ends. To take a crude example, two persons with different metabolic rates and consuming the same amount of food will quite possibly achieve rather different levels of nourishment. Insofar as being well nourished is an important end, their actual achievements will be different, despite the congruence of their command over the *means* of achieving nourishment. As it happens, "poverty lines" have typically been defined in developing countries in the light of the "requirements" of some basic commodities, in particular food, and the inter-personal as well as the intra-personal variability in the relationship between food and nourishment have been, in this context, a major problem to deal with.[5]

Ultimately, the assessment of development achieved cannot be a matter only of quantification of the *means* of that achievement. The concept of development has to take note of the actual achievements themselves. The assessment of development has to go well beyond GNP information, *even when* the other difficulties referred to earlier (such as distributional variation, presence of externalities and non-marketabilities, imperfect price mechanisms, etc.) were somehow overcome.

3. Characteristics, functionings, and living

Insofar as development is concerned with the achievement of a better life, the focus of development analysis has to include the nature of the life that people succeed in living. This incorporates, of course, the *length* of the life itself, and thus life expectancy data have an immediate relevance to the living standard and through that to the concept of development. But the nature of the life that people succeed in living in each period is also a matter of importance. People value their ability to do certain things and to achieve certain types of beings (such as being well nourished, being free from avoidable morbidity, being able to move about as desired, and so on). These "doings" and "beings" may be generically called "functionings" of a person.

The well-being of a person can be seen as an evaluation of the functionings achieved by that person. This approach has been implicitly used by Adam Smith (1776) and Karl Marx (1844) in particular, and more recently in the literature on

---

[5]For arguments on different sides of this debate, see Bardhan (1974), Sukhatme (1977), Srinivasan (1982), Lipton (1983), Gopalan (1983), Dasgupta and Ray (1986), Kakwani (1986), Osmani (1987).

"the quality of life" [see, for example, Morris (1979), Streeten (1981)].[6] It can be more explicitly developed, conceptually defended, and empirically applied [on this see Sen (1980, 1985a)]. The functioning achievements are, of course, causally related to commodity possession and use, and thus the constituent elements of the GNP do enter the *determination* of functioning achievements. Indeed, these elements are the means of which the functionings are the ends – a point of view clearly presented by Aristotle in *Nicomachean Ethics* and *Politics*.

In recent departures in consumer theory, developed by Gorman (1956, 1976) and Lancaster (1966, 1971), commodities are viewed in terms of their characteristics. This is clearly a move in the right direction as far as well-being is concerned, since the functionings achieved by a person relate to the characteristics of the commodities used. On the other hand, no index of characteristics as such could possibly serve as an indicator of the achievements of a person, since the conversion of characteristics into functionings can and does vary from person to person. Characteristics of commodities are impersonal in a way that functionings cannot be, since the latter are features of *persons*, whereas the former are features of *commodities*. The relationships between commodities, characteristics, and functionings, and the sources of variations in their interconnections, have been discussed elsewhere [see Sen (1980, 1985a, 1985b)].

The achievement of functionings depends not only on the commodities owned by the person in question, but also on the availability of public goods, and the possibility of using private goods freely provided by the state. Such achievements as being healthy, being well-nourished, being literate, etc. would depend naturally also on the public provisions of health services, medical facilities, educational arrangements, and so on. In recognizing this, there is no need yet to enter into the debate, which is important but need not be pursued here, as to whether provision by the state is a cost-effective way of enhancing the relevant functionings involved. That debate about development strategy will involve logistic and engineering issues, which require careful assessment. What is being pointed out here is the importance of judging development in terms of *functionings achieved*, and of seeing in that light the availability and use of the *means* to those functionings (in the form of possession of commodities, availability of public goods, and so on).

4. Freedom and capability

One of the functionings that may be thought to be particularly important in assessing the nature of development is the freedom to choose. Sometimes this

[6]See also Sen (1973, 1985b), Adelman (1975), Scanlon (1975), Gwatkin, Wilcox and Wray (1980), Floud and Wachter (1982), Fogel, Engerman and Trussell (1982), Gopalan (1983), Panikar and Soman (1984), UNICEF (1986), Chen (1986), Williams (1987).

concept is used in a rather narrow and limited way, so that the *actual* freedom to choose is not assessed, but instead the focus is on whether there are *restraints* imposed by others that hinder the actual freedom. That "negative" perspective, much pursued in the libertarian literature, does have, of course, philosophical standing of its own [see Hayek (1960), Berlin (1969), Nozick (1974)]. However, what is important to recognize in the present context is the fact that the "negative" emphasis on the absence of restraint is part of a moral approach that does not judge the goodness of a society in terms of the actual qualities of life *achieved* by the members of the society, and concentrates instead on the correctness of the *processes* through which these and other achievements come about. It is possible to debate whether the particular insistence on *processes* that do not involve such restraint is, in fact, as convincing as it clearly is to some exponents of this point of view. But in the present context, we need not enter into that large and important debate. It is sufficient here to note that as far as the living standards of the people are concerned, there is no escape from focusing on *achievements*, and processes come into all this mainly as means to and antecedents of those achievements, rather than being *independently* valuable in this context.

However, the *positive* freedom to be able to choose is, in fact, an important functioning on its own rights. Two persons who have identical achievements of *other* functionings may not still be seen as enjoying the same level of well-being if one of the two has no option to choose any other bundle of functionings, whereas the second person has significant options. Being able to freely choose to lead a particular life may be a point of a richer description of the life we lead, including the choices we are able to make [on this perspective, see Sen (1985a)].

A person's capability can be seen as the set of alternative functioning n-tuples any one of which the person can choose. One way of introducing the importance of freedom in the determination of well-being is to see well-being as a function not only of the actual functioning achievement, but also of the capability set from which that n-tuple of functionings is chosen. In this way of formally characterizing the problem, the list of functionings need not include "choosing" as such, but the value of choosing will be reflected in the evaluation by making that evaluation depend both on the chosen n-tuple of functionings, *and* on the nature and the range of the capability set itself.

There are difficult analytical problems involved in the evaluation of a set, in the light of the freedom it offers [on this see Koopmans (1964), Kreps (1979), Sen (1985b)]. But insofar as the assessment of the quality of life and of development achievements involves these considerations, it is important not to lose sight of this perspective, even though it may not be immediately possible to make extensive use of this approach in actual empirical exercises.

A different way of looking at this problem involves incorporating the freedom to choose in the nature of the functionings themselves by defining them in a "refined" way [see Sen (1985a)]. Choosing to do x when one could have chosen any member of a set S, can be defined as a "refined functioning" x/S. The point can be brought out by considering the functioning of "fasting". When a person fasts he is clearly starving, but the nature of that functioning includes the choice *not* to so starve. A person who has no option but to starve (because, say, of his extreme poverty) cannot be said to be fasting. In assessing the achievements of the persons and of the society, the distinction between fasting and willy-nilly starving may well be very important. The route of "refined functionings", taking note of substantive exercise of choice, provides one particular way of incorporating the aspect of freedom in the assessment of functionings.

5. Weights and rankings

It should be clear that the perspective of functionings and capabilities specifies a *space* in which evaluation is to take place, rather than proposing one particular formula for evaluation. The exercise has to begin with an identification of valuable functionings. In the context of economic development, there might well be considerable agreement as to what functionings are valuable, even though there might be disagreement on the *relative* values to be attached to the different functionings. When an agreed list has been arrived at, the approach of "dominance" provides a *minimal* partial order on that space (in terms of greater achievement in *every* respect).

To go further than this will require more articulate evaluation functions. But these evaluations need not be based on a unique set of "indifference curves". The relative values may be specified as belonging to particular ranges, and corresponding to such specification of ranges, the overall ranking may be a partial order more extensive than the minimal dominance order but probably well short of a complete ordering. As the ranges of relative values are narrowed, the partial ordering will be extended. The mathematical technology involved in such evaluation (based on "intersection partial orderings") has been extensively used in other contexts [see, for example, Sen (1970), Blackorby (1975), Fine (1975), Basu (1979)]. The important thing to note here is that the problem of evaluation need not be seen in an all-or-nothing way. It is possible to extend the partial order by narrowing the ranges of weights, and how far one can go on the basis of agreement on evaluation will depend contingently on the nature of the exercise in question.

Even the specification of the space of functionings and capabilities does, however, have considerable cutting power. Achievements of real income and opulence may differ quite substantially from that of functionings and capabilities. To give just one example, in a comparison of the states in India, Kerala always figures as one of the poorest, in terms of GNP per head. On the other hand, in terms of many of the more important functionings, including living long, being educated, etc. Kerala does better than any other Indian state. Given this contrast, it is interesting to ask whether Kerala should be seen as having *more* achievement *or* rather *less* than the other Indian states. This relates to a question of considerable importance to the formulation of the concept of development. The argument for placing Kerala at the high end, rather than the low end, turns on the evaluation of functionings and capabilities as the right approach to development.

A crude assessment of functionings and capabilities in terms only of a few indicators like longevity, literacy, etc. will, of course, be inadequate and have to be revised and extended, but the exercise can be systematically done if and only if the concept of development is seen in terms of ends rather than means. As it happens, use of information regarding *morbidity* detracts somewhat from Kerala's high record, since the extent of illness seems to be rather large in Kerala, in comparison with some other Indian states, even after taking note of the greater "awareness" of health conditions in a population that is more educated and better served by public health services [on this see Pankar and Soman (1984), Kumar (1987)]. The adoption of the perspective of functionings and capabilities will call for a great deal of empirical as well as theoretical work being done within that general format.

As was argued earlier, that format is, of course, an old one in economics, even though the focus on opulence on the one hand and utility on the other has tended to deflect attention from that fundamental concern. Aside from discussions by Aristotle, Smith, and Marx, to which reference was made earlier, it should be mentioned that ad hoc uses of this perspective can be found extensively in the economic literature. In many planning exercises, the specification of objectives has included a clear recognition of the importance of certain functionings, e.g. in the specification of a "minimum level of living" [see Pant (1962)]. The literature on development indicators has also brought in some of these functionings, along with many other types of variables [see, for example, Adelman and Morris (1973), Adelman (1975), Kakwani (1981), Streeten (1981)].

The literature on "basic needs" also relates to this question, since the specification of basic needs of commodities has to be related to the recognition of their role in the achievement of functionings. Even though the *space* in which the basic needs have typically been specified has been that of commodities rather than of functionings and capabilities, the motivation clearly does relate to attaching importance to the latter [see, for example, Streeten (1981), and Streeten et al. (1981)].

The literature on basic needs has been growing rapidly in the recent years, but clear discussions of this question can be found even in Pigou's classic book *Economics of Welfare* (1952). Of course, Pigou related his focus on the command over a minimal basket of commodities to the utilitarian perspective, whereas in the modern literature quite often the foundational features have not been specified. It is arguable that these foundational questions are ultimately quite important for the concept of development, and it is precisely in that context that the capability approach provides a different strategy of assessment, more clearly geared to the evaluation of living as such rather than merely of the happiness generated by that living (as in the utilitarian approach). This is not the occasion to pursue the philosophical differences further [I have tried to do this elsewhere; Sen (1985a)], but there is no escape from recognizing the importance of this foundational question underlying the concept of development.

6. Values, instruments, and objects

One of the difficulties in adequately characterizing the concept of development arises from the essential role of evaluation in that concept. What is or is not regarded as a case of "development" depends inescapably on the notion of what things are valuable to promote.[7] The dependence of the concept of development on evaluation becomes a problem to the extent that (1) the valuation functions accepted by different people differ from each other, and (2) the process of change involved in development alters the valuations of the people involved. These two problems may be called respectively " value-heterogeneity" and " value-endogeneity".

The problem of value-heterogeneity was already addressed earlier in the context of valuations of functionings and capabilities. It was pointed out that even when there are disagreements on the relative values to be attached to different functionings and capabilities, it is still possible to get uncontroversial partial orderings, based minimally on "dominance", but more extensively on "intersections" of the class of acceptable valuation functions. It is, of course, a matter of substantive normative analysis to argue in favor of some valuation functions against others, and insofar as the ranges of disagreement could be reduced through this means, the scope and reach of "intersection partial orderings" can be correspondingly enhanced.

Much of traditional development economics has proceeded on the basis of implicitly assuming a fairly large intersection of valuations related to objects of development. Even though the original discussions of economic development had tended to concentrate on the GNP and real income as such, the evaluation underlying that approach was implicitly based on assuming a widespread agreement on the *ends* to which real income and opulence are *means*. The shift in the focus of attention to basic needs, quality of life, and functionings and capabilities in general, would not change the assumed agreement on the underlying basis of

---

[7]On this general question, see Marglin and Marglin (1986).

development analysis. The problem of value-heterogeneity is undoubtedly serious, but it is by no means absurd to think that the actual extent of agreement is indeed quite large. Most of the debates on development policy have tended to concentrate on the relationship between policy instruments and *agreed* ends (accepted in the analysis of policy).

It is, however, possible that a more explicit characterization of well-being and of people's freedom to achieve what they would value achieving will increase the demand for data and information in the conceptualization of development. For example, the scope for using more demographic and health-related information is certainly great in assessing the real achievements of development, and recent works dealing with the past as well as the present have outlined the necessity of seeking this type of information, neglected in traditional development analysis.[8]

It is possible that once these informational needs are recognized, there might again emerge a fair degree of consensus on what is to be valued and how. On the other hand, it is also possible that there might be much disagreement regarding the respective importance of different aspects of well-being. Some of these differences might involve scientific argumentation as to the precise role of different variables in human functioning. For example, whether an expansion of body size related to the process of economic development is an achievement of importance can be disputed in terms of the alleged presence or absence of relations between body size and performance. The conversion of nutrients into body characteristics *and* the role of body characteristics in achieving valuable functionings both call for close scrutiny.[9]

Other disputes may turn not on factual relations, but on what is to be regarded as an important part of a valuable life and how valuable it is. It would be idle to pretend that disputes on the relative importance of different types of functionings can be fully resolved on the basis of scientific argument alone. It is, therefore, particularly important to build into the concept of development the possibility of persistent incompleteness in ranking. Seeing the agreed ranking as the intersection of the partly divergent valuation functions must, of necessity, entail this.

The value-endogeneity problem raises issues of a somewhat different kind from those raised by value-heterogeneity. With value-heterogeneity the intersection partial ordering may have to be silent on some comparisons, but insofar as judgements are possible, they can be made on the basis of a *given* valuation function (whether or not complete). Value-endogeneity, on the other hand, raises what is, in some ways, a deeper problem, to wit, the *dependence* of the valuation function on the thing that is being valued. The process of development may bring about changes in what is regarded as valuable and what weights are attached to

[8] See, in particular, Sen (1973, 1985b), Floud and Wachter (1982), Fogel, Engerman and Trussell (1982), Gopalan (1983), Panikar and Soman (1984), UNICEF (1986), Williams (1987).
[9] For different views on this subject, see, for example, Sukhatme (1977), Srinivasan (1982), Gopalan (1983), Fogel (1986), Dasgupta and Ray (1986), Kakwani (1986), Osmani (1987).

these objects. There are complex philosophical issues involved in judging changed conditions, when those changes bring about alterations in the values attached to these conditions.[10]

However, in this problem too there is a possibility of using an "intersection" technique. A change may be judged to be an improvement if it is superior *both* in terms of the antecedent values *and* subsequent values, i.e. prospectively better than the available alternatives and also retrospectively better than the rejected alternatives. In this case, there may be at least a pragmatic argument in favor of regarding this to be a genuine improvement, even though a purist might doubt whether such judgements can at all be taken as definitive when they are *generally* volatile (even though not, as it happens, in a way that affects the judgement of *this particular* change). Even this pragmatic justification will not obtain if the judgements based on antecedent values differ on the particular issue under discussion from those based on subsequent ones. It is possible for a change to be regarded as worse in terms of the earlier values, but better in terms of valuations made after the event.

In the more philosophical literature, the case for seeing valuations as having a certain measure of objectivity has increasingly gained ground compared with the situation that obtained some decades ago.[11] The "objectivist" position is, in fact, in line with very old traditions in ethics and political economy (going back at least to Aristotle), even though it was extremely unfashionable at the time development economics emerged as a subject, when the dominant schools of methodology were "positivism" of various types. The "objectivist" position would tend to support the possibility of resolving the conflicts involved in intertemporal changes in values by rational assessment.

These foundational issues will not be purused further here. It is sufficient for the present purpose to note that no matter what view is taken of the nature of valuation, the practical problems of making judgement in the situation of value-heterogeneity and value-endogeneity must be enormous. Even if these differences could in principle be resolved through rational assessment, the possibility of actually resolving these differences in practice may be severely limited. Given that fact, the necessity of settling for partial orders in response to value-endogeneity as well as value-heterogeneity is, to some extent, inescapable.

Explicitly facing these problems of valuation has some advantages which should be emphasized. First, separating out relatively uncontroversial judgements from the controversial ones related to value-heterogeneity and value-endogeneity, helps to clarify what can be asserted with some confidence, and what can be said only with much greater hesitation. A lot of the debates on policy making in the

---

[10] For an interesting discussion of this question, see Elster (1979, 1983). Some similar issues are raised in consumer theory when tastes are taken as endogenous [see, for example, von Weizsacker (1971), Pollak (1978)]. See also Hirschman (1970).

[11] See in particular, McDowell (1981), Nagel (1980, 1986), Hurley (1985), Wiggins (1985).

context of economic development relates to valuation problems that are not unduly problematic. Whether state intervention or reliance on the market may be better means of enhancing living conditions is, of course, both important and controversial, but the controversy has typically centered, rightly, on the relationship between means and achievements, rather than on differences in valuation. By explicitly facing the sources of the difficulties in valuation, it is possible to give those debates a deeper foundation, without compromising the broad motivation underlying development economics.

Second, in some parts of the development literature, values have been treated as if they are simply *instrumental* to economic development, rather than the ultimate basis of judging the nature of development itself. For example, encouraging the valuation of profits and that of enterprise has often been seen as good *means* of development. Certainly, in terms of the dependence of economic growth on particular motivations these propositions can be helpfully presented and assessed. On the other hand, it is also important to recognize that values are not *just* instruments, but also views about what should or should not be promoted. This dual role of values – both important and neither sacrificable – was recognized clearly enough by pioneers of modern economics, including Adam Smith (1776, 1790) and Karl Marx (1844, 1875). The foundational role of values can be neglected in favor of an instrumental view only by trivializing the basis of the concept of development.

7. Conclusion

The concept of development is by no means unproblematic. The different problems underlying the concept have become clearer over the years on the basis of conceptual discussions as well as from insights emerging from empirical work. Insofar as these problems have become clearer, something of substance has in fact been achieved, and the demise of the brashness which characterized the initiation of development economics need not be seen entirely as a loss. A clearer recognition of the difficulties and problems is certainly a step in the direction of enhancing our ability to tackle them.

Work on valuational problems will undoubtedly continue. Meanwhile, the agreed valuations in the form of emphasizing the importance of certain basic achievements in life make it possible for us to pursue practical debates on policy and action on the basis of an acceptable valuational foundation. Since many of these debates relate to matters of life and death, well-being and illness, happiness and misery, freedom and vulnerability, the underlying objectives are perspicuous enough and command broad agreement. Work on development economics need not await a complete "solution" of the concept of development.

24   *A. Sen*

References

Adelman, I. (1975) 'Development economics – a reassessment of goals', *American Economic Review, Papers and Proceedings*, 65.
Adelman, I. and C.T. Morris (1973) *Economic growth and social equity in developing countries*. Stanford: Stanford University Press.
Allardt, E. (1981) 'Experiences from the comparative Scandinavian welfare study, with a bibliography of the project', *European Journal of Political Research*, 9.
Anand, S. and C. Harris (1986) 'Food and living standard: implications for food strategies', WIDER, Helsinki, mimeo.
Baran, P. (1957) *Political economy of growth*. New York: Monthly Review Press.
Bardhan, P.K. (1974) 'On the incidence of poverty in rural India in the sixties', in: T.N. Srinivasan and P.K. Bardhan, eds., *Poverty and income distribution in India*. Calcutta: Statistical Publishing Society.
Basu, K. (1979) *Revealed preference of government*. Cambridge: Cambridge University Press.
Bauer, P.T. (1971) *Dissent on development*. London: Weidenfeld and Nicholson.
Berlin, I. (1969) *Four essays on liberty*. Oxford: Clarendon Press.
Blackorby, C. (1975) 'Degrees of cardinality and aggregate partial ordering', *Econometrica*, 43.
Chen. L.C. (1986) 'Primary health care in developing countries: Overcoming operational, technical, and social barriers', *Lancet*, 2.
Dasgupta, A.K. (1954) 'Keynesian economics and underdeveloped countries', *Economic Weekly*, 6 (January 26). Reprinted in *Planning and economic growth*. London: Allen & Unwin (1965).
Dasgupta, P. (1982) *The control of resources*. Oxford: Blackwells.
Dasgupta, P. and G. Heal (1979) *Economic theory and exhaustible resources*. London: James Nisbet; Cambridge: Cambridge University Press.
Dasgupta, P. and D. Ray (1986) 'Adapting to undernutrition: Clinical evidence and its implications', WIDER, Helsinki, working paper. Forthcoming in Drèze and Sen (1988).
Datta, B. (1952) *Economics of industrialization*. Calcutta: World Press.
Dobb, M.H. (1951) *Some aspects of economic development*. Dehli: Dehli School of Economics.
Drèze, J. and A. Sen (1988) *Hunger: Economic and policy*. Oxford: Clarendon Press. To be published.
Elster, J. (1979) *Ulysses and the sirens*. Cambridge: Cambridge University Press.
Elster, J. (1983) *Sour grapes*. Cambridge: Cambridge University Press.
Erikson, R., E.J. Hansen, S. Ringen, and H. Uusitalo (1986) *The Scandinavian way: Welfare state and welfare research*. Forthcoming.
Fine, B. (1975) "A note on 'interpersonal comparisons and partial comparability'", *Econometrica*, 43.
Floud, R. and K.W. Wachter (1982) 'Poverty and physical stature: Evidence on the standard of living of London boys 1770–1870', *Social Science History*, 6.
Fogel, R.W. (1986) 'Nutrition and the decline in mortality since 1700: Some additional preliminary findings', National Bureau of Economic Research, Cambridge MA, working paper 182.
Fogel, R.W., S.L. Engerman, and J. Trussell (1982) 'Exploring the use of data on height: The analysis of long-term trends in nutrition, labour productivity', *Social Science History*, 6.
Gopalan, C. (1983) 'Measurement of undernutrition: Biological considerations', *Economic and Political Weekly*, 19 (April 9).
Gorman, W.M. (1956) 'The demand for related goods', Iowa Experimental Station, Ames, IA, journal paper J3129.
Gorman, W.M. (1976) 'Tricks with utility function', in: M.J. Artis and A.R. Nobay, eds., *Essays in economic analysis*. Cambridge: Cambridge University Press.
Grant, J.P. (1978) *Disparity reduction rates in social indicators*. Washington, DC: Overseas Development Council.
Gwatkin, D.R., J.R. Wilcox, and J.D. Wray (1980) 'The policy implications of field experience in primary health and nutrition', *Social Science and Medicine*, 14C.
Hayek, F.A. (1960) *The constitution of liberty*. London: Routledge & Kegan Paul.
Hicks, J.R. (1965) *Capital and growth*. Oxford: Clarendon Press.
Hirschman, A.O. (1958) *The strategy of economic development*. New Haven: Yale University Press.
Hirschman, A.O. (1970) *Exit, voice and loyalty*. Cambridge, MA: Harvard University Press.
Honderich, T., ed. (1985) *Morality and objectivity*. London: Routledge.

Hull, C.H., ed. (1899) *The economic writings of Sir William Petty*. Cambridge: Cambridge University Press.

Hurley, S. (1985) 'Objectivity and disagreement', in: T. Honderich (1985).

Kakwani, N.C. (1981) 'Welfare measures: An international comparison', *Journal of Development Economics*, 8.

Kakwani, N.C. (1986) 'On measuring undernutrition', WIDER, Helsinki, working paper. Forthcoming in *Oxford Economic Papers*.

Koopmans, T.C. (1964) 'On the flexibility of future preferences', in: M.W. Shelly and G.L. Bryan, eds., *Human judgements and optimality*. New York: Wiley.

Kreps, D.M. (1979) "A representation theorem for 'preference for flexibility'", *Econometrica*, 47.

Kumar, B.G. (1987) 'Poverty and public policy : Government intervention and levels of living in Kerala, India', D. Phil. dissertation, Oxford University. To be published.

Lancaster, K.J. (1966) 'A new approach to consumer theory', *Journal of Political Economy*, 74.

Lancaster, K.J. (1971) *Consumer demand: A new approach*. New York: Columbia University Press.

Lewis, W.A. (1955) *The theory of economic growth*. Homewood, IL: Irwin.

Lipton, M. (1983) *Poverty, undernutrition and hunger*, World Bank Staff Working Paper. Washington, DC: World Bank.

McDowell, J. (1981) 'Noncognitivism and rule-following', in: S.H. Holtzman and C.M. Leich, eds., *Wittgenstein: To follow a rule*. London: Routledge & Kegan Paul.

McMurrin, S. (1980) *Tanner lectures on human values*, vol. I. Cambridge: Cambridge University Press.

Mandelbaum (Martin), K. (1945) *The industrialization of backward areas*. Oxford: Blackwell.

Marglin, F. and S. Marglin, eds. (1986) 'Development and technological transformation in traditional societies: Alternative approachers', papers presented at a WIDER conference. To be published.

Marx, K. (1844) *The economic and philosophic manuscript of 1844*, English translation. London: Lawrence & Wishart.

Marx, K. (1875) *Critique of the Gotha programme*, English translation. New York: International Publishers.

Morris, M.D. (1979) *Measuring the conditions of the world's poor: The physical quality of life index*. Oxford: Pergamon.

Nagel, T. (1980) 'The limits of objectivity', in: S. McMurrin (1980).

Nagel, T. (1986). *The view from nowhere*. Oxford: Clarendon Press.

Nordhaus, W. and J. Tobin (1972) 'Is growth obsolete?', in: National Bureau of Economic Research, *Economic growth: Fiftieth anniversary colloquium*. New York: NBER.

Nozick, R. (1974) *Anarchy, state and utopia*. Oxford: Blackwell.

Nurkse, R. (1953) *Problems of capital formation in underdeveloped countries*. Oxford: Blackwell.

Osmani, S.R. (1987) 'Nutrition and the economics of food', WIDER, Helsinki, working paper. Forthcoming in Drèze and Sen (1988).

Panikar, P.G.K. and C.R. Soman (1984) *Health status of Kerala*. Trivandrum: Centre for Development Studies.

Pant, P. et al. (1962) *Perspective of development 1961–1976. Implication of planning for a minimum level of living*. New Delhi: Planning Commission of India.

Parfit, D. (1984) *Reasons and persons*. Oxford: Clarendon Press.

Petty, W. (1676) *Political arithmetick*. Republished in: C.H. Hull (1899).

Pigou, A.C. (1952) *The economics of welfare*, 4th ed., with eight new appendices. London: Macmillan.

Pollak, R.A. (1978) 'Endogenous tastes in demand and welfare analysis', *American Economic Review, Papers and Proceedings*, 68.

Rosenstein-Rodan, P. (1943) 'Problems of industrialization in Eastern and Southeastern Europe', *Economic Journal*, 53.

Scanlon, T.M. (1975) 'Preference and urgency', *Journal of Philosophy*, 73.

Sen, A.K. (1970) 'Interpersonal aggregation and partial comparability', *Econometrica*, 38; 'A correction', *Econometrica*, 40.

Sen, A.K. (1973) 'On the development of basic income indicators to supplement GNP measures', *Economic Bulletin for Asia and the Far East (United Nations)*, 24.

Sen, A.K. (1980) 'Equality of what?', in: S. McMurrin (1980).

Sen, A.K. (1985a) 'Well-being, agency and freedom: The Dewey lectures 1984', *Journal of Philosophy*, 82.

Sen, A.K. (1985b) *Commodities and capabilities*. Amsterdam: North-Holland.

Singer, H.W. (1952) 'The mechanics of economic development', *Indian Economic Review*. Reprinted in: A.N. Agarwala and A.P. Singh, eds., *The economics of underdevelopment*. London: Oxford University Press.

Smith, A. (1776) *An inquiry into the nature and causes of the wealth of nations*. Republished; edited by R.H. Campbell and A.S. Skinner. Oxford: Clarendon Press (1976).

Smith, A. (1790) *The theory of moral sentiments*, rev. ed. Republished; edited by D.D. Raphael and A.L. Macfie. Oxford: Clarendon Press (1975).

Srinivasan, T.N. (1982) 'Hunger: Defining it, estimating its global incidence and alleviating it', in: D. Gale Johnson and E. Schuh, eds., *Role of markets in the world food economy*.

Stewart, F. (1985) *Planning to meet basic needs*. London: Macmillan.

Streeten, P. (1981) *Development perspectives*. London: Macmillan.

Streeten, P. et al. (1981) *First things first: Meeting basic needs in developing countries*. New York: Oxford University Press.

Sukhatme, P.V. (1977) *Nutrition and poverty*. New Delhi: Indian Agricultural Research Institute.

UNICEF (1986) *The state of the world's children 1986*. New York: United Nations.

Usher, D. (1968) *The price mechanism and the meaning of national income statistics*. Oxford: Clarendon Press.

Usher, D. (1976) 'The measurement of real income', *Review of Income and Wealth*, 22.

Van Herwaarden, F.G. and A. Kapteyn (1981) 'Empirical comparison of the shape of welfare functions', *European Economic Review*, 15.

Van Praag, B.M.S. (1978) 'The perception of welfare inequality', *European Economic Review*, 10.

von Weizsacker, C.C. (1971) 'Notes on endogenous changes in tastes', *Journal of Economic Theory*, 3.

Wiggins, D. (1985) 'Claims of need', in Honderich (1985).

Williams, A. (1987) 'What is wealth and who creates it?', York University, mimeo.

World Bank (1986) *World Development Report 1986*. New York: Oxford University Press.

[6]

Famines

AMARTYA SEN*
Oxford University

*Text of the first Annual Lecture of the Development Studies Association,
delivered in Reading, England, on 21 September 1979.*

Summary. – This is a text of the first Annual Lecture of the Development Studies Association.
It investigates a variety of issues that arise in famine analysis, covering identification, causation
and prevention. The rejection of the food availability approach is combined with exploration of
the 'entitlement approach' presented by the author in an earlier contribution in the *Cambridge
Journal of Economics*, Vol. 1 (1977). Four recent famines as well as some famous historical
ones are examined in the light of the entitlement approach. Aside from throwing light on the
causes and cures of famines, the entitlement approach also permits us to distinguish between
various types of famines all of which share the feature of a common *predicament* of a mass of
people but which do not share the same *causal* mechanism, nor invite the same *response*. Famine
analysis, it is shown, requires more structure than the traditional approaches are able to provide.

1.

Economics has been called the dismal science. But it may not be quite dismal enough. While famines ravaging one country or another – killing millions and ruining many more – clearly have much to do with economics, famine analysis has typically been left to the journalist, the agriculturist, the epidemiologist, the general administrator and – recently – the new clan of disaster experts. Within their own domains of interest, these famine analysts have done an excellent job, and there is a tremendous wealth of material dealing with actual famine experience which economists can use if they so choose. This applies not merely to modern famines, but also to those in the past, and some of the 19th century were illuminatingly studied by those who had to deal with them. In particular, the British imperial administrators produced some great *famine reports* (in addition to producing – some would say – some great *famines*).

While economists have not typically expended much time on famines as such, the administrator's *reading* of economic theory has often played a decisive role in the choice of public policy. Adam Smith in particular, has cast his shadow over famines in Ireland, India and China, and Robert Malthus, who actually did produce a neat little piece on food shortage[1] as a follow up of his essay on population, provided cunning justification of administrative policies which from the commonsense point of view seemed remarkably uncunning.

When, in 1812, the Governor of Bombay turned down a proposal of interfering with the market mechanism in dealing with a famine that was developing in Gujarat, he explained: 'The digression of the celebrated author of the *Wealth of Nations* concerning Corn-trade . . . and particularly as far as respects the *inland Trader*, is forcibly and irresistibly applicable to every state of society where merchants or dealers in grain may be established.'[2] Warren Hastings, who was an interventionist (not merely *vis-à-vis* the Begums of Oudh), was later rapped on the knuckles by Colonel Baird-Smith, for using public channels to move food into Bengal in the famine of 1783. Colonel Baird-Smith accused Hastings of not having understood his Adam Smith, making the condescending remark that Hastings could hardly be expected to understand so soon (in 1783) 'the first dawn of the revolution of thought on such questions produced ultimately by the publication of Adam Smith's *Wealth of Nations* in 1776'.[3] Leslie Melville, the Company civil servant, commented on a later incident of deplorable neglect of the economist's valuable thoughts when discussing 'an order issued by an Indian Magistrate, fixing a maximum price of

---
* For helpful discussion, I am most grateful to Keith Griffin, Judith Heyer, Roger Hay and Felix Paukert.

grain in a particular town': 'I was immediately satisfied (as was the fact), that the authority who issued it, could never have attended, however negligently, the lectures of Mr Malthus.'[4] While failure to attend Mr Malthus's lectures would have been, I imagine, quite a common vice in India, classical political economy did play a major role in providing justification for non-interventionist policies in many of the Indian famines in the 19th century, as it did in Ireland as well.[5] I shall have something to say on this policy question, but before that I would like to take up the question of *causation* of famines.

On the subject of causation, the view that has certainly dominated most studies of famines is one that centres on *food availability decline* — FAD for short. This is a rather obvious view to take, and while many economists, including Malthus, adhered to such a diagnosis, it would be surprising if non-economists would not have also arrived at the same thought rather effortlessly. If people are dying for want of food, it would seem natural to think that there must be a shortage of food availability. This would fail to be the case only if, it might appear, food is somehow denied to people by a deliberate policy.

It may be recalled that in Bernard Shaw's *Man and Superman*, the Irish-American Mr Malone, Hector's father, explains to his English daughter-in-law the distinction between 'famine' and 'starvation'.

> Malone: Me father died of starvation in the black 47. Maybe you've heard of it?
> Violet: The famine?
> Malone: No, the starvation. When a country is full of food and exporting it, there can be no famine.[6]

Malone's statement raises three interesting and important questions — all of which I would like to pursue in this lecture. First, there is the question as to whether famines can take place without any substantial decline in food availability per head, i.e. the question of the correctness of what I have been calling the FAD view. Second, Malone speaks of food being exported out of Ireland during the famine. I shall call this the issue of 'food *counter-movement*'. Finally, there is the point about the distinction between famine and starvation. The former, presumably, is the result of some kind of a 'natural' occurrence involving genuine food shortage while the latter is the result of some deliberate action in starving people to death or to migrate. This concerns the *mechanism* through which people are deprived of food.

2.

How does FAD fare as an approach to famines? The answer seems to be: not very well. While several famines recently have been interpreted in the FAD light, arguing that food availability did go down sharply leading to the respective famines, a closer examination shows that this has often not been the case at all. I shall presently take up four different cases of recent famines which are interesting to study, but would like first to make two preliminary remarks.

First, even without looking for empirical evidence, it should be clear that the FAD view *need not* be correct. Famine is a characteristic of some people not *having* enough food; it is not a characteristic of there *being* not enough food. While the latter *can* be a cause of the former, it is one of many possible causes, and indeed *may or may not* be associated with famines. Food supply statements say things about *commodities* as such, while statements about famines are concerned with the *relationship* between persons and commodities. To understand famines, we need to go into this relationship.

Second, that the FAD view *need not* be correct is not merely clear, it *has been* clear for a very long time to people who have tried to look beyond their first thoughts on famines. Before political economists are written off as overlooking the obvious, it is worth recalling David Ricardo's reaction to a FAD argument contained in his notes for a speech in Parliament in 1822. (It was written by Ricardo in the third person *as if* reported in Hansard, though it was not delivered in Parliament in that form, and was not thus reported in Hansard.)

> But says the honble. gentn. the people are dying for want of food in Ireland, and the farmers are said to be suffering from superabundance. In these two propositions the honble. gentn. thinks there is a manifest contradiction, but he Mr R could not agree with him in thinking so. Where was the contradiction in supposing that in a country where wages were regulated mainly by the price of potatoes the people should be suffering the greatest distress if the potato crop failed and their wages were inadequate to purchase the dearer commodity corn? From whence was the money to come to enable them to purchase the grain however abundant it might [be] if its price far exceeds that of potatoes. He Mr Ricardo should not think it absurd or contradictory to maintain that in such a country as England where the food of the people was corn, there might be an abundance of that grain and such low prices as not to afford a remuneration to the

grower, and yet that the people might be in distress and not able for want of employment to buy it, but in Ireland the case was much stronger and in that country there should be no doubt there might be a glut of corn, and a starving people.[7]

Clearly, the interesting question is not so much whether famines *can* happen even when there is no food availability shortage, but whether typically famines *are* in fact associated with food availability decline. Also *when* food availability decline *is* associated with the development of famine conditions, does FAD provide a good approach to understanding why famine conditions have developed?

In fact, in the case of most of the great famines in history, the FAD hypothesis cannot be easily rejected on the basis of the available evidence, and in some cases there *is* evidence of a substantial food availability decline.[8] Even the great Irish famines of the 1840s had that feature, and the collapse of the potato crops did make a substantial dent on food availability in Ireland. The issue of food *exports* out of Ireland is, of course, a separate one, which would have to be discussed, since export of some goods is no proof of there being enough of that good for the population. However, temporal association with food availability decline does not settle the issue of the usefulness of the FAD approach for understanding the great historical famines, and I shall come back to this question later. Before that I would like to report on the food availability picture in the four recent famines to which I referred earlier.

3.

The four famines considered are from two parts of the world, in particular Bengal and Ethiopia, the famines in question being: (1) the Great Bengal famine of 1943; (2) the Ethiopian famine – centred in the province of Wollo – of 1973; (3) the Ethiopian famine – centred in the province of Harerghe – of 1974; and (4) the Bangladesh famine of 1974. These are certainly among the biggest famines in recent years, with the Great Bengal famine arguably the largest in this century, causing the death of around 3 million people.[9]

I have shown elsewhere that the FAD approach can be firmly rejected in the case of the Great Bengal famine.[10] While the food availability did go down in 1943 compared with the year immediately preceding, it was substantially higher than in 1941 when there was no hint of a famine. The total availability in the

famine year was around 11% higher than in 1941, and the *per capita* availability 9% higher. There was nothing like a famine in 1941. And yet while these figures stood high, people fell and perished. The explanation has to be sought in something other than FAD.

The position in Ethiopia in 1973 is a bit more complicated. The food output did fall very substantially in the province of Wollo, where the famine was severest, but it did not fall by much for Ethiopia as a whole. In fact, the *per capita* availability of calories has been estimated to have been fairly normal in 1973, about the same as in the preceding years.[11] The question that arises in this case is one of the appropriate unit: Ethiopia *or* Wollo? I shall postpone this question until a bit more wherewithal for answering this question has been presented, and will come back to it later.

In the following year, there was a noticeable shortfall of food availability both in Ethiopia as a whole and in Harerghe – our focus province – so that the FAD hypothesis is not contradicted by either piece of food statistics.

Finally, in the Bangladesh famine of 1974, rice output as well as food availability per head were higher than in any other year during 1971 – 1975, and still the famine hit precisely in the peak availability year.[12] If we look back on the inter-district pattern, again the famine districts – Rangpur, Mymensingh, Sylhet – seem to have been relatively better supplied with food grains, and also had substantial increases in rice output – the chief food – in 1974 compared with 1973.[13]

To take a quick tally, in two cases out of the four studied, the FAD approach gets contradicted firmly, while there is no rejection of FAD in one case, and some interpretative ambiguity in the fourth.

4.

I move now from questioning FAD to discussing an alternative line of attack, which I have called the entitlement approach. This sees starvation as arising from failure on the part of groups of people to establish entitlement over a requisite amount of food. What a person is entitled to in a given society is constrained by a collection of relationships covering the legal system (e.g. ownership laws), the political system (e.g. presence or absence of social security or right to work), economic forces (including those of the market), as well as social and cultural influences (e.g. the family's system of sharing incomes and food). In a private ownership economy, the entitlement relationships can be conveniently split into two broad categories of influences, viz. *endowment*, covering a person's basic ownership situation, and *exchange entitlement mapping*, specifying for each endowment the set of alternative commodity bundles that the person in question can command, through using the means of exchange that are available in the economy. This is not the occasion to go into the technical details of these relationships, which have been presented elsewhere,[14] but I would like to mention that 'exchange' for this purpose includes all ways of changing ownership over one bundle to ownership over another, and this includes production as well as trade.

Our ability to command food depends on what we own and what we can get by exchanging what we own. If a peasant slides into starvation because he has lost the land he owned (say, because of debt settlement), it is a case of an entitlement loss arising from an endowment loss. On the other hand, if a barber has to starve because there is a sharp decline in the demand for haircuts (as, incidentally, is quite common in rural famines), this is a case of entitlement loss traceable not to endowment changes but to a collapse of the exchange entitlement mapping.

The entitlement approach takes the line that one can understand the development of famines by examining how the entitlements change *within* the system of entitlement relations operating in the economy. Before proceeding further, it may be useful to diagnose some possible influences which the entitlement approach denies or ignores. The first is the role of *choice* in the most immediate and narrow sense. If a person has not got enough food, this can' be *either* because he did not have the *ability* to command that food, or because he *chose* not to exercise that ability. The entitlement approach concentrates solidly on the ability side of the story.

This may not be quite as trivial or noncontroversial as it might at first sound. One of the frequent lines of analysis of famines concentrates on people's unwillingness to consume unfamiliar food. Charles Edward Trevelyan, the Head of the Treasury at the time of the Irish famines of the 1840s, had complained: 'There is scarcely a woman of the peasant class in the West of Ireland whose culinary art exceeds the boiling of a potato'.[15] However, the introduction of corn-meal while meeting with initial resistance — including being named 'Peel's brimstone' in honour of the Prime Minister — was soon a great success, as anything would have been with a starving population.

More recently, Dom Moraes, the distinguished poet, has produced the following extraordinary version of the Bengal famine of 1943:

> . . . in India in the 1940s there was a famine in Bengal and millions of people died. During the famine, the British brought in a large amount of wheat. Now, the people of Bengal are traditionally rice eaters and they would not change their eating habits; they literally starved to death in front of shops and mobile units where wheat was available. Education must reach such people.[16]

In contrast with Moraes's analysis, other accounts — including that of the official Famine Inquiry Commission — speak of gigantic queues for trying to get relatively small amounts of food distributed free.[17] And there is indeed no evidence whatsoever of people starving because of unwillingness to change food habits. People dying in front of shops full of food, which is true, has to be seen in terms of failure of entitlement rather than of choice.

A second point concerns the concentration of the entitlement approach on *legally valid* procedures. If food is snatched away from people by some illegal means, the entitlement approach will not be able to catch this. In so far as historical periods of turmoil and disorder have led to starvation through such illegal deprivations, the entitlement approach will not be a useful guide to employ. There is a hint of this even in Mr Malone's account of British rule in Ireland. The entitlement approach concentrates instead on legal means, and views starvation and famines as essentially law-consistent deprivations under the economic, political, legal system in operation in that country at that time. Most recent famines have, in fact, taken place under very orderly circumstances — this applies to the Irish famine as well, despite occasional looting and obstructions. When people died of starvation in front of well-stocked shops in Bengal in 1943 the powerful arm of the law was there to protect the property rights of those who had food or the ability to command it. There is typically nothing illegal about the process that leads up to famine deaths. That is the line that the entitlement approach explores.

A third distinction concerns the denial that famines must be linked invariably to non-entitlement variables such as the total food supply in the country. If the total food supply were to affect starvation, this can happen — according to the entitlement approach — only through changing people's entitlement positions. The most important denial made by the entitlement approach is, therefore, of simple analysis of famines in terms of 'too many people, too little food'. In contrast, David Ricardo's state-

ment, quoted earlier, fits well within the entitlement approach, even though one could dispute
the specifics of it, e.g. Ricardo's potato theory
of wages, and ignoring other aspects of the entitlement relations.

5.

I do not want to go here into the technical
characterization of entitlement relations and
the forces governing its changes. But it is
important to distinguish between two different types of entitlement failures – a contrast
that differs somewhat from the distinction
made earlier between endowment loss and
unfavourable shifts in the exchange entitlement
mapping. The distinction I now want to consider is between *direct* entitlement failure and
trade entitlement failure. Some people produce
the food that they themselves eat, and a failure
of production, e.g. a failure of rice crop for a
rice-growing peasant, would directly predispose
them to starvation. This I shall call a *direct*
entitlement failure. In contrast, most people
acquire food by trade, and their starvation can
arise from the failure of their trade entitlement
either because of endowment loss *or* because of
worse terms of trade (or indeed failure to sell
or buy). This dependence on trade for survival
is a characteristic not merely of tinkers, tailors,
soldiers and watchful sailors, but also of lawyers, doctors and businessmen. Their food command is dependent on the precise nature of the
trade relationships.

It may be useful to bring in the contrast
with the FAD approach in the context of this
distinction. A trade entitlement failure can arise
from many causes, of which a decline in food
availability – affecting trade relations – is
only one. A glut of cash crops, a decline in the
demand for particular services, a general excess
demand for foodgrains, all can put adequate
food beyond the reach of particular classes
or groups of people, leading to starvation and
famines.

So much for trade entitlements. It might
look as if *direct* entitlement failure is more
closely connected with FAD. But this is not the
case either. If the output from my farm falls
sharply because of some local calamity, but the
food supply in the market is unaffected or even
increased, I – the peasant – shall still be forced
towards starvation. What keeps me from hunger
is not the food supply in the country or the
region or even in the local market, but my
ability to establish command over food through
the systems of entitlement in operation. As a

peasant I get this directly from the food I grow.
I am, of course, free to buy food in the market,
but what do I buy it with? The crop failure will
not merely affect my direct food command,
but also my main source of entitlement.

When there is a general crop failure, the
element of food availability decline and that
of direct entitlement decline are both present,
but they are quite distinct entities. Moving food
into a region in which the crop has failed may
do rather little for the local peasants unless
some means are devised for them to have the
ability to exercise some trade entitlement.

Essentially, such a general crop failure in a
peasant economy is primarily a direct entitlement failure, and the role of food availability
decline is a subsidiary one, making it even
more difficult for the peasant to acquire food,
which is difficult enough anyway thanks to
their lacking things with which food can be
traded. Typically, on these occasions, markets
for land, livestock and other assets also tend
to collapse, and the shortage of food clearly
plays a role here in reducing the value of non-
food assets. But all this is subsequent to the
primary story which is one of direct entitlement failure of the peasants who rely on food
grown by themselves.

6.

Two comments may be made here on matters that were postponed earlier. First, even
though many historical famines might have
been associated with food availability decline,
a discriminating analysis would have to distinguish between famines *caused* by FAD and
those caused by *direct* entitlement decline
(possibly supplemented by trade entitlement
difficulties made worse by shortage of food).
Indeed, for peasant economies, the direct
entitlement story goes through much more
easily than the *impersonal* tale of food availability decline.

Second, in a situation of direct entitlement
failure, food availability in shops may not go
down very much even when total food availability sharply goes down. When during the
Irish famine in late 1846, people were starving,
Major Parker, the local Relief Inspector sent
the following report on December 21st from
Skibbereen: 'On Saturday, notwithstanding all
this distress, there was a market plentifully
supplied with meat, bread, fish, in short everything.'[18] Similar reports from all over Ireland
made Trevelyan insist that all the 'resources' of
the country should be, as he put it, 'drawn out'.

In fact, however, the apparently paradoxical situation had arisen from a decline in entitlement in excess of the supply of food. That situation is, in fact, quite a common occurrence in famines. What has to be guaranteed to prevent starvation is not food availability but food entitlement.

7.

I am in a position now to return to the unresolved issue of food availability in the Ethiopian famine in 1973 in the province of Wollo. As was noted before, there was little overall food availability decline in Ethiopia, but a sharp reduction in Wollo. For Wollo peasants, this would have been a *direct* entitlement failure and that clearly was the first step towards starvation. The question arises then as to why the Wollo agricultural population could not *buy* food, and in this context one has to examine the choice of the market unit for analysing availability: Ethiopia *or* Wollo? One interpretation would be that they were unable to buy food since food could not be moved to Wollo from other — more plentiful — regions. It is, of course, well-known that the transport system in Wollo was underdeveloped, and this lends plausibility to the story that the starvation in Wollo was due to food availability decline in Wollo specifically.

I do not think, however, that this story is sustainable. First of all, while the transport system in Wollo is underdeveloped, two highways run through it, and the Ethiopian north-south highway linking Addis Ababa to Asmara runs right through the area most affected by the famine. In fact, the early reports of the famine came from travellers being stopped on this highway, and later when famine relief camps were set up, they concentrated on the region around the highway not merely because of supply advantages, but also because of the geographical focus of the famine. Underdeveloped roads will not explain why food did not move into this region of acute starvation.

Second, there were confirmed reports of food moving *out of* Wollo into Addis and Asmara throughout the period of the famine, rather like in Ireland. While there was also some food moving in, the existence of outward movement of food from Wollo would indicate that something other than food availability would have also fallen in Wollo.

Third, the price of food in Dessie, the main market in Wollo, was hardly higher in the famine year than in preceding years.[19] Even

from other regions, such as Raya and Kobo — most affected by the famine — whatever price information we have indicates little evidence of a sharp rise. Wollo seems to have experienced a major famine with an almost unchanged price level of foodgrains.

All this taken together would confirm the view that what prevented the Wollo population from having enough food to eat was not the transport difficulty of getting food into Wollo from the rest of Ethiopia, but the inability of the Wollo population to command food through the market entitlement system. The entitlement failure applies directly to the farmers — both tenant and rist-owners — and indirectly to farm servants, dependents and others evicted by farmers, and also to those elsewhere the demand for whose products went down sharply as a result of the agricultural population's inability to buy urban goods and services. If this analysis is accepted, then the score against the FAD view is clearly three out of four.

8.

The Wollo famine can be described as a *slump* famine. So was the Great Irish famine. In contrast, the Great Bengal famine of 1943 was a *boom* famine. Food output did not fall very much anywhere, and in general was quite high. But the economy — fed by immense war-related expenditures — was subjected to powerful expansion of demand in general, and demand for food in particular.

I have presented a detailed analysis of the happenings elsewhere, but what seems to me to be the central issue can be understood in terms of a highly simplified model. In a poor community take the poorest section, say, the bottom 20% of the population, and double the money income of *half* of that group, keeping the money income of the rest unchanged. In the short run prices of food will now rise sharply, since the lucky half of the poorest group will now fill their part-filled bellies. While this might affect the food consumption of other groups as well, the group that will be pushed towards starvation will be the *remaining* half of the poorest community which will face higher prices with unchanged money income. Something of this nature happened in the economy of Bengal in 1943. Expansionary forces worked very unevenly, helping the urban areas, especially Calcutta, and some rural areas in which military construction took place, or war-related industries and activities expanded. But the bulk of rural Bengal faced sharply rising prices with money incomes that were not at all comparably higher. Speculative withdrawal of rice supply at a later stage added fuel to the fire of this unequal expansion which was *already* causing misery to many.[20]

The most affected groups were the rural labourers, particularly agricultural labourers, but the shifts also affected other groups in the rural economy selling services and crafts to the local market. The exchange entitlement mappings took deep plunges, forcing these occupation groups into starvation. The story is made grimmer by the military policy of destroying large boats in the coastal region of Bengal — fearing the arrival of the Japanese (who, incidentally, refused to come for *other* reasons) — and also the removal of rice stocks from three districts — again with the object of starving the elusive Japanese. These added to the entitlement decline, and indeed the fishermen and the river transporters were the two most affected groups in proportionate terms, but this was an added impetus in a movement that was leading to a famine anyway, affecting primarily the large population of landless rural labourers all over Bengal.

Since the famine was largely a result of trade entitlement failure rather than of direct entitlement failure, the groups that suffered least were those whose trade entitlements were *guaranteed*, and those who did not *need* to purchase rice. The former included the population of Calcutta protected by a system of rationing of food at heavily subsidized prices, and the latter included peasants and share-croppers who, while poor, were the least affected group in the rural economy of Bengal. If the Wollo famine was a slump famine with direct entitlement failure, the Bengal famine was a boom famine with trade entitlement failure, arising from shifts in the market powers of different groups.

largely over. While the decline in food availability was delayed, the reduction of employment and rice-buying power of wages were immediate. The most affected group again was rural labour, even though there was more distress among peasants and share-croppers in the Bangladesh famine of 1974 than in the Bengal famine of 1943, and many peasants and share-croppers did suffer from flood-based destructions.

The 1974 famine in Harerghe in Ethiopia concentrated on the pastoralists, particularly the Ogaden Somali and Issa Somali herdsmen. There was a sharp decline in the animal stock due to drought. This endowment loss was worsened by a precipitate fall in the terms of trade between animals and grain, affecting the herdsmen who rely on buying cheaper calories from grains by selling animals. Grains being an 'inferior' good *vis-à-vis* animal products, the demand for them *increased* as the herdsmen got impoverished, adding to the deterioration of the animal–grains terms of trade. Thus an endowment failure (animals as stocks), a direct entitlement failure (animals as food) and a trade entitlement failure (grains commanded by selling animals) can all be seen in the Harerghe famine. While, as was mentioned earlier, there was also some general food availability decline in Ethiopia and particularly in Harerghe, it seems more natural to relate the starvation of the herdsmen to these entitlement variations. On the other hand, the food availability fall did clearly contribute to the worsening of terms of trade of animals *vis-à-vis* grains, along with other forces, including demand shift in favour of foodgrains with impoverishment of the herdsmen. The Afar community of herdsmen in Wollo had suffered similarly, in 1973, but their distress was further increased by another entitlement shift, viz. the loss of some of their best grazing grounds in the Awash valley due to expansion of commercial agriculture.

9.

The Bangladesh famine of 1974 had a mixture of boom and slump characteristics. Certainly the overall inflationary tendency fed the rise in rice price. But the floods during June–September of 1974 also sharply reduced the demand for labour, leading to unemployment and making the wages fall behind the increase in rice price. The food output did of course go down as a result of the floods when the *aman* crop was harvested around November 1974–January 1975, but by then the famine was

10.

I turn now, very briefly, to some policy issues. There has been a good deal of discussion recently about the so-called 'world food crisis'. The focus of attention has centred on the availability of food, both through adequate production as well as through international trade. There have been proposals of international insurance systems to guarantee that a country should not suffer a big decline in food availability if its crop were to fail.

There is much merit in these discussions,

since food availability is certainly among the influences affecting starvation. But there are reasons for disquiet about this focus on food, and the importance attached tó it to the exclusion of other variables. If the entitlement approach is accepted, then the focus has to be on that combination of economic, political, social and – ultimately – legal arrangements that affect people's entitlement to food. Food supply will be a part of the story but no more than that, and it has to be borne in mind that some of the recent major famines have taken place in favourable food supply situations, sometimes even in peak food supply situations.

The entitlement approach suggests concentration on such policy variables as social security, employment guarantees, terms of trade between non-food and food (especially between labour power and food), and the totality of rights that govern people's economic life. Policies both of long-run nutritional improvements as well as of short-run famine avoidance and relief have to take note of these different influences on food deprivation. A focus on the ratio of food supply to population hides more than it reveals, and this has persistently deranged public policy over the centuries. In fact, as I have argued elsewhere, the gigantic Bengal famine was not anticipated – not even recognized when it came – largely because of the overwhelming preoccupation with the statistics of food availability per head.[21]

The issue of intervention vs free market obviously relates to this question. A focus on food availability tends to produce the anticipation that a free market would encourage food movement into deficit areas, and the best that the government could do would be to leave things to the private trader. Such a policy is not entirely dismissable when the famine is a boom famine like the Bengal famine of 1943. Interprovincial restrictions in food movement certainly did add to the pressure on foodgrains supply in Bengal arising from a severely expansionary demand situation, and I do not doubt that the suffering would have been less if there were free movements of rice into Bengal at that time. Unhappily, for once the Raj departed from its traditional free market policy, and that was clearly the worst moment to stifle private trade especially without making any systematic arrangement for public movement of foodgrains between the provinces. Given the absence of an all-India food policy, which came into effect only *after* the famine, it clearly would have been better not to stifle private trade, and here a leaf might well have been taken from the book of Adam Smith which caused such a

rampage in the preceding centuries. Free food movement would not have guaranteed food to the Bengali rural labourer, but could have somewhat lessened the worsening of his terms of trade through checking the rise in food prices.

The situation, however, is entirely different when one is dealing with a slump famine. There, food *counter-movements* are perfectly possible and indeed quite common, since the food supply – even if low – may be in excess of what the population of that country or region can establish entitlement for in a competitive market. Food did not move much into Wollo, and quite a bit moved out of it. In the Bangladesh famine of 1974, there was evidence of food going out into India, and while the quantification of this remains difficult, the occurrence of such counter-movements cannot be dismissed. In China, the British refusal to stop rice exports from famine-affected Hunan – a slump famine it was – caused an uprising in 1906, and later a similar thing occurred leading to the famous Changsha rice riots of 1910.[22] During the Great Irish Famine, ship after ship laden with wheat, oats, cattle, pigs, eggs and butter sailed from Limerick, sailing down the Shannon from a starving country to one with plenty of food. A non-interventionist policy does nothing to take note of the fact that entitlement declines would encourage food to move out even when there is acute shortage.

Sincere and well-meaning believers in the market mechanism were often disappointed by the failure of private trade to bring food into famine affected regions. During the Orissa famine of 1865–1866, Ravenshaw, the distinguished Commissioner of Cuttock division, expressed great disappointment that private trade did not bring in much food from outside which would have occurred since 'under all ordinary rules of political economy the urgent demand for grain in the Cuttock division *ought to have created* a supply from other and more favoured parts'.[23] The fact is, however, that political economy says no such thing and the pulls of market can hardly be identified with acute needs when not backed by entitlement relations of economic or legal kinds.

11.

The main purpose of my discussion has been to draw attention to this variety of issues that arise in famine analysis, covering identification, causation and prevention. The rejection of the food availability approach seems overdue. It predicts badly, and even when starvation is temporally associated with famines, it does not offer explanation as to why one group starves and another does not. Indeed, the FAD approach fails altogether to go into the crucial issues in famine analysis, viz. the relationship between people and food, and instead it keeps brandishing one piece of inert statistics.

Famine analysis requires more structure, and I have tried to argue that the entitlement ap-

proach provides that. It also permits us to distinguish between various different types of famines all of which share the feature of a common *predicament* of a mass of people but which do not share the same *causal* mechanism. It is in the study of the various aspects of entitlement relations that, in my judgement, the most fruitful fields of famine analysis can be found.

NOTES

1. *An Investigation of the Cause of the Present High Price of Provisions* (1800).

2. Quoted by S. Ambirajan, *Classical Political Economy and British Policy in India* (Cambridge: Cambridge University Press, 1978), p. 71, which provides an interesting study of the influence of classical political economy on famine policy in India (among other things). See also S. Rashid, 'The policy of laissez-faire during scarcities', *Economic Journal*, forthcoming.

3. *Parliamentary Papers*, H. C. 29, Vol. 40, Session 1862; quoted by Ambirajan (1978), *op. cit.*, p. 75.

4. *Remarks on the East India Bill* (London: 1833), p. 26; quoted by Ambirajan (1978), *op. cit.*, p. 77.

5. See C. Woodham-Smith, *The Great Hunger: Ireland 1845−9* (London: Hamish Hamilton, 1962; New English Library edition, 1975).

6. Bernard Shaw, *Man and Superman* (1903; Penguin Books edition, 1946), p. 196.

7. *The Works and Correspondence of David Ricardo*, edited by P. Sraffa with the collaboration of M. H. Dobb, Vol. 5 (Cambridge: Cambridge University Press, 1971), pp. 234−235.

8. See, for example, G. B. Masefield, *Famine: Its Prevention and Relief* (London: Oxford University Press, 1963); B. M. Bhatia, *Famines in India: 1860−1965* (Bombay: Asia Publishing House, 2nd ed., 1967).

9. See my 'Famine mortality: a study of the Bengal Famine', in E. Hobsbawm *et al.* (eds.), *Peasants in History* (Calcutta: Oxford University Press, 1980), a volume in memory of Daniel Thorner.

10. For a more detailed analysis, see my 'Starvation and exchange entitlement: a general approach and its application to the Great Bengal famine', *Cambridge Journal of Economics*, Vol. 1 (1977).

11. See my 'Ingredients of famine analysis: availability and entitlements', Working Paper No. 210, Department of Economics, Cornell University (October 1979).

12. See Sen (1979), *op. cit.* My analysis of the Bangladesh famine draws heavily on the pioneering study by Mohiuddin Alamgir, 'Famine 1974: political economy of mass starvation in Bangladesh', 1979.

13. See Alamgir (1979), *op. cit.*

14. See Sen (1979), *op. cit.* There is a more comprehensive exploration to be found in Appendices A and B of my manuscript *Poverty and Famines*, prepared for the ILO World Employment Programme, to be published by Oxford University Press.

15. Quoted in Woodham-Smith (1975), *op. cit.*, p. 71.

16. Dom Moraes, 'The dimensions of the problem: comment', in S. Aziz (ed.), *Hunger, Politics and Markets: The Real Issues in the Food Crisis* (New York: NY Press, 1975).

17. See Government of India, Famine Inquiry Commission, *Report on Bengal*, (New Delhi: 1945). See also T. Das, *Bengal Famine 1943* (Calcutta University Press, 1949); and K. C. Ghosh, *Famines in Bengal 1770−1943* (Calcutta: Indian Associated Publishers, 1943).

18. See Woodham-Smith (1975), *op. cit.*, p. 159.

19. See Sen (1979), *op. cit.* My analysis is based on data of the National Bank of Ethiopia and of the Ethiopian Grain Agency, and I am most grateful to Julius Holt for directing me to these unpublished data.

20. See Sen (1977), *op. cit.* and also Chap. 6 and note B of my manuscript *Poverty and Famines* (1980), *op. cit.*

21. See Sen (1977), *op. cit.*

22. See J. W. Esherick, *Reform and Revolution in China* (Berkeley: University of California Press, 1976).

23. See Ambirajan (1978), *op. cit.*, p. 76; italics added. See also Ajit Ghose, 'Short-term changes in income distribution in poor agrarian economies: a study of famines with reference to the Indian subcontinent', mimeographed, Queen Elizabeth House, Oxford (1979).

Poverty Is Powerlessness and Voicelessness

Deepa Narayan

"Nobody hears the poor. It is the rich who are being heard."—a discussion group of poor men and women, Egypt
⋙

"Poverty is humiliation, the sense of being dependent and of being forced to accept rudeness, insults, and indifference when we seek help."—a poor woman, Latvia
⋙

"When the poor and rich compete for services, the rich will always get priority."—a discussion group of poor men and women, Kenya

THE WORLD LOOKS different when viewed through the eyes of a poor person. In preparation for the *World Development Report 2000/2001: Attacking Poverty*, the World Bank conducted a research study that brought together the experiences of over 60,000 poor women and men from 60 countries around the world. Using open-ended qualitative and participatory research techniques, the *Voices of the Poor* study aimed to understand poverty from the perspective of poor people and to illuminate the human experience behind the poverty statistics.

The study establishes, first, that poverty is multidimensional and has important non-economic dimensions; second, that poverty is always specific to a location and a social group, and awareness of these specifics is essential to the design of policies and programs intended to attack poverty; and third, that despite differences in the way poverty is experienced by different groups and in different places, there are striking commonalities in the experience of poverty in very different countries, from Russia to Brazil, Nigeria to Indonesia. Poor people's lives are characterized by powerlessness and voicelessness, which limit their choices and define the quality of their interactions with employers, markets, the state, and even nongovernmental organizations (NGOs). Institutions both formal and informal mediate and limit poor people's access to opportunities.

These findings challenge all those committed to working for poverty reduction.

The realities of poor people's lives must inform policymaking at macro as well as micro levels.

Multidimensional nature of poverty

When poor people speak about well-being, they speak about the material, social, physical, psychological, and spiritual dimensions, in addition to security and the freedom of choice and action. In Ethiopia, an older woman said, "a better life for me is to be healthy and peaceful and to live in love without hunger." In Russia, "well-being is life free from daily worries about lack of money." A Brazilian said well-being is achieved "when there is cohesion, no quarrels, no hard feelings, happiness, peace with life." In Thailand, well-being was simply defined as "happiness: it is found in peace and harmony in the mind and in the community."

Conversely, poverty and ill-being are the lack of material well-being, insecurity, social isolation, psychological distress, and lack of freedom of choice and action. Not having enough to eat or possessing any assets to cope with shocks were mentioned over and over again. A poor woman in Egypt said, "a poor person is a person who does not own anything that provides him with a permanent source of living. If he has a permanent source of income, he will not ask for other people's assistance." With few exceptions, poor people reported that insecurity and unpredictability of life have increased in the past few years. In Russia, a poor man said, "every day I am afraid of the next." A poor woman in a *favela* (slum) in Brazil said, "there is no control over anything, at any hour a gun could go off, especially at night." Poor people also stated that, unlike the rich, they did not have the luxury of long-term planning horizons. As a poor woman in Bulgaria put it, "to be poor means to live from day to day, you have no money, no hope." The new poor in the former Soviet Union countries, who had no previous experience with poverty, often expressed shame, anger, and hopelessness in discussing their present conditions.

Poverty is specific to place and social group

Even within communities, poor people's priorities and experiences can be different, depending on their gender, age, marital status, and ethnicity. The plight of widows emerged as distinct from that of other social groups, particularly in Africa and Asia. Irrespective of the number of years of marriage, widows often found themselves thrown out of households and destitute overnight. The experience of one middle-aged woman speaks for widows in other parts of Africa and Asia: "when my husband died, my in-laws told me to get out. So I came to town and slept on the pavement." In Latin America, indigenous groups and those of African descent spoke about discrimination, whether in trying to get loans or buying food in the local markets or in their interactions with their children's schools.

Powerlessness and voicelessness

The defining experiences of poor people involve highly limited choices and an inability to make themselves heard or to influence or control what happens to them. Powerlessness results from multiple, interlocking disadvantages, which, in combination, make it extremely difficult for poor people to escape poverty (see figure on page 20). By and large, poor people say that insecurity of life has increased and they have not been able to take advantage of new opportunities because of corruption and a lack of connections, assets, finance, information, and skills.

Many poor people define poverty as the inability to exercise control over their lives. Old men in Nigeria say, "if you want to do something and have no power to do it, it is *taluchi/* poverty." Limited resources force poor people to think in terms of very short time horizons. "You can't think of the future because you can only see how to survive in the present," says a group of young adults in Ecuador. Poor people are often forced to make agonizing choices: feed the family or send children to school; buy medicine for a sick family member or feed the rest of the family; take a dangerous job or starve. In Brazil, drawing the connection between power, control, and well-being, a poor woman says, "the rich man is the one who says I am going to do it, and does it." The poor, in contrast, cannot fulfill their wishes or develop their capacities.

Low self-confidence both results from poverty and increases powerlessness and isolation from opportunity. A group of young men in Bower Bank, Jamaica, rank low self-confidence as the second biggest impact of poverty. "Poverty makes us not believe in ourselves; we hardly leave the community. Not only are we not educated but we don't have a street-wise education."

Quality of interactions with institutions

Poor people's powerlessness and voicelessness are most clearly evident in the quality of their interactions with the formal and informal institutions on which they depend for their survival. Institutions mediate their access to resources and opportunities. But the individuals with whom they must interact in the private sector, state, and, to a much lesser extent, civil society are often exclusionary, rude, and uncaring, as well as corrupt and exploitative. Poor people end up depending on their own informal networks of kin and friends for survival and solace.

Most poor people, particularly women, survive in the informal sector through a patchwork of low-paying, temporary, seasonal, and, often, backbreaking jobs with little security and no guarantee of payment. Whether in Russia or Bolivia or India, poor people say that they often do not get paid when they complete a job and have no recourse to justice. In Russia, a man cries that he has been paid in mayonnaise and vodka when what he needs is cash to buy medicines for his sick daughter. In Malawi, poor fishermen tell of their powerlessness to negotiate a reasonable wage with boat owners: "The problem is that these boat owners know that we are starving, and so we would accept any little wages they would offer to us because they know we are very desperate . . . we want to save our children from dying." In

Dimensions of powerlessness and ill-being

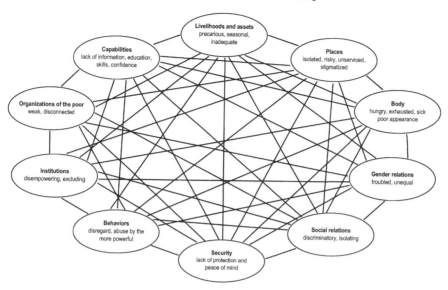

Bulgaria, women over 25 report finding it difficult to find employment, while younger women report that sexual favors are expected from them in exchange for jobs. In Cambodia, a poor woman said, "poverty means working for more than 18 hours a day, but still not earning enough to feed myself, my husband, and our two children."

Although some government programs are excellent and some officials are highly praised, these are the exceptions. In general, poor people report finding it difficult to take advantage of government programs, whether for loans, education, or health care, or for child, disability, or old-age benefits. They give detailed descriptions of the amounts and frequency of the unofficial payments they are required to make for government services. They speak of teachers who do not teach, doctors who do not show up or who want to see patients for a fee in their private clinics, nurses who extract payments even to register patients. They complain of loan officers who deduct 20–50 percent of loans as "processing fees," policemen who are oppressors rather than protectors, and justice that is available only to the rich. All are commonplace occurrences in poor people's lives. Poor people long for government officials who listen, can be trusted, do not lie, and are respectful even when they cannot help.

Nongovernmental and religious organizations are valued where they exist. However, they, too, are often seen as not accountable or as refusing to listen to the poor. Religious organizations are also faulted for excluding people of other denominations from their beneficence, thereby sowing seeds of disunity in communities.

In many countries, although more poor women are working outside the home to boost household incomes with their earnings, they are not necessarily experiencing greater autonomy, empowerment, or involvement in decisionmaking in households or communities. Where changes have occurred, for example in communities in Bangladesh and Brazil, civil society groups have played important roles, providing resources, skills training, and counseling to women and women's solidarity groups. Nonetheless, the asymmetry of power within the household remains deeply entrenched, as indicated by widespread violence against women. Physical violence against women was reported in 93 percent of the communities visited. Domestic violence was reported in every community in Eastern Europe and Central Asia where the issue was discussed. In the words of a poor woman in Bulgaria, "women must take care of everything and to top it all off, get beaten up every night if he comes home drunk."

The challenge ahead

"A person doesn't have the strength or power to change anything, but if the overall system changed, things would be better."—a poor man in Sarajevo, Bosnia and Herzegovina

Poor people are not the problem. Nor is the culture of poverty. Poor people work hard, are remarkably resourceful, and show grit and determination in providing for their families. All those committed to poverty reduction must ask themselves three questions: How can we build on what already works, design institutions, and change institutional character so that they support poor people's own initiatives to lift themselves out of poverty? How can poor people's connectivity with institutions be increased so that they are heard and represented in programs and policymaking at the local, national, and global levels? How can the knowledge, resources, and power at the local, national, and global levels be used to support poor people's own efforts?

Changing mindsets. The mindset of professional and technical experts must change. Instead of assuming they know what's best, they must strive to understand poor people's realities. They must be willing to listen; to understand poor people's knowledge, priorities, and actions; and then to use their technical knowledge to respond to poor people's concerns, whether at the local, national, or global levels. They must routinely ask what is happening within households and communities, so that macro and micro policy interventions designed to support women, men, or children have the desired impact. Participation in policy decisionmaking must be broad based.

Investing in poor people's assets. Poor people need assets to reduce their vulnerability. Just as the definitions of poverty are multidimensional, so are the assets poor people need to move out of poverty. Five kinds of assets are particularly important in an overall context of powerlessness.

First is the *body*, often a poor person's only asset. Frequently, it is weak, hungry, exhausted, and poor in appearance. For it to remain an asset rather than a liability requires measures to protect the health of the poor: provision of health care, water, sanitation, and energy-saving services that poor people can access and afford and are willing to use.

A second asset is *organizational ability.* Those who can organize and mobilize get their voices heard and their interests represented. The rich are organized and connected, the poor invariably are not. They depend primarily on their own informal and fragmented networks. Strong networks and membership-based organizations extending beyond the family and immediate community are essential to help poor people gain access to other assets and resources.

A third asset is *information.* While it is commonly recognized that information is power, poor people are cut off from information about their rights as workers, pensioners, and citizens, as well as about jobs, resources, and assistance programs. The experience of social entrepreneurs shows that new information technologies—the internet and cellular telephones—can be used to connect poor people to each other and to markets and governments, increasing their bargaining power. The experience of Bangladesh's Grameen Bank, which makes loans to rural, landless, often illiterate, poor women for the purchase of cellular telephones, shows that poor people in these villages, armed with information about market prices, are able to negotiate better prices for their goods with middlemen. Owning telephones is also transforming the social status of the "Grameen phone ladies."

Deepa Narayan is Lead Social Development Specialist in the World Bank's Poverty Reduction and Economic Management Network.

A fourth asset is *education.* Faced with harsh realities, many poor parents cannot afford to send their children to school or keep them in school. Almost everywhere, poor people want to educate their children but calculate that the returns to their investment are unrewarding. Strategies must be found that change the cost-benefit outcomes for poor people of investing in their children's education. These include providing scholarship programs for girls and boys and, when needed, compensating parents for the lost labor of their children.

Ideas and entrepreneurship constitute the fifth asset. At the national and global levels, there are laws that seek to protect intellectual property rights. In a rapidly globalizing world, poor people's knowledge, whether of plants or traditional healing or building practices, needs protection so that they too can be the beneficiaries of their ideas and practices. Their property rights need to be registered.

There are banks, trusts, and venture capital to support rich people's ideas and entrepreneurship but not poor people's ideas and entrepreneurship. Financial services, venture capital funds, and micro insurance programs are needed to capitalize the ideas and initiatives of poor people, who work primarily in the informal sector.

Changing governance. Poor people know that their very survival depends on the resources controlled by others. With few options, they remain silent witnesses to exploitation and wrongdoing even when invited to speak out. As a poor man in Uzbekistan put it, "a dog won't betray its master." Examples of corruption and poor governance pervade poor people's lives. Change requires investment in reforms to make governments effective, participatory, transparent, and accountable to citizens. Strong networks of poor people's organizations and a strong civil society are required for effective governance at the local, national, and global levels. Let a poor man from Argentina have the final word: *"If we aren't organized and don't unite, we can't ask for anything."* **F&D**

This article is based on findings reported in three publications: Deepa Narayan, Robert Chambers, Meera Shah, and Patti Petesch, 1999, Global Synthesis, Consultations with the Poor *(Washington: World Bank); Deepa Narayan with Raj Patel, Kai Schafft, Anne Rademacher, and Sarah Koch-Schulte, 2000,* Voices of the Poor: Can Anyone Hear Us? *(New York: Oxford University Press for the World Bank); Deepa Narayan, Robert Chambers, Meera Shah, and Patti Petesch, 2000,* Voices of the Poor: Crying Out for Change *(New York: Oxford University Press for the World Bank). All are posted at* http://www.worldbank.org/poverty/voices/reports.htm. *The last two volumes can be ordered on the World Bank's external website* (www.worldbank.org/publications) *or by telephone (1-800-645-7247).*

[8]

ON THE ETHICS OF DEVELOPMENT PLANNING

DENIS GOULET
Overseas Development Council

I

Development itself poses ancient ethical questions faced by all societies: What are the nature and foundations of the good life? What is the basis for justice in societal relations? What posture should societies adopt towards nature and that second nature called technology? These questions are rendered specifically developmental by the modern context, characterized by the following traits: the gigantic scale of basic operations; their technical complexity, with the minute division of labor ensuing therefrom; the interdependencies which link all societies—local, regional, national, or international; and an ever-shortening time lag between social stimuli, in the form of proposed or imposed changes, and the responses societies must make to survive or preserve their integrity. The combination of these traits places in jeopardy the validity of all traditional answers to these questions.

Ethical reflection on social problems takes place at four distinct levels (Goulet, 1965:77-80): (1) general ends; (2) specific criteria to identify the institutions and procedures which embody these ends in concrete situations; (3) clusters (or systems) of means taken as wholes; and (4) individual means, taken separately. Little disagreement arises over general goals or values—level (1)—since everyone favors these: peace, justice, freedom, and equity. Even warmongers declare that the reason they fight is to create conditions which make peace possible. Or tyrants declare that their repression is necessary to assure the minimum level of order without which freedom cannot survive. At level (2) (criteria to determine when general goals are present) ideological and value divergence abounds. To illustrate, Marxists will claim that freedom is meaningless in the absence of economic equality, whereas liberals retort that freedom flourishes only if such democratic institutions as multiple parties and free elections can thrive. The third level (cluster of instru-

26   STUDIES IN COMPARATIVE INTERNATIONAL DEVELOPMENT

ments for governing society), is most important to social change agents. Development planning itself is such a system of means, as are technology policy, international aid, or financing schemes. The fourth level (means taken in isolation) is relatively conflict-free because such means are often morally neutral techniques which can be put to good or evil uses. Debate in development ethics is located mainly at the two middle levels—(2) and (3)—criteria for desirable change and strategies of implementation.

Genuine ethics can never be mere discourse as to ends and means, but rather critical reflection on the value content of one's personal and social action. Although many ethicists rest content with passing judgment on the ends and means employed by others—politicians, businessmen, or planners—such an extrinsic approach is worthless; development ethics must penetrate the dynamics of social action and become a veritable "means of the means." Any society's values as to what are essential needs and what basic relationships are precious directly condition its choice of goals and its use of means. Clarity about ends is presupposed; but no less important is the realistic acceptance of sacrifices which must be paid so as to gain these ends. How can one promote human dignity unless one refers to social conditions which foster or crush dignity— endemic disease, let us say, or the abdication of national culture to qualify for international funding? And what is the precise relationship between dignity, a spiritual good, and the material and social conditions which support it? To insist upon precise criteria and measures for comparing sacrifices to be made in defense of ethical values establishes the difference between true ethical strategies and mere moralism. Since ethical strategies have their genesis in a social matrix, one must inquire into the sources whence such strategies derive their content.

Content of Ethical Strategies for World Development

There are two sources whence ethical strategies for world development draw their content: the goal and the dynamic processes of development itself.

Goals

One must first look at goals: Which common values do all societies seek? Three such goals are sought by all individuals and societies: optimum life sustenance, esteem, and freedom.

ON THE ETHICS OF DEVELOPMENT PLANNING   27

Optimum life sustenance. Sane people everywhere nurture and cherish life. Even where human sacrifices were offered to propitiate jealous gods or where female infanticide was practiced by parents desiring sons, the rationale for such violation of life was its alleged contribution to overall vitality in community or family. It is because no one disputes the importance of life-sustaining goods that consensus exists over one important goal of development: to prolong lives and render them less stunted by disease or exposure to nature's elements. Longer human life can appear desirable only after it appears possible. So long as people remain convinced that it is the will of the gods that children die or that to combat disease with artificial means is to revolt against nature, they will accept brutish reality with equanimity. What shocks them is the first discovery that physically stunted lives are so unnecessary; health agents and technicians have brought to the most remote areas of the world proof that human life can be prolonged. The very acceptance of average life expectancy as a general index of development reflects the centrality of life sustenance as a goal of development. No culture has separated sustenance of physical life from nourishment of the spirit. Accordingly, sustenance itself must be viewed in larger terms, as an instrumental good.

Esteem. All persons and societies seek esteem, identity, and respect. They need to be accepted as beings of worth for their own sakes and on their own terms. Notwithstanding their own profound sense of self-esteem, materially poor societies suffer greatly in their contacts with technologically advanced societies for the simple reason that material prosperity has now become so widely accepted as the touchstone of worthiness. And esteem, in today's world, is conferred mainly on those who possess material and technical abundance.

So long as esteem was conferred on grounds other than material achievement, the world's masses could resign themselves to poverty and maintain their self-esteem. Once the prevailing image of the good life came to center on material welfare, it became difficult for the poor to feel respected. The reason is that some measure of recognition by others is essential to preserve a modicum of self-respect. Nineteenth-century Japan embraced industrialization largely to avoid humiliation by technologically superior "barbarians." Similarly, today's Third World seeks development, in great measure, in order to gain the esteem denied to societies living in a state of "underdevelopment." Because mass

28   STUDIES IN COMPARATIVE INTERNATIONAL DEVELOPMENT

poverty cuts them off from recognition, they are ready to pay a high price to gain "development."

Freedom. A third universal component of the good life is the twofold freedom—*from* undue constraints and *for* fulfillment, however defined. Though countless meanings attach to the word *freedom*, at the very least it signifies some range of choices for societies and their members, along with the minimization of constraints, external though not necessarily internal, in the pursuit of desired goods. Not that all peoples wish to govern themselves or determine their own economic future, or that they can bear the insecurities that come with freedom. For, as Fromm (1963) observes, most humans try to escape from freedom so as to meet their deeper need for security. Yet even security must be viewed as freedom *from* unforeseen dangers, albeit it is not necessarily freedom *for* exploration, actualization, or spiritual growth. At least in minimal terms, development for many is a search for freedom from the servitudes of ignorance, misery, and exploitation by others. But ethical strategies need to look beyond goals to the development process itself as an additional source of their value content.

Dynamism of Development Processes

Like its goals, the dynamisms of development's processes lend ethical strategies their content. Three such dynamisms are worth examining: social conflict, political imagery, and the vital nexus which links values to overall development strategies and to specific policies.

The dynamism of social conflict. Peace and order need to be rooted in justice; hence peace is not genuine if underdevelopment, with its train of exploitation, misery, and injustice, continues. Several years ago the Vatican created a global Secretariat for Justice and Peace. This misleading name spreads the illusion that justice implies peace or that peace insures justice. On the contrary, the dialectics of world development breeds great tension between peace and justice. Development is no harmonious process, but one of struggle and contradiction. Yet much conventional wisdom still preaches the merits of gradual social change. The language of incrementalism is now widely criticized in the Third World, however, as a conceptual superstructure aimed at diluting development's thrust toward liberation from cultural, economic, political, and technological dependency.

At bottom, two competing viewpoints on development vie for adherents: domestication and liberation (Goulet, 1971a; Goulet and Hudson, 1971:13-72). Both approaches generate social conflict, domestically and internationally. The technocratic consumerist vision (domestication) adopted by many countries almost everywhere gives birth to revolutionary opposition and to a repressive apparatus to keep popular forces under control. Revolutionary models, in turn, threaten powerful vested interests willing to fight to obstruct change. Even in the best of circumstances, the development process is laden with a high potential for domestic conflict.

What of international conflict? Can world peace be managed? Most Western specialists of international relations assign to superpowers the primary responsibility for containing nuclear armaments and avoiding nuclear war. They urge a policy of opposition by big powers to limited wars of liberation lest these upset precarious balances of power or violate spheres of influence. Inasmuch as wars of national liberation can also revolutionize internal social structures, global peace managers are led to veto liberation models of development. The American, and, I suspect, the Soviet public are socialized into equating peace with avoiding nuclear warfare and with keeping the lid on potentially explosive revolutionary wars. We face a true dilemma here: if peace means stabilizing the present world order, and if that order is radically unjust, then a contradiction exists between the demands of justice and those of peace. It remains true that a real danger exists that uncontrolled violence may annihilate the race or destroy the very institutional fabric whence a new order is to be built even if the old is destroyed.

The long-term mission of the peacemaker, from the perspective of developmental justice, is to destroy the prior legitimacy enjoyed by the forces of institutional violence. Those who make this their priority can then, without losing their moral credentials, engage in the task of devising revolutionary strategies whose use of destructive violence is truly minimal.

Creative utopianism as realistic policies. Like social conflict, politics is an indispensable instrument for achieving development. What content does politics supply to ethical strategies for development? No answer is possible unless we first recognize that the very requirements of development refute the dictum that "politics is the art of the possible." This

30   STUDIES IN COMPARATIVE INTERNATIONAL DEVELOPMENT

formulation sets limits within which power can be juggled; it defines the range of possibilities in ways congenial to some status quo and it brands those who move outside these borders as "utopian" or "subversive" (Fals Borda, 1969). Within many underdeveloped societies, established orders are structurally unjust. This is the reason why politics must become the "art of creating new possibilities" in order to alter these structures.

Political development is conventionally defined as a political system's growing capacity to process new and expanding demands, treated as input, and to produce a widening array of problem-solving decisions, viewed as output. Missing in this perspective is the recognition that even efficient power is no self-validating end. Power exists for a purpose other than legitimizing particular interests or arbitrating among conflicting demands. Politics is the art of rationally managing power in the service of the common welfare. Plato, Aristotle, and other ancient theorists, it is true, defined the common good uncritically in ways which reinforced particular interests, as for example those of propertied classes. Worse still, their frank idealism led them to take their historically conditioned norms as culturally universal. The demystification of political idealism launched by Machiavelli and completed by Marx has proven salutary; it invalidates all prescriptive politics formulated in purely ideal terms divorced from historical conditions. Nevertheless, even Marx refused to take existing power categories as givens, or to condone Hegel's glorification of the state as the incarnation of the Absolute. On the contrary, Marx denounced all existing political power as immoral because it represented minority interests, not a common good. He wanted in its place a form of power incarnating the majority interests of proletarians considered as the latent bearers of universal human values. He thus indirectly confirmed the normative view of political power defended long before by Plato and Aristotle. Power is justified by its use; ultimately, the only valid use of power is the construction of a common good which transcends the mere aggregation or arbitration of particular goods.

Normative strategies profile the frontiers of new political possibilities. Development ethics, in particular, plays the four related roles of evaluation, critique, pedagogy, and norm-setting. I cannot here repeat the analysis made elsewhere (Goulet, 1971b:337-41) of these roles. The crucial point is that even when they are rejected by wielders of power, norms affect their decisions, directly or indirectly. Among competing notions of change one usually finds some version of the "salvation by increased productivity" image versus the "salvation by redistribution" image. For holders of the first view, social injustice and poverty can be abolished by harnessing society's energies to solving problems. Defenders of the second view, despair of the capacity of the ground rules operative in their societies to satisfy the needs of the exploited. The choice between gradualist and nongradualist solutions to social problems requires the intervention of human will. Shakespeare is right: The wish *is* father of the thought. One can predict with surprising statistical accuracy that those in whose interest it is to cherish a gradualist image of change will, by and large, do so. Conversely, those who can gain most by adopting a nongradualist image of change will probably do so, provided their level of consciousness has reached a certain critical threshold. The impasse is only on rare occasions broken by those small numbers of people who are willing to settle issues in broader terms than those dictated by their limited interests or those of their nation, social class, profession, or ideological sect. Basic values are tightly linked to development strategies and specific policies; the nexus of these three is a third source of content for development ethics.

The vital nexus: values, strategies, policies. Nowhere is national development strategy so overtly related to basic values professed by society as in the People's Republic of China (Lin, 1975). After Mao's forces gained power in 1948, a large society had to be mobilized and countless institutional problems solved: a viable educational system created, access to modern technology gained, and health services provided to all. If we are to heed the words of the Chinese themselves, the key to their success has been the creation of a shared value system based on solidarity, revolutionary consciousness, and the primacy of moral over material incentives.[1] Their value options place a normative premium on austerity over affluence, on equality over privilege, on "serving the people" as a motivational principle over individual competition. To a considerable degree, investment strategies express these relative priorities: agriculture over industry, human resources over infrastructure, credit to local communes over tax incentives to outside firms, and small technology over mass techniques.

Ideological preferences of any national society are linked to its development strategy. If a nation chooses a capitalist path to development, with its implications of integration to the world market, certain incompatible values will necessarily fall by the wayside: a high degree of self-reliance, a notion of efficiency which internalizes social justice in

32   STUDIES IN COMPARATIVE INTERNATIONAL DEVELOPMENT

distribution and participation. On the other hand, if a decentralized communitarian or socialist approach to development is adopted on ideological grounds, gains in economic independence will tend to be rated higher than mere efficiency, greater social justice in land tenure higher than increased output, at least in initial stages.

If we introduce a third element in the equation, specific policy, the vital nexus tightens. Suitable illustrations can be found in the realm of technology. Technology policy is not to be guided merely by considerations of technical efficiency, aspirations after modernity, or the pure imitation of technological pioneers. On the contrary, technological decision making should flow from the basic value options which have presided over the choice of a development strategy. By way of illustration, if Tanzania seriously preaches self-reliant development, building on the traditional values of its largely rural population, its technology policy should, in its main lines, provide incentives to ''soft'' technologies aimed at increasing productivity via labor-intensive tools optimizing local resources with little dependence on outside expertise. To take another case, we may consider Algeria's commitment to reaching full industrial capacity to satisfy internal as well as export markets. This strategic choice likewise points the way to certain technology policies: know-how will be imported from various sources to build up native capacity, national technicians will be quickly trained to render them competitive, and coordinated bargaining postures will be adopted vis-à-vis foreign suppliers.

This essay has already moved away from general principles in ethics to their application in a specific domain: value conflicts in technology transfers. The shift is quite a natural one, for as the Brazilian economist Celso Furtado (1966) explains, ''Technology transfer is not some neutral technological act, it is a value-laden political act.''

II

Value Conflicts in Technology Transfers

Technology as a Two-Edged Sword

Historians have described the special circumstances which gave birth to technology in Western Europe and its areas of influence. They conclude that the modern technological mentality is an exceptional expression of societal response to the challenges of nature: it is a latecomer on the historical scene and an untypical phenomenon.

At its given level of information-processing capability and effective access to resources, any society formulates a "rational" strategy for survival and for optimizing its primary values. Modern technology, as it impinges upon many societies, standardizes their "existence rationality" in accord with its preferred definitions of efficiency, rationality, and problem solving. Modernization is not the presence of factories but a new outlook on factories. In modern societies technology comes to be viewed as normal, whereas in nonmodern societies both technology and factories are alien to experiential landscapes. The road to modernity does pass through technology. As John Montgomery (1974:16) puts it: "Modern man really wants to be modern. He has imparted to that desire the conviction of a philosophy of life. He is committed to technology, and he believes he can use it to correct its own evils."

Technology, the bearer of values. What values does technology transmit? The first value embedded in Western technology is a particular approach to rationality. For the technological mind, to be rational means to view any phenomenon as amenable to disaggregation into parts which can be put together again. The cognitive task of technology is not what older traditions called truth; instead, technologists are interested in verification and control. Epistemologically, the scientific mind set, which constitutes the underpinnings of technology, has proceeded to a reductionist substitution of verifiability for truth. Expressed geographically, the West brought the East the ability to change things, to extract more out of nature, to organize human efforts so as to get results. But for many in the East the mythical level[2] is no less real than the historical level. Accordingly, it may be wrong for Westerners to assume that historical reality is somehow more real than myth simply because myth cannot be verified empirically and does not confer direct control over nature. But the West also has need of transcendent myths and symbols; and perhaps the reason why Western societies are so prone to spurious symbolical manipulation is that they operate in a vacuum of such genuine myths. This vulnerability is not accidental, inasmuch as reductionist rationality is inherent in Western technology.

A second value vectored by technology is the cult of efficiency, expressed in industrial terms by productivity. Whereas production looks to final output, productivity points to a relationship, some ratio between what goes in and what comes out. One judges productivity by comparing

34   STUDIES IN COMPARATIVE INTERNATIONAL DEVELOPMENT

the amount of labor, capital, machinery, or time invested with the volume, weight, or value of what results. Whoever measures productivity draws lines as to what goes inside and what is kept outside the efficiency calculus. To use the language favored by economists, the key question is: Which externalities does one choose to internalize?

An example from traditional society may help. In 1958 I lived with two Bedouin tribes in the Sahara—the Ouled Sidi-Aissa and the Ouled Sidi-Cheikh—whose judgments of efficiency reflected their Muslim belief system. Their view of an efficient way to work was one that allowed them time to make Koranic prayers seven times daily, and that limited expenditure of energy during fasting periods. These tribes had internalized religious values in their assessment of an efficient way to work in still other ways. The efficient path was not to lead their flocks to pasture via the shortest route, with the fewest interruptions possible, but one that induced them to practice Koranic hospitality toward the poor along the way. Clearly, there exist divergent criteria for defining efficiency in technological and other societies.

A third value component of Western technology is its predilection for problem solving. Technologists do not gaze upon nature so as to discover harmony with it; they seek to manipulate and dominate it. A similar difference emerges in the social realm between the attitude of the problem solver and that of the "problematizer." The latter term is drawn from Brazilian educator Paulo Freire,[3] who states that one can know the social world to be transformed only to the extent that one problematizes the natural and historical reality in which one is immersed. Problematizing is the antithesis of problem solving, a stance wherein an expert steps back from reality, analyzes it into component parts, devises ways to solve difficulties in the most efficient way, and then dictates policy. Such problem solving, according to Freire, distorts the reality of experience by reducing it solely to those dimensions which can be treated as mere difficulties to be solved. To problematize, on the other hand, is to engage an entire populace in the task of codifying its total reality into symbols which generate critical consciousness and empower them to change their relations with nature and social forces. Problem solvers remain mere outside viewers who break wholes into parts; problematizers know themselves to be part of a totality which can be transformed only if they change themselves. Three main values are channelled by technology: a reductionist form of rationality, a closed efficiency calculus, and a bias for problem solving. What values, we must now ask, does technology destroy or weaken?

ON THE ETHICS OF DEVELOPMENT PLANNING   35

Technology, the destroyer of values. Technologists do not deliberately plan to destroy old values, nor even to implant new values directly. Their overt aim is to solve problems more efficiently or to improve the quality of products and processes. But technologists do much more than destroy prior values: they fracture the delicate bond which weaves the totality of values in premodern societies into meaningful patterns.

A close bond exists in nontechnological societies between normative and meaing values (Goulet, 1971c). "What ought to be done" in any domain—family relations, work, exchange, dealing with others— relates to the symbols society uses to explain the meaning of life and death. But no such nexus or unifying vision of life's total meaning, is to be found in developed societies; a plurality of meaning values is tolerated. To illustrate, devout Mormon businessmen obey the same professional ethic as their atheistic counterparts, even if their belief or meaning systems are radically opposed. Whereas in traditional societies work is a cosmic art, in developed societies it is but a specialized function.

Technology challenges prevailing normative values in traditional societies by proposing to do things differently: to plant crops, educate children, or practice hygiene. Technology also suggests new purposes for human effort: to earn money, obtain a bigger house or more food, gain geographical mobility. By challenging extant norms, the stimuli channelled by technology breed crises: Should members of society act as before or change their norms and ways? Since traditional norms of behavior are derived from a given universe of explanations, when norms are threatened by technology, that belief system is also attacked.

Once this link is shattered, affected societies are left with two options, both unpleasant. The first is to hold fast to meanings even if these now contradict norms of behavior governing daily activity. Such fragmentation is traumatic to beings accustomed to attach cosmic, if not mystical, significance to simple actions carried out in the home, in the field, or on the pathways. Not only is a serious social identity problem posed, but new behavior tends to be either totally rejected or uncritically internalized, often with damaging effects. Hence, the first option is to live in a state of cultural fragmentation.

Another choice is theoretically open to societies touched by technology: to create a new synthesis of meaning and normative values. From the very nature of the case, such a creation is beyond their capacities. How can communities undergoing their first experience of modern technology develop a new value synthesis when modern nations themselves, after two centuries of contact with science and technique, have

36   STUDIES IN COMPARATIVE INTERNATIONAL DEVELOPMENT

proven unable to find a wisdom to match their sciences? As Danilo Dolci
(1968:51) explains, "We have become experts when it comes to
machinery, but we are still novices in dealing with organisms." Pre-
technological societies lack that familiarity with science and technology
which might enable them to create a new synthesis. Once they receive
new techniques, they have no realistic hope of preserving unity in their
world of values. They are doomed to value disruption; the delicate
balance between acquisitive desires and effective access to resources has
been shattered. This balance finds expression in the facetious phrase:
"One shouldn't want what one can't get." The psychology of needs in
traditional societies has always been based on this principle. It was
frankly recognized that all members have acquisitive desires for things
and for benefits associated with persons. Often men "owned" wives in
much the same way they owned houses, goats, or jewelry. Most pre-
technological societies lived in ecological conditions wherein material
abundance for all was impossible. The state of productive arts was
rudimentary, and effective access to resources, free from harassment by
enemies or from natural catastrophes, was limited. If group survival was
to be assured, and if disruptive conflict among members of the group
was to be mitigated, it became necessary—and therefore morally
good!—for individuals to curb their acquisitive instincts. Not that all
acquisitive instincts were illegitimate or that none could gain for themselves more than a pro rata share of total available goods. The contrary
proved true. Although social values legitimized the need of all for
minimum food, shelter, sexual satisfaction, access to arable lands,
fishing grounds, or hunting areas, most societies assigned greater material rewards, prestige, and influence to certain classes enjoying hierarchical, functional, or charismatic superiority. It was deemed right for
some to accumulate wealth while others had to be content with bare
survival. Nevertheless, the poor identified vicariously with the wealth
and display of their community's privileged members. The crucial
norm, in such social structures, was not the license granted to the few to
expand their acquisition, but the general constraint on acquisitiveness
imposed on the many. And the rationale for "putting brakes on desire"
was that under no conceivable circumstances could enough resources be
available to allow all to desire, and to obtain, much more. Hence social
norms and symbols restricted the instincts of accumulation.

Technology introduces a new dynamism of desire which legitimizes a
general drive toward acquisitiveness. It thereby alters the existence
rationality of societies, their strategy to optimize survival in ways which

preserve meaning, esteem, and freedom. Beyond these broad areas of value conflicts, it is worth examining five more limited conflict zones engendered by the transfer of technology.

Conflict Arenas in Technology Transfer

A first tension arises from the way different actors view technology. Personnel in corporations, consulting firms, or business schools view technology as a marketable commodity. Technology, they say, costs money to produce; it is a product to be sold, not a free good such as air or water were in preecology days. Officials in governments, international agencies, and voluntary aid organizations, in turn, tend to speak of technology, not as a marketable commodity, but as a free good. They rhetorically affirm the Third World's right to share in the pool of scientific and technological knowledge. This divergence in perceptions gives rise to serious conflicts.

Ritchie-Calder (1973:11) analyzes why the advantages of latecomers to technology are largely fictious.

It is true that one does not have to re-invent the wheel in order to ride a bicycle. It is true that each country that undertakes the modernization of its economy relies partly on the heritage of others. It is also true that there is a great deal of knowledge and know-how freely available for transmission from one country to another but many of the less-developed countries do not know how to go shopping in the super-market of science (Nobel laureate Patrick Blackett's phrase) nor how to get the free samples or generally available technology. The term "transfer" in this sense is a euphemism because technology and know-how is being bought and sold like a commodity, but there is no world market nor a world exchange nor world prices for technology. The "latecomers" in this case are like spectators arriving at the last moment at a cup final and having to buy tickets from speculators at excessive prices.

A second conflict opposes the economics of growth to demands for social justice. Most technology transfers reinforce the consumer patterns of upper and middle classes in underdeveloped countries, those who buy and sell on the world market. Disregarding this fact, the standard argument invoked to justify importing technology asserts that it can abolish the misery of the poor.

Furtado (1973) sees a direct correlation between the "basket of consumer goods" a national economy produces and the patterns of class divisions one finds in that nation. Development, he explains, is distorted unless three activities are organically integrated into the national economy: the production of a basket of goods, capital accumulation, and

38   STUDIES IN COMPARATIVE INTERNATIONAL DEVELOPMENT

technical progress. *Organically integrated* means that outside resources play a minor role and that the basic locus of decision making is national. If a nation pays no attention to social justice, the cheapest and most efficient way for it to acquire technology is indeed through the channel of multinational corporations. In absolute terms this choice is terribly expensive; relatively speaking, it is the quickest and most efficient way to become technologically competitive in the world market. If, on the contrary, a nation values greater social justice and seeks to produce goods to meet the needs of its poor majorities, then what may appear as the cheapest and most efficient route for achieving technological maturity does violence to its development objectives. Technology transfers tend to increase social inequalities, because multinational managers and their clients favor products, processes, and technologies which satisfy the wants of the relatively rich, not the needs of the poor.

A third tension pits the desire of less developed countries to gain relative autonomy against the high costs of imported technology. José Bejarano (1971), vice president for Latin America of Xerox Corporation, declares that most Third World countries desperately need technology to abolish mass misery within their borders but lack the infrastructure to produce it. But, he continues, technological research is so expensive that leaders of these nations would be "well-advised to recognize that solutions to technological problems are beyond their means. Officials of emerging countries can best foster technological development by enlisting the aid of the international business enterprise."

The threat to autonomy posed by technology can be gauged by suggestions made recently regarding multinational business, the main carrier of modern technology. Political scientist Franklin Tugwell (1972) argues that "soft states won't make it"; therefore, enlightened leaders should subcontract the running of their nations to multinational corporations. Others urge that MNCs be given votes in the United Nations in recognition of their de facto sovereignty. Still others, evoking the global character of MNCs, call for the creation of a kind of Vatican City to provide an international charter for corporations, preferably in some pleasant, sea-lapped Caribbean island (*Center Report*, 1971). Corporations so chartered would be exempt from tax jurisdictions of their host countries. There is ample room for value conflicts around Bejarano's statement.

A fourth polarity is the tendency of technology to standardize for the sake of efficiency, of economies of scale, and of keeping research and

ON THE ETHICS OF DEVELOPMENT PLANNING   39

development costs down. This drive counters the aspirations of most less developed countries to preserve cultural diversity. One must nonetheless beware of adopting a mausoleum outlook on cultural values and diversity. Culture needs to find expression, not only in language, fine arts, local garb, and colorful markets, but also in the practical arts—in diverse work patterns, in differentiated tools and products.

Economist John White (1972), of the Institute of Development Studies in Sussex, dramatizes the issue in these words:

> Benefit is subjectively perceived and if one simply aggregates the perceptions of individual members of society one becomes lost in conflicts and inconsistencies. Hence, the paradoxically reactionary emphasis on changing attitudes which is the age-old response of the bureaucratic paternalist to a situation in which he finds himself exposed to uncomfortable challenges . . . . If people do not like the taste of new wheat, the bureaucrat decides that people's tastes must be changed, whereas simpletons like myself think that it might be more logical to change the taste of the wheat.

It is no doubt more logical to change the taste of the wheat, but in order to do so, one must actively resist the tendency technology displays towards standardization.

A fifth polarity is the contradiction arising from too exclusive a search for so-called appropriate or intermediate technology: inexpensive, labor-intensive, and small-scale (Schumacher, 1973). Although intermediate technology is cheaper and generates more employment than so-called high technology, most leaders do not want their nations to be, or to seem to be, second-rate, militarily or technically. No matter how expensive or wasteful "high" technology is, they want to have it in order to "be modern," even if they plan never to use the technology acquired, especially the military hardware. Wisdom in national leaders consists in making appropriate choices of a whole gamut of technologies for varying purposes.

Mainland China offers an illustration of the principle of multiple criteria of appropriateness. One must note seriously the nation's formal commitment to associating workers and students to the production process, to disseminating inventiveness, and to assuring full employment. Recent studies indicate that the Chinese favor capital-intensive, high-quality control, and modern technologies in capital goods industries (Heyman, 1974; Dean, 1972; Needham, 1975; Sobin, 1972; Reynolds, 1974; Rifkin and Kaplinsky, 1973; Ishikawa, 1972; Oldham, 1973). For these industries front-line technology is the watchword. In secondary industries, on the contrary, manufacturing consumer goods—food, textiles, bicycles, sewing machines—efficiency is sacrificed to maximize employment and worker participation in production and research decisions. Here is an example of an appropriate choice of several technologies in the light of larger social values.

Whatever the final judgment one passes on the merits of China's vast experiment with technology, one lesson emerges from its policy. Chinese leaders constantly declare that, for them, values command politics (the primary value is to construct revolutionary consciousness); politics (which includes ethics) commands economics; and economics commands technique. To command does not mean to ignore constraints; hence the dialectic of trial and error is given wide play. The relevant point is that appropriate technology embraces a whole range of technologies whose degree of appropriateness is judged sector by sector, industry by industry, and product by product, in line with development strategies flowing from central value options (Goulet, 1975).

Conclusion

Any ethic—of development, of social practice, or of cultural reconstruction—is simultaneously an ethic of goals and a "means of the means." No extrinsic grafting of norms can truly work; norms must be drawn from the inner dynamisms of each arena in which they operate. At stake is the difference between hollow moralism and genuine ethical strategies.

Social planners are prey to the same temptations which have beset other intellectuals at all times: to adopt roles which are personally gratifying but which fall short of their obligation to a new humanity in gestation.[4] Classically, these roles have been: counselor to the prince; the pure specialist in pursuit of apolitical goals; the faithful servant of a committed cause; and the free-lancer with varying degrees of sympathy for some political party or movement.

Counselors to the prince abdicate their critical spirit. Pure technicists live outside history and buttress whatever powers presently enjoy influence. Committed intellectuals, if they accept party or movement discipline uncritically, become someone else's ideologue or, if they remain true to their critical vocation, get expelled or marginalized as heretics. As for free-floating independent spirits, no real human community of need recognizes itself in their voice.

Planners and other intellectuals find it so difficult to create a true professional ethic because they are crafters of words, ideas, and models.

ON THE ETHICS OF DEVELOPMENT PLANNING 41

Consequently, they are timid about plunging into the heartland reality of ethics as existential power, and not as moral verbalism or conceptualism. Ethicists themselves constantly vacillate between ethical paralysis or compromise in the face of power, and energetic creativity newly released whenever they catch a faint glimpse of the power of ethics itself. Unless ethicists or social planners are ethically purified and achieve consistency in their ethical praxis, they cannot believe in the power of ethics to counter the power of wealth, of politics, of bureaucratic inertia, of defeatism, of social pathology. Such power can be won by a Gandhi, a Martin Luther King, a Danilo Dolci; it can never be institutionalized. But those others who lack ethical grandeur will inevitably lose hope in the face of larger powers, and accept compromises which strip their own ethics of its latent power.

This essay links ethics to value conflicts in technology because technology has now become the major resource of development. Paradoxically, it is also the chief instrument used by industrially advanced countries to domesticate Third World development and by totalitarian Third World leaders to subdue their own populations. Technology is the prime arena where cultures and subcultures will survive or be crushed.[5] The old convergence argument stated that industrialization will eventually blur the lines between capitalism and socialism. The argument now takes on a completely new dimension framed in two questions: Is there really only one technological culture, in which a truly human ethics has no place? And, can any culture harness technology to human ends?

NOTES

This paper was originally presented at the Graduate School of Social Planning, University of Puerto Rico, April 2, 1975.

1. For a less favorable reading of the Chinese "development strategy," the reader is referred to Berger (1974:150-65) and Ellul (1972:71, 303-13). Both view China with alarm as epitomizing a society ruled by the imperatives of propagandistic technology.

2. "Myth" is understood here in the religious and metaphysical sense of a comprehensive view of reality and mystery as central to human existence. It is apparent, on the other hand, that Western societies possess their own myths in the Sorelian sense: a frantic adherence to such goals as progress, quantitative growth, the advancement of science, the cult of celebrity, success defined in terms of "making it," etc.

3. The term appears throughout Freire's work. His major writings in English are listed under References. An interesting evaluative study of Freire's work has been done by John Albert Bugbee (1973).

42   STUDIES IN COMPARATIVE INTERNATIONAL DEVELOPMENT

4. I am grateful to the Argentine scholar Marcos Kaplan for illuminating discussions and unpublished notes on the roles of intellectuals in social change.

5. This theme is discussed further in Goulet's forthcoming book.

REFERENCES

BEJARANO, JOSE R.
    1971   "Let the Multinationals Help." New York Times (December 5).
BERGER, PETER L.
    1974   Pyramids of Sacrifice: Political Ethics and Social Change. New York: Basic Books.
BUGBEE, JOHN ALBERT
    1973   On the Quality of the Moral Partisanship of the Pedagogy of Paulo Freire. Ann
            Arbor: Michigan University Microfilms.
Center Report
    1971   "Will Businessmen Unite the World? A Discussion with Arnold Toynbee, Orville
            Freeman, Aurelio Peccei, and Eldridge Haines." Center Report (April):8-10.
DEAN, GENEVIEVE
    1972   "A Note on the Sources of Technical Innovations in the People's Republic of
            China." Journal of Development Studies 9 (October): 187-99.
DOLCI, DANILO
    1968   "Mafia-Client Politics." Saturday Review (July 6).
ELLUL, JACQUES
    1972   Propaganda. New York: Knopf.
FALS BORDA, ORLANDO
    1969   Subversion and Social Change in Colombia. New York: Columbia University Press.
FREIRE, PAULO
    1970a   Pedagogy of the Oppressed. New York: Herder and Herder.
    1970b   Cultural Action for Freedom. Cambridge, Mass.: Center for the Study of Develop-
            ment and Social Change.
    1973   Education for Critical Consciousness. New York: Seabury Press.
FROMM, ERICH
    1963   Escape From Freedom. New York: Holt, Rinehart and Winston.
FURTADO, CELSO
    1966   "Les conditions d'efficacité du transfert des techniques." Développement et Civili-
            sations 26 (June): 21-22.
    1973   "The Brazilian 'Model' of Development." In Charles K. Wilber (ed.), The Politi-
            cal Economy of Development and Underdevelopment. New York: Random House.
GOULET, DENIS
    1965   Etica del Desarrollo. Barcelona/Montevideo: Editorial Estela/IEPAL.
    1971a   "Development . . . or Liberation?" International Development Review 13 (Sep-
            tember): 6-10.
    1971b   The Cruel Choice. New York: Atheneum.
    1971c   "An Ethical Model for the Study of Values." Harvard Educational Review 41
            (May): 205-27.
    1975   "The Paradox of Technology Transfer." Bulletin of the Atomic Scientists 31
            (June): 39-46.
    Forth- Technology Transfers and Development: A Study in Value Conflicts.
    coming
GOULET, DENIS, and MICHAEL HUDSON
    1971   The Myth of Aid. New York: IDOC North America.
HEYMANN, HANS, Jr.
    1974   China's Approach to Technology Acquisition: Part III—Summary Observations.
            Santa Monica: Rand Corporation (unpublished report).
ISHIKAWA, SHIGERU
    1972   "A Note on the Choice of Technology in China." Journal of Development Studies 9
            (October): 161-86.

ON THE ETHICS OF DEVELOPMENT PLANNING 43

LIN, PAUL T.K.
  1975   "Development Guided by Values: Comments on China's Road and Its Implications." In Saul H. Mendlovitz (ed.), On the Creation of a Just World Order. New York: Free Press.
MONTGOMERY, JOHN D.
  1974   Making and Implementing Development Decisions. Cambridge, Mass.: MIT Press.
NEEDHAM, JOSEPH
  1975   "History and Human Values: A Chinese Perspective for World Science and Technology." Paper presented at the Canadian Association of Asian Studies Annual Conference (May).
OLDHAM, C.H.G.
  1973   "Science and Technology Policies." In Michael Oksenberg (ed.), China's Developmental Experience. New York: Academy of Political Science.
REYNOLDS, LLOYD G.
  1974   "China's Economy: A View from the Grass Roots." Challenge 17 (March-April): 12-20.
RIFKIN, SUSAN B., and RAPHAEL KAPLINSKY
  1973   "Health Strategy and Development Planning: Lessons from the People's Republic of China." Journal of Development Studies 9 (January): 213-32.
RITCHIE-CALDER, LORD
  1973   "Role of Modern Science and Technology in the Development of Nations." United Nations Document E/5238/Add.1 (January).
SCHUMACHER, E.F.
  1973   Small is Beautiful: A Study of Economics as if People Mattered. New York: Harper Torchbooks.
SOBIN, JULIAN M.
  1972   "Pilgrimage to the Canton Fair." Columbia Journal of World Business 7 (November-December): 88-91.
TUGWELL, FRANKLIN
  1972   "The 'Soft States' Can't Make it." Center Report (December): 15-17.
WHITE, JOHN
  1972   "What is Development?" Hammamet (Tunisia): Unpublished paper (April).

[9]

Development Experts: The One-Eyed Giants

DENIS GOULET

University of Notre Dame

Summary. – 'One-eyed giants' lack wisdom: they consider non-scientific modes of rationality retrograde.

Exceptions: For Lebret development is cultural and spiritual as well as economic and political. Gandhi favours 'production by the masses' over mass-production. *Secularism* (reducing all value to earthly ones) is bad but *secularization* (taking earthly values as decisive) is good.

Non-instrumental treatment derives development goals from within latent dynamisms in religion. *Instrumental* treatment treats tradition as means to 'modernity'.

The *'coefficient of secular commitment'* describes the varying religious rationales for working in history. Religions should reinforce secular commitment by linking morality to ultimate meanings.

Authentic development summons persons and societies to 'make history while witnessing to transcendence'.

The white man, says Laurens Van Der Post, came into Africa (and Asia and America for that matter) like a one-eyed giant, bringing with him the characteristic split and blindness which were at once his strength, his torment, and his ruin. . . . The one-eyed giant had science without wisdom, and he broke in upon ancient civilizations which (like the medieval West) had wisdom without science: wisdom which transcends and unites, wisdom which dwells in body and soul together and which, more by means of myth, or rite, of contemplation, than by scientific experiment, opens the door to a life in which the individual is not lost in the cosmos and in society but found in them. Wisdom which made all life sacred and meaningful – even that which later ages came to call secular and profane.[1]

1. INTRODUCTION

In a recent essay Godfrey Gunatilleke, Director of Sri Lanka's Centre for Development Studies (Marga Institute), pleads for a comprehensive view of development which recognizes the importance of religious values. He laments that 'political and religio-cultural components are not kept in the field of vision' of experts and are left outside 'the development strategy itself'. Why this monumental omission?

The reluctance of current development thinking to engage in a discussion of these issues ultimately has its roots in a system of cognition, a structure of knowledge which is partial and incomplete. In the development strategies that are propagated it is always the pursuit of material well-being, it is the socio-economic component of development which has primacy. Underlying this bias are the European ideologies of social change and the cognitive systems which grew out of the industrial revolution and enthroned the economistic view of society and man.[2]

This reductionist approach to knowledge leads most development specialists to become one-eyed giants: scientists lacking wisdom. They analyse, prescribe and act *as if* man could live by bread alone, *as if* human destiny could be stripped to its material dimensions alone. Small wonder, then, that developers have, in society after society, made 'things fall apart' (to cite the title of Achebe's novel) or launched fragile communities on what Kane calls the 'Ambiguous Adventure'. Yet, as I have noted elsewhere:

High indices of suicide in 'developed' countries have often blinded observers to the truth that material sufficiency, or abundance, may be less essential – even for survival – than is the presence of *meaning*. In order to survive one must want to survive, but how can one want to survive unless life has a meaning? Accordingly, having a meaningful existence may well be the most basic of all human needs.[3]

Falk judges that 'awe and mystery are as integral to human experience as bread and reason'.[4] After evaluating most approaches to global and national problem-solving, Falk concludes that '[N]o amount of tinkering can fix up the present international system. . . . the future prospects of the human species depend upon internalizing an essentially religious perspective, sufficient to transform secular outlooks that now dominate the destiny of the planet'.[5]

Most persons in developing countries still find in religious beliefs, symbols, practices and mysteries their primary source of meaning. Moreover, they instinctively sense that neither the promise of material paradise, nor the glorification of political processes can abolish life's tragic dimensions – suffering, death, wasted talents and hopelessness.[6]

Within advanced industrial countries one also detects a thirst for something more than purely material happiness. The editorial writers of London's *The Economist* evoked these aspirations while commenting on the conclave that elected Pope John Paul I (the present pontiff's short-lived predecessor) on 26 August 1978. These worldly-wise and politically hard-headed writers noted that the church ought to stand out 'as a Christian beacon in a secular world which may be starting to re-examine its wish to be secular'.[7] Three weeks later they added that the:

> . . . late-twentieth century world, with its urge to openness and equality, is also a world which is starting to think that its recent preoccupation with the material aspects of life may be incomplete. It therefore needs a church, Catholic, Orthodox, Protestant or whatever, prepared to carry the banner for the non-material aspects, and to insist that some kinds of truth – the non-political kinds – are objective and permanent.[8]

Growing pleas for a richer and less homogeneous universe of values provide a context for the present article, whose aims are threefold: (1) to recall exceptions to the general neglect of religion by development writers; (2) to distinguish two modes (instrumental and non-instrumental) of handling values in social change theory and practice; and (3) to examine how religious belief systems are vectors of different 'coefficients of insertion in time and history'.

2. EXCEPTIONS

As early as 1942 Lebret and his associates published their *Manifesto for a Human Economy*[9] calling for patterns of development that would satisfy the needs of 'all in man and all men' ('tout l'homme et tous les hommes', to use Perroux's phrase). Their vision of the human needs to be satisfied by authentic development embraced recreational, aesthetic and religious needs –including societal openness to the deepest levels of mystery and transcendence. Material welfare, effective social institutions, political modernity and technical problem-solving should all be subordinated to what Lebret called 'the human ascent',[10] the conquest by every person and community, via successive approximations, of a more human and more humane form of life. Such a conquest, Lebret argues, can only result from a 'revolution in solidarity'[11] binding local groups to the world community in patterns of interdependence founded on mutuality and cooperation, not on domination and exploitation.[12] From its inception Economy and Humanism raised the banner of a comprehensive view of development. In 1971 I paraphrased that movement's view of authentic development in the following terms:

> What is conventionally termed development – dynamic economic performance, modern institutions, the availability of abundant goods and services – is simply one possibility, among many, of development in a broader, more critical, sense. Authentic development aims at the full realization of human capabilities: men and women become makers of their own histories, personal and societal. They free themselves from every servitude imposed by nature or by oppressive systems, they achieve wisdom in their mastery over nature and over their own wants, they create new webs of solidarity based not on domination but on reciprocity among themselves, they achieve a rich symbiosis between contemplation and transforming action, between efficiency and free expression. This total concept of development can perhaps best be expressed as the 'human ascent' – the ascent of all men in their integral humanity, including the economic, biological, psychological, social, cultural, ideological, spiritual, mystical, and transcendental dimensions.
>
> It follows from this view of authentic development that innovation can be good only if it is judged by the concerned populace to be compatible with its image of the good life and the good society.[13]

Although most development scholars have neglected the role of religion in development processes, other noteworthy exceptions are also to be found. One recalls such books as Banfield's *The Moral Basis of a Backward Society* (1959); French economist Jacques Austruy's *L'Islam Face au Développement Economique* (1961); that edited by the late Kalman Silvert, a political scientist, *Churches and States, the Religious Institution and Modernization* (1967); the work edited by Smith on *Religion and*

Political Modernization (1974); and that same author's *Religion and Political Development* (1970); Bruneau's *The Political Transformation of the Brazilian Catholic Church* (1974); Gamer's *The Developing Nations, A Comparative Perspective* (1976). Also important were the numerous productions emanating from the pen of sociologists like Bellah or anthropologists like Geertz. Notwithstanding these significant exceptions, however, it remains true that the vast majority of development authors have paid scant attention to religious values in their writings. In short, they deserve Gunatilleke's condemnation.

Most development authors and practitioners have simply assumed that religious beliefs incarnate a superstitious or retrograde approach to knowledge and reflect an uncritical cast of mind incompatible with the demands of modern rationality. For them, progress has meant not only secularization but secularism as well.[14]

Marxist revolutionary theorists, in turn, understandably brand religion as the ally of reaction, the enemy of radical power shifts. Nevertheless, the overt social commitment of Latin American 'theologians of liberation' (Gutierrez, Perez, Assmann, Segundo, Emilio Castro, Bonino, Arroyo, Dussel *et al.*), allied to the resounding testimony given by revolutionary priests such as Torres or Lain, undermine such simplistic judgements. While dedicating a school in Cuba honouring the memory of the slain Camilo Torres, Fidel Castro declared that if the Christian Church ever threw its support to the Latin American revolutionary movement, that movement would prove invincible.

Even non-revolutionary development experts have recently had their complacent bias toward secularism overthrown by two forces. The first is the powerful anti-elitist thrust now emerging in development discourse: 'experts' find it increasingly difficult to justify imposing their solutions and values on people who must pay the price of their prescriptions.[15] As greater legitimacy is assigned to self-reliant strategies which build from within traditional values, planners, administrators and politicians have had to acknowledge that it is their own intellectual elitism and cognitive arrogance which nurture a sustained bias against the religiosity of the people in whose benefit they allegedly decide, prescribe or act. Indeed, the very bankruptcy of conventional development models propels even conservative development experts into the search for alternative development strategies. Such explorations have usually led

them to confess, at least implicitly, the truth of the admonition issued in 1962 by the late econometrician, Max Millikan. Millikan insisted that good planning ought to be 'the presentation of certain key alternatives to the community in ways which will help shape the evolution of the community's value system'.[16] But how can agronomists, demographers, or educators 'help shape the evolution of the community's value system' if they ignore or disparage the religious dimensions of those values?

Within 'developed' countries as well, social commentators and politicians have likewise grown uneasy over the failure of purely secular images of happiness and the good life to satisfy people. During his year-end interview with *New York Times* columnist James Reston in 1978, Zbiegniew Brzyzinski, the US president's national security adviser, explained that:

> The crisis of contemporary democracy associated with inflation is a product of a culture in which 5 per cent more of material goods per annum is the definition of happiness. People are discovering that it isn't. . . . Ultimately, every human being, once he reaches the stage of self-consciousness, wants to feel that there is some inner and deeper meaning to his existence than just being and consuming, and once he begins to feel that way, he wants his social organization to correspond to that feeling; whereas some aspects of our social organization, the vulgar and crass commercialism, correspond largely only to the desires of the stomach, in a figurative sense, to the consumptive (sic!) ethic. I think modern man is discovering this isn't enough.[17]

The American sociologist, Daniel Bell, author of the well-known *The Post-Industrial Society*, states that 'The real problem of *modernity* is the problem of belief. To use an unfashionable term, it is a spiritual crisis, since the new anchorages have proved illusory and the old ones have become submerged.'[18]

The year 1979 brought shock waves even to the staunchest secular political observers, obliging them to revise their views as to the importance of religion in social change. When Iran's Shah was overthrown and replaced by a theocratic ruler, everyone suddenly wanted instant understanding of Islam and of its impact on political and economic affairs.[19]

When interviewed by the Iranian *Communications and Development Review*,[20] Lerner was asked to assess his earlier work, *The Passing of Traditional Society* (1958). He noted a sharp difference between attitudes found in Iran in 1958 and 1977. Earlier it was 'psychic mobility' — the capacity of peasants, shopkeepers and housewives to imagine new roles, futures and lives for themselves — which acted as the motor force galvanizing their energies to pursue development, which they equated with progress. Twenty years later, Lerner informs us the prevailing attitude is not psychic mobility but ambivalence, a profound sense of conflict regarding the benefits and evils accompanying development. Lerner now prefers to use the neutral term 'change' to 'development': his reason is that change can be either good or bad, whereas 'development' implies the progressive unfolding of something which is good or better than what came before.

Now that conventional development wisdoms are being radically questioned even by their former adepts, it is essential to look more closely at the role played by traditions and indigenous values in development. The large majority of Third-World populations, especially peasants who are economically and technologically underprivileged, cling to traditional values anchored in religious meaning systems. Even traditional Chinese philosophy long regarded as non-theistic and secular, carries quasi-religious overtones, with its injunctions to observe filial piety and respect the 'celestial' order. Therefore, to study the interaction between religion and social change is no idle endeavour. On the contrary, the new regard for values bears directly on the formulation of strategies by which suitable developmental changes can be proposed. In the process, however, one must avoid a purely instrumental treatment of values.

3. HOW TO TREAT VALUES?

What does it mean to say that religious and other indigenous values must not be treated by change agents in a purely *instrumental* fashion? The answer is that such values are not to be viewed *primarily* as mere means – aids or obstacles – to the achievement of goals derived from sources outside the value systems in question. Even development agents who are sensitive to local values usually derive their goals from outside these values: from development models or the common assumptions of their respective scientific disciplines. Thus, a demographer will strive to 'harness' local values to his objective of promoting contraception or achieving zero population growth. Similarly, the agronomist will search for a traditional practice upon which to 'graft' his recommendation to use chemical pesticides. Similarly, the community organizer will 'mobilize' a population for political ends around traditionally cherished symbols. All three cases illustrate an

'instrumental' treatment of local values. Obviously, this approach is also frequently used by national leaders, politicians or technocrats.

The anthropologist Louis Dupree describes the instrumental use of Islamic beliefs and practices made by Afghanistan's Prime Minister Mohammad Daoud Khan in the 1950s. The example he gives constitutes an almost 'pure case' of the politically 'instrumental' use of religion in the quest for development.

> During the Afghan national holidays (Jeshn) in August of 1959, the government of Prime Minister Mohammad Daoud Khan, who had seized power from his uncle in a bloodless 1953 coup, informally ended purdah (the isolation of women) and the chowdry of burqa (Afghan version of the veil). The king, cabinet, high-ranking military officers, and members of the royal family stood before the march past of the army and the fly past of the air force as they had in past years – but with a radical difference. Their wives stood beside them unveiled. The thousands of villagers and tribesmen (including many religious leaders) in the crowd were stunned, some genuinely shocked. Amanullah [the ruler of Afghanistan, 1919–1929] had tried the same thing, but without the support of the army. In addition, he had issued a royal firman (proclamation) which made unveiling obligatory. The 1959 unveiling, however, was technically voluntary. The king did not issue a firman, and only high government officials were actually forced to display their unveiled wives in public, to set an example for the masses.
>
> The immediate result of the voluntary unveiling could have been easily predicted. A delegation of leading religious leaders in the country demanded and received an audience with Prime Minister Daoud, whom they accused of being anti-Islamic, of having succumbed to the influence of the Isai'ites (American Christians) and Kafirs (heathen Russians).
>
> Prime Minister Daoud, normally not a patient man, waited until the mullahs vented their spleens, and then calmly informed the delegation that the removal of the veil was not anti-Islamic, and that if the venerable religious leaders could find anything in the Qur'an which definitely demanded that women be kept in purdah, he would be the first to return his wife and daughters to the harem. Daoud knew he stood on firm theological ground, for several young Afghan lawyers had carefully checked the Qur'an.[21]

Daoud had unmistakeably drawn his goals from his vision of modernity; he was, in effect, 'using' religion to engineer popular compliance with his modernization programme. It is precisely such an instrumental approach which must be avoided by sensitive national leaders and external change agents alike.

The more justifiable stance, I submit, is the *non-instrumental* one whose initial postulate holds that traditional values (including religious beliefs and practices) harbour within them a latent dynamism which, when properly respected, can serve as the springboard for modes of development which are more humane than those drawn from outside paradigms. When development builds from indigenous values it exacts lower social costs and imposes less human suffering and cultural destruction than when it copies outside models. This is so because indigenously-rooted values are the matrix whence people derive meaning in their lives, a sense of identity and cultural integrity, and the experience of continuity with their environment and their past even in the midst of change.[22] A non-instrumental treatment of values draws its development goals from within the value system to which living communities still adhere. A sound development strategy doubtless requires that these values be critically re-examined in the light of modern diagnoses of human needs to have improved nutrition or greater security against the ravages of nature or the uncertainties of unplanned production. This re-examination of old values leads to the formulation of goals for a development appropriate to the populace in question. The Overseas Development Council, a non-governmental research institute located in Washington, D.C., will soon publish a book on *Traditions and Indigenous Values in Development*. The work contains theoretical essays and case studies prepared by commissioned authors from Sri Lanka, India, Peru, Paraguay, Colombia, Tanzania and the United States. The book's culturally diverse authors concur in the view that traditional value systems contain within them both strengths and weaknesses. Therefore, a proper strategy presupposes a collective debate around how these strengths, whether visible or latent, can best be harnessed to achieve humane developmental goals consonant with what is best in those values. The first task is to define development goals themselves; only afterwards does one instrumentally 'use' local institutions or traditional strengths found in the value system to galvanize people into action. Such a normatively sequential procedure is the one advocated by Gandhi when he promoted a form of village development founded on traditional Hindu values. Nevertheless, he was discerning in his appraisal of ancient values, not hesitating to reject untouchability and, at least implicitly, the caste system as a whole. Although Gandhi is often portrayed by Westerners as a traditionalist, he introduced modern rational critique to Hindu consciousness, insisting that his countrymen reject the Brahmins' claim to be the sole

valid interpreters of the sacred writings. Instead, Gandhi taught, they should employ their reasoning powers to discover whether logical consistency and correspondance could be found between the Brahmins' teachings and reality critically observed. What Gandhi sought was a harmonious blend between traditional belief and modern rationality.

Parallel efforts have more recently been made by Islamic theorists and practitioners in their search for dynamic approaches to developmental problem-solving within the boundaries of their own religious traditions. Western politicians, investors, consultants, lawyers and journalists are now displaying a keen interest in the workings of so-called 'Islamic banks' in Saudi Arabia, Kuwait and other countries.[23] Because the Koran condemns interest as sinful usury, Islamic banks neither pay interest to depositors nor charge it to borrowers. Nevertheless, the banks need to operate as viable economic enterprises; therefore, the banks spread the risks flowing from their borrowing and lending. They receive a share of the profits realized by their borrowers and, in turn, proportionate shares of these profits are then distributed to their depositors. Technically and ethically speaking, such payments do not constitute interest (that is, an automatic fee charged for the use of money). Islamic bankers claim that they are simply facilitating the institutional circulation of money in ways which generate productive activities. Their example shows how a religious norm can alter a 'modern' practice, instead of itself being shaped by the dictates of modernity.

Students of comparative development know, of course, that religions, like traditional and indigenous values, come in all varieties and shapes. For this reason it becomes essential to identify the coefficient of insertion in secular matters inherent in any religious value system.

4. THE COEFFICIENT OF SECULAR COMMITMENT

By stigmatizing religion as 'the opium of the masses' Marx sought to hasten the demise of 'religious alienation' which turned men away from the tasks of building history on earth. Other-worldly Gods and paradises, Marx complained, poisoned men's minds by adorning them with dreams of celestial bliss. He denounced religion for abolishing history by making human destiny reside outside history. Religious doctrines, he thundered, negate true humanism and perpetuate injustice by offering promises of happiness to people who remain alienated. With the same passion Breton, the French surrealist poet, branded Jesus Christ as 'that enternal thief of human energies'. No contemporary religious believers can ignore the challenge to their values posed, not only by Marx or Breton, but by secularization and secularism everywhere. The central question they must answer is whether any religion can supply men and women of our day with a convincing rationale for building up history even as they strive to bear witness to transcendence?[24] Stated differently, can any religion preach a humanistic philosophy of history which, no less compellingly than does Marxism, incites faith in the future of the world while making of commitment to today's historical tasks an inescapable duty?

The key to the answer is suggested by comparing the 'coefficient of secular commitment' contained in Marxism with that contained in de Chardin's exegesis of Christianity. Limitations of space rule out a repetition here of the argument I have presented in an earlier essay.[25] But two points are worth noting: (1) that the coefficient of insertion can be applied to *all* religions; and (2) that a few key arenas of religion can be examined with a view to determining how 'serious' about historical commitment any religion (more precisely, any interpretative stream within a religion) is.

The first vital arena is the way in which religious doctrine views earthly life itself: is human life simply a means to some paradise beyond this world, or is it rather an end endowed with its own dignity and worth? The Christian philosopher Jacques Maritain (in *Integral Humanism*, first published in 1936), struggled to define, on behalf of pluralistic and secular twentieth-century societies, a paradigm of humanism which considered art, political advance, cultural progress, scientific achievement and ethical maturation as 'infravalent' ends. By infravalent ends, he understood not mere means to some other-worldly ends, but rather goals having their own terminal value although they rank on a lower order of dignity than the supreme ultimate goals (eternal union with a loving God together with all other creatures). Accordingly, Maritain distinguished between humanisms which were anthropocentric (man-centred) and theocentric (God-centred). Both philosophies were humanistic because they took human values and human achievements as worthy in themselves and not simply because they served higher purposes. Value was assigned to material existence for its own sake, and not simply as a stepping-stone to moral

virtue or to some celestial reward. Given such a perspective, the ethical 'goodness' of persons is to be judged, not primarily in terms of their subjective intentions, but rather according to their objective contributions toward the betterment of human life. Religious believers — Hindu, Buddhist, Christian or Muslim — are summoned to work on behalf of more rational and equitable economic structures, not because involvement in these arenas is the precondition for religion or God to triumph, but because that involvement is an urgent human duty bearing on tasks which are precious in their own right. To scorn creatures, in short, is to despise their Creator.

De Chardin once compared a contemporary pagan with a 'true Christian humanist'. The former, he says, loves the earth in order to enjoy it; the latter, *loving it no less*, does so to make it purer and draw from it the strength to escape from it. For de Chardin, however, this escape is not a flight from reality but the opening, or the 'issue', which alone confers final meaning on the cosmos.[26] De Chardin held that no pretext, however subtle or 'spiritual' it may appear, justifies inertia in religious believers faced with an array of pressing secular tasks to accomplish: knowledge and wisdom to be gained, greater justice to be forged, creativity and creation to be unleashed, political fraternity to be instituted and comprehensive human development to be progressively achieved.

A second arena in which a religion's coefficient in secular affairs may be judged is eschatology — the 'last things' or the final destiny of human effort. If gods are thought of as dramatic saviours who 'bail out humanity' in spite of its sins and errors, humans will be powerfully motivated to 'sin by omission' in the face of their ecological responsibilities, their duty to reduce armaments, their summons to abolish misery and exploitation everywhere. What is crucial, therefore, is the connection between religiously inspired commitment to human tasks and the 'final redemption,' 'nirvana', 'bliss', or 'absorption into Brahman–Atman'. If a religion is to possess a high coefficient of insertion in history, that connection must be intrinsic and essential, not extrinsic or accidental. This means that, as the poet and novelist Nikos Kazantzakis put it, we humans must help God save us. And by helping Him save us, we thereby also save Him.

The new breed of Latin American 'theologians of liberation'[27] have repudiated all purely spiritualistic conceptions of religion which justify passivity in the presence of oppressive structures. Their writings and the inspired by, them are especially important to students of development. Liberation theologians embrace the creative tensions which exist between fidelity to the demands of religious mystery, and the exigencies of full involvement in the creation of history — scientific and artistic work, political struggle, building a just and prosperous economy, changing social structures to meet human needs, and evolving moral norms in the face of rapidly changing circumstances. Building history and witnessing to transcendence, as these theologians understand the terms, are co-extensive with that sound and comprehensive view of development called for by Gunatilleke in earlier pages.

No less than other traditional meaning systems can religions turn away from the challenges posed to them by secularization and, more particularly, by the requirements of instituting just forms of national and global development. Therefore, a key strategic question emerges, namely: HOW are change strategies aimed at development to be *proposed* (and not *imposed*) to a populace whose traditional interpretation of its own religious value system may display a lower coefficient of insertion in history than might otherwise be possible without violating the essential tenets of that religion itself? The answer lies in what elsewhere I have called 'existence rationality'.[28] Existence rationality is the process by which any human society applies a conscious strategy for realizing its goals (survival, the defence of its identity and cultural integrity, the protection of possibilities for its members to attain what they understand to be the 'good life' etc.), given that society's ability to process information, and given the effective access it has to resources. All existence rationalities contain an inner core of values which must not be sacrificed, along with an outer periphery where, at least in principle, alteration is admissible. Even the narrow existence rationalities of 'traditional' societies offer considerable scope for change, on condition that proposed alterations reinforce the dominant strategy adopted by the society in question to assure its life-sustenance, minimum esteem (self-esteem and out-group esteem), freedom from unwanted constraints and modes of fulfilment of its own choosing (all of these are core values). As several authors note,[29] traditional value systems — which usually include a rich religious content — harbour a latent dynamism for change. If this dynamism is respected and activated by sound strategies of proposed social change or problem-solving, traditional values themselves can become the driving force of desired development. It is essential that change strategies respect the inner core of a value system's existence rationality: frontal attacks must not be mounted against the values contained in that core. Instead, efforts at transformation should concentrate on the latent flexibilities located at the outer margins of the existence rationality in question.

Independently of the strategy adopted, however, the *legitimacy* of change agents is vital. Although time is lacking here for a full discussion of the question, the central point is that most (all?) religions harbour within them, at least latently, a relatively high coefficient of commitment to human tasks, even those which require great changes in symbols, social organization and normative values. Hence, it is a mistake to assume that development is incompatible with religion. On the contrary, mutually respectful encounters between religious values and sound plans usually prove beneficial to both sides. In the process alienating interpretations of religion lose their legitimacy and development models are challenged to become more humane and to open themselves to a fuller gamut of values, not excluding those which thrust human endeavours into domains of mystery and transcendental meaning.

Recent experience in Catholic Latin America suggests that, notwithstanding initial misgivings, no basic resistance is offered to well-designed population control programmes, if these are part of a broader strategy to bring economic and social improvement and a wider range of personal choices to poor populations. More importantly, all traces of upper-class manipulation of lower-class-peoples' need to find social security and joy in numerous progeny must be purged.

I have evoked the duty of building history in ways which leave history itself open to transcendence. In a world of plural religions, philosophies and modes of knowledge, there exists no single predetermined channel to transcendence.[30] The late Herbert Marcuse took transcendence to mean the refusal to be satisfied with what is an ineradicable faith in the capacity, and the duty, of humans to go beyond the limitations of their present conditions. For millions of religious believers — Christians, Muslims, Hindus and others — transcendence points to a life after this life, a universe beneath and beyond this material world, which alone confers full and final meaning to all human efforts deployed in time. Whether historical life be viewed as a testing ground for separating the virtuous from the wicked, or simply as a tragic confirmation of the finiteness of all material things, what matters most are the precise links postulated between this-worldly existence and the transcendent reality which is the object of religious faith. Is transcendence something so qualitatively *other* that nothing accomplished in historical time has any direct or proportionate relationship to the higher values? Or, on the contrary, does one's image of transcendence make of collective human effort in time the very prerequisite of triumphant divine intervention as the final crowning of history? In the second 'way of the spirit', human effort is not alienated from human tasks by pointing toward transcendence; on the contrary, it draws from its orientation to values beyond itself a new dignity, urgency and depth. To this extent, therefore, it is a powerfully developmental force: for it is the vector of a high coefficient of secular commitment.

5. CONCLUSION

Development specialists no less than spiritual teachers would do well to heed the warning issued by the contemporary French spiritual writer, René Voillaume:

Christianity is at the moment exposed to two temptations, faced as it is with a world drawn almost in spite of itself into the ever more rapid and impetuous advance of a civilization based on technical achievement, which tends to enslave humanity and shut it up within the bounds of a purely earthly kingdom; first there is the temptation to separate the destiny of christendom from that of the world by a movement of withdrawal, Christians retreating into a 'small residue' living in expectation of the advent of the spiritual reign of

Jesus in their souls and in the life to come. This goes with a desire to extend the contemplative's way of life, set apart by vocation, to the whole community of the faithful. And on the other hand there is the temptation for the Christian to commit himself with his whole being to all sorts of scientific, economic, social and political activities, so as to bring Christian influence to bear on the structure of tomorrow's world, at the possible cost of reducing Christianity to being no more than the best solution to worldly problems, de facto if not de jure, and losing the sense of a spiritual kingdom, of the transcendent nature of Christ's mission, of worship, and of the divine supernatural destiny of all humanity.

A Christian must not succumb to either of these temptations, but must overcome them by transcending both, in a full realization of his vocation as man and son of God.[31]

A growing chorus of voices, in rich and poor countries alike, proclaim that full human development is not possible without regard for essential religious values. These voices assert that achievements in political, social, economic, technical, artistic and scientific realms do not exhaust the creativity, beauty or triumphs of which human beings are capable. Development's pressing imperatives will doubtless oblige religious practitioners to change many of their ancient symbols and practices. And conversely, it is to be hoped, the resiliency of critically tested religious value systems will invite development experts to enrich their own diagnoses and prescriptions for action. Both categories of one-eyed giants may perhaps come to acknowledge that they need each other if they are, jointly, to gain a wisdom to match modern sciences.

NOTES

1. T. Merton, *Gandhi on Non-Violence* (New York: New Directions, 1965), p. 1. His reference is to Van Der Post's *The Dark Eye in Africa* (New York: William Morrow, 1955), pp. 118–124.

2. G. Gunatilleke, 'The interior dimension', *International Development Review*, Vol. 21, No. 1 (1979/1), p. 4.

3. D. Goulet, 'Strategies for meeting human needs', in M. E. Jegen and C. K. Wilber (eds.), *Growth with Equity* (New York: Paulist Press, 1979), p. 49.

4. R. Falk, 'Satisfying human needs in a world of sovereign states: rhetoric, reality and vision', in J. Gremillion and W. Ryan (eds.), *World Faiths and the New World Order* (Washington, D.C.: Interreligious Peace Colloquium, 1978), p. 136.

5. *ibid.*, pp. 134, 136.

6. Cf. J.-M. Domenach, *Le Retour du Tragique* (Paris: Editions du Seuil, 1963).

7. Editorial, 'The keys to Rome', *The Economist* (12 August 1978), p. 9.

8. Editorial, 'John Paul's agenda', *The Economist* (2 September 1978), p. 13.

9. L. J. Lebret and R. Moreux, *Manifeste d'Economie et Humanisme* (Marseille: Economie et Humanisme, 1942).

10. L. J. Lebret, *Montée Humaine* (Paris: Les Editions Ouvrières, 1951).

11. L. J. Lebret, *Développement = Révolution Solidaire* (Paris: Les Editions Ouvrières, 1967).

12. Cf. K. Kumar (ed.), *Bonds Without Bondage:*

Explorations in Transcultural Interactions (Honolulu: University Press of Hawaii, 1979). Cf. D. Goulet, 'World interdependence: verbal smokescreen or new ethic?' (Washington, D.C.: Overseas Development Council, Development Paper No. 21, 1976).

13. D. Goulet, 'An ethical model for the study of values', *Harvard Educational Review*, Vol. 41, No. 2 (May 1971), pp. 206–207.

14. *Secularization* is the process whereby this-worldly values are increasingly taken as decisive in human affairs and as meriting the full energies and attentions of societies' members. *Secularism*, in contrast, is a philosophical stance –whether theoretical or practical – which reduces the world of values or of worthwhile pursuits to secular matters. Not surprisingly, many religious figures –including Gandhi, Archbishop Camara of north-east Brazil or the late philosopher-scientist Teilhard de Chardin – endorse the secularization process while rejecting secularism. On this see A. T. van Leeuwen, *Prophecy in a Technocratic Era* (New York: Charles Scribner's, 1968), pp. 56–67.

15. Human pain and value destruction in development are central themes in P. L. Berger's *Pyramids of Sacrifice* (New York: Basic Books, 1974).

16. M. F. Millikan, 'The planning process and planning objectives in developing countries', in *Organization, Planning, and Programming for Economic Development* (Washington, D.C.: US Government Printing Office, 1962), p. 33.

17. J. Reston, 'Interview with Brzyzinski', *Washington Star* (Sunday, 31 December 1978), Section E, p. E-4.

18. D. Bell, *The Cultural Contradictions of Capitalism* (New York: Basic Books, 1976), pp. 28–29.

19. For an introduction to these issues see E. W. Said, *Orientalism* (New York: Pantheon, 1978); also M. Abdul-Rauf, *The Islamic Doctrine of Economics and Contemporary Economic Thought* (Washington, D.C.: American Enterprise Institute for Public Policy Research, 1979).

20. 'An interview with Daniel Lerner', *Communications and Development Review*, Vol. 1, Nos. 2 and 3 (Summer/autumn 1977), p. 5.

21. L. Dupree. 'The political uses of religion: Afghanistan', in K. H. Silvert (ed.), *Churches and States, The*

Religious Institution and Modernization (New York: American Universities Field Staff, 1967), pp. 195–214.

22. The need for continuity is cogently argued by British sociologist P. Marris in *Loss and Change* (New York: Patheon, 1974).

23. 'Basic Islamic principles will shape Iran's economy in post-revolutionary era', *Business International*, Weekly report to managers of worldwide operations (New York: 16 March 1979), pp. 81–84. In June 1979 the Chase Manhattan Bank sponsored a conference for businessmen on 'The reemergence of Islamic Law'. On this see the *Washington Post*, Metro section (Monday, 14 May 1979), p. C-1. For a scholarly treatment of Islamic approaches to finance, technology and economics see Z. Sardar, *Science, Technology and Development in the Muslim World* (London: Croom Helm, 1977).

24. D. Goulet, *A New Moral Order* (Maryknoll, New York: Orbis Books, 1974), final chapter entitled 'Makers of History or Witnesses to Transcendence?'.

25. D. A. Goulet, 'Secular history and teleology', *World Justice*, Vol. 8, No. 1 (September 1966), pp. 5–18.

26. M. B. Madaule, 'La personne dans la perspective Teilhardienne', in *Essais sur Teilhard de Chardin*, Collective editors (Paris: Fayard, 1962), p. 76.

27. G. Gutierrez, *A Theology of Liberation* (Maryknoll, New York: Orbis Books, 1973); cf. J. L. Segundo, *The Liberation of Theology* (Maryknoll, New York: Orbis Books, 1976).

28. D. Goulet, *The Cruel Choice* (New York: Atheneum, 1971), Chapter 9, 'Existence Rationality and the Dynamics of Value Change', pp. 187–214.

29. L. Rudolph and S. Rudolph, *The Modernity of Tradition* (Chicago: University of Chicago Press, 1967); M. B. Ghali, *Tradition for the Future* (Oxford, England: Alden Press, 1972); and R. E. Gamer, *The Developing Nations: A Comparative Perspective* (Boston: Allyn & Bacon, 1976).

30. H. W. Richardson and D. R. Cutler, *Transcendence* (Boston: Beacon Press, 1969).

31. R. Voillaume, *Au Coeur des Masses* (Paris: Cerf, 1965), p. 532. Translation mine.

[10]

DEVELOPMENT AS PRACTICE IN A LIBERAL CAPITALIST WORLD

ALAN THOMAS*

Development Policy and Practice, The Open University, Milton Keynes, UK

Abstract: As we enter the 21st century, a dominant trend in development thinking makes it refer specifically to the practice of development agencies. However, to accept this as *the* main meaning of development would carry the dangers of losing the complexity and ambiguity of development, of underplaying the importance of vision and of historical process, and of limiting development to actions and policies aimed at reducing poverty in poor countries. It is important to challenge this restricted view of what development is. At the same time, the current prime importance of practice within the development field should be recognized and development practice should be taken more seriously from the point of view of theory building. Focused work on notions such as accountability, trusteeship and public action would help here, as would work on building up a tradition of critical practice analogous to that in Organization Development.

1 INTRODUCTION

This paper is based around the proposition that, as we enter the 21st century, a dominant trend in development thinking restricts it to a rather limited meaning, referring specifically to the practice of development agencies. While recognizing the value of the work of these agencies in attempting to combat poverty, the paper explores the dangers of allowing this to become accepted as *the* main meaning of development. However, it also argues that the current prime importance of practice within the development field should be recognized and hence that development practice should be taken more seriously from the point of view of theory building.

This brief paper does not attempt to review the considerable literature on development. It simply raises some issues which I believe are worthy of consideration. It draws heavily on certain arguments developed by Cowen and Shenton (1996) in their book on *Doctrines of Development*, which discusses the history of the idea of development. Since Mike Cowen's recent death it seems

* Correspondence to: Alan Thomas, Development Policy and Practice, Centre for Complexity and Change, Faculty of Technology, The Open University, Walton Hall, Milton Keynes, MK7 6AA, UK. E-mail: a.r.thomas@open.ac.uk

particularly important to work through some of the implications of the insights in his and Shenton's analysis.

The current context for development is liberal capitalism as the dominant mode of social organization and the basis for globalization. Indeed, liberal capitalism is so dominant that there appears to be no question of wholesale social transformation in any other direction. As a result, development appears no longer to be mainly about the transformation of the economic and social basis of societies, and is now often thought of in terms of dealing with problems rather than searching for grand alternatives. Development has always been an ambiguous idea, on the one hand being virtually synonymous with 'progress' and on the other referring to intentional efforts to 'ameliorate the disordered faults of progress' (Cowen and Shenton, 1996, p. 7). However, at present there is little debate in development circles about the direction or form of 'progress' in the more 'advanced' countries, despite the differences between types of capitalism — US, European and East Asian. Perhaps there is an unspoken acceptance of Fukuyama's (1992) 'end of history' argument and hence of the idea that the only end result of development in the first sense is globalized liberal capitalism, its regional variations being of relatively little significance. This leaves the danger that the second meaning of development will become institutionalized as the prime meaning.

Indeed, at present, what are publicly visible as 'development agencies' are mostly engaged either in attempts to reduce poverty (and improve health, education, gender equality and environmental degradation) or in humanitarian relief to mitigate the effects of internal wars and other disasters. Thus the practice of activities such as these has become the substance of development in many parts of the world.

The proposition that the dominant sense in which development is used is that of development as practice is not one that can be demonstrated conclusively. The question is one of usage and power rather than of trying to show which meaning is the 'correct' one. It is impossible to avoid the contradictions behind the idea of development by laying down a single, simple definition of one's own. As Cowen and Shenton point out (1996, p. 4): 'Development comes to be defined in a multiplicity of ways because there are a multiplicity of "developers" who are entrusted with the task of development.' And only some of this multiplicity have sufficient power for their interpretation of 'development' to be effectively imposed on others.

'Developers' might include governments in poor and middle-income countries, human rights organizations, international people's movements, and many other agencies. However, the most powerful 'developers' of others are the multilateral development agencies on the one hand and state agencies such as those of the United States and its allies on the other, and these tend to refer to development in terms of alleviating problems. This approach is epitomized by the Declaration adopted at the United Nations World Summit on Social Development in Copenhagen in 1995, which includes the adoption of the aim of reducing by half by 2015 the proportion of people living in extreme poverty. Similar targets have been agreed during the 1990s, at conferences where these powerful agencies were strongly represented, with respect to reducing infant and maternal mortality rates, achieving universal primary education, access to reproductive health services, minimizing gender inequality and reversing environmental degradation. These are now referred to as the International Development Targets. The Copenhagen Declaration also explicitly endorses the global market system while recognizing the need to intervene in this system 'to the necessary extent' in order to prevent or correct its failures.

The rest of this paper is devoted to taking further the proposition that development practice has come to be the dominant meaning of development. First, I discuss how the end of the Cold War has led to the dominance of the idea of development as practice and then I explore a little more closely how this is a limited view of development. I go on to how the axes of debate on development are quite different now compared to previous debates, relating them to the various competing views of development. Then in the last two sections I look at two major implications of the proposition which lead in different directions. There is the need to react to the danger that the dominance of the idea of development as practice may lead to this becoming accepted as effectively the only meaning of development. This makes it imperative to contest this meaning by promoting the other senses of the term. The other implication is quite different. Recognizing the importance of the idea of development as practice implies building on it by researching it, theorizing about it, and so on. This points to the importance of work on aspects of agency in the study of development, including particularly questions of trusteeship and of accountability.

2 DEVELOPMENT SINCE THE COLD WAR

The Cold War has receded into history remarkably quickly. It has become clear that our previous concentration on development as a post World War Two phenomenon taking place in the 'Third World' was a limited view shaped by Cold War thinking. There are several ways in which development could mean something different as we enter the 21st century from what it meant for most of the second half of the twentieth, though this paper suggests its meaning has become limited once again, in another way.

First, development can no longer be seen in terms of competing capitalist and communist (or state socialist) models, since 'capitalism has won'. Second, the notion that development refers specifically to part of the world, the 'underdeveloped' or 'Third' world where the competition between the two models takes place, as well as the possibility of searching for a third alternative, makes no sense now that the 'Second World' has mostly collapsed. One might like to suggest that development, if it continues to have meaning as we enter the 21st century, should apply to processes which occur, or fail to occur, at all levels anywhere in the world, from the individual up to the global. Indeed, massive economic and social transformations are occurring currently in much of the world, particularly China and the rest of East and Southeast Asia and to some extent India. Nevertheless, the dominant usage of development refers to the practice of development agencies intervening in global capitalism to alleviate poverty and other problems, so that development is still applied mainly to certain, other, parts of the world, namely those defined as 'poor'. Thus the British Department for International Development, for example, uses the notion of poverty focus in such a way that there is a danger of development appearing to apply only to certain of the world's poorest countries — and not to those parts of the world experiencing the most far-reaching transformation.

Third, the demise of the state socialist model of development makes it even more essential for development to be analysed in relation to capitalism. Possibilities for development now have to be related to the current realities of global capitalism, and indeed the combination of capitalist industrialization with liberal democracy is widely accepted as the only viable model of social organization. Fukuyama (1995), for example, writes:

> Today virtually all advanced countries have adopted, or are trying to adopt, liberal democratic political institutions, and a great number have simultaneously moved in the direction of market-oriented economics and integration into the global capitalist division of labour.
> ... As modern technology unfolds, it shapes modern economies in a coherent fashion, interlocking them in a vast global economy. The increasing complexity and information intensity of modern life at the same time renders centralized economic planning extremely difficult. The enormous prosperity created by technology-driven capitalism, in turn, serves as an incubator for a liberal regime of universal and equal rights, in which the struggle for recognition of human dignity culminates. ... [T]he world's advanced countries have no alternative model of political and economic organization other than democratic capitalism to which they can aspire (Fukuyama, 1995, pp. 3–4).

As a corollary to viewing development today in relation to the dominance of global liberal capitalism, the history of development should be viewed over the whole period of the domination of the industrial capitalist system, rather than only in relation to the polarized post-war world political order of the Cold War. According to Cowen and Shenton (1996), the era of industrial capitalism has also been the period of the 'modern doctrine of development'. They suggest that the latter was invented in the first half of the nineteenth century precisely to control the social disruptions caused by the unchecked 'development' of capitalism.

Here we run up the ambiguity of the term 'development'. Capitalism had been 'developing' for several centuries up to this point, continues to 'develop' to this day, and can be expected to 'develop' into the future. Indeed, an absolutely crucial aspect of capitalism is that it is intrinsically dynamic; it tends to build on itself and grow or 'develop' from within. This 'immanent' development should be clearly differentiated from the 'intentional development' which forms the deliberate policy and actions of states and development agencies, and which I am arguing is currently the dominant meaning given to the term. Cowen and Shenton also argue that development should be conceptually differentiated from progress. They point out that in the preceding centuries progress had been thought of as an immanent process, in that human society was conceived as moving inexorably to a higher and higher stage of civilization. There had always been casualties of this 'progress', as with those agricultural producers dispossessed by the 'enclosures' of the early seventeenth century in Britain. Only when this 'progress' moved to the stage of industrial capitalism did the poverty, unemployment and human misery caused threaten to bring about social disorder on a scale which necessitated 'intentional constructive activity' (Cowen and Shenton, 1996). This was when intentional development was invented.

> Industrial production and organization was accepted ... to be a historically given part of the movement towards an organic, positive or natural stage of society in Europe. The burden of development was to compensate for the negative propensities of capitalism through the reconstruction of social order. To

develop, then, was to ameliorate the social misery which arose out of the immanent process of capitalist growth (Cowen and Shenton, 1996, p. 116).

Writers of the post-development school are clearly referring to intentional development or development as practice when they suggest that the 'era of development' began with Harry S. Truman's inaugural address as President of the United States in January 1949 (Esteva, 1992), and that development 'did not work' so that now 'it is time to dismantle this mental structure' (W. Sachs, 1992, p. 1). Esteva is clear that the concept of development was not new, having been used and debated in many ways for at least 150 years. It was Truman's promotion of a 'program of development' as a way of maintaining United States hegemony which he suggests ushered in a new era, one in which the idea of development became of central importance at a global level.

In fact, to Truman development was only part of a strategy for the containment of communism. The era which began with Truman's inauguration would be better described as the era of the Cold War than the 'era of development'. For the next forty years development was the subject of competing theories in the context of the global clash between capitalism and communism. The post-development writers have done us a service in drawing attention to development as 'practice' or 'programme', but they are inaccurate in suggesting this usage of the term to be characteristic of the Cold War era. It is better to follow Cowen and Shenton in considering intentional development as having formed part of the policies of powerful global actors ever since the first half of the nineteenth century. In fact I suggest that it is particularly since the *end* of the Cold War that this sense of development has become the dominant one.

3 PRACTICE AS A LIMITED VIEW OF DEVELOPMENT

By arguing that the dominant meaning of development has come to reside in the idea of development as practice, I am suggesting that development has taken on a meaning which is limited in several ways.

First, it focuses on only one of the three main senses of the term 'development' which are distinguished in my discussion of *Meanings and Views of Development* (Thomas, 2000). These are:

(i)   as a *vision, description or measure of the state of being of a desirable society*;
(ii) as an *historical process of social change* in which societies are transformed over long periods;
(iii) as consisting of *deliberate efforts aimed at improvement* on the part of various agencies, including governments, all kinds of organizations and social movements.

It appears that as we enter the 21st century the third sense of the term has become dominant. Thus development has come to have a rather tautological meaning, referring not to a desired state or the process of social change which might achieve it, but simply to whatever is done in the name of development, and development is now used to mean *practice* more than vision or process.

Second, while the dominant notion of development as practice cannot exclude ideas of development as vision and as process completely, it is limited in that it incorporates rather simplistic versions of these. When development means simply what development agencies do then the vision of development tends to be reduced to targets and the process of development to techniques. The targets may be extremely ambitious, as with the Copenhagen Declaration target mentioned above for halving the proportion of the world's population in extreme poverty by 2015, and the techniques may be relatively sophisticated, as with the plethora of good practice guidelines on the running of micro-finance programmes or the widespread use of logical framework planning. It may also be argued that there is still room for considerable debate about the underlying assumptions on which the agencies base their calculations that certain policies will lead to desired results, and that these assumptions in turn must be based on some broad theory of social change. Nevertheless, targets are inherently unidimensional and as such represent a very limited vision of social transformation, while the application of techniques designed to achieve such targets tends to simplify theory to the idea that large-scale social change may be achieved straightforwardly by deliberate actions, or even that poverty reduction may be achieved by targeting the poor without the need for broader social change, and thus provides an equally limited view of the historical process of development.

Thirdly, considering development as practice tends to limit consideration to cases of the deliberate application of policies aimed at poverty reduction by leading international development agencies. However, it is important to learn from the examples of China and other East Asian and Southeast Asian countries which are certainly developing, but not simply in response to the practice of international development agencies. Of course, these countries generally have strong states which should be regarded as development agencies in their own right, so that these could also be thought of as examples of development as practice. Nevertheless there remains the danger that focusing on the poverty reduction policies of international agencies will restrict attention to the poorest countries, since this is where these policies are focused, even though countries which remain poor are by definition not likely to provide lessons about the successful application of development policies.

Generally, the notion of development as practice fails to capture the complexity and ambiguity of development. Even the apparently simple definition given by Chambers (1997), for whom development means just 'good change', already embodies a degree of ambiguity. The two words combine quite different ideas deriving from different senses in which the term 'development' is used. 'Good' implies a vision of a desirable society, something to aim at, a state of being with certain positive attributes which can be measured so that we can talk of 'more' or 'less' development. 'Change', on the other hand, is a process, which may entail disruption of established patterns of living.

There are several further points about the idea of development which go beyond simply 'good change' and which together show it to be an inherently ambiguous concept. First of all, development implies an all-encompassing change, not just an improvement in one aspect. Second, development is not just a question of a once-off process of change to something better, but implies a process which builds on itself, where change is continuous and where improvements build on previous improvements. Third, development is a matter of changes occurring at the level of social change and at the level of the individual human being at one and the same time. Changes in society have implications for the people who live in that society, and, conversely changes in how people think, interact, make their livings and perceive themselves form the basis for changes in society. Finally, development is not always seen positively. These points often go together, in that what some see as a general improvement may have losers as well as winners, and if social change is all-encompassing and continuous then the implication is that previous ways of life may be swept away, with the loss of positive as well as negative features.

However, the dominant usage of development tends to deny this complexity and ambiguity. For example, reducing development to a question of targets and of deliberate policies aimed at alleviating problems directly leaves aside questions about whether such change can indeed be achieved without what Schumpeter called 'creative destruction'. Again, since development agencies are often involved in emergency relief, this also comes to form part of what development is taken to mean, even though here there is nothing of the 'all-encompassing change, not just an improvement in one aspect', or 'process which builds on itself, where change is continuous and where improvements build on previous improvements'. We can declare that development *should* mean these things, but if we lack the power to impose such views development in practice means what development agencies do, and this is much more restricted.

4 NEW AXES OF DEBATE ON DEVELOPMENT

The suggestion that development in its dominant meaning is now somewhat restricted and refers mainly to practice does not mean that debates and disagreements about development have ceased. However, the main axes of debate have shifted from opposition between major theoretical positions or models of social transformation to differences about the form and extent of intervention or which agencies have the right to intervene.

Although the clash between capitalism and communism now seems to have been resolved in favour of capitalism, there remain basic differences in how development is seen to relate to capitalism. Competing views of development may be characterized as development *of*, *alongside* or *against* capitalism. Table 1 (from Thomas, 2000) summarizes these in terms of their visions, theories of social change, and views on the role and agents of development.

At one extreme there is neo-liberalism (or market liberalism), for which the immanent development of capitalism is sufficient. A number of essentially different views, concerned with underlying social and economic structures and which see development as involving changes in these structures, are grouped under the heading structuralism. These views tend to be associated with advocating state planning and are generally out of favour as far as development practice is concerned. Then there is 'interventionism', which sees the need for intentional development alongside capitalism. There are others who reject both capitalism and state planning and look for alternatives in different models of development, in particular what is variously termed 'another development' or 'people-centred development'. Finally there is the post-development school, which rejects the whole notion of development.

It would be useful, and neat, to be able to write that each of the columns in Table 1 constitutes a coherent theory of development. However, in practice things are less clear-cut than that. First, the dividing-lines between the columns only represent one person's attempt to simplify and to bring out the most important differences between

780   *A. Thomas*

Table 1. Summary of the main views of development (Thomas, 2000, p. 43)

	Development *of* capitalism	Development *alongside* capitalism		Development *against* capitalism		Rejection of development
	Neo-liberalism	Interventionism		Structuralism	'Alternative' (people-centred) development	'Post-development'
		'Market efficiency'	'Governing the market'			
Vision: desirable 'developed' state	Liberal capitalism (modern industrial society and liberal democracy)	(plus achieving basic social/environmental goals)		Modern industrial society (but not capitalist)	All people and groups realise their potential	['development' is *not* desirable]
Theory of social change	Internal dynamic of capitalism	Need to remove 'barriers' to modernization	Change can be deliberately directed	Struggle between classes (and other interests)	[not clear]	[not clear]
Role of 'development'	Immanent process within capitalism	To 'ameliorate the disordered faults of [capitalist] progress'		Comprehensive planning/transformation of society	Process of individual and group empowerment	A 'hoax' which strengthened US hegemony
Agents of development	Individual entrepreneurs	Development agencies or 'trustees' of development (states, NGOs, international organizations)		Collective action (generally through the state)	Individuals, social movements	Development agencies

views. In fact some of the views identified overlap, labels are not agreed and some of the protagonists might distinguish their views from others in quite different ways. Second, not all the views represented in Table 1 are complete theories of development. For example, the 'alternative development' school is strong on vision but weak on any theory of social change which might help explain how this vision might be achieved. Conversely, certain structuralist views concentrate on explaining social change but fail to offer any clear prescriptions.

However, the columns of Table 1 can be used to see how the main debates about development have shifted. As is well-known, neo-liberalism was dominant in the 1980s, and could be seen as a reaction against the structuralist views which had achieved widespread credence in the 1960s and 1970s. Thus a major debate in development thinking was between these two views, which nevertheless shared important areas of commonality. Both saw development mainly in terms of broad historical social change, and did not offer detailed prescriptions for what development agencies should do. The main area of disagreement was between the neo-liberal insistence on the materialist motivations of individuals and the self-regulating market and the structuralist view of the importance of social solidarity, class and collective forms of action. Since the only examples of large-scale collective action for development have occurred through the state, this opposition tended to be represented as *market versus state* or *profit versus planning*.

In the 1990s, with the demise of the Soviet Union and the general discrediting of comprehensive state planning as a vehicle for development, structuralist thinking fell even further out of favour, particularly with development agencies in respect of their policies towards the poorest countries. However, the ideal of a totally free global market society as envisaged by crude versions of neo-liberalism is also demonstrably bankrupt (Hobsbawm, 1994). The evident chaos caused by the attempt to let capitalism 'develop' itself in the ex-Soviet Union, together with the increases in inequity, poverty, environmental degradation and wars has led the World Bank and other agencies to modify their position considerably from the neo-liberal 'Washington consensus' of the 1980s.

Hence those with a degree of power in various development agencies today are all interventionists of some description. This is true equally for those who welcome Fukuyama's position on the lack of any realistic alternative to liberal capitalism expressed in the quote above and for those who deplore it but feel obliged to accept it nevertheless. The consensus among the world's decision-makers and academics regards global industrial capitalism as a fact of 21st century life, while at the same time perceiving a need for non-market intervention — or 'intentional development' to 'ameliorate' its 'disordered faults'. This includes intervention by the state and actions by other development agencies, including the World Bank itself, which go well beyond simply ensuring the conditions for market competition. The main area of debate in what may be called 'mainstream' development circles is no longer 'market versus state' but about the form and degree of intervention.

There are debates about whether intervention should be minimal or far-reaching, and about the role of intervention with respect to capitalism. On the one hand there are those for whom poverty, pollution, violence and so on are only problems insofar as they threaten the proper working of the capitalist system. However, they recognize that the answer is not simply to try to remove all obstacles to the self-regulation of the market, but that these problems need dealing with at least to the extent that they are kept under control. On the other hand, others see capitalism as dynamic and productive but dangerous if it is not controlled. From this point of view social goals need to be addressed directly and the market must be stringently regulated in order for development goals to be achieved. Kaplinsky (1998) has referred to the former as the *market efficiency* view of intervention, and the latter as *governing the market.*

All the versions of interventionism envision the state and other development agencies as taking on the job of intentional development required. As noted, these form the current 'mainstream' of development. The set of ideas grouped together under the labels 'another development' or 'people-centred development' are a reaction against this. In particular they reject the notion that others should determine what is required for people's development. This is a current of thought that places emphasis on people themselves as agents of development, solving their own problems individually or through local organizations and networks.

It has to be admitted that there is little if any theory as to how such dreams could be replicated on a large scale, and how the kind of social change could be brought about that would safeguard them for the future. However, throughout the 1990s there has been a growing consensus on the need to look more closely at the potential for local groups and individuals to be involved as their own development agents, if only because of the manifest failure of the main theoretical perspectives on development to deliver major improvements in living conditions to the world's poorest individuals and communities.

From the point of view of this paper, it should be noted that both sides of the debate between 'mainstream' interventionism and people-centred development concentrate on development as practice. The debate is about whether development should be done on behalf of others or whether people should somehow be empowered to 'develop themselves'.

5 CONTESTING THE DOMINANT VIEW OF DEVELOPMENT AS PRACTICE

It is important to accept that the dominant meaning of development is indeed restricted to practice or intervention in the context of liberal capitalism. Only then can we move on, either to contest that meaning or to work through the implications.

However, if the dominant meaning attributed to development derives from the usage of powerful agencies, how can those with less power contest this meaning? Fortunately, it is not clear that power over usage is monolithic. There have certainly been moments when powerful agencies have been influenced to adopt concepts originating in civil society or with apparently less powerful agencies. For example, the notions of sustainable development, of gender in development, of participatory development, have all gained widespread credence beyond the groups or movements where they originated. The fact that development currently means the practice of development is certainly open to challenge, for example by new development theorists or by those propounding new visions for development, though this challenge does not appear to be strong at the moment.

Contesting the idea of development as practice means emphasizing development as vision or historical process or both. One potential source of challenge in terms of vision is 'people-centred' development, including, for example, Korten's vision of 'authentic' development based on principles of justice, sustainability and inclusiveness (Korten, 1995), and the idea that development means not just combating or ameliorating poverty but restoring or enhancing basic human capabilities and freedoms. As noted above, this vision is also about practice: people should be enabled (or 'empowered') to take direct action to meet their own needs. However, this vision of empowerment involves more than practice, since it implies redistributing power and transforming institutions (Friedmann, 1996). It leads in the potentially extremely fruitful direction of considering development in terms of 'effective appropriation of human rights by all' (I. Sachs, 2000, p. 95). A final important aspect of this alternative development vision is cultural diversity. If people and communities are empowered to develop themselves and demand their rights, it follows that they will do so in distinctively different ways.

When we move from vision to considering historical process, we find that there is no clear model for how 'people-centred' development, based on the realization of human potential in diverse ways, might build on itself to create a self-reproducing process of social change throughout a whole society over a long period. We need to look elsewhere for a theoretical challenge to the notion that liberal capitalism and global market society constitute the only future for humanity and hence for a challenge to development only as intervention within this context. One important source of challenging ideas in this area is the work of Karl Polanyi (1944/1957), who disputed the idea that the development of capitalism accords to some kind of natural historical law, arguing that the conditions for global capitalism have constantly to be promoted by those political forces which favour them. He characterized the historical processes by which global capitalism has been established as a struggle between two 'movements': one trying to achieve the commoditization of land, labour and economic organization by force; the other attempting to 'protect' these three elements. It was not a question of the natural workings of the market itself against government, but two competing movements, representing capitalist interests and those adversely affected by capitalism respectively, struggling for influence within government.

It is instructive to attempt to interpret some recent history of development in similar terms. For example, trade unions have long been engaged in trying to protect the collective interests of workers and up to the 1960s and 1970s were increasingly successful in doing so. Up to that time also, in less developed countries there were a large number of state interventions regulating the relation between the national economy and the international. LDCs typically maintained exchange rate and credit controls, tariffs, and import controls. States commonly imposed direct price controls and quality standards; they also employ different types of incentives such as preferential tax treatment for reinvestment in certain areas of production. Not only in LDCs but in advanced capitalist countries as well, many public goods and especially public services were, and are, supplied directly by state agencies. Also, almost all countries have at least some services provided universally, as with the National Health Service and basic educational provision in the UK, and the basic food provisioning policies of the Sri Lankan governments since independence. These can all be seen as the result of interests outside and within governments succeeding in restricting the force and scope of capitalism.

On the other hand, since the early 1980s pro-market interests have made headway. Particularly during the 1980s, many Southern states competed to attract investment from transnational corporations by making a virtue of their tough anti-union legislation. Structural adjustment programmes, promoted by the World Bank and the International Monetary Fund (IMF), have effectively forced many LDCs to become almost completely open to overseas ownership of enterprises through foreign investment. Under the so-called 'Washington consensus' both these multilateral agencies and others such as the United States Agency for International Development (USAID) agreed on a range of policies such as minimizing state intervention in the economy, privatization of any previously state-owned industries, and a reduction in state provision of services. These policies were not only followed at home but pushed on to LDCs. Rather than being an inevitable consequence of global market forces, they can be seen as the result of a political movement advancing the conditions for capitalism to 'develop' further at the global level.

Polanyi saw the two movements as operating within the context of states, such as the British state, although the system of industrial capitalism which they were trying to promote or restrain was attaining global influence. As we enter the 21st century we can interpret events in terms of two similar movements at global level, struggling over the commodification not only of land and labour but also of knowledge and even life itself, epitomized by the clash between various NGOs and 'people's organizations' and corporate interests at the World Trade Organization meeting in Seattle in November 1999.

6 THE IMPLICATIONS OF ACCEPTING THAT DEVELOPMENT HAS COME TO MEAN PRACTICE

At the same time as challenging the tendency for development only to mean practice, it is important to take development as practice very seriously, and to work out some of the implications. If development is simply what development agencies do, then we may ask what are development agencies and what entitles them to the name. Cowen and Shenton suggest that there is a basic 'problem of development' which arises because development as a process of improvement which builds on itself also causes destruction, and those adversely affected are generally powerless to help themselves. As a response to this problem, at the same time as the invention of 'intentional development' the concept of 'trusteeship' was also brought into use. Trusteeship means that one agency is 'entrusted' with acting on behalf of another, in this case to try to ensure the 'development' of the other. Cowen and Shenton define it as 'the intent which is expressed, by one source of agency, to develop the capacities of another. It is what binds the process of development to the intent of development' (1996, p. x): Trusteeship may be taken on by an agency on another's behalf without 'the other' asking to 'be developed' or even being aware that the intention to 'develop' them is there.

Originally trusteeship was generally exercized by states on behalf of their societies or by colonial states on behalf of the colonized. Since attaining independence many ex-colonial states continued to assume trusteeship over the development of their peoples, and until the 1970s the idea of the state as the sole legitimate agency of development retained strong currency. More recently a variety of agencies can be seen as claiming trusteeship over the development of others, or even over the development of global society as a whole, including a variety of local, national and international NGOs as well as international organizations such as the World Bank, IMF and others including the United Nations and its agencies. One might even see the range of agencies involved including large private corporations, to the extent that their power over populations and communities often rivals that of states and international agencies, and their interests also are served by promoting development in order to forestall widespread social disruption. This puts corporate responsibility alongside rights on the agenda for development debate in the new century, as indeed it already has been by various agencies including Britain's Department for International Development.

Two questions have to be asked about any agency which claims trusteeship for the development of others. Does it have legitimacy to act on their behalf? And does it have the power and capacity to do so? For almost the whole of the period since the 'invention' of intentional development, the state has claimed both the right and the might to develop its people. However, the idea of the 'developmental state' now only clearly applies to a small number of cases (Leftwich, 1994), and even there it can no longer be regarded as the *sole* source of development action. Nevertheless, particularly in East and South East Asia and to some extent in Latin America, there are relatively strong states which maintain trusteeship over the development of their populations, and even the weaker states of Africa cannot be discounted as legitimate development agencies. In addition, community and local organizations are here to stay alongside national governments and international organizations as agents of national development. Thus there is a plethora of agencies claiming trusteeship in some form, but no clear successor to the developmental state. The same is the case when one starts to think in terms of world development rather than development within the boundaries of nation states. Hence the question of the inter-organizational relations between the agencies (Robinson *et al.*, 2000) takes on a huge importance, and in particular the rather poorly conceptualized notion of *partnership*. It is easier to see development globally as the joint responsibility of a number of agencies each having a part to play in global governance, and thus working together as partners in intentional development, than to envisage a single global state taking on the role of trusteeship for world development.

A third question about trusteeship asks which interests are represented by a development agency. Can the interests of those being developed be represented through the actions of an agency 'entrusted' with acting on their behalf? The very notion of trusteeship depends on being able to answer 'Yes' to this question. However, there are those, particularly those seeking 'alternative development' who see this answer as impossible. Banuri, for example writes that if development means 'what "we" can do for "them"' then it is just a 'licence' for imperial intervention (Banuri, 1990, p. 96). For these the answer is to reject the notion of trusteeship. People should become the agents of their own development.

The idea of people becoming their own development agents raises enormous questions about political feasibility as well as the question whether it is really possible to avoid the notion of trusteeship in this way. Surely empowerment cannot be achieved without being promoted by some powerful agent allied with those to be empowered? Perhaps some form of people's movement might fill the role of this agent, but even then the leadership of that movement would be taking on a trusteeship role in a way. A more general problem is how those with the role of trustee or development agent can be made to continue to align their interests at least to some extent with the interests of those 'being developed'. This is a question about how to design accountability into sustainable institutional systems.

Finally, taking development as practice seriously implies researching and theorizing about ·'intentional development', including questions about action and problems of trusteeship. Research might include empirical investigation of the effects of interventions designed to have certain developmental effects, as well as the organizational rationales which led the agencies concerned to undertake the interventions. It would have to take into account strong states in poor countries as well as community, local and international agencies as sources of intervention. In most cases it is unlikely that in actuality the desired results will follow linearly from the policies and practices designed to bring them about. Analysing the role of such intentional development and of other social forces in the changes which actually occur could be done in terms of Polanyi's conflicting movements.

New theory could include work on what is involved in action for development at the global level, and on the ambiguity of the 'developer' or 'trustee' role. The former could involve analysing the implications of extending the notion of 'public action' (Drèze and Sen, 1989; Mackintosh, 1992), with its two aspects of meeting public need and simultaneously contesting what is to be regarded as such a need, to global development.

The latter could lead to a strand of development studies analogous to work in Organization Development (OD), where the role of change agent is subject to critical analysis, those involved in such roles practice self-awareness and a critical theory of action research has been built up. The field of development in the broader sense used throughout this paper needs to build up its own tradition of critical practice in a similar way.

REFERENCES

Banuri T. 1990. Modernisation and its discontents: a cultural perspective on the theories of development. In *Dominating Knowledge*, Marglin F, Marglin S (eds). Clarendon Press: Oxford.

Chambers R. 1997. *Whose Reality Counts? Putting the First Last*. Intermediate Technology Publications: London.

Cowen M, Shenton R. 1996. *Doctrines of Development*. Routledge: London.

Drèze J, Sen A. 1989. *Hunger and Public Action*. Clarendon Press: Oxford.

Esteva G. 1992. Development. In *The Development Dictionary: A Guide to Knowledge as Power*, Sachs W (ed). Zed Books: London; 6–25.

Friedmann J. 1996. Rethinking poverty: empowerment and citizen rights. *International Social Science Journal*. UNESCO **148**.

Fukuyama F. 1992. *The End of History and the Last Man*. Penguin: Harmondsworth.

Fukuyama F. 1995. *Trust: The Social Virtues and the Creation of Prosperity*. Penguin: Harmondsworth.

Hobsbawm E. 1994. *The Age of Extremes: A History of the World, 1914–91*. Pantheon Books: New York.

Kaplinsky R. 1998. If you want to get somewhere else, you must run at least twice as fast as that. In *The roots of the East Asian Crisis*, East Asia conference, 13–14 July; Institute of Development Studies, Brighton.

Korten D. 1995. Steps towards people-centred development: vision and strategies. In *Government-NGO Relations in Asia: Prospects and Challenges for People-centred Development*, Heyzer N, Riker JV, Quizon AB (eds); 165–189.

Leftwich A. 1994. Governance, the state and the politics of development. *Development and Change* **25**(2): 363–386.

Mackintosh M. 1992. Introduction. In *Development Policy and Public Action*, Wuyts M, Mackintosh M, Hewitt T (eds). Oxford University Press: Oxford; 1–9.

Polanyi K. 1944. *The Great Transformation*. Beacon Press: Boston republished 1957.

Robinson D, Hewitt T, Harriss J (eds). 2000. *Managing Development: Understanding Inter-Organizational Relationships*. Sage: London.

Sachs I. 2000. *Understanding Development: People, Markets and the State in Mixed Economies*. Oxford University Press: New Delhi.

Sachs W (ed.). 1992. *The Development Dictionary: A Guide to Knowledge as Power*. Zed Books: London.

Thomas A. 2000. Meanings, views of development. In *Poverty, Development in the 1990s*, Allen T, Thomas A (eds). Oxford University Press, The Open University: Oxford, Milton Keynes; 23–48.

Part III
Ethical Principles:
Needs, Capabilities, Rights

[11]

Development and human needs
Manfred Max-Neef

Latin America: crisis and perplexity

In creating the future, there is either the risk of making errors of perception, or of making errors of action. Concerning perception, two serious mistakes are often made. The first is to believe that the Latin American crisis can be ascribed principally to an external crisis. The second, stemming from the first, is to assume that our depression is just a passing historical circumstance. Although it is true that external conditions do considerably influence dependent and vulnerable economies like ours, it is, none the less, also probable that a recovery of the capitalistic economy in the North will not affect significantly our own recovery.

It would be a delusion to base a strategy for future development on the expansion of exports of primary products. Very simply, indicators suggest that the bulk of primary products will be affected, for different reasons, by unfavourable terms of trade. Moreover, others are already being replaced by more efficient substitutes. Another strategy based on the diversification of exports, that is, of manufactured goods, would inevitably come up against the protectionist policies of the powers in the North. Also, to assume a type of development which is nurtured by external contributions of capital is ruled out altogether on account of the serious and insoluble condition of indebtedness in which we are forced to live.

In our opinion, the future lies in mustering all our energy to design imaginative but viable alternatives. The conditions for these alternatives seem to be quite clear. The two schools of economic thought which have prevailed in the Latin American setting, neo-liberal monetarism and the more inter-ventionist state-centered developmentalism promoted by the Economic Commission for Latin America, these have not been able to satisfy the legitimate needs of the Latin American masses. A new perspective is called for which aims at an adequate satisfaction of human needs. Furthermore, if future development cannot be sustained through the expansion of exports or through substantial injection of foreign capital, an alternative development must generate a capacity for greater self-reliance.

We are proposing an orientation which would enable us to create conditions for a new praxis based on Human Scale Development. Such development is focused and based on the satisfaction of fundamental human needs, on the generation of growing levels of self-reliance, and on the construction of organic articulations of people with nature and technology, of global processes with local activity, of the personal with the social, of planning with autonomy, and of civil society with the state, where 'articulation' is taken to mean the construction of coherent and consistent relations of balanced interdependence among given elements.

Human needs, self-reliance and organic articulations are the pillars which

198   *Human needs and aspirations*

support Human Scale Development. However, these pillars must be sustained on a solid foundation which is the creation of those conditions where people are the protagonists in their future. If people are to be the main actors in Human Scale Development both the diversity as well as the autonomy of the spaces in which they act must be respected. Attaining the transformation of an object-person into a subject-person in the process of development is, among other things, a problem of scale. There is no possibility for the active participation of people in gigantic systems which are hierarchically organized and where decisions flow from the top down to the bottom.

Human Scale Development assumes a direct and participatory democracy. This form of democracy nurtures those conditions which will help to transform the traditional, semi-paternalistic role of the Latin American State into a role of encouraging creative solutions flowing from the bottom upwards. This is more consistent with the real expectations of the people.

I wish to emphasize at this point the democratic nature of the alternative proposed. Instead of relying on stereotyped ideological options, this document advocates the need to: develop processes of economic and political decentralization; strengthen genuine democratic institutions; and encourage increasing autonomy in the emerging social movements.

The creation of a political order which can represent the needs and interests of a heterogeneous people is a challenge to both the state and civil society. The most pressing question, not only for a democratic state but also for a society based on a democratic culture, is how to respect and encourage diversity rather than control it. In this regard, development must nurture local spaces, facilitate micro-organizations and support the multiplicity of cultural matrixes comprising civil society. This type of development must rediscover, consolidate and integrate the diverse collective identities that make up the social body.

Processes which nurture diversity and increase social participation and control over the environment are decisive in the articulation of projects to expand national autonomy and distribute the fruits of economic development more equitably. Hence, it is essential to prevent the increasing atomization of social movements, cultural identities and communities. To articulate these movements, identities, strategies and social demands in global proposals is not possible through the programmes of homogenization which have characterized the Latin American political tradition. It requires, on the part of the state, new institutional mechanisms capable of reconciling participation with heterogeneity. It also requires more active forms of representation, and greater translucency in the practices of the public sector.

It is not the purpose of this document to propose a state model that promotes Human Scale Development. Rather, our emphasis is on empowering civil society to nurture this form of development. This is not to minimize the importance of the state but to develop further the potential role of social actors, of social participation and of local communities. Our preoccupation is a 'social democracy' or rather a 'democracy of day-to-day living' which does not imply a lack of concern for 'political democracy' but a firm belief that only by rediscovering the 'molecular' composition of the social fabric (micro-organizations, local spaces, human-scale relations) is a political order founded on a democratic culture made possible. We believe that in order to avoid the atomization and the exclusion of people – be it in political, social or cultural terms – it is absolutely necessary to generate new ways of conceiving and practising politics. Thus, this document attempts to open up a space for critical reflection on the way we live and, more importantly, on the urgent need to develop a new political praxis.

Development and human needs

This new praxis starts from a theory of human needs for development. Human needs must be understood as a system; that is, all human needs are interrelated and interactive. With the sole exception of the need of subsistence, that is, to remain alive, no hierarchies exist within the system. On the contrary, simultaneities, complementarities and trade-offs are characteristics of the process of needs satisfaction.

Needs and satisfiers

As the literature in this area demonstrates, human needs can be classified according to many criteria. We have organized human needs into two categories: existential and axiological, which we have combined and displayed in a matrix (see Table 7.1, pp. 206–7). This allows us to demonstrate the interaction of, on the one hand, the needs of Being, Having, Doing and Inter-acting; and, on the other hand, the needs of Subsistence, Protection, Affection, Understanding, Participation, Creation, Leisure, Identity and Freedom.

From the classification proposed it follows that, for instance, food and shelter must not be seen as needs, but as satisfiers of the fundamental need for Subsistence. In much the same way, education (either formal or informal), study, investigation, early stimulation and meditation are satisfiers of the need for Understanding. The curative systems, preventive systems and health schemes in general are satisfiers of the need for Protection.

There is no one-to-one correspondence between needs and satisfiers. A satisfier may contribute simultaneously to the satisfaction of different needs, or conversely, a need may require various satisfiers in order to be met. Not even these relations are fixed. They may vary according to time, place and circumstance. For example, a mother breast-feeding her baby is simul-taneously satisfying the infant's needs for Subsistence, Protection, Affection and Identity. The situation is obviously different if the baby is fed in a more mechanical fashion.

Having established a difference between the concepts of needs and satisfiers it is possible to state two postulates: first, fundamental human needs are finite, few and classifiable; and second, fundamental human needs (such as those contained in the system proposed) are the same in all cultures and in all historical periods. What changes, both over time and through cultures, is the way or the means by which the needs are satisfied.

Each economic, social and political system adopts different methods for the satisfaction of the same fundamental human needs. In every system they are satisfied (or not satisfied) through the generation (or non-generation) of different types of satisfiers. We may go as far as to say that one of the aspects that define a culture is its choice of satisfiers. Whether a person belongs to a consumerist or to an ascetic society, his/her fundamental human needs are the same. What changes is his/her choice of the quantity and quality of satisfiers. In short, what is culturally determined are not the fundamental human needs, but the satisfiers for those needs. Cultural change is, among other things, the consequence of dropping traditional satisfiers for the purpose of adopting new or different ones.

It must be added that each need can be satisfied at different levels and with different intensities. Furthermore, needs are satisfied within three contexts: (1) with regard to oneself *(Eigenwelt)*; (2) with regard to the social group *(Mitwelt)*; and (3) with regard to the environment *(Umwelt)*. The quality and intensity, not only of the levels, but also of contexts will depend on time, place and circumstances.

Poverties and pathologies

The proposed perspective allows for a reinterpretation of the concept of poverty. The traditional concept of poverty is limited and restricted, since it refers exclusively to the predicaments of people who may be classified below a certain income threshold. This concept is strictly economistic. It is suggested here that we should speak not of poverty, but of poverties. In fact, any fundamental human need that is not adequately satisfied, reveals a human poverty. Some examples are: poverty of subsistence (due to insufficient income, food, shelter, etc.), of protection (due to bad health systems, violence, arms race, etc.), of affection (due to authoritarianism, oppression, exploitative relations with the natural environment, etc.), of understanding (due to poor quality of education), of participation (due to marginalization of and discrimination against women, children and minorities), of identity (due to imposition of alien values upon local and regional cultures, forced migration, political exile, etc.). But poverties are not only poverties. Much more than that, *each poverty generates pathologies*. This is the crux of our discourse.

In the Latin American context examples of persistent economic pathologies are unemployment, external debt and hyperinflation. Common political pathologies are fear, violence, marginalization and exile. Our challenge consists of recognizing and assessing these pathologies generated by diverse socio-economic political systems, with every system creating in its own way obstacles to the satisfaction of one or more needs. A further challenge is to develop and fulfil dialogue in pursuit of a constructive interpretation of the issues and solutions raised here. These challenges form the basis for an ongoing programme of participatory action research which has blossomed in hundreds of communities in Latin America since *Human Scale Development* was published.

Deprivation and potential

The very essence of human beings is expressed palpably through needs in their twofold character: as deprivation and as potential. Understood as much more than mere survival, needs bring out the constant tension between deprivation and potential which is so peculiar to human beings.

Needs, narrowly conceived as deprivation, are often restricted to that which is merely physiological and as such the sensation that 'something which is lacking is acutely felt'. However, to the degree that needs engage, motivate and mobilize people, they are a potential and eventually may become a resource. The need to participate is a potential for participation, just as the need for affection is a potential for affection.

To approach the human being through needs enables us to build a bridge between a philosophical anthropology and a political option: this appears to have been the motivation behind the intellectual efforts of, for example, Karl Marx and Abraham Maslow. To understand human beings in terms of needs, that is, conceived as deprivation and potential, will prevent any reduction of the human being into a category of a restricted existence.

Human needs and society

If we wish to define and assess an environment in the light of human needs, it is not sufficient to understand the opportunities that exist for groups or individuals to actualize their needs. It is necessary to analyse to what extent the environment represses, tolerates or stimulates opportunities. How accessible, creative or flexible is that environment? The most important question is how far people are able to influence the structures that affect their opportunities.

Satisfiers and economic goods

It is the satisfiers which define the prevailing mode that a culture or a society ascribes to needs. *Satisfiers are not the available economic goods.* They are related, instead, to everything which, by virtue of representing forms of Being, Having, Doing, and Interacting, contributes to the actualization of human needs. Satisfiers may include, among other things, forms of organization, political structures, social practices, subjective conditions, values and norms, spaces, contexts, modes, types of behaviour and attitudes, all of which are in a permanent state of tension between consolidation and change.

For example, the availability of food is a satisfier of the need for Protection in much the same way that a family structure might be. Likewise, a political order may be a satisfier of the need for Participation. The same satisfier can actualize different needs in different time periods.

The reason that a satisfier may have diverse effects in various contexts is due to the following: the breadth of the goods generated; how they are generated; and how consumption is organized. Understood as objects or artifacts which make it possible to increase or decrease the efficiency of a satisfier, goods have become determinant elements within industrial civilization. In industrial capitalism, the production of economic goods along with the system of allocating them has conditioned the type of satisfiers that predominate.

While a satisfier is in an *ultimate sense* the way in which a need is expressed, goods are in a *strict sense* the means by which individuals will empower the satisfiers to meet their needs. When, however, the form of production and consumption of goods makes goods an end in themselves, then the alleged satisfaction of a need impairs its capacity to create potential. This creates the conditions for entrenching an alienated society engaged in a productivity race lacking any sense at all. Life, then, is placed at the service of artifacts, rather than artifacts at the service of life. The question of the quality of life is overshadowed by our obsession to increase productivity.

Within this perspective, the construction of a human economy poses an important theoretical challenge, namely, to understand fully the dialectic between needs, satisfiers and economic goods. This is necessary in order to conceive forms of economic organization in which goods empower satisfiers to meet fully and consistently fundamental human needs.

This situation compels us to rethink the social context of human needs in a radically different way from the manner in which it has been approached by social planners and designers of policies for development. It is not only a question of having to relate to goods and services but also to relate them to social practices, forms of organization, political models and values. All of these have an impact on the ways in which needs are expressed.

In a critical theory of society, it is not sufficient to specify the predominant satisfiers and economic goods produced within that society. They must be understood as products which are the result of historical factors and consequently, liable to change. Thus, it is necessary to retrace the process of reflection and creation that conditions the interaction between needs, satisfiers and economic goods.

The vindication of subjectivity

To assume a direct relation between needs and economic goods has allowed us to develop a discipline of economics that presumes itself to be objective, a mechanistic discipline in which the central tenet implies that needs manifest themselves through demand which, in turn, is determined by individual preferences for the goods produced. To include satisfiers within the framework of economic analysis involves vindicating the world of the 'subjective', over and above mere preferences for objects and artifacts.

We can explain how needs are met: our own and those of others in our milieu, family, friends, members of the community, cultural groups, the economic system, the socio-political system, the nation and so on. We can try to understand how satisfiers and predominant economic goods are related in our environment to the manner in which we emotionally express our needs. We can detect how satisfiers and the availability of goods constrain, distort or enhance the quality of our lives. On this basis, we can think of viable ways to organize and distribute the satisfiers and goods so that they nurture the process of actualizing needs and reduce the possibilities of frustration.

The ways in which we experience our needs, hence the quality of our lives, is, ultimately, subjective. When the object of study is the relation between human beings and society, the universality of the subjective cannot be ignored. Any attempt to observe the life of human beings must recognize the social character of subjectivity. It is not impossible to advance judgements about the subjective. Yet there is a great fear of the consequences of such a reflection. Economic theory is a clear example of this. From the neoclassical economists to the monetarists, the notion of preferences is used to avoid the issue of needs. This perspective reveals an acute reluctance to discuss the subjective-universal. This is particularly true if it is a question of taking a stand in favour of a free-market economy. Preferences belong to the realm of the subjective-particular and, therefore, are not a threat to the assumptions that underlie the rationale of the market. Whereas to speak of fundamental human needs compels us to focus our attention from the outset on the subjective-universal.

The way in which needs are expressed through satisfiers varies according to historical period and culture. The social and economic relations, defined by historical and cultural circumstances, are concerned with the subjective and the objective. Hence, *satisfiers are what render needs historical and cultural, and economic goods are their material manifestation.*

The evolution of human needs

Owing to the dirth of empirical evidence, it is impossible to state with absolute certainty that the fundamental human needs are historically and culturally constant. However, there is nothing that prevents us from speaking of their socio-universal character because people everywhere want to satisfy their needs. In reflecting on the nine fundamental needs proposed in this document, common sense, along with some socio-cultural sensitivity, surely points to the fact that the needs for Subsistence, Protection, Affection, Understanding, Participation, Creation and Leisure have existed since the origins of *homo habilis* and, undoubtedly, since the appearance of *homo sapiens*.

Probably at a later stage of evolution the need for Identity appeared and, at a much later date, the need for Freedom. In much the same way, it is likely that in the future the need for Transcendence, which is not included in our proposal, as we do not yet consider it universal, will become as universal as the

204   *Human needs and aspirations*

other needs. It seems legitimate, then, to assume that fundamental human needs change with the pace of evolution. That is to say, at a very slow rate. Therefore, fundamental human needs are not only universal but are also entwined with the evolution of the species. They follow a single track.

Satisfiers behave in two ways: they are modified according to the rhythm of history and vary according to culture and circumstance. Economic goods (artifacts, technologies) behave in three different ways: they are modified according to episodic rhythms (vogues, fashions) and diversify according to cultures and, within those cultures, according to social strata.

In summary, perhaps we may say that fundamental human needs are essential attributes related to human evolution; satisfiers are forms of Being, Having, Doing and Interacting, related to structures; and economic goods are objects related to particular historical moments.

Evolutionary, structural and episodic changes take place at different paces and rhythms. The movement of history places the human being in an increasingly unrhythmical and unsynchronized domain in which human concerns are neglected more and more. In the present moment, this situation has become extreme.

The speed of production and the diversification of objects have become ends in themselves and as such are no longer able to satisfy any need whatsoever. People have grown more dependent on this sytem of production but, at the same time, more alienated from it.

It is only in some of the regions marginalized by the crisis and in those groups which defy the prevailing styles of development, that autonomous processes are generated in which satisfiers and economic goods become subordinated once again to the actualization of human needs. It is in these sectors that we can find examples of synergic types of behaviour which offer a potential response to the crisis which looms over us.

A matrix of needs and satisfiers

The interrelationship between needs, satisfiers and economic goods is permanent and dynamic. A dialectic relationship exists among them. If economic goods are capable of affecting the efficiency of the satisfiers, the latter will be determinant in generating and creating the former. Through this reciprocal causation, they become both part and definition of a culture which, in turn, delimits the style of development.

As Table 7.1 indicates, satisfiers can be organized within the grids of a matrix which, on the one hand, classifies needs according to the existential categories of Being, Having, Doing and Interacting, and, on the other hand, according to the axiological categories of Subsistence, Protection, Affection, Understanding, Participation, Creation, Recreation, Identity and Freedom. This matrix is neither normative nor conclusive. It merely gives an example of possible types of satisfiers. In fact, this matrix of satisfiers, if completed by individuals or groups from diverse cultures and in different historical moments, might vary considerably.

An examination of the different fields in the matrix with their possible satisfiers demonstrates clearly that many of the satisfiers can give rise to different economic goods. If we take, for instance, field 15, showing different ways of Doing to actualize the need for Understanding, we see that it includes satisfiers such as investigating, studying, experimenting, educating, analysing, meditating and interpreting. These satisfiers give rise to economic goods, depending on the culture and the resources, such as books, laboratory instruments, tools, computers and other artifacts. The function of these goods is to empower the *Doing of Understanding.*

Examples of satisfiers and their attributes

The matrix presented is only an example and in no way exhausts the number of possible satisfiers. Because satisfiers have various characteristics, we suggest for analytical purposes five types that may be identified, namely (1) violators or destroyers, (2) pseudo-satisfiers, (3) inhibiting satisfiers, (4) singular satisfiers, and (5) synergic satisfiers (see Tables 7.2 to 7.6).

The first four categories of satisfiers are exogenous to civil society as they are usually imposed, induced, ritualized or institutionalized. In this sense, they are satisfiers which have been traditionally generated at the top and advocated for all. On the other hand endogenous satisfiers derive from liberating processes which are the outcome of acts of volition generated by the community at the grass roots level. It is this that makes them anti-authoritarian, even though in some cases they may originate in processes promoted by the state.

One of the important aims of Human Scale Development is to affect change in the nature of the Latin American State. It should move from its traditional role as a generator of satisfiers which are exogenous to civil society, to a stimulator and creator of processes arising from the bottom upwards. Particularly, given the tremendously restrictive conditions which the current crisis imposes on us, an increase in the levels of local, regional, and national self-reliance should be deemed a priority. This objective can be met through the generation of synergic processes at all levels of society.

The fact that several of the satisfiers offered as examples do not appear in the matrix is due to the fact that the tables are more specific. It must be borne in mind that the matrix is merely illustrative and not normative.

Application of the matrix

The schema proposed can be used for purposes of diagnosis, planning, assessment and evaluation. The matrix of needs and satisfiers may serve, at a preliminary stage, as a participative exercise of self-diagnosis for groups located within a local space. Through a process of regular dialogue – preferably with the presence of a facilitator acting as a catalysing element – the group may gradually begin to characterize itself by filling in the corresponding

Table 7.1 Matrix of needs and satisfiers*

Needs according to axiological categories	Being	Having	Doing	Interacting
			Needs according to existential categories	
Subsistence	1/ Physical health, mental health, equilibrium, sense of humour, adaptability	2/ Food, shelter, work	3/ Feed, procreate, rest, work	4/ Living environment, social setting
Protection	5/ Care, adaptability, autonomy, equilibrium, solidarity	6/ Insurance systems, savings, social security, health systems, rights, family, work	7/ Co-operate, prevent, plan, take care of, cure, help	8/ Living space, social environment, dwelling
Affection	9/ Self-esteem, solidarity, respect, tolerance, generosity, receptiveness, passion, determination, sensuality, sense of humour	10/ Friendships, family, partnerships, relationships with nature	11/ Make love, caress, express emotions, share, take care of, cultivate, appreciate	12/ Privacy, intimacy, home, spaces of togetherness
Understanding	13/ Critical conscience, receptiveness, curiosity, astonishment, discipline, intuition, rationality	14/ Literature, teachers, method, educational policies, communication policies	15/ Investigate, study, experiment, educate, analyse, meditate	16/ Settings of formative interaction, schools, universities, academies, groups, communities, family

Participation	17/ Adaptability, receptiveness, solidarity, willingness, determination, dedication, respect, passion, sense of humour	18/ Rights, responsibilities, duties, privileges, work	19/ Become affiliated, co-operate, propose, share, dissent, obey, interact, agree on, express opinions	20/ Settings of participative interaction, parties, associations, churches, communities, neighbourhoods, family
Leisure	21/ Curiosity, receptiveness, imagination, recklessness, sense of humour, tranquility, sensuality	22/ Games, spectacles, clubs, parties, peace of mind	23/ Day-dream, brood, dream, recall old times, give way to fantasies, remember, relax, have fun, play	24/ Privacy, intimacy, spaces of closeness, free time, surroundings, landscapes
Creation	25/ Passion, determination, intuition, imagination, boldness, rationality, autonomy, inventiveness, curiosity	26/ Abilities, skills, method, work	27/ Work, invent, build, design, compose, interpret	28/ Productive and feedback settings, workshops, cultural groups, audiences, spaces for expression, temporal freedom
Identity	29/ Sense of belonging, consistency, differentiation, self-esteem, assertiveness	30/ Symbols, language, religions, habits, customs, reference groups, sexuality, values, norms, historical memory, work	31/ Commit oneself, integrate oneself, confront, decide on, get to know oneself, recognize oneself, actualize oneself, grow	32/ Social rhythms, everyday settings, settings which one belongs to, maturation stages
Freedom	33/ Autonomy, self-esteem, determination, passion, assertiveness, open-mindedness, boldness, rebelliousness, tolerance	34/ Equal rights	35/ Dissent, choose, be different from, run risks, develop awareness, commit oneself, disobey	36/ Temporal/spatial plasticity

* The column of BEING registers *attributes*, personal or collective, that are expressed as nouns. The column of HAVING registers *institutions*, *norms*, *mechanisms*, *tools* (not in a material sense), *laws*, etc. that can be expressed in one or more words. The column of DOING registers *actions*, personal or collective, that can be expressed as verbs. The column of INTERACTING registers *locations* and *milieus* (as times and spaces). It stands for the Spanish ESTAR or the German BEFINDEN, in the sense of time and space. Since there is no corresponding word in English, INTERACTING was chosen *à faut de mieux*.

208   *Human needs and aspirations*

Table 7.2   Violators and destructors*

Supposed satisfier	Need to be supposedly satisfied	Needs whose satisfaction it impairs
1. Arms race	Protection	Subsistence, Affection, Participation, Freedom
2. Exile	Protection	Affection, Participation, Identity, Freedom
3. National security doctrine	Protection	Subsistence, Identity, Affection, Understanding, Participation, Freedom
4. Censorship	Protection	Understanding, Participation, Leisure, Creation, Identity, Freedom
5. Bureaucracy	Protection	Understanding, Affection, Participation, Creation, Identity, Freedom
6. Authoritarianism	Protection	Affection, Understanding, Participation, Creation, Identity, Freedom

* Violators or destructors are elements of a paradoxical effect. Applied under the pretext of satisfying a given need, they not only annihilate the possibility of its satisfaction, but they also render the adequate satisfaction of other needs impossible. They seem to be especially related to the need for protection.

Table 7.3   Pseudo-satisfiers*

Satisfier	Need which it seemingly satisfies
1. Mechanistic medicine: 'A pill for every ill'	Protection
2. Over-exploitation of natural resources	Subsistence
3. Chauvinistic nationalism	Identity
4. Formal democracy	Participation
5. Stereotypes	Understanding
6. Aggregate economic indicators	Understanding
7. Cultural control	Creation
8. Prostitution	Affection
9. Status symbols	Identity
10. Obsessive productivity with a bias to efficiency	Subsistence
11. Indoctrination	Understanding
12. Charity	Subsistence
13. Fashions and fads	Identity

* Pseudo-satisfiers are elements which stimulate a false sensation of satisfying a given need. Though they lack the aggressiveness of violators, they may, on occasion, annul, in the medium term, the possibility of satisfying the need they were originally aimed at.

Table 7.4 Inhibiting satisfiers*

Satisfier	Need	Needs, whose satisfaction is inhibited
1. Paternalism	Protection	Understanding, Participation, Freedom, Identity
2. Over-protective family	Protection	Affection, Understanding, Participation, Leisure, Identity, Freedom
3. Taylorist-type of production	Subsistence	Understanding, Participation, Creation, Identity, Freedom
4. Authoritarian classroom	Understanding	Participation, Creation, Identity, Freedom
5. Messianisms (Millennarisms)	Identity·	Protection, Understanding, Participation, Freedom
6. Unlimited permissiveness	Freedom	Protection, Affection, Identity, Participation
7. Obsessive economic competitiveness	Freedom	Subsistence, Protection, Affection, Participation, Leisure
8. Commercial television	Leisure	Understanding, Creation, Identity

* Inhibiting satisfiers are those which by the way in which they satisfy (generally over-satisfy) a given need seriously impair the possibility of satisfying other needs.

Table 7.5 Singular satisfiers*

Satisfier	Need which it satisfies
1. Programmes to provide food	Subsistence
2. Welfare programmes to provide dwelling	Subsistence
3. Curative medicine	Subsistence
4. Insurance systems	Protection
5. Professional armies	Protection
6. Ballot	Participation
7. Sports spectacles	Leisure
8. Nationality	Identity
9. Guided tours	Leisure
10. Gifts	Affection

* Singular satisfiers are those which aim at the satisfaction of a single need and are, therefore, neutral as regards the satisfaction of other needs. They are very characteristic of development and co-operation schemes and programmes.

210   *Human needs and aspirations*

Table 7.6   Synergic satisfiers*

Satisfier	Need	Needs, whose satisfaction it stimulates
1. Breast-feeding	Subsistence	Protection, Affection, Identity
2. Self-managed production	Subsistence	Understanding, Participation, Creation, Identity, Freedom
3. Popular education	Understanding	Protection, Participation, Creation, Identity, Freedom
4. Democratic community organizations	Participation	Protection, Affection, Leisure, Creation, Identity, Freedom
5. Barefoot medicine	Protection	Subsistence, Understanding, Participation
6. Barefoot banking	Protection	Subsistence, Participation, Creation, Freedom
7. Democratic trade unions	Protection	Understanding, Participation, Identity
8. Direct democracy	Participation	Protection, Understanding, Identity, Freedom
9. Educational games	Leisure	Understanding, Creation
10. Self-managed house-building programmes	Subsistence	Understanding, Participation
11. Preventive medicine	Protection	Understanding, Participation, Subsistence
12. Meditation	Understanding	Leisure, Creation, Identity
13. Cultural television	Leisure	Understanding

* Synergic satisfiers are those which, by the way in which they satisfy a given need, stimulate and contribute to the simultaneous satisfaction of other needs.

fields. A method of accomplishing this is described in some detail elsewhere (Max-Neef *et al.* 1989: 40–3).

The outcome of the exercise will enable the group to become aware of both its deprivations and potentialities. After diagnosing its current reality, it may repeat the exercise in propositional terms; that is, identifying which satisfiers would be required to fully meet the fundamental needs of the group. As the satisfiers are selected with increasing levels of specificity, they should be discussed critically by the group in terms of their characteristics and attributes, in order to determine if they are – or should be – generated exogenously or endogenously, that is by the community itself. Such an analysis will demonstrate the potential capacity for local self-reliance. The same analysis of proposed satisfiers will enable the group to assess not only whether their positive effects are singular or synergic, but also whether the negative effects are violators, inhibiting satisfiers, or pseudo-satisfiers. The next stage of reflection of the group is to determine whether access exists to the necessary economic goods and material resources.

The proposed exercise has a twofold value. First, it makes it possible to identify at a local level a strategy for development aimed at the actualization of human needs. Second, it is an educational, creative and participatory exercise that brings about a state of deep critical awareness; that is to say, the method is, in itself, a generator of synergic effects.

The technique described is not restricted only to an analysis of local spaces. It is likewise applicable at regional and national levels. In local spaces it can be a broad based participation process where those representing the interest of the economic, political and social domains of the community may express their ideas.

At a regional level the exercise should be undertaken by a carefully chosen team which not only represents the different domains of endeavour, but also, by virtue of its representative nature, combines both public and private interests. At the national level it is essential that the task should be approached in a transdisciplinary manner because of the complexity of the issues.

Development geared to the satisfaction of fundamental human needs cannot, by definition, be structured from the top downwards. It cannot be imposed either by law or by decree. It can only emanate directly from the actions, expectations and creative and critical awareness of the protagonists themselves. Instead of being the traditional objects of development, people must take a leading role in development. The anti-authoritarian nature of Human Scale Development does not involve making the conflict between state and civil society more acute. On the contrary, it attempts to prove, through the method proposed, that the state can assume a role which encourages synergic processes at the local, regional and national levels.

Implications for development

From the linear to the systemic approach

Fundamental human needs must be understood as a system, the dynamics of which does not obey hierarchical linearities. This means that, on the one hand, no need is *per se* more important than any other; and, on the other hand, that there is no fixed order of precedence in the actualization of needs (that need B, for instance, can only be met after need A has been satisfied). Simultaneities, complementarities and trade-offs are characteristic of the system's behaviour. There are, however, limits to this generalization. A pre-systemic threshold must be recognized, below which the feeling of a certain deprivation may be so severe, that the urge to satisfy the given need may paralyse and overshadow any other impulse or alternative.

The case of subsistence may serve to illustrate this clearly. When the possibilities of satisfying this need are severely impaired, all other needs remain blocked and a single and intense drive prevails. But such a situation does not hold true only in the case of subsistence. It is equally relevant in the case of other needs. Suffice it to say, that total lack of affection, or the loss of identity, may lead people to extremes of self-destruction.

Whether to follow the assumptions of linearity or the systemic assumptions is such an important choice that it will determine the resulting style of development.

If linearity is favoured, the development strategy will most probably establish its priorities according to the observed poverty of subsistence. Programmes of social assistance will be implemented as a means of tackling poverty as it is conventionally understood. Needs will be interpreted exclusively as deprivations and, at best, the satisfiers that the system may generate will correspond to those identified here as singular. Last, but not least, linear assumptions will stimulate accumulation regardless of people's human development. Paradoxically this option results in a circular cumulative causation (in the sense of Myrdal) and, thus, the poor remain poor inasmuch as their dependence on exogenously generated satisfiers increases.

If one opts for the systemic assumptions, the development strategy will favour endogenously generated synergic satisfiers. Needs will be understood simultaneously as deprivations and potentials, thus allowing for the elimination of the vicious circle of poverty.

It follows from the above that the way in which needs are understood, and the role and attributes ascribed to the possible satisfiers, *are absolutely definitive*, in determining a development strategy.

From efficiency to synergy

To interpret development as here proposed, implies a change in the prevailing economic rationale. It compels us, among other things, to undertake a critical and rigorous revision of the concept of efficiency. This concept is often associated with notions such as the maximization of productivity and of profits, the ambiguity of both terms notwithstanding. If we stretch economic criteria to the most alienated extreme of instrumental reasoning, productivity appears quite inefficient. In fact, by overemphasizing the need for Subsistence, it sacrifices other needs and so ends up threatening Subsistence itself.

The dominant development discourses also associate efficiency with the conversion of labour into capital, with the formalization of economic activities, with the indiscriminate absorption of the newest technologies and, of course, with the maximization of growth rates. In the eyes of many, development consists of achieving the material living standards of the most industrialized countries, in order for people to have access to a growing array of goods (artifacts) which become increasingly more diversified.

Human Scale Development does not exclude conventional goals such as economic growth, so that all persons may have access to required goods and services. However, the difference with respect to the prevailing development styles lies in considering the aims of development not only as points of arrival, but as components of the process itself. In other words, fundamental human needs can and must be realized from the outset and throughout the entire process of development. In this manner the realization of needs becomes, instead of a goal, the motor of development itself. This is possible only inasmuch as the development strategy proves to be capable of stimulating the permanent generation of synergic satisfiers.

To integrate the harmonious realization of human needs into the process of development gives everyone the possibility of experiencing that development from its very outset. This may give rise to a healthy, self-reliant and partici-pative development, capable of creating the foundations for a social order within which economic growth, solidarity and the growth of all men and women as whole persons can be reconciled.

The exercise described here has, as already stated, received an enthusiastic response from hundreds of different communities in Latin America, from local grass-roots groups working in a specified locality (the majority), to seminars of academics, to meetings of government officials. For the grass-roots especially the process permits a clarification of the realities of their socio-economic-cultural situation. It gives an opportunity to free the creative imagination, similar to the 'Future Workshops' devised by Robert Jungk (Jungk and Mullert 1988). Thence the required bridges between the (negative) present and (positive) future can be identified. Finally the group, which will by then have engendered a considerable degree of self-knowledge, can proceed to a consideration of specific self-reliant development strategies and projects, resources that can be mobilized and outside support that can be enlisted. Although the HSD exercise was developed with a Third World context in mind, there is nothing that invalidates it for use in any society. In an industrial context the need of subsistence will be less pressing, of course, and one can expect many other differences across different cultures and situations. However, because the 'development crisis' is perceived as most acute in the Third World, one can expect the methodology to be most employed there, as indeed is the case with the take-up in Latin America. Most importantly, it defines a frame within which the relatively recent explosion of self-organized community action in Third World countries, as identified in, for example, Schneider (1988) or Pradervand (1989), can orient itself towards holistic, need-satisfying endeavour.

However, as Max-Neef, Elizalde and Hopenhayn recognize, 'grass-roots self-mobilisation is not enough', and the second half of their document is devoted to discussion as to how this can be related constructively to macro-social processes, which is also one of the subjects in the final part of this book. There is a need for all actors in the formal development process, from inter-governmental institutions to national governments to municipal authorities and all the economists, planners and officials whom they employ, and irrespective of whether their prime focus is environment, development or

214   *Human needs and aspirations*

employment, to recognize the primacy of local wishes and realities and to find ways of helping them to be realized. This applies especially when the needs are being articulated by those whom development professionals characterize as 'poor'.

Bibliography

Jungk, R. and Mullert, N. (1988) *Future Workshops: How to Create Desirable Futures*, Institute for Social Inventions: London.
Max-Neef, M., Elizalde, A. and Hopenhayn, M. (1986) 'Desarollo a Escala Humana: una opcion para el futuro', *Development Dialogue*, Dag Hammarskjöld Foundation, Uppsala, Sweden.
―――― ――― and ――― (1989) 'Human scale development: an option for the future', *Development Dialogue*, 1989(1): 5–81. (English translation of Max-Neef *et al*. 1986.).
Myrdal, G. (1978) 'Institutional Economics', *Journal of Economic Issues* 12: 771–83.
Pradervand, P. (1989) *Listening to Africa: Developing Africa from the Grassroots*, Praeger: Westport, CT.
Schneider, B. (1988) *The Barefoot Revolution*, IT Publications: London.

[12]

Women's Capabilities and Social Justice*

MARTHA NUSSBAUM

Martha Nussbaum is the Ernst Freund Distinguished Service Professor of Law and Ethics, Department of Philosophy, Law School, and Divinity School, The University of Chicago, IL, USA

We come from our family's house to live in our husband's house. If we mention <u>our</u> name in this house, they say, "Oh, that is <u>another</u> family". Yet when it comes to working, they say, "What you earn is ours, because you are in <u>this</u> family's house", or "because you are working on <u>this</u> family's land. Let the land be registered in our names, so that we will not always feel like we are in someone else's family". (Santokbehn, agricultural laborer, Ahmedabad)

In your joint family, I am known as the second daughter-in-law. All these years I have known myself as no more than that. Today, after fifteen years, as I stand alone by the sea, I know that I have another identity, which is my relationship with the universe and its creator. That gives me the courage to write this letter as myself, not as the second daughter-in-law of your family ... I am not one to die easily. That is what I want to say in this letter. (Rabindranath Tagore, 'Letter from a Wife', 1914)

We not only want a piece of the pie, we also want to choose the flavor, and to know how to make it ourselves. (Ela Bhatt, founder, Self-Employed Women's Association (SEWA), 1992)

Development and sex equality

Women in much of the world lack support for fundamental functions of a human life. They are less well nourished than men, less healthy, and more vulnerable to physical violence and sexual abuse. They are much less likely than men to be literate, and still less likely to have pre-professional or technical education. Should they attempt to enter the workplace, they face greater obstacles, including intimidation from family or spouse, sex discrimi-

---

* The present article is closely related to the arguments of my book *Women and Human Development: The Capabilities Approach* (Nussbaum, 2000a, Introduction and chapter 1); those who would like more extensive versions of my arguments (and more empirical material, focusing on India) can find them there. For earlier articulations of my views on capabilities, see Nussbaum (1988, 1990, 1992, 1993, 1995a,b, 1997a,b, 1999, chapter 1, pp. 29-54).

M. Nussbaum

nation in hiring, and sexual harassment in the workplace — all, frequently, without effective legal recourse. Similar obstacles often impede their effective participation in political life. In many nations, women are not full equals under the law: they do not have the same property rights as men, the same rights to make a contract, the same rights of association, mobility, and religious liberty.[1] Burdened, often, with the 'double day' of taxing employment and full responsibility for housework and child care, they lack opportunities for play and the cultivation of their imaginative and cognitive faculties. All these factors take their toll on emotional well-being: women have fewer opportunities than men to live free from fear and to enjoy rewarding types of love — especially when, as often, they are married without choice in childhood and have no recourse from a bad marriage. In all these ways, unequal social and political circumstances give women unequal human capabilities.

One might sum all this up by saying that, all too often, women are not treated as ends in their own right, persons with a dignity that deserves respect from laws and institutions. Instead, they are treated as mere instruments of the ends of others — reproducers, caregivers, sexual outlets, agents of a family's general prosperity. Sometimes this instrumental value is strongly positive; sometimes it may actually be negative. A girl child's natal family frequently treats her as dispensable, seeing that she will leave anyhow and will not support parents in their old age. Along the way to her inevitable departure, she will involve the family in the considerable expense of dowry and wedding festivities. What use would it be, then, to care for her health and education in the same way that one would care for that of a boy? What wonder that the birth of a girl is often an occasion for sorrow rather than for rejoicing? As the old Indian proverb[2] puts it, 'A daughter born, To husband or death, She's already gone'.[3]

Nor is the marital home likely to be a place of end-like respect for such a daughter, although here her instrumental value may become positive. Her in-laws are likely to see her as a mere adjunct of a beloved son, a means to (especially male) grandchildren, an addition to the number of household workers, perhaps as a device to extract money in dowry payments from her parents. Even when she is not abused, she is unlikely to be treated with warmth, nor is her education likely to be fostered. Should her husband prove kind, he can be a buffer between her and the demands of his parents. Should he prove unkind, the woman is likely to have no recourse from abuse in the marital family, and no good exit options. Her natal family will probably refuse to have her back, she probably has no employment-related skills, and the law is not very interested in her predicament. Should the husband die, her situation is likely to become still worse, given the stigma attached to widowhood in many parts of the world. A tool whose purpose is gone: that is what a widow is, and that is rather like being dead.

These are not rare cases of unusual crime, but common realities. According to the 1999 *Human Development Report* of the United Nations Development Programme (UNDP), there is no country that treats its women as well as its men, according to a complex measure that includes life

Women and Social Justice

expectancy, wealth, and education (United Nations Development Programme, 1999). Developing countries, however, present especially urgent problems. Gender inequality is strongly correlated with poverty.[4] When poverty combines with gender inequality, the result is acute failure of central human capabilities. In the group of 'medium human development' countries taken as a whole, the male adult literacy rate is 83.3%, as against 67.3% for women; in the 'low human development countries', the rate is 57.2% for males and 35.8% for females. School enrollment percentages (combining all three levels) are, in the medium development countries, 60% for females and 68% for males; in the low human development countries, they are 33% for females and 44% for males. In terms of real Gross Domestic Product per capita, women control $2220 as against $4414 for men in the medium development countries, and the comparative values in the low human development countries are $691 for women and $1277 for men. We do not yet have reliable statistics for rape, domestic violence, and sexual harassment because, in many countries, little attention is paid to domestic violence and sexual harassment, rape within marriage is not counted as a crime, and even stranger-rape is so rarely punished that many women are deterred from reporting the crime.[5]

If we turn to the very basic area of health and nutrition, there is pervasive evidence of discrimination against females in many nations of the developing world. It is standardly believed that, where equal nutrition and health care are present, women live, on average, slightly longer than men: thus, we would expect a sex ratio of something like 102.2 women to 100 men (the actual sex ratio of Sub-Saharan Africa[6]). Many countries have a far lower sex ratio: India's, for example, is 92.7 women to 100 men, the lowest sex ratio since the census began early in this century. If we study such ratios and ask the question, 'How many more women than are now present in Country C would be there if they had the same sex ratio as Sub-Saharan Africa?', we get a figure that economist Amartya Sen has graphically called the number of 'missing women'. There are many millions of missing women in the world today.[7] Using this rough index, the number of missing women in Southeast Asia is 2.4 million, in Latin America 4.4 million, in North Africa 2.4 million, in Iran 1.4 million, in China 44.0 million, in Bangladesh 3.7 million, in India 36.7 million, in Pakistan 5.2 million, and in West Asia it is 4.3 million. If we now consider the ratio of the number of missing women to the number of actual women in a country, we obtain: Pakistan, 12.9%; India, 9.5%; Bangladesh, 8.7%; China, 8.6%; Iran, 8.5%; West Asia, 7.8%; North Africa, 3.9%; Latin America, 2.2%; and SouthEast Asia, 1.2%. In India, not only is the mortality differential especially sharp among children (girls dying in far greater numbers than boys), the higher mortality rate of women compared with men applies to all age groups until their late thirties (Drèze and Sen, 1989, p. 52). In some regions, the discrepancy is far greater than the national average: in rural Bihar, for example, a non-governmental organization has counted heads and arrived at the astonishing figure of 75 females to 100 males (Srinivasan, Adithi, Patna, Bihar, personal communication).

221

M. Nussbaum

One area of life that contributes especially greatly to women's inequality is the area of care. Women are the world's primary, and usually only, caregivers for people in a condition of extreme dependency: young children, the elderly, and those whose physical or mental handicaps make them incapable of the relative (and often temporary) independence that characterizes so-called 'normal' human lives. Women perform this crucial work, often, without pay and without recognition that it is work. At the same time, the fact that they need to spend long hours caring for the physical needs of others makes it more difficult for them to do what they want to do in other areas of life, including employment, citizenship, play and self-expression (Folbre, 1999; Harrington, 1999; Kittay, 1999; Williams, 1999).

Women, in short, lack essential support for leading lives that are fully human. This lack of support is frequently caused by them being women. Thus, even when they live in a constitutional democracy such as India, where they are equals in theory, they are second-class citizens in reality.

The capabilities approach: an overview

I shall argue that international political and economic thought should be feminist, attentive (among other things) to the special problems women face because of sex in more or less every nation in the world, problems without an understanding of which general issues of poverty and development cannot be well confronted. An approach to international development should be assessed for its ability to recognize these problems and to make recommendations for their solution. I shall propose and defend one such approach, one that seems to me to do better in this area than other prominent alternatives. My version of this approach is philosophical, and I shall try to show why we need philosophical theorizing in order to approach these problems well (see Nussbaum, 1998a,b; 2000b). It is also based on a cross-cultural normative account of central human capabilities, closely allied to a form of political liberalism; one of my primary tasks will be to defend this type of cross-cultural normative approach as a valuable basis from which to approach the problems of women in the developing world. Finally, I shall also try to show that my version of the capabilities approach, while attractive for many reasons, has special advantages when we are approaching the special problems faced by women: both intellectually and practically, there is a strong link between a concern for gender justice and reasons we might have to turn to the capabilities approach.

The aim of my project as a whole is to provide the philosophical underpinning for an account of basic constitutional principles that should be respected and implemented by the governments of all nations, as a bare minimum of what respect for human dignity requires. I shall argue that the best approach to this idea of a basic social minimum is provided by an approach that focuses on 'human capabilities', i.e. what people are actually able to do and to be — in a way, informed by an intuitive idea of a life that is worthy of the dignity of the human being. I shall identify a list of 'central human capabilities', setting them in the context of a type of 'political liberalism' that makes them specifically political goals and presents them in a manner free of any specific metaphysical grounding. In this way, I argue, the capabilities can be the object of an 'overlapping consensus' among people who otherwise have very different comprehensive conceptions of the good.[8] I shall also argue that the capabilities in question should be pursued for each and every person, treating each as an end and none as mere tools of the ends of others: thus, I adopt a 'principle of each person's capability', based on a 'principle of each person as end'. Women have all too often been treated as the supporters of the ends of others, rather than as ends in their own right; thus, this principle has particular critical force with regard to women's lives. Finally, my approach uses the idea of a 'threshold level of each capability', beneath which it is held that truly human functioning is not available to citizens; the social goal should be understood in terms of getting citizens above this capability threshold.

The capabilities approach has another related, weaker, use. It specifies a space within which 'comparisons of life quality' (how well people are doing) are most revealingly made among nations. Used in this way, as in the *Human Development Reports*, it is a rival to other standard measures, such as Gross National Product (GNP) per capita and utility. This role for the conception is significant, since we are not likely to make progress toward a good conception of the social minimum if we do not first get the space of comparison right. We may also use the approach in this weaker way to compare one nation with another, even when we are unwilling to go further and use the approach as the philosophical basis for fundamental constitutional principles establishing a social minimum or threshold. On the other hand, the comparative use of capabilities is ultimately not much use without a determinate normative conception that will tell us what to make of what we find in our comparative study. Most conceptions of quality of life measurement in development economics are implicitly harnessed to a normative theory of the proper social goal (wealth maximization, utility maximization, etc.), and this one is so explicitly harnessed. The primary task of my argument will be to move beyond the merely comparative use of capabilities to the construction of a normative political proposal that is a partial theory of justice.

The capabilities approach is fully universal: the capabilities in question are important for each and every citizen, in each and every nation, and each is to be treated as an end. Women in developing nations are important to the project in two ways: as people who suffer pervasively from acute capability failure, and also as people whose situation provides an interesting test of this and other approaches, showing us the problems they solve or fail to solve. Defects in standard GNP and utility-based approaches can be well understood by keeping the problems of such women in view; but of course women's problems are urgent in their own right, and it may be hoped that a focus on them will help compensate for earlier neglect of sex equality in development economics and in the international human rights movement.

M. Nussbaum

The need for cross-cultural norms

Should we be looking for a set of cross-cultural norms in the first place, where women's opportunities are concerned? Obviously enough, women are already doing that, in many areas. To take just one example, women laboring in the informal sector, for example, are increasingly organizing on an international level to set goals and priorities.[9] Many other examples are provided by the international human rights movement and international agreements such as Convention on the Elimination of all forms of Discrimination Against Women (CEDAW). But this process is controversial, both intellectually and politically. Where do these normatives categories come from, it will be asked? And how can they be justified as appropriate ones for cultures that have traditionally used different normative categories? Now, of course, no critical social theory confines itself to the categories of each culture's daily life. If it did, it probably could not perform its special task as critical theory, which involves the systematization and critical scrutiny of intuitions that in daily life are often unexamined. Theory gives people a set of terms with which to criticize abuses that otherwise might lurk nameless in the background. Terms such as 'sexual harassment' and 'hostile work environment' give us some obvious examples of this point. But, even if one defends theory as valuable for practice, it may still be problematic to use concepts that originate in one culture to describe and assess realities in another — and all the more problematic if the culture described has been colonized and oppressed by the describer's culture. Attempts by international feminists today to use a universal language of justice, human rights, or human functioning to assess lives like those of Vasanti and Jayamma is bound to encounter charges of Westernizing and colonizing — even when the universal categories are introduced by feminists who live and work within the nation in question itself. For, it is standardly said, such women are alienated from their culture, and are faddishly aping a Western political agenda. The minute they become critics, it is said, they cease to belong to their own culture and become puppets of the Western elite.[10]

We should begin by asking whose interests are served by the implicit nostalgic image of a happy harmonious culture, and whose resistance and misery are being effaced. Describing her mother's difficult life, Indian feminist philosopher Uma Narayan writes, "One thing I want to say to all who would dismiss my feminist criticisms of my culture, using my 'Westernization' as a lash, is that my mother's pain too has rustled among the pages of all those books I have read that partly constitute my 'Westernization', and has crept into all the suitcases I have ever packed for my several exiles". This same pain is evident in the united voice of protest that has emerged from international women's meetings such as those in Vienna and Beijing, where a remarkable degree of agreement was found across cultures concerning fundamental rights for women.

Nonetheless, when we advance a set of universal norms in connection with women's equality, we will also face three more sincere and respectable objections, which must be honestly confronted. First, one hears what I shall

Women and Social Justice

call the 'argument from culture'. Traditional cultures, the argument goes, contain their own norms of what women's lives should be: frequently norms of female modesty, deference, obedience, and self-sacrifice. Feminists should not assume without argument that those are bad norms, incapable of constructing good and flourishing lives for women. By contrast, the norms proposed by feminists seem to this opponent suspiciously 'Western', because they involve an emphasis on choice and opportunity.

My full answer to this argument will emerge from the proposal I shall make, which certainly does not preclude any woman's choice to lead a traditional life, so long as she does so with certain economic and political opportunities firmly in place. But we should begin by emphasizing that the notion of tradition used in the argument is far too simple. Cultures are scenes of debate and contestation. They contain dominant voices, and they also contain the voices of women, which have not always been heard. It would be implausible to suggest that the many groups working to improve the employment conditions of women in the informal sector, for example, are brainwashing women into striving for economic opportunities: clearly, they provide means to ends women already want, and a context of female solidarity within which to pursue those ends. Where they do alter existing preferences, they typically do so by giving women a richer sense of both their possibilities and their equal worth, in a way that looks more like a self-realization (as Tagore's heroine vividly states) than like brainwashing. Indeed, what may possibly be 'Western' is the arrogant supposition that choice and economic agency are solely Western values!

Another general point should be stressed: cultures are dynamic, and change is a very basic element in all of them. Contrasts between West and non-West often depict Western cultures as dynamic, critical, modernizing, while Eastern cultures are identified with their oldest elements, as if these do not change or encounter contestation. Looking at the relationship between her grandmother's way of life and her own, Narayan (1997, p. 26) comments, "I find it impossible to describe 'our traditional way of life' without seeing change as a constitutive element, affecting transformations that become 'invisible' in their taken-for-grantedness". Criticism too is profoundly indigenous to virtually all cultures,[11] but to none more so than to the culture of India, that extremely argumentative nation.[12] To cite just one famous and typical example, Bengali religious thinker Rammohun Roy, imagining the horrors of death, singles out as especially terrible the fact that "everyone will contest your views, and you will not be able to reply".[13] This is also Indian culture.

In short, because cultures are scenes of debate, appealing to culture give us questions rather than answers. It certainly does not show that cross-cultural norms are a bad answer to those questions.

Let us now consider the argument that I shall call the 'argument from the good of diversity'. This argument reminds us that our world is rich in part because we do not all agree on a single set of practices and norms. We think the world's different languages have worth and beauty, and that it is a bad thing, diminishing the expressive resources of human life generally, if

M. Nussbaum

any language should cease to exist. So, too, cultural norms have their own distinctive beauty; the world risks becoming impoverished as it becomes more homogeneous.

Here, we should distinguish two claims the objector might be making. She might be claiming that diversity is good as such; or she might simply be saying that there are problems with the values of economic efficiency and consumerism that are increasingly dominating our interlocking world. This second claim, of course, does not yet say anything against cross-cultural norms; it just suggests that their content should be critical of some dominant economic norms. So the real challenge to our enterprise lies in the first claim. To meet it, we must ask how far cultural diversity really is like linguistic diversity. The trouble with the analogy is that languages do not harm people, and cultural practices frequently do. We could think that threatened languages such as Cornish and Breton should be preserved, without thinking the same about domestic violence: it is not worth preserving simply because it is there and very old. In the end, then, the objection does not undermine the search for cross-cultural norms, it requires it: for what it invites us to ask is whether the cultural values in question are among the ones worth preserving, and this entails at least a very general cross-cultural framework of assessment, one that will tell us when we are better off letting a practice die out.

Finally, we have the 'argument from paternalism'. This argument says that when we use a set of cross-cultural norms as benchmarks for the world's varied societies, we show too little respect for people's freedom as agents (and, in a related way, their role as democratic citizens). People are the best judges of what is good for them and, if we say that their own choices are not good for them, we treat them like children. This is an important point, and one that any viable cross-cultural proposal should bear firmly in mind. But it hardly seems incompatible with the endorsement of cross-cultural norms. Indeed, it appears to endorse explicitly at least some cross-cultural norms, such as the political liberties and other opportunities for choice. Thinking about paternalism gives us a strong reason to respect the variety of ways citizens actually choose to lead their lives in a pluralistic society, and therefore to seek a set of cross-cultural norms that protect freedom and choice of the most significant sorts. But this means that we will naturally value religious toleration, associative freedom, and the other major liberties. These liberties are themselves cross-cultural norms, and they are not compatible with views that many real people and societies hold.

We can make a further claim: many existing value systems are themselves highly paternalistic, particularly toward women. They treat them as unequal under the law, as lacking full civil capacity, and as not having the property rights, associative liberties, and employment rights of males. If we encounter a system like this, it is in one sense paternalistic to say, sorry, which is unacceptable under the universal norms of equality and liberty that we would like to defend. In that way, any bill of rights is 'paternalistic' vis-à-vis families, or groups, or practices, or even pieces of legislation that treat people with insufficient or unequal respect. The Indian Constitution, for example, is in that sense paternalistic when it tells people that it is from now on illegal to use caste or sex as grounds of discrimination. But that is hardly a good argument against fundamental constitutional rights or, more generally, against opposing the attempts of some people to tyrannize over others. We dislike paternalism, insofar as we do, because there is something else that we like; namely, liberty of choice in fundamental matters. It is fully consistent to reject some forms of paternalism while supporting those that underwrite these basic values.

Neither does the protection of choice require only a formal defense of basic liberties. The various liberties of choice have material preconditions, in whose absence there is merely a simulacrum of choice. Many women who have, in a sense, the 'choice' to go to school simply cannot do so: the economic circumstances of their lives makes this impossible. Women who 'can' have economic independence, in the sense that no law prevents them, may be prevented simply by lacking assets, or access to credit. In short, liberty is not just a matter of having rights on paper, it requires being in a material position to exercise those rights. And this requires resources. The state that is going to guarantee people rights effectively is going to have to recognize norms beyond the small menu of basic rights: it will have to take a stand about the re-distribution of wealth and income, about employment, land rights, health, and education. If we think that these norms are important cross-culturally, we will need to take an international position on pushing toward these goals. That requires yet more universalism and, in a sense, paternalism; but we could hardly say that the many women who live in abusive or repressive marriages, with no assets and no opportunity to seek employment outside the home, are especially free to do as they wish.

The argument from paternalism indicates, then, that we should prefer a cross-cultural normative account that focuses on empowerment and opportunity, leaving people plenty of space to determine their course in life once those opportunities are secured to them. It does not give us any good reason to reject the whole idea of cross-cultural norms, and some strong reasons why we should seek such norms, including in our account not only the basic liberties, but also forms of economic empowerment that are crucial in making the liberties truly available to people. The argument also suggests one thing more: that the account we search for should seek empowerment and opportunity for each and every person, respecting each as an end, rather than simply as the agent or supporter of ends of others. Women are too often treated as members of an organic unit such as the family or the community is supposed to be, and their interests subordinated to the larger goals of that unit, which means, typically, those of its male members. However, the impressive economic growth of a region means nothing to women whose husbands deprived them of control over household income. We need to consider not just the aggregate, whether in a region or in a family; we need to consider the distribution of resources and opportunities to each person, thinking of each as worthy of regard in her own right.

M. Nussbaum

Traditional economic approaches to development: the need for human norms

Another way of seeing why cross-cultural norms are badly needed in the international policy arena is to consider what the alternative has typically been. Prior to the shift in thinking that is associated with the work of Amartya Sen[14] and with the *Human Development Reports* of the United Nations Development Programme (1993–1996),[15] the most prevalent approach to measuring quality of life in a nation used to be simply to ask about GNP per capita. This approach tries to weasel out of making any cross-cultural claims about what has value — although, notice, it does assume the universal value of opulence. What it omits, however, is much more significant. We are not even told about the distribution of wealth and income, and countries with similar aggregate figures can exhibit great distributional variations. (Thus, South Africa always did very well among developing nations, despite its enormous inequalities and violations of basic justice.) Circus girl Sissy Jupe, in Dickens' novel *Hard Times*, already saw the problem with this absence of normative concern for distribution. She says that her economics lesson did not tell her "who has got the money and whether any of it is mine".[16] So, too, with women around the world: the fact that one nation or region is, in general, more prosperous than another is only a part of the story: it does not tell us what the government has done for women in various social classes, or how they are doing. To know that, we would need to look at their lives. But then we need to specify, beyond distribution of wealth and income itself, what parts of lives we ought to look at — such as life expectancy, infant mortality, educational opportunities, health care, employment opportunities, land rights, political liberties. Seeing what is absent from the GNP account nudges us sharply in the direction of mapping out these and other basic goods in a universal way, so that we can use the list of basic goods to compare quality of life across societies.

A further problem with all resource-based approaches, even those that are sensitive to distribution, is that individuals vary in their ability to convert resources into functionings. (This is the problem that has been stressed for some time by Amartya Sen in his writings about the capabilities approach.) Some of these differences are straightforwardly physical. Nutritional needs vary with age, occupation, and sex. A pregnant or lactating woman needs more nutrients than a non-pregnant woman. A child needs more protein than an adult. A person whose limbs work well needs few resources to be mobile, whereas a person with paralyzed limbs needs many more resources to achieve the same level of mobility. Many such variations can escape our notice if we live in a prosperous nation that can afford to bring all individuals to a high level of physical attainment; in the developing world, we must be highly alert to these variations in need. Again, some of the pertinent variations are social, connected with traditional hierarchies. If we wish to bring all citizens of a nation to the same level of educational attainment, we will need to devote more resources to those who encounter obstacles from traditional hierarchy or prejudice: thus, women's literacy will prove more expensive than men's literacy in many parts of the world. If we operate only with an index of resources, we will frequently re-inforce inequalities that are highly relevant to well-being. As my examples suggest, women's lives are especially likely to raise these problems: therefore, any approach that is to deal adequately with women's issues must be able to deal well with these variations.

If we turn from resource-based approaches to preference-based approaches, we encounter another set of difficulties.[17] Such approaches have one salient advantage over the GNP approach: they look at people, and assess the role of resources as they figure in improving actual people's lives. But users of such approaches typically assume without argument that the way to assess the role of resources in people's lives is simply to ask them about the satisfaction of their current preferences. The problem with this idea is that preferences are not exogenous, given independently of economic and social conditions. They are, at least in part, constructed by those conditions. Women often have no preference for economic independence before they learn about avenues through which women like them might pursue this goal; nor do they think of themselves as citizens with rights that were being ignored, before they learn of their rights and are encouraged to believe in their equal worth. All of these ideas, and the preferences based on them, frequently take shape for women in programs of education sponsored by women's organizations of various types. Men's preferences, too, are socially shaped and often misshaped. Men frequently have a strong preference that their wives should do all the child care and all the housework — often in addition to working an 8-hour day. Such preferences are also not fixed in the nature of things: they are constructed by social traditions of privilege and subordination. Thus, a preference-based approach typically will re-inforce inequalities, especially those inequalities that are entrenched enough to have crept into people very desires. Once again, although this is a fully general problem, it has special pertinence to women's lives. Women have especially often been deprived of education and information, which are necessary, if by no means sufficient, to make preferences a reliable indicator of what public policy should pursue. They have also often been socialized to believe that a lower living standard is what is right and fitting for them, and that some great human goods (for example, education, political participation) are not for them at all. They may be under considerable social pressure to say they are satisfied without such things: and yet we should not hastily conclude that public policy should not work to extend these functions to women. In short, looking at women's lives helps us see the inadequacy of traditional approaches; and the urgency of women's problems gives us a very strong motivation to prefer a non-traditional approach.

Human dignity and human capabilities

I shall now argue that a reasonable answer to all these concerns, capable of giving good guidance to governments establishing basic constitutional prin-

M. Nussbaum

ciples and to international agencies assessing the quality of life, is given by
a version of the 'capabilities approach' — an approach to quality of life
assessment pioneered within economics by Amartya Sen, and by now highly
influential through the *Human Development Reports* of the UNDP. My own
version of this approach is in several ways different from that of Sen;[18] I shall
simply lay out my view as I would currently defend it.

The central question asked by the capabilities approach is not 'How
satisfied is this woman?' or even 'How much in the way of resources is she
able to command?'. It is, instead, 'What is she actually able to do and to be?'.
Taking a stand for political purposes on a working list of functions that
would appear to be of central importance in human life, users of this
approach ask, Is the person capable of this, or not? They ask not only about
the person's satisfaction with what she does, but about what she does and
what she is in a position to do (what her opportunities and liberties are).
They ask not just about the resources that are present, but about how those
do or do not go to work, enabling the woman to function.

To introduce the intuitive idea behind the approach, it is useful to start
from this passage of Marx's 1844 *Economic and Philosophical Manuscripts*,
written at a time when he was reading Aristotle and was profoundly
influenced by Aristotelian ideas of human capability and functioning:

> It is obvious that the <u>human</u> eye gratifies itself in a way different
> from the crude, non-human eye; the human <u>ear</u> different from the
> crude ear, etc. … The <u>sense</u> caught up in crude practical need has
> only a <u>restricted</u> sense. For the starving man, it is not the human
> form of food that exists, but only its abstract being as food; it could
> just as well be there in its crudest form, and it would be impossible
> to say wherein this feeding activity differs from that of <u>animals</u>.

Marx here singles out certain human functions, eating and the use of the
senses, that seem to have a particular centrality in any life one might live.
He then claims that there is something that it is to be able to perform these
activities in a fully human way — by which he means a way infused by
reasoning and sociability. But human beings do not automatically have the
opportunity to perform their human functions in a fully human way. Some
conditions in which people live, conditions of starvation or of educational
deprivation, bring it about that a being that is human has to live in an animal
way. Of course, what he is saying is that these conditions are unacceptable
and should be changed.

Similarly, the intuitive idea behind my version of the capabilities
approach is twofold. First, there are certain functions that are particularly
central in human life, in the sense that their presence or absence is typically
understood to be a mark of the presence or absence of human life. Second,
and this is what Marx found in Aristotle, that it is something to do these
functions in a truly human way, not a merely animal way. We judge,
frequently enough, that a life has been so impoverished that it is not worthy
of the dignity of the human being, that it is a life in which one goes on
living, but more or less like an animal, not being able to develop and

Women and Social Justice

exercise one's human powers. In Marx's example, a starving person just grabs at the food in order to survive, and the many social and rational ingredients of human feeding cannot make their appearance. Similarly, the senses of a human being can operate at a merely animal level — if they are not cultivated by appropriate education, by leisure for play and self-expression, by valuable associations with others — and we should add to the list some items that Marx probably would not endorse, such as expressive and associational liberty, and the freedom of worship. The core idea seems to be that of the human being as a dignified free being who shapes his/her own life, rather than being passively shaped or pushed around by the world in the manner of a flock or herd animal.

At one extreme, we may judge that the absence of capability for a central function is so acute that the person is not really a human being at all, or any longer — as in the case of certain very severe forms of mental disability or senile dementia. But I am less interested in that boundary (important though it is for medical ethics) than in a higher one, the level at which a person's capability is 'truly human', i.e. 'worthy' of a human being. The idea thus contains a notion of human worth or dignity.

Notice that the approach makes each person a bearer of value, and an end. Marx, like his bourgeois forebears, holds that it is profoundly wrong to subordinate the ends of some individuals to those of others. That is at the core of what exploitation is, to treat a person as a mere object for the use of others. What this approach is after is a society in which individuals are treated as each worthy of regard, and in which each has been put in a position to live really humanly.

I think we can produce an account of these necessary elements of truly human functioning that commands a broad cross-cultural consensus, a list that can be endorsed for political purposes by people who otherwise have very different views of what a complete good life for a human being would be. The list is supposed to provide a focus for quality of life assessment and for political planning, and it aims to select capabilities that are of central importance, whatever else the person pursues. They therefore have a special claim to be supported for political purposes in a pluralistic society.[19]

The list represents the result of years of cross-cultural discussion,[20] and comparisons between earlier and later versions will show that the input of other voices has shaped its content in many ways. It remains open-ended and humble; it can always be contested and remade. Neither does it deny that the items on the list are to some extent differently constructed by different societies. Indeed, part of the idea of the list is that its members can be more concretely specified in accordance with local beliefs and circumstances. Here is the current version of the list.

Central human functional capabilities

(1) *Life.* Being able to live to the end of a human life of normal length; not dying prematurely or before one's life is so reduced as to be not worth living.

231

M. Nussbaum

(2) *Bodily Health*. Being able to have good health, including reproductive health;[21] to be adequately nourished; to have adequate shelter.

(3) *Bodily Integrity*. Being able to move freely from place to place; to be secure against violent assault, including sexual assault and domestic violence; having opportunities for sexual satisfaction and for choice in matters of reproduction.

(4) *Senses, Imagination, and Thought*. Being able to use the senses, to imagine, think, and reason — and to do these things in a 'truly human' way, a way informed and cultivated by an adequate education, including, but by no means limited to, literacy and basic mathematical and scientific training. Being able to use imagination and thought in connection with experiencing and producing works and events of one's own choice, religious, literary, musical, and so forth. Being able to use one's mind in ways protected by guarantees of freedom of expression with respect to both political and artistic speech, and freedom of religious exercise. Being able to have pleasurable experiences, and to avoid non-necessary pain.

(5) *Emotions*. Being able to have attachments to things and people outside ourselves; to love those who love and care for us, to grieve at their absence; in general, to love, to grieve, to experience longing, gratitude, and justified anger. Not having one's emotional development blighted by fear and anxiety. (Supporting this capability means supporting forms of human association that can be shown to be crucial in their development.)

(6) *Practical Reason*. Being able to form a conception of the good and to engage in critical reflection about the planning of one's life. (This entails protection for the liberty of conscience.)

(7) *Affiliation*

  (A) Being able to live with and toward others, to recognize and show concern for other human beings, to engage in various forms of social interaction; to be able to imagine the situation of another and to have compassion for that situation; to have the capability for both justice and friendship. (Protecting this capability means protecting institutions that constitute and nourish such forms of affiliation, and also protecting the freedom of assembly and political speech.)

  (B) Having the social bases of self-respect and non-humiliation; being able to be treated as a dignified being whose worth is equal to that of others. This entails protections against discrimination on the basis of race, sex, sexual orientation, religion, caste, ethnicity, or national origin.

(8) *Other Species*. Being able to live with concern for and in relation to animals, plants, and the world of nature.

(9) *Play*. Being able to laugh, to play, to enjoy recreational activities.

Women and Social Justice

(10) *Control over one's Environment*

- (A) *Political.* Being able to participate effectively in political choices that govern one's life; having the right of political participation, protections of free speech and association.
- (B) *Material.* Being able to hold property (both land and movable goods); having the right to seek employment on an equal basis with others; having the freedom from unwarranted search and seizure. In work, being able to work as a human being, exercising practical reason and entering into meaningful relationships of mutual recognition with other workers.

The list is, emphatically, a list of separate components. We cannot satisfy the need for one of them by giving people a larger amount of another one. All are of central importance and all are distinct in quality. The irreducible plurality of the list limits the trade-offs that it will be reasonable to make, and thus limits the applicability of quantitative cost–benefit analysis. At the same time, the items on the list are related to one another in many complex ways. One of the most effective ways of promoting women's control over their environment, and their effective right of political participation, is to promote women's literacy. Women who can seek employment outside the home have more resources in protecting their bodily integrity from assaults within it. Such facts give us still more reason not to promote one capability at the expense of the others.

Among the capabilities, two (practical reason and affiliation) stand out as of special importance, since they both organize and suffuse all the others, making their pursuit truly human. To use one's senses in a way not infused by the characteristically human use of thought and planning is to use them in an incompletely human manner. Tagore's heroine, summarizing her decision to leave her husband, says "I found myself beautiful as a free human mind". This idea of herself infuses all her other functions. At the same time, to reason for oneself without at all considering the circumstances and needs of others is, again, to behave in an incompletely human way.

The basic intuition from which the capability approach begins, in the political arena, is that human abilities exert a moral claim that they should be developed. Human beings are creatures such that, provided with the right educational and material support, they can become fully capable of these human functions, i.e. they are creatures with certain lower-level capabilities (that I call 'basic capabilities'[22]) to perform the functions in question. When these capabilities are deprived of the nourishment that would transform them into the high-level capabilities that figure on my list, they are fruitless, cut off, in some way but a shadow of themselves. If a turtle were given a life that afforded a merely animal level of functioning, we would have no indignation, no sense of waste and tragedy. When a human being is given a life that blights powers of human action and expression, that does give us a sense of waste and tragedy — the tragedy expressed, for example, in Tagore's heroine's statement to her husband, when she says, "I am not one to die easily". In her view, a life without dignity and choice, a

M. Nussbaum

life in which she can be no more than an appendage, was a type of death of her humanity.

Notice that the approach makes each person a bearer of value, and an end. Marx, like his bourgeois forebears, holds that it is profoundly wrong to subordinate the ends of some individuals to those of others. That is at the core of what exploitation is, to treat a person as a mere object for the use of others. Thus, it will be just as repugnant to this Aristotelian/Marxian approach as to a bourgeois philosophy to foster a good for society considered as an organic whole, where this does not involve the fostering of the good of persons taken one by one. Thus, it will be insufficient to promote the good of 'the community' or 'the family', where that leaves intact gross asymmetries of capability among community or family members. Women are especially likely to be the losers when the good of a group is promoted as such, without asking about hierarchies of power and opportunity internal to the group. The capabilities approach insists on pressing that question. What the approach is after is a society in which persons are treated as each worthy of regard, and in which each has been put in a position to live really humanly. (That is where the idea of a threshold comes in: we say that beneath a certain level of capability, in each area, a person has not been enabled to live in a truly human way.) We may call this the 'principle of each person as end', which can be further articulated as a 'principle of each person's capability': the capabilities sought are sought for each and every person, not, in the first instance, for groups or families or states or other corporate bodies. Such bodies may be extremely important in promoting human capabilities, and in this way they may deservedly gain our support: but it is because of what they do for people that they are so worthy, and the ultimate political goal is always the promotion of the capabilities of each person.[23]

We begin, then, with a sense of the worth and dignity of basic human powers, thinking of them as claims to a chance for functioning, claims that give rise to correlated social and political duties. In fact, there are three different types of capabilities that play a role in the analysis. First, there are 'basic capabilities': the innate equipment of individuals that is the necessary basis for developing the more advanced capability, and a ground of moral concern. Second, there are 'internal capabilities': states of the person herself that are, so far as the person herself is concerned, sufficient conditions for the exercise of the requisite functions. A woman who has not suffered genital mutilation has the 'internal capability' for sexual pleasure; most adult human beings everywhere have the 'internal capability' for religious freedom and the freedom of speech. Finally, there are 'combined capabilities', which may be defined as internal capabilities combined with suitable external conditions for the exercise of the function. A woman who is not mutilated, but who has been widowed as a child and is forbidden to make another marriage has the internal but not the combined capability for sexual expression (and, in most such cases, for employment, and political participation) (see Chen, 1995, 1999). Citizens of repressive non-democratic regimes have the internal but not the combined capability to exercise

Women and Social Justice

thought and speech in accordance with their conscience. The list, then, is a list of 'combined capabilities'. To realize one of the items on the list entails not only promoting appropriate development of people's internal powers, but also preparing the environment so that it is favorable for the exercise of practical reason and the other major functions.

Functioning and capability

I have spoken both of functioning and of capability. How are they related? Getting clear about this is crucial in defining the relation of the 'capabilities approach' to our concerns about paternalism and pluralism. For, if we were to take functioning itself as the goal of public policy, a liberal pluralist would rightly judge that we were precluding many choices that citizens may make in accordance with their own conceptions of the good. A deeply religious person may prefer not to be well-nourished, but to engage in strenuous fasting. Whether for religious or for other reasons, a person may prefer a celibate life to one containing sexual expression. A person may prefer to work with an intense dedication that precludes recreation and play. Am I declaring, by my very use of the list, that these are not fully human or flourishing lives? And am I instructing government to nudge or push people into functioning of the requisite sort, no matter what they prefer?

It is important that the answer to this question is no. Capability, not functioning, is the appropriate political goal. This is so because of the very great importance the approach attaches to practical reason, as a good that both suffuses all the other functions, making them fully human, and also figures, itself, as a central function on the list. The person with plenty of food may always choose to fast, but there is a great difference between fasting and starving, and it is this difference that we wish to capture. Again, the person who has normal opportunities for sexual satisfaction can always choose a life of celibacy, and the approach says nothing against this. What it does speak against (for example) is the practice of female genital mutilation, which deprives individuals of the opportunity to choose sexual functioning (and indeed, the opportunity to choose celibacy as well) (Nussbaum, 1999, Chapters 3 and 4). A person who has opportunities for play can always choose a workaholic life; again, there is a great difference between that chosen life and a life constrained by insufficient maximum-hour protections and/or the 'double day' that makes women unable to play in many parts of the world.

Once again, we must stress that the objective is to be understood in terms of 'combined capabilities'. To secure a capability to a person, it is not sufficient to produce good internal states of readiness to act. It is also necessary to prepare the material and institutional environment so that people are actually able to function. Women burdened by the 'double day' may be internally incapable of play; if, for example, they have been kept indoors and zealously guarded since infancy, married at age 6, and forbidden to engage in the kind of imaginative exploration of the environment that male children standardly enjoy. Young girls in poor areas of rural Rajasthan,

M. Nussbaum

India, for example, have great difficulty learning to play in an educational
program run by local activists, because their capacity for play has not been
nourished early in childhood. On the other hand, there are also many
women in the world who are perfectly capable of play in the internal sense,
but who are unable to play because of the crushing demands of the 'double
day'. Such a woman does not have the 'combined capability' for play in the
sense intended by the list. Capability is thus a demanding notion. In its focus
on the environment of choice, it is highly attentive to the goal of functioning, and instructs governments to keep it always in view. On the other hand,
it does not push people into functioning: once the stage is fully set, the
choice is theirs.

Capabilities and care

All human beings begin their lives as helpless children; if they live long
enough, they are likely to end their lives in helplessness, whether physical
or also mental. During the prime of life, most human beings encounter
periods of extreme dependency; and some human beings remain dependent
on the daily bodily care of others throughout their lives. Of course, putting
it this way suggests, absurdly, that 'normal' human beings do not depend on
others for bodily care and survival; but political thought should recognize
that some phases of life, and some lives, generate more profound dependency than others.

The capabilities approach, more Aristotelian than Kantian, sees human
beings from the first as animal beings whose lives are characterized by
profound neediness as well as by dignity. It addresses the issue of care in
many ways: under 'life', it is stressed that people should be enabled to
complete a 'normal' human lifespan; under 'health' and 'bodily integrity',
the needs of different phases of life are implicitly recognized; 'sense',
'emotions', and 'affiliation' also target needs that vary with the stage of life.
'Affiliation' is of particular importance, since it mentions the need for both
compassion and self-respect, and it also mentions non-discrimination. What
we see, then, is that care must be provided in such a way that the capability
for self-respect of the receiver is not injured, and also in such a way that the
care-giver is not exploited and discriminated against on account of performing that role. In other words, a good society must arrange to provide care
for those in a condition of extreme dependency, without exploiting women
as they have traditionally been exploited, and thus depriving them of other
important capabilities. This huge problem will rightly shape the way states
think about all the other capabilities.[24]

The capabilities approach has a great advantage in this area over
traditional liberal approaches that use the idea of a social contract. Such
approaches typically generate basic political principles from a hypothetical
contract situation in which all participants are independent adults. John
Rawls, for example, uses the phrase "fully cooperating members of society
over a complete life".[25] But, of course, no human being is that. The fiction
also distorts the choice of principles in a central way, effacing the issue of

Women and Social Justice

extreme dependency and care from the agenda of the contracting parties, when they choose the principles that shape society's basic structure. And yet, such a fundamental issue cannot well be postponed for later consideration, since it profoundly shapes the way social institutions will be designed.[26] The capabilities approach, using a different concept of the human being, one that builds in need and dependency into the first phases of political thinking, is better suited to good deliberation on this urgent set of issues.

Capabilities and human rights

Earlier versions of the list appeared to diverge from approaches common in the human rights movement by not giving as large a place to the traditional political rights and liberties, although the need to incorporate them was stressed from the start. This version of the list corrects that defect of emphasis.[27] The political liberties have a central importance in making well-being human. A society that aims at well-being while overriding these has delivered to its members an incompletely human level of satisfaction. As Amartya Sen (1994) has recently written, "Political rights are important not only for the fulfillment of needs, they are crucial also for the formulation of needs. And this idea relates, in the end, to the respect that we owe each other as fellow human beings".[28] There are many reasons to think that political liberties have an instrumental role in preventing material disaster (in particular, famine; Sen, 1981), and in promoting economic well-being. But their role is not merely instrumental: they are valuable in their own right.

Thus, capabilities as I conceive them have a very close relationship to human rights, as understood in contemporary international discussions. In effect, they cover the terrain covered by both the so-called 'first-generation rights' (political and civil liberties) and the so-called 'second-generation rights' (economic and social rights). They also play a similar role, providing the philosophical underpinning for basic constitutional principles. Because the language of rights is well established, the defender of capabilities needs to show what is added by this new language.[29]

The idea of human rights is by no means a crystal-clear idea. Rights have been understood in many different ways, and difficult theoretical questions are frequently obscured by the use of rights language, which can give the illusion of agreement where there is deep philosophical disagreement. People differ about what the 'basis' of a rights claim is: rationality, sentience, and mere life have all had their defenders. They differ, too, about whether rights are prepolitical or artifacts of laws and institutions. (Kant held the latter view, although the dominant human rights tradition has held the former.) They differ about whether rights belong only to individual persons, or also to groups. They differ about whether rights are to be regarded as side-constraints on goal-promoting action, or rather as one part of the social goal that is being promoted. They differ, again, about the relationship between rights and duties: if A has a right to S, then does this mean that

237

there is always someone who has a duty to provide S, and how shall we decide who that someone is? They differ, finally, about what rights are to be understood as rights 'to'. Are human rights primarily rights to be treated in certain ways? Rights to a certain level of achieved well-being? Rights to resources with which one may pursue one's life plan? Rights to certain opportunities and capacities with which one may make choices about one's life plan?

The account of central capabilities has the advantage, it seems to me, of taking clear positions on these disputed issues, while stating clearly what the motivating concerns are and what the goal is. Bernard Williams (1987, p. 100) put this point eloquently, commenting on Sen's 1987 Tanner Lectures:

> I am not very happy myself with taking rights as the starting point. The notion of a basic human right seems to me obscure enough, and I would rather come at it from the perspective of basic human capabilities. I would prefer capabilities to do the work, and if we are going to have a language or rhetoric of rights, to have it delivered from them, rather than the other way round.

As Williams says, however, the relationship between the two concepts needs further scrutiny, given the dominance of rights language in the international development world.

In some areas, I would argue that the best way of thinking about what rights are is to see them as 'combined capabilities'. The right to political participation, the right to religious free exercise, the right of free speech — these and others are all best thought of as capacities to function. In other words, to secure a right to a citizen in these areas is to put them in a position of combined capability to function in that area. (Of course, there is another sense of 'right' that is more like my 'basic capabilities': people have a right to religious freedom just in virtue of being human, even if the state they live in has not guaranteed them this freedom.) By defining rights in terms of combined capabilities, we make it clear that a people in country C do not really have the right to political participation just because this language exists on paper: they really have this right only if there are effective measures to make people truly capable of political exercise. Women in many nations have a nominal right of political participation without having this right in the sense of capability: for example, they may be threatened with violence should they leave the home. In short, thinking in terms of capability gives us a benchmark as we think about what it is really to secure a right to someone.

There is another set of rights, largely those in the area of property and economic advantage, which seem analytically different in their relationship to capabilities. Take, for example, the right to shelter and housing. These are rights that can be analyzed in a number of distinct ways: in terms of resources, or utility (satisfaction), or capabilities. (Once again, we must distinguish between the claim that 'A has a right to shelter' — which frequently refers to A's moral claim in virtue of being human, with what I

Women and Social Justice

call 'basic capabilities' — from the statement that 'Country C gives its citizens the right to shelter'. It is the second sentence whose analysis I am discussing here.) Here again, however, it seems valuable to understand these rights in terms of capabilities. If we think of the right to shelter as a right to a certain amount of resources, then we get into the very problem I discussed in the section 'The need for cross-cultural norms': giving resources to people does not always bring differently situated people up to the same level of capability to function. The utility-based analysis also encounters a problem: traditionally, deprived people may be satisfied with a very low living standard, believing that this is all they have any hope of getting. A capabilities analysis, by contrast, looks at how people are actually enabled to live. Analyzing economic and material rights in terms of capabilities thus enables us to clearly set forth a rationale we have for spending unequal amounts of money on the disadvantaged, or creating special programs to assist their transition to full capability.

The language of capabilities has one further advantage over the language of rights: it is not strongly linked to one particular cultural and historical tradition, as the language of rights is believed to be. This belief is not very accurate: although the term 'rights' is associated with the European Enlightenment, its component ideas have deep roots in many traditions.[30] Where India is concerned, for example, even apart from the recent validation of rights language in Indian legal and constitutional traditions, the salient component ideas have deep roots in far earlier areas of Indian thought — in ideas of religious toleration developed since the edicts of Ashoka in the third century BC, in the thought about Hindu/Muslim relations in the Moghul Empire, and, of course, in many progressive and humanist thinkers of the nineteenth and twentieth centuries, who certainly cannot be described as simply Westernizers, with no respect for their own traditions.[31] Tagore portrays the conception of freedom used by the young wife in his story as having ancient Indian origins, in the quest of Rajput queen Meerabai for joyful self-expression. The idea of herself as 'a free human mind' is represented as one that she derives, not from any external infusion, but from a combination of experience and history.

So 'rights' are not exclusively Western, in the sense that matters most; they can be endorsed from a variety of perspectives. Nonetheless, the language of capabilities enables us to bypass this troublesome debate. When we speak simply of what people are actually able to do and to be, we do not even give the appearance of privileging a Western idea. Ideas of activity and ability are everywhere, and there is no culture in which people do not ask themselves what they are able to do, what opportunities they have for functioning.

If we have the language of capabilities, do we also need the language of rights? The language of rights still plays, I believe, four important roles in public discourse, despite its unsatisfactory features. When used in the first way, as in the sentence 'A has a right to have the basic political liberties secured to her by her government', this sentence reminds us that people have justified and urgent claims to certain types of urgent treatment, no

M. Nussbaum

matter what the world around them has done about that. I have suggested that this role of rights language lies very close to what I have called 'basic capabilities', in the sense that the justification for saying that people have such natural rights usually proceeds by pointing to some capability-like feature of persons (rationality, language) that they actually have on at least a rudimentary level. I actually think that, without such a justification, the appeal to rights is quite mysterious. On the other hand, there is no doubt that one might recognize the basic capabilities of people and yet still deny that this entails that they have rights in the sense of justified claims to certain types of treatment. We know that this inference has not been made through a great deal of the world's history. So appealing to rights communicates more than does the bare appeal to basic capabilities, which does no work all by itself, without any further ethical argument of the sort I have supplied. Rights language indicates that we do have such an argument and that we draw strong normative conclusions from the fact of the basic capabilities.

Even at the second level, when we are talking about rights guaranteed by the state, the language of rights places great emphasis on the importance and the basic role of these spheres of ability. To say, 'Here's a list of things that people ought to be able to do and to be' has only a vague normative resonance. To say, 'Here is a list of fundamental rights', is more rhetorically direct. It tells people right away that we are dealing with an especially urgent set of functions, backed up by a sense of the justified claim that all humans have to such things, in virtue of being human.

Third, rights language has value because of the emphasis it places on people's choice and autonomy. The language of capabilities, as I have said, was designed to leave room for choice, and to communicate the idea that there is a big difference between pushing people into functioning in ways you consider valuable and leaving the choice up to them. But there are approaches using an Aristotelian language of functioning and capability that do not emphasize liberty in the way that my approach does: Marxist Aristotelianism and some forms of Catholic Thomist Aristotelianism are illiberal in this sense. If we have the language of rights in play as well, I think it helps us to lay extra emphasis on the important fact that the appropriate political goal is the ability of people to choose to function in certain ways, not simply their actual functionings.

Finally, in the areas where we disagree about the proper analysis of rights talk — where the claims of utility, resources, and capabilities are still being worked out — the language of rights preserves a sense of the terrain of agreement, while we continue to deliberate about the proper type of analysis at the more specific level.

Capabilities as goals for women's development

I have argued that legitimate concerns for diversity, pluralism and personal freedom are not incompatible with the recognition of cross-cultural norms, and indeed that cross-cultural norms are actually required if we are to protect diversity, pluralism, and freedom, treating each human being as an agent and an end. The best way to hold all these concerns together, I have argued, is to formulate the norms as a set of capabilities for fully human functioning, emphasizing the fact that capabilities protect, and do not close off, spheres of human freedom.

Used to evaluate the lives of women who are struggling for equality in many different countries, developing and developed, the capabilities framework does not, I believe, look like an alien importation: it squares pretty well with demands women are already making in many global and national political contexts. It might, therefore, seem superfluous to put these items on a list: why not just let women decide what they will demand in each case? To answer that question, we should point out that the international development debate is already using a normative language. Where the capabilities approach has not caught on, as it has in the *Human Development Reports*, a much less adequate theoretical language still prevails, whether it is the language of preference satisfaction or the language of economic growth. We need the capabilities approach as a humanly rich alternative to these inadequate theories of human development.

Of course the capabilities approach supplies norms for human development in general, not just for women's development. Women's issues, however, are not only worthy of focus because of their remarkable urgency; they also help us see more clearly the inadequacy of various other approaches to development more generally, and the reasons for preferring the capabilities approach. 'Preference-based approaches' do not enable us to criticize preferences that have been shaped by a legacy of injustice and hierarchy: men's preferences for dominance and for being taken care of, women's preferences for a low level of attainment when that is the only life they know and think possible. The 'capabilities approach', by contrast, looks at what women are actually able to do and to be, undeterred by the fact that oppressed and uneducated women may say, or even think, that some of these capabilities are not for them. 'Resource-based approaches', similarly, have a bias in the direction of protecting the *status quo*, in that they do not take account of the special needs for aid that some groups may have on account of their subordinate status: we have to spend more on them to bring them up to the same level of capability. This fact the capabilities approach sees clearly, and it directs us to make a basic threshold level of capability the goal for all citizens.[32] 'Human rights approaches' are close allies of the capabilities approach, because they take a stand on certain fundamental entitlements of citizens, and they hold that these may be demanded as a matter of basic justice. In relation to these approaches, however, the capabilities approach is both more definite, specifying clearly what it means to secure a 'right' to someone and, more comprehensively, spelling out explicitly certain rights that are of special importance to women, but which have not until recently been included in international human rights documents.

The capabilities approach may seem to have one disadvantage, in comparison with these other approaches: it seems difficult to measure

241

M. Nussbaum

human capabilities. If this difficulty arises already when we think about such obvious issues as health and mobility, it most surely arises in a perplexing form for my own list, which has added so many apparently intangible items, such as development of the imagination, and the conditions of emotional health. We know, however, that anything worth measuring, in human quality of life, is difficult to measure. Resource-based approaches simply substitute something easy to measure for what really ought to be measured, a heap of stuff for the richness of human functioning. Preference-based approaches do even worse, because they not only do not measure what ought to be measured, they also get into quagmires of their own, concerning how to aggregate preferences — and whether there is any way of doing that task that does not run afoul of the difficulties shown in the social choice literature. The capabilities approach as so far developed in the *Human Development Reports* is admittedly not perfect: years of schooling, everyone would admit, are an imperfect proxy for education. We may expect that any proxies we find as we include more capabilities in the study will be highly imperfect also, especially if it is data supplied by the nations that we need to rely on. On the other hand, we are at least working in the right place and looking at the right thing; over time, as data-gathering responds to our concerns, we may also expect increasingly adequate information, and better ways of aggregating that information. As has already happened with human rights approaches, we need to rely on the ingenuity of those who suffer from deprivation: they will help us find ways to describe, and even to quantify, their predicament.

Women all over the world have lacked support for central human functions, and that lack of support is to some extent caused by them being women. But women, like men — and unlike rocks and trees, and even horses and dogs — have the potential to become capable of these human functions, given sufficient nutrition, education, and other support. That is why their unequal failure in capability is a problem of justice. It is up to all human beings to solve this problem. I claim that the capabilities approach, and a list of the central capabilities, give us good guidance as we pursue this difficult task.

Notes

1 For examples of these inequalities, see Nussbaum (2000a, Chapter 3; 1997c, 1999).
2 Throughout this paper, as in my book, I focus particularly on India, because I believe it is more helpful to study one situation in some detail than to pull in examples from all over the place without their context. But the problems described are ubiquitous.
3 For an excellent discussion of these attitudes, see Bagchi (1997).
4 Among the four countries ranking lowest in the gender-adjusted development index (GDI) (Niger, Ethiopia, Burkina Faso, and Burundi — no ranking being given for Sierra Leone because of insufficient data), three are among the bottom four on the Human Poverty Index (HPI), a complex measure including low life expectancy, deprivation in education, malnutrition, and lack of access to safe water and health services (the bottom four being Sierra Leone, Niger, Ethiopia, and Burkina Faso — Burundi is 15 places higher) (see United Nations Development Programme (1999), pp. 140–141, 146–148). Among the four developing countries ranking highest in the HPI (Barbados, Trinidad and

Women and Social Justice

Tobago, Uruguay, and Costa Rica), all have high rankings on the GDI (Barbados, 27; Uruguay, 36; Costa Rica, 42; and Trinidad and Tobago, 44).

5 On India, see the special report on rape in *India Abroad*, 10 July 1998. According to the latest statistics, one woman is raped every 54 minutes in India, and rape cases have increased 32% between 1990 and 1997. Even if some of this increase is due to more reporting, it is unlikely that it all is, because there are many deterrents to reporting. A woman's sexual history and social class is sure to be used against her in court, medical evidence is rarely taken promptly, police typically delay in processing complaints, and therefore convictions are extremely difficult to secure. Penile penetration is still a necessary element of rape in Indian law, and thus cases involving forced oral sex, for example, cannot be prosecuted as rape. Rape cases are also expensive to prosecute, and there is currently no free legal aid for rape victims. In a sample of 105 cases of rape that actually went to court (in a study conducted by Sakshi, a Delhi-based non-governmental organization), only 17 resulted in convictions.

6 Sub-Saharan Africa was chosen as the 'baseline' because it might be thought inappropriate to compare developed with developing countries. Europe and North America have an even higher ratio of women to men: about 105/100. Sub-Saharan Africa's relatively high female/male ratio, compared with other parts of the developing world, is very likely explained by the central role women play in productive economic activity, which gives women a claim to food in time of scarcity. For a classic study of this issue, see Boserup (1970). For a set of valuable responses to Boserup's work, see Tinker (1990).

7 The statistics in this paragraph are taken from Drèze and Sen (1989, 1995, chapter 7). Sen's estimated total number of missing women is 100 million; the India chapter discusses alternative estimates.

8 The terms 'political liberalism', 'overlapping consensus', and 'comprehensive conception' are used as by Rawls (1996).

9 See *Women in Informal Employment: Globalizing and Organizing*, publication of a public seminar, April 1999, in Ottowa, Canada; the steering committee of WIEGO includes Ela Bhatt of SEWA, and Martha Chen, who has been a leading participant in discussions of the 'capabilities approach' at the World Institute for Development Economics Research, in the 'quality of life' project directed by myself and Amartya Sen (see Sen, 1983, 1995a).

10 See the excellent discussion of these attacks in the essay 'Contesting Cultures' (Narayan, 1997).

11 For one fascinating example of this point, together with a general critique of communitarian fantasies of cultural peace and homogeneity, see Kniss (1997).

12 For a general discussion, with many references, see Nussbaum and Sen (1989, pp. 299–325).

13 Cited by Amartya Sen, in speech at the Conference on The Challenge of Modern Democracy, The University of Chicago, April 1998.

14 The initial statement is in Sen (1980), reprinted in Sen (1982). See also Sen (1984, 1985a,b, 1992, 1993, 1995b) and Drèze and Sen (1989, 1995).

15 For related approaches in economics, see Dasgupta (1993), Agarwal (1994), Alkire (1999), Anand and Harris (1994), Stewart (1996), Pattanaik (1980), Desai (1990), and Chakraborty (1996). For discussion of the approach, see Aman (1991), Basu, Pattanaik and Suzumura (1995).

16 See the discussion of this example in Nussbaum and Sen (1993).

17 Nussbaum (2000a, Chapter 2) gives an extensive account of economic preference-based approaches, arguing that they are defective without reliance on a substantive list of goals such as that provided by the capabilities approach. Again, this is a theme that has repeatedly been stressed by Sen in his writings on the topic (see Nussbaum, 1998a,b, 2000b).

18 See Nussbaum (2000a, Chapter 1) for an account of these differences.

19 Obviously, I am thinking of the political more broadly than do many theorists in the Western liberal tradition, for whom the nation-state remains the basic unit. I am envisaging not only domestic deliberations, but also cross-cultural quality of life assessments and other forms of international deliberation and planning.

M. Nussbaum

20 For some examples of the academic part of these discussions, see the papers by Roop Rekha Verma, Martha A. Chen, Nkiru Nzegwu, Margarita Valdes, and Xiaorong Li in Nussbaum (1995b).

21 The 1994 International Conference on Population and Development (ICPD) adopted a definition of reproductive health that fits well with the intuitive idea of truly human functioning that guides this list: "Reproductive health is a state of complete physical, mental and social well-being and not merely the absence of disease or infirmity, in all matters relating to the reproductive system and its processes. Reproductive health therefore implies that people are able to have a satisfying and safe sex life and that they have the capability to reproduce and the freedom to decide if, when, and how often to do so". The definition goes on say that it also implies information and access to family planning methods of their choice. A brief summary of the ICPD's recommendations, adopted by the Panel on Reproductive Health of the Committee on Population, established by the National Research Council specifies three requirements of reproductive health: "1. Every sex act should be free of coercion and infection. 2. Every pregnancy should be intended. 3. Every birth should be health" (see Tsui *et al.*, 1997).

22 See the fuller discussion in Nussbaum (2000a, Chapter 1).

23 Nussbaum (2000a, Chapters 3 and 4) confronts the difficult issues raised by religion and the family for this approach.

24 See the varied proposals in Kittay (1999), Folbre (1999), Harrington (1999) and Williams (1999), and also 'The Future of Feminist Liberalism', a Presidential Address to the Central Division of the American Philosophical Association, 22 April 2000, by Nussbaum to be published in *Proceedings and Addresses of the American Philosophical Association*.

25 A frequent phrase from Rawls (1996). For detailed discussion of Rawls' views on this question, see Nussbaum (2000c) and 'The Future of Feminist Liberalism' (see note 24).

26 See the excellent argument in Kittay (1999).

27 Not all political approaches that use an Aristotelian idea of functioning and capability are freedom-focused in this way; thus, Aristotle was an inspiration for Marx, and also for many Catholic conservative thinkers. Among historical approaches using Aristotle, my approach lies closest to that of the British social-democratic thinkers T. H. Green, in the latter half of the nineteenth century (pioneer of compulsory education in Britain), and Ernest Barker, in the first half of the twentieth.

28 Compare Rawls (1996, pp. 187–188), which connects freedom and need in a related way.

29 The material of this section is further developed in Nussbaum (1997b).

30 On both India and China, see Sen (1997a) and Taylor (1999).

31 See Sen (1997a). On Tagore, see Sen (1997b) and Bardhan (1990). For the language of rights in the Indian independence struggles, see Nehru, *Autobiography*, 612.

32 That is my account of the political goal: one might, of course, retain the capabilities approach while defining the goal differently — in terms, for example, of complete capability equality. I recommend the threshold only as a 'partial theory of justice', not a complete theory. If all citizens are over the threshold, my account does not yet take a stand on what distributive principle should govern at that point.

References

Agarwal, Bina (1994) *A Field of One's Own: Gender and Land Rights in South Asia*, Cambridge University Press, Cambridge.

Alkire, Sabina (1999) 'Operationalizing Amartya Sen's capability approach to human development: a framework for identifying valuable capabilities', D. Phil. Dissertation, Oxford University.

Aman, K. (Ed.) (1991) *Ethical Principles for Development: needs, capabilities or rights*, Montclair State University Press, Montclair, NJ.

Anand, Sudhir and Harris, Chris (1994) 'Choosing a welfare indicator', *American Economic Association Papers and Proceedings*, 84, pp. 226–249.

Women and Social Justice

Bagchi, Jasodhara (1997) *Loved and Unloved: the girl-child in the Indian family*, Stree, Calcutta.

Bardhan, Kalpana (1990) 'Introduction', *Of Women, Outcastes, Peasants and Rebels*, University of California Press, Berkeley.

Basu, Kaushik, Pattanaik, Prasamta and Suzumura, Kōtarō (Eds) (1995) *Choice, Welfare, and Development: a festschrift in honour of Amartya K. Sen*, Clarendon Press, Oxford.

Boserup, Esther (1970) *Women's Role in Economic Development*, St. Martin's Press, New York (second edition, 1986, Gower Publishing, Aldershot).

Chakraborty, Achin (1996) 'The concept and measurement of the standard of living', Ph.D. Thesis, University of California at Riverside.

Chen, Martha A. (1995) 'A matter of survival: women's right to employment in India and Bangladesh', in Martha Nussbaum and Jonathan Glover (Eds), *Women, Culture, and Development*, Clarendon Press, Oxford, pp. 37–57.

Chen, Martha A. (1999) *Perpetual Mourning: widowhood in rural India*, Oxford University Press and University of Pennsylvania Press, Delhi and Philadelphia, PA.

Dasgupta, Partha (1993) *An Inquiry Into Well-Being and Destitution*, Clarendon Press, Oxford.

Desai, Meghnad (1990) 'Poverty and capability: towards an empirically implementable measure', *Suntory-Toyota International Centre Discussion Paper No. 27*, London School of Economics Development Economics Research Program.

Drèze, Jean and Sen, Amartya (1989) *Hunger and Public Action*, Clarendon Press, Oxford.

Drèze, Jean and Sen, Amartya (1995) *India: economic development and social opportunity*, Oxford University Press, Delhi.

Folbre, Nancy (1999) 'Care and the global economy', background paper for *Human Development Report* 1999, unpublished.

Harrington, Mona (1999) *Care and Equality: inventing a new family politics*, Knopf, New York.

Kittay, Eva (1999) *Love's Labor: essays on women, equality, and dependency*, Routledge, New York.

Kniss, Fred (1997) *Disquiet in the Land: cultural conflict in American Mennonite communities*, Rutgers University Press, New Brunswick, NJ.

Narayan, Uma (1997) *Dislocating Cultures: identities, traditions, and Third World feminism*, Routledge, New York.

Nussbaum, Martha (1988) 'Nature, function, and capability: Aristotle on political distribution', *Oxford Studies in Ancient Philosophy Supplement*, I, pp. 145–184.

Nussbaum, Martha (1990) 'Aristotelian social democracy', in R. Douglass Bruce, Gerall Mara and Henry Richardson (Eds), *Liberalism and the Good*, Routledge, New York, pp. 203–252.

Nussbaum, Martha (1992) 'Human functioning and social justice: in defense of aristotelian essentialism', *Political Theory*, 20, pp. 202–246.

Nussbaum, Martha (1993) 'Non-relative virtues: an Aristotelian approach', in Martha Nussbaum and Amartya Sen (Eds), *The Quality of Life*, Clarendon Press, Oxford.

Nussbaum, Martha (1995a) 'Aristotle on human nature and the foundations of ethics', in James Edward John Altham and Ross Harrison (Eds), *World, Mind and Ethics: Essays on the Ethical Philosophy of Bernard Williams*, Cambridge University Press, Cambridge, pp. 86–131.

Nussbaum, Martha (1995b) 'Human capabilities, female human beings', in Martha Nussbaum and Jonathan Glover (Eds), *Women, Culture, and Development*, Clarendon Press, Oxford, pp. 61–104.

Nussbaum, Martha (1997a) 'The good as discipline, the good as freedom', in David A. Crocker and Toby Linden (Eds), *Ethics of Consumption: The Good Life, Justice, and Global Stewardship*, Rowman and Littlefield, Lanham, MD, pp. 312–411.

Nussbaum, Martha (1997b) 'Capabilities and human rights, *Fordham Law Review*, 66, pp. 273–300.

Nussbaum, Martha (1997c) 'Religion and women's human rights', in Paul Weithman (Ed.), *Religion and Contemporary Liberalism*, University of Notre Dame Press, Notre Dame, pp. 93–137.

M. Nussbaum

Nussbaum, Martha (1998a) 'Public philosophy and international feminism', *Ethics* 108, pp. 770–804.

Nussbaum, Martha (1998b) 'Still worthy of praise: a response to Richard A. Posner, the problematics of moral and legal theory', *Harvard Law Review*, 111, pp. 1776–1795.

Nussbaum, Martha (Ed.) (1999) 'Women and cultural universals', *Sex and Social Justice*, Oxford University Press, New York.

Nussbaum, Martha (2000a) *Women and Human Development: The Capabilities Approach*, Cambridge University Press, Cambridge and New York.

Nussbaum, Martha (2000b) 'Why practice needs ethical theory: particularism, principle, and bad behavior', in Steven Burton (Ed.), *The Path of the Law in the Twentieth Century*, Cambridge University Press, Cambridge, pp. 50–86.

Nussbaum, Martha (2000c) 'Rawls and feminism', in Samuel Freeman (Ed.), *The Cambridge Companion to Rawls* (forthcoming).

Nussbaum, Martha and Sen, Amartya (1989) 'Internal criticism and indian rationalist traditions', in Michael Krausz (Ed.), *Relativism: interpretation and confrontation*, University of Notre Dame Press, Notre Dame, pp. 299–325.

Nussbaum, Martha and Sen, Amartya (Eds) (1993) 'Introduction', *The Quality of Life*, Clarendon Press, Oxford.

Pattanaik, Prasanta (1980) 'Cultural indicators of well-being: some conceptual issues', in *UNESCO, World Culture Report: culture, creativity, and markets*, UNESCO Publishing, Paris, pp. 333–339.

Rawls, John (1996) *Political Liberalism* (expanded paper edition), Columbia University Press, New York.

Sen, Amartya (1980) 'Equality of What?', in Sterling McMurrin (Ed.), *Tanner Lectures on Human Values 1*, Cambridge University Press, Cambridge.

Sen, Amartya (1981) *Poverty and Famines: an essay on entitlement and deprivation*, Clarendon Press, Oxford.

Sen, Amartya (1982) *Choice, Welfare, and Measurement*, Basil Blackwell and MIT Press, Oxford and Cambridge, MA.

Sen, Amartya (1983) *A Quiet Revolution: women in transition in rural Bangladesh*, Schenkman, Cambridge, MA.

Sen, Amartya (1984) *Resources, Values, and Development*, Basil Blackwell and MIT Press, Oxford and Cambridge, MA.

Sen, Amartya (1985a) *Commodities and Capabilities*, North-Holland, Amsterdam.

Sen, Amartya (1985b) 'Well-being, agency, and freedom: the Dewey lectures 1984', *The Journal of Philosophy*, 82, pp. 169–221.

Sen, Amartya (1992) *Inequality Reexamined*, Clarendon Press and Harvard University Press, Oxford and Cambridge, MA.

Sen, Amartya (1993) 'Capability and well-being', in Martha Nussbaum and Amartya Sen (Eds), *The Quality of Life*, Clarendon Press, Oxford, pp. 30–53.

Sen, Amartya (1994) 'Freedoms and needs', *The New Republic*, 10/17 January 1994, pp. 31–38

Sen, Amartya (1995a) 'A matter of survival: women's right to work in India and Bangladesh', in Martha Nussbaum and Jonathan Glover (Eds), *Women, Culture, and Development*, Clarendon Press, Oxford.

Sen, Amartya (1995b) 'Gender inequality and theories of justice', in J. Glover and Martha Nussbaum (Eds.), *Women, Culture, and Development*, Clarendon Press, Oxford, pp. 153–198.

Sen, Amartya (1997a) 'Human rights and Asian values', *The New Republic*, 14/21 July, pp. 33–41.

Sen, Amartya (1997b) *New York Review of Books*, June.

Stewart, Frances (1996) 'Basic needs, capabilities, and human development', in Avner Offer (Ed.), *In Pursuit of the Quality of Life*, Oxford University Press, Oxford.

Taylor, Charles (1999) 'Conditions of an unforced consensus on human rights', in Joanne R. Bauer and Daniel A. Bell (Eds), *The East Asian Challenge for Human Rights*, Cambridge University Press, Cambridge.

Women and Social Justice

Tinker, Irene (Ed.) (1990) *Persistent Inequalities*, Oxford University Press, New York.

Tsui, Amy O., Wasserheit, Judith N. and Haaga, John G. (Eds) (1997) *Reproductive Health in Developing Countries*, National Academy Press, Washington, DC, p. 14.

United Nations Development Programme (1993–1996) *Human Development Reports 1993, 1994, 1995, 1996, 1999*, UNDP, New York.

United Nations Development Programme (1999) *Human Development Report*, UNDP, Oxford University Press, Oxford and New York.

Williams, Bernard (1987) 'The standard of living: interests and capabilities', in Geoffrey Hawthorne (Ed.), *The Standard of Living*, Cambridge University Press, Cambridge.

Williams, Joan (1999) *Unbending Gender: why family and work conflict and what to do about it*, Oxford University Press, New York.

[13]

What is the capability approach?
Its core, rationale, partners and dangers

Des Gasper*

Institute of Social Studies, P.O. Box 29776, 2502 LT The Hague, Netherlands

Abstract

The paper specifies the core elements of Amartya Sen's capability approach to socio-economic valuation. It analyzes recent formulations by some of Sen's close associates, in addition to his own work, and identifies important variants, obscurities and tensions, as well as the key rationale and value-added of the approach. The approach is placed within a system of partner discourses, notably the broader 'human development' approach. The paper then shows issues faced in operationalization, and dangers that overly vague specification of the approach's rationale and commitments could lead to questionable choices in practical use.

JEL classification: I310; D630; B590

Keywords: Capability approach; Well-being (subjective and objective); Freedom; Human agency; Amartya Sen; Economic and social evaluation; Human development

1. What do we mean by the capability approach—and does it matter?

A difficulty in discussing and teaching the capability approach lies in knowing what it is. What does it contain, defined in what way? What does it not contain? Is it simply a proposition about an appropriate space in which social arrangements should be evaluated (Alkire, 2005a), or does it, for example, include implied conceptions of the good (Deneulin, 2002) and of human personhood (Giovanola, 2005)? How does it relate to 'development as freedom' and the human development approach? Do they stand and fall together, or are they separable?

For years the closest to an integrated statement of the capability approach has been a standard length paper by Amartya Sen from the late 1980s, published later in the volume *The Quality of Life* (1993). At that stage, Sen was presenting an approach in socio-economic valuation that gives an alternative to measurement of income, expenditure or satisfaction. Since

---

* Tel.: +31 70 426 0558; fax: +31 70 426 0799.
  E-mail address: gasper@iss.nl.

336   *D. Gasper / The Journal of Socio-Economics 36 (2007) 335–359*

then the capability approach (CA) has grown enormously. It contains ambiguities and unclear boundaries. Sen has not presented an updated equivalent statement; and the collection of his key relevant papers since 1984 remains in process. His ideas continue to evolve, as seen in moves in preferred language from 'capability', through (positive) 'freedoms', to 'the opportunity- and process-aspects of freedom'. Martha Nussbaum has provided, like Sen, various papers and lecture series, but for her quite distinct 'capabilities' approach. There too we await a com- prehensive presentation that was promised in *Women and Human Development* (Nussbaum, 2000).

Here is the easiest ambiguity to clarify: 'the capability approach' refers to Sen's work, and 'the capabilities approach' to Nussbaum's (see, e.g., Nussbaum, 2000; Gasper, 1997). Yet even their close associate Hilary Putnam writes of the 'capabilities approach' (2002, p. vii) when he in fact refers to Sen's work. 'Capability' is the full set of attainable alternative lives that face a person; it is a counterpart to the conventional microeconomics notion of an opportunity set defined in commodities space, but is instead defined in the space of functionings. 'Capabilities', in contrast, conveys a more concrete focus on specific attainable functionings in a life, and connects to ordinary language's reference to persons' skills and powers and the current business jargon of 'core capabilities'.

Other matters of specification are more difficult. Since Sen's capability approach has been self-consciously lightly explicitly specified, it can as Robeyns (2000, 2003) noted, be variously elaborated. Further, as it spreads in a variety of fields of practice it naturally evolves. Adjust- ments, extensions, partnerships and working simplifications are required. Some that are made may endanger the rationale of the approach; for example, if GDP per capita is reinstated as the supposed measure (or proxy) for human freedoms/capabilities in a supposedly separate sphere of 'material aspects of welfare' (e.g., Kuklys and Robeyns, 2004). Elsewhere, subjective well-being measures may become re-endorsed (see the discussion in Teschl and Comim, 2005). We need a formulation of the approach which reflects its rationale and can adequately guide its applications, elaborations and evolution.

This paper offers a specification of current core elements of the capability approach from Sen. The purpose is not to fix CA, which should be encouraged to grow; instead it is to pro- mote growth, through aiding self-awareness, clarity and learning. I have taken into account and critically analyze a series of recent formulations published by some of Sen's close asso- ciates (e.g., Alkire, 2002, 2005a; Robeyns, 2000, 2005; Kuklys and Robeyns, 2004). Section 2 begins with the approach's rationale based in the problematique of well-being and the attrac- tions of emphasizing human agency. Section 3 looks at the component features of the CA as an evaluation approach, to show how it is more than merely a criterion. The larger task of specifying underlying assumptions of the approach as a contribution in normatively oriented humanistic social science, for example its stances on methodology and personhood, is left for another occasion. Section 4 locates and anchors CA within a system of partner or cognate discourses from the human development family. Section 5 looks at how CA's abstracted con- cepts fare in practice. Section 6 reviews the main arguments and the dangers that face CA, not least that vague specification can bring overconfidence and misguided choices in operationaliza- tion.

Does vagueness about the content of the capability approach and about how it relates to other bodies of work – human development, human security, 'development as freedom', Sen's work as a whole – really matter? Underdefinition allows everyone to perceive space for themselves in a project. It gives, fittingly, a lot of freedom for people of varied backgrounds to grow out from a small kernel in diverse ways, according to their interests and skills. Nussbaum's more

D. Gasper / The Journal of Socio-Economics 36 (2007) 335–359   337

specific sister version perhaps shows the risks and resistance to identifying areas where one must in practice make choices and then proposing some specific choices. But underdefinition also has disadvantages for a research programme: the programme remains hard to communicate, to teach, to use with at least some potential cooperators and to assess and therefore improve. It remains unpersuasive to those who look for clarity, let alone precision. The risk increases that 'anything goes' during the inevitable simplifications in operationalization. In policy programmes too, lack of clarity on core principles allows all to claim the CA mantle yet may only briefly defer divisions.

2. Rationale of the capability approach

Sen's approach arose from dissatisfaction with subjective states and command over resources as concepts or measures of well-being or advantage; and from the wish for a concept that presents persons as reasoning agents with the right to make choices.

2.1. The well-being problematique

Four main considerations, then, support the capability approach:

1. The capability approach captures the intuitively attractive idea that people should be equal with respect to effective freedom and so has some initial plausibility.

2. Because it is attentive to the fact that preferences and values are sometimes adaptive, it compares favourably with views that focus on "subjective" achievements.

3. Because it is attentive to issues of responsibility and diversity of aims, it contrasts favourably with views that focus on achievements (however understood).

4. Because it is attentive to diversity in abilities to transform means into achievements, it is preferable to views that focus on equality of means (Cohen, 1993, p. 7).

Reflecting on what would be a normatively relevant concept of (in)equality, Sen had asked 'equality of what?'. He compared various concepts of advantage—in other words, concepts of the 'what' whose distribution we evaluate. He argued that normative priority could neither attach to (a) satisfactions, because these subjective outcomes are too dependent on personality, acculturation, prior expectations and other framing factors; nor, more generally, to (b) any other sort of outcome, because outcomes depend on how well people have used their opportunities; nor to (c) any sort of input or means, because their sufficiency and relevance varies according to the nature of the person concerned. Instead priority should be given to (d) the effective freedoms which people have to achieve prioritized outcomes.

Settling on a focus by finding arguments in its favour and arguments against each alternative, leaves open the possibility that strong arguments also exist against the category that has been placed at the end of the line waiting to collect the prize. Qizilbash (1997) pointed out, for example, that effective freedoms depend partly on a person's capacities built up through his/her own efforts, so that lack of capability does not necessarily establish a claim against others. Therefore, whether capability has normative priority or is simply one more normatively relevant category remains open for discussion. We return to this in Section 3. In practice, the capability approach gives normative priority to capability; otherwise why call it 'the capability approach'?

Cohen's 'four main considerations' are reflected in Figs. 1 and 2. Fig. 1 indicates the classic problematique around well-being. Economic 'inputs' to living (notably possessions and

220

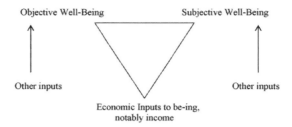

Fig. 1. The well-being puzzle triangle: inputs and outcomes (*source:* Gasper, 2005a).

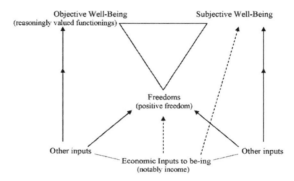

Fig. 2. Sen's addition of attention to potential outcomes.

income) have patchy relationships to both objective well-being (OWB: achievement/functionings in non-feelings dimensions that are reflectively valued as important, e.g., physical and mental health, longevity, security) and subjective well-being (SWB: feelings of happiness, satisfaction or fulfilment).[1] In addition, subjective and objective well-being in these senses are not well correlated. Hence, the sides of the triangle are not marked by arrows. Reasons include: that well-being is fundamentally influenced by not only economic inputs (money and things directly obtainable with money), but also 'non-economic' factors such as family relations, friendships, beliefs, purposeful activity, exercise and health, and so on; that sometimes economic inputs have no significant or sustained direct impact on objective- or even subjective well-being; and that acquiring more economic inputs is quite often indirectly competitive with maintaining or increasing the relevant 'non-economic' factors or inputs (Gasper, 2005a).

Sen extended this discussion by adding the category of potentials to that of achievements; specifically, potential functionings, not actual functionings as measured in studies of objective

---

[1] If one dropped the 'non-feelings' condition for 'objective well-being' then the SWB and OWB categories would overlap, when feelings of happiness and satisfaction are amongst the reflective priorities of the mandated decision-maker. If, further, the mandated decision-maker is a person choosing for herself, then OWB overlaps in character also with reflectively considered as opposed to directly felt SWB, without necessarily being identical to it. We will see not only these aspects, but also others, in Sen's capability notion. 'Subjective' refers here to what is being measured, not how it is measured: SWB research has found that SWB can be reliably measured, including by self-report. That is a separate question from whether the feelings are a good reflection of a person's situation.

D. Gasper / The Journal of Socio-Economics 36 (2007) 335–359 339

well-being in most work on social indicators and quality of life. As shown in Fig. 2, inputs contribute to opportunities for achieving functionings and satisfactions but do not guarantee their achievement.[2] Whether opportunities promote well-being depends on how they are used. Sen expects that freedoms conduce to both objective and subjective well-being but that the outcomes are not guaranteed, and he anyway grants freedoms an independent normative status.

The non-guaranteed links in Fig. 2 concern not only those along the sides of the triangle, notably the use of freedoms. The middle bottom arrow is not reliable. The operation of an economic system, and the generation of economic inputs to being, can not only compete against maintenance of other inputs vital for well-being, but also can contribute to un-freedoms through moulding of preferences. Jon Elster rather than Sen has emphasized this: 'There certainly comes a point beyond which the frustrating search for material welfare no longer represents a liberation from adaptive preferences, but rather an enslavement to addictive preferences' (Elster, 1982, p. 233).

Sen's capability approach originated then in a wish for welfare economics to join other social and human sciences (including health sciences) in looking at OWB, not merely at the economic inputs to living or at SWB. The dissatisfaction with SWB arose not only from adaptive preferences (when people come to take hardship for granted or luxury for granted), but also from the wider range of framing factors that influence SWB by moulding preferences and satisfactions, from infancy onwards, even if preferences become somewhat more fixed in adulthood. The dissatisfaction applies therefore even for reflectively reasoningly discursively self-assessed SWB, not only for directly experienced happiness, even if less so.[3]

Within OWB, Sen focused in a novel way. He focuses primarily, at least in his theoretical writing, on 'capability' – access to OWB – rather than on OWB achievement. This capability category is a complex hybrid. It is not an SWB variant, since even if self-assessed it concerns not feelings but instead options for achievement; and like all variants of the potentially misleadingly named OWB category, it is normative, for it involves an accounting in terms of normatively prioritized aspects of being. But it is not a standard OWB measure, at least not in Sen's theoretical writings. It means the access to those functionings 'which people have reason to value'. Which people? What constitutes reason? We will come to this later.

2.2. The 'agency' emphasis in this approach to well-being

'The capability approach captures the intuitively attractive idea that people should be equal with respect to effective freedom', said Cohen (1993, p. 7). The idea attracts because it uses a picture of persons as agents who have their own goals (including not only for themselves), make their own choices, and are not mere receptacles for resource-inputs and satisfaction; who, in Aristotelian language, live through the exercise of practical reason.

The focus on freedom covers the process aspect of freedom, not only the opportunity aspect of freedom. The 'capability' label that Sen chose for the latter aspect might not then be adequate as label for the whole approach; indeed he for a while switched to a large extent to freedom language. However, while not amending his opportunity freedom definition of capability and never refining

---

[2] Direct connections could exist from the holding of economic inputs through to subjective well-being if ownership is a source of satisfaction (hence the long dotted line in Fig. 2); and then through to objective well-being, if say subjective satisfaction is good for health.

[3] The procedural contrast between these types of (hedonic) SWB is not identical to Ryan and Deci's (2001) widely used substantive contrast between eudaimonic and hedonic well-being. The latter means feelings of happiness; the former concerns feelings of meaningfulness, purposefulness and fulfilment.

340   *D. Gasper / The Journal of Socio-Economics 36 (2007) 335–359*

usage in the way that Nussbaum does to distinguish different aspects of capability, Sen's concern for agency has been protected by the connotations of the term 'capability', connotations which Nussbaum makes explicit. One cannot have capability in the sense of opportunity freedom if one lacks capability in the agency senses, of capacity and skills to think and act.

3. Specification: capability approach or capability criterion? Features of 'the' capability approach as a valuation approach

I suggest that the approach has six major features, although it is ambiguous about the fourth and the sixth.[4]

1. An orientation to use a broad variety of sources of information.
2. A language, with novel categories, to describe that variety.
3. A prioritization amongst categories, notably the prioritization of capability. In an extreme variant, only capability matters.
4. A principle that the prioritization of capabilities for individuals is to be reasoned.
5. A principle that prioritization for groups is to be by public debate and democratic decision.
6. The categories of basic capabilities and threshold levels.

Standing at the margin of the approach is the idea of a list of basic capabilities.

3.1. Feature 1—orientation to a broad variety of sources of information

The first feature is the principle that there are more types of information relevant for the assessment of well-being and quality of life than those considered in mainstream economics (people's assets, incomes, purchases and stated or imputed levels of satisfaction or preference-fulfilment). The root of the capability approach is an insistence on referring to a wide range of types of information, notably about how people actually live – what they do and are – and their freedom—what they are able to do and be. Sen further stresses that besides (possible) outcomes we must consider the inter-personal distribution of outcomes, persons' rights and other features of the decision situation.

Sometimes this first feature is downgraded in use, if the focus narrows to only capability. Sometimes it is emphasized, as when Comim (2005) reviews reasons whether to bring back in the much more easily measured SWB category.

Taking into account more types of information is no breakthrough for the capability approach. It has been done since at least the 1960s, in enormous streams of work on social indicators, quality of life and varieties of subjective well-being. Sen's contribution is instead to help to focus, organize and rationalize that work. Vitally, he has '(la)belled the cat' of conventional policy economics literature, by drawing out and naming its utilitarian elements and assumptions, and showing how it excludes swathes of relevant information.[5] He then builds an alternative approach to valuation, grounded in an explicit philosophical perspective. He has highlighted the alternative by giving

---

[4] This section elaborates and refines the specification in Gasper (2004b, Chapter 7); and draws also on Gasper (2002) and Gasper and van Staveren (2003).

[5] To 'bell the cat' means, in English, to identify and make noticeable a potential menace—as by putting a bell around the neck of a cat.

it a name and a distinctive language; this profiles the approach and its categories and assists cumulative work. The approach thus certainly contains also features 2 and 3 below: a language, within which a concept of capability is given evaluative priority.

3.2. Feature 2: A set of categories

Sen's family of categories constitutes a language for discussing this wider range of considerations. He added several concepts to those conventional in micro- and welfare economics (income, goods and utility). One could list each new concept as a distinct component of the approach; but since they are interlinked we should treat them as a family, a language. The main concepts are as follows:

Functionings are components of how a person lives—for example, one's health status, or arguing about one's rights. Together a set (or *n*-tuple) of such functionings makes up a person's life. A person's *capability* is (definition I): the set of alternative *n*-tuples of functionings she could attain ('capability set'), in other words, the alternative lives open to her, the extent of her positive freedom; or (definition II): the valuation of her positive freedom, her access to OWB, based on the range and quality of attainable reasonably valued outcomes she has to choose between. Sen has generally used definition I, but with constant stress on 'the capability to achieve valuable functionings' (Sen, 1993, p. 31) and on judgement of opportunity freedom according to the opportunities to attain what 'one has reason to value' (e.g., Sen, 2002, p. 519). Leading exponents such as Alkire and Robeyns in their recent expositions adopt definition II, which gives 'capability' a selective, value-guided character; as, implicitly, does the UN definition of development as expansion of capabilities. Expanded opportunities for life-paths which are reasonably disvalued do not raise 'capability' by definition II.[6]

Capabilities in the plural refers for Sen to the particular functionings that may be attainable for a person; for example, the ability to speak up about one's rights. Sen argues that an agent's situation can be relevantly evaluated in a number of ways: (1) by her own valued functionings ('*well-being achievement*'), not merely her utility (satisfaction or preference fulfilment, actual or imputed); (2) by the outcomes in terms of her values, including for other people, beings and things ('*agency achievement*'); and by what she is *able* to achieve, both in terms of her own well-being (3-'*well-being freedom*') and of her actual values (4-'*agency freedom*'), including her values for other people, beings and things. His primary category of capability was well-being freedom, which concerns the functionings that a person can herself attain.

3.3. Feature 3: a stance concerning which levels have ethical priority

Sen and most other proponents of the capability approach seem to typically rank spaces in which to measure well-being and equity as follows (in descending order):

(i) capability (as personal well-being freedom), the valuation of the set of life-paths a person *could* follow; placed first because of a priority to freedom and self-responsibility;

---

[6] Robeyns: 'the freedoms or *valuable* opportunities (capabilities) to lead the kind of lives they want to lead' (Robeyns, 2005, p. 95; emphasis added); and Alkire: 'Capability refers to a person or group's freedom to promote or achieve *valuable* functionings' (Alkire, 2005a, p. 121; emphasis added). However, Alkire's next sentence cites Sen using definition I ('[Capability] represents the various combinations of functionings that the the person can achieve', Sen, 1992, p. 40), and we find almost identical formulations by Sen in *Development as Freedom* (Sen, 1999, p. 75) and *On Economic Inequality* (Sen and Foster, 1998, p. 200).

(ii) (valued) functionings: how people *actually* live;
(iii) (1) utility, whether interpreted as declared feelings of satisfaction, or the fulfilment of preferences, or the fact of choice: all these are placed lower, because choices and preferences may have been formed without much reflection or in situations of deprivation of exposure, information or options. We cannot presume a person's satisfaction from her choices, since agents do not only make conscious and error-free choices. Despite these dangers, satisfaction can still be treated as a significant type of functioning; (2) goods/commodities used—this criterion is ranked low because goods/commodities are means not ends, and because different people have different needs and wants.

Sometimes proponents declare that the CA involves only commitment to capability as a relevant space, not to its priority, but they commonly then elsewhere accord it priority, as is implied by the very name 'Capability Approach'. Sen himself often acknowledges the relevance of several types of information (see, e.g., Sen, 2002, pp. 83–84), but typically gives priority to capability (e.g., Sen, 1999, pp. 3, 76). Alkire starts cautiously: 'If equality is to be demanded in any space – and most theories of justice advocate equality in some space – it is to be demanded in the space of capabilities' (Alkire, 2005a, p. 122).[7] Then she asserts priority: 'social states should be defined *primarily* in the space of human capabilities' (Alkire, 2005a, p. 125; emphasis added). Comim is unambiguous: priority to capability space provides the '"normative anchor" for assessing HWB [human well-being, and] is at the core of the contribution of the CA, that does more than simply argue for a broader informational space in making normative evaluations' (Comim, 2005, p. 165).

Three possible more detailed formulations deserve mention.

3.3.1. Feature 3 – variant B: priority to capability as a policy rule

The normative priority given to capability could be interpreted as a policy rule to give people freedom and 'let them make their own mistakes', rather than as an evaluative rule that 'capabilities deserve more value-weighting than do functionings'. Capability (WBF) is then seen as an appropriate measure of advantage, of how advantaged a person is, rather than of well-being (WBA), even though it might well contribute to the latter. In contrast, functionings concern well-being. The very term 'functioning' better matches 'being'. Such a policy rule is not relevant for children, but becomes more so as they learn and mature.

3.3.2. Feature 3 –variant C: a claim that we should look only at the capability level

This more extreme version of feature 3 is not the mainstream but is quite widespread in discussion of human development, seen in formulations like 'development is the expansion of capabilities'. For Alkire (2005a, p. 117): 'according to the capability approach, *the* objective of both justice and poverty reduction (for example) should be to expand the freedom that deprived people have to enjoy "valuable beings and doings"' (emphasis added). Sen sometimes has similar formulations (e.g., 'The issue ultimately, is what freedom does have a person have …'; Sen, 2000, p. 29). But he appears overwhelmingly a pluralist: e.g., 'happiness is of obvious and direct relevance to well-being, [although] it is inadequate as a [sole] representation of well-being' (Sen, 1985, p. 189). Comim argues that subjective information should be attended to because the spirit

---

[7] 'The space of capabilities' in fact covers two spaces: those of well-being freedom and agency freedom. Alkire earlier lists also well-being achievement and agency achievement when referring to 'the internal plurality of capability space' (Alkire, 2005a, p. 122), but would not strictly include these achievement spaces as capability spaces.

D. Gasper / The Journal of Socio-Economics 36 (2007) 335–359   343

of the capability approach is to use multiple types of information, not just one (Comim, 2005, p. 231).

3.3.3. Feature 3 – variant D: prioritizing should be situation-dependent, not situation-independent

For Robeyns, in judging people's advantage, one should look at 'the space of functionings and/or capabilities, depending on the issue at hand' (Robeyns, 2005, p. 103). This is Sen's usual style. Which space is relevant and has priority will depend on the case. In relation to 'young children or the mentally disabled' or 'all situations of extreme material and bodily deprivation in very poor societies or communities' – a series of enormously important contexts – the space of functionings is often more appropriate (Robeyns, 2005, p. 101).

3.4. Feature 4: priority capabilities are those which 'people have reason to value'

When we come to prioritize amongst capabilities, for a person, the criterion is: priority to 'what people have reason to value'. This feature contains two, potentially competitive, principles: an emphasis on reason, and a liberal valuation that people should choose for themselves. Competition between them arises when people choose in poorly reasoned ways. 'Reason' carries here the connotation of 'good reason' or 'well-reasoned', otherwise the phrase 'have reason to' would be superfluous: 'what people value' would suffice. It does not connote that good reasoning can draw one conclusion only.

The potential tension between principles of reason and own-choice is more veiled when we talk of 'people', 'we' and 'they', rather than of 'individuals', 'a person', 'one' or 'she'. It remains unspecified whether in a group process authorized agents will draw reasoned conclusions for others. Sen sometimes writes 'what we value' (e.g., Sen, 1993, p. 31), which is on its own ambiguous: Is there to be multi-person valuation of each person's state? Is he referring on to cases of public debate about public policy? Robeyns rightly observes that: 'the capability approach is clearly a theory within the liberal school of thought in political philosophy' (Robeyns, 2005, p. 95); liberalism is though a large kingdom of species. Sen has throughout his career been insistently a reflective liberal, propounding that valuation is to be a reflective informed exercise, not simply assertion of whatever one currently directly feels; it is to be value judgement in the true sense. He characteristically writes of what 'one has reason to value' (e.g., Sen, 1999, p. 74), and his most famous book could strictly be called 'Development as Reasoned Freedom'. One implication, pursued especially by Nussbaum, concerns the importance of capabilities *for* valuing, including capabilities for reasoning.

So common, however, is the variant formulation which dissolves the tension by dropping the words 'have reason to', that we must note it separately.

3.4.1. Feature 4 – variant B: priority capabilities are those which people value, or even simply want

Alkire presents an unqualified liberal variant—'the capability approach is a proposition, and the proposition is this: that social arrangements should be evaluated according to the extent of freedom people have to promote or achieve functionings they value' (Alkire, 2005a, p. 122), the 'freedoms to do and be what they value' (p. 125). Evaluation is to be by the people themselves, no one else; and by what they value, not necessarily have reason to value. Robeyns presents a yet more liberal formulation: 'What is ultimately important is that people have the freedoms or valuable opportunities (capabilities) to lead the kind of lives they *want* to lead, to do what they want to do and be the person they want to be' (Robeyns, 2005, p. 95; emphasis added). Undesirable wants – for example, to suppress women or blacks or immigrants or non-co-religionists – disappear here from view.

Part of the rationale for the CA was that SWB is an unreliable yardstick. The more that CA reintroduces preferences into its evaluative calculus, as the principle for selecting and prioritizing capabilities, the more it must face the issues of adaptive and moulded preferences (see, e.g., Teschl and Comim, 2005). The implication should be at least to emphasize informed and educated preference and capable choice—issues examined by authors such as Brandt (1979), Nussbaum (2000) and Scitovsky (1992), but perhaps not yet sufficiently mainstreamed in the capability approach.

Taking distance from individuals' direct preferences and felt utility reflects that the capability approach is a language in and for public policy discourse. Given that it works at a policy level with a capability currency, how to operationalize ideas such as informed and educated preferences about capabilities, in multi-person and intra- and inter-organizational settings, is not automatically obvious. This leads us to features 5 and 6.

3.5. Feature 5: public procedures for prioritizing and threshold-setting

Sen incorporates a stress on public discussion and decision procedures for prioritizing which and whose capabilities (e.g., Sen, 1999, p. 148). This is for where a criterion of 'whatever people have reason to value' in individual deliberations does not suffice—where markets, complemented by adequate support for capacities in information receipt and assessment, preference assessment, and decision-making, cannot satisfactorily handle society's choices; in other words, for the classic realms of public goods and public policy. Public discussion is also important for educating the preferences at work in markets.

Robeyns notes that 'In Sen's case, it is not at all clear how these processes of public reasoning and democracy are going to take place . . . at present not enough work seems to have been carried out on the kind of democratic institutions that the "capability approach in practice" would require' (Robeyns, 2005, pp. 106–107). One of the approach's relatively empty boxes is called democracy. Not coincidentally, we saw that the distinction between features 4 and 5 is often blurred. Since the approach is quintessentially a public policy approach – for individuals are unlikely to decide against their own preferences – feature 5 is more central: group decision-making for groups, not for solitary individuals. It requires more evidence-based attention to forms of democracy, not only wishful thinking.

3.6. Feature 6: a category, and even a list, of basic capabilities

Pre-set lists of priority capabilities could be competitive with feature 5, public procedures for prioritization; lists could, however, emerge from such procedures. Sen makes no such formal list, unlike Nussbaum. But in practice, Sen and the HDRs use notions of *basic capabilities* (basic for survival or dignity) and *required thresholds* for minimum necessary attainment (e.g., Anand and Sen, 2000, p. 85; and in the HDRs' specification of equity). His list of five basic 'instrumental freedoms' is also not so different (Sen, 1999, p. 38ff.). As Stewart and Deneulin note, 'In practical work, Sen [accepts] that to be healthy, well nourished, and educated are basic capabilities, which, presumably, he would argue, would always get democratic support. In effect, this shifts the approach to one that is almost identical with the BN [basic needs approach]', except that it is has much broader scope and a more elaborate philosophical foundation (Stewart and Deneulin, 2002, p. 64).

D. Gasper / The Journal of Socio-Economics 36 (2007) 335–359   345

		PURPORTEDLY DEFINITIVE	PURPORTEDLY INDICATIVE
EXACT	Complete (relative to the specified purpose)	*Some religious systems*	
	Incomplete	*Some other religious systems*	*Millennium Development Goals[23]*
VAGUE	Complete (relative to the specified purpose)	*Nussbaum's list as sometimes presented*	*Nussbaum's list as occasionally presented*
	Incomplete	*Universal Declaration of Human Rights*	*Nussbaum should redefine thus*

Fig. 3. Types of lists of priorities, with illustrations.

The problem is this. In human history the health, nourishment and education of all groups of the population do not always receive democratic support: some groups can be, unnecessarily, excluded—vicitimized for example on grounds of ethnicity, caste or religion. Feature 6 guards against those cases where agents' reasoning leads or is led towards behaviour seriously damaging to the agents or to others. The function of a notion and list of basics is to entrench – perhaps in a constitution or bill of rights – and protect some fundamentals against the incursions of power. Feature 6 reduces to feature 5 if 'basic' is only a label for the priorities chosen through feature 5's procedures within a political community. We refer though to something more: to a special priority category that has an entrenched status, a moral and constitutional precedence, above the normal political deliberations: the set of rights that cannot be taken away, even by an ordinary majority.

Sen thus works in reality with: (a) a category of 'basic capabilities'; (b) an incomplete list of basic capabilities, not derived by bottom-up democratic decision-making; and (c) an acceptance of the idea of more extensive lists, provided that they are derived by democratic decision-making case-by-case in each era in each political community. This recognition will not remove all the disagreement with Nussbaum over lists, especially if Sen holds to an idealized notion of democracy; but it does considerably limit it. Conversely, Nussbaum's rather too sweeping advocacy of a list does not exhaust the case for lists.

Much disagreement can be removed by better distinguishing types of list. Lists come in many types: as proposed definitive statements or as indicative suggestions; as exact prescriptions or as requiring local interpretation; as purportedly complete or explicitly partial statements (see Fig. 3). Insofar as a priorities list is vague, incomplete or, especially, indicative then it becomes more compatible with feature 5: democratic political process. Arguably, Nussbaum should redefine her proposed list further in that direction, to make it more relevant. Still, there are limits to that direction: a list of basic capabilities that did not at all constrain ordinary political process would have no point. The purpose of a list such as Nussbaum's, like the Universal Declaration of Human Rights, is precisely to set limits. She may confuse that valid and essential role with the question of the appropriate form for her individual contribution to the debate, where a stress on its indicative nature would be more effective (Gasper, 2003).

Let us distinguish then at least: (1) lists of basic capabilities that constrain the operation of a state, that are set domestically, and for example included in the national constitution; (2) a list of basic capabilities that constrains states, set internationally, incomplete but covering central priorities for, say, health and education; such as perhaps in the MDGs; and (3) a list of basic capabilities, set internationally to constrain states, and extensive in scope, such as Nussbaum's or – more extensive still – the Universal Declaration of 1948.

3.7. Review

Several points arise from the specification exercise.

First, the capability approach would hardly deserve to be called an approach if it consisted of a single feature, whether a catholic stance on types of information (feature 1) or a normative prioritization of just one type (feature 3). In the latter case, we should speak only of the capability criterion, not of an approach. It is the attempt to approach policy realities that merits the term 'capability *approach*'. This occurs through features 4–6, which are thus integral parts of the 'approach'.

Second, the approach not only contains multiple features but allows of various selections and combinations of the features. So we find various versions in use. We could easily therefore talk of capability approaches, rather than of 'the' CA.

Third, some of the features are potentially in tension, internally or with each other: feature 1 calls for broad information while feature 3 calls for normative priority to (and sometimes even a sole focus on) capability; feature 4 calls for both reason and value; feature 6 tries to limit or structure the space for the political determination of priorities that was introduced by feature 5. The tensions are not necessarily failings but reflect the realities of policy practice and attempts to construct a balanced system. The conflicting pulls increase the scope for very different versions of the approach.

Lastly, the tensions have sometimes been managed by vagueness or ambiguity. Proponents can adopt an elastic specification: sometimes only feature 1 is avowed, to indicate modesty and wide relevance, but at other times several or all features are embraced, to indicate the approach's power. Fleurbaey is not the only reader who feels 'some ambiguity in Sen's formulation in [*Development as Freedom*] about whether his proposal is more a useful framework within which debates can take place, or a particular approach which must be defended against rivals' (Fleurbaey, 2002, p. 73). It could be more helpful to clearly distinguish and work with both constructs, indeed with several variants, rather than struggle on with supposedly one, in reality vague and confusing entity. The point applies on a larger scale too, beyond the six features we mentioned. Alkire, after equating the CA with feature 3 ('the capability approach is a proposition . . .'; (Alkire, 2005a, p. 122) cited with variant 4B earlier) suggests 'that further developments of the capability approach should consider [Sen's other] conceptual writings and should not restrict attention to the bare definitions of capability and functioning and the proposition already outlined' (Alkire, 2005a, p. 123). She sees the approach as providing relevant categories across many related areas, while leaving specific weighting and application to informed participants (p. 128).

The six features we discussed have been those in the foreground of the capability approach led by Sen. To look at its background assumptions, concerning methodology, personhood and value would require another paper or papers.[8] Here, in Section 5 we will look instead at the core concept

---

[8] A start is made in Gasper (2002), sections 5 and 6, and Gasper (2003). The latter paper contrasts Sen's and Nussbaum's approaches by reference to their positions in a series of background dimensions.

of capability (part of feature 2) and at the exercise of moving from an abstracted and notional entity through to choices in the real world. In doing so we will touch further on features 3–6 – priority ranking of spaces; and priority ranking of capabilities by reason, preference, political process and/or the political institutionalization of an entrenched category of 'basics' – though not in terms of their philosophical status, but as elements in the exercise of connecting the capability concept to practice. Before that, Section 4 connects the capability approach to some closely related discourses.

4. Partners: capability 'approach' or human development approach? Locating and anchoring the CA within a set of cognate discourses

4.1. 'Development as Freedom'

Two other features might arguably be added to the list of main features in the capability approach. They figure centrally in Sen's work of the past decade, notably in the book *Development as Freedom*.

One is the category of 'process freedom'. Sen's capability concept concerns 'opportunity freedom': the range of favourably valued life opportunities which are attainable for a person. It refers to attainable end-states. Process freedom concerns the person's role in decision-making. Alkire (2005b) suggests that we should in general describe and compare alternatives in terms of both criteria.[9] Formally speaking, however, Sen considers process freedom as outside his conception of capability. It falls outside the capability approach, but within a wider theoretical construction—'development as freedom'. If Sen adopted a richer conceptualization of capability, like Nussbaum's which includes attention to the potentials and skills which are the basis of agency, it would feel natural to still include process freedom concerns under the capability approach heading.

Development as Freedom and the associated work contain more than a normative definition of development as freedom and a re-labelling of the capability criterion as 'opportunity freedom'. Unlike CA, it essays also an explanatory theory of development: that the path to development is freedom. If development is defined as freedom, risk of tautology looms; similarly, if we judge whether people were really free by reference to when they developed. Substantively, emphasis is placed on five proposed key 'instrumental freedoms' and their hypothesized complementarity as a set of factors that contain a normative and explanatory core of good human development. The five are: political freedoms; economic facilities; social opportunities; transparency guarantees; and protective security (Sen, 1999, pp. 38–40). This model is a second candidate for addition to our specification of key features of the capability approach. But it goes beyond evaluation, and one can wait to see if it wins much support and endures. At present, it could figure as part of a distinctly labelled special variant.

Various commentators now argue that the label 'the capability approach' is inadequate. Segal (1998) suggested instead 'the functioning and capability approach'; for not only is functioning nearly always the operational proxy for capability, it also has normative significance in itself, including for most CA proponents. Robeyns (2005) proposes as we saw a priority status for

---

[9] She notes however that process freedom would not be a central concern in many vital cases involving young children (nutrition, immunization and primary school attendance) (Alkire, 2005b, p. 8).

348   *D. Gasper / The Journal of Socio-Economics 36 (2007) 335–359*

functionings in a huge swathe of work, on grounds of inherent appropriateness not only of practical ease. David Crocker has suggested that we refer instead to 'the agency approach', since Sen's framework stresses the agent's capacity to formulate and pursue reasoned objectives. Sen for a while preferred the 'development as freedom' label for popular audiences. That encountered significant criticism, and Sen has stayed instead with the label 'Capability' in the name of the new Human Development and Capability Association. This paper focuses accordingly.

4.2. Human development and human security

How does Sen's CA fit into the larger story of work on human development? The Human Development Approach (HDA) bears the imprints of Mahbub ul Haq, Paul Streeten, Richard Jolly and others, not only of Sen, although he is the main progenitor of many aspects, including the Human Development Index and recent attempts to connect to human rights and culture. Both approaches are deliberately specified in a broad-brush, open way. Sen describes the Human Development Approach as not a Hinayana (Little Vehicle) but a Mahayana (Great Vehicle) school, one that readily accomodates many variants. Its Human Security offspring is equally broad, which has brought some vagueness and confusion in usage.

Sen's CA is an evaluation approach. The HDA is much more, being also an approach to explanation and to policy, which uses CA as an evaluation approach and as one guide to identify what is important to explain and to include in a policy framework. HDA likewise includes Sen's entitlements analysis as part of its explanatory armoury, for investigating issues indicated as normatively important. Thus, not only has HDA broadened the range of objectives routinely considered in development debate and planning, but also it broadens the scope of analyses and breaks out from conventional disciplinary and national boundaries. Epitomized by the work of, e.g., Haq (1999), it attempts 'joined-up thinking' not distorted by those boundaries (Gasper and Truong, 2005). In addition, the HD approach takes a step towards 'joined-up feeling', for its field of valuative reference is all humans, wheresoever in the world.

Its sibling or offspring, Human Security discourse goes further, by a focus on securing the basics of decent human lives, through attention to stability, peace and sufficiency for all. This more concrete focus strengthens its roles in promoting fellow-feeling, motivation and action (Gasper, 2005b). The Human Security elaboration of thinking about human development and capabilities is less risk-prone than the highly generalized 'Development as Freedom' path, in which dangers of inappropriate operationalization of the capability approach are heightened (Gasper and van Staveren, 2003).

Dreze and Sen's joint work (1989, 2002) provides a happier balance. Writing in particular policy contexts with which they are closely familiar, Dreze and Sen make judicious practical choices about balancing different factors in explanation, about operationalization and measurement, value priorities, and choice of policy means. The wider range of values used in evaluation still has a unifying focus, on how individuals live and can live. This focus energizes and guides the work. Firstly, in choice of topic, we see a priority attention to human issues of hunger, longevity, health, abilities to understand and communicate, security and freedom. Secondly, along the pathways of analysis, attention goes to the distinctive situations of different groups (such as different occupational groups' access to food, and women's and girls' access to health services), and causes and effects are traced through – regardless of disciplinary tradition – to people's functionings and capabilities. Thirdly, the data analysis is led by concern for socio-economic significance above only statistical significance (McCloskey and Ziliak, 1996). Fourthly, in policy design, the focus on clear high-level ends brings an innovative and broad perspective on means – thus for example, the

D. Gasper / The Journal of Socio-Economics 36 (2007) 335–359 349

capability approach gives much attention 'to inputs other than food as determinants of nutritional functioning and capability' (Dreze and Sen, 1989, p. 44) – and an orientation to employing 'an adequate plurality' of policy means in order to respect the specific capability determinants of specific groups (Dreze and Sen, 1989, p. 102). Lastly, the need to respect, promote and employ human agency is a continuing illuminating theme in the policy analysis: in the stress on women's education, which has now become standard worldwide; in the demonstration of the greater longrun efficacy of education and discussion than coercion in population policy; and in showing how a democratic culture of public information can 'help citizens to take an interest in the lives of each other' (Dreze and Sen, 2002, p. 378), which underlies democracies' lesser proneness to famine.

For the new Human Development and Capability Association, which defines human development largely in terms of capability, 'Human Development and Security Association' might have been a title with more information content. It would have pointed to the aspects that the sister discourse of human security adds (Gasper, 2005b). 'Capability' remains though the highlighted label. What, one must then check, is the capability 'approach' an approach to? If it sees itself as an approach to the understanding, evaluation and promotion of human well-being, then the label 'Human Development and Capability' is agreeable and encouraging. It brings an onus on the capability approach to continue to extend and adapt.

5. Operationalization: from the purity of concepts to the demands of practice

5.1. Operationalization

The operationalization of an approach includes its institutionalization and its conversion into feasible procedures of application, sometimes including quantification. Both institutionalization and application involve adaptations to fit specific contexts. Sometimes adaptation involves simplification but equally often it requires complication, instead or in addition.

In looking at experiences in development policy with the dissemination of new policy-related approaches, McNeill (2006) finds three standard dangers. First, fatal conceptual fuzziness may emerge as all and sundry take up and twist the approach's terms. Second, sometimes in reaction, academics far from the policy frontline can over-refine the approach and the debate, rendering it arcane and remote to potential users. Third, as 'practical men' go their own way in operationalization, the approach can become bastardized and lose its rationale. McNeill thinks that the Human Development approach has been spared somewhat from the first danger, evisceration of meaning, because it has had a focus and edge through being explicitly opposed to taking economic growth as top priority. In addition, its concepts have a fairly rich theoretical basis from the capability approach. Similarly, it has fared relatively well on the third front because its theoreticians have been involved with operationalization too.

Looking more narrowly, at the capability approach, one might be less sanguine. The approach may not have been worked out yet as carefully as it requires, perhaps because of tendencies to become a sect, a church, something that Haq warned against. We do not, it is true, require sharp definitions for all purposes. Often major advances occur despite obscurities, as seen in the history of economic theory with terms like 'utility' and 'value'. The very vagueness can draw in people from diverse backgrounds. We do need sufficient contrast with existing concepts in order to steer attention in new directions. The capability concept and criterion serve at least as procedural injunctions: look at reasoningly valued opportunities rather than at (only) outcomes or unassessed opportunities, and keep this in mind to guide the judgements that are involved in practice. Problems

350   *D. Gasper / The Journal of Socio-Economics 36 (2007) 335–359*

arise though when basic issues of rationale and formulation are not sufficiently considered before or during practice, 'operationalization'. Dangers in leaving the capability approach vague and highly flexible could include failure to develop and refine theory, and proneness to operationalize by reversion to familiar, conservative forms that are not consistent with the approach's rationale. Operationalization could become dominated by:

- economism, as in a notion of a separate sphere of 'economic welfare';
- unreflective liberalism, as in a tendency to weaken the 'have reason to value' clause, into just 'value' or 'want', and to adopt unreflective versions of SWB;
- a preoccupation with quantification above institutionalization, despite the interest in democracy;
- considerations of ease of availability of data (such as with SWB statements).

Several of these dangers may arise with the Human Development Index. An approach that began by distancing itself from GNP per capita, here brings that into its popularly perceived core. While granting the other strengths of the Index – calculability, palatability and a vivid message – this is a serious price to pay, for it tacitly undermines the capability approach's original rationale.[10] An input category (income) whose relation to both subjective well-being and (other) valued functionings has been shown to be often very weak and unreliable, becomes reinstated as one supposed aspect of well-being or as a good proxy for that aspect (Gasper, 2005a). Hopefully that tendency will be well countered in other work.

Let us look at key problems that arise in trying to work with the concept of 'capability' and at the available responses.

5.2. The central concept: capability—problems and dangers

Several aspects of Sen's 'capability' concept make it difficult to work with. The concept draws on but diverges from everyday language. As a result, a number of notions need to be distinguished, as Nussbaum does: (a) inborn potentials, or P-capabilities, (b) trained potentials which constitute skills, abilities and aptitudes, or S-capabilities, and (c) Sen's sense, attainable outcomes or O-capabilities, which are the joint implications of environmental opportunities and a person's abilities.[11] Everyday language mostly uses sense (b), but Sen has not elaborated his vocabulary to make this clear, nor related his usage to the different vocabulary in fields of education and training.[12] Although Nussbaum's labels for the concepts of capability are prone to being misunderstood, this is remediable. We discuss next four aspects that are more difficult.

First, 'capability' is a hypothetical concept, and the notion of 'attainable' is hard to specify. Second, 'capability' must in use be an evaluative concept for we need to focus on attainable *favourably valued* functionings *n*-tuples, not simply all attainable *n*-tuples. The set of favourably

---

[10] The Human Development Index in fact applies a major discount to per capita incomes above the international average, but this is not known to its main audiences and anyway does not obviate the main objections to GNP figures as welfare measures: that, besides ignoring distribution, they count as benefits: (1) huge ranges of things which are costs and (2) things whose growth displaces non-monetized things that would have been of greater benefit.

[11] P: potential; S: skill, O: option or opportunity; see Gasper (1997, 2002, 2003).

[12] Note, for example, a substantial body of work in British vocation-oriented education which called itself 'the capabilities approach', and the Latin American work on 'capacitation' (introduced in Carmen, 2000).

valued opportunities is however hard to identify or compare. Third, it is an unusual intermediary between OWB and SWB concepts, though closer to the former than the latter, which are descriptive concepts about the feelings attached to actual functionings. Fourth, it has two versions: well-being freedom and agency freedom; and draws on the appeal of the latter while being mostly elaborated in terms of the former.

5.3. The elusiveness of an opportunity concept

The capability concept concerns attainable opportunities. It refers to what could be, to the future. It lacks an explicit time-dimension: implicitly well-being freedom refers to the rest of an agent's life, and agency freedom refers to the rest of history, if the agent cares for subsequent generations, subsequent life and non-life, or ongoing general causes. Long extended chains in capability analysis are indeed not merely possible, they are the rule. Perhaps the most central capabilities concern health and those conveyed through education. Both cases involve long extended processes.[13]

Since 'capabilities are an inherently prospective idea .... This interpretation brings in the issue of the uncertainty of current and future alternatives. What matters for the measurement of capabilities is not only the possibility, but also the *probability* to achieve an *n*-tuple of functionings. This raises, in turn, other questions such as the proper time horizon in the evaluation of capabilities and the opportunity to allow for varying time horizons for different functionings' (Brandolini and D'Alessio, 2000, p. 14). Harder yet, questions arise about the meaning of 'can achieve'. 'Can achieve' under what assumptions about the rest of the world? 'Can attain' when we take into account the person's mental frailties (Harrison, 2001, p. 15)?

If we could formulate such hypothetical scenarios, perhaps using fuzzy set concepts, how could we plausibly estimate them? How can one say what are the life-opportunities open to a specific person?

> The knowledge of capability sets required for judging whether [a science teacher's] capability set is better or worse than someone else's requires information that is simply unavailable. It is not a conventional problem of asymmetric information—as though the science teacher knows his capability set, but lacks appropriate incentives for revealing it. The problem is that he has no access to it.
>
> Indeed the problem is not merely epistemological. Why suppose that people face determinate capability sets, that there is a determinate answer to the question: What would have happened had the teacher decided to stick with physics, or try his hand as an actor? Whatever the metaphysics of the case, our evidence never reaches the full range of alternatives lying within reach, but extends to actual functioning and a limited range of counterfactual variations (Cohen, 1993, p. 9).[14]

In this situation one can only proceed by using simplifying and standardizing assumptions. In particular, one might have to look at representative standard individuals, not idiosyncratic real individuals, and use standard human values, not idiosyncratic individual preferences.

---

[13] This contributes to the syndrome wherein health (a set of functionings) and education (a set of inputs, or of S-capabilities) become each referred to as (O-) capabilities. For example, Robeyns (2005, pp. 95–96), '[The capability approach] asks whether [1a] people are being healthy [*a functioning*], and whether the means or resources necessary for [1b] this *capability* are present ... It asks whether [2a] people are well-nourished [*a functioning*], and whether the conditions for [2b] this *capability* ... are being met' (italics and enumeration added).

[14] Another version of the passage is published in Cohen (1995, p. 287); this version is more forceful.

5.4. Can the capability concept only be practicably operationalized in terms of standard human values?

'Capability' refers not to all the opportunities the person (or group) has but to all those which she (/it) 'has reason to value'. This makes the approach's call for equality of effective freedom difficult to interpret, other than in the adapted but workable form of a call for universal attainment of target levels of basic freedoms. A call for equality of capability concerns equality of access to reasoningly valued functionings, whether valued by the individual or by some legitimate social process (features 4 and 5). But when individuals do the valuation of their situations then they each value different functionings and the criterion of equality becomes in practice unworkable, warns Thomas Pogge. Similarly, to demand 'equality in the space of capabilities' may not be relevant if we see capability as agency freedom rather than own well-being freedom. How can we specify equality not in terms of ability to achieve own well-being but in terms of ability to achieve one's goals? Equality in fulfilling one's ambitions? What of the person who has none, versus the person whose ambitions are immense? The approach has insisted that it is not restricted to basic capabilities alone, but concludes Pogge, in both principle and in practice 'What matters for capability theorists is each person's ability to promote typical or standard human ends—and not: each person's ability to promote his or her own particular ends' (Pogge, 2003, p. 34). This is the logic behind the MDGs and some other variants of feature 6: that universal possession of a set of basic capabilities is both a more operational and a more appropriate criterion.

5.5. An objective well-being category ... that is operationalized via SWB measures?

In a group decision context, especially in a public policy context, almost inevitably much valuing is done by representatives and/or experts for others, and an operational concept of capability inclines even more towards OWB rather than SWB. Even in the private context, judgements of 'capability' will partner judgements of OWB, since they concern reasoningly valued options not direct feelings. Fig. 4 indicates this.[15] Covering also well-being judgements for or in a collectivity, the table indicates three different capability measures, shown in bold. Three other italicized cells have some flavour as measures of capability.

We saw that the concept of capability as opportunity freedom arose out of dissatisfaction with SWB as a valuative measure. Interestingly, some recent work within the capability approach considers rehabilitating SWB: direct personal valuations of one's life (see, Comim, 2005; Teschl and Comim, 2005). This is motivated by the attractions of SWB as a readily operationalizable measure, liberal inclinations, and hope that SWB's limitations can be eliminated.

Adaptive preference concerns not only the adjustment of preferences 'downwards' to cope with scarcity, which is the case of consolation (Comim, 2005, p. 165), but also adjustment 'upwards' in face of plenty, which is the case of jading, and in addition and more generally the moulding of preferences.[16] SWB literature does not show the absence or rarity of adaptive preference (Teschl and Comim, 2005, p. 232), but its ubiquity, as in the steadily corroborated 'Easterlin paradox',

---

[15] As in SWB studies, we take what-is-assessed, not assessment by self/others, as the master dimension for distinguishing SWB and OWB; thus, the horizontal dimension not the vertical dimension in Fig. 4.

[16] Probably at least as important as (1) adjustment downwards of aspirations by the poor, are (2) adjustment upwards of aspirations by those who enter markets and are moulded by new influences, and (3) content shifts in aspirations, rather than gross 'upwards'/'downwards' shifts—for example, decline in aspiration in spheres of religion and family interaction while aspirations for monetarily related achievement increase.

D. Gasper / The Journal of Socio-Economics 36 (2007) 335–359 353

WELL-BEING JUDGEMENTS FOR AN INDIVIDUAL (QOL = quality of life)	BY FEELINGS (asking: how does the person feel?)	BY BOTH FEELINGS AND NON-FEELINGS	BY NON-FEELINGS (asking: what can and does the person do?)
SELF-JUDGEMENT – IMMEDIATE	1 – Standard hedonic SWB	5 – In some QOL studies (usually just as one component of QOL)	9 – In some QOL studies (usually just as one component of QOL)
SELF JUDGEMENT – REFLECTIVE	2 – Reflective hedonic SWB; and eudaimonic SWB	6 – In some QOL studies (usually just as one component of QOL). *(Only a part capability measure since it is not only about attainable options)*	**10 – In some QOL studies (usually just as one...).** ***Example: Sen's capability category (since it concerns attainable options)***
EXTERNAL JUDGEMENT – FROM GROUP DISCUSSION	3 - Also an SWB category but hardly relevant	*7 - An OWB conception*	***11 - Another OWB- (and capability-) conception***
EXTERNAL MEASURE -- FROM EXTERNAL AUTHORITY	4 - Externally/ scientifically judged SWB	*8 - Another OWB conception*	***12 - Typical OWB- (and another capability-) conception***

Fig. 4. Well-being judgements for an individual.

and more generally in cultural moulding.[17] One recent survey for example identified Nigerians as the happiest people in the world; another cites several Latin American countries similarly. In Easterlin-paradox behaviour, the jaded affluent report no sustained improvement in felt well-being when their incomes grow beyond around US\$ 15,000 per capita per annum. Research has found that real income, particularly above that level, is not a good predictor of SWB over time although it has better predictive power cross-sectionally (richer people are happier than poorer people in

---

[17] SWB research shows also considerable unreliability in people's memories of their past felt well-being.

a given country at a given time; cf. Teschl and Comim, 2005, pp. 237, 242).[18] Arguably, part of the explanation is not only that people beyond US$ 15,000 per annum become inured to and unappreciative of good living, but that the content of what they can obtain with money beyond that level is not what, consciously or unconsciously, they find important for good living. But there is still abundant evidence of adaptive preference.[19] Whether preference adaptations are functional and desirable or not (Comim, 2005, pp. 165–166) is a different matter from whether SWB is a good or bad measure of wellbeing. Adaptation is often functional but it renders SWB a flawed measure of wellbeing for public purposes.

5.6. 'Agency' and 'well-being' variants of capability: SWB as an agency freedom proxy?

Sen has two concepts of O-capability: 'well-being freedom', a person's attainable life alternatives, which can be valued in terms of those features in her own life which she values or disvalues; and 'agency freedom', the futures attainable by the person, described in terms of those features of existence (her own or anyone or anything else's) which she (dis)values. 'Agency freedom' could perhaps better be called goal-capability. While the capability approach is operationalized in terms of well-being freedom, much of its appeal may come from 'agency freedom', which is however peculiarly difficult to operationalize.

No problem arises if the two types of capability are highly and reliably correlated. But a reason for having two sets of capability concept is because they are liable to diverge. Some of Sen's examples concern situations where agency achievement and own well-being achievement are not well correlated: (i) the wife and mother who willingly subordinates her own well-being to the expectations and interests of her husband and family; and (ii) the political hunger-striker who damages her well-being in order to promote other valued goals. One can add: (iii) the consumer addicted to excess who undermines the futures of her children and grandchildren. In the first and third cases one asks how much effective freedom the agent in fact had.

Both SWB and OWB can reflect the other goals that individuals value besides their own direct well-being; the progress of a person's wider causes can influence both her happiness and her health. SWB in particular could reflect agency achievement, which perhaps explains some of the observed divergences between the movements of economic variables, OWB and SWB (Gasper, 2005a). To return to SWB as a capability measure is, as we saw, tempting: the measure is readily available and has liberal credentials. Teschl and Comim further propose that 'given greater freedom, Sen assumes that the influence of adaptive preference formation (APF) would be much reduced in the creation of people's values and wants' (Teschl and Comim, 2005, p. 235).[20] Is such an assumption, whether or not in fact made by Sen, plausible? How much greater freedom, and reduced how much? Will it justify rehabilitation of SWB as a capability measure for a significant set of cases?

The proposition about the impact of freedom on APF could be sustainable as a tautology when freedom is defined accordingly, but otherwise SWB research does not seem to support this set of views. The many strong factors that distort measurement of SWB and influence the feelings of

---

[18] The 'dynamic life-span perspective' would seem to endorse rather than refute the 'hedonic treadmill' (Teschl and Comim, 2005, p. 239): jading or satiation of existing preferences frequently leads to emergence of new interests, and new activity, to attain the same level of fulfilment that had earlier wilted.

[19] See, e.g., Easterbrook (2004).

[20] The quotation they provide says only: 'Greater freedom enhances the ability of people to help themselves and to influence the world, and these matters are central to the process of development' (Sen, 1999, p. 18).

SWB that we seek to measure are ubiquitous, as parts of socialization and the pursuit of goals. They can affect not only standard hedonic SWB measures but also eudaimonic SWB measures. In addition, while measurement approaches exist to counter the distortions in measurement and the contortions of feeling, measures that strongly modulate, regulate and distance subjectivity might perhaps better be described as OWB measures. Further, SWB would be a candidate proxy for agency achievement not agency freedom. Freedom not matched by achievement would often be a source of frustration, subjective ill-being, so that agency freedom and SWB can easily move in opposite directions. Income is an alternative measure of agency freedom, but extremely imperfect since so much of life passes outside the reach of money or can be undermined by it. The appeal of GNP to many governments as a performance measure is indeed not as a societal well-being measure but as a measure of power: power to acquire arms, properties, personnel and other sources of more power.

So, whether SWB is a good variable with which to reflect agency concerns is questionable. SWB still has genuine claims to attention on grounds of inherent significance (Gasper, 2004a). As in many contemporary studies of quality of life, we can simply include an SWB dimension (or dimensions) as one (or more) dimension(s) in the larger set of relevant dimensions, and add ways of measuring both ability to choose and engagement in choice.

Faced with this panoply of complications in turning Sen's capability notion into something to work with, one compares the alternatives or reduced forms. Cohen (1995) and Pogge (2003) advise that we look instead at Rawlsian primary goods, except in extreme cases of destitution or disability where Sen's arguments against a focus on means in order to assess advantage and disadvantage have special force. Fleurbaey (2002) advises that we measure functionings – as in practice is nearly always done – but including the functioning of choosing; Sen (2002) counsels him to add the functioning of having choices. Others advise in effect that we follow the MDG strategy, a modified capability approach but with a strong focus on primary goods. Finally, one might conclude that the key empirical and policy foci, besides functionings, are 'S-capabilities' – people's skills and powers – rather than, or in addition to, what people notionally can attain.

5.7. Institutionalization

The points so far arise from looking at conceptual and epistemological obstacles, not yet at political and organizational obstacles. Let us return to feature 5, that prioritizations should come through public reason and debate, and specifically through participation and democratic choice.[21] Given the legions and diversity of relevant capabilities, and the constraints to making political choice processes simultaneously feasible, participatory and equitable, workable operationalizations of capability analysis may be very simplified in this area too. One should remember though that complex tasks can be adapted into series of simplified feasible tasks within complex systems.

Feature 6, a list of priority capabilities, is one attempt to be realistic about institutionalization. According to Robeyns, Nussbaum's emphasis on a list is part of a focus on what 'citizens have a right to demand from their government (Nussbaum, 2003). Sen's capability approach, in contrast, need not be so focused on claims on the government, due to its wider scope. . . . Nussbaum has been criticized for her belief in a benevolent government' (Robeyns, 2005, p. 105). In reality, legal constitutions exist more to constrain and steer governments than because of belief in their

---

[21] Deneulin (2005) warns that Sen has used the three terms public debate, participation and democracy loosely and interchangeably.

benevolence. Further, the demands advanced through a legal system, including demands to be enforced by government if that is required by the constitution or other laws, include claims against any and all members of the society, not only claims against government. Nussbaum has a theory of politics in which states and societies have complex institutional structures and democracy is not reducible to direct democracy and continuous plebiscites. Stress on public discourse and rational scrutiny must be combined with understandings of political power and organizational process and structure, including the roles for constitutional and other constraints on power.

6. Conclusions

Sen's capability approach arose from a dissatisfaction with both of subjective states and command over resources as concepts or measures of well-being or advantage, and from the wish for a concept that presents persons as reasoners with the right to make choices; in sum, from concerns for people as diverse, thinking, adaptive agents (Section 2).

The approach contains six characteristic elements: (1) a broad orientation in valuation to use more sources of information than only information on outcomes, let alone only monetizable outcomes; (2) a language – of 'capability', 'functionings' and so on – with which to insightfully structure such information; (3) a normative prioritization, to one degree or other, of the category of capability, in making decisions; (4) a reliance on reasoned valuation by persons in ordering their own capabilities, real or potential; (5) a reliance on reasoned democratic discussion by groups in ordering and selecting between opportunities for the group; and (6) elements that could set limits on the prioritizations permissible through features 4 and 5, including a category, and possibly a list of, basic capabilities. Section 3 concluded that in order to be an 'approach' the capability approach must contain more than a concept and a criterion; and that it indeed contains additional ideas about prioritization through reasoned valuation, public debate and legitimate and democratic process. Amongst the relevant possible products of such valuation, debate and process, we can say, are the Universal Declaration of Human Rights and the MDGs.

The catholic stance on types of information (feature 1) and the normative prioritization of one type (feature 3) are combined with an attempt to face policy realities through features 4–6. Features 1 and 6 are not novel; features 2 and 3 are much more so; as are – in an economics context – features 4 and 5 with their stress on reflection and debate as opposed to assumptions of given, fully-formed and fixed preferences or of 'de gustibus non est disputandum' ('tastes are not open to discussion', the classical tag repeated by Gary Becker).

Over time, the approach's concern for human agency has brought increasing stress on process freedom and feature 4, making one's own choices, and/or on feature 5, participation in group choices; but feature 5 remains seriously underdeveloped.

We saw a number of tensions within the set: between features 1 and 3, within feature 4 and between features 4–6. The tensions are not necessarily failings but reflect realities of policy practice and attempts to construct a balanced system. Tension between features 5 and 6 can be mitigated by refined specification of the character of a list of proposed priority (/'basic') capabilities.

The tensions between, and different emphases on, these diverse elements lead to various different versions, even as presented by the same author or by authors who think they are in agreement. A shared stance that capability is a relevant informational space in evaluation is far from constituting a shared approach. Managing the tensions occurs partly through vagueness and ambiguity, which is problematic. To distinguish and work with several variants, each perhaps adapted to a different context, could be more useful, including for testing and amendment.

D. Gasper / The Journal of Socio-Economics 36 (2007) 335–359 357

Tensions and dangers increase as we move from theorization to operationalization (Section 5). Sen's capability concept is peculiarly hard to operationalize, for it concerns hypothetical attainments of (in practice, favourably valued) functionings n-tuples, and is an unusual intermediary concept, a type of OWB with an SWB flavour. Major simplifications may be required in operationalization, with a danger of inappropriate reductions when the approach's rationale is not kept clear.[22]

An example of inappropriate reduction is use of the notion of a separate sphere of 'economic welfare', for which per capita GNP is supposedly a satisfactory indicator. Such an operationalization tacitly undermines the original rationale of the capability approach.

A second example of distortion or transformation in much operationalization is the weakening of feature 4's clause 'have reason to value', into just 'value' or 'want', and adoption of unreflective versions of SWB as measures of advantage. The paradox arises that an approach which arose by distancing itself from SWB sometimes now re-allies with it, as supposedly a good measure of agency achievement (or even agency freedom) or as liberally sound. This could be more than a mere fine-tuning of the balance between CA's well-being orientation and agency orientation, for the CA's very rationale lay in a distinction between considered and unconsidered lives, between reasoningly valued as opposed to directly felt well-being.

The MDGs and similar basic-capabilities-list formulations are also drastically simplified operationalizations, but potentially defensible. From feature 3's injunction to approach development and equality with strong reference to capability, they focus appropriately on representative standard individuals, and priority aspects of access or functioning in terms of universal basic values, not idiosyncratic personal features or wishes. They form a workable point of attention, usable to put pressure on real governments and hold them accountable.

Overall, the approach's additional ideas about prioritization (features 4 and 5, even feature 6) are underdeveloped. To go beyond the familiar – that what matters is the content of living and the amounts and distribution of effective freedom, not the amounts of income and expenditure – the capability approach has to connect to more theoretical apparatus and empirical basis (see, e.g., Deneulin, 2006), not only implicit residues from liberal economics and philosophy.

This conclusion is endorsed, not refuted, by the thriving state of capability studies. The required theoretical and empirical deepening is being attempted. Compared to a decade back, we see a major research effort, a scientific association, regular conferences at which many disciplines, nationalities and topics are seriously represented, and policymaker attention not only within the UN system but some influence in many countries and even in the World Bank. There was a danger that the capability approach's success in being quickly adopted by the bigger approach to which it contributes – the human development approach – would freeze it at an immature stage. On balance however the bigger approach seems now to instil required energy, urgency, and sense of proportion.

References

Alkire, S., 2002. Valuing Freedoms. Oxford Univ. Press, Oxford.
Alkire, S., 2005a. Why the capability approach? Journal of Human Development 6 (1), 115–133.
Alkire, S., 2005b. Measuring the Freedom Aspects of Capabilities. Mimeo.
Anand, S., Sen, A., 2000. The income component of the human development index. Journal of Human Development 1 (1), 83–106.

---

[22] Comim (2007) gives a helpful survey of measurement options which is aware of this.

358   *D. Gasper / The Journal of Socio-Economics 36 (2007) 335–359*

Brandolini, A., D'Alessio, G., 2000 Measuring well-being in the functioning space. Paper for Conference of International Association for Research in Income and Wealth, Krakow, Poland, August 2000.

Brandt, R., 1979. A Theory of the Good and the Right. Clarendon, Oxford.

Carmen, R., 2000. Prima Mangiare, Pois Filosofare. Journal of International Development 12 (7), 1019–1030.

Cohen, J., 1993. Lecture Notes on the Capability Approach. MIT, Cambridge, MA.

Cohen, J., 1995. Review of Sen's *Inequality Reexamined*. Journal of Philosophy, 275–288.

Comim, F., 2005. Capabilities and happiness: potential synergies. Review of Social Economy LXIII (2), 161–176.

Comim, F., 2007. Measuring capabilities. In: Alkire, S., Comim, F., Qizilbash, M. (Eds.), The Capability Approach: Concepts, Measures and Applications. Cambridge Univ. Press.

Deneulin, S., 2002. Perfectionism, paternalism and liberalism in Sen and Nussbaum's capability approach. Review of Political Economy 14 (4), 497–518.

Deneulin, S., 2005. Promoting human freedoms under conditions of inequalities: a procedural framework. Journal of Human Development 6 (1), 75–92.

Deneulin, S., 2006. The Capability Approach and the Praxis of Development. Basingstoke, Palgrave.

Dreze, J., Sen, A., 1989. Hunger and Public Action. Clarendon, Oxford.

Dreze, J., Sen, A., 2002. India: Development and Participation. Oxford Univ. Press, Delhi.

Easterbrook, G., 2004. The Progress Paradox—How Life Gets Better While People Feel Worse. Random House, New York.

Elster, J., 1982. Sour grapes. In: Sen, A., Williams, B. (Eds.), Utilitarianism and Beyond. Cambridge U.P., Cambridge, pp. 219–238.

Fleurbaey, M., 2002. Development, capabilities, and freedom. Studies in Comparative International Development 37 (2), 71–77.

Gasper, D., 1997. Sen's capabilities approach and Nussbaum's capabilities ethic. Journal of International Development 9 (2), 281–302.

Gasper, D., 2002. Is Sen's capability approach an adequate basis for considering human development? Review of Political Economy 14 (4), 435–461.

Gasper, D., 2003. Nussbaum's capabilities approach in perspective—purposes, methods and sources for an ethics of human development. Working Paper 379. Institute of Social Studies, The Hague (www.iss.nl).

Gasper, D., 2004a. Human well-being: concepts and conceptualizations. WIDER Discussion Paper 2004–06. WIDER (Helsinki), UN University; and Working Paper 388. Institute of Social Studies, The Hague (www.iss.nl).

Gasper, D., 2004b. The Ethics of Development: From Economism to Human Development. Edinburgh University Press, Edinburgh. South Asia Edition: Sage, Delhi, 2005.

Gasper, D., 2005a. Subjective and objective well-being in relation to economic inputs: puzzles and responses. Review of Social Economy LXIII (2), 177–206.

Gasper, D., 2005b. Securing humanity—situating 'human security' as concept and discourse. Journal of Human Development 6 (2), 221–245.

Gasper, D., van Staveren, I., 2003. Development as freedom—and as what else? Feminist Economics 9 (2–3), 137–161.

Gasper, D., Truong, T.-D., 2005. Deepening development ethics—from economism to human development to human security. European Journal of Development Research 17 (3), 372–384.

Giovanola, B., 2005. Personhood and human richness: good and well-being in the capability approach and beyond. Review of Social Economy LXIII (2), 249–267.

Haq, M.ul, 1999. Reflections on Human Development, second ed. Oxford Univ. Press, Delhi.

Harrison, M., 2001. From theory to measurement: some issues raised in operationalizing Professor Sen's capability approach. Paper Presented to Conference on the Capability Approach, St. Edmund's College, Cambridge, June 2001.

Kuklys, W., Robeyns, I., 2004. Sen's capability approach to welfare economics. Cambridge Working Paper in Economics 0415.

McCloskey, D., Ziliak, S., 1996. The standard error of regression. Journal of Economic Literature 34, 97–114.

McNeill, D., 2006. 'Human Development'—the power of the idea. Journal of Human Development, in press.

Nussbaum, M., 2000. Women and Human Development. Kali for Women, Delhi/Cambridge Univ. Press, Cambridge.

Nussbaum, M., 2003. Capabilities as fundamental entitlements: Sen and social justice. Feminist Economics 9 (2/3), 33–59.

Pogge, T., 2003. Can the Capability Approach be Justified? (http://aran.univ-pau.fr/ee/page3.html).

Putnam, H., 2002. The Collapse of the Fact/Value Dichotomy and Other Essays. Harvard Univ. Press, Cambridge, MA.

Qizilbash, M., 1997. A weakness of the capability approach with respect to gender justice. Journal of International Development 9 (2), 251–262.

Robeyns, I., 2000. An unworkable idea or a promising alternative? Sen's capability approach re-examined. Discussion Paper 00.30. Centre for Economic Studies, University of Leuven.

D. Gasper / The Journal of Socio-Economics 36 (2007) 335–359   359

Robeyns, I., 2003. Sen's capability approach and gender inequality: selecting relevant capabilities. Feminist Economics 9 (2–3), 61–92.

Robeyns, I., 2005. The capability approach—a theoretical survey. Journal of Human Development 6 (1), 93–114.

Ryan, R.M., Deci, E.L., 2001. On happiness and human potentials: a review of research on hedonic and eudaimonic well-being. Annual Reviews in Psychology 52, 141–166.

Scitovsky, T., 1992. The Joyless Economy, second ed. Oxford Univ. Press, New York.

Segal, J., 1998. Living at a high economic standard: a functionings analysis. In: Crocker, D., Linden, T. (Eds.), Ethics of Consumption. Rowman & Littlefield, Lanham, MD, pp. 342–365.

Sen, A., 1985. Well-being, agency and freedom. Journal of Philosophy 82, 169–221.

Sen, A., 1993. Capability and well-being. In: Nussbaum, M., Sen, A. (Eds.), The Quality of Life. Clarendon, Oxford, pp. 30–53.

Sen, A., 1999. Development as Freedom. Oxford University Press, New York.

Sen, A., 2000. Social exclusion: concept, application, and scrutiny. Social Development Paper No. 1. Office of Environment and Social Development, Manila, Asian Development Bank.

Sen, A., 2002. Rationality and Freedom. Belknap, Cambridge, MA.

Sen, A., Foster, J., 1998. On Economic Inequality, expanded ed. Oxford University Press, Delhi.

Stewart, F., Deneulin, S., 2002. Amartya Sen's contribution to development thinking. Studies in Comparative International Development 37 (2), 61–70.

Teschl, M., Comim, F., 2005. Adaptive preferences and capabilities: some preliminary conceptual explorations. Review of Social Economy LXIII (2), 229–247.

[14]

Development, Common Foes and Shared Values

MOZAFFAR QIZILBASH

School of Economic and Social Studies, University of East Anglia, Norwich NR4 7TJ, UK

There is considerable common ground among various positions—involving needs, capabilities, prudential values and basic goods—in the literature about advantage and development. The well-known debate about the relative merits of various spaces relating to advantage, associated with Amartya Sen, has tended to obscure this point. Differences among the relevant positions often have to do with the context in which they are developed, or strategies involved in dealing with common foes, rather than any fundamental divergence in values. The various lists of the components of advantage that these positions offer can, to some degree, be seen as relating to different levels in our concern about the quality of life. To this degree, they can be reconciled, and Sen's capability approach simply highlights an important level. Furthermore, both differences, as well as convergence, in the various lists, may be consistent with shared values.

It will not have escaped the reader that this book is informed by a belief in the ability of people from different cultures to share certain common values and to agree on some common commitments. Amartya Sen (1999, p. 244)

1. Introduction

Many of those involved in debates about development and the quality of life express the conviction that there is scope for considerable agreement amongst people from many cultures over values and norms. The lines from Amartya Sen's *Development as Freedom* at the beginning of this paper articulate just this conviction. Sen has also argued that development is best thought of in terms of an expansion in 'capabilities' or 'positive freedoms'. He has contrasted this view with various others involving resources, basic needs, Rawls's 'primary goods' *inter alia*. Indeed, differences, rather than agreement, amongst protagonists of these various views are often rehearsed in Sen's work.

In this paper, I suggest that much of this debate fails to acknowledge the

The author is very grateful to Sabina Alkire, David Clark, Des Gasper and two anonymous referees for very helpful comments on a preliminary version of this paper, which was presented at a meeting at St. Edmund's College, Cambridge, in March 2001. He is also grateful to Flavio Comin and Angels Varea for hosting the meeting, and to David Clark for organising it. Any errors in the paper are his. E-mail: m.qizilbash@uea.ac.uk

common ground amongst these views. Differences among the various intellectual positions involved often have, I argue, little to do with fundamental
differences in value, and often emerge from differences relating to context and
strategic concerns. The intellectual positions I shall focus on are: capability
views, prudential value theories, and views involving notions of 'basic goods'
and 'basic needs'. An examination of the differences among these positions may
actually *deepen* our understanding of the quality of life, and help us to see how
they may, potentially, be reconciled. The common ground among these views is
explored in Section 1. In Section 2, it is argued that many of the differences
among these views relate to the context in which they have been developed and
applied, as well as strategic concerns. Reasons for, and forms of, convergence
among the various views are examined in Section 3. Section 4 concludes.

2. Common Ground and Common Foes

There is considerable common ground among some of those involved in debates
about development and the quality of life. I shall focus on four varieties of
positions. These are: (1) capability views associated with Amartya Sen and
Martha Nussbaum; (2) prudential value list theories associated with James
Griffin; (3) views involving 'basic goods' associated with John Finnis and his
co-authors; and (4) basic need views, which have many advocates (see Doyal &
Gough, 1991; Streeten *et al.*, 1981; Gasper, 1995). It is worth noting at the outset
that these views are not necessarily mutually exclusive. Nussbaum's capability
view often includes a list of basic capabilities that are thought of as basic human
needs; my variation (Qizilbash, 1996a, 1996b, 1997a, 1997b, 1998) on Griffin's
prudential value account lists various basic values that are associated with basic
human needs and capacities; and Sabina Alkire and Rufus Black try to 'complete' Amartya Sen's capability approach with Finnis's account of basic goods
(Alkire & Black, 1997, pp. 267–269; Alkire, 1999). Basic need views can also
make room for basic capabilities. So Doyal & Gough (1991, p. 156) attempt to
'integrate Sen's framework within … [their] own.'

   The first area of common ground is so obvious that it hardly needs
expression. All these views have a central concern with *human beings* and the
quality of human lives. It is inevitable that it is just these accounts, that have
become most closely associated with the turn in the development debate which
has tended to focus on human beings, and 'human development' (UNDP, various
years; Haq, 1995). Some differences among the various views may have to do
with, what Sen terms, the 'space', or informational base, of evaluation (i.e.
whether it is need, capability, or well-being which is the focal variable). Such
differences may be distinct from differences in what are thought to be the central
components of, and differences of emphasis on particular aspects of, good lives.

   The second obvious area of common ground follows directly from the first.
Inasmuch as there is a central concern with human beings, these accounts, are
addressed to all human beings.[1] To this degree, these views, are *universalist*.

---

[1] Of course, there can be differences in the actual account of what it is to be human.

Differences of value among individuals and cultures are typically taken very seriously in all these accounts, but all these positions suppose that differences among individuals, cultures and nations, are not so deep as to undermine the possibility of some shared space of human concerns or interests.

The third area of common ground involves the plurality of components of good lives. All these views suppose that there are a number of components of good lives, and that these cannot be reduced to a single component. They thus articulate the irreducibility of the components of the good life. I refer to this irreducibility (following Qizilbash, 1997a, p. 264) as *component pluralism*. These views thus encounter difficulties when it comes to the construction of an overall index of well-being or development, which takes all the various components into account. Some of them suppose that the irreducibility of values or components relates to some sort of fundamental 'incommensurability of values' and others suppose it does not (Qizilbash, 1997a; Nussbaum, 1995a, pp. 85–86; Alkire & Black, 1997, p. 269). Since component pluralism emerges in all these views, they all need to list the components of the good or of 'advantage' (a list of needs, values, goods or capabilities) when it comes to some concrete case of evaluation.

The common ground among these various views means that they have common foes. First, the focus on human beings means that it can be argued that views of development that have a human focus are 'anthropocentric' (Dower, 2000). They may thus fail to give intrinsic importance to the environment and non-human animals. Secondly, the universalism that comes with a focus on human beings means that these views come under attack from those who think that there are no universal values. Relativists and communitarians might reject these views, on the grounds that the universalism of reach that is claimed by these views involves nothing other than an 'ethnocentric' and Western picture of what it is to be human (or of a good human life), which is being imposed on other cultures. These two lines of argument can, of course, be combined forcefully, since it can be argued that the focus on humans (which involves 'anthropocentrism') is part of a Western viewpoint (which involves 'ethnocentrism') so that such views of well-being and development are a Western export that distorts the process of change in certain developing countries. Finally, all these views are opposed to *monism of value*. Monism of value is the view that there is only a single value that all other values can be reduced to. The most influential version of monism is thought to be classic utilitarianism, as propounded by Jeremy Bentham, with happiness the only 'super-value' to which all others were reducible.[2] If monism were true there would be no need to list different values, needs or goods.

The common ground among these various views is on matters of deep significance. The commitments to the quality of human lives, to universalism and to component pluralism each have very important implications for the way in which these views can be applied and developed. However, it is also on the background of this common ground and in responding to common foes that a

---

[2] See Bentham (1996). Doubt has been recently expressed about whether Bentham really held this view. See Warke (2000).

466   *Mozaffar Qizilbash*

number of the significant differences among these approaches come out. First, despite a fundamental concern with the quality of human lives, these views have different accounts of, or different focuses in their accounts of, the quality of life. Secondly, differences can arise because of the various ways in which they respond to their common foes. So, for example, there are different ways of dealing with the charges levelled by relativists. Basic needs theorists might, for example, argue that human needs are the key aspects of the human condition on which we can all agree, and act jointly (Doyal & Gough, 1991, p. 75; Goulet, 1995, p. 38; Gasper, 1995, p. 17 and 1996, p. 24). Prudential value theorists and capability theorists sometimes go further and claim that there are several other aspects of well-being that are common to all human beings (Qizilbash, 1996a; Nussbaum, 1995a, 2000). Thirdly, there may be different reasons given for the particular claim to which each view is committed. So, for example, the particular reason for rejecting value monism for one view might be that values are 'incommensurable'—in the sense that there are limits to the trade-offs that can be made between values (Nussbaum, 1995a, pp. 85–6; 2000)—while, in another view, some values might be thought to be 'commensurable'—in the sense of being 'comparable' (see Griffin, 1986; Qizilbash, 1997a).[3] However, given the commitment to component pluralism, it is unsurprising that the possibility of incommensurability becomes a central issue these positions have to respond to, especially when the issue of measuring the quality of life is involved. Inasmuch as these approaches deal in different ways with the various issues, which must emerge for all of them, their common ground tends to be obscured.

It is worth comparing the various accounts that are under consideration with one that is often treated as belonging to the same general category. This is John Rawls's account of primary goods, as it has been developed in various versions of his account of justice, from *A Theory of Justice* to *Political Liberalism*. Rawls's theory does not actually share the common ground the above views hold. In the earlier version of the theory, expounded in *A Theory of Justice* (Rawls, 1972), the primary goods were the sorts of things that all rational persons desired, whatever their conception of the good, because they were all-purpose means. Primary goods were thus not the components of a good life, but the sorts of things that people needed to pursue valuable lives. The reason why Rawls is not primarily concerned with the quality of life is that his theory is primarily concerned with *agreement*: it provides a contractarian theory of justice. Nonetheless, since the primary goods are all-purpose means for the pursuit of any rational life plan, there is a sense in which they are needs.[4] So even if some primary goods (such as income and wealth) are not *basic* human needs, they can be characterised as the needs of rational persons, in the early Rawls. The theory was, to this degree, universalist, but not primarily focused on the quality of human lives. The primary goods were given by a list. So one can

---

[3] Part of the problem is that different people have different ways of using the notion of 'incommensurability'. See Qizilbash (1997a).

[4] While this point comes out more clearly in the later Rawls, it is already explicit in the revised version, which Rawls prepared for the 1975 German edition of his *A Theory of Justice*. See Rawls (1999a, p. xiii).

think of the early Rawls as endorsing a plural set of needs (i.e. holding to component pluralism). He can thus be seen as sharing considerable ground with the positions described above.

In later versions of the theory, primary goods lay the foundations for social unity among citizens in a liberal democracy (Rawls, 1982, 1993). Citizens are thought of as free and equal inasmuch as they have two 'moral powers'. These are the power to have a conception of the right, and the power to have and pursue a conception of the good. Primary goods are now conceived of as the goods needed to exercise these powers. The primary goods are: (1) the basic liberties, given by a further list (Rawls, 1993, pp. 289–299); (2) freedom of movement, freedom of association and freedom of occupational choice against a background of diverse opportunities; (3) powers and prerogatives of office and positions of responsibility in political and economic institutions; (4) income and wealth; and (5) the social bases of self-respect. Rawls (1993) has dropped the claim to universality, and has argued that his theory only applies to liberal democracies. Primary goods emerge as citizen's needs in such societies, and are—for the later Rawls—the basis of an 'overlapping consensus' amongst citizens with differing conceptions of the good, who all share a common conception of justice. This overlapping consensus is one of the central elements of his 'political liberalism'. So in the later Rawls, primary goods are not *human* needs as such. They are the needs of citizens in certain polities. Rawls has, thus, moved further away from the views discussed above. Nonetheless, Rawls's views have been highly influential in this literature, especially on Martha Nussbaum's most recent versions of her capability approach, which attempt to develop her version of political liberalism.

3. Differences of Value, Strategy and Context

There are, thus, important areas of common ground among some accounts of well-being and development. However, there are also well-known differences among the various accounts. Some may be about what is the best account of well being, or the quality of life, or advantage. I shall refer to these as *differences in the account of advantage*. These can, to some degree, be distinguished from different strategies for dealing with their common foes, and differences that relate to the context of application.[5] Since many of these accounts furnish us with lists of the elements of advantage, it is natural to look at differences in the proposed lists. It is at this level then that, on the face of it, these views no longer seem to share common ground. This is one way of looking at differences in lists, but those differences might relate to differences in the context of application or to strategic differences.

We can learn something by looking at Amartya Sen's capability approach. Sen's first well-known work to focus on the concept of capability related to an

---

[5] Obviously there may be some overlap because there may be some differences in various accounts of advantage which arise because of context, or issues relating to strategy.

468   *Mozaffar Qizilbash*

important question about egalitarian justice (Sen, 1980).[6] The capability approach has subsequently become very influential in the fields of development and the quality of life *inter alia*. The approach has enormous scope. Sen argues that the quality of life is best understood in terms of what people *can* do or be and that development is best thought of in terms of an expansion of (valuable) capabilities. He uses the term 'functionings' to refer to states of the person—to 'beings and doings'—and the vector (or *n*-tuple) of functionings one can achieve is one's 'capability set'. A person's capability set thus tells us what she can do or be, and to this degree reflects her 'positive freedom'. Sen does not typically go beyond listing some rather 'basic capabilities', and while he does also refer to other more sophisticated capabilities, he gives no definitive list (see Crocker, 1995; Qizilbash, 1998). He tells us that: '[s]ome functionings are very elementary, such as being adequately nourished, being in good health, etc, and these may be strongly valued by *all*, for obvious reasons. Others may be more complex, but still *widely* valued, such as achieving self-respect or being socially integrated' (Sen, 1993, p. 31; italics added). The thought here seems to be that while *everyone* values some elementary functionings, others may only be *widely* endorsed. One reason for not giving a definitive list of valuable functionings (and a list of capabilities, inasmuch as these relate to the ability to achieve the relevant functionings) is that not everyone would agree on all the elements of the list. That is, it is due to the possibility of differences in people's views of advantage that a full list is not endorsed. Indeed, this is also the reason that Sen gives for not endorsing a full or complete account of value in his advocacy of the capability approach. He explains this point in a response to Martha Nussbaum (1988).[7] Nussbaum has argued that there are important reasons why Sen's incompleteness makes his approach vulnerable. Just as people might adapt their preferences to deprived circumstances, people might, in Nussbaum's view, adapt their list of capabilities to deprivation. In his response, Sen tells us that he wants his approach to be consistent with '[q]uite different specific approaches to value' (Sen, 1993, p. 48). The thought is that even if people disagree about particular objects of value, they may all agree on certain 'spaces of value'—such as capability and functioning. Here, Sen's reason for retreating to agreement on a space of, rather than objects of, value is related to Rawls's reasons for a focus on primary goods. Indeed, in making the case for not filling out a complete account of capabilities, and 'pausing' at an incomplete account, Sen echoes Rawls. He writes that: '[i]f reasoned agreement is seen as an important foundational quality central to political and social ethics, then the pause is not hard to understand' (Sen, 1993, p. 48). However, despite this concern with agreement, Sen's approach is not developed in the spirit of contractarian theory, as is Rawls's.[8] The concern with agreement does, nonetheless, lead Sen (1992, pp. 46–47) to argue for certain methods (involving a 'dominance partial order'

---

[6] The question was about what egalitarians ought to aim to equalize, and the lecture was given at Stanford University in 1979.

[7] Nussbaum (2000, p. 77) herself has given up the possibility of a complete account of capabilities; the list she has recently offered is only partial.

[8] Robert Sugden has made this point. See Sugden (1993).

and the 'intersection approach') in dealing with issues relating to the valuation and weighting of capabilities and functionings. These methods involve focusing on cases where there is agreement over the set of valued capabilities selected and about the weight (or priority) that is given to each. Sen's concern with 'agency' (see, for example, Sen, 1992, pp. 57–60)—which involves a concern with people realising their values or objectives though their own efforts—also suggests that he would prefer that people had the freedom to formulate their own lists of capabilities. The incompleteness of the capability approach allows them that freedom.

The fact that Sen does not give a definitive list of capabilities and functionings thus has to do, in part, with the possibility of differences in people's views of advantage. However, there are other reasons why Sen does not give a definitive list of capabilities. In part, this is because of the great variety of contexts in which the approach can be developed and used. In his discussion in *Development as Freedom*, Sen writes that '[a] general approach can be used in many different ways, depending on the context and the information that is available. It is this combination of foundational analysis and pragmatic use that gives the capability approach its extensive reach' (Sen, 1999, p. 86). The reason for keeping the approach general thus has to do with the multiplicity of possible contexts of application. And according to the context in which the approach is used, different lists of capabilities might be relevant. Sen tells us that: '[i]n dealing with extreme poverty in developing economies, we may be able to go a fairly long distance with a relatively small number of centrally important functionings and the corresponding basic capabilities .... In other contexts ... the list may have to be much longer and much more diverse' (Sen, 1993, p. 31).

In marked contrast to Sen, Martha Nussbaum (1990, 1992, 1995a, 1998, 1999, 2000) has developed a very long list of capabilities, which are relevant to the evaluation of the quality of life. The list has changed over the years, but there is much continuity also (Deneulin, 2002). Nussbaum's initial articulation of the capability approach came, like Sen's, in the context of a debate relating to equality and distribution (Nussbaum, 1988). Since then, the list has been developed in articulating an Aristotelian view of the good, which can be used in discussions relating to feminism and development, in two important recent works—*Sex and Social Justice* (Nussbaum, 1999) and *Women and Human Development* (Nussbaum, 2000)—which bring together, and revise, many recent papers and lectures. Nussbaum's specific list of capabilities has been the subject of much discussion (Alkire & Black, 1997; Alkire, 1999; Clark, 2000a, 2000b; Deneulin, 2002). The list is very long, and the capabilities are listed under various categories. Two of these categories—practical reason and affiliation— are thought of as being especially important in organising the rest (Nussbaum, 1995b). Table 1 gives some of the capabilities in her most recent version of the list (Nussbaum, 2000, pp. 78–80). In this table, all the categories and a selection of the relevant capabilities under each category are listed.

Part of the reason for the divergence between Sen's variation of the capability approach and Nussbaum's has to do with the specific tasks for which the approach is being used. Nussbaum wants to use this approach to criticise

470   *Mozaffar Qizilbash*

Table 1. A selection of Nussbaum's central human functional capabilities

1	Life	Being able to live to the end of a human life of normal length
2	Bodily health	Being able to have good health including reproductive health
3	Bodily integrity	Being able to move freely from place to place
4	Senses, imagination and thought	Being able to use the senses, to imagine and reason—and to do these things in a truly human way, a way informed and cultivated by an adequate education, including, but by no means limited to literacy and basic mathematical and scientific training
5	Emotions	Being able to have attachments to things and persons outside ourselves
6	Practical reason	Being able to form a conception of the good and to engage in critical reflection about planning one's life
7	Affiliation	(a) Being able to live with and toward others, to recognise and show concern for other human beings; (b) having the social bases of self-respect; being able to be treated as a dignified being whose worth is equal to that of others
8	Other Species	Being able to live with concern for, and in relation to, animals, plants and the world of nature
9	Play	Being able to laugh, to play, to enjoy recreational activities
10	Control over one's environment	(A) *Political,* being able to participate effectively in political choices that govern one's life; having the right of political participation, protections of free speech and association (B) *Material,* Being able to hold property (both land and movable goods), not just formally but in terms of real opportunity; having property rights on an equal basis with others

Source: Nussbaum (2000, pp. 78–80).

moral norms in various contexts. If she did not explicitly list the various capabilities that relate to some realm of a good life—say bodily integrity—Nussbaum would not be able to criticise some specific norm or practice, such as female circumcision. Such criticism is, for her, a central part of the goal of philosophical writing. Without a list, her approach would lack any critical 'bite'. Her approach makes her very vulnerable to criticism along the lines that her list is not universal, and that it does not take account of individual and cultural differences. Sen has strategic reasons for wanting to avoid this criticism. Furthermore, the task of criticism of social norms is less central to Sen's project than it is to Nussbaum's.[9]

Given her general strategy, Nussbaum inevitably spends a great deal of effort defending universalism—against relativists—and showing that her approach can allow for considerable individual and cultural variations in views of the good life.[10] Her approach to this issue involves allowing the list of capabilities to be open-ended and allowing for multiple specifications by different people, and in different contexts. She thus allows her list to be *vague*—inasmuch as it can be specified in different ways—but nonetheless it gives a list of distinct capabilities—it is *thick*. In the more recent versions of this approach, Nussbaum goes further still and suggests that this list can form the foundation for political principles that will form the basis of a Rawlsian overlapping consensus (Nussbaum, 2000, p. 76). Unlike Rawls's proposal—which is only for a list of the components of advantage for an overlapping consensus within liberal democracies—Nussbaum's proposal is for an international consensus not limited to liberal democracies.[11] Nussbaum has thus again moved further than Sen, at least in articulating a more full, although still partial, theory of justice, where Sen has, in general, left his views more incomplete (Sen, 1999, pp. 286–287). In short, Nussbaum's advocacy of a specific list of capabilities has a great deal to do with the goals, and the context, of her writing. It is unlikely that Sen would argue much with her specific list of capabilities, but his approach can be used with alternative substantive accounts of value (Alkire & Black, 1997; Alkire, 1999) and that is just what he wants. However, the differences between Sen's and Nussbaum's strategies in developing the capability approach has left each open to criticism. Nussbaum can be criticised for adopting a controversial account of the good—which is where Sen parts company with her—and Sen can be criticised for giving a very incomplete account of valuable functionings—which is where Nussbaum parts company with him (Qizilbash, 1998; Alkire & Black, 1997, p. 268; Nussbaum, 2000, pp. 12–13). There seems to be no 'third way' between 'excessive incompleteness' (Nussbaum's complaint about Sen) and 'excessive specification' (Sen's complaint about Nussbaum).

It is worth comparing the strategies that Nussbaum and Sen employ with those of James Griffin (1996). Like Nussbaum and Sen, Griffin is concerned with how to develop an account of well-being that is sensitive to differences in the variety of things people value. Like Nussbaum, Griffin wants to use his account of well-being to play a part in thinking about ethical beliefs and moral norms (Griffin, 1996), and like Sen he is concerned with the traditional questions in economics and philosophy: can we make meaningful interpersonal comparisons of well-being in public policy and how ought we to make such comparisons

---

[9] I do not mean to suggest that Sen never criticises norms. He clearly does criticise norms, such as those that are involved in gender injustice. See, for example, Sen (1999, Chapter 8). My claim is only that the criticism of norms is less central to Sen's project(s) than it is to Nussbaum's.

[10] Until recently, Sen has not spent much time defending universalism. His recent contributions include Sen (1998), although Sen (1999) clearly moves in this direction too.

[11] Rawls has extended his view to deal with issues of international justice, but this does not involve the idea of primary goods as the basis of unity. See Rawls (1999b).

472   *Mozaffar Qizilbash*

(Griffin, 1991; Qizilbash, 1997a)? Like Nussbaum and Sen, Griffin's account is universalist, it is about human well-being, and it involves multiple components. So Griffin's view shares with the capability approach the common ground that was identified in Section 1. However, Griffin's account focuses on values and deals with the variety of views of the good in a different way.

Griffin's starting point is the idea of 'prudential values', which he thinks of as the sorts of thing that make a distinctively human life go better. In deliberation about such values one focuses directly on what makes for a good *human* life, and thus abstracts from what makes *my* or *your* life go well. There is thus a tendency to avoid the rather specific things that we each value—such as specific activities or states of mind—which would nonetheless count among Sen's valuable functionings. For example, playing tennis makes my life better, and is a valuable functioning for me. However, it might not make your life better. You might instead enjoy mountain climbing. In spite of this difference in what makes my life better and your life better, we may both think and agree that 'enjoyment' is a value: for you mountain climbing is enjoyable, for me playing tennis is enjoyable. Enjoyment is thus a candidate for a prudential value: the sort of thing that makes a *human* life better, not just your or my particular life better. Now take some other functioning, or 'being'. Suppose being a lawyer makes my life better and being an academic makes yours better. Pursuing these careers successfully fulfils, or gives meaning to, our lives. If so, we can say that, despite our differences, there is some value that makes our lives better, something like 'making something of one's life'. Griffin uses a term of art, 'accomplishment', for this value. These examples show how even if we have different lists of valuable functionings, we may nonetheless share some prudential values. This point applies to differences in lists of functionings that arise due to both individual and cultural differences.

A recent version of Griffin's list of prudential values (Griffin, 1996, pp. 29–30) is the following: (1) accomplishment; (2) the components of a characteristically human existence (autonomy, liberty, basic capabilities, minimum material provision and freedom from great pain and anxiety); (3) understanding; (4) enjoyment; and (5) deep personal relations. One distinction that is important in Griffin's approach to dealing with individual differences is that between 'value-token' and 'value-type'. Accomplishment and enjoyment are value-types. They refer to values that make for a good life. Value-tokens, by contrast, refer to the actual form in which the value is realised. So, for example, if I accomplish my lifetime ambition by writing a ninth symphony, 'writing a ninth symphony' is a value-token and 'accomplishment' is a value-type that is realised in the writing. It is because some value-types are realised in just about all good human lives, despite the variety of good lives, that it makes sense to talk of *human* values. Griffin needs a list of such values for his purposes, which relate to issues such as interpersonal comparisons of well-being, ethical beliefs and human rights amongst others (Griffin, 1986, 1996, 2000). However, unlike Nussbaum, his list is very short.

Griffin's list is, in some respects, determined by the context in which he is working. He admits that the list might be incomplete and may need revision (Griffin, 1996, p. 28). He has nonetheless used much the same list with very limited variations for many years (see Griffin, 1977). He is also open to the possibility that his list may be one about which there is disagreement (Griffin,1996, p. 30). However, since his aim is not to ground morality on agreement, this is not a serious problem for him. It can, nonetheless, be argued that a variation on this list might form the basis of agreement among people with different conceptions of the good (Qizilbash,1997a, p. 266). When it is applied in the development context, the list of prudential values typically includes the stuff of basic needs in much more detail. Griffin covers these, in his shorthand, with 'minimum material provision'. That shorthand is inappropriate, or unhelpful, in the context of development, as well as many other contexts. In the development context, the following variation on Griffin's list, which I have used elsewhere (see Qizilbash, 1996a, 1997a, 1997b, 1998), might be more appropriate. It involves adding: (1) minimum levels of health, nutrition, shelter, sanitation, rest and security; (2) certain basic mental and physical capacities and literacy; (3) self-respect and aspiration, to some of Griffin's values (autonomy, liberty, understanding, enjoyment and accomplishment) and replacing 'deep personal relations' with 'significant personal relations and some participation in social life'. The list becomes longer when it is developed in this way. Comparing the two lists of prudential values, it is clear that context, rather than any fundamental differences in the account of advantage, plays a decisive role in determining the length and content of the two lists.

John Finnis's list of 'basic goods' (or again 'reasons for action' or 'components of well-being') is, for the most part, individuated at the same level of abstraction as Griffin's prudential values. For this reason, Finnis allows for the same possibilities for coping with individual and cultural differences. Here is the list in his book *Natural Law and Natural Rights* (Finnis, 1979, pp. 86–89): (1) life; (2) knowledge; (3) play; (4) aesthetic experience; (5) sociability; (6) practical reasonableness; and (7) religion. In a variation on this list in co-authored work with Germain Grisez and Joseph Boyle (Grisez *et al.*, 1987), 'play' is replaced by 'some excellence in work and play'. Finnis, like Griffin, is not interested in the morality or politics of agreement. His view is developed in a context similar to the one in which Griffin and Nussbaum work—moral philosophy and jurisprudence.

While Finnis's list is similar to Griffin's in some respects, there are differences in the two lists that may have to do with differences in the account of advantage. Both the list in *Natural Law and Natural Rights* and the list articulated in his work with Grisez and Boyle include items that *seem to* reflect a religious view of the world, which may not be shared by everyone.[12] So Finnis lists 'religion', which he thinks of in terms of 'the establishment and maintenance of proper relationships between oneself ... and the divine' (Finnis, 1979, p. 88) and in his co-authored work in terms of 'harmony with some more-than-human source of meaning and value' (Grisez *et al.*, 1987, p. 108). The problem

---

[12] Grisez *et al.* (1987) argue that religious commitment is necessary to achieve integral human fulfilment. In their account, this argument comes out of a reading of Aristotle and Aquinas. However, there is reason to worry that such views are not consistent with a liberal point of view. Nussbaum (1998) expresses this worry in a discussion of views that she thinks of as broadly similar to Finnis's.

here is that some people (e.g. various humanists[13]) find their source of meaning entirely in other human beings. There may, thus, be some doubt about whether religion really is a basic good, or value. So listing goods at this level of generality does not, *in itself* guarantee that they are shared values about which agreement is likely. If one is looking for a value or good that is more inclusive, one might settle for something like 'finding meaning or purpose in life', and leave open the particular way anyone finds meaning or purpose. A concern with shared values leads one, perhaps, to aim at generality as well as inclusivity in the selection of the objects of value. Of course, Finnis is not, himself, interested in agreement. So this may not be a valid criticism of his position *as such*. Nonetheless, what this shows is that the possibility of shared values requires that the values are not just individuated at a general level, but that they are the sorts of things that make *any* human life better.

4. Convergence, Shared Values and Different Levels of Concern

While there may be some disagreement about the particular items on lists of the components of the quality of life or advantage (which leads Sen to avoid articulating a definitive list) there also seems to be some convergence. This has been especially evident in Nussbaum's recent articulation of her list of capabilities, as well as in more recent variations on the list of prudential values. So, for example, Nussbaum's list of capabilities now includes items that seem to have been influenced by John Rawls's list of primary goods. Rawls lists the 'social bases of self-respect' as one of his primary goods, and Nussbaum's list of capabilities includes 'having the social bases of self-respect'. My variation on Griffin's list of prudential values includes 'self-respect'. Griffin lists the components of a distinctively human existence, which include 'basic capabilities' (Griffin, 1996, p. 29). The ability to achieve self-respect, and the ability to appear in public without shame are also capabilities that Sen often mentions.

This sort of convergence suggests that there is some bedrock of shared values around which the various lists are structured. Take another value that is often cited, and which sometimes goes under different names: friendship or significant relations with others. This can, at one level, enter as a component of well-being (for Griffin and Finnis), and there can be a list of capabilities related to it (the capabilities that Nussbaum associates with affiliation and the emotions), and so on. So the lists might be operating at different levels of our concern with the quality of life. If this is the case, many of these lists might be reconcilable.

One way of attempting to separate out the different levels of our concern with the quality of life involves four levels. They are: level one, the means for a good life (needs, primary goods and resources); level two, opportunities or

---

[13] Humanism is a broad category, which covers many views not just Western ones (e.g. that associated with Comte). Nussbaum and Sen mention a variety of Indian forms of atheism in Nussbaum & Sen (1989) and Clark mentions an African variation of humanism –*ubuntu*– in his discussion of South Africa (Clark, 2000b).

abilities for leading a good life (capability); level three, the value-types that constitute a good life (prudential values/basic goods); and level four, valuable functionings (which may be value-tokens) constitutive of a good life. Convergence in the various lists of needs, capabilities, prudential values and so on—which are thought of as falling at these different levels—would then only be likely to arise if there are some shared values (at level three) which make for a good life, since such values provide a common grounding for items listed at levels one, two and four. The debate about whether it is need, or capability, or values, or functionings that crucially matter may then be something of a red-herring. Each of these is relevant to the analysis of the quality of life, and there may even be some consensus over this. In this view, the attraction of the capability approach derives primarily from the fact that it highlights an important level in our concern with the quality of life, which has not received enough attention in much of mainstream economics—particularly welfare economics—and moral philosophy. This is one way of thinking about Sen's contribution in arguing for the space of capability. The reason that the space of capability may command considerable consensus has perhaps to do with the fact that it picks up on an important level. Without information at that level, our analysis of the quality of life is impoverished. However, the debate about which space is crucial can be misleading. All the spaces—needs, capabilities, functionings and values (both value-tokens and value-types)—are important. This is perhaps why Sen has increasingly emphasised the importance of a broad informational base for normative judgements and of capability information as one part of that base in more recent defences of his view (Sen, 1993, pp. 48–49; 1999, pp. 57–67).

However, there is another tendency in this literature. It looks as if one author, being influenced by another, takes an item from the other's list and makes room for it in his or her own list. That certainly seems to be what is happening when Nussbaum includes a capability relating to the social bases of self-respect on her list. She appears to be accepting Rawls's insight, which she wishes to accommodate in her capability approach. Sen's inspiration for listing the 'ability to appear in public without shame' of course takes its inspiration from Adam Smith (Sen, 1984a, p. 333), and Nussbaum's list is heavily influenced by Aristotle.[14] So it is not just that these authors are influenced by each other, they clearly have several influences. Nonetheless, they do seem to be influenced by each other. So while Sen was influenced by basic need views in some of his earlier papers on the capability approach (such as 'Goods and People') while noting the limitations of such accounts (Sen, 1984a, pp. 513–15), some more recent basic need accounts, such as that of Doyal & Gough (1991), attempt to allow for the insights of Sen's framework. Inasmuch as each approach needs to cover the whole range of components of the quality of life, each

---

[14] Nussbaum began her work on the capability approach with a paper (Nussbaum, 1988) that is about how best to understand Aristotle's writings on justice. The early versions of her list (e.g. the versions in Nussbaum, 1990 and 1992) are explicitly (neo-)Aristotelian. Her more recent versions of the list are supposed to be the basis of an overlapping consensus, but nonetheless the list is much the same (with small changes) over the years. On this see Deneulin (2002).

476   *Mozaffar Qizilbash*

account seems to be parasitic on the insights of others. This tendency also leads to convergence in lists.

It is also worth noting that divergence in some of the lists may not necessarily signal a divergence in fundamental values. So, for example, one might have agreement about the value 'enjoyment', and different people have different valuable functionings on their various lists (with differences reflecting interpersonal variations in the things people find enjoyable) and different valuable capabilities (if the relevant capabilities relate to the different particular things people find enjoyable). The different valuable functionings may in turn imply different needs. So there is a case for thinking that it is at the most general level—the level of values or basic goods—that convergence about the components of advantage is likely to occur. This suggests that if we care about consensus among people with different conceptions of the good life, we ought to be concerned with values individuated at a general level.

This suggestion reverses the standard presumption, which is that we are likely to have consensus about the means, or capabilities, for pursuing or realising values, and thus ought to avoid a focus on the values themselves. It is that presumption that leads Sen to aim at agreement on the space of capabilities, rather than a specific list of valuable functionings or capabilities. So it is an odd suggestion, especially for those who are wedded to Sen's view, as well as those influenced by the Rawlsian account of primary goods, and by Nussbaum's list of central human capabilities. Nussbaum states that to deal with variations in people's views of the good life, one ought to focus on capabilities rather than on functionings, which constitute good living. She makes this claim for the simple reason that anyone insisting on the space of functionings would seem to impose her specific view of the good life on others (Nussbaum, 2000, p. 87). This seems plausible—certain valuable functionings are among the more specific things that make particular lives good. These will differ among people, because many of them are value-tokens. So for a list of capabilities to be agreed on, it must work at the level of broad value-types. For example, if it is enjoyment that is the relevant value, then it must be the ability to enjoy oneself that is likely to be agreed on, rather than the ability to do any specific thing, such as enjoy recreational activities (which Nussbaum cites) or to play tennis or to climb mountains. This suggests an alternative way of understanding Sen's claim that 'elementary' functionings might be endorsed by all, whereas complex functionings might only command wide endorsement. If 'elementary functionings' relate to the achievement of value-types (e.g. achieving understanding) and 'complex functionings' relate to achievement of value-tokens (e.g. understanding how to use a computer, or understanding the proof of some theorem), it is more likely that there will be agreement about elementary functionings than about complex ones. If there are shared values which underpin the various lists, listing capabilities for elementary functioning—in this sense—allows us the possibility for a 'third way' between Sen's incompleteness and Nussbaum's overspecificity. The notion of a 'complex functioning' used here is different from Sen's since, for Sen, 'achieving self-respect' is a complex functioning and, on the proposed notion of 'complex functioning', achieving self-respect is not such a functioning: it is elementary if self-respect is a general value-type. By contrast, Sen's 'appearing in public without shame' is a complex functioning, on this account, inasmuch as it relates to a value-token.

There is, nonetheless, some support, even in Nussbaum's own writing, for the view that it is values at the most general level that ground consensus. In the first chapter of *Women and Human Development* (entitled 'In Defence of Universal Values'), in a discussion of cultural relativism she writes:

> But it is one thing to say that we need local knowledge to understand the problems women face ... It is quite another to claim that certain *very general values*, such as the dignity of the person, the integrity of the body, basic political rights and liberties, basic economic opportunities and so forth, are not appropriate norms to be used in assessing women's lives in developing countries (Nussbaum, 2000, p. 41, emphasis added).

Nussbaum's claim here seems to be that, in spite of cultural differences, certain general values (or norms) are relevant anywhere. Inevitably, these values are rather close to some of the elements in the list of prudential values as well as the list of basic goods, and it is also these rather general values that guide Nussbaum in arriving at the full list of capabilities in the relevant chapter. The value 'dignity' is clearly guiding her when she lists, 'having the social bases of self-respect' and 'being able to be treated as a dignified being'.

Separating out the various levels that seem relevant for analysis of the quality of life then seems to be a promising way of proceeding if one wants to understand differences in the various lists. However, there is a potential flaw in this approach. This relates to the tendency (mentioned earlier in this section) for each author to borrow from, or be influenced by, the others. Consider Griffin's account of prudential values. This might seem to be the account to go for if one is interested in attempting to look for rather general values. However, Griffin lists minimum material provision under his prudential value, 'the components of human existence', and he also lists basic capabilities amongst these components. Comparing the components of the different lists, we now seem to have prudential values at different levels. Minimum material provision might fall at the level of needs or primary goods (level one), while basic capabilities might fall in the capability category (level two), and accomplishment, freedom and understanding would fall under general values (level three). Indeed, it is only because the notion of a 'prudential value' is individuated at such a broad level (so that it relates to the things that make a human life better) that it can cover objects that seem to fall at different levels. However, there is another factor operating here: the different levels identified are not easy to separate. Having certain basic abilities is both constitutive of certain opportunities for good living, as well as being partly constitutive of good living. It might be constitutive of well-being to the degree that it makes one an agent, for example. The same can be said of some of the basic needs: being minimally adequately nourished, or healthy, is both necessary for one to be able to live a good life as well as being, in part, constitutive of a good life.[15] So, there is a problem about separating the

---

[15] It is not hard to see that, in such cases, it is often also hard to distinguish intrinsic and instrumental value. The distinction between instrumental and intrinsic value thus may have limited use in this context. See Alkire & Black (1997) and Alkire (1999) for a contrary view.

different levels that are relevant to thinking about the quality of life in the way that has been attempted above. This point helps clarify another reason why we have so much convergence in the lists. Even with different foundational concepts (primary goods, capabilities, etc) one might end up with convergence in the various lists because the different levels (means, opportunities, well-being etc) which are relevant to the quality of life (which the different foundational concepts pick up on) are not easily separated.

It is, of course, not just Griffin's view that involves trying to capture items that fall at each of the different levels. The capability approach, in both Sen's and Nussbaum's hands, involves items that are capabilities, as well as function-ings, and treats some capabilities as either basic needs (on Nussbaum's account of 'basic capabilities') or related to basic needs (in Sen's account). So Nussbaum and Sen effectively attempt to cover three of the four levels. Furthermore, Nussbaum does list a set of categories under which each of the capabilities is listed. These are clearly items that relate to general values, or dimensions of value, and thus fall at level three. So her capability list does effectively cover all the levels listed above. The same sort of strategy can be found in Doyal & Gough's theory of human need. While there is only one focal variable—need—in their account, Doyal & Gough differentiate between various levels of need. So there are two 'basic needs' on their view (physical health and autonomy) and a list of further 'intermediate needs' (food and water, housing, a non-hazardous working environment, health care and so on) which are requirements for basic need satisfaction. Liberty is also included in their account, but as a societal precondition for need satisfaction (Doyal & Gough, 1991, p. 225).

We are thus left with the conclusion that while the various lists look as if they relate to different levels of our concern with the quality of life, this is not always true. In fact, most of the lists under consideration occupy more than one of the levels of concern. Indeed, that is a major reason for the convergence in lists. Attempting to distinguish levels of concern about the quality of life while being aware that they overlap should nonetheless help in our analysis of the quality of life. This is not merely for analytical convenience. The process of transforming resources or primary goods into capabilities and values is, in itself, of concern for those who care about the quality of life. The debate about which space to focus on has obscured this rather basic issue.

5. Conclusions

Sen has been greatly involved in the debate about the various spaces that matter in analysing the quality of life. This debate has sometimes tended to obscure the common ground among various views involving needs, values and capabilities. Differences among these views often have to do with considerations of strategy and context rather than fundamental differences in values. Furthermore, the various lists of the stuff of advantage can be reconciled if the various levels of our concern about the quality of life are separated out—to the extent that this is possible. Divergences in the various lists do not necessarily reflect differences in values, while convergence in the lists that are offered may arise even if the lists actually appear to be of rather different sorts of things. Both convergence and divergence are thus consistent with shared values at the most general level.

References

Alkire, S. (1999) Operationalising Amartya Sen's capability approach, DPhil Thesis, University of Oxford.

Alkire S. & Black, R. (1997) A practical reasoning theory of development ethics: furthering the capabilities approach, *Journal of International Development,* 9, pp. 263–279.

Bentham, J. (1996) *An Introduction to the Principles of Morals & Legislation*; an authoritative edition of J. H. Burns & H. L. A. Hart in the series: *The Collected Works of Jeremy Bentham* (Oxford, Clarendon Press).

Clark, D. A. (2000a) Conceptualising development, PhD Thesis, University of Cambridge.

Clark, D.A. (2000b) Perceptions of development: some evidence from the Western Cape, SALDRU Working Paper no. 88, Southern Africa Labour and Development Research Unit, Cape Town.

Crocker, D. (1995), Functioning and capability: the foundations of Sen's and Nussbaum's development ethic, Part 2, in: M. C. Nussbaum & Jonathan Glover (Eds) *Women, Culture and Development* (Oxford, Clarendon Press), pp. 153–198.

Deneulin, S. (2002) Perfectionism, paternalism and liberalism in the theory of human development and in Sen and Nussbaum's capability approach, *Review of Political Economy,* 14.

Dower, N. (2000) Human development—friend or foe to environmental ethics? *Environmental Values,* 9, pp. 39–54.

Doyal, L. & Gough, I. (1991) *A Theory of Human Need* (London, Macmillan).

Finnis, J. (1979) *Natural Law and Natural Rights* (Oxford, Oxford University Press).

Gasper, D. (1995) Needs and basic needs as conceptual foundation for 'Human Development', Paper presented at the ESRC Development Economics Study Group, Leicester University, 24–25 March 1995.

Gasper, D. (1996) Needs and basic needs: a clarification of meanings, levels and different streams of work, Working Paper no. 210, Institute of Social Studies, The Hague.

Goulet, D. (1995) *Development Ethics. A guide to theory and practice* (London, Zed).

Griffin, J. P. (1977) Are there incommensurable values? *Philosophy and Public Affairs,* 7, pp. 39–59.

Griffin, J. P. (1986) *Well-Being: its meaning, measurement and moral importance* (Oxford, Clarendon Press).

Griffin, J. P. (1991) Against the taste model, in: J. Elster & J. E. Roemer (Eds), *Interpersonal Comparisons of Well-Being* (Cambridge, Cambridge University Press), pp. 45–69.

Griffin, J. P. (1996) *Value Judgement* (Oxford, Clarendon Press).

Griffin, J.P. (2000) Discrepancies between the best philosophical account of human rights and the international law of human rights, *Proceedings of the Aristotelian Society,* 74, pp. 1–28.

Grisez, G., Boyle, J. & Finnis, J. (1987) Practical principles, moral truth and ultimate ends, *American Journal of Jurisprudence,* 32, pp. 99–151.

Haq, M. (1995) *Reflections on Human Development* (Oxford, Oxford University Press).

Nussbaum, M. C. (1988) Nature, function and capability: Aristotle on political distribution, *Oxford Studies in Ancient Philosophy,* 6, Supplementary Volume, pp. 145–184.

Nussbaum, M. C. (1990) Aristotelian social democracy, in: B. Doulglass, G. Mara & H. Richardson (Eds) *Liberalism and the Good* (London, Routledge), pp. 203–252.

Nussbaum, M. C. (1992) Human functioning and social justice. In defence of Aristotelian essentialism, *Political Theory,* 20, pp. 202–246.

Nussbaum, M. C. (1995a) Human capabilities, female human beings, in: M. C. Nussbaum & J. Glover (Eds) *Women, Culture and Development* (Oxford, Clarendon Press), pp. 61–104.

Nussbaum, M. C. (1995b) Aristotle on human nature and the foundations of ethics, in: J. E. J. Altham & R. Harrison (Eds) *World, Mind and Ethics: Essays on the Ethical Philosophy of Bernard Williams* (Cambridge, UK, Cambridge University Press), pp. 86–131.

480   *Mozaffar Qizilbash*

Nussbaum, M. C. (1998) The good as discipline, as freedom, in: D. A. Crocker & T. Linden (Eds), *Ethics of Consumption: the good life, justice and global stewardship* (London, Rowman and Littlefield), pp. 312–341.

Nussbaum, M. C. (1999) *Sex and Social Justice* (Oxford, Oxford University Press).

Nussbaum, M. C. (2000) *Women and Human Development: the capabilities approach* (Cambridge, Cambridge University Press).

Nussbaum, M. C. & Sen, A. K. (1989) Internal criticism and Indian rationalist traditions, in: M. Krauz (Ed.), *Relativism* (Notre Dame, Notre Dame University Press), pp. 299–325.

Qizilbash, M. (1996a) Ethical development, *World Development*, 24, pp. 1209–1221.

Qizilbash, M. (1996b) Capabilities, well-being and human development: a survey, *Journal of Development Studies*, 33, pp. 143–162.

Qizilbash, M. (1997a) Needs, incommensurability and well-being, *Review of Political Economy*, 9, pp. 261–276.

Qizilbash, M. (1997b) Pluralism and well-being indices, *World Development*, 25, pp. 2009–2026.

Qizilbash, M. (1998) The concept of well-being, *Economics and Philosophy*, 14, pp. 51–73.

Rawls, J. (1972) *A Theory of Justice* (Oxford, Oxford University Press).

Rawls, J. (1982) Social unity and primary goods, in: A. K. Sen and B. A. O. Williams (Eds), *Utilitarianism and Beyond* (Cambridge, Cambridge University Press), pp. 159–185.

Rawls, J. (1993) *Political Liberalism* (New York, Columbia University Press).

Rawls, J. (1999a) *A Theory of Justice,* Revised Edition (Oxford, Oxford University Press).

Rawls, J. (1999b) *The Law of Peoples* (Cambridge, MA, Harvard University Press).

Sen, A.K. (1980) Equality of what? in: A. K. Sen, 1982, *Choice, Welfare and Measurement* (Oxford, Blackwell), pp. 353–369.

Sen, A. K. (1984a) *Resources, Values and Development* (Oxford, Blackwell).

Sen, A. K. (1984b) Goods and People, in: A. K. Sen, 1984, *Resources, Values and Development,* (Oxford, Blackwell), pp. 509–532.

Sen, A. K. (1990) Justice: means versus freedom, *Philosophy and Public Affairs*, 19, pp. 111–121.

Sen, A. K.(1992) *Inequality Reexamined* (Oxford, Clarendon Press).

Sen, A. K. (1993) Capability and well-being, in: M. C. Nussbaum & A. K. Sen (Eds), *The Quality of Life* (Oxford, Clarendon Press), pp. 30–55.

Sen, A. K. (1998) *Reason Before Identity: the Romanes Lecture* (Oxford: Oxford University Press).

Sen, A. K. (1999) *Development as Freedom* (Oxford, Oxford University Press).

Streeten, P. with Burki, S.J., Haq, M., Hicks, N. & Stewart, F. (1981) *First Things First: meeting basic needs in developing countries* (Oxford, Oxford University Press).

Sugden, R. (1993) Welfare, resources and capabilities: a review of *Inequality Reexamined* by Amartya Sen, *Journal of Economic Literature,* 31, pp. 1947–1962.

United Nations Development Programme (Various Years) *Human Development Report* (New York, Oxford University Press).

Warke, T. (2000) Multi-dimensional utility and the index number problem: Jeremy Bentham, J. S. Mill and qualitative hedonism, *Utilitas*, 12, pp. 176–203.

[15]

A deliberative ethic for development

A Nepalese journey from Bourdieu through Kant to Dewey and Habermas

John Cameron and Hemant Ojha

School of Development Studies, University of East Anglia, Norwich, UK

Abstract

Purpose – The purpose of this paper is to explore the possibility of a procedural deliberative alternative to an atomistic conception of individuals and an economic logic of markets or a priori universal lists, as ethical foundation for evaluating socio-economic change.

Design/methodology/approach – To develop this argument, the paper combines a modified Kantian categorical imperative with deliberative ethics drawing on the writings of Habermas and Dewey. The journey through the European Enlightenment thought of Kant to the contemporary thought of Habermas and Bourdieu aims at mapping continuity and change in key themes in development ethics. These ideas are then given practical application in a case-study of the people-forestry interface in Nepal.

Findings – The paper shows how Kantian non-deception links to Habermas' notion of communicative action and Dewey's notion of cooperative inquiry, and how Kantian non-coercion links to the inclusion of subaltern voices. While the paper proposes that more open deliberative processes can potentially produce ethical gains, it also identifies an idealistic risk in this position. Bourdieu's thinking is utilised to reveal limitations on improving deliberative processes where there are powerful mechanisms reproducing inequalities.

Practical implications – The paper makes the case for greater attention being given to exploring deliberative processes as a prerequisite for ethical developmental actions.

Originality/value – The paper brings together authors who rarely feature in the development studies discourse and applies their ideas to a practical case study.

Keywords Ethics, Sustainable development, Forestry, Nepal

Paper type Research paper

Introduction

This paper explores the possibility of centre-staging deliberative processes in development ethics. We seek to show how this approach can throw light on the challenges in both improving the lives of vulnerable people in the world and conserving the natural environment. We offer a framework for a procedural ethics which is culturally "thin" enough for all to own it and which excludes no position where good reason is sustained in open deliberation. On this basis, we offer an assessment of deliberative processes (which qualitatively differ from, and go beyond, participatory processes) in a case study of the people/forestry interface in Nepal.

The paper combines our ongoing empirical research on forest/people interactions in Nepal (Ojha and Timsina, 2006; Ojha *et al.*, 2006; Ojha, 2006b), with ideas of Habermas (on deliberation and communicative action), Dewey (on cooperative inquiry) and Bourdieu (on *doxa* and *habitus*) and our previous work on Kantian ethics (Cameron, 1999). Figure 1 outlines how we draw on and link the theoretical sources. The paper

A deliberative ethic for development   67

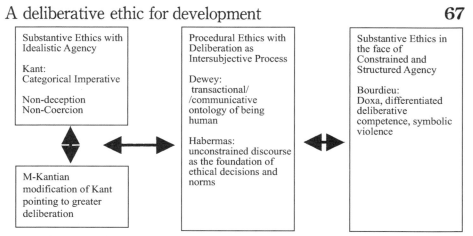

Figure 1. A conceptual map linking substantive and deliberative ethical ideas

then moves from the theoretical through to a case study of people/nature interactions in Nepal.

Current ethical and political practice after the collapse of the USSR is largely within a neoliberal order, but the global order has found no ideological consensus, and there are numerous claimants to truth about improving the human condition. While many practical challenges are being organised against the neo-liberal ordering of the world (as reflected in street rallies concurrent with major policy events of the globalisation giants such as World Trade Organisation (WTO)), there is a general problem of conceptualising ends and means for improving human quality of life. Responses to the challenge of thinking through improvement in the human condition have recently drifted into a culturally rich, ethically ambiguous relativism, though that is not without its critics (Bauhn, 1998; Bauman, 1998). Post-modernist relativists in the North are jostling for recognition with more absolutist claimants from various parts of the South, including from Islam, Hinduism, Confucianism, and various branches of Christianity.

Our argument is organised as follows. In the next section, we introduce the work of Pierre Bourdieu (1930-2002) to analyse a structural model that delimits the potential for fully open deliberative ethics. The main input from Bourdieu is that deliberation is itself a process of enacting more entrenched forms of violence which he calls symbolic violence, enacted through the very process of language and communication, and that genuine deliberation is possible when crisis arises in the symbolic structure of society, forcing the habituated actions of people to be brought under discursive deliberation. From this relatively pessimistic position we move to Kant's categorical imperative, as a universalist, substantive ethical position, and then modify this Kantian position to take account of a number of factors, notably an unequal distribution of power (Cameron, 1999).

We use these ideas to move towards a design for a procedural ethics that applies conscious human agency to development practice. We particularly draw on John Dewey's notions of transactional inquiry and democracy as a learning process, and Jurgen Habermas's discourse ethics and deliberative basis for arriving at moral restraints for collective life. Dewey (1859-1952) provides a strong ontological basis for understanding communicative human co-existence. This is expanded by Habermas (1929-), searching for grounds for the democratic legitimacy of social norms or governance by recourse to both private and public autonomy as co-original, rather than mutually exclusive. Figure 1 shows how we locate Dewey and Habermas between the rationalist position of Kant and the structuralist approach of Bourdieu.

Our case study is based on Nepal's community forestry (CF) policy and practice, which we see as a complex interaction among diverse groups of social agents, mainly local people, techno-bureaucrats, and development agencies. Throughout the modern history of Nepal, forests have been a highly contested space – both materially and symbolically – for a broad range of actors. Whereas forest was traditionally a resource for subsistence livelihoods, subsequent intervention by state functionaries, business groups and Western conservationists and developmentalists have made the forest a very complex ground of conflict and deliberation. As forest was the hub of conservation and local livelihoods in a highly fragile Himalayan environment where some of the world's poorest groups (at least in material wealth) live, rapid ethical shifts in development thinking have been found in the policy and practice of forest governance. In Nepal's field of forest/people interface, one can find the world's most progressive legislation recognising local people's rights over forest, and at the same time, a highly stratified society in which certain groups of elites control the resources without facing much resistance and deliberative challenge from the ordinary people.

Using Bourdieu's concepts as a foundation for a realistic procedural ethics

Bourdieu's ideas are introduced here to meet a concern that deliberation needs to be purged of the utopian idealism of appealing solely to free moral agency supposedly persuadable by well intentioned texts claiming to be universally rational. The case of Nepal CF practice suggests that despite intensive developmental efforts in institutionalising participatory processes, supported by very progressive legislation, non-deliberative decision processes continue both at local community level and national policy levels. There is a recurrent problem of control of decision spheres by people who enjoy greater symbolic privileges in the deliberative setting, often drawing on specific social locations in terms of caste, class, formal political positions and gender (Malla, 2001; Ojha *et al.*, 2006). The presupposition of completely free and equal moral agency prior to deliberation is unrealistic. Bourdieu warns us that deliberation as an ethical practice should be seen in the context of these imperfections.

The reality of ethical conservatism in contexts of reproduced grave inequalities and socio-ecological non-sustainability can be conceptualised using Bourdieu's theoretical framework. We use Bourdieu's idea of social fields as relatively independent arenas of social practice and negotiation. Human agents, according to Bourdieu, seek legitimacy through accumulation of symbolic capitals. Study of how symbolic power is gained and exercised can provide important insights into how certain ethical patterns reproduce, within restricted spaces for deliberation, and provide opportunities for deception and violence, thus reproducing chronic social inequality (Hallett, 2003; Swartz, 2003). The symbolic basis of domination provides important guidelines to understand the dynamics of deliberative deficits and social inequality. Bourdieu's chief concern is that neither "forced choice" nor "consent" can fully explain deliberative deficits. Bourdieu (2001, p. 37) argues:

> The effect of symbolic domination (whether ethnic, gender, cultural, or linguistic) is exerted ... through the schemes of perception, appreciation and action that are constitutive of *habitus*, ... below the level of the decisions of consciousness and the controls of the will.

A deliberative ethic for development   **69**

Therefore, *habitus* is patterned behaviour that delimits free choice – including ethical choices.

A pattern in which deliberative practices are frustrated or dominated does not mean that people have chosen this situation willingly. The dominated contribute, often unwittingly, sometimes resignedly, to their own domination by non-deliberative decision-making. This acceptance can take form as emotions:

> ... shame, humiliation, timidity, anxiety, guilt – or passions and sentiments – love, admiration, respect. ... The passions of dominated *habitus* ... are not of the kind that can be suspended by a simple effort of will, founded on a liberatory awakening of consciousness (Bourdieu, 2001, p. 39)

This is because "they are deeply embedded in the form of dispositions" (Bourdieu, 2001, p. 39). The distribution of symbolic capital is crucial to understanding the acceptance of unequal access to decision-making (Crossley, 2004).

The other related challenge concerns the possibility for human agents with diversity of capitals to engage in open deliberation. If human agents are situated according to the structural logic of a social field, actualised by the relations between *habitus* and field, then how can agents in different social locations engage in deliberation? The way one speaks and behaves varies systematically from one social location to another, and people with different ethical beliefs do not normally meet in the social exchange processes, and therefore are less likely to engage in deliberation. This threatens the normative ideal of deliberation that says state officials, politicians and the marginalised citizens should engage together in political decisions (Hayward, 2004). Aware of such challenges, deliberative theories are pushing out their conceptual boundaries to include deliberative activism (Young, 2003; Fung, 2005).

Bourdieu notes two types of constraint on high quality deliberation. First, the practice of deliberation itself is impregnated with a strategic orientation, as seemingly disinterested actions are in fact interested ones (centred on the protection and accumulation of economic, cultural, symbolic and political capitals in their various forms). Second, even the calculated interests of social agents are inscribed within certain sets of deeply held assumptions and values, which he calls *doxa*, deposited historically in a pattern of habituses, working in particular fields of day to day practices (Swartz, 1997; Crossley, 2004)). The concept of *doxa* is used to capture the worldview of ideas and rules that people bring to any field of action. In our usage the concept of *habitus* includes the part of *doxa* that constitute ethical rules, but also includes socially acceptable deviance from those ideal doxic rules.

Engagement with Bourdieu thus helps us to connect deeply held beliefs (*doxa*) and observable practices (*habitus*) in particular social fields – in which some people are more advantaged than others in terms of symbolic and cultural capitals as well as of deliberative dispositions. As a result of differences in these internal and external competencies, some are systematically advantaged over others in the processes of deliberation and cooperative inquiry.

Bourdieu (1991, pp. 127-8) proposes substantive social conditions for the emergence of deliberation. As the social order draws its permanence from the tacit acceptance of the agents:

> ... politics begins, strictly speaking, with the denunciation of this tacit contract of adherence to the established order which defines *doxa*; in other words, political subversion presupposes

cognitive subversion ... But heretical break with the established order ... presupposes a conjuncture of critical discourse and an objective crisis, capable of disrupting the close correspondence between the incorporated structures and the objective structures which produce them, and of instituting a practical epoche, [in other words] a suspension of the initial adherence to the established order.

Bourdieu himself sees some possibilities of opening up deliberation in circumstances that might be broadly characterised as crises. The concept of crisis is vital to introducing active human agency to the more passive structures in Bourdieu and can potentially throw light on the dynamics and changes in deliberative processes. Crisis can originate, for example, when experiences of nature fail to match expectations of stability in natural processes over a significant period of time. Such experiences can include both unforeseen volatility and perverse trends – that is issues of both uncertainty and non-sustainability. Crises shift decision-making from structural habit to conscious agency. The existing predominant form of symbolic power may become unstable due to dissonance between the regularities of the field and on the other hand the schemes of perceptions and thought of the *habitus* groups. This may lead to an awareness of symbolic violence, on the part of both dominated and dominant, and the former may start undergoing an active process of reflection, faster than the latter. The process of recognition once triggered may move at accelerated pace, as an uncovering of an element of *doxa* that has hitherto legitimated symbolic violence may lead to further and faster uncovering of the deeper level *doxa*. Critical self reflexivity then becomes a source of transformation which Bourdieu recognises (Wacquant, 2004). Thus, transformation can involve shifts in both procedural and substantive ethical stances.

In another paper, we have explored the field of people/forest interactions in Nepal to give insights into continuity and change in deliberative processes (Ojha *et al.*, 2006). That research explored the case of forestry development in Nepal in which *habitus* and *doxa* of international actors, forest bureaucrats, local elites and members of poor and marginalised groups interface in the nation's widely acclaimed CF programme. The deficits in deliberative processes that we identify are explained by the interplay of bureaucratic, elitist and marginalised worldviews (*doxa*), and the corresponding inequality in the distribution of cultural, symbolic and economic resources essential to exercise communicative agency in processes of more open deliberation.

We examine how this interplay is unlikely to produce substantive or procedural ethical gains in terms of diminished coercion and deception or higher quality deliberative processes because of the absence of crisis. We conceptualise an ensemble of political and cultural practices within the discursive territory of "sustainable forestry" as a Bourdieuian social field, in which a complex pattern of human agencies and subcultures operate to generate observable practices (Ojha, 2006b). An ethical assessment of deliberative processes in the field suggests that participatory processes in practice have ended up with conservative outcomes – in terms of further embedding of violence, corruption and deception in increasingly less visible ways – such as professionalisation, extension of expert authority, and the proclamation of egalitarian legal-ethical imperatives for all members of a community without addressing the extremely hierarchical relations between and within agencies in Nepalese society.

To conclude this section, we suggest three levels of decision-making practices derived from Bourdieu, each involving *doxa-habitus*-deliberation tensions:

A deliberative ethic for development   **71**

(1) *Practices that proceed largely within existing doxic rules and relations of power, which are largely mis-recognised.* Deliberative processes here are confined to attempts to sort out minor operational cases by using widely accepted rules, e.g. fines for collecting grazing materials out of season.

(2) *Practices that move from doxic rules to habitus pragmatics and bring power relations under rational critiques.* Here intermediate deliberative processes attempt to sort out tensions between *habitus* positions by using practically oriented ethics, e.g. penalties for not providing household labour for forest maintenance by richer households.

(3) *Practices brought fully into the discursive domain, with fundamental relations of power brought under critique.* A major rift or dissonance between practices and field takes us beyond manageability through *habitus* pragmatics and challenges the language and symbolic boundaries/structures of deliberation, e.g. when evidence emerges of bribes being paid to forest department officials by commercial loggers.

All three levels interact, with accumulations of tensions at one level overflowing into the next, higher level, but in the absence of a generalised crisis the deficits in deliberative processes will be reproduced – albeit possibly involving increased use of physical violence.

Kantian categorical imperative as a thin substantive foundation for development ethics

Immanuel Kant (1724-1804) lived through the heart of the European Enlightenment and in globally tumultuous times. He proposed a universalist ethic: a categorical imperative for all people, independent of their cultural orientation. From an instrumentalist position, he can be seen as arguing that, if people wish to constitute an indefinitely sustainable society, then they rationally must accept a categorical ethical imperative to create a social order in which nobody is coerced or deceived. This categorical imperative of non-coercion and non-deception applies even to a society of devils, as no social order can survive the precariousness and uncertainties of living where killing and lying are a continuing threat to life and contract (Cameron, 1999).

At a time when development debates are becoming increasingly concerned with violence and corruption as key elements in damaging human well-being, the claim that non-coercion and non-deception are foundational principles of rights and obligations for all human beings in all societies provides a promising philosophical focus in the search for principles for normative development theory. In an earlier paper, Cameron applied a modified view of Kant's ethical imperative to suggest two mappings – one from the non-fulfillment of the principle of non-deception through to the social experience of corruption, and the other from non-fulfillment of the principle of non-coercion through to the social experience of violence (Cameron, 1999). The modified Kantianism (m-Kantianism) proposed by Cameron (1999) argues that the Kantian ethical categorical imperative to non-deception and non-coercion can play a role as a universalistic foundation for development evaluation, provided it is adjusted to meet the following major interconnected challenges:

- Moving to cover not only individual but also group interactions.
- Linking rights to obligations.

- Dealing with action at a distance through institutions.
- Taking account of unequal economic, cultural and political resources/wealth.
- Recognising variations between societies and groups in thick values.
- Including time as an explicit factor, taking account of duration, non-reversibility, uncertainty, and sustainability.

These challenges make enactment of the Kantian ethical imperative in human social practice extremely complex and require exploration of the procedural and practical dimensions in different social contexts. In rural Nepal, where people earn a living partly from the forests, we can see violence and corruption enacted by individuals working on behalf of the state (techno-bureaucrats) or those who draw on traditionally legitimate forms of power (such as local elites). The thick social institutions which help in the coordination and collective action around forest governance are themselves sites of domination and violence. Allocation of forest and land resources to local feudal lords, and then coopting peasants in order to extract rents, has been a common phenomenon in Nepal's modern history (Regmi, 1977), and this system of relations of production still dominates the current pattern of institutions and social relations. Also, cultural differentiation in terms of caste, gender and ethnicity further complicates the possibility of non-deceptive practices. At least what is now clear by 2006 is that a neo-liberal marketisation of forest governance is not a feasible alternative to these collective institutions of coordination and control. But the problem of domination remains. The problem becomes further entrenched when we move from small communities to larger geographic scales – and it is increasingly appreciated that we need an ethic of environmental governance at even global scale – as we have to deal with diverse social values with regard to environment. While Kantian ethics help us to see the problem of ethical practice in terms of a categorical imperative, it falls short of showing how non-deception and non-coercion can actually be enacted in the complex reality.

The categorical imperative is intended to be universal and apply to all human beings at all points in time. The modified version here lacks Kant's original optimism in that it admits issues of unequal power. Patterns of inequality in power will vary between societies and thus ethical behaviour will be sensitive to context. A society with a highly unequal distribution of power and a related capacity to use coercion and deception to reproduce that inequality will have a different ethic of resistance compared to a more equal society, in which coercion and deception can be more readily reduced through improved deliberative processes. The challenge is that even the processes of ethical improvement in governance practices – such as CF in Nepal – are often driven by Western assumptions, and tend to limit their practices of governance to establishment of groups and institutional structures, which in reality stand on the basis of existing structures of inequality which sustain deception and coercion.

Given current awareness in development studies for the physical environment, a complete ethical position must include a position on "nature." Here, too Kant provides insights. His approach to the people/nature relationship is summarised in *The Critique of Judgement,* where he discusses nature in terms of its power over people:

A deliberative ethic for development

... threatening rock, thunderclouds piled up [to] the vault of heaven, borne along with flashes and peals, volcanoes in all their violence of destruction, hurricanes leaving desolation in their track, the boundless ocean rising with rebellious force, the high waterfall of some mighty river, and the like, make our power of resistance of trifling moment in comparison with their might. ... [They] raise the forces of the soul above the height of the vulgar commonplace and discover within us a power of resistance of quite another kind, which gives us courage to be able to measure ourselves against the seeming omnipotence of nature (Kant, 1989, pp. 10-1).

Kant envisages insecure contexts in which fearful people are rendered passive by dread and compares them with securer contexts in which such natural forces are experienced as sublime. In securer contexts, people can appreciate their capacity for reason as a distinct capability that exists in contrast to the emotional sensation of the sublime. Reason becomes more valued because of the natural. People can then turn reason back towards nature and attempt to reduce it to scientific laws. But the raw emotional essence of the natural does not disappear in this process. Kant's ethical categorical imperative is based on reason, but nature is crucial to the valuation of that reason and hence a lively natural world with its moments of the sublime is vital to Kantian ethics. A person who is unaware of the eye of the tiger will not value calm reflection and deliberation as much as a person who has experienced the insecurity of that moment. If nature is totally tamed then human ethical consciousness becomes less not more. In the same way, consciousness for Hegel's bondsman, who knows fear of loss of life and associated interdependence, is likely to be more developed than for the master. Even for the austere Kant, nature has significance for his ethics in inducing a humility that makes ethical behaviour more likely and deliberative closure more difficult.

In terms of both people/people and people/nature relationships, m-Kantian thinking pushes the discourse on development ethics towards non-closure and procedural rather than substantive ethical conclusions. Our position seeks to move from a thin substantive starting point, through the implied procedural ethical concerns, towards procedural arrangements to improve deliberation in the direction of less deception and coercion in specific social contexts.

Neo-liberals and m-Kantians can share doubts about the nature of the State, bureaucratic allocation of resources and bureaucratic accountability. The neo-liberal structural adjustment approach seeks to marketise away these problems of bureaucratic economics and politics, while the m-Kantian seeks to deliberate them away. Which is the better approach to critical questions on conservation of a habitable physical environment, widespread addictive narcotic production and use, and inadequate personal and public safety has become a crucial issue. The neo-liberal approach to development which marginalises and individualises such issues is already on the defensive and is likely to remain so. To face such issues, the m-Kantian position demands that the concepts of democracy, participation, access and accountability be problematised and theorised as developmental keywords and rescued from formalistic use in multi-party electoral and bureaucratic paradigms.

The Kantian categorical imperative to non-deception is crucial to understanding deliberative deficits. The sense of having been deceived can be aroused by many experiences. The simplest situation involves direct misrepresentation of a piece of information by one agent to another agent. More complex are situations in which one agent has reason to expect one form of behaviour but receives another.

Effective agency is undermined by both experiences and, when such experiences are common in a society, the viability and sustainability of the social order can be chronically, if not mortally, undermined.

Undermining of agency may involve a combination of deception and violence. German society between 1925 and 1945 provides a telling case-study suggesting such an interaction. Owings (1993) uses ethnographic methodology, including recall from as long as 60 years previously, to attempt to understand the range of women's responses in the Germany of that time. These women were not directly threatened by Nazi deceptions regarding superiority and inferiority among social groups. Owings suggests that women took a wide range of positions with respect to the rise of Nazism. The range included: willingness to accept authority (legitimated by emphasis on nationalism and motherhood, and enforced by self-and family-preservation); perceived powerlessness to oppose Nazism socially (despite examples of individual courage in assisting other individuals and following Communist Party or other discipline); and crises of explicit moral choice when the price of following one option was probable death, so that women instead lived with guilt in a context of uncertainty over "reality."

This uncertainty over the violent reality relied upon removal by the Nazis at an early stage of agencies concerned with transparency and accountability, thus increasing the potential for deception. The extension of violence was more gradual and secretive right up to the final solution from 1942. Women from a variety of positions who were asked about violence in Germany during 1933-1939 might well have argued it had decreased, at a time when potential for carrying through unprecedented violence was being developed. Some would even have claimed the level of economic deception had decreased with the repression of "Jewish" businesses (Owings, 1993).

Societies possess multiple ethical codes for limiting coercive and deceptive behaviour in political, civil society, and market relationships. But such codes not only involve ethical rules (analogous to Bourdieu's *doxa*), they also include reasons/ justifications for apparent breaches of each code (as one part of what Bourdieu calls *habitus*). Multiple codes of behaviour in a society with differing degrees of formality generate multiple potential forms of coercion and deception and protestations that coercion and deception were not present. For instance, a common form of deception is to claim to be acting within one code when *de facto* operating with reference to another. Also each of the codes may have its own dynamics leading to redefinitions of acceptable behaviour within each code and modifying the interaction between codes. Thus, mapping from the Kantian categorical imperative of non-coercion and non-deception to actual required behaviour is a complex process. Nevertheless, in m-Kantian terms, this preliminary overview suggests there may be ways to assess whether a society is moving towards less or more coercion and deception, utilising Bourdieu's concepts.

The existence of corruption and violence at their present levels has implications for any intellectual project that is concerned with the possibilities of progress in the quality of human life. The m-Kantian position attempts to give that project conceptual depth. It aspires towards a universal, global ethics, but leaves much room for sensitive analysis of local variations in the meanings and patterns of coercion and deception. The m-Kantian methodology is inevitably discursive, inclusive and critically aware of power relations, unequal power structures, and the power poverty of some people. Corruption and violence, both at the individual and, particularly, at the mass levels, are

A deliberative ethic for development   **75**

outcomes of unequal or uncertain power relationships. Varying mixtures of inequality and uncertainty in a power relationship can induce different forms of violence and different potentials for corruption.

To bring corruption and physical violence to the centre of development studies, as major causes of low quality of human life, requires explicit attention to the specific nature of deception and coercion at a societal level and the decision-making space for limiting them. Policies to place people as ends and agents, rather than as means and victims/clients/customers/human capital, require concern with the means and processes of policy formulation and implementation and explicit evaluation of interactions and relationships. With m-Kantian development objectives, the policy process from identification to evaluation should over time become more transparent, less opaque. Rights to information and public inquiry procedures become a development issue, not an optional extra or a transaction cost to be minimised.

Many of the people in grass-roots organisations concerned with development will suspect this m-Kantian approach of being politically utopian as much as economically unrealistic. They would argue that day-to-day exercise of power is based on structures where power is centralised and multi-form and any proposal to more equally distribute power will meet uncompromising resistance in depth across the whole range of economic, cultural and political experience. If this analysis is accepted, which concludes that the agency of large groups of people is structurally hindered and their claims undermined and repressed, then the m-Kantian approach becomes a variant on a Hegel-Marx approach (Hegel, 1966) to society and consciousness. The process of asserting claims to agency by those to whom it is denied is developmentally progressive and justifiable. m-Kantians must argue though that such a political revolution should be carried out using means that respect the categorical imperatives of non-coercion and non-deception.

There is much work to be done in developing means of communication and indicators that allow patterns of whole lives, including coercion and deception, to be understood sensitively at all levels of aggregation and to omit no sub-group of people. Networks with the ability to communicate patterns of others' lives to people remote from that experience are needed. Universal literacy in, and access to, the written and electronic media is an important objective. Facilitating unstructured, non-commercial, mutually reflective, cultural contact has a vital role to play.

Numerous practical experiments on local scales in self-defence, democracy, participation, access and accountability and environmental conservation need to be more widely communicated, and their impacts on corruption and violence, deception and coercion, and environmental degradation can be evaluated. We can then also move beyond the defensive language of rights to be not deceived and coerced, into the language of obligations to positively advance less deception and coercion.

Improved deliberation as an ethical process: Habermas and Dewey

The work of Onora O'Neill (1941-) helps us to bridge from Kant to Habermas. Her interpretation of Kant's thinking emphasises both interdependence and communication as key human characteristics (O'Neill, 1986, 1990, 1996). Habermas's "discourse ethics" requires that all those affected by ethical norms to coordinate and guide collective action of social agents must deliberate together without coercion and deception over the possibility and the content of the norms. As he argues "Only those norms can claim to be valid that meet (or could meet) with the approval of all affected in their capacity as participants in a practical discourse" (Habermas, 1990). Since, for him, private and public autonomy are co-original (Habermas, 1996, p. 129), one leading to the other, social agents in an ethical community "have to" engage in communicative interactions to arrive at understanding so that both the individual and collective gains are maximised (Haller, 1994, p. 111).

This suggests that resolving the practical problems of poor and marginalised people in a degrading natural environment involves creating conditions through which they can engage in discursive deliberation free from coercion and deception. The optimistic belief is that high quality deliberation will address structural constraints on deprived people's participation. Two dimensions need to be identified – one of ensuring free and non-coerced communication of emotions, feelings and information; and secondly, recognition of uncertainty and complexity, and of the need for experiential learning over time, testing and exploring ideas in the real world setting. Seen from this ethical perspective, even the well-recognised participatory process of Nepal CF suffers from major deliberative deficits. Let us take an example:

> In a CFUG [Community Forest User Group] with a pole stage Sal forest, foresters advised the group to undertake thinning so that the Sal trees[1] grow faster. The group is close to Kathmandu valley, and because of easy road access, many of the smallholder farmers in the area have started to cultivate vegetables as cash crops, such as beans, cucumber and others, which need small supporting sticks. Before a CFUG was organised, the forest was *de facto* open access and the farmers could collect sticks without any restrictions. But after the establishment of [a] CFUG in mid-1990, technical forestry staff developed a forest management plan which prescribed clearing of all bushes/inferior species in the Sal forest. When the bushes were cleared, the forest became clean monoculture of Sal trees as per the wishes of the forest officials. But [the] majority of the land-poor farmers who were trying to earn a living through the production of cash crops had no supply of small sticks from the forest. On an average, each household needs about 1,000 sticks per year. This means that the forest could have better remained as bushy and shrubby for them but they could not argue against official forestry knowledge during planning and decision-making. This illustrates how government forestry knowledge is being imposed, without any deliberative interaction with local citizens (Ojha, 2006b).

The case illustrates that deliberative ethics is distorted by unequal power between technical experts and ordinary people. Still the concept of deliberation points to directions of more ethical practice – if farmers were allowed to participate in the process of identifying and designing the strategies of forest management, the outcomes could have been more ethical. Here, the Kantian notion of non-coercion and deception needs to be enlarged, to recognise a Habermasian domain of communicative action.

Deliberative governance is inspired by Habermas's notion of seeking communicative rationality in power relationships. This is a form of rationality, beyond a scientific or technical conception of reason employed by humans to understand the physical world (Habermas, 1971, 1987). When free and equal subjects deliberate, they transform each other and a new form of rationality emerges in the communicative interaction (Dryzek, 2000). Habermas's main thesis is that only those norms are valid that meet with the approval of all affected in their capacity as participants in a practical discourse. This rationality redefines democratic legitimacy, ethics, and decision-making processes. From the perspective of communicative rationality, political agency (or citizenship) is an intersubjective enterprise, as people

A deliberative ethic for development   **77**

are connected to diverse networks of communication in society. In that sense, they are not autonomous rational beings in themselves, as the ways through which they understand, interpret and channel resources are mediated by intersubjective processes. This reasoning questions aggregative models of liberal governance, which merely add up individual preferences without regard to deliberative principles and collective ethics (Chambers, 1996; Dryzek, 2000).

Deliberation is a conscious exercise of communicative competence by social beings to understand, negotiate and transform human relations and ethical norms. It is a "social process" involving communication of reasons, arguments, rhetoric, humour, emotion, testimony, story-telling, and gossip (Dryzek, 2000, p. 1). Such communicative practices do not just make governance possible but changes in them can be constitutive of improved governance. Both Habermas and Dewey claim that most problems of governance are associated with distortions in communication among the social agents engaged in ethical discourse (Bohman, 1999; Bohman, 2002). Difficulties exist in dependability of communication and mutual intelligibility (Dewey and Bentley, 1949, p. v), and there is always a possibility of communication getting distorted, especially when humans have to engage in situations of differences and conflicts.

In Bourdieu's terms, deliberation has doxic procedural ethical rules, differentiable from the substantive rules of *habitus* in a particular field. These procedural ethical rules admit uncertainty, risk, and existence of power (otherwise there would be no need for deliberation). As such they must have elements of being open-ended in outcomes, discursive in style, evidence-based in legitimacy, and also providing room for emotions to flow.

While the Habermasian view is too exclusively preoccupied with normative framing of deliberation, ideas of Dewey highlight the ontological value of deliberation. Dewey's ontological stance, on a communicative basis for understanding being human, emphasises that human relationships are in a continuous process of creation (Dewey, 1966, p. 3). Dewey distinguishes between "transactional" and "interactional" processes. Whereas the interactional processes assume that individuals have an autonomous existence before interaction, transactional processes envisage the creation of both individuals and groups in society through the processes of transmission (Dewey and Bentley, 1949). Dewey's conclusion is that "when communicative processes are involved, we find in them something very different from physiological process; the transactional inspection must be made to display what takes place, and neither the particles of physics nor those of physiology will serve" (Dewey and Bentley, 1949, p. 134). From Dewey, we argue that an atomistic conception of purely autonomous individuals is not adequate to understand ethical actions. An alternative is to start analysis from the complex social interactions surrounding practical problem situations of ethics.

Another aspect in which Dewey complements Habermas is the dynamic notion of learning through experience, rather than transcendental deliberation. Dewey considers social practices as central to collective learning, experimentation and democracy. Every social practice is based on a practical rational ethics that can give rise to individual variations. This resonates with the Habermasian idea of deliberation as a process of transforming preferences through interaction, and Bourdieu's fuzzy practical logic in social action (the knowledge of a coach is never applied exactly into practice by a player, who has his or her own technique of playing). But nevertheless, in everyday language and means of communication, we can observe the primacy of the collective in shaping the private.

One of the crucial questions which treatises on ethics should address is how power can be an ethical action, as human collectivities are always coordinated through some relations of power. The history of human society shows that there has been a recurring question as to how individuals and groups can constitute ethical relations of power. The question of legitimacy becomes even more critical when there is general recognition of a crisis and a need to transform existing relations of power from one form to another (such as from a feudal society to a democratic society). Whereas Dewey argued for democracy as cooperative inquiry by concerned citizens, his ideas are sometimes criticised for being too instrumental (Festenstein, 1997). Habermas's discursive conception of "radical democracy" does not designate a specific institutional form but a social and epistemological ideal of a "self-controlled learning process," with freely participating subjects (Festenstein, 1997). Both Habermas and Dewey thus provide a normative basis of organising power but both depend heavily on confidence in universal, open communicative processes, without reference to contextual, complex patterns of inequality. To qualify that over-confidence we suggest utilising Bourdieu's more structuralist ideas as a counterweight to Habermas's and Dewey's optimism.

Reflections on forestry policies and practices of Nepal from the 1970s to today

As introduced in previous sections of this paper, Nepal's CF does not consist of harmonious village communities managing forest areas in isolation from the entire society. The forestry practice of local communities is a result of a complex web of relations within themselves, and between them and a range of non-local social agents, who take various positions in the field of CF and thus affect, and are affected by, the practices of forest management and decision-making. Although it started as a donor-supported program by government in the late 1980s, CF has emerged as a distinct social field with numerous actors engaged in the reciprocal relations of exchanging various forms of economic, cultural and symbolic resources, and at the same time having differentiated social positions, enduring dispositions, cognitive frames, and diverse motivations. Over the past 25 years, the range of actors engaged within the field of CF has consistently increased, especially after the enactment of a multi-party political system in 1990 and a devolutionary forest law in 1995. Actors engage in different ways – producing policy ideas, disseminating technical ideas and information, mediating conflicts and the like. They together constitute a topography of social space.

During the early 1980s, Nepal's mountains were perceived widely as a site of environmental and livelihoods crisis – deforestation and soil erosion were seen as affecting water flows and the livelihood resources base locally and beyond (Eckholm, 1976). Around the same time, a global environmental movement was gathering momentum, using the language of crisis to emphasise the environmental costs of continuity and the need for change. The Nepal Himalaya then became a matter of concern internationally. Technical environmental experts emphasised a technical scientific rationality, highlighting the rates, nature and dynamics of environmental degradation in "ultra-conservationist" fashion (Blaikie and Muldavin, 2004).

A deliberative ethic for development   **79**

The discourse on Nepal's forests thus went beyond the political boundary of Nepal, and international agencies started to deliberate over how the field could be addressed.

Expatriate "experts" came to Nepal and the number of environmental scientists working in Nepal increased following the 1980s Stockholm conference on Environment and Development. Richer countries now had a new mandate to intervene in the physical environments of poorer countries, to replace their powers in the colonial period. Initially, both Nepalese foresters and foreign technical experts emphasised government controlled plantation/afforestation as the solution. These experts could not understand local people's negative responses to their recommendations as they were working from a technocratic rationality. Local citizens were allowed very little deliberative space to define problems and propose solutions. This is why many of the plantations undertaken as a quick-fix technical solution were not successful – they intruded into the pre-existing systems of resource use decided in local deliberative processes, leading to strong local resistance (such as defying fences, continued grazing, and even uprooting of seedlings). But this local resistance forced experts and bureaucrats to reflect (Table I). The experts then began to relocate priorities from technical to socio-political dimensions, including to issues of local deliberative processes (Gilmour and Fisher, 1991).

After a series of deliberative interactions, new rules were created to authorise local communities to take control over forests. But in the 1980s a political regime with very constrained deliberative processes was in place: the partyless panchayat[2] system with limited civic participation in political decision-making. The process of decentralisation of forest control was confined to local Panchayats, the local bodies of the Panchayat political system that was directly controlled and dictated by the King. This allowed local elites to capture control over the forests (Panchayat forests), working closely with local bureaucrats and largely acting on their technical advice, though lubricated by regular corruption and occasional violence (for forceful exclusion of the forest-dependent poor). This, in modified Kantian terms, can be seen as a deceptive move by the Royalist government to coopt local elites around Panchayati politics, and thus to dissipate their possible resentment against community resource management.

A more genuinely decentralised form of governance emerged following a popular struggle for multi-party democracy in 1990. Community Forest User Groups (CFUGs) were recognised as independent local groups to manage designated forest areas. In 2005, there were about 15,000 CFUGs nationally, with more independence over resource control. But there remain persistent questions of equity and democratic practice, mainly because of a thin notion of democratic accountability and a consequent deliberative gap in the relations between people and political leaders. Under this liberal governance framework, forest bureaucrats have exercised tremendous symbolic power not only as scientists but also as *haakim* or patrons (Ojha, 2006a). Malla (2001) reports a compelling case of the persistence of "patron-client" relations between the forest bureaucrats and local elites, and the peasant forest users, despite the change in forest policies. Just providing greater independence to local groups proved ineffective as there seems to be a lack of concurrent discursive politics to tackle issues of exclusion and inequality. The political field and the field of CF are not linked adequately, and the latter has again been subjected to technocratic dispositions emphasising the formation of CFUGs and quantitative assessment of resource stocks, at the cost of deliberative

	Kant	m-Kantian	Habermas/Dewey	Bourdieu
Concepts and themes	Non-deception, non-coercion	Corruption, violence, need for deliberation, inequality	Communication, deliberation	*Doxa*, differentiated deliberative competence, symbolic violence
Nepal case	Reveals how practices of forest governance are marked by the ubiquity of unethical practices in terms of both non-coercion and deception. But this position gives little insight into how they can be reformulated	Demonstrates a more pronounced critique of unethical practice and points to the need for deliberation. Fails to demonstrate a procedural strategy of ethical practice	Provides a more visible direction for ethical improvement in terms of countering deliberative deficit. Offers some evidence of causal relations between deliberation and justice outcomes – such as from policies to support community based management and civil society institutions to safeguard civic rights and challenge technocratic *doxa*, but there remains a huge deficit on deliberation. Challenges to this deliberative ethical strategy include: the idea seems too idealistic and constrained by unequal deliberative competence of the social agents involved	The idealism of deliberation is purged to provide deeper analytical insights into when/how deliberation can lead to reproduction or transformation. Currently, deliberation in forest governance is structured around the languages of techno-bureaucrats and the participatory/deliberative gains are not free from symbolic violence

Table I.
Overview of Nepal
forestry case seen from
different ethical
perspectives

A deliberative ethic for development 81

transformation of *doxa*. But there are better practical instances at local level that show that when political forums are widened within and around CFUGs, the scope for deliberative transformation of inequitable practices and rules is expanded (Timsina *et al.*, 2004; Banjade and Ojha, 2005).

Local Nepalese societies have dense networks of institutions and associated symbolic ethical *doxa* and patterns of *habitus* which provide challenges and opportunities for deliberation. Institutions of caste and gender are particularly challenging for deliberative improvement as they differentiate citizens into structurally very unequal groupings. Ethnic diversity can add to cultural richness and social learning (Young, 1997) but when it crosscuts with inequality, the deliberative challenge is suppressed. More open deliberative practices within local societies as well as between those societies and the wider world could produce both procedural and substantive ethical gains. But CF still tends to be viewed in isolation from civil society socio-cultural systems, and their ethical *doxa* is instead guided by a thin logic of modernist scientism and its claims to ethical neutrality (Scott, 1998; Nightingale, 2005).

In addition to the discourse on community management, the neo-liberal *doxa* emphasising the desirability (in terms of both efficiency and ethics) of moving control of forests towards "autonomous individuals" and market forces (in a neo-liberal sense) is still present in Nepal (Shrestha, 1999). Politicians and technocrats tend to ally in favour of privatisation of commercial forest resources. Civil society has time and again vehemently questioned the application of such ideology in governing Nepal's forests (Shrestha, 1999). Deliberation over the use of forest resources is thus ethically threatening for elite interests. This is consistent with a retreat from the language of ecological crisis.

Forestry at local level is related to non-local and global processes through the exchange of economic and symbolic capitals. WTO policies on trade affect the market prices and markets for medicinal plants and other forest products which local CFUGs produce (US $26 million was earned in 1995 from the trade in non-timber forest resources). This means CFUGs not only acquire resources to become local autonomous practitioners, but also become participants in the global discourse on global trading rules. Emergence of a nation-wide federation of CFUGs in the mid-1990s is an indication of the ability of Nepalese people to build institutions to play this role. The Federation of Community Forest Users, Nepal (FECOFUN) has actively promoted local agendas of users at national and international levels.

Although CFUGs were declared independent entities in the Forest Act of 1993, several subsequent actions of government tended to undermine the power of CFUGs (Britt, 2001). FECOFUN sought to safeguard their rights by participating in the national debate. Deliberative gains were still being challenged by *doxa* sceptical of deliberative rationality and its associated ethical challenges (Ojha and Timsina, 2006). For instance, more aggressive emphasis on conservation in the 1990s tended to emphasise a need for coercion to protect those resources. FECOFUN's contribution in the national debate was crucial in bringing the views of local forest users into national and international policy discourse. There will be continuing instances in which the debate over control of forests is threatened with capture by bureaucrats and technical experts using deception and coercion, and marginalisation of deliberative processes. In one instance, for example, a FECOFUN activist was offered a grant by a bilateral forestry project if he would stop publicly criticising the project approach (personal communication with national FECOFUN activist).

A law or rule is often not implementable in practice, as practices are not determined by formal rules if these compete with powerful dispositions of habituses in the field. The Forest Act 1993 recognised the rights and authorities of CFUGs, but the behaviour of state forest officials has distorted the law markedly in practice (Dhital *et al.*, 2002; Lachapelle *et al.*, 2004; Timsina *et al.*, 2004). FECOFUN's public criticisms of the technocratic dispositions of foresters and its work to politicise forest governance issues have provided much evidence of these distortions.

Such experiments in changing deliberative governance seek to engage a wide range of people with diverse interests, capacities and positions, communicating in the field of forestry practices, critiquing each other, challenging each others' *doxa*, exchanging different forms of capitals, formulating and refining their *habitus* patterning (Table II). Procedural ethical gains can be made from the resulting significant, mutually reinforcing, challenges to deceptive practices including:

- Increased sensitivity to corruption; Maoist threat to bribery (Seddon and Hussain, 2002).

- Growing value of more scientific cultural capital (which gives scope for becoming independent consultants rather than traditional bureaucrats).

Table II. Civil society challenges for more deliberative processes over forestry in Nepal

Civil society institutions seeking greater access to communicative deliberation on forest resources	Foundational *doxa* being challenged and ethical implications	Symbolic capital aspects of *habitus* being questioned
National Forestry Organisation	Neo-liberal marketisation. Technocratic closure in terms of universal scientific knowledge Regulatory authoritarianism Questioning of ethical *doxa* that tolerate state corruption and violence	Autonomous individualism "Expert" judgements Bureaucratic authority
Community Forestry User Groups	Technocratic closure in terms of local environmental knowledge Corruption Questioning of ethical *doxa* of scientific ethical neutrality/ superiority	"Expert" judgements Contempt for the "peasantry"
Local more excluded people	Cultural closure and claimed right to exploit resources Questioning of ethical *doxa* of Hindu caste superiority legitimating deception and coercion	Caste and gender legitimacy
Professional NGOs	Liberal-constitutionalist and technocratic state Questioning of ethical *doxa* of individual liberty	"Hakim" culture of bureaucrats and respect of political agency of citizens

A deliberative ethic for development   **83**

- Mass media and local revelations of limits of "expert" technical knowledge and competence.
- Social and political science oriented research into use of techno-bureaucratic power in relation to forests (of which this paper is part).
- Local people challenging the *haakim* – such as by not using the formal greeting *Namaste*.
- Ordinary citizens learning the language of the foresters in order to subvert it.
- Radical challenge to development failures of the past four decades (including the Maoist threat).
- Emergence of more politically engaged civil society both in forestry and the national political field.
- Political limits of national developmentalist *doxa* being revealed by radical NGOs (Ojha, 2006a).

In the conclusion section, we will reflect on the potential for continuing change.

But overall, the history of recent forestry activities in Nepal reveals a continuing ethical deficit in both substantive and procedural terms. Deception and coercion have continued despite claims of increased popular participation. Attempts to improve deliberative processes have had limited local and national impact, less than the effects of the Maoist rising with its own *doxa* and *habitus* practices and associated ethics on who can deliberate. The degree of success of Nepal CF in reversing Himalayan environmental degradation must be weighed against deliberative failures resulting from the imposition of a *doxa* with its own ethical dimension legitimating a technocratic, conservationist *habitus*. This demands reframing of public debate both in procedural and substantive terms – procedurally to enhance the agency of the poor and marginalised groups to effectively participate, and substantively to expose deceptive elements in the claims to ethical authority on the part of the dominant technocratic *habitus*, and the associated element of deception utilised to reproduce social inequality.

Conclusion

The pessimistic tone of our conclusions to the case study raises the question of whether the framework we are offering here is doomed to find acute structural deliberative deficits in any field where patterns of mutually reinforcing inequalities persist over time. But we do see opportunities for conscious agency improving deliberative processes and associated procedural ethics. Our framework allows both for continuing (and even deepening) deficits and for improvement. Elements of Kantian deception can be found in any dominant *doxa* wherever gross inequalities are rationalised as being natural and inevitable. These deceptions seek to close deliberation on the reasons for inequalities. Where this closure is challenged, deceptions are exposed and demands for more open deliberation cannot be suppressed by symbolic violence alone. Then more open deliberation or increasing physical coercion may result. The key to shifting from symbolic to physical violence or more open deliberation lies in the concept of crisis.

Crisis can originate when nature dramatically challenges a psycho-social reality, when experiences fail to match doxic expectations of stability in natural processes. The Kantian contemplation of the sublime in nature is relevant here in terms of the capacity of nature to shock the rational into deeper reflection. In less elevated terms, the natural environment still has the capacity for surprise and for forcing a fundamental review of what it means to be human. Despite all the external proclamations of crisis in the Himalayan/Gangetic Plain eco-system this has not been the experiential reality of the mass of households with average sized landholdings in Nepal (Blaikie *et al.*, 2002).

Crisis can also emerge from exposure by intellectuals and activists of systematic hypocrisy, between avowed doxic ethical rules and actual performance in a field, that cannot be accepted as mere variations within *habitus* practices. The intellectual leadership of the Maoist rising can be seen as having revealed an unacceptable degree of deception by the nationally powerful elite, deception in which external donors have been complicit.

Seen through the lens offered in this paper, there is a potential for a more deliberatively open, and hence more procedurally ethical, direction of change in Nepal. But the challenge to the patterns of *doxa* and *habitus* that have reproduced deliberative deficits is not being driven by a common cause in conserving a vulnerable environment; rather by the Maoist movement's exposure of the dominant national *doxa*, and of the elite's claims to be developmental in the interest of the mass of the Nepalese people, as essentially deceptive in modified Kantian terms.

We see this as a complex crisis with a strong ethical aspect, in which more open local deliberation would be a rational response, rather than a class war seeking to exclude those complicit in previous exclusions as the Maoists claim. The situation in Nepal in 2006 is confused, and vulnerable at national and local levels to moves towards increasing physical coercion rather than to reducing deception. The modified Kantian categorical imperative then predicts a vicious rather than virtuous spiral and the situation may move beyond both Bourdieu's reproductive structures and Dewey and Habermas' free will, into bloody chaos. There is a window of opportunity for human agency acting to reduce deliberative deficits at local level but it may be rapidly bricked up if those seeking office at the national level attempt to close down local deliberative processes through electoral or dictatorial means. The most likely outcome then would be that the technocratic *doxa*, possibly in military uniform, will eventually reassert itself and an opportunity for procedural ethical gain will be lost.

Notes

1. Sal is a high value timber species found in South Asia. Much of the Colonial Indian silviculture was focused on Sal forest management, developing models of management that maximized timber.

2. The panchayat system was headed directly by the king. It had three tiers of elected body of panchayat politicians – village panchayat, district panchayat and national panchayat. Despite elections, the real power was derived from the monarchy.

References

Banjade, M. and Ojha, H. (2005), "Facilitating deliberative governance: innovations from Nepal's community forestry – a case of Karmapunaya", *The Forestry Chronicle*, Vol. 81 No. 3, pp. 403-8.

Bauhn, P. (1998), "Universal rights and the historical context", *European Journal of Development Research*, Vol. 10 No. 2, pp. 19-32.

A deliberative ethic for development   **85**

Bauman, Z. (1998), "On universal morality and the morality of universalism", *European Journal of Development Research*, Vol. 10 No. 2, pp. 7-18.

Blaikie, P. and Muldavin, J. (2004), "The politics of environmental policy with a Himalayan example", *Asia Pacific Issues*, East-West Center, Hawaii.

Blaikie, P., Cameron, J. and Seddon, D. (2002), "Understanding 20 years of change in west-central Nepal: continuity and change in lives and ideas", *World Development*, Vol. 30 No. 7, pp. 1255-70.

Bohman, J. (1999), "Democracy as inquiry, inquiry as democratic: pragmatism, social science, and the cognitive division of labor", *American Journal of Political Science*, Vol. 43 No. 2, pp. 590-607.

Bohman, J. (2002), "How to make a social science practical: pragmatism, critical social science and multiperspectival theory", *Millennium: Journal of International Studies*, Vol. 31 No. 3, pp. 499-524.

Bourdieu, P. (1991), *Language and Symbolic Power*, Polity, Cambridge, MA.

Bourdieu, P. (2001), *Masculine Domination*, Polity, Cambridge, MA.

Britt, C. (2001), "Mixed signals and government orders: the problem of on-again off-again community forestry policy", *Forests, Trees and People Newsletter*, No. 45, pp. 29-33.

Cameron, J. (1999), "Kant's Categorical Imperative as a Foundation for Development Studies and Action", *European Journal of Development Research*, Vol. 11 No. 2, pp. 23-43.

Chambers, S. (1996), *Reasonable Democracy: Jurgen Habermas and the Politics of Discourse*, Cornell University Press, Ithaca and London.

Crossley, N. (2004), "On systematically distorted communication: Bourdieu and the socio-analysis of publics", *The Sociological Review*, Vol. 52, pp. 88-112.

Dewey, J. (1916/1966), *Democracy and Education: An Introduction to the Philosophy of Education*, The Free Press, New York, NY.

Dewey, J. and Bentley, A.F. (1949), *Knowing and the Known*, Greenwood Press, Westport, CT.

Dhital, N., Paudel, K.P. and Ojha, H. (2002), *Inventory of Community Forests in Nepal: Problems and Opportunities*, ForestAction and Livelihoods and Forestry Programme, Kathmandu.

Dryzek, J.S. (2000), *Deliberative Democracy and Beyond: Liberals, Critics, Contestations*, Oxford University Press, Oxford.

Eckholm, E.P. (1976), *Losing Ground: Environmental Stress and World Food Prospects*, W W Norton, New York, NY.

Festenstein, M. (1997), *Pragmatism and Political Theory*, Polity Press, Cambridge, MA.

Fung, A. (2005), "Deliberation before revolution: toward an ethics of deliberative democracy in an unjust world", *Political Theory*, Vol. 33 No. 2, pp. 397-419.

Gilmour, D.A. and Fisher, R.J. (1991), *Villagers, Forests and Foresters: The Philosophy Process and Practice of Community Forestry in Nepal*, Sahayogi Press, Kathmandu.

Habermas, J. (1971), *Knowledge and Human Interests*, Beacon Press, Boston, MA.

Habermas, J. (1987), *The Theory of Communicative Action: Lifeworld and System – A Critique of Functionalist Reason*, Polity Press, Cambridge, MA.

Habermas, J. (1990), "Discourse ethics: notes on a program of philosophical justification", in Benhabib, S. and Dallmayr, F. (Eds), *The Communicative Ethics Controversy*, MIT Press, Cambridge, MA.

Habermas, J. (1996), *Between Facts and Norms – Contributions to a Discourse Theory of Law and Democracy*, MIT Press, Cambridge, MA.

Haller, M. (1994), *The Past as Future – Jurgen Habermas Interviewed*, Polity, Cambridge, MA, (Translated and edited by Max Pensky).

Hallett, T. (2003), "Symbolic power and organizational culture", *Sociological Theory*, Vol. 21 No. 2, pp. 128-49.

Hayward, C.R. (2004), "*Doxa* and deliberation", *Critical Review of International Social and Political Philosophy*, Vol. 7 No. 1, pp. 1-24.

Hegel, G. (1966), *The Phenomenology of Mind*, George Allen and Unwin Ltd., London.

Kant, I. (1989), *The Critique of Judgement*, Clarendon Press, Oxford.

Lachapelle, P.R., Smith, P.D. and McCool, S.F. (2004), "Access to power or genuine empowerment? An analysis of three community forest groups in Nepal", *Human Ecology*, Vol. 11 No. 1, pp. 1-12.

Malla, Y.B. (2001), "Changing policies and the persistence of patron-client relations in Nepal: stakeholders' responses to changes in forest policies", *Environmental History*, Vol. 6 No. 2, pp. 287-307.

Nightingale, A. (2005), "The experts taught us all we know: professionalization and knowledge in Nepalese community forestry", *Antipode*, Vol. 37, pp. 581-604.

O'Neill, O. (1986), *Faces of Hunger*, George Allen and Unwin, London.

O'Neill, O. (1990), "Justice, gender and international boundaries", *British Journal of Political Science*, Vol. 20, pp. 439-59.

O'Neill, O. (1996), *Towards Justice and Virtue*, Cambridge University Press, Cambridge, MA.

Ojha, H. (2006a), "Techno-bureaucratic *doxa* and challenges for deliberative governance: the case of community forestry policy and practice in Nepal", manuscript.

Ojha, H. (2006b), "Development as symbolic violence? The case of community forestry in Nepal", manuscript.

Ojha, H. and Timsina, N. (2006), *From Grassroots to Policy Deliberation – The Case of Federation of Forest User Groups in Nepal*, Forest Action, Kathmandu.

Ojha, H., Timsina, N., Khanal, D. and Cameron, J. (2006), "Deliberation in environmental governance – the case of forest policy making in Nepal", manuscript.

Owings, A. (1993), *Frauen: German Women Recall the Third Reich*, Penguin, London.

Regmi, M.C. (1977), *Land Ownership in Nepal*, Adroit, Delhi.

Scott, J. (1998), *Seeing Like a State: How Certain Schemes to Improve the Human Condition Have Failed*, Yale University Press, New Haven, CT.

Seddon, D. and Hussain, K. (2002), "The consequences of conflict: livelihoods and development in Nepal", Working Paper 185, Overseas Development Group, Norwich.

Shrestha, K. (1999), "Community forestry in danger", *Forests, Trees and People Newsletter*, Vol. 38, pp. 33-4.

Swartz, D.L. (1997), *Culture and Power: The Sociology of Pierre Bourdieu*, University of Chicago Press, Chicago, IL.

Swartz, D.L. (2003), "Drawing inspiration from Bourdieu's sociology of symbolic Power", *Theory and Society*, Vol. 32 Nos 5-6, pp. 519-28.

Timsina, N., Luintel, H., Bhandari, K. and Thapaliya, A. (2004), "Action and learning: an approach for facilitating change in knowledge-power relationship in community forestry", *Journal of Forest and Livelihood*, Vol. 4 No. 1, pp. 5-12.

Wacquant, L. (2004), "Critical thought as solvent of *doxa*", *Constellations*, Vol. 11 No. 1, pp. 97-101.

A deliberative ethic for development   **87**

Young, I.M. (1997), "Difference as a resource for democratic communication", in Bohman, J. and Rehg, W. (Eds), *Deliberative Democracy: Essays on Reason and Politics*, MIT Press, Cambridge, MA, pp. 383-406.

Young, I.M. (2003), "Activist challenges to deliberative democracy", in Fishkin, J.S. and Lasslett, P. (Eds), *Debating Deliberative Democracy*, Blackwell, Oxford, pp. 102-20.

Further reading

Bourdieu, P. (1998), *Practical Reason: On The theory of Action*, Polity, Cambridge, MA.

Habermas, J. (1990b), "Discourse ethics: notes on a program of philosophical justification", in Habermas, J. (Ed.), *Moral Consciousness and Communicative Action*, trans. Lenhardt, C., Nicholsen, S.W, MIT Press, Cambridge, MA, pp. 43-115.

Timsina, N., Ojha, H. and Paudel, K.P. (2004), "Deliberative governance and public sphere: a reflection on Nepal's community forestry 1997-2004", paper presented at Fourth National Workshop on Community Forestry, Department of Forestry, Kathmandu, Nepal.

Corresponding author

John Cameron can be contacted at: john.cameron@uea.ac.uk

[16]

The Right to Development and Its Corresponding Obligations
David Beetham

"And he said, Now, this schoolroom is a Nation. And in this nation there are fifty millions of money. Isn't this a prosperous nation? Girl number twenty, isn't this a prosperous nation, and a'n't you in a thriving state?" . . .

"I said I didn't know. I thought I couldn't know whether it was a prosperous nation or not, and whether I was in a thriving state or not, unless I knew who had got the money, and whether any of it was mine. But that had nothing to do with it. It was not in the figures at all. . . ."

"That was a great mistake of yours," observed Louisa.

– Charles Dickens, *Hard Times*

Definition of the Right to Development

This chapter is concerned with the duties, obligations, or responsibilities that are entailed by the right to development. Critical to this discussion is a clear conception of what that right involves and how it should be defined. As I am no expert on the subject of development, my primary qualification for addressing this issue must be whatever advantage exists in approaching the subject with a fresh pair of eyes. I hope that this confession will serve to explain, if not excuse, a certain skepticism on my part, not about the right to development itself, but about the dangers of conceptual inflation, or "terminological creep," to which the right seems to me intrinsically prone, especially under the pressure to achieve a political consensus among different state parties. My preference is to apply Occam's Razor to narrow the definition of the right to a minimum core meaning, which is clearly distinct from other human rights, rather than inclusive of them all, or the sum of the interrelationships among them.

In light of this approach, I find some merit in concentrating on the original idea of a nation's or people's right to economic development, however much this may require further explication in its relation to individual human rights. In my understanding, the right to development was first formulated by representatives from developing countries, particularly though not exclusively from francophone Africa, and was intimately linked to two demands: first, for a new international order, which would be more favorable to the economic development of less developed countries, and, second, for the full control by peoples over their own natural wealth and resources.[1] Both demands find a place in the 1986 UN Declaration on the Right to Development (Articles 1 and 3), although their impact is somewhat blunted by the comprehensive list of other articles.[2]

The right to development was originally asserted as a claim against the developed countries, in the context of what was perceived as a perpetuation of colonialism

1   Laurent Meillan, "Le Droit au Développement et les Nations Unies: Quelques Réflexions," *Droit en Quart Monde*, No. 34 (January 2003), p. 14.
2   Ian Brownlie and Guy S. Goodwin-Gill (eds.) *Basic Documents on Human Rights*, 4th Edition (Oxford: Oxford University Press, 2002), pp. 845-851.

through economic domination and exploitation. In its more strident formulations, the collective right to development was defined as a right specific to the Third World, and was counterposed to the individual human rights championed by the developed countries. A typical example is the statement of the foreign minister of Senegal, Doudou Thiam, in an economic conference of the group of 77 in 1967: "Il s'agit de dénoncer le vieux pacte colonial, dont la situation actuelle n'est encore que le pro-longement. De lui substituer un droit nouveau. De même que l'on a proclamé dans les Nations développées pour les individus le droit à l'instruction, à la santé, au tra-vail, nous devons proclamer, ici, hautement, pour les Nations du tiers-monde le droit au développement."[3]

This antithesis between a collective right to development and the human rights of the individual has subsequently been firmly rejected, and rightly so. It appears that the link between a nation's or people's right to economic development and individual human rights is now firmly established through two key propositions:

> 1) Without economic development, the resource constraints that limit the realization of human rights for a country's people cannot be overcome. This proposition applies as much to civil and political rights (provision of police forces, courts, legal aid, and so forth) as to economic, social, and cultural rights. This proposition is phrased carefully, so as to avoid the claim that economic development is a *necessary condition* for realizing individual human rights. As the Limburg principles on economic, social, and cultural rights insist, for example, lack of resources should never be used by states as an excuse for not progressing with a human rights program: "the obligation of progres-sive achievement exists independently of the increase in resources; it requires effective use of resources available."[4] Yet it would be difficult to contest the proposition that a condition of economic underdevel-opment and societal impoverishment constitutes a severe limitation on the range of human rights that can be effectively realized. In a re-cent article, Professor Sengupta steers a careful course through these divergent currents. "The resource constraint," he writes, "may not be quite binding if the implementation of any one human right is con-sidered in isolation. But it may be quite severely binding for any pro-gramme trying to implement all the rights." And he asserts again later: "A reduction in income poverty is almost always associated with growth. . . .With regard to the non-income variables . . . it is possible at a given moment to raise these values by reallocating the resources within a given level of income. But this cannot be sustainable, even in the medium term, without an increase in the availability of re-sources."[5]

---

3   Meillan, *supra*, note 1. [Eds. translation: "Our task is to denounce the old colonial compact and to replace it with a new right. In the same way that developed countries proclaimed individual rights to ed-ucation, health and work, we must claim here, loud and clear, that the nations of the Third World have the right to development."]
4   Limburg Principles on the Implementation of the International Covenant on Economic, Social and Cultural Rights, *Human Rights Quarterly*, 9, (1987), pp. 122-135, para. 23.
5   Arjun K. Sengupta, "On the Theory and Practice of the Right to Development," *Human Rights Quarterly*, Vol. 24 (2002), pp. 887-888.

Although an increase in resources may be realized through assistance from international donors, the only secure way to a sustainable and continuing increase in resources for a country, and to expanded economic opportunities for its citizens, is through its own economic development. Indeed, a progressive overcoming of a condition of one-sided economic dependency is what the right to development is surely about.

2) The second proposition about the relation between economic development and individual human rights qualifies the first. Not any and every process of economic development will serve to protect and enhance the human rights of a country's population, but only one that is directed toward the more equitable distribution of economic opportunities and resources. Being in a thriving nation, to use Dickens' terminology, means nothing to those who are not themselves thriving. Dickens' irony was directed not only at the socially divisive consequences of industrial "development," but even more at the schoolroom teachings of political economy that legitimized them. It has taken the experience of similarly extreme liberal economic doctrines by a much later generation to revive the realization that economic development as such can be accompanied by intensified inequalities and social exclusions of all kinds.[6]

In this context, the right to development signifies the right to a form of economic development which serves to expand the human rights of a country's people, and, through doing so, enhances their own capacity to contribute to society's further development. For the individual, it signifies the right to share in society's economic development. This second proposition, then, posits a reciprocal relation between economic development and the realization of individual human rights, not just a causal link in one direction.

My summary, then, of what I take to be the key components of the right to development in the human rights literature (both texts and commentaries) is the following: the right to development, as a nation's or people's right to economic development, is something distinct from the different individual rights of the international human rights covenants, but also intimately connected with them, both as a crucial means to, and as a product of, their progressive realization.

Inflationary Tendencies in the Concept

To elucidate and justify this relatively narrow interpretation of the right to development, one might consider inflationary tendencies found in the literature, which extend the concept well beyond this core meaning, with a corresponding danger of losing clarity of focus. Two tendencies in particular contribute to this inflation. The first trades on an ambiguity in the term "development," as between an economic process at the societal level, and the personal development of the individual. Both meanings are of course well established in scientific discourse and everyday usage

---

6 For example, UNDP, *Human Development Report 1996* (New York: Oxford University Press, 1996); Amartya K. Sen, *Development as Freedom* (Oxford: Oxford University Press, 1999).

alike; and it could well be said that the all round development of the individual constitutes the aim of any human rights agenda. However, because a term in common usage has many different meanings does not justify including them all in the corresponding human right. To make the personal development of the individual into a separate human right, say, as the sum of all other human rights, is to lose an important critical focus in the right to development. Note that I am making a clear distinction here between an individual's right to share in society's economic development (which is implicit in what has already been said above) and a separate "right to personal development."

One thing that encourages the inclusion of the latter is a certain unease about the status of collective rights in a human rights canon that has the dignity of the individual as its focus and rationale.[7] Yet, if we unpack the idea of a collective right, we find that it has two essential components. The first is that it is a right that can only be asserted and exercised collectively, by and on behalf of a *determinate group* of people (as opposed to an indeterminate group, in such terms as freedom of association, assembly, and so forth). Such are the rights of peoples to self-determination, of indigenous peoples to live as a distinct people, and of national minorities to protect their own distinctive language and culture — so, too, is it a nation's or people's right to economic development. The second is that the right in question counts as a "right" only because of the value that it has to the *individuals* in the group, and because, correspondingly, a violation of the right is damaging to the individual members of the group and to their individual well-being or dignity.

A collective right, in other words, necessarily has both a collective and an individual dimension. It is worth adding at this point that, when I use the term "nation" or "people" as subjects of the right to development, I am giving the terms no more weight than simply "those people sharing a common state and subject to its legal jurisdiction." Radical theorists of globalization and radical cosmopolitans alike would argue that only individuals can be proper subjects of a right to economic development, though for different reasons: the former, because in their view the state has, as a matter of fact, lost all power to determine its own economic policy; the latter, more normatively, because neither the state nor the nation can have any special moral significance in a scheme of global justice.[8] For neither set of theorists could people grouped as a nation have any significance as subjects of a right to development.

To counter such views does not entail believing that the division of the human race into separate states is the best of all conceivable arrangements. It is enough to acknowledge 1) that, as the world is arranged, states have a deeply embedded existence; 2) that they are still a prime locus, alongside the international level, for the creation of binding policies and regulations that matter for their citizens' well-being; and 3) that, as a result, members of a state have some special rights and responsibilities in relation to one another, which they do not have toward non-members, and

---

7   Meillan, *supra* note 11.
8   See, for example, Brian Barry, "Statism and Nationalism: a Cosmopolitan Critique," in Ian Shapiro and Lea Brilmayer (eds.), *Global Justice: Nomos XLI* (New York: New York University Press, 1999), pp. 12-66.

which give people grouped as a "nation" or "people" a normative as well as practical significance. These considerations do not entail assigning any deep metaphysical or primordial significance to the idea of national identity, and they hold sufficiently, regardless of the arbitrariness of any particular state boundaries.

If one inflationary tendency, then, in the right to development, lies in its extension to embrace an individual right to personal development, a second derives from the development studies literature and its conception of societal development as a multifaceted process. So the preamble to the 1986 UN Declaration declares that "development is a comprehensive economic, social cultural and political process," a phrase which is repeated in Article 1 of the Declaration itself. Indeed, that article continues expansively: development so understood is a condition "in which all human rights and fundamental freedoms can be fully realized."[9] Development at the societal level is indeed a multifaceted process, but it does not follow that all these facets should be included equally in the "right to development." Again, there seems to be a high price to be paid in a loss of focus by extending the right beyond the original conception of a right to *economic* development. Narrowing the concept may well be controversial, but two considerations for doing so seem to be compelling:

> 1) The centrality of resource constraints as an obstacle to realizing human rights, and of economic development in overcoming or at least mitigating these constraints, is critical. It is this centrality that defines both the distinctiveness of the right to development from the sum of individual rights and also its connection to them. When one reads the depressing litany from across the developing world of increases in infant mortality, in lost schooling, in the loss of food security, in the incidence of preventable disease, and so on, it is hard not to conclude that a condition of economic underdevelopment or distorted development lies at their root. To be sure, other factors are involved, and many of them are listed in the articles of the UN Declaration. Yet the issue of economic development is surely both paramount and general.

> 2) The more the right to development is expanded to include all possible aspects of development, the more difficult it becomes to specify what would count as a violation or infringement of the right, since almost anything might count as such, and the responsibility for not fulfilling it becomes correspondingly diffuse and unidentifiable. The UN Committee on Economic, Social and Cultural Rights has labored long and hard in trying to specify, for each right of the Covenant, "an absolute minimum entitlement in the absence of which a state party is to be considered to be in violation of its obligations."[10] It has recognized the need to do so for the rights to be taken seriously and for the responsibility for protecting them to be both clearly assignable and realizable. A broad and multifaceted conception of the right to development moves us in the opposite direction and makes assigning

---

9   Ian Brownlie and Guy S. Goodwin-Gill, *supra*, note 2, pp. 848-849.
10   Philip Alston, "Out of the Abyss: The Challenge Confronting the New UN Committee on Economic, Social and Cultural Rights," *Human Rights Quarterly* 9, 332-381 (1987), p. 353.

the responsibilities that correspond to the right impossible because they are virtually unlimited. By the same token, almost any government anywhere could claim that they were contributing to the right to development in some aspect or another. In sum, a wide definition of the right to development provides a convenient excuse for the evasion of responsibility.

Since the subject of this chapter is about defining obligations, the second consideration above is especially relevant to my purpose. If we can concentrate on *economic* development, then it at least becomes possible to specify what would count as a violation or infringement of the right to development. It would occur where 1) a government's policies or institutions are such as to damage the economic development of its people, or to encourage a markedly unequal form of that development, or 2) policies or institutions at the international level are such as to damage a country's economic development or to encourage a markedly unequal form of that development.

This is a large enough agenda to be sure. Yet at least it has the merit of identifying potential responsible agents and the kinds of responsibility that might be relevant for securing a right to development. This brings me to the main subject of the chapter.

Obligations Not to Damage or Harm

The previous section argued for a concept of the right to development, which would enable us to specify clearly what would count in principle as a violation or infringement of the right and who the responsible agents might be. These agents are governments, and their corresponding obligation is not to initiate or support policies or institutional arrangements, whether domestic or international, which systematically damage any country's economic development or encourage a markedly unequal form of that development. These are not the only obligations governments have; as with all human rights, they also have positive duties to "aid and protect."[11] However, the merit of specifying what would count as a violation or infringement of a country's right to economic development is that it concentrates attention on what everyone would agree to be a compelling obligation — not to cause damage or harm. Certainly, as with all public policy, there is room for disagreement about what exactly causes any particular damage or harm and whether such damage might be justifiable if it could be shown to be necessary to some much greater good. But it would be difficult to contest the principle that the first duty of governments, as of citizens also, is not to cause damage or harm. Since the application of this principle in relation to the right to development raises different issues at the domestic and international levels, I shall treat each separately, beginning with the international level, since it increasingly conditions the room for maneuver of domestic economic policy.

The language of responsibility in international development policy and literature is almost always couched in terms of positive duties — to give aid, assistance, and so

---

11   Henry Shue, *Basic Rights* (Princeton, NJ: Princeton University Press, 1980), p. 53.

forth, especially to the less developed countries. Article 4.2 of the UN Declaration points out that "sustained action is required to promote more rapid development of developing countries. As a complement to the efforts of developing countries, effective international cooperation is essential in providing those countries with appropriate means and facilities to foster their comprehensive development."[12] Such positive assistance is of course essential, and it remains a scandal that so few countries manage to attain even the modest UN goal of 0.7 percent of GDP devoted to this purpose. Yet the very language and policies of development assistance or "cooperation" tend to reinforce a relationship of one-sided dependency between the developed and developing worlds, and convey an image of benevolence on the part of developed countries that obscures the fact that they also pursue or support international policies that inflict considerable damage on developing countries. The idea of a violation or infringement of the right to development focuses our attention on this damage and on the failure in a primary obligation not to cause damage or harm. There are a number of significant reasons for considering the matter this way:

> 1) There is universal agreement on the obligation not to damage or harm others, whatever the relationship (or lack of it) in which we stand to them. This consideration is argued forcefully by Thomas Pogge in his latest book, *World Poverty and Human Rights*: "Our starting point . . . (is the) deeply entrenched view that any moral duty not to wrong another person, or not to harm him unduly, is much weightier than any corresponding duty to protect him against like wrongs from other sources."[13] Actually, I think Pogge overstates the case and does so because he wants to carry the argument over poverty to those who subscribe to the liberal tenet that the only general duties we owe to others are duties not to harm, not duties to aid. As I have argued elsewhere, I believe that this liberal distinction is ultimately arbitrary, since both sets of duties find their justification in the same underlying principle, namely, the supreme value that we attach to individual well-being and autonomy and the equal worth of all human beings.[14] Given, however, that so many people believe that the duty not to harm is indeed much weightier, demonstrating that the relations between developed and developing countries breach this duty constitutes a powerful and potentially far-reaching argument. As Pogge says elsewhere, "we are not bystanders who find ourselves confronted with foreign deprivations whose origins are wholly unconnected to ourselves."[15]

> 2) Providing evidence of damage to development or infringements of the right to development sets the practice of development assistance in a different moral light. Some theorists of international justice would argue that the damage inflicted turns the duty to give aid from a "duty of benevolence" to a much more compelling "duty of justice,"

---

12 Brownlie and Goodwin-Gill, *supra*, note 2, p. 850.
13 Thomas W. Pogge, *World Poverty and Human Rights* (Cambridge: Polity Press, 2002), p. 132.
14. David Beetham, *Democracy and Human Rights* (Cambridge: Polity Press, 1999), pp. 125-129.
15 Thomas W. Pogge, (ed.), *Global Justice* (Oxford: Blackwell, 2001), p. 14.

since it serves as a form of compensation for damage inflicted.[16] I think this move is mistaken, since it implies that, if the source of harm or damage were to be removed, the duty to provide aid would be much less morally compelling. Yet considerations of justice would still apply, regardless of any damage caused, whether we derive such considerations from the extension of Rawlsian principles of justice to the international sphere (as in the pathbreaking work of 1979 by Charles Beitz)[17] or, as I myself would prefer, from the injustice entailed by the failure to realize basic human rights in a world of abundance. However, even though the duties to provide development assistance are morally compelling anyway, there is no doubt that the assistance itself appears in a very different moral light if the "donors" are also implicated in policies which damage that same development. Who can fail to be shocked by calculations that show that the cost to Southern producers from Northern subsidy and protectionist regimes is many times greater than the value of the same governments' combined development assistance? Furthermore, those calculations do not include the value of all the other economic transfers from developing to developed countries.

3) Considering the matter from this point of view links the discussion on the right to development firmly with the burgeoning critical literature on the arrangements of the international economic system and the institutions and policies that sustain them — the so-called global economic architecture. The argument here is that significant features of these arrangements and the rules governing them — on trade, finance, investment, the environment — systematically disadvantage the poorest countries and damage their economic development, further intensifying global inequalities. This happens because the structure of the international economic institutions accords much greater decisional power to the governments of the developed countries, to the extent that they should be considered largely responsible for the global economic arrangements which these institutions endorse.

Two objections to this last argument are worth considering before I review the empirical evidence in support of it. The first objection is that all countries, even the least developed ones, gain more than they lose from their membership in the international economic order and are therefore better off than they would be outside it in some form of "autarchy." Even if such a proposition could be proved, it is simply beside the point. The issue is not whether economic relations between countries, taken as a whole or in principle, are a good or bad thing. It is whether those features that are particularly damaging to developing countries could be other than they are, and therefore subject to a change of policy by those with the power to effect it. Loose talk

---

16   See, for example, A. Dobson, *Justice and the Environment* (Oxford: Oxford University Press, 1998), and J. Lichtenberg, "National Boundaries and Moral Boundaries, a Cosmopolitan View," in P. G. Brown and H. Shue (eds.), *Boundaries: National Autonomy and its Limits* (Totowa, NJ: Rowman, 1981), pp. 79-100.
17   Charles Beitz, *Political Theory and International Relations* (Princeton, NJ: Princeton University Press, 1979).

about "globalization" may convey the impression that the pattern of international economic relations is an unstoppable force of nature, but actually it is structured and sustained by political decision, including decisions about what *not* to regulate, as well as what to regulate, and how to do so.[18]

A second objection is that, since developing countries are members of the international organizations in question and take part in their proceedings, they thereby demonstrate consent to the decisions that flow from them. And consent legitimates the outcomes, whatever their balance of advantages and disadvantages may be. This objection, however, is no more tenable than the first. It is notorious that in many of the relevant organizations (for example, IMF, World Bank) formal voting power is massively weighted in favor of the developed countries. And even where it is not (for example, WTO) their decisional power is still disproportionate because of huge inequalities in the resources available for research and preparation of negotiating positions, and in the relative costs to the respective parties of not reaching agreement, or of opting out altogether. Although consent obtained under conditions of inequality may convey the appearance of legitimacy, it does not meet the normative criteria established by the tradition of liberal political philosophy, which requires an original equality between the contracting parties if the outcomes are to be considered at all fair or just.[19] The recent refusal of developing countries to reach agreement at Cancun shows how prejudicial to them was the trade deal on offer, but it also exposed for all to see the inequity of the relations among the respective parties.

What, then, is the state of the evidence about the damage that is caused to the economic development of developing countries by significant and avoidable features of international economic arrangements? Here, I shall confine myself to brief summaries in three key areas — trade, finance, and the environment. What is significant is the convergence of evidence and argument on these issues between those who might be termed "insiders," such as George Soros[20] and Joseph Stiglitz,[21] with more longstanding opponents of current international economic arrangements, such as Naomi Klein[22] or George Monbiot.[23]

Trade

- Developed countries use their bargaining power to open up Third World markets to their goods, while maintaining tariffs and subsidies that damage developing countries' producers, especially in agriculture and textiles.

- Northern governments underwrite and enforce international contracts which distort development needs (for example, arms and construction) or

---

18 Paul Q. Hirst and Grahame Thompson, *Globalization in Question: The International Economy and the Possibilities of Governance* (Cambridge: Polity Press, 1996), Chapter 1.
19 John Rawls, *A Theory of Justice* (Oxford: Oxford University, 1971).
20 George Soros, *On Globalization* (Oxford: Public Affairs, 2002).
21 Joseph Stiglitz, *Globalization and its Discontents* (London: Allen Lane, 2002); and Joseph Stiglitz, *The Roaring Nineties: Seeds of Destruction* (London: Allen Lane, 2003).
22 Naomi Klein, *Fences and Windows* (London: Flamingo, 2002).
23 Geroge Monbiot, *The Age of Consent* (London: Flamingo, 2003).

saddle countries with excessive long-term payments (for example, power generation and other public utilities).

■ Technology patents, including patents on naturally occurring foods and drugs, enable Northern companies to extract large and continuing transfers from developing countries.

■ Transfer pricing enables multinational companies to avoid taxation in all jurisdictions, but it has a particularly heavy impact on countries with limited state budgets.

According to Soros,[24] "Trade liberalization all too often fails to live up to its promise. . . . Western countries pushed trade liberalization for the products they exported, but at the same time continued to protect those sectors in which competition from developing countries might have threatened their economies." Stiglitz comments that "(t)he critics are right in claiming that the WTO is biased in favor of the rich countries and multinational corporations."[25]

Finance

■ The high cost of credit for home-grown firms in developing countries increases the difficulties that they face in competing with international companies.

■ Capital market liberalization has impeded economic growth and made countries vulnerable to speculative flows, which can create or exacerbate financial crises.

■ IMF policies for countries in financial crisis have been contractionary and damaging to the public sector, burdening countries with long-term pay ments at inflated rates of interest while exacerbating the contagion effects of crisis on other countries.

Soros observes that ". . . financial markets are inherently unstable and the playing field is inherently uneven . . . Emerging market economies are suffering from capital outflows and higher borrowing costs,"[26] while Stieglitz purports that ". . . if IMF policies had simply failed to accomplish the full potential of development, that would have been bad enough. But the failures in many places have set back the development agenda."[27]

The Environment

■ Global warming, largely caused by developed countries and responsible for an intensification and frequency of extreme events such as drought and flooding, impacts particularly severely on developing countries and on populations at the margin of subsistence.

■ Demand from Northern consumers leads to rapid depletion of non-renewable natural resources in developing countries (oil, minerals,

---

24 George Soros, *On Globalization* (Oxford: Public Affairs, 2002), p. 33.
25 Joseph Stiglitz, *Globalization and its Discontents* (London: Allen Lane, 2002), p. 60.
26 Soros, *supra*, note 19, p. 123.
27 Stiglitz, *supra*, note 20, p. 76.

hardwood, fish stocks, and so forth), often causing local environmental pollution and damaging traditional livelihoods.

- The lower capacity for effective environmental regulation in developing countries is widely exploited by Northern companies and colluded in by their governments.

Lonergan posits that ". . . until there is recognition that those countries which have not caused these problems are indeed the ones that are going to suffer most, the outlook, I think, for many countries . . . is very bleak."[28]

What is being claimed here is not that the consequences of countries' increased insertion into the global economy are all negative. It is rather that those features that are particularly damaging for the economies of developing countries could be made less detrimental through a change in policy or regulation, and that the governments of developed countries must take the major share of responsibility for their persistence. International economic relations in the 1990s, concludes Joseph Stiglitz in his latest book, were "built by brute force, by dictating inappropriate conditions in the midst of crisis, by bullying, by imposing unfair trade treaties or by pursuing hypocritical trade policies — all of which are part of the hegemonic legacy that the US established in the 1990s but seem to have become worse in the next administration."[29]

National Priorities and International Obligations

The right to development of developing countries, then, is seriously infringed by international arrangements that have been initiated or sustained by the governments of developed countries, in breach of a basic obligation not to cause harm or damage to others. This happens because, as Pogge observes, "our representatives in international negotiations do not consider the interests of the global poor as part of their mandate. They are exclusively devoted to shaping each such agreement in the best interests of the people and corporations of their own country."[30] Many people would argue that they are right to do so. We share a common citizenship and many other characteristics with our fellow nationals, they argue, and are linked to them by bonds of mutual recognition and mutual responsibility. It is therefore right that both we and the governments that represent us should give priority to the needs and interests of fellow nationals over those of other nations, with whom we do not stand in any special relationship.

This common-sense viewpoint has formed the subject of lively philosophical debate between so-called "cosmopolitans" and "communitarians," the former contending that the principles of justice require that "everyone should count for one" regardless of where they live, and the latter contending, in turn, that principles of justice can apply only within bounded political communities, in which there exist strong ties of mutual recognition and an acknowledged reciprocity of obligations.[31]

28 Stephen Lonergan, "UN early warning and assessment centre, Nairobi," quoted in *The Guardian*, August 11, 2003, p. 8.
29 Joseph Stiglitz, *The Roaring Nineties: Seeds of Destruction* (London: Allen Lane, 2003).
30 Pogge, *supra*, note 12, p. 20.
31 Shapiro, I. and Brilmayer, L. (eds.), *Global Justice: Nomos XLI* (New York: New York University Press, 1999).

Neither position, however, if taken to an extreme, looks remotely plausible. We cannot ignore or eliminate the special responsibilities that we recognize and owe to our fellow nationals, yet neither can we make these the limits of our moral concern or obligation in an increasingly interconnected and interdependent world. As Samuel Scheffler has observed, we confront here "two ideas — the idea of special responsibilities and the idea of global justice — which are evidently in tension with each other . . . yet each of these ideas is rooted in values that occupy a central place in the moral outlook of many people."[32] How we might reconcile this tension, or which idea we should give priority to when they conflict, Scheffler does not consider. Yet it is one of the central questions to which any theory of human rights and their corresponding obligations has to provide a convincing answer.

What we are looking for, then, is a clear principle that will enable us to determine when, and under what circumstances, those who live in developed countries (and the governments that represent us) would be justified, indeed required, to give priority to international obligations over special responsibilities to fellow nationals, given that we must acknowledge the force of both. Two ideas may help us here. One is advanced in the recent writings of Peter Singer, who has relaxed the heroic stringency of his earlier work to accommodate the moral limitations of ordinary mortals, though his basic starting point is the same — a version of the marginal utility principle. Since the gap between living standards in the developed and developing countries is so enormous, he argues, and since relatively small sums which would only add to the marginal superfluities of the well-off would transform the lives of the impoverished, it must be justified, indeed morally required, for transfers to be made from the former to the latter, since no significant damage would be done to their basic interests or the fulfillment of their special duties to family, friends, and others by doing so. And such transfers should be set at the point which, if generalized, would enable the minimum needs of everyone for "enough to eat, clean water to drink, shelter from the elements and basic health care" to be met.[33]

This is a clear and persuasive idea in principle, except to those who acknowledge no positive duties to aid whatsoever. It serves to identify the nature of the transfers at issue, from the marginal disposable income of those whose living requirements and special responsibilities are already met and the limits of such transfers — the point where the most basic human rights are satisfied for all. It represents, we could say, a minimal, rather than a maximal, conception of international justice. Singer weakens his argument for those who take special responsibilities to co-nationals seriously with his contention that such transfers *between* countries should take priority over transfers *within* countries.[34] He provides no evidence that these are in competition with one another; rather, both are in competition with a relatively small amount of marginal expenditure of the large numbers of the well-off. Indeed, what evidence

---

32   Samuel Scheffler, "The Conflict between Justice and Responsibility," in Shapiro and Brilmayer, *supra*, note 28, pp. 86-115 (1999), p. 102.
33   Peter Singer, *One World: the Ethics of Globalization* (New Haven: Yale University Press, 2002), Chapter 5.
34   *Ibid.*, pp. 174-175.

there is indicates that those countries which come closest to achieving UN targets for development assistance (the Nordic ones) are also the ones that operate the most re-distributive policies domestically. In other words, the principles of national and international justice are mutually reinforcing in practice, rather than conflictual.[35]

Singer is primarily concerned with the issue of aid and with specifying positive duties of assistance, both by individuals and governments, to those in greatest need. Yet the right to development, as I have conceived it, looks at the obverse side of the coin, at the damage done to societies' economic development by the arrangements of the international economic order. Here a second idea seems particularly relevant for deciding between the respective claims of international justice and the special responsibilities due to co-nationals. It is advanced by Thomas Pogge in Chapter Five of his latest book, where he discusses "the bounds of nationalism." In this chapter he sets out a hierarchy of obligations, with "negative duties not to wrong (unduly harm) others" at the top. When it is a question of other kinds of duty, he argues, such as the duties to aid and protect, then "it is morally more important to attend to the needs of our compatriots than to give like assistance to foreigners." When we come to negative duties, however, the distinction between compatriots and foreigners (or between those to whom we are specially connected and third parties) becomes arbitrary, and avoiding harm to third parties must "trump" any duties to aid and protect, even those with whom we stand in a special relationship.[36]

The relevance of this principle to infringements of the right to development should be evident. Yet there are two problems with the principle as it stands, neither of which Pogge addresses. The first is a classic conceptual conundrum, to the effect that not to provide protection where we have the clear responsibility and capacity to do so is equivalent to harming, so Pogge's basic distinctions will not withstand close examination. A more practical objection is that, if governments of the developed countries were to reverse most of the policies mentioned in the previous section as being particularly damaging to developing countries, it would harm some of their own nationals and their businesses in the process. The point at issue, therefore, is not so much to distinguish among different kinds of obligation as it is how to assess the relative harms involved, to nationals and non-nationals respectively, in maintaining current policies or changing them.

By this criterion, one may thus conclude that Western nationals would experience less harm in both numbers and degree as a result of changing the policies in question than developing countries would from maintaining them. The damage to those from developed countries would be incurred by those most able to sustain it; when this is not the case, however, the governments involved have the resources to provide forms of transitional assistance that are not so externally damaging as current subsidies and protectionism. In other words, we have here the obverse of Singer's marginal utility principle; we could call it the "relative sustainability of harms" principle. And here

---

35 Charles Jones, *Global Justice: Defending Cosmopolitanism* (Oxford: Oxford University Press, 1999), Chapter 6.
36 Thomas Pogge, *supra*, note 12, pp. 132-133.

the concept of the right to development could be invoked to give support to this principle: Whereas the harms incurred clearly damage the economic development of developing countries, the same could not be said of the harms that would be incurred by already developed countries from a change in the relevant policies.

We thus have two robust principles for determining where the claims of international justice should override any special responsibilities owed to co-nationals and where international obligations should override domestic ones, whether on the part of citizens or their governments. One is the marginal utility principle, which endorses an overriding positive obligation to provide assistance to satisfy basic human rights from the discretionary expenditure of the well-off. The second is what I have called the "relative sustainability of harms" principle, which requires the elimination of international policies that damage the economic development of developing countries as an obligation that is prior to avoiding harms that might occur to nationals of already developed countries by doing so. The strong support that it provides for this second principle, in my estimation, gives the idea of the right to development its special distinctiveness and normative force within the human rights agenda.

The fact that governments in the main do not acknowledge these principles or act according to them does not render them invalid or utopian. Yet, in confronting the world as it is, those campaigning for changes in the international economic order and for greater protection for human rights should be clear about their grounds for doing so and should be able to answer deep-seated objections, one of the most pervasive of which is that governments are expected to give priority to the interests of their own nationals. Few individuals will come out publicly and say that they are against human rights, but many will challenge the corresponding obligations which are necessary if these rights are actually to be realized. Being clear about the justification for these obligations is a necessary starting point for any effective response.

At the same time, we need to understand why governments and their publics do not give these obligations the weight that they merit. Two kinds of reasons are usually advanced. One points to the moral limitations of the average citizen of the developed countries. Our moral sensibilities, it is argued, change more slowly than the world around us, and the pace of globalization has outstripped the capacity of nation-centered moralities to adapt to an expanded universe of interdependency.[37] A less generous version identifies a malign effect of neo-liberal economics, which has been to legitimate self-interest-maximizing behavior throughout public life. One consequence has been a perceived resistance to increases in taxation, with development assistance budgets declining proportionately as a result; or, where governments have increased them (as recently in the UK) they have done so only "by stealth." Yet the level of support for international NGOs suggests that public attitudes are more complex in reality, and that open and serious public debate about official aid budgets would be beneficial. Opinion surveys quoted by Peter Singer show that, although most US citizens think that the percentage of the federal budget spent on official aid is between 10 and 20 times higher than it actually is, they nevertheless believe that

---

37 Lichtenberg, *supra*, note 15, pp. 94-95.

it should be reduced. The figure that they find appropriate to "cut" it to, however, is more than five times what is actually being spent — a sum that is, in any case, a small fraction of the projected annual *increase* in the US military budget for 2003 and successive years.[38]

This brings us to a second kind of explanation, which is more relevant to Western governments' failure to end the damage done to developing countries by international economic arrangements. This is, not surprisingly, that these governments are in hock to their own producer and financial interests, on whose monetary support they rely to meet the costs of their own re-election, and who are consequently given priority and preferential access in the formation of government policy. Although this relationship finds its most extreme manifestation with the current U.S. administration, it is evident to a greater or lesser extent in all the developed countries. It demonstrates a close link between the failure to meet their international obligations abroad and the distortions to which the democratic process is subject at home.[39]

Prospects for changing this balance of moral and political forces may seem distant, but they are not hopeless. Recent years have witnessed the development of an increasingly vocal international public opinion, in which progressive forces in both developing and developed countries have combined to campaign for changes to the international economic order, with some modest successes to their credit. The emergence of a new bloc of developing countries at Cancun, under the leadership of Brazil, China, and India, may signal a turning point as significant as the development of trade unionism in the industrial era. A clearly focused "right to development" could provide a unifying rubric for the different agendas of this movement and would have a much more critical purchase than simplistic slogans of anti-globalization.

Infringements of the Right to Development by Domestic Governments

The focus thus far has been on the damage to economic development caused by international economic arrangements. An earlier section, however, identified the other source of infringements to the right to development as coming from the policies and institutions of a country's own government. Some commentators find it convenient to lay the onus for the poor economic development of developing countries on their own governments' corruption and other deficiencies, which divert attention from the responsibility of the rest of the world. Yet there is no doubting that domestic governments share some of the responsibility for economic under-development and that authoritarian regimes that are major human rights violators are among the most damaging in this respect as well.

It is at this point that the agendas for economic development and democratization converge. Other contributors to this book have written eloquently about this connection,[40] to which I will add a few remarks.

---

38 Singer, *supra*, note 33, pp. 182-185.
39 Greg Palast, *The Best Democracy Money Can Buy* (London: Robinson, 2003).
40 Sen, *supra*, note 6, Chapter 6.

First, electoral democracy on its own is insufficient either to diminish the scale of corruption or to prevent "elite capture" of the democratic process. Indeed, the costs of electoral campaigning can serve to consolidate both. With rare exceptions, the kind of economic development indicated by the "right to development" requires both strong institutions of public accountability and the emergence of political parties committed to an at least modestly redistributive and socially empowering agenda.[41]

Second, Western governments must take some of the blame for the emergence of authoritarian regimes in developing countries. In the past they have either actively encouraged or colluded in the establishment of many of them. In the present, they maintain international arrangements which allow such regimes to plunder their countries' resources and saddle their peoples with debt burdens stretching into the distant future. Here, the right of peoples to "full sovereignty over all their natural wealth and resources," pronounced in Article 1 of the UN Declaration, has proved to be something of a two-edged sword. Conceived initially to protect against neo-colonial exploitation, it overlooks the possibility that the product of such resources might be appropriated by their own ruling elites. Indeed, there is increasing evidence that the possession of substantial natural resources, especially mineral resources, diminishes the prospects for economic development, by maximizing elite discretion over the process of rent distribution, and that such resources provide a fertile soil for "coups, civil wars, oppression and corruption."[42]

At this point, it is important to insist that the rights encompassed by the right to development belong to peoples rather than to governments and that there are circumstances in which, as with any human right, they may have to be asserted on behalf of people against their own governments.[43] At what point a people may need external assistance or intervention to help protect their rights, and what form this intervention should take, are among the most pressing — and also divisive — issues in international politics today. One reason for their divisiveness is that, as this chapter has argued, we inhabit two different worlds simultaneously, each with its own distinct morality. On the one hand is the world of sovereign nation states, with the claims of nationhood, self-determination, and the normative primacy of co-nationals. On the other hand is the emerging supra-national order, with the claims of human rights, transnational justice, and universal equality. The language of the UN Declaration reflects both these worlds. Thus it emphasizes sovereignty, self-determination, and the rights of nations to their own resources and to freedom from foreign interference. At the same time, it insists on responsibilities and obligations that transcend national boundaries and that require institutions that can work only by limiting national sovereignty. How we negotiate the tensions between these two worlds and their respective moralities is the key to establishing a coherent right to development and its corresponding obligations.

---

41   David Beetham, *Democracy and Human Rights* (Cambridge: Polity Press, 1999), Chaper 5.
42   Pogge, *supra*, note 12, pp. 163-164.
43   Allan Rosas, "The Right to Development," in Asbjørn Eide, Catarina Krause and Allan Rosas (eds.), *Economic, Social and Cultural Rights* (Dordrecht: Martinus Nijhoff, 1995), pp. 247-255.

Conclusion

To make a human right realizable or effective requires not only identifying who the appropriate agents are who have an obligation for upholding the right, but also specifying what would count as an infringement of the right in question so that the scope of that obligation can be determined. I have argued that to do this for the right to development requires narrowing its definitional scope to "a nation's or people's right to economic development." An infringement or violation of this right can be said to occur "when a government initiates or supports policies or institutional arrangements, whether domestic or international, which systematically damage any country's economic development, or encourage a markedly unequal form of that development." The obligation not to act in this way ties in with a widespread conviction that we should not cause damage or harm to others. In the central part of the chapter, I examine the damage that is caused to the economic development of developing countries by current international economic arrangements, and I identify principles that will help determine when governments should give priority to international obligations over the interests of their nationals, where these conflict. Tensions between international and national moralities are explored further in the context of regimes that damage their own countries' economic development and the problems of how to address them. I conclude that, given a narrowing of definitional focus and an effective resolution of the tension between universalist and nation-centric normative demands, the right to development can serve as a coherent reference point for campaigns to reform international institutions and policies.

Part IV
Methodologies

[17]

Approaches to Evaluation of Development Interventions: The Importance of World and Life Views

ROLAND HOKSBERGEN
Calvin College, Grand Rapids, Michigan

Summary. — Differences in approaches to evaluation have been prevalent in the literature since social cost-benefit methods fell from favor in many circles in the early 1970s. Such differences are especially evident when the US AID approach is compared with the approaches of many organizations in the growing private voluntary community.

This paper argues that differing approaches to evaluation often reflect basic disagreements in alternative world and life views. To support this claim, it examines the world and life view and associated notion of the good embedded in the US AID approach (as evidenced in AID's current evaluation program) and compares this approach both with a "humanist" alternative and with the approach of Church World Service, an influential Christian private voluntary organization.

Whenever an outside agent intervenes in the development process with the intention of instigating positive change, it becomes wise for that agent periodically to step back and evaluate the effects of the intervention. Evaluation, however, is not simple. In fact, it is often a troublesome undertaking for it forces clear and precise thinking. Above all, it requires a clearly understood position as to the character of the good, because without such a position evaluation becomes an arbitrary and unconvincing exercise. Unfortunately, in recent times evaluators of development activities have often found it imprudent to state clearly their notion of the good because, once out in the open, many are likely to disagree. Perhaps it is for this reason that there is a pronounced tendency in development evaluations either to accept a very limited and noncontroversial, but also incomplete, notion of the good (e.g., it is good for life expectancy to be high), or to accept implicitly a particular, perhaps controversial, notion of the good without any clear statement of that notion. Either way, the notion of the good against which the development intervention is being evaluated is unacceptably fuzzy.

This tendency results largely from the criticism that has been launched against social cost-benefit methods of evaluation. At least a generation of development economists has been raised with the idea that social cost-benefit evaluation (SCBE) is

the most appropriate method for evaluating development interventions. Originally this method was touted as being neutral, or value-free, for it purportedly measured only the efficiency of a project in obtaining some good that had been selected prior to and external to the cost-benefit method. If this were true, then evaluators need not concern themselves with whether the objectives were ultimately good, only with whether they were being achieved. But thanks to the work of Marglin, Stewart, Squire and VanderTak, Mishan, Pearce and Nash, and others,[1] it is now widely recognized that it is impossible for SCBE to be perfectly neutral. Value judgments are inevitably made in SCBE. In particular, these authors pointed out that SCBE must necessarily make a value judgment, either explicitly or implicitly, on the equity of the distribution of benefits and costs. Such a judgment is based on some, often unspoken, notion of the good.

What I will argue, however, is that the notion of the good contained within social cost-benefit evaluation goes much deeper than is generally recognized. The notion of the good and the values permeating SCBE involve much more than the now long-discussed equity considerations. Instead, being part of the neoclassical paradigm of economics, SCBE is based on the world and life view that gives rise to the entire network of neoclassical analysis.[2] It is in part from this world and life view that the notion of the good contained within SCBE and the entire neoclassical paradigm arises.

It is important to understand better this relationship between the world and life view and approaches to evaluation because much of the evaluation literature does not clearly state the meaning of development upon which evaluation is based. As a consequence, there is a significant amount of disagreement on proper evaluation procedures. People within the UN, US AID, the OECD, and the private voluntary community have come out with a number of different approaches to evaluation and often find themselves at odds with each other.[3] Much of the disagreement centers around issues that range beyond technical and procedural matters.

The paper will proceed in the following way. The first section will bring out the relationship between the world and life view that stands behind all neoclassical analysis and the notion of the good (or judgments of value) contained within SCBE. The second part will briefly consider the approach to project evaluation of the US Agency for International Development (AID) and argue that, although SCBE is not explicitly employed, the notion of the good implicit in AID evaluations is the same as that permeating the neoclassical paradigm. The third section will go beyond the neoclassical tradition to show how different world and life views have a major impact on what are considered to be appropriate approaches to development and the evaluations of intervention in the development process.

1. THE NEOCLASSICAL WORLD AND LIFE VIEW AND THE NOTION OF THE GOOD IN SCBE

It has been commonplace since the Enlightenment to believe that science is and must be objective, that is to say, unhindered by "subjective" and unsubstantiable world and life views. But this overreaction to religious influence on scientific study is now being tempered by a renewed interest in the legitimate role of metaphysics or world and life views in science, especially social science. In the recent literature on methodology of economics, for example, a discussion of the importance of the world and life view has become increasingly prominent. Larry Dwyer has recently written that

. . . since all knowledge claims presuppose historically relative values, interests, and classification schemes, science is done from what might be called

a *Weltanschauung* or *Lebenswelt*. This conceptual perspective shapes the interests of the scientist and determines the questions he asks, the problems he attempts to solve, the answers he deems acceptable, the assumptions underlying his theorizing, his perception of "the facts," the hypotheses he proposes to account for such facts, the standards by which he assesses the fruitfulness of competing theories, the language in which he formulates his results, the categories in terms of which his experiences are organized, and so on.[4]

Or, as Royall Brandis has argued, "we cannot escape from value judgments because we must hold some world-view before we can select the axioms of the theory by which we organize empirical data. Our axioms are based on our world-view."[5] Such statements made by economists are the fruit of new developments in the philosophy of science which are restoring the world and life view to a legitimate role in scientific inquiry.[6]

It is my position that the world and life view is closely associated with the notion of the good embedded in a particular scientific paradigm. When development interventions are evaluated, the evaluation also occurs within the context of some particular scientific paradigm and on the basis of the notion of the good permeating the paradigm. What must be argued, therefore, is that SCBE, an element of the neoclassical paradigm, is infused with a particular notion of the good consistent with the world and life view that stands behind all of neoclassical analysis.

Let us consider this at greater length. It seems to me that neoclassical economics, of which SCBE is one branch, is founded on a world and life view made up of the following four propositions:

1. Human nature is such that humans are:
   a. Self-interested.
   b. Rational. That is, they know their own interest and choose from among a variety of means in order to maximize that interest.

2. The purpose of human life is for individuals to pursue happiness as they themselves define it.

3. The social world is a gathering of individuals who compete with each other under conditions of scarcity to achieve self-interested ends. As in the natural world with physical entities, in the social world, too, there are forces at work that move economic agents toward equilibrium positions.

To be considered a neoclassical, one must either accept the preceding empirically unverifiable and unfalsifiable statements or, barring overt acceptance, conduct scientific inquiry with methods based thereon.[7] To state it simply, neoclassicals *believe* that humans are rational maximizers of their own self-interest and that humans act in a rational world characterized by forces which move things toward equilibrium.[8] The first two propositions contain the motivating force in economic life (satisfaction of self-interest), and the third proposition spells out the context in which that force works itself out.

It seems fairly clear that judgments of value, of a particular notion of the good, are directly implied by propositions one and two of the world and life view. If the purpose of life is for individuals to pursue happiness and if they self-interestedly pursue this happiness, then it would certainly be good if individuals received what they wanted. Here is the basic notion of the good permeating all of neoclassical economics, that individuals should get as much as possible of what they want. Other value judgments of the neoclassical paradigm either qualify what types of individual wants will be considered or are derivative from this basic value judgment. That this basic position is, in fact, a judgment of value, or of the good, is a point willingly granted by Pearce and Nash, two proponents of SCBE. They argue that there are two basic judgments in any SCBE and the first of these is "that individual preferences should count."[9] Why should individual preferences count? For no other reason than that, according to the world and life view, the purpose of life is fulfilled only through the satisfaction of individual wants. SCBE will thus ignore group dynamics and focus on the effects of an intervention on individual satisfaction.

Pearce and Nash also agree that SCBE necessarily makes a value judgment on distributional equity.[10] But this value judgment is rather superficial, for it is external to the neoclassical paradigm. It is (regrettably) necessary for the conduct of welfare economics and SCBE, but the paradigm itself says nothing about it. Because it is external, however, it often obstructs our view of the more fundamental value judgments, those deeply embedded in the paradigm itself. These other value judgments, along with the basic value judgment, are summarized below;

1. Individuals should get what they want.
2. Competitive market equilibrium is the ideal economic situation.
   a. Competitive market institutions should be established whenever and wherever possible.
   b. Shadow prices or market prices should be used to determine value.
3. Means and ends should be completely

bifurcated into two mutually exclusive categories.
4. Means and ends should be measured quantitatively.

The second value judgment derives from elements one and three of the world and life view and from the basic value judgment that individual preferences should count. If one takes the core ideas of individualism, rationality and the social context of harmony from diverse and conflicting interests, along with a goodly number of limiting assumptions, it can be shown that competitive equilibrium maximizes the value of consumption and is therefore the best of all possible economic situations. As Harberger has said, given that the objective of economic activity is increased aggregate consumption, then

> . . . we all agree that in a world in which all markets worked perfectly, and were completely undistorted, the pursuit of this objective would entail the maximization of the excess benefits over costs, at market prices.[11]

The second value judgment is thus a different sort than the first, because it is conditional on the first. It does not stand alone. Competitive market equilibrium is good, in part, because it allows the greatest number of individual wants to be satisfied. But it is more than this as well, for this value judgment is also determined by the world and life view. Without the third proposition of the world and life view, such a judgment could not be made, for then some other economic condition could be found to satisfy individual wants as well. The world and life view prohibits such a discovery. Competitive market equilibrium is also good, therefore, because the world and life view insists that only this condition can be ideal.

The notion of competitive equilibrium carries out two basic functions: it serves as an ideal to be strived for, and it serves as a standard by which to measure the real value of current economic conditions. Because it serves as an ideal to be strived for, it leads directly to the value judgment that wherever competitive markets do not exist or are weak, they should be instituted or promoted. Wherever markets do not exist, the natural competitiveness of human beings will be channeled into other nonproductive directions, and it would be better to establish markets where this competitiveness and self-interest seeking behavior could be channeled into mutually satisfying activities. Wherever markets are weak, distortions arising from monopoly power or from government interference are sure to reduce the value of actual consumption below what it could be. Therefore, one should do what is possible to get rid of the distortions and promote perfectly competitive markets so that the ideal competitive equilibrium can be achieved.

Because competitive market equilibrium acts also as a standard against which to measure the goodness of the current economic situation, it gives the value of products and resources used in any production activity. Since the tradeoffs realized in the theoretical competitive market equilibrium are the optimal tradeoffs (i.e., recognizing the true value), then the prices resulting from these tradeoffs are used to show the true value of the goods currently being produced and the resources currently being employed.[12]

The third and fourth value judgments do not spring directly from the world and life view. Instead, they make the paradigm based thereon operational. The separation of means and ends is not strictly required by the world and life view itself, but it is an operational requirement, for without it the paradigm could generate no meaningful research or study. If means and ends were not mutually exclusive, then neoclassical economics would be nothing more than a huge tautology, a simple statement that humans do what they do because they wish to do it. There could be, for example, no inquiry into how satisfaction is maximized by choosing among various means. If some activity (e.g., production or consumption) could be both means and end, then one could not determine which part is which. As Jerome Rothenberg concedes, the intermixing of means "does violence to our paradigm and to the cost-benefit approach which depends on it."[13]

This is a judgment of value because it results in the designation of consumption as the end, and therefore the "good," to be achieved. In so doing, any process or means for obtaining higher consumption is prohibited from possessing some inherent good in and of itself. The splitting of economic activities into means and ends thus, by its very nature, promotes and encourages the achievement of a particular notion of the good. It may be an operational necessity, but it is also a judgment of value.

With means and ends separated, it becomes operationally convenient to measure quantitatively the satisfaction given by the particular ends and the dissatisfaction (costs) resulting from employing the various means. In this way, it becomes possible to measure how much better one situation is than another, for one can compare numbers instead of concepts or ideas. Things that are apparently incommensurable thus become commensurable through the use of numbers.

This is, of course, evident in SCBE where every cost and benefit is put into money figures, but it is also evident in many other branches of neoclassical analysis, even when money values are not used. If money values are unavailable or irrelevant, quantified units will take their place.

Exactly why neoclassical economics has become so enamored of quantification is hard to say. It is not required by the world and life view, nor is it absolutely necessary for conducting research within the paradigm, as is the case with the previous value judgment. Probably the most likely reason that it has taken such a central role is that neoclassical economics has, in general, adopted the methodological practices prescribed by logical positivism. For the logical positivist, precision and "objectivity" are held in highest regard; and there is, on this view, no more precise or objective unit than a number.

Whatever the case, neoclassical economics certainly encourages quantification. The emphasis on quantification also adds another element to the particular notion of the good found in neoclassical economics and in SCBE. While the third value judgment separates means and ends, the fourth value judgment tells us to focus on means and ends that can be quantified. One practical outcome of this is that neoclassical economics heavily emphasizes "things" over such areas of life as interpersonal relationships, education, cultural affairs, family, workplace organization, etc. Things are countable, while the quality of these other spheres of human life is not. What generally occurs in neoclassical economics is that these other areas of important human activity are shunted off into the corner of *ceteris paribus* and are not considered relevant. The trouble with this is that in the field of development especially, such areas are treated more often as obstacles to be removed or overcome than as other important and independently good areas of life. To the extent that this occurs, a particular notion of the good, one that focuses on quantifiable inputs and outputs, is embedded in the paradigm and in SCBE.

Thus, within SCBE and within neoclassical economics, there are judgments of value that are rooted in a fundamental world and life view. There are also judgments of value that operate in concert with the world and life view and allow the neoclassical approach to be operational. Together these judgments make up the neoclassical position on the character of the good; and when a development intervention is planned, implemented, and evaluated, it is done on the basis of these clearly defined standards.

2. THE US AID APPROACH TO EVALUATION

Although it is interesting in its own right to uncover the particular notion of the good inherent in SCBE and neoclassical economics, it is also important to notice that SCBE does not have as many committed adherents as it once did. In fact, as the thought on development shifted in the 1970s to such areas as dependency theory, Basic Needs development, self-reliance, etc., development interventions became ever smaller in size and much more diverse than they had been; and SCBE seemed less and less appropriate all the time. What has emerged in recent years is a great diversity among development agents in their approaches to development and to evaluation. Different agencies understand development in different ways, and they propose to evaluate their efforts with different methods. As this has occurred, the moorings of the different approaches to development have become less well-defined, and there seems to be no new concensus on either development or evaluation coming to the fore.

One of the interesting developments in this trend has been the relationship in the US between US AID and the nation's private voluntary community. AID was mandated in 1973 to work toward a closer relationship with the private voluntary community, and certainly it has done so. But AID and the private agencies often do not see eye to eye. In general, AID has tried to get the much smaller private agencies to conform to standard AID procedures of project planning, design, implementation, monitoring, and evaluation. To these overtures, however, the private agencies have responded with some ambivalence. They too wished for greater cooperation, but they were very uneasy about adopting the AID approach to development and particularly to their methods of project evaluation.[14] In particular, the logical framework matrix developed and promoted by AID caused them great problems. As John Sommer points out.

> . . . the logframe appeared to represent everything the majority of voluntary agencies did not: scientific exactitudes in a world of amorphous imponderables, and the triumph of statistics and computers over what were seen as fuzzy-headed do-gooder mentalities. . . . Many felt that this overly quantitative approach failed to recognize the human elements in their programming.[15]

What seems to be the problem is that much of the current unease and uncertainty about evaluation is founded upon deeper issues than just those about data collection methods, monitoring procedures, etc. Instead, it is based on a concern that the data generally collected and the focus of the entire program are misguided.

The uneasiness, I believe, is based on differences deriving from the distinct world and life views that underpin the approaches to evaluation. Even though AID has in the late 1970s shed its close ties with rigid cost-benefit evaluation, the Agency still saw (and sees) development and project evaluation from a well-defined neoclassical perspective. It is this neoclassical perspective, with associated world and life view, that people in these agencies find so objectionable.

What this section will do is point out how the position on the character of the good contained within neoclassical economics and SCBE is by and large the same position permeating the approach to development and evaluation of AID. The next section will then consider the approaches of one prominent private agency and of some "humanist" theorists and will through this comparison show the fundamental importance of the world and life view for the evaluation of development interventions.

In the late 1970s AID began a concerted effort to rigorously evaluate their work. In the 1960s, AID had adopted the use of SCBE, but in the early 1970s development theory moved toward a Basic Needs approach and in 1973 Congress passed the landmark "New Directions" legislation. In this new environment, SCBA fell from favor in both the larger development community and in AID. For a short period in the mid-1970s the evaluation program at AID floundered.[16] But the renewed efforts in the later 1970s spawned the logical framework (logframe) methods of planning, implementing, monitoring, and evaluating projects, and also led to the impact evaluation program begun in 1979 and still in operation today.[17] This program relies heavily on the logframe approach and seeks to restore consistency and reputability to the evaluation of foreign assistance passing through AID.

It is this series of impact evaluations that will receive attention in this section. The evaluation series contains five types of studies: Program Evaluation Discussion Papers, Project Impact Evaluations, Program Evaluation Reports, Special Evaluation Studies and Studies on Evaluation Methods. All of these studies are oriented toward discovering what works and what does not. The centerpiece of the series is the impact evaluations, of which there were 50 as of December 1983. The discussion papers are designed to raise important issues for consideration in the actual impact evaluations, and the program evaluations are summaries of a number of impact evaluations conducted in one given area (e.g., irrigation, nutrition). The few studies on evaluation methods are designed to help evaluators learn how to gather data with which to assess impact. Finally, the special studies deal with broad areas of concern that do not really fit into any one impact area, but are nonetheless important to the agency. This program began in 1979 and has once again brought some consistency to development project evaluation at AID. This paper will focus on the project impact evaluations.

The AID evaluation effort tends to group projects according to their primary activity. The bulk of these evaluations (40 out of 50) is taken up with projects designed to improve rural roads (8), local agricultural research capacity (8), rural irrigation facilities (7), potable water supplies (7), local education (6), and rural electrification (4). Other evaluations are spread fairly evenly over such areas as P.L. 480 food aid, institution building, health and nutrition, and private sector development. Summary program evaluations have been written for projects in agriculture research, irrigation, rural roads, potable water, and food aid. Discussion papers and special studies are spread evenly over the whole group, each area with one or two of each type of study (the private sector is the exception here with nine recently completed special studies).

Although there are exceptions (in particular the impact of education projects), the vast preponderance of material exhibits with striking regularity the same value judgments found in SCBE. The evaluations focus on individual gain rather than on interpersonal and group relationships; they encourage and applaud the establishment or extension of market institutions; they neatly separate means from ends; and they focus heavily on quantified or quantifiable variables. This is not to argue that the AID evaluations present a strikingly unified picture. They do not, for whenever this many documents are written by many different people, as is the case in this series, perfect consistency cannot be expected. Nevertheless, in spite of the exceptions, some of which are discussed below, the evaluation material does present an overall picture that is clearly of the same foundations as is SCBE.

Because it would be impossible to discuss at length each category of projects, the discussion will center around the rural roads project and the projects designed to improve potable water supplies and/or to improve health and nutrition. These latter projects are grouped because most of the potable water projects are designed to improve health by improving both water quality and quantity. These two groupings are chosen

because they are good representatives of the entire batch of evaluations and because they are different sorts of projects. Whereas rural roads projects are designed to improve agricultural production and therefore rural income, the water and health projects are derived more from the agency's Basic Needs orientation. Of these, the latter may be of greater interest, because it was this sort of project, one without a clear market relationship, that caused evaluators a lot of difficulty in the mid-1970s.

As one considers the extent to which the neoclassical value judgments are present in the evaluations, it is well to remember that, in general, explicit value judgments are seldom made (except with regard to equity). This is consistent with the neoclassical position on objectivity and neutrality. The evaluations do not make statements that give a clear understanding as to their notion of the good. Instead, evaluators prefer to use broad and imprecise terms like "rural development" or "quality of life," without specifying exactly what is meant by them. Still, the context of the evaluations implies the same value judgments already discussed.

(a) *Individualism*

Both types of projects are oriented toward essentially individual concerns. The roads projects are designed primarily to increase the personal income of local people and the health projects are designed to improve the physical health, again, of individuals. Beyond this immediately obvious orientation, however, is greater and more penetrating evidence of the individualism value judgment.

In the roads project evaluations, for example, there is repeated favorable mention of local participation and group decision-making structures. But, upon close scrutiny, one finds that in each case these structures are expected to lead to the greater satisfaction of individual wants. The Philippines evaluation notes that greater community involvement would have "brought more benefits to the rural poor."[18] The Colombia evaluation points out that village cohesiveness has improved, and this has helped the community to lobby the government more successfully for electricity, water, and other services.[19] In both cases, village involvement is good because it *leads to* benefits for the individuals, not because group involvement or village cohesiveness is good by some other standard.

In the health and water project evaluations, four of the five water projects are supposed to go beyond basic health improvements to the improvement of a more general "quality of life."

One of the main benefits here is time saved. With the time saved, the water gatherers, usually women, now have free time to engage in other activities. Activities typically mentioned are leisure, child care, income-generating production, and community involvement.[20] What is important here, and what the evaluations emphasize, is that the women are able to exercise choice from a new and broader range of alternatives. Because the range of alternatives is increased, the quality of life is improved.

Another way the individualism value judgment frequently arises in all 50 evaluations is in their treatment of women. Women are seen in the evaluations not so much as part of a legitimate social–cultural system, but as individuals with legitimate personal needs and preferences. Wherever women are allowed greater satisfaction of personal wants, and wherever their own voice becomes more powerful in decision-making, the project is applauded. Women are thus individuals whose personal wants are worthy of satisfaction, not functioning members of an alternative legitimate social–cultural system.

The emphasis on women is particularly evident in the health and water project evaluations. One powerful example of this is found in the Peru water project evaluation;

> An additional benefit not mentioned by the women was the opportunity to actively participate in community functions. In their initial meetings with the villagers the CARE staff emphasized the importance of including women in every phase of the project. Many women took part in the town meetings and two women were selected as members of the Administrative Juntas. This was a tremendous breakthrough for the women in this traditionally "macho" culture. Had the water supplies provided no other services to the village, it would seem that they were justified solely for the impact they had on women.[21]

There is nowhere in the evaluation any argument denying the legitimacy of this "traditionally 'macho' culture," and yet it is presumed to be flawed. Why is it so obvious to these evaluators and others that the local culture is unduly oppressive of women?[22] It is because women are individuals, and as individuals women have rights and legitimate preferences, just as much as other individuals in society do. If the preferences of women (as individuals) are increasingly satisfied, the impact is assessed as positive. No consideration is given in these evaluations to what this does to the broader social–cultural context.

(b) *Market promotion and market prices*

Whereas the rural roads evaluations evidence a

strong commitment to markets and the use of market prices, the health/water projects tend not to. The rural roads evaluations do not explicitly state that markets must replace current economic structures. Rather, they seem to assume that markets are good and comment only on how well the establishment of markets is progressing. The health/water evaluations, on the other hand, seem to take for granted that health, nutrition and water projects are naturally run by some public agency. To this extent, these evaluations downplay one very important neoclassical value judgment. Nevertheless, in a Special Study on how to evaluate health projects, the author argues that the only reason health/water evaluations have not emphasized the market and market prices is because it has been practically very difficult to assess the market value of health services. New procedures, he claims, are overcoming these deficiencies.[23]

The primary goal of the roads project is to increase rural incomes. The way this is to be achieved is largely through the reduction in transport costs. Two reasons are given why these costs should fall. First, because of easier access, the journeys to markets will take less time and be less wearing on animals and machines. Second, if a competitive transport industry develops on the road, then farmgate prices will be bid up by haulers anxious to gain the available business. In six of the seven rural roads evaluations (only seven of eight were available), explicit attention is paid to the reduction in transport costs, for both of the above reasons, as the key to higher incomes. The following passage from the Thailand study is typical;

> Among the more readily quantifiable effects of the road are the cost of transportation and relative prices at different locations. This is shown, for example, in Sisaket Province where the average cost of transporting paddy rice from villages to a nearby market fell nearly 30 percent after a road was opened. In Sakon Nakhon Province it was found that the average differential between the price of rice at the farm and the market fell more than 40 percent. The fall in price differential may reflect increased competition among traders as well as the decline in trasport costs.[24]

There is also another market related reason for farmer incomes to increase, and this is that higher profit margins should lead to increased production. Higher production, according to neoclassical theory, is the normal response of a self-interested and rational entrepreneur to high profits. This is the expected motivation for increased production in all seven evaluations. The Colombia evaluation states, for example, that

The keystone of this success was the sharp reduction in transport costs following the switch from animal to motorized transportation. As transport costs fell, economic incentives increased and production rose without changes in policy or such services as agricultural extension. When it was in the farmers' interest to grow more, they grew more; in rural Colombia at least, they did not have to be taught or exhorted to do so.[25]

The increased sale of cash crops for market sale is a recurrent theme throughout the evaluations, and the advent of increased market awareness and market activity is loudly applauded.

Several of the evaluations go still further. They not only applaud the improvement of markets in agricultural produce, but also praise the development of commercial activity not directly related to agriculture. All seven of the evaluations report on the development of nonagricultural commercial activity in the region of the road project. The more general business activity had increased, the more successful was the project. Quoting from the Thailand evaluation;

> Motorcycle and automobile agencies have sprung up with the advent of ARD (accelerated rural development) roads. Movie theatres, restaurants and hotels are being built in most of these towns. New stores of all kinds, especially those selling farm supplies, have opened in all major towns. . . . Retail stores selling a wide range of consumer goods have proliferated along with wholesale establishments in the larger towns.[26]

In the health/water evaluations, on the other hand, the development of market behavior receives little attention, and market prices are not used as a basic measure of value. But, according to David Dunlop, this is only because the state of health evaluation techniques is still quite primitive. Dunlop notes that most health evaluations currently use cost-effectiveness techniques. But this is a second-best alternative;

> The primary problem with such an approach is the general lack of comparative situations. Without reasonable comparative situations, it is difficult to determine the relative cost-effectiveness of the intervention under review.[27]

This approach is used, he says, only because there is as of yet no reliable way to establish true market prices. So even though the health/water evaluations do not make much of markets, there are strong currents underneath the surface that say this is only due to practical difficulties of establishing the appropriate markets.

The second half of the competitive market value judgment, that goods should be valued according to market prices, is the preferred approach of Dunlop. But the evaluations themselves show no great attention to this matter. In the rural roads evaluations, however, increased income is the goal and since income is earned according to the prices paid for the produce on the market, the magnitude of project impact is determined by market prices. The health/water evaluations do not value according to market prices or shadow prices, but Dunlop argues this is only because of practical inability, not because of theoretical impropriety.

(c) *The separation of means and ends*

In both sets of evaluations, there is convincing evidence that processes (or means) are only worth the ends they generate. In the roads evaluations, for instance, increased consumption resulting from increased incomes is the final goal, and rural roads are the means to attain this. If, however, rural roads do not generate at least the same high levels of increased income as do, say, agricultural research projects, then rural road building will fall out of favor. Or, again, if roads do achieve high gains in income and one approach to constructing roads results in more roads than another, then the first approach will be chosen. Whatever gives the greatest gains in income is the favored process. The same is true for the health/water projects. The approach that generates the greatest improvements in health is automatically rated the best. The process is not valued.

One area where the value judgment associated with this separation becomes apparent is in the treatment of community involvement in the projects. Consider, for example, the Thailand roads project. The evaluators think highly of this project, and its success is attributed largely to the fact that it was conceived of and organized by the Thai people instead of by AID personnel. Because this project is so successful, the evaluators consider the issue of replicability. The final paragraph of the evaluation contains the following statement;

> Lastly, in Thailand and elsewhere, AID might benefit from the experience implicit in its association with ARD. Our evaluation suggests that success came from long-term AID support of efforts to implement a project that the Thai had conceived, rather than from the efficient implementation of an AID project with Thai consent and counterpart assistance.[28]

In the Panama water project, evaluators note that "carefully planned efforts to secure the involvement and commitment of community residents contributed to the success of the piped water systems."[29] Notice that in neither case is success equated in any way with the fact that community members are involved in the process. Rather, in the first case success "came from" this process, and the second case the process "contributed to" the project's success. In both situations, the means of involving locals holds no independent value.

Contrast these evaluations with the Honduras roads evaluation and the Senegal health project, both of which also encouraged local participation. In Honduras, AID wanted to experiment by establishing community organizations and promoting community involvement in the road construction. Unfortunately, this approach led to major delays in the construction of the roads. The result was that the mission dropped the experiment.

> By 1977, three years after the project was signed, the mission and the GOH (Government of Honduras) decided to make up for lost time by abandoning the road construction experiment and using the capital intensive approach. Construction was further streamlined with elimination of the plans to create community awareness about the road and to develop a local maintenance capability.[30]

The Senegal evaluation has this to say about local control and participation in project management:

> There are those who argue that this "hands off" style of management is preferable since it assures that the local bureaucracy and the villagers will regard the project as theirs, and take responsibility for it. . . . This may be true, but if the project collapses, as it threatens to do, what has the "hands off" style accomplished?[31]

The evaluation then makes a statement that clearly shows the importance of achieving the ends, no matter what the process: "The basic rule should be that the project has to work, no matter what the management style, otherwise everyone loses."[32]

In both cases local involvement is encouraged until it is discovered that it just does not "work" very well. Roads needed to be built and they were not; physical health needed to be improved and it was not. The process of involving local people in decision-making and management is given no value on its own. In Thailand and Panama it worked, so it is promoted. In Honduras and Senegal it did not, so it is scrapped.

(d) *Quantification*

Probably the best indicator of the emphasis on quantified variables is the frequent lament in all project evaluations that good quantitative baseline data are not available. According to the Thailand water project evaluation, for example,

> No baseline data was ever gathered for the purpose of measuring impact, nor do health statistics exist . . . from which judgments about impact can be made.[33]

Evaluators are forced, as a result, to rely on their own subjective impressions;

> Despite the absence of confirming statistics, the increased availability of water appears to have fostered sanitary practices that have had beneficial health impacts, including decreased skin disease and diarrhea.[34]

No hard and fast data have been gathered, but the results are still put in quantifiable terms.

On the other hand, three of the seven roads evaluations are concerned with impacts that seem not to be quantifiable at all; religious life, political participation, social structure, and national unity. These impact areas are discussed in the Thailand, Colombia, and Liberia rural roads evaluations. Only in the Thailand roads evaluation, however, where national unity and political participation are important concerns, do such qualitative concerns enjoy prominence.[35] In the Liberia and Colombia roads evaluations, although nonquantifiable impacts are considered, they are mentioned more in passing than as central parts of the evaluations. As such, they are not very important to the overall evaluation.

For the health/water projects, since health is conceived as physical health, it becomes relatively easy to center on quantifiable indicators of that health. Life expectancy, infant mortality, incidence of disease, and caloric intake are all indicators of physical health and all are quantifiable.[36] In none of the health/water evaluations is there mention of any final impact that is not quantified or quantifiable. Only in the discussion of appropriate means, as with the management style of Senegal's health project, are nonquantifiable variables considered.

Another indication of the value judgment of quantification is that the health/water projects all eventually refer to the various inputs in terms of money cost. When inputs are measured this way, the means are also ultimately quantified.[37] In the end, AID can compare the quantified benefits with the money cost and decide whether the project is worthy of replication.

In the roads evaluations, projects are typically divided into two categories, economic and social. On the economic side, by far the most discussed category, there is unambiguous improvement if crop yields and farmer incomes increase. Such impacts are, of course, quantifiable and comprise the bulk of concern in the evaluations. Even on the social side, including such areas as health, education, and migration, impacts are assessed in quantitative terms. Only the Thailand evaluation with its political focus, and the Colombia and Liberia evaluations pay any noticeable attention to nonquantifiable impact. There are exceptions, but the vast majority of both sets of evaluations considers both inputs and outputs in quantifiable terms.

In many respects, then, AID evaluations are laden with the same value judgments that are embedded within neoclassical economics and SCBE. The reasons some development groups and agencies find this so objectionable will become evident as two alternative approaches to evaluation are now presented.

3. ALTERNATIVE APPROACHES TO EVALUATION — ALTERNATIVE WORLD AND LIFE VIEWS

(a) *A humanist alternative*

The first alternative is presented by W. Haque, N. Mehta, A. Rahman, and P. Wignaraja in a 1977 edition of *Development Dialogue*.[38] The approach to evaluation suggested by them is radically different than the one taken by AID, and it embodies a notion of the good radically opposed to that of the neoclassicals. The differences arise largely because Haque *et al*. hold to a world and life view that is also radically different from that of the neoclassicals.

Haque *et al*. begin their discussion of evaluation as follows:

> . . . we have outlined principles for initiating a rural development project whose fundamental objective is to enhance the political status of the exploited in a village. We have indicated that irrespective of who initiates such a project, its evolution must be seen as a self-generating process in which subsequent stages are built on the collective experience of the previous ones. For this, collective experience needs to be periodically assessed and systematized. This is the task of evaluation of the project as we see it.
>
> In this sense, evaluation is simultaneously a part of the internal dynamics of the project and an assessment of progress from the standpoint of the world view from which its fundamental objective is derived.[39]

Evaluation is thus part of the development process itself and is necessarily conducted by participants in the development project. In addition, as boldly stated above, the evaluation is to assess progress in the context of a particular

world view. In opposition, then, to neoclassicals, Haque *et al*. are not uncomfortable with recognizing their allegiance to a certain world and life view.[40]

Based on this world view (discussed in detail shortly), the authors argue, evaluation should proceed to discover if certain "values" are being achieved. The particular values most important for the evaluation will depend on the historical context of the village, for it would not be realistic to pursue an advanced value from a primitive historical condition. Nevertheless, the evaluation should proceed through four basic steps.[41] First, it should ask if the "basic institution," a forum where village members get together to discuss problems and take action, has been suitably established. If so, then evaluators should proceed to assess progress in the economic base, in attitudes of the people and in self-administration and momentum.

In evaluating the economic base, values for consideration are as follows: (1) the achievement of material gain, (2) fairness in distribution of material benefits, (3) the accumulation of collectively owned assets, (4) expansion of the project to other people and other areas, and (5) establishment of linkages and communication with other villages that are engaging in such development projects.

Attitudes that should be encouraged and evaluated are the following: (1) a sense of community solidarity, (2) democratic values (i.e., "a respect for each other's views and a desire not to impose decisions on others but to try to arrive at consensus"), (3) a spirit of cooperation, (4) a collective spirit, (5) a creative spirit, and (6) a spirit of collective self-reliance.

Under self-administration and momentum, participants in the project should improve their administrative skills, new leaders should be generated from within, and the project should become less and less dependent on outsiders for its motivating force.

Once the assessment of progress toward achieving these values is obtained, the evaluation should then proceed to the third and fourth steps by answering two yet more fundamental questions. In the words of the authors:

> The basic question to ask is whether, as a result of progress being made in the several dimensions discussed above, a change is taking place in the *social consciousness* of the target group. The development of social consciousness . . . consists of (a) an understanding of exploitation in the society and (b) liberation from psychological dependence on the exploiters which makes exploitation possible . . . .
>
> Finally, there is the question of the fundamental

task — enhancement of *political power* of the target group.[42]

The ultimate objective, then, that evaluators must be concerned with is whether the poor, exploited, and psychologically dependent rural folk are gaining political power. In each stage of a project, there must be movement toward this objective if the project is to be judged successful.

This approach to evaluation is clearly opposed to that of AID and it embodies judgments of value that are also at odds with the AID approach. Haque *et al.* have a very clear and well-defined notion of the good that includes all the values presented above and culminates in the judgment that the improved political status of the exploited masses is the ultimate concern.

For the sake of direct comparison let us consider for a moment how Haque *et al.* stand with respect to the value judgments found in the neoclassical paradigm. With respect to individualism, Haque *et al.* argue that this is one of the evils to be overcome. They believe one of the basic tasks of development is "liberation from the narrowness of individualistic thinking and the creation of the collective spirit."[43] Or again,

> Creation of a collective personality is one of the most important tasks before a mass democracy. It represents a higher stage of human evolution, rising above the narrow individualistic striving which formed the basis of the old society.[44]

Ideally, as development proceeds individual wants will be consistent with and even molded by the collective personality. Under such conditions, it would be good to satisfy them. But, if they run contrary to the collective spirit or collective personality, it would be harmful if they were fulfilled.

Although the authors never denounce markets openly, it is nonetheless apparent that the establishment of competitive markets would be anathema to their approach. Collective activity, collective decision-making, and consensus-reaching are valued in this approach and any incipient competitive forces would undermine these valued processes. What also is clear is that, ideally, productive activity would become more and more collectively planned as the society developed. The inculcation of collective values is a most important step in the development process, and once this is achieved, economic planning activities will naturally flow out of collective activity.[45] Competitive markets and market prices would presumably play little or no role in the progressive society.

The authors also see means and ends differently than do those of neoclassical leanings. Development is seen here as a process, the precise objective of which is uncertain. In fact, one of the primary ends of development is the process of development itself. Thus, there is no clear distinction between the ends and the means.

> Social change is not a discrete sequence of target-attaining, but a continuous process where the ends are inseparable from the means. A change which appears "progressive" in the abstract may nevertheless alienate the masses further, or give them distorted interests in it, if it is accomplished by, say, a bureaucratic method. For this reason the method employed for the thrust, and for that matter for any change, must be so chosen as to naturally generate the desired institutions and cultures.[46]

Haque *et al.* would never, as did the AID evaluators, say that "the basic rule should be that the project has to work, no matter what the management style." For the method, the means, the process is every bit as important as the tangible product generated by the process.

Quantification, while seen as useful in some cases, receives nowhere the same degree of emphasis as it does with the AID approach. Almost all the values cited above as valuation criteria are inherently qualitative rather than quantitative. This does not mean that quantitative indicators are useless, only that they are to be restricted.

> Being evolutionary, the project develops in stages. In some phases the development may be "quantitative" only, being growth of the same or similar form of activity in terms of increase in participation, the size of investment, diversification of activity, multiplication of the project in other areas, etc.[47]

But more important changes are qualitative changes which occur "when a higher form of cooperation is initiated."[48] Quantitative measures are thus not totally disparaged, but they are restricted to areas of importance secondary to the more important qualitative changes.

Why do Haque *et al.* espouse such a different set of value judgments, a different notion of the good, than do neoclassical thinkers? It is because they begin from fundamentally different foundations, that is, from different world and life views. From their distinct foundational springboards, each group jumps off into an entirely different universe of concepts, theories, facts, data, language, etc. The notion of the good is different because they see the world and life in totally different ways. Coming from their distinct world and life view, Haque *et al.*, in direct opposition to the neoclassical approach, conclude that individualism is to be overcome, competitive markets are to be spurned, means and ends are inextricably intertwined, and quantification is useful only in a secondary role to qualitative concerns. Their notion of the good arises not so much from objective experience, but, as with the neoclassicals, from a number of empirically unverifiable and unfalsifiable statements about the nature of the world and about the nature and purpose of life.

This is, of course, begging the question of what the world and life view of Haque *et al.* actually is. Working backward from the notion of the good evident in this approach, and also taking into account the language and the context in which the discussion takes place, I suggest that the core of the world and life view would contain the following three propositions:

1. Human beings are malleable social creatures who both adapt to and create their social environments.
2. The purpose of life is to work toward the enhancement of both individual and collective personality.
3. Both the biological world and the human social world are engaged in a process of historical evolution that moves them progressively toward higher stages of order.

These propositions, I would argue, are accepted by these authors, and perhaps other radical theorists, on faith. There is absolutely no empirical evidence that could be adduced that would result in any of these propositions being jettisoned. They are simply to be believed.

It is from such a world and life view that Haque *et al.* derive the notion that the purpose of a development project is to motivate malleable humans to transcend their current state of evolution and work to create the environments in which their individual and collective personalities can be enhanced. This is how social evolution proceeds. At present, Haque *et al.* would argue, the power wielded by some allows them to repress the creative potential of the poor and powerless. It is the purpose of a development project, therefore, to discover the sources of such "contradictions" and try to get the society as a whole to move itself to a higher evolutionary state, one in which the creative potential of all is allowed to unfold.

Consider once again some of the value judgments made in the radical approach to evaluation. Material goods are important for Haque *et al.* and the question to ask is why? Neoclassicals would say they are important because individuals want them. But the humanist approach has a different answer.

> Since this development (i.e. the unfolding of creative potential) requires improvement in the material conditions of living so as to fulfil physiological and psychic needs, the role of accumulation in the process of augmentation of production forces via technical progress and expansion of capacity becomes crucial. Without accumulation, man lives on a subsistence or low level of physio-psychic conditions.[49]

Material goods are not the end of development, but they are goods necessary for development. They are facilitators of development; they allow creative potential to unfold. Thus, the answer goes right back to propositions two and three of the world and life view.

The attitudinal criteria provide another powerful illustration. Why is it, say, that a sense of community solidarity and democratic values are encouraged to develop? First, because humans are malleable they are able to change and attitudes therefore can be changed. Second, because in order for individual and collective personality to be enhanced people have to develop attitudes that allow the group to coalesce and work together. Mutual respect and group affinity, along with attitudes that permit a collective procedure for making decisions are important attitudes to encourage. Again, the ultimate answer clearly is and must be given in the context of the world and life view.

Finally, why is it important for the humanist approach that social consciousness be raised? Again, the answer derives from the world and life view. Social consciousness must be raised because people have been molded by their historical environment, and they must learn that they are not only to be molded by the environment, but that they can also mold it. Therefore, they must learn of the sources of their current powerlessness and begin to take hold of their own destiny. As they do so, they will work to enhance the colective personality and thereby help move society to ever higher evolutionary stages.

(b) *The alternative of one Christian private voluntary organization*

Having looked at neoclassical and humanist approaches to evaluation and their relationships with their respective world and life views, consider now the approach of Church World Service (CWS), a Christian development agency. CWS is the development arm of the US National Council of Churches (NCC), an affiliation of a large number of Protestant denominations in the US. The NCC itself is affiliated with the global World Council of Churches. CWS is, therefore, an explicitly Christian agency and operates out of a world and life view different from either of the previous two.

As with Haque *et al.*, CWS is not uncomfortable with admitting both that it holds to a particular world and life view, and that it analyzes social problems and works toward solutions within the context of that world and life view. It is a continual effort on the part of CWS to make their development work consistent with their fundamental world and life view. For this reason, CWS has written position papers and working papers that try to work out the implications of its basic world and life view for its various activities.

In one such position paper, "The Nature of Church World Service," the point is made that God is the creator of the world, the director of the universe, and the ultimate source of guidance for people here on earth. God created humans perfect, in his own image, but they fell into sin and brought upon themselves the problems that humans have experienced ever since the fall of Adam and Eve.

> As bearer of the God image, man/women is also a responsible being, able to choose between good and evil, right and wrong, obedience to God or obedience to self, which is the source sin of all other sin. Man/women, in the use of that freedom, chose/ chooses self-obedience and is sinner. Sin results in alienation, estrangement, conflict.[50]

But God, in his goodness, did not leave humans to dwell in their self-inflicted misery.

> One can in fact observe that the whole biblical story from Genesis to Revelation, and indeed the entire history of Israel and the Church, represent a struggle to bring humanity, creation and the Creator into the kind of all-inclusive reconciliation signified in the word shalom.[51]

The major event in this struggle was the death and resurrection of Jesus Christ, God's son, who came to earth as a man both to pay the price for human sin and to give humanity a new hope for the world to come. In his death and resurrection, Christ conquered sin forever, and

> . . . he is already sovereign of all created existence . . . ., but the brutal alienating forces of pride and selfishness have not yet come under his submission.[52]

Thus, misery is not yet removed from our presence, and it never will be until Christ comes again. How then are humans to conduct their lives?

> . . . in Christ's forgiving grace we keep pressing forward toward the call of God in Christ Jesus, seeking to be more like his new humanity and less like the old from which he has set us free.[53]

As humans struggle toward this new humanity, this "shalom," it must be recognized that

> . . . God's eternal purpose was established in creation itself, and moves toward fulfillment. All of creation is moving not just toward an end, but toward that purpose. Its full dimensions are not yet clear, but it is understood as God-like-ness.
>
> To be in serving community is to accept the call to participate in that purpose. That call is judgment and is hope, for the future is God's.[54]

Based on the foregoing, the world and life view of CWS seems to contain at least the following propositions:

1. God created all that exists, and he created humans in his own image.
2. God created a perfect world which, through human choice, fell into sin.
3. God is at work redeeming his fallen world, and righteous humans are both witnesses to the new "shalom" and transforming agents.
4. The purpose of human life is to participate in God's purpose, that is, to obey him.

Again, there is nothing in the empirical world which tells CWS that these propositions are true. The people at CWS simply believe them; they are the springboard into the analysis of world problems and to their solution.

But what does such a world and life view mean for development and for evaluation? CWS understands it to mean that world poverty and inhumane living conditions are products of sin and that Christians must work toward restoring the shalom that is God's community. CWS interprets this as enhancing the "quality of life" of people everywhere. According to CWS,

> CWS's theological perspective leads it to affirm that a life of quality results when fundamental moral and ethical values are manifested in and promoted by the social, political, economic and personal dimensions of life.[55]

In addition to this, a life of quality is possible when physical necessities of life are available, spiritual fulfillment is realized, people engage in purposeful activity, people participate in decisions that affect their own lives, and peace, security and harmony reign in individuals, communities, and nations.[56] Finally, CWS believes justice and sustainability are important elements in the quality of life. Justice here is more than equitable distribution, for "when justice prevails, power is used for sharing and caring, not for economic, political and social exploitation of others."[57] Sustainability refers to the belief that humans must seek to live in shalom, not only with other people, but also with the creation at large. Human activity must therefore preserve the resources God has given in his creation to the whole of humanity.

This understanding of the quality of life is also CWS's understanding of the good. It will define the purpose and character of any development activity, and it will also be the standard against which CWS evaluates its activities. As with the humanist alternative, production activities are only part of the development picture. When development projects are designed and evaluated, therefore, the whole range of important elements in a life of quality are considered.

Unlike the previous two approaches, CWS has not developed a comprehensive approach to evaluation. With the AID approach, the evaluation methods are clear, while the world and life view is obscure. With CWS, it is just the opposite; the world and life view gets a fair amount of attention, but evaluation procedures have not yet been well worked out. Nevertheless, there are some CWS working papers on evaluation that shed some light on CWS thinking on evaluation.[58]

For example, because the CWS approach to development places such a high emphasis on participation, on the inculcation of values, on the shalom community, it is interested in much more than just the attainment of concrete objectives.

> For CWS, the object under evaluation is the development process underway, not development projects *per se*. This implies that judgments, about growth in self-reliance, exercise of local initiative, or qualities of organizational capabilities are equally, or perhaps more important than, the success of projects with respect to stated objectives. It implies that evaluation will center around people rather than forms.[59]

Development, more than anything, is a process by which people come to an understanding of the shalom community God intended them to live in. Any stated objectives that are to be achieved in a project, while very important, are nevertheless either subordinate to, or of equal value with, the building up of the community, that is, with the process of development.

> Effectiveness or efficiency are not the sole criteria for evaluation of CWS related programs, ... it is the process rather than activity or results that is being evaluated.[60]

Whereas for AID it does not seem important who conducts an evaluation, as long as they are knowledgeable and know how to obtain and assess the right data, and whereas for Haque *et al.* the evaluation is to be conducted by the participants themselves, CWS takes the middle ground and claims it is important for both

insiders and outsiders to be involved in the evaluation.

> Evaluation of CWS related programs requires assessment by project participants as well as by project sponsors in order to be complete. Comprehensive evaluation includes information and judgments from "internal" and from "external" sources.[61]

Because process is basic, it is important for participants to be involved. But because participants, too, are partially blinded by sin, and because "external" sources are part of the broader Christian commuunity, their insights are also crucial. Such outsiders are to be people well versed in the Christian world and life view.

Because CWS sees humanity in the context of God's call to follow him and to be part of his plan of restoration, it also recognizes that different people find themselves at different places on their pilgrimages to God's shalom. For this reason project design will depend much on the local situation and evaluation approaches will likewise differ.

> Evaluation can take place at a variety of levels and with varying degrees of formality. . . . The character of an evaluation will be shaped by the special circumstances it's designed to address.[62]

Above all, CWS believes evaluation is important to assess its work in the kingdom of God, to assess its service in the community that God has established. Perhaps the most important part of this is restoring the broken relationships that have resulted from human sin. In keeping with this task of restoration CWS believes that

> . . . the purpose of evaluation is growth in understanding in order to strengthen relationships among Christian colleague agencies. Understanding, not control, is the objective of CWS in evaluation.[63]

The real purpose of evaluation is to help build up the community through mutual understanding.

4. CONCLUSION

AID is an influential actor in the world's development picture, but it has its own particular view of what development is, how development interventions should be conducted, and how they should be evaluated. Haque *et al.* present a humanist alternative that is radically opposed to that of AID. CWS offers a third approach that sees the problems and solutions in yet a third light. Many of their differences arise not because one or the other side has not carefully examined the available evidence, nor because one side or the other is infected with "false consciousness" or unscientific ideology, but because all three approaches simply start from different premises about what life is all about and how the world is put together. All three groups have internally respectable positions once one accepts the propositions of their respective world and life views. If, however, one does not accept the world and life view, neither will one agree with the notion of the good embedded in the associated approach to evaluation. Most likely one will reject the whole paradigm. Once the world and life view is rejected there is no amount of empirical evidence that could be presented that would prove the truth or validity of the paradigm.

For some this may be a troubling view, for if taken to extremes it may mean we are in for times of ever-increasing polarization. Certainly the polarization between Marxist and neoclassical capitalist approaches to economics and society is already well advanced. And, because there is large number of widely held world and life views, perhaps the polarization will worsen. I do not believe, however, that such is inevitable, for there is common ground in many of the world and life views and, consequently, in how people believe society ought to live together and ought to develop.

On the other hand, what I am certain of is that development theorists cannot go on pretending that science is objective from some ultimate standpoint. We cannot continue under the assumption that world and life views have no relevance for social scientific inquiry or that we do our work without some particular notion of the good embedded therein. Nor can we await the day when the methods of scientific inquiry (e.g., hypothesis testing) will lend empirical credence to one world and life view over against another. By its very nature, the world and life view is not open to such review.

In the development of societies the recognition of the foundational world and life views is particularly important because everybody seems to know what the people of Third World countries *ought* to be doing. Such "knowledge" derives from some very basic faith statements that give character to one's entire range of knowledge and determine, in large measure, how development ought to be promoted and how it ought to be evaluated. It should be no surprise, then, that agencies like AID and those of the private voluntary community do not see eye to eye on these issues. They simply cannot if they hold true to their own basic convictions. What is most important at the present is that we recognize the source of many of these disagreements and go on from there.

NOTES

1. Marglin (1977); Stewart (1975); Squire and VanderTak (1975); Mishan (1980); Pearce and Nash (1981); Green and Waitzman (1980).

2. A world and life view is here taken to mean a set of empirically unverifiable or unfalsifiable basic statements about the nature of the world and about the nature and purpose of life.

3. Compare, for example, the following works: United Nations (1978); US Agency for International Development (1981); Murelius (1981); Pietro (1983). For an analysis of several approaches to evaluation, which makes a similar argument to the one made here, see Elzinga (1981).

4. Dwyer (1982) p. 76.

5. Brandis (1963), pp. 47–48. Other writers who have introduced the world and life view into discussions on methodology include Duhs (1982), McKenzie (1981), and Katouzian (1980).

6. It might be argued that Thomas S. Kuhn and Imre Lakatos laid the groundwork for the reintroduction of the world and life view into the disucssion on methodology, even though they themselves did not consider the idea. By introducing the ideas of "paradigm" and "scientific research programs," they left the door open to the reinstatement of the world and life view as the foundation of scientific work. For example, Lakatos' "hard core" is hardly distinguishable from a world and life view. Though neither Kuhn nor Lakatos is much concerned with methodology of social science as opposed to physical science, it is in the social sciences that the introduction of the world and life view makes the most immediate sense. For more on this, see Thomas (1979).

7. Many contend that they do not ultimately "believe" these propositions, only that they accept them and some logically consistent and consequent propositions as "useful assumptions" in the conduct of their work. From a philosophy of science perspective, however, such a position is wholly untenable, the product of shoddy methodology. In the philosophy of science, it is known as instrumentalism and receives a severe denunciation from Imre Lakatos: "instrumentalism is a degenerate version of (conventionalism), based on a mere philosophical muddle caused by a lack of

elementary logical competence." Quoted in Caldwell (1982), p. 52.

8. Reading recently an article on Friedman and Monetarism, I came unexpectedly upon the following statement: "Friedman takes consistent optimization as an article of faith." In other words, it is part of his world and life view. Hoover (1984), p. 69.

9. Pearce and Nash (1981), p. 10.

10. *Ibid.*

11. Harberger (1977), p. 228.

12. According to Sassone and Schaffer (1978), if markets exist for every good, if there are no distortions, and if all markets are in competitive equilibrium, "then economic theory has established this very important result: all goods have market prices, and the market prices are exactly equal to the corresponding shadow prices (true social values)" (p. 58). In practice, neoclassicals cannot be absolutely sure when markets are in competitive equilibrium. In full-blown SCBE, attempts are usually made to establish suitable shadow prices. In smaller scale evaluations, however, it is common to accept actual market prices as acceptable approximations.

13. Rothenberg (1975), p. 57. For example, if the production activity of human labor would be more than just a means — say, if work were good in and of itself regardless of the final product — then it would be impossible for the neoclassical to discover how much individual wants are satisfied by the activity. The ends and the means would be all mixed together, and it would be impossible to speak of the value of the product and cost of the resources independently.

14. See, for example American Council of Voluntary Agencies for Foreign Services, Inc. Reports on three workshops held in 1981 and 1982.

15. Sommer (1977), p. 82.

16. Several AID reviews of evaluations from this period show the confused nature of the AID evaluation program. See, for example, Berry *et al.* (1980), p. xii, or Crawford and Barclay (1982), p. 39.

17. The logframe provides four important elements for effective project management in the AID context; a causal-hierarchy of inputs, outputs, purpose, and higher goal; hypotheses about means–ends linkages; articulated assumptions about external influences; and verifiable progress indicators. See Turner (1976), pp. 26–30.

18. Levy *et al.* (1980), p. ix.

19. VanRaalte *et al.* (1979), p. 10.

20. Meehan *et al.* (1982), p. 8; Haratani *et al.* (1981), p. 8; Chetwynd *et al.*, (1981), p. 10.

21. Haratani *et al.*, (1981), pp. 8–9.

22. See, for example, Meehan *et al.* (1982), p. 8; Gilmore *et al.* (1980), p. 10; or for rural roads, Roberts *et al.* (1982), pp. 15–16.

23. Dunlop (1982), p. 14.

24. Moore *et al.* (1980), p. 10.

25. VanRaalte *et al.* (1979), p. vi.

26. Moore *et al.* (1980), p. 12.

27. Dunlop (1982), p. 14.

28. Moore *et al.* (1980), p. 61.

29. Meehan *et al.* (1982), p. 15.

30. Hamilton (1981), p. 10.

31. Weber *et al.* (1980), p. 7.

32. *Ibid.*

33. Dworkin and Pillsbury, *et al.* (1980), p. 7.

34. *Ibid.*, p. 8.

35. In Thailand, one of the initial motivations of the project was to curb the communist insurgency in isolated villages. Although the thrust of the project is to increase rural incomes, evaluators take note of how loyalty among the Thai villagers to the present government has increased. They mention the enthusiastic political participation and the enhanced religious life. The important thing here seems to be that roads have led to increased participation of isolated Thai people in the life of the nation. The project thus succeeded in promoting a more cohesive body of people. See Moore *et al.* (1980).

36. The Panama water project (Meehan *et al.* 1982), is exemplary in its reliance on quantifiable indicators. See especially the project logframe in the Appendix.

37. Of the eight available evaluations the four successful ones calculate the cost per beneficiary of the project. See Dworkin and Pillsbury *et al.* (1980), p. 6; Haratani *et al.* (1981), p. 13; Meehan *et al.* (1982), p. 14; and Gilmore *et al.* (1980), p. 12. For the unsuccessful projects, since no benefits were generated, cost calculations are not so important, because the cost-effectiveness ratio would be infinity in all cases anyway.

38. This "humanist" alternative is presented in Haque *et al.* (1977), pp. 1–137.

39. *Ibid.*, p. 8.

40. Haque *et al.* (1977), however, have a different notion of a world view than is understood in this paper. I argue that the world and life view precedes and gives a foundation to the scientific paradigm, while Haque *et al.* seem to argue that a world view is based on scientific

inquiry. "We have also taken the world view that society is not a homogeneous entity, and that social relations are characterized by contradictions. This world view is based on scientific knowledge already existing" (p. 71). It is characteristic for both neoclassicals and radical humanists to believe that their respective approaches are the "objective" and scientifically correct views. The view presented in this paper counters such thinking.

41. The following material on evaluation is from pp. 126–131.

42. *Ibid.*, pp. 129–130.

43. *Ibid.*, p. 51.

44. *Ibid.*, p. 57.

45. *Ibid.*, p. 62.

46. *Ibid.*, p. 50.

47. *Ibid.*, p. 123.

48. *Ibid.*, p. 123.

49. *Ibid.*, p. 14.

50. Church World Services (n.d.), p. 1.

51. Lara-Braud and Schlachtenhaufen (1974), p. 1.

52. *Ibid.*, p. 2.

53. *Ibid.*

54. Church World Service (n.d.), p. 3.

55. *Ibid.*, p. 4.

56. *Ibid.*

57. *Ibid.*, p. 5.

58. Church World Service (1977).

59. *Ibid.*, pp. 1–2.

60. *Ibid.*, p. 6.

61. *Ibid.*, p. 3.

62. *Ibid.*, p. 6.

63. *Ibid.*, p. 1.

REFERENCES

American Council of Voluntary Agencies for Foreign Service, Inc., "Approaches to Evaluation," Reports on three workshops held in 1981 and 1982.

Berry, Leonard *et al.*, "The impact of irrigation on development: Issues for a comprehensive evaluation study," US AID Program Evaluation Discussion Paper No. 9 (October 1980).

Brandis, Royall, "Value judgements and economic science, " *Quarterly Journal of Economics and Business*, Vol. 3, No. 2 (1963).

Caldwell, Bruce, *Beyond Positivism: Economic Methodology in the Twentieth Century* (London: Allen & Unwin, 1982).

Chetwynd, Eric Jr. *et al.*, "Korea potable water systems project: Lessons from experience," AID Project Impact Evaluation Report No. 20 (May 1981).

Church World Service, "Program and project evaluation," Working Paper No. 8 (May 1977).

Church World Service, "The nature of Church World Service" (New York: n.d.).

Crawford, Paul R., and A. H. Barclay, Jr., "AID experience in agricultural research: A review of project evaluations," US AID Program Evaluation Discussion Paper No. 13 (May 1982).

Duhs, L. A., "Why economists disagree: The Philosophy of irreconcilability," *Journal of Economic Issues*, Vol. 16, No. 2 (March 1982), pp. 221–236.

Dunlop, David, "Toward a health project evaluation framework," AID Evaluation Special Study No. 8 (June 1982).

Dworkin, Daniel M., and Barbara L. K. Pillsbury *et al.*, "The potable water project in rural Thailand," AID Project Impact Evaluation Report No. 3 (May 1980).

Dwyer, Larry, "The alleged value-neutrality of economics: An alternate view," *Journal of Economic Issues*, Vol. 16, No. 1 (March 1982).

Elzinga, Aant, "Evaluating and evaluation game: On the methodology of project evalaution, with special reference to development cooperation" (A SAREC Report, 1981).

Gilmore, Judith *et al.*, "Morocco: Food aid and nutrition education," AID Project Impact Evaluation Report No. 8 (August 1980).

Green, Mark, and Norman Waitzman, "Cost, benefit and class," *Working Papers for a New Society*, Vol. 7, No. 3 (May-June 1980), pp. 39–51.

Hamilton, John, "Honduras rural roads: Old directions and new," AID Project Impact Evaluation Report No. 17 (January 1981).

Haque, W. *et al.*, "Toward a theory of rural development," *Development Dialogue*, Vol. 2 (1977).

Haratani, Joseph *et al.*, "Peru: CARE OPG water health services project," AID Project Impact Evaluation Report No. 24 (October 1981).

Harberger, Arnold C., "On the UNIDO guidelines for social project evaluation," in Hugh Schwarz and Richard Berney (Eds.), *Social and Economic Dimensions of Project Evaluation* (Washington D.C.: Inter-American Development Bank, 1977).

Hoover, Kevin D., "Two types of monetarism," *Journal of Economic Literature*, Vol. 22, No. 1 (March 1984).

Katouzian, Homa, *Ideology and Method in Economics*, (New York: New York University Press, 1980).

Lara-Braud, Jorge, and Harold Schlachtenaufen, "Theological Position Paper for Church World Service," CWS Working Paper No. 1 (10 June 1974).

Levy, Irvin *et al.*, "Philippines: Rural Roads I and II," Project Impact Evaluation Report No. 18 (March 1981).

Marglin, Stephen A., "The essential of the UNIDO approach to benefit-cost analysis," in Hugh Schwarz and Richard Berney (Eds.), *Social and Economic Dimensions of Project Evaluation* (Washington: Inter-American Development Bank, 1977), pp. 199–210.

McKenzie, Richard B., "The necessary normative context of positive economics," *Journal of Economic Issues*, Vol. 15, No. 3. (September 1981), pp. 704–719.

Meehan, Robert *et al.*, "Panama: Rural water," AID Project Impact Evaluation Report No. 32 (May 1982).

Mishan, E. J., "How valid are economic evaluations of allocative changes?", *Journal of Economic Issues*, Vol. 14, No. 1 (March 1980).

Moore, Frank J. *et al.*, "Rural roads in Thailand," AID project Impact Evaluation Report No. 13 (December 1980).

Murelius, Olof, *An Institutional Approach to Project Analysis in Developing Countries* (Paris: OECD, 1981).

Pearce, D. W., and C. A. Nash. *The Social Appraisal of Projects* (New York: John Wiley, 1981).

Piertro, Daniel, *Evaluation Sourcebook: For Private and Voluntary Organizations* (New York: American Council for Voluntary Organizations in Foreign Services, 1983).

Roberts, John E. *et al.*, "Kenya: Rural roads," AID Project Impact Evaluation Report No. 26 (January 1982).

Rothenberg, Jerome, "Cost-benefit analysis: A methodological exposition," in Marcia Guttentag and Elmer L. Struening (Eds.), *Handbook of Evaluation Research*, Vol. 2 (Beverly Hills: Sage, 1975).

Sassone, Peter G., and William A. Schaffer, *Cost-Benefit Analysis: A Handbook* (New York: Academic Press, 1978).

Sommer, John, *Beyond Charity: US Voluntary Aid for a Changing World* (Washington D.C.: Overseas Development Council, 1977).

Squire, Lyn, and Herman G. VanderTak, *Economic Analysis of Projects* (Baltimore: Johns Hopkins University, 1975).

Stewart, Frances, "A note on social cost-benefit analysis and class conflict in LDCs," *World Development*, Vol. 3, No. 2 (January 1975).

Thomas, David, *Naturalism and Social Science: A Post-Empiricist Philosophy of Science* (Cambridge: Cambridge University Press, 1979).

Turner, Herbert, "Principles and methods of program evaluation," *International Development Review*, Vol. 3 (1976).

United Nations, *Systematic Monitoring and Evaluation of Integrated Development Programs: A Source Book* (New York: UN, 1978).

US Agency for International Development, *Evaluation Handbook: 2nd Edition* (Washington D.C.: USAID, 1981).

VanRaalte, G. R. *et al.*, "Colombia: Small farmer market access," AID Project Impact Evaluation Report No. 1 (December 1979).

Weber, Richard *et al.*, "Senegal: The Sine Saloum rural health care project," AID Project Impact Evaluation Report No. 9 (October 1980).

[18]

The Implications and Value Added of a Rights-Based Approach

Jakob Kirkemann Hansen and Hans-Otto Sano

Introduction

The past seven years or so have seen a remarkable growth in the interest in and pro-motion of what has been termed a "rights-based approach," (RBA) in which goals and processes of international assistance reflect the principles and norms embodied in the international human rights instruments.

Rights-based approaches are not necessarily confined to development activities, but they have received particular attention within this sphere. Efforts to reinforce human rights and democratization as a cross-cutting or important element in devel-opment work have without any doubt contributed to the fact that rights-based approaches have become almost exclusively related to the field of development. It must be emphasized, however, that such approaches could well become integral elements in other efforts of planned and institutional change, say in developed coun-tries.

We see rights-based approaches primarily as a means of integrating human rights principles and aspirations into measures of planned and institutional change. An im-portant caveat — and one that we seek to keep in focus throughout this chapter — is that rights-based approaches are not, and should not be, applied to all economic, social, political, and institutional change. Human rights principles are relevant in the field of development, and human rights should permeate development efforts, but there are certainly areas of the development universe where human rights may have a lesser role to play in determining what is done and not done.

This is then a crucial point of departure of this chapter: Rights-based approaches will imply a different design of development interventions, but not of all develop-ment interventions. There is a certain caution which needs to be asserted in making a rights-based approach a panacea for all development efforts.

The increased attention to a rights-based approach has taken place in an interna-tional human rights climate where the importance of economic, social, and cultural rights is being reconfirmed; where poverty is repeatedly being stated as a denial of human rights; and where there is a growing consensus that the current human rights challenge has gone beyond standard setting and has become one of implementation. These changes are matched, in part, by the development world through an accept-ance of human rights as a legitimate concern for international assistance and a view that development assistance should remain poverty-focused in deed as well as in words. Development interventions should be human-centered and process oriented with concepts of empowerment, accountability, and participation as common currency.

In this chapter we examine the emergence of rights-based approaches to development and explore the aims, implications, and value of adopting the approach. The rationale of a rights-based approach is that human rights and development are interconnected and that it "adds value" to this relationship. But what exactly is the value added and what policy or institutional changes are implied? In addressing these questions, the chapter takes its point of departure in existing notions and practices of rights-based approaches and examines and clarifies the conceptual elements and modes of operationalization. It critically examines the inherent assumptions, strengths, and weaknesses in order to suggest ways to make a rights-based approach operational in development assistance.

Much uncertainty exists on the interpretation of what a rights-based approach may imply for donors and beneficiaries of development aid. This chapter is inspired by an objective of addressing this uncertainty. In seeking realistic ways of making human rights succeed in development assistance, we hope to clarify some of the prevailing questions.

The first section of this chapter traces origins of rights-based approaches and examines positions of relevant actors and agencies in order to show the variety of definitions that exists.

The second section examines the policies and practices of development agencies that define their work according to the principles of a rights-based approach. These principles are universality, indivisibility, accountability, participation, empowerment, and non-discrimination.

The third section asks what the underlying assumptions of rights-based approaches are. How are they justified? What are the strengths and weaknesses of these approaches? To what degree are the inherent assumptions and propositions sound? Based on this examination, an operational definition is proposed.

The final and concluding section of the chapter discusses the value-added dimensions of the rights-based approach and its limitations.

Background

At a conference in 2000, the High Commissioner for Human Rights stated that:

> Poverty eradication without empowerment is unsustainable. Social integration without minority rights is unimaginable. Gender equality without women's rights is illusory. Full employment without workers' rights may be no more than a promise of sweatshops, exploitation and slavery. The logic of human rights in development is inescapable.[1]

A rights-based approach to development shares this logic, or more specifically, would be the operational expression of it.

---

1   Mary Robinson, United Nations High Commissioner for Human Rights at International Conference, "Stopping the Economic Exploitation of Children: New Approaches to Fighting Poverty As a Means of Implementing Human Rights?" (Hattingen, Germany: February 22-24, 2000).

However, the exact nature of the logic is not clear. Indeed, it could be said that the role played by the interrelationship between human rights and development has been contested almost since the adoption of the Universal Declaration of Human Rights in 1948 (UDHR). Later, contestation erupted about the right to development, and disputes arose on the interrelationship between categories of rights, whether political and civil rights could be sacrificed for development or whether any development had to be foregone by a political system based on the respect of the rights. Discussion on the interrelationship not only became entangled in the politics of decolonisation but also quickly became a point of confrontation in the Cold War. The human rights regime was seen as questioning the sovereignty of states, and it was often asked if there was an underlying liberal-capitalist agenda being attached to the imposition of human rights in development.[2]

Discounting the purely political reasons for various blocs taking their respective positions, many challenged the justification of economic and social rights, and thus important linkages between human rights and development. Economic and social rights were disputed on the grounds that they were collective rights; that they confused goals and rights by entailing positive obligations that could not realistically be fulfilled; and that they identified no specific duty holder — in sum, they lacked the cogency and justiciability that were argued to be intrinsic to the nature of human rights.[3]

In fact, human rights and development remained two separate spheres institutionally and operationally well into the 1980s, and the recent rapprochement between them rests on a number of events or advances, politically, conceptually, and institutionally which have come together to create the circumstances that imbue the logic of a rights-based approach with its rationale.

While the drafters of the UDHR might have imagined a close interrelationship between economic, social, cultural, civil, and political rights, as well as between these rights and development, controversy during the drafting process codified these rights in two separate treaties and placed development in a different sphere altogether. The adoption in 1986 of the Declaration on the Right to Development can be seen as an attempt to realign development with human rights and emphasize the interrelationship of human rights as envisaged by the UDHR. In its preamble, the Declaration held that human rights and development were inter- dependent. It further stated that the right to development is "an inalienable right by virtue of which every human person and all peoples are entitled to participate in, contribute to, and enjoy economic, social, cultural and political development, in which all human rights and fundamental freedoms can be realised."[4] It went on to provide that "the human person is the central subject of development and should be an active participant and beneficiary to the right to development."[5] The main duty-holder of the right to develop-

---

2 Kevin Boyle, *Stock-taking on Human Rights: The World Conference on Human Rights* (Vienna: 1993), pp. 89 ff., i. In David Beetham (ed.), *Politics and Human Rights* (Oxford: Blackwell, 1995), pp. 79-95.
3 David Beetham, *Democracy and Human Rights* (Cambridge: Polity Press, 1999), p. 115.
4 Declaration on the Right to Development, adopted by the General Assembly Resolution 41/128, of December 4, 1986.
5 *Ibid.*

ment remained the state, but much more emphasis s placed on the obligations of the international community to facilitate development and effectively remove obstacles for the realization of the right to development.

A change in the international political climate was necessary before the issues raised by the right to development again came to the fore. With the demise of the Soviet Union, a new global order started to emerge based on principles of democratization, participation, and international cooperation. A new sense of international commitment could be discerned, together with a recognition of the need to strengthen the international community in a globalized world, where the challenges to be addressed stretched beyond the bounds of any single nation state.

In this new political environment, many of the old divisions were laid to rest, and human rights gained a new prominence in international politics.[6] Targets for development, first set forth during noteworthy conferences and summits of the 1990s,[7] were later adopted at the Millennium Assembly of the United Nations and elaborated in concrete terms in the Millennium Report. The Millennium Development Goals are often referred to as reflecting a rights-based approach, especially by UN organs. In human rights terms, however, the Vienna Declaration of 1993, establishing an agenda for the new world order, was more significant and underscored the indivisibility and equal priority of all rights — economic, social, cultural, civil, and political. Not least, it recognized that democracy, development, and human rights are interdependent and mutually reinforcing.[8]

With these political changes, the relationship between human rights and development started to move from being conceptual toward being intentional, in the sense that key actors within the development community started to integrate human rights concerns into their mandates and policies. Thus, the 1990s saw a host of supportive statements on the interdependence of development and human rights, especially in terms of policy declarations on the need for further integration, mainstreaming, collaboration, and analysis. In response to this new interest, an Independent Expert on the Right to Development was appointed in 1998 and started to define the scope and nature of the right to development. Efforts were intensified to clarify the content of economic and social rights.

If the post-Cold War political climate recharged the human rights agenda and confirmed the interdependence between human rights and development, it was the conceptual work around economic, social, and cultural rights that provided much of the normative elements needed to operationalize the relationship in terms of rights. The general comments of the Committee on Economic, Social, and Cultural Rights and documents such as the Maastricht Guidelines and Limburg Principles have done

---

6 Hans-Otto Sano, *Good Governance, Accountability and Human Rights*, in Hans-Otto Sano, Gudmundur Alfredsson, and Robin Clapp G. Alfredson (eds.), *Human Rights and Good Governance*, (The Hague: Martinus Nijhoff, 2002), pp. 123-146.
7 Notably, these were the *Rio Conference on Environment and Development* in 1993, the 1994 UN *International Conference in Cairo on Population and Development* in Cairo, the 1993 *World Conference on Human Rights* in Vienna, and the *Copenhagen Social Summit* in 1995.
8 General Assembly, Vienna Declaration, and Programme of Action, UN Doc. A/CONF.157/23 (July 12, 1993).

much to dilute the stark contrast between civil and political rights on the one hand, and economic and social rights on the other. The focus on economic and social rights also devolved the traditional attention from a strict state-centered human rights regime toward other duty-bearers and sparked the elaboration of new methods and means of accountability that went beyond strict legal procedures — a development that was important in operationalizing a rights-based approach.

Another trend in international relations emphasizing the role of human rights was the reform process of the UN that started in 1997, in which human rights were reconfirmed as a key priority of the UN. Accordingly, human rights became a cross-cutting issue for the four main fields[9] of the UN. The call of the Secretary-General on all entities of the UN to mainstream human rights into their activities represented a political endorsement and heightened interest in a rights-based approach. Through the 1990s, the relationship between human rights and development moved from an academic acknowledgement toward a growing willingness to operationalize these intentions.

A final set of influences in support of a rights-based approach to development was a movement from a growth-centered to a more human- and poverty-centered agenda of development. Already during the 1970s, the idea had emerged that development should be directed toward basic needs. Other concepts started to surface that highlighted the importance of gender and vulnerability in development, the value of participation and ownership for effective sustainability, and the "holistic nature" of poverty. Even more important was the introduction of the concept of good governance by the World Bank during the late 1980s. While initial definitions of the concept were mainly technical and apolitical, it implied a re-emergence of the state as a central actor within the development paradigm. These conceptual innovations not only highlighted a number of issues already central to human rights, but also led to the development of tools and practices that have influenced subsequent attempts to integrate human rights into development activities.

Defining a Rights-based Approach

The Office of the High Commissioner for Human Rights (OHCHR) has defined a rights-based approach in the following manner: "A rights-based approach to development is a conceptual framework for the process of human development that is normatively based on international human rights standards and operationally directed to promoting and protecting human rights . . . ."

Furthermore: "A rights-based approach to development includes the following elements:

- express linkage to rights
- accountability
- empowerment

---

9   Peace and security; economic and social affairs; development cooperation; and humanitarian affairs. See Secretary General's Report, *Renewing the United Nations: A Programme for Reform.* UN Doc. (A/51/950) (July 14, 1997).

- participation
- non-discrimination and attention to vulnerable groups."[10]

The definition adopted by OHCHR, which is also used by other UN members like the UNDP, can be compared to a definition used by Care International, which states:

> For CARE, a rights-based approach deliberately and explicitly focuses on people achieving the minimum conditions for living with dignity. It does so by exposing the roots of vulnerability and marginalization and expanding the range of responses. It empowers people to claim their rights and fulfil their responsibilities. A rights-based approach recognizes poor, displaced, and war-affected people as having inherent rights essential to livelihood security — rights that are validated by international law.[11]

Both of the definitions quoted relate a rights-based approach to a particular type of development: a focus on poverty, equity, or marginalized groups and a focus on rights-related empowerment and participation. For Care International, however, a rights-based approach is not tied narrowly to human rights. For OHCHR, there is a strong emphasis on non-discrimination and accountability.

The major distinction between these two definitions is, therefore, that the former may focus equally on duty-holders and on rights-claimants inasmuch as this definition emphasizes accountability, while the latter has a point of departure in rights-based empowerment — that is, in the claims of the rights-holders. Both of the definitions imply, however, that a rights-based approach presupposes a particular character of development — that is, one based on equity, poverty eradication, participation, and empowerment. Interpreted in this way, a rights-based approach becomes an integral element of a human development approach characterized by key concepts such as participation, empowerment, and support for vulnerable and marginal groups.[12]

In commenting on the relationship between a human development approach and a rights-based approach, Arjun Sengupta, the Independent Expert on the Right to Development appointed by the UN Commission on Human Rights argues that:

> The human rights approach to development added a further dimension to development thinking. While the human development approach aims at realizing individuals' freedom by making enhancement of their capabilities the goal of development policy, the human rights approach focuses on the claims that individuals have on the conduct of State and other agents to secure their capabilities and freedoms.[13]

---

10   Available at www.unhchr.ch/development/approaches.html.
11   CARE statement on "A Rights-Based Approach to Achieving HLS," ALMIS # 5250, November 2000, quoted in CARE, *Promoting Rights and Responsibilities* (June 2001), p. 11. Available at http://www.interaction.org/files.cgi/2496_Analysis_of_RBA_Definitions1.pdf. (Accessed November 12, 2005.)
12   The human development approach became a strategy of organizations organizations such as UNDP and UNICEF during the late 1980s and early 1990s. Development with a human face, based on conceptions of human capability, poverty eradication, participation, environmental safe-guards, and gendered empowerment were characteristic traits.
13   Commission on Human Rights, Open-Ended Working Group on the Right to Development. *Fourth Report of the Independent Expert on the Right to Development*, Arjun Sengupta, submitted in accordance with the Committee Resolution 2001/9, UN Doc. E/CN.4/2002/WG18.2 (December 20, 2001).

Added to this perspective of claiming rights, however, the more recent thinking on rights-based development emphasizes the accountability of the duty-holders.

There are, therefore, three possible criteria defining a rights-based approach:

- A rights-based approach makes explicit reference to human rights achievement as an integral part of the objectives of development. This is what is expressed in the definition of OHCHR when "express linkage to human rights" is mentioned.[14] Inherent in this interpretation is that human rights achievement can be understood as one among several other objectives of development.

- A rights-based approach is a framework for the process of human development, operationally directed to promoting and protecting human rights. Thus, while goals other than rights-based goals can be involved in a rights-based approach, the latter must still be associated with a kind of development that reinforces human development and human rights; thus, dimensions of accountability of duty-holders will often be in focus in rights-based approaches.

- A rights-based approach empowers people to claim their rights. This criterion anchors a rights-based approach with empowerment of right-holders. Some actors such as Care International do not refer to human rights, but to rights in general.

As evident from the definitions above, these options are often mixed. What is characteristic of the definitions introduced above is the reference to substantive contents such as accountability, participation, empowerment, and anti-poverty — in short, the emphasis on a human development agenda combined with an emphasis on rights. Among these combined definitions between the normative and non-normative contents, however, it is not clear which principle is the prevailing one.

In the discussion below, we seek to clarify this balance by looking more closely into the assumptions of a rights-based approach.

The Scope of Rights-Based Development

One major question is the scope of rights-based development. How far does it extend in terms of reorganizing development interventions and support? To what degree should development agencies in general incorporate the notion?

In interpreting the right to development, the UN's Independent Expert on the Right to Development establishes a close linkage between a rights-based approach and the right to development. In his third report, the Independent Expert states:

---

14   ODI, the Overseas Development Institute, earlier defined a rights-based approach accordingly: "A rights-based approach to development sets the achievement of human rights as an objective of development policy" (1999). Compared to the formulation of OHCHR, the ODI formulation is more restrictive inasmuch as realization of human rights is set as the goal and objective of development policy. Interpreted in this way, human rights realization will define what development policy should be. The later formulation of OHCHR provides for a less rigorous way of implementing a rights-based approach.

> Regarding the right to development as a human right implies two things, especially when that right refers to a process of development. First, the realization of each human right and of all of them together has to be carried out in a rights-based manner, as a participatory, accountable and transparent process with equity in decision-making and sharing of the fruits of the process while maintaining respect for civil and political rights. Secondly, the objectives of development should be expressed in terms of claims or entitlements of rights-holders which duty-bearers must protect and promote in accordance with international human rights standards of equity and justice.[15]

The assumption here that the objectives of development should be expressed in terms of claims or entitlements of rights-holders which duty-bearers must protect and promote, represents a quest for restructuring development processes, including the granting of development aid: Objectives of development have to be put in rights terms.

According to this understanding, however, the Independent Expert is promoting a very broad — and not, in our view, realistic — model that expects rights-based approaches to guide all development efforts. A similar rights-based approach was once suggested by André Frankovits and Patrick Earle, of the Human Rights Council of Australia, who argue that: "In effect, human rights and development are not distinct separate spheres. Development should in fact be seen as a subset of human rights."[16]

This position can be read as a grand scheme for the restructuring of development assistance according to human rights norms and instruments. Some human rights scholars tend to argue that the traditional development model has failed and that it has had a negative or detrimental impact on poor or marginalized populations. One question remains important, however: Can a rights-based framework remedy the structural or institutional ailments of the developing world? Or more specifically, when development policies have failed, is it because of a failure to include a rights framework, or is it because of political interference, corrupt state leaders and institutions, inadequate resources or capacity, or local class or political struggles?

Our view that a broad and all-encompassing approach is not realistic is partly based on an understanding of existing practices of development, where only a few cases of rights-based approaches prevail. More important, however, is our contention that a reorganization of development programs according to an all encompassing rights-based pattern must be based on a realistic assumption of real value-added in incorporating a human rights approach in all corners of development thinking. It cannot be based only on a normative interpretation.

---

15 Commission on Human Rights, Working Group on the Right to Development. *Report of the Independent Expert on the Right to Development,* Arjun Sengupta, pursuant to General Assembly Resolution 54/175 and Commission on Human Rights Resolution E/CN.4/Res/2000/5. UN Doc. E/CN.4/2000/WG.18/CRP/1 (2000), p. 8.
16 André Frankovits and Patrick Earle, *The Rights Way to Development: A Human Rights Approach to Development Assistance, Policy and Practice* (Maroubra: The Human Rights Council of Australia, Inc., 2001), p. 25.

Operational Strategies for the Application of Rights-Based Approaches

The Relationship Between Concepts and Operationalization

One critique of rights-based approaches concerns the alleged discrepancy between human rights principles and the reality of rights. Bas de Gaay Fortman states that while "the whole world appears to have a mouth full of human rights, in terms of implementation one might still speak of a crisis."[17] He argues that the basic weakness of human rights is that they are mainly proclaimed rather than implemented.[18]

Surely, that the reality does not correspond to the law does not necessarily remove the relevance of the law. Indeed, as Jack Donnelly has brilliantly argued, the paradox of rights is that the fewer you possess, the more important they become.[19]

Another, more serious aspect of the critique, is purported by Peter Uvin, arguing that rights-based approaches introduce little more than "rhetorical, feel good change"[20] or serve as "a fig leaf for the continuation of status quo,"[21] with little to offer in the way of operational practice. As always, it is refreshing when someone points out that the emperor has no clothes. While acknowledging the discrepancy between the conceptual and operational level of rights-based approaches, however, we posit that the discrepancy between the normative and the operational level stems not from conceptual sinister motives, but rather from the fact that rights-based approaches originate from legal principles, which are still in the process of being inscribed into practice.

Common Principles of Rights-Based Approaches?

A critique of rights-based approaches calls attention to the importance of their operational implications and questions whether they will change the reality of those in need. Hence, we ask: What does a rights-based approach have to offer current development paradigms? What kind of changes do rights-based organizations propose? How are program areas changed?

The ways in which organizations conceptualize a rights-based approach differ, as has been noted, and these differences become even more apparent when one examines how organizations operationalize the approach. Variations are unavoidable — and indeed necessary — for organizations operating with different mandates, programs, and implementation capabilities. For an approach where central values are said to be coherence, transparency, and an increased possibility for coordination, some consistency might, however, be warranted.

Despite these differences, it is possible to discern a number of common constituent elements or principles within the various applications of a rights-based

---

17 Bas de Gaay Fortman, "'Rights-Based Approaches': Any New Thing Under the Sun?" IDEA Newsletter (December 2000).
18 *Ibid.*
19 Jack Donnelly, *Universal Human Rights in Theory and Practice* (New York: Cornell University Press, 2002).
20 Peter Uvin, *On High Moral Ground: The Incorporation of Human Rights by the Development Enterprise*, p. 1. Available at http://fletcher.tufts.edu/praxis/archives/xvii/Uvin.pdf.
21 *Ibid.*

approach. While the terms may vary, most organizations emphasize principles such as universality, interdependence between rights, accountability, participation, non-discrimination, and empowerment.[22] A closer examination of these principles and how they have been interpreted and translated into practice follows.[23]

Universality

In human rights terms, universality relates to the foundational principle of the Universal Declaration, stating that "recognition of the inherent dignity and of the equal and inalienable rights of all members of the human family is the foundation of freedom, justice and peace in the world." A broad understanding of the principle could translate needs into rights held by "all people, everywhere, and at all times," simply by virtue of being human. It implies both an aspiration, namely that the enjoyment of rights should become universal (and thus, areas with an identified rights deficit should be targeted), and an obligation, namely that all individuals should be treated as holders of rights. In essence, then, by being a question of rights rather than charity, development transforms itself into a matter of justice.[24]

These principles were promoted by the UN Secretary General as one of the defining aspects of a rights-based approach:

> A rights-based approach to development describes situations not simply in terms of human needs, or of development requirements, but in terms of society's obligations to respond to the inalienable rights of individuals. It empowers people to demand justice as a right, not as a charity and gives communities the moral basis from which to claim international assistance where needed.[25]

Similar statements can be found by others who support a rights-based approach. UNDP notes that the vision of a rights-based approach is "to secure the freedom, well-being and dignity of all people everywhere."[26] UNICEF explicitly adopts universality as an overall guiding principle,[27] and both Oxfam and Sida express similar notions on the universal normative relevance and on the need to view development "beneficiaries" as rights-holders.[28]

Formally, the principle of universality within a rights-based approach has been argued to mean that all development programming should have the objective of

---

22   Craig G. Mokhiber, *Human Rights in Development: What, Why and How* (Geneva: UN OHCHR, 2000).

23   It is important to note that when we refer to "operationalize" or other terms relating to operationalization, we are primarily referring to intentions, guidelines, and action plans; we are not determining how or if these have been carried out in practice. In general, a number of organizations applying a rights-based approach have not moved beyond the intentional or piloting phase.

24   Stephen Marks, *The Human Rights Framework for Development: Five Approaches.* UNDP Global Forum on World Development, October 2000.

25   Annual Report of the Secretary-General on the Work of the Organization, UN Doc. A/53/1 (August 1998).

26   UNDP, *Poverty Reduction and Human Rights: A Practice Note* (June 2003).

27   UNICEF, *A Human Rights Approach to UNICEF Programming for Children and Women – What It Is, and Some Changes It Will Bring,* UNICEF Doc. CF/EXD/1998-04 (April 21, 1998). Available at http://www.coe-dmha.org/UNICEF/HPT_IntroReading01.htm.

28   Sida, *Democracy and Human Rights in Swedish Development Cooperation* (February 1999). Available at http://www.sweden.gov.se/content/1/c6/02/04/00/ab9c2080.pdf.

improving human rights. In real terms a universal application of human rights as the explicit goal of development may test the relevance of their application and many rights-based organizations take more implicit strategies for the promotion of human rights. In general, initiatives taken to promote the universality of human rights fall within three categories, ranging from the most to the least explicit: 1) promotion of a specific human right, 2) building the capacity of human rights-relevant institutions, and 3) promotion of human rights values or the creation of an enabling environment.

OHCHR argues for the first of these approaches, stating that "the explicit reference to rights as the objective of development and the establishment of express links to international, regional and national human rights instruments is a crucial element of a rights-based approach." This argument has been supported mainly by NGOs, such as Oxfam, but also by UNICEF, which define their programs in terms of the promotion of specific rights or classes of rights.

UNDP and Sida define the relationship mainly at the policy level and confine rights objectives to specific projects targeting primarily the two later categories.[29] These types of initiatives have been taken up generally by classical development organizations, thus broadening the agenda of what would be considered "development territory." UNDP continues to be concerned with classical good governance issues as well as with participation and empowerment in terms of creating an enabling environment for human rights, and its projects now also include support to parliaments, ombudsman, and national human rights institutions.[30] The approach taken is primarily an add-on approach, which does not necessarily explicitly target human rights within specific programs and projects.

Indivisibility

The principle of indivisibility of rights was strongly supported by the Vienna Declaration and by the Independent Expert on the Right to Development and has become an important element of a rights-based approach. In its positive form the principle denotes that a sustainable advancement of any right will depend on a similar advancement of all other rights. A negative reading of the principle stresses that no right should be pursued to the detriment of any others. The OHCHR defines the principle by stating:

> Rights-based approaches are comprehensive in their consideration of the full range of indivisible, interdependent and interrelated rights: civil, cultural, economic, political and social. This calls for a development framework with sectors that mirror internationally guaranteed rights, thus covering, for example, health, education, housing, justice administration, personal security and political participation."[31]

---

29 A third practice may be observed in organizations that adopt programs using the vocabulary of rights, but referring to what is arguably self-styled rights, a practice that may potentially undermine the carefully devised universal system.
30 UNDP, *Integrating Human Rights with Sustainable Human Development: A Policy Document* (New York: UNDP, 1998); UNDP, *A Human Rights-Based Approach to Development Programming in UNDP – Adding the Missing Link* (New York: UNDP, 2001).
31 Mokhiber, *supra*, note 22.

In general what the principle brings to development is a focus on the need for "holistic" programming or a comprehensive development agenda. Organizations operationalize a rights-based approach through a number of changes, including instituting:

- new areas of programming,
- new modes of analysis,
- increased coordination, and
- ground rules for development.

A comprehensive mode of development planning involves the adoption of new program areas focusing on non-economic aspects of poverty reduction. Most rights-based organizations stress the need for inter-sectoral strategies and approaches and the need to establish synergies among different program types. UNDP emphasizes that a rights-based approach requires particular attention to institution building, democratic support, and legal and policy reform. However, little attention is paid to how laws and social norms affect target groups of UNDP programming,[32] and changes are, in practice, related primarily to good governance programming. Sida emphasizes support for elections, media support, and judicial capacity-building programs as an immediate effect of the introduction of a rights-based approach.[33] UNICEF also emphasizes the need for holistic programming but stresses the corresponding need for integrated strategies combining advocacy, communication, and capacity and partnership building.[34] On the basis of their adoption of a rights-based approach, Oxfam has defined completely new program types, including a particular program on equitable participation in political, economic, and social policy- and decision-making.[35]

Holistic programming will call for new and more comprehensive situation analysis for program preparation. Additionally, acknowledging that few organizations can cover the full spectrum of rights, all organizations recognize that operationalizing comprehensive programs will require more coordination with other organizations. For UNDP, this is being done through the Common Country Assessment/UN Development Assistance Framework (CCA/UNDAF) procedures,[36] but otherwise, few organizations elaborate how this requirement is to be put into practice.

The final implication of the principle of indivisibility — that no program should act to the detriment of any human rights — has been explored in policies of only a few donors. UNDP, however, has developed a formal check list to avoid programming that may violate human rights. NORAD has also included this in its *Handbook on Human Rights Assessment.*[37] It seems surprising, however, that this dimension, which has been extensively considered within the humanitarian field, has not been explored more within rights-based development programming.

---

32 UNDP, *Poverty Reduction and Human Rights: A Practice Note* (June 2003).
33 Sida, *supra*, note 28.
34 Available at http://coe-dmha.org/Unicef/HPT_IntroReading01.htm.
35 Oxfam, *Strategic Plan 2001-2004* (Oxford: Oxfam International, 2001).
36 UNDP, *supra*, note 32.
37 NORAD, *Handbook in Human Rights Assessment* (February 2001).

Accountability

Accountability may be the principle where a rights-based approach distinguishes itself most clearly from other approaches to development. The principle is obviously a common requirement for all development activities. What is special about accountability within a rights-based framework, however, is that the principle is legalistic and focuses on how to transform rights-holders from being passive recipients of aid to being empowered claimants.

Once needs are transformed into rights, downward accountability is emphasized, along with accountability to donors.[38] Accountability within a rights-based framework focuses on organizational accountability and accountability between duty-bearer and rights-holder. This implies attention to new modes of account-ability such as laws, policies, institutions, administrative procedures, and other mechanisms of redress.[39]

The UN agencies mirror the definition of the OHCHR, and most other rights-based organizations also identify the same principles as central to increasing accountability. The operationalization of these principles, however, differs. Most initiatives group around three sets of activities:

- Analysis focusing on rights-holders and duty-bearers,
- Increasing the accountability of duty-holders, and
- Strengthening organizational procedures for accountability.

As noted, increasing accountability in programming to a large extent evolves around a focus on the relation between duty-bearers and rights-holders. As noted by Carolin Moser and Andy Norton, a potential limitation of a human rights perspective on accountability is the overriding focus on state-citizen relationships as the basis of obligations and corresponding rights.[40] The expansion of duty-holders to include the full range of relevant actors, such as individuals, states, local organizations and authorities, private companies, aid donors, and international institutions, is a necessary trait of a rights-based approach, but also one that points to the difficulty in keeping a strictly legally centered approach when exporting the rights-based ideals into a broader development agenda.

In general, various strategies are taken depending on the nature of the duty-bearer and the mandates of the rights-based organization. UNDP, thus, continues to work primarily with state accountability and applies what can be termed a capacity-development perspective. The focus of UNDP in this regard is not human rights, but rather the added value to development. UNDP states that "without a sound legal framework, without an independent and honest judiciary, economic and social development risks collapse."[41] In increasing the accountability of duty-holders, the

---

38 This should not be taken to imply that rights-based development does not require accountability toward donors.
39 *Ibid.*
40 Caroline Moser and Andy Norton, *To Claim Our Rights: Livelihood, Security and Sustainable Development* (London: Overseas Development Institute, 2001).
41 UNDP, *The Application of a Human Rights Approach to Development: What Is the Added Value?* Available at http://www.undp.org/governance/docshurist/rightsapproach.doc.

human rights framework offers a stronger and more stringent system for target setting and benchmarks.

Oxfam's strategy focuses less on capacity building of duty-holders than on global advocacy for human rights. They thus take the more confrontational role associated with traditional human rights work.[42] They also are more concerned with a related aspect of accountability –namely, strengthening the ability of individuals and civil society to claim and monitor rights. This dimension will be further examined in relation to the principle of empowerment below.

Lastly, a rights-based approach is generally acknowledged to require accountability not only to outcomes, but also to the processes of development. This naturally applies to all stakeholders, but also to the aid organization itself. OHCHR notes the need of rights-based organizations to pay "due attention to issues of accessibility, including to development processes, institutions, information and redress or complaints mechanisms."[43] While few organizations go as far, most organizations seek to enhance accountability by focusing on increased participation of beneficiaries and acknowledge the need for institutional accountability in terms of management based on organizational efficiency, openness, and accountability.

Participation, Non-Discrimination, and Empowerment

Participation, non-discrimination, and empowerment are distinct principles, but the consequences for rights-based organizations overlap somewhat. As these principles are not specific to a rights-based approach, it is important to identify their specific contributions to this approach.

Participation

In instrumental terms, participation enables people to make effective decisions on issues affecting their own lives. Rights-based approaches require "a high degree of participation, including from communities, civil society, minorities, indigenous peoples, women and others. Such participation must be 'active, free, and meaningful,' so that mere formal or 'ceremonial' contacts with beneficiaries are not sufficient."[44]

Participation should be seen as intrinsic to the process of development, and, understood as the broader aim of creating public participation, should itself be seen as one of the objectives of development. Initiatives to operationalize this principle fall within two categories: 1) increasing participation in programming and 2) increasing public participation through programming (see non-discrimination).

Increasing participation within programming relates primarily to a number of requirements to project cycle management. Aid organizations emphasize that participation must include all phases of programming, including formulation, implementation, and monitoring. The second aspect focuses especially on strength-

---

42 Oxfam, *Strategic Plan 2001-2004* (Oxford: Oxfam International, 2001).
43 Mokhiber, *supra*, note 22.
44 OHCHR, *What Is a Rights-Based Approach?* Available at http://www.unhchr.ch/development/approaches-04.html.

ening the involvement of media, interest groups, or civil society in public decision-making. Oxfam goes further and focuses also on international issues of participation, such as advocacy efforts on equitable access and the need for reform of the international decision-making bodies.

Non-Discrimination

Access to public decision-making by minorities or vulnerable groups is an important dimension of participation in development. Non-discrimination implies "[g]iving particular attention to discrimination, equality, equity and vulnerable groups. These groups include women, minorities, indigenous peoples and prisoners, but there is no universal checklist of who is most vulnerable in every given context."[45]

Discrimination goes beyond the economic sphere and emphasizes how laws, polices, or administrative practices may create or combat structural discrimination. A rights-based approach highlights the fact that a great deal of poverty originates from political, social, cultural, or institutional discriminatory practices — both overt and covert — at the international, national, and local levels. Operational implications relate primarily to methodological requirements and targeting the vulnerable.

The need to identify the vulnerable population in development programs is noted by all organizations examined in this chapter. UNDP notes that programs should account for those whom they reach as well as those whom they do not.[46] Targeting the vulnerable is generally seen as an issue of mainstreaming non-discrimination across all aspects of programming and creating mechanisms of inclusion and empowerment.

Empowerment

The last aspect of a rights-based approach is the emphasis of the principle of empowerment. The central premise of the principle is that development should not be understood simply as a process of improving people's incomes through economic growth, but also as a process of expanding the fundamental choices and freedoms of people. Empowerment emphasizes the need to target root causes of poverty, often related to non-economic or structural problems or, as in the above, simply to the absence of human rights. According to OHCHR,

> Rights-based approaches give preference to strategies for empowerment over charitable responses. They focus on beneficiaries as the owners of rights and the directors of development, and emphasize the human person as the centre of the development process. The goal is to give people the power, capacities, capabilities and access needed to change their own lives, improve their own communities and influence their own destinies.[47]

---

45 Mokhiber, *supra*, note 22.
46 UNDP, *supra*, note 32.
47 Mokhiber, *supra*, note 22.

The operationalization of empowerment in practice relates to the sum of the initiatives taken in relation to the principles above; however, the principle may be categorized by relating it primarily to two sets of initiatives — focusing on non-economic aspects of poverty, and enhancing people's ability to claim their rights.

This conception of empowerment is inspired by Amartya Sen's understanding of capability. Economic development represents only one of many ways to expand empowerment and human freedom.

Empowerment also implies people's capacity to claim and exercise their rights effectively. Sida focuses on a broad notion of fostering participation as the basis of empowering individuals and civil society.[48] UNDP elaborates that accountability, to be effective, needs to be demanded, and thus requires the empowerment of claimholders and the inclusion of civil society.

UNICEF underscores the need to pay attention to the root causes of poverty or vulnerability and promote empowerment, understood as the capacity of people to enjoy or claim their rights. For them this implies addressing the multiple causes of a given situation, including attention to the legislative frame and integrating strategies of advocacy and capacity building.[49]

Whereas UNDP often talks more generally about creating an "enabling environment," Oxfam works more directly with strengthening the ability of groups to demand social justice.[50] Oxfam adds an international perspective by also stressing the need to establish and implement "fair rules for the global economy,"[51] thus noting that in a globalized economy, many issues that affect local communities reach beyond national borders.

Principles, Assumptions, and Implications of a Rights-Based Approach

At two levels, it is necessary to explore more profoundly what the core dimensions of a rights-based approach are: First, it is necessary to examine how a rights-based approach relates to the right to development. Secondly, it is important to examine what the key principles and implications of the approach are when exposed in the development field.

Justifying a Rights-Based Approach in Development

The deliberations and strategizing of a rights-based approach have been based so far on concerns with current development practices, but many of the concerns raised are of a general and unfocused nature. A document by OHCHR refers to the "essentially pragmatic and empiricist approach of development professionals" and the inherent instrumentalist propositions of such an approach, which is then contrasted

48   Sida, *Democratic Governance: Four Reports on Democratic Governance in International development Cooperation Summary* (February 2003). Available at http://www.sida.se/shared/jsp/download.jsp?f=SIDA2950en_webb.pdf&a=2880.
49   UNICEF, *Human Rights for Children and Women: How UNICEF Helps Make Them a Reality* (New York: UNICEF, 1999).
50   Oxfam, *supra*, note 42.
51   *Ibid.*

with a normative-legal one.[52] Structural adjustment policies and donor conditionality — that is, the imposition of policy benchmarks that the developing state should achieve as a condition of receiving loans and assistance — are often seen by human rights experts to be a dominant trait of past development policies. Such policies are believed to exacerbate already existing biases of an overriding economistic policy.[53]

It can, however, be argued that human rights agencies, in devising their respective rights-based approaches, have been more concerned with the human rights prism than with a more thorough exploration of development thinking. Thus, the basic principles discussed in section four are characterized by general human rights concerns rather than by development concerns. This could mean that a better understanding of the value added of a rights-based approach might be hampered by the fact that its basic tenets have not really been exposed to the development context. This seems particularly true as regards the insertion of key concepts like universality and indivisibility.

Figure 1, elaborated by Siddiq Osmani, illustrates a particular understanding of the origins and genealogy of RBA and its relationship to the right to development.[54] The diagram shows that a human rights approach to development derives from two sources — from development and from human rights activities. The human rights approach to development leads, in turn, to the implementation or realization of the right to development.

In our opinion, there are two principal objections to the figure as it stands, however. First, the figure presupposes that the right to development has been formulated based on development experiences. This is the case only to a limited degree. The right to development hardly expresses any strong interpretation of learning from development work except as regards very general notions about the North-South relationship.

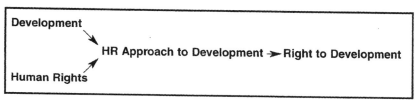

Figure 1. Human Rights-Based Approach to Development

Secondly, the figure can be interpreted to mean that a rights-based approach to development precedes the right to development in chronological terms. Such an interpretation would, however, be problematic inasmuch as the right to development and rights-based approaches have been interpreted on parallel tracks, so to speak.

---

52 Craig Mushier, *Human Rights in Development; What, Why, How* (Geneva: OHCHR, 2000). Available at http://www.vivatinternational.org/1%20POVERTY%20ERADICATION/human_rights_in_ devt.htm.
53 Frankovits and Earle, *supra*, note 16, p. 36. See also Patrick Van Weerelt, *The Application of a Human Rights Approach to Development: What Is the Added Value?* (New York: UNDP, 2000).
54 The figure was presented at the Nobel Symposium in Oslo, October 2003.

As an alternative, we have tried to use the model of Figure 1 as a source of inspiration for Figure 2. This latter figure sketches two parallel tracks that have occurred almost simultaneously. Development and human rights programs have engendered a common inspiration, namely the concept of a human rights-based approach to development. This approach is currently inspiring new practices of rights-based approaches among donors as well as among international NGOs and local NGOs.

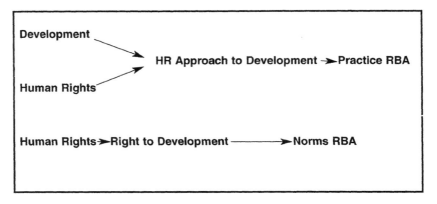

Figure 2. Practice and Norms, Rights-Based Approach to Development

A parallel process (as adopted, for example, by the Independent Expert of the Human Rights Commission[55]) is a normative one that is inspired by the right to development. OHCHR and UNDP have also been involved in a normative understanding of rights-based development.

The model stresses that there are normative as well as practical dimensions in justifying a rights-based approach. Implicit in the normative track is an assumption that RBA derives from discourses on the right to development.

One major challenge of the broader application of a rights-based approach is, therefore, to explore the linkages between normative and practical concerns of the development context — that is, to facilitate a strong dialogue between development experiences and human rights norms about development. The norms inherent in the Declaration on the Right to Development have to be incorporated in practical de-

---

55 Interestingly, the first report elaborated by the Independent Expert does not refer to a rights-based approach; see *UN Economic and Social Council, Commission on Human Rights* (1999). *Study on the Current State of Progress in the Implementation of the Right to Development*, submitted by Arjun K. Sengupta, Independent Expert, *Pursuant to Commission Resolution 1998/72 and General Assembly 53/155*. Only in later reports does the Independent Expert refer specifically to a rights-based approach. In the second report, it was stressed that "...the rights approach to development is not the same thing as realizing the right to development" (see UN Doc. E/CN.4/2000.WG.18/CRP.1 (September 2000), p. 4), while in the third report, it was stated that "...the realization of each human right and all of them together has to be carried out in a rights-based manner..." (see UN Doc. E/CN.4/2001/WG.18/2 [January 2001], p. 8). The tendency in the writings of the Independent Expert has been to strengthen the linkages between the right to development and rights-based approaches; see also Margot E. Salomon and Arjun Sengupta, *The Right to Development: Obligations of States and the Rights of Minorities and Indigenous Peoples* (London: Minority Rights Group International, 2003).

velopment efforts as part of a mainstreaming effort. It would, however, be premature to argue that this has already happened in development thinking and practices.

Four Constituent Elements of a Rights-Based Approach

The question of where the meeting points of normative and practical thinking are in the development context begs deeper theoretical work than is possible here. An examination of rights-based principles, however, reveals four obvious areas: in the development of values and application of norms of justice, in structures and institutions of power and governance, in the integration of the rule of law and legality in development, and in the analysis of poverty and entitlements.

These four points draw on the examination of normative principles above but seek to elucidate four constituent principles of a rights-based approach and their implications in the development field. In their implementation of a rights-based approach, NGOs tend to define their strategies not far from these principles.[56] Table 1 summarizes the principles and some of their major implications.

The first principle is that development efforts would benefit from being anchored in the normative or legal domain, typically international human rights law, but organizations like Care International should be careful to relate a rights-based approach only to international human rights law. The implication of this principle is that normative-legal entitlements become constituent elements of development policy.[57]

The second principle is well known and one of the most well argued in a rights-based framework. It serves analytical purposes, but its strongest implication may be to emphasize the accountability of duty-bearers and thus provide a means for linking human rights to governance development programs. Accountability in a rights-based sense defines an accountability of duty-bearers to human rights.

The third principle links the focus on justice and rights. The role of human rights in combating poverty has gained growing attention in the UN by the UNDP human development agenda, as well as through the growing focus on poverty by the OHCHR and UNESCO.

The last principle addresses how economic policies supported by development institutions may do human rights harm. For instance, structural adjustment policies have implied that public sector spending was cut, with adverse human rights implications. The implication here is that human rights establishes a bottom line, a set of minimum standards below which narrow economistic and political rationality

---

56 See, for instance, a checklist developed by Oxfam UK in use during 2003 to assess whether a rights-based approach is pursued:
- Do we focus on people's rights?
- Do we concentrate on worst violations and most vulnerable people?
- Do we support people to demand their rights?
- Do we strengthen accountability of governments for rights?
- Do we fight discrimination and promote equality?

57 OHCHR argues that human rights professionals generally work within a clearly defined normative legal policy framework. They thus tend to be highly skeptical of instrumentalist arguments. Craig Mokhiber, *Human Rights in Development; What, Why, How* (Geneva: OHCHR, 2000). Available at http://www.vivatinternational.org/1%20POVERTY%20ERADICATION/human_rights_in_devt.htm.

Table 1.

Principle 1	Principle 2	Principle 3	Principle 4
Development efforts based on clearly defined normative principles, including those of international human rights law, bring more just and sustainable development.	Rights-based development brings a clear division of responsibility based on a framework of rights-holders and duty-bearers.	Individual and group entitlements and rights are crucial in the creation of equity, non-discrimination, and well-being.	Human rights trump political and economic expediency.
Implication	**Implication**	**Implication**	**Implication**
Legal entitlements, including those of international law, must become constituent concerns of development policy.	There are clear gains in terms of good governance in applying a frame-work where accountability plays a crucial role.	Rights-based empowerment is an effective means for combating poverty and redressing prevailing unjust power and eco-nomic structures.	Do no human rights harm! Mainstream human rights in development.

cannot be allowed to move. Thus, the principle of "do no human rights harm" refers to the establishment of minimum conditions which have to be respected.

Conclusions

Interpretations of a rights-based approach have evolved conceptually before being operationally developed. Currently, UN agencies, donors, and NGOs operating at the international and local levels are involved in a process of operationalization. Such processes demand a clearer and more feasible conceptualization as well as an under-standing of the value added of the approach compared with other approaches.

According to the analysis above, the implications of a rights-based approach are analytical and substantive. At the analytical level, a rights framework will imply a dif-ferent analysis emphasizing not only a focus on rights and empowerment, but also a different focus on accountability and governance.

At the substantive level, a rights-based approach implies a focus on rights rather than needs, a focus on rights-based advocacy, capacity development in relation to rights implementation, and the "do not harm" principle. A rights-based approach has implications for bench-marking and monitoring — not least for performance assessment in relation to human rights respect, empowerment, accountability, and institutional capacity building — including institutional development to seek redress in cases of human rights violations. Non-discrimination and targeting of vulnerable groups should also be included in rights-based performance measurements, but the methods of non-discrimination are not yet well developed.

The analysis above indicates, too, what a rights-based approach is and what it is not. While part of the rights discourse tends to focus on participation, empowerment, and accountability — that is, themes that are recurrent also in the development field — the specific marks of a rights-based approach are three characteristics that may be performed in combination or separately:

- programs and projects are developed according to human rights law and principles;

- programs and projects have objectives of rights realization and rights empowerment; and

- programs and projects are defined with components of human rights accountability.

A rights-based framework may not have equal relevance in all spheres of development thinking. The extent to which rights-based approaches deal specifically with human rights issues or human rights-relevant institutions could serve as an important litmus test. In sum, four dimensions of potential contributions of a rights-based approach in development exist:

1) the foundation in universally accepted norms and legal standards, a fact with strong implications in terms of accountability and governance;

2) the force of legality, which strengthens sustainability;

3) the notion of justice forcefully inherent in human rights thinking, with strong implications for efforts of combating poverty and marginalization; and

4) the prospects of defining minimum standards in assessments of no harm done.

A rights-based approach includes normative as well as practical sources of inspiration and is applicable in four fields of development: 1) governance, 2) rule of law, legal change, and access to justice, 3) poverty, vulnerability, and discrimination, and 4) safeguard policies.

At the practical level, we think that a dialogue between development and human rights advocates may be more fruitful than confrontation as a tool to advance and consolidate a rights-based approach. Experiences are being gained now in the field. Learning from these experiences is important to conceptualize and consolidate a rights-based approach.

[19]

HUMAN SECURITY—NATIONAL PERSPECTIVES AND GLOBAL AGENDAS: INSIGHTS FROM NATIONAL HUMAN DEVELOPMENT REPORTS[§]

RICHARD JOLLY[1][*][†] and DEEPAYAN BASU RAY[2][‡]

[1]*University of Sussex, Brighton, UK*

[2]*Aid Policy, Oxford Policy Management, Oxford, UK*

Abstract: Since its introduction in UNDP's Human Development Report 1994, 'human security' has been a topic of lively debate. The purpose of this paper is to explore empirically how human security has been treated in National Human Development Reports (NHDRs), produced in 13 countries since 1997 with different definitions and points of focus. We use an inductive approach to examine how these stand up to the criticisms levelled in the literature against broader concepts of human security. The NHDRs of Afghanistan, Latvia, Macedonia and Bangladesh are of particular interest, both because of their rich analysis and because of the originality of the methodology they use. The paper concludes that broader definitions of human security are operational for both analysis and policy making. Limits to define a core of high-priority concerns with human security can be set *after* exploring the concerns of people in specific situations rather than before.

Keywords: human security; national human development reports; Afghanistan; Latvia; Macedonia; Bangladesh

1 INTRODUCTION

Despite the obvious fact that the term 'security' means very many different things to very many different people, the practice of *security-making* has been alarmingly narrow in scope. To a large extent, policy as well as academic discussions in the post-Cold War era continued to prescribe numerous permutations of the same cocktail of military force and financial aid to

---

*Correspondence to: Richard Jolly, Research Associate, Institute of Development Studies, University of Sussex, Brighton BN1 9RE. E-mail: r.jolly@ids.ac.uk

[†]Research Associate.

[‡]Assistant Consultant.

[§]This paper is a synopsis and update of a more comprehensive report prepared by the authors in 2006 for the UNDP Human Development Report Office (Jolly & Basu Ray, 2006).

address questions of 'national' security. Experiences of Iraq, Israel and Sri Lanka and much of Sub-Saharan Africa suggest that security needs to be conceived as a much broader issue than merely a matter of defence and the use of armed forces to enforce peace.

Yet moves to adopt conceptualisations of security within a wider socio-economic and political context have been slow. Several major reports on international policy in the last few years have presented human security as a frame of reference for policy analysis and proposals but their attempts to re-conceptualise security have met with a cautious or sceptical reception in some parts of the academic and policy worlds. In the changing world context, this response seems limited and over-cautious. Perhaps the explanation Keynes (1964) gave for the opposition by economists to the General Theory applies here once more. 'The ideas . . .are extremely simple and should be obvious. The difficulty lies, not in the new ideas, but in escaping from the old ones, which ramify, for those brought up as most of us have been, into every corner of our minds'. (Keynes, 1964).

The United Nations Development Programme's Human Development Report (1993) introduced the concept of human security as a shift from the security of the state by the military protection of a country's borders to the security of people by a variety of measures to protect people from a diversity of threats.[1] Human security was therefore people-centred, multi-dimensional, interconnected and universal. The following year, the HDR 1994 defined human security as '. . .the safety from such chronic threats as hunger, disease and repression and; protection from sudden and hurtful disruptions in the patterns of daily lives, whether in homes, jobs or communities' (UNDP, 1994). It elaborated the need for a variety of actions to respond to these problems, including measures of disarmament to free up resources to make the new actions possible.

Notwithstanding academic caution, the human security framework as a policy tool has increasingly been gaining currency within policy circles since 1994. One significant step in this was the constitution by the UN Secretary General of the Commission on Human Security (CHS), which produced the landmark study, *Human Security Now* (2003). Other significant statements include the adoption of a human security framework for the report by the UN Secretary General Kofi Annan's 2004 High Level Panel on Threats, Challenges and Change (TCC, 2004), and his subsequent report entitled *In Larger Freedom–Towards Security Development, and Freedom for All* (Annan, 2005).

This paper focuses on the UNDP's National Human Development Reports (NHDRs), which have become an invaluable tool for exploring aspects of human development in specific national situations. The 550 or so national-level reports have generated a substantial body of literature using country-specific data to assess the status of human development within countries. Thus far, a human security perspective has been a main theme in at least a dozen NHDRs. Typically, these reports have been prepared in one or other of three broad settings:

- by countries which have just emerged from conflict;
- by countries grappling with lingering but still major elements of national (and in some cases, regional) insecurity from military causes; and
- by countries in the midst of fundamental socio-political and economic transition.

It is in cases such as these that the strengths of the UNDP's broad perspectives on human security have shone through. It has provided a frame for multi-dimensional analysis of

---

[1]The HDR 1993 first introduced the human security concept, stating that "new concepts of human security must stress the security of people, not only of nations. (UNDP, 1993, p. 2).

human security at country level—and of the interconnected factors which underlie insecurity. Analyses have also focused on how different forms of insecurity are perceived and of the policy measures available to deal with them.

National perspectives on human security and the policy proposals they lead to also do much to answer the critics of the human security framework. The critics appear to focus on five difficulties with the concept:

- Human security, they argue, merely involves renaming problems which have already been recognised in other contexts and which already have perfectly good names. What is gained by combining them together under a new label? (Ayoob, 1997)
- Human security does not have any definite parameters, therefore anything and everything could be considered as a risk to security (Paris, 2001).
- Human security, when broadened to include issues like climate change and health, complicates the international machinery for reaching decisions or taking action in relation to the threats identified.[2]
- Human security risks engaging the military in issues best tackled through non-military means (Knudsen, 2001).
- Human security under the UN risks raising hopes about the UN's capacity, which it cannot fulfil.

This paper responds to each of these criticisms by highlighting the policy-related impacts defined in the NHDRs. The paper concludes that the UNDP concept of human security, when applied at national level, is both robust in providing answers to criticisms, and operationally useful in identifying policy measures and action to tackle serious problems of insecurity of people within the countries concerned.

In this paper, we use the term 'human security' in a broad sense. We focus on the insecurities felt subjectively by people or experienced objectively by them. We do not set limits in advance on the types of insecurities that we consider as dimensions of 'human security', but rather let the focus and range emerge from the situation or analysis. But we do recognise the need in any situation to determine priorities among the different and various insecurities identified—especially if one is to make policy that seeks to improve 'human security' in the situation being analysed and with limited resources.

This approach fits well with the analysis given by Des Gasper (2005) in his paper summarising the various alternatives used to define human security in recent articles and debate. Gasper brings out the contrasts and overlaps among the different definitions: the narrowest relating to personal physical security alone; a broader but still specific one being based on basic needs; a somewhat broader one being related to UNDP's list of goods; and the broadest being related to Amartya Sen's capability approach. Gasper also considers three types of threat: from being below some basic (static) level of provision; from instability through falling below some required minimum level of security; and from instability combined with starting below some basic level of provision and capabilities. The notion of falling below some level of human development links closely with Sen's distinction that human development is about the process of increasing levels of human development while human security focuses on avoiding the downside risks of falling below some level of human development already achieved.

Consistent with our broad perspective, we use the term 'human security' in this paper to encompass potentially all these approaches. Our purpose is not to define in advance human

---

[2]For more information see Ayoob (1997), Paris (2001), Deudney (2001), and Owens and Arneil (1999).

460   *R. Jolly and D. Basu Ray*

security, but to see how actual analysis of situations on the ground in fact treats the concept—in the countries analysed in the NHDRs under review. We are also interested in whether a broader view of human security stands up in practice to the criticisms levelled against these broader definitions in the literature.

2   ANTECEDENTS AND DEFINITIONS OF HUMAN SECURITY

Human security has evolved from both a shift in policy-making towards more people-centred approaches and the need to develop more relevant tools of analysis to achieve this. By the end of the Cold War, theoretical narratives which characterised international relations (IRs) began to prove increasingly inadequate. The post-Cold War era presented a fundamental challenge to the supremacy and efficacy of an international state-based system. Trans-national, intra-state factors and socio-economic conditions now demand far greater consideration within the security calculus than ever before.

Following the demise of the Cold War order, debates about the metamorphosis of the international system began to emerge within IRs, many centred on the very concept of security. Recognising the analytical weaknesses of traditional and orthodox theories led the way for a process of critical self-reflection, outside academia and within.[3] A sustained argument emerged which called for a widening of the levels of analysis of the concept of security to better explain causes and sources of insecurity in an increasingly destabilised international system.[4] The need to bring economic, social and environmental causes of conflict into analysis of insecurity was also argued prolifically by the academics who later came to be known as the Copenhagen School (Knudsen, 2001).

The human security framework was one of the new alternatives to emerge from this process of reflection. Mahbub ul Haq used the Human Development Reports to explore human security as a dimension of human development (HDR, 1993, 1994). James Busumtwi-Sam related human security to 'extended notions of security [which] attempt to broaden the scope horizontally by the inclusion or 'securitisation' of issues not confined to military threats (poverty, inequality, environmental degradation, human rights and so on) and deepen the domain vertically by shifting from a focus on the state/nation as the object of security to include the security of individuals and groups' (Busumtwi-Sam, 2002, p. 255). Caroline Thomas included in human security the provision of 'basic material needs' and 'emancipation from oppressive power structures—be they global, national or local in origin and scope' (Thomas, 1999). Gary King and Christopher J. L. Murray's definition of human security through the rubric of development and poverty provided another intriguing example of the depth of the process of contextualisation that the concept can provide. They defined 'an individual's human security as his or her expectation of years of life without experiencing the state of generalised poverty. Population human security is then an aggregation of individuals' human security' (2001–2002).

The common thread in each of these definitions concerns the need to contextualise the experiences of insecurity, and develop policy responses based on this more nuanced understanding. Human security is primarily an analytical tool which focuses on the provision of security for the individual, not the state. Exploring options aimed at mitigating

---

[3]For more information, see Walt (1991), Booth (1991), Homer-Dixon, (1991), Walker (1997), Dalby (1997) and Buzan (1998).
[4]For further discussion, see Buzan (1998) and Stoett (1999).

threats to the insecurity of individuals thus becomes a central goal of policy recommendations and actions. In line with the expanded definition of security, the causes of insecurity are subsequently broadened to include threats to socio-economic and political conditions, food, health, environmental, community and personal safety. Policy initiatives generated through the application of this human security framework have incorporated considerations far beyond the traditional focus on military force, greatly reducing the emphasis on armies, if not replacing them altogether.

In this ideal setting, action to achieve human security becomes the aggregation of the various measures required to prevent or mitigate each and every factor that contributes to insecurity. In practice, there is a need to focus on a core of insecurities within each specific context. A country-by-country approach, as with the NHDRs, helps to do this.

For example attaining human security in Afghanistan can and should involve policies which address human rights, poverty, basic needs, trans-national crime and democratic governance. The human security needs of the people of Nigeria could and probably would include protection from regional conflicts, socio-economic exploitation, civil unrest stemming from ethnic identities, poverty and public health issues such as HIV/AIDS and tuberculosis. Each of these cases therefore represents national sub-sets of human security, linked together by a common condition of insecurity—which manifests itself in decidedly different terms of reference for both Afghanistan and Nigeria. A human security framework makes it possible to develop a core of policies for each case which can address the most important specific insecurities identified in each situation.

3 CRITICS OF HUMAN SECURITY THINKING

Many eminent academics and practitioners in the field of IRs retain reservations about the very concept of human security.[5] Their doubts focus particularly on the five points set out earlier. The five points comprise important challenges but ones to which we believe there are cogent answers. We will therefore address the five objections in order, drawing on specific elements from the NHDRs that have focused on HS in order to illustrate the flexibility, adaptability and comparative advantage of the HS methodological framework. As will be evident by the end, human security is a framework already being utilised and its list of positive accomplishments is growing.

- Does HS do more than merely rename issues and bring them together under the new label of human security?

Yes, the concept most certainly does do more than simply rename old problems. The NHDRs and a large body of recent analysis of insecurities are proof of this. Human security places a great deal of emphasis on considering a wider range of linkages between non-traditional threats to security, both in analysis and in the development of policy initiatives. Since the end of the Cold War, the need to consider wider linkages has been argued in a growing number of policy documents and other publications. The recent Report of the UN Secretary General's High Level Panel on Threats, Challenges and Change puts it most clearly (TCC, 2004): 'Today, more than ever before, threats are interrelated and

---

[5]For further discussion, see Ayoob (1997), Paris (2001), Foong-Khong (2001) and MacFarlane and Foong-Khong (2006).

462   *R. Jolly and D. Basu Ray*

a threat to one is a threat to all. The mutual vulnerability of weak and strong has never been clearer'. The Panel's report elaborates: 'Development and security are inextricably linked. A more secure world is only possible if poor countries are given the chance to develop. Extreme poverty and infectious diseases threaten many people directly, but they also provide a fertile breeding ground for other threats, including civil conflict. Even people in rich countries will be more secure if their Governments help poor countries to defeat poverty and disease by meeting the Millennium Development Goals' (TCC, 2004).

This is much more than simply renaming. It is a recognition of the interrelated causes and interrelated actions required to deal with them, to prevent them arising and control them when they do. As already noted, it is this inherent interconnectedness that orthodox approaches to security are unable or unwilling to address. Human security's methodological framework is posited on analysis of causal processes. As a result, it becomes possible to address any given threat-based scenario, because the limiting boundaries inherent in most analytical traditions within IRs are not present. Unless one wishes to argue there is no significant interconnectedness, the case for taking account of these wider interactions and consequences seems overwhelming.

The complexity of the different types and causes of insecurities, and notably of terrorism, raises similar issues, more sharply in the present global context. The causes are indeed complex and diverse and subsequently difficult to analyse. But complexity is no reason not to explore the interacting causes as best as one can. Given the repeated failure of the neo-realist strategy to beat terrorism into submission, is it not high time that alternatives are considered?

The country situations analysed in the NHDRs further illustrate this point. The NHDRs on human security do much more than simply rename existing problems. These reports provide new analytical traction by treating the various elements of human security together rather than analysing them separately. Our study involved a careful review of the 13 NHDRs which dealt specifically with human security. The reports covered the following countries: Afghanistan, Bulgaria, East Timor, Estonia, Kyrgyzstan, Latvia, Lesotho, Macedonia, Moldova, Mozambique, Philippines, Sierra Leone and the Solomon Islands.

This review left us in no doubt that most of the NHDRs do much more than give new names to old problems. The problems identified have a number of dimensions and are new or original in traditional approaches to security and often even in terms of the human security literature. Almost all the reports develop links between military security, human security and development as an integrated whole. The Afghanistan report, for instance, brings out the need for a broad approach to human security issues as an essential component of peace, reconstruction and development. The Latvian report shows how in the minds of citizens a complex range of insecurities are felt and identified, which need action, many not as single separable elements or sectors but in an interrelated way, certainly as part of an integrated strategy. The Macedonian report shows the special needs for giving attention to a broad range of new security issues as part of the transition to a market system. All these considerations go far beyond the renaming of accepted issues of either development strategy or traditional views of 'national security'.

In fact, most of the policy recommendations put forth by these reports take into consideration a very wide range of factors affecting security, both the security of persons and of states. The Solomon Island report pin-points the need to reshape education policies and, specifically, the content of school curricula, as one of the first steps to meaningful conflict prevention (UNDP, 2002c). The Macedonian NHDR focuses on strengthening health systems and environmental regulation as a means of addressing the security concerns of the citizens of the country (UNDP, 2001). The Bangladesh human security report considers an extensive set of justice-sector reforms to address the security needs of its population (UNDP, 2002a) Through the human security framework, the multiplicity of experiences of insecurity are given greater consideration than what is found in traditional approaches to mitigating insecurity.

- By not setting pre-determined boundaries and parameters, and considering anything and everything a risk to security, does the concept of human security leave policy makers without direction, and academics without clear analytical and comparative tools?

This particular objection highlights both the rigidity with which traditional concepts of security are understood in IRs, as well as the most fundamental strength that human security has to offer. In a state-centric model, security has very specific implications and connotations. Threats are assessed by their implications for structures, territorial boundaries and, most importantly, state 'interests'. But, as history has repeatedly shown, the interpretation of state interests often mimics the power and privileges of those in positions of economic and political advantage. In this situation, it is difficult to accept that securing the state ensures protection of all individuals and their interests.

Given the numerous challenges arising in the post-Cold War world, the state-centric model appears to be flawed and misdirected in its inability to respond effectively. The impacts of terrorism, disease and pandemics, globalisation and environmental disasters on the state-centric international system lead one to consider alternative broader assessments of security. No longer can a threat-based approach in which threats continue to be defined according to the interest of the state be considered adequate. In today's world, the well-being of the individual requires a far more complex set of considerations than was considered necessary within earlier state-based definitions of security. The very reason that, for an Afghani citizen, the specifics of security are drastically different from those of a Latvian citizen, requires an immediate re-formulation of the very definition of security.

The human security approach strives to contextualise this understanding of security in order to develop appropriate policy responses. The NHDR reports show that such a process is entirely possible, and reveals a far more comprehensive picture of the security needs and situations of individuals than a state-based approach would do. In surveys conducted as part of the NHDR exercises, Latvians were asked to rank their perception of some 30 general threats to their security as well as some 30 threats to their security at a personal level. The former covered such threats as armed or ethnic conflict in Latvia, nuclear threats, the spread of narcotics and organised crime to the rise of HIV/AIDS, environmental pollution, global warming and economic instability through high inflation and devaluation. The threats to security at the personal level ranged from the risks of becoming seriously ill with insufficient resources to pay for treatment, being unable to support oneself and having an inadequate pension to threats to personal security from being physically abused or sexually assaulted, being robbed or falling victim to organised crime. The surveys were based on interviews of about 1000 permanent residents of Latvia over the age of 18 years.

The surveys revealed that health risks and the inability to pay for medical care were felt to be of primary personal importance, ranked more important than terrorism or armed conflict (UNDP, 2002/2003). A similar finding applied to the perception of general threats, where organised crime, HIV/AIDS and economic instabilities were ranked much higher than the risk of armed or ethnic conflict and occupation. That is not to say that the more traditional security issues do not deserve any consideration. It does suggest,

464   *R. Jolly and D. Basu Ray*

however, that a reconsideration of priorities is needed, with more attention to the positive trade-offs which might follow from reallocating resources and attention from traditional measures of military security to those felt by the population to be more directly related to the aspects of human security which directly affect their lives. It is important to remember that many of the respondents lived in highly unstable and conflict-prone environments.

This picture is substantiated by the Solomon Islands NHDR, for example which found that the most pressing cause of insecurity was a combination of poverty—affecting access to food, eucation and employment—and unstable and corrupt governance. The report also noted the growing challenge of containing health-related insecurities linked with malaria, tuberculosis and maternal health (UNDP, 2002c).

The situation of civil war in Sierra Leone offered a good example of the 'value-added' of using a human security approach. Traditional security analysis in Sierra Leone has, amongst other factors, focussed on conflict mediation, disarmament, peacekeeping and the role of donor agencies in facilitating the rebuilding process.[6] A human security perspective provided a more comprehensive picture of both the causes of the conflict, as well as a focussed plan for the rebuilding of the country. The Sierra Leone NHDR entitled 'From Conflict to Human Security' noted the following:

> Economic security has been lost through loss of income and employment. Food security has deteriorated due to decrease in food production in conjunction with loss of income which connotes lack of economic access to food. Increased incidence of diseases and reduced access to health facilities have implied reduced health security. Environmental security has suffered as a result of damage to the environment. Personal security has been affected in diverse ways including exposure to violence from the fighting and increased crime rates. Deterioration in community security has occurred when sometimes members of entire communities have been threatened. Lastly, political security has also suffered as basic human rights have been violated (UNDP, 1998b).

The need to analyse linkages in the context of policy responses is immediately evident through human security's analytical framework. This process also enables another important feature of policy analysis, and that is the setting of benchmarks. Because of the linkages between human security and human development, it is possible to create policies to mitigate insecurity that simultaneously promote sustainable human development. The key recommendations of the Afghanistan NHDR also take into account these fundamental linkages between physical security and human development. For instance, when discussing security sector reform and reintegration of former combatants in Afghanistan, the report notes that 'Disarmament, however, needs to be carried out within a context of employment creation and alternative livelihoods. An ill-planned Disarmament, Demobilisation and Reintegration (DDR) approach, involving no long-term plan for employment of disarmed persons and no training for security personnel to replace them, may be more dangerous than no strategy at all' (UNDP, 2004).

As mentioned earlier, the strength of UNDP's human security framework is its ability to engage with discussions of non-state security, interconnect these and discussions of state security and focus the analysis to those specific issues critical to the understanding of

---

[6]For further discussion of the Sierra Leone conflict, see Berman (2000), Chawla (2000), Hagman, (2002) and Grant (2005).

insecurity in a particular case. Both Sierra Leone and Afghanistan have the challenge of rebuilding state and society. The path each needs to take is however drastically different. Given the conditions in each country, policy initiatives require (a) a major degree of flexibility; (b) the ability to measure and assess progress and success; and (c) targeted solutions to specific developmental and security challenges. The ability to highlight issues and set priorities—to 'securitise' agendas—is particularly relevant in these cases. For instance, the need to substitute livelihoods from agriculture in place of opium production is of crucial importance in Afghanistan, whereas this is not a major security-threatening experience for Sierra Leone. On the other hand, effective environmental control and natural resource mobilisation are of far more strategic importance in Sierra Leone than Afghanistan.

Whereas the objectors to a human security language and framework are right to point out that there are no definitive parameters for setting the boundaries to human security, experience shows that the concept can be limited to a central core of issues in particular contexts. Doing this enables one to concentrate on high-priority issues which offer greater dividends than following rigid definitions of traditional threats to security. By broadening the concept of security and allowing for specific experiences to be addressed within a framework of action and analysis, human security enables a substantive and comprehensive engagement with factors of insecurity as experienced by individuals around the world.

- By broadening the security calculus to include issues like climate change and threats from disease, doesn't human security complicate the international machinery for reaching decisions or taking action in relation to the threats identified?

There will indeed be difficulties. Decision making and implementation of a much broader approach will neither be easy nor always fit easily within conventional thinking and procedures. On the other hand, if the causes of insecurity have broadened, if new issues of human security have displaced traditional threats, it would be absurd to continue along old routes, rather than finding new ways to deal with new problems.

What would be the key elements in such a broader approach? We would name four:

- In order to set the objectives and priorities of human security, there is a need to analyse the complex of national and international factors affecting human security of people in each country.
- One also needs to seek information about the viewpoints and rankings of the various threats to human security of the main groups of the population within the country.
- In such an analysis, one needs to consider motivations as well as objectives and strategy.
- And one needs to give explicit consideration to new and changing threats to national stability and human security. (In Afghanistan, these would currently include warlordism, the narco-mafia and international groups committed to destabilise the country.)

Climate change is a perfect example of this need to broaden considerations. Whereas scientific and economic arguments often fall into opposing sides of the debate, the human security perspective encourages a critical analysis of the potential human impacts of the problem. Aside from the scientific predictions, it is clear from events in 2005 that fragile livelihoods are at the mercy of volatile environmental changes. As the South Asian Tsunami, the drought in Niger and the change in the Amazon's ecosystem have clearly demonstrated, the livelihoods of countless millions—inevitably the most vulnerable members of society—suffer new threats and require new actions to better protect their security.

The NHDRs recognise the importance of analysing cross-cutting issues comprehensively, as well as to develop policies for protection as well as prevention. Current strategy in Afghanistan, for instance, falls short of the NHDR recommended strategies through its failure to approach issues such as terrorism and environmental security with a sufficiently comprehensive and holistic view of human security. As a result, in Afghanistan today, 'Reinforcement of the mutually beneficial interests of big business, and political and military power holders, is spawning unregulated, informal and illicit markets that are undermining the agendas of reconstruction and development' (UNDP, 2004). Given this context, the report goes on to state that 'The challenge to design and deliver a coherent national strategic framework for social protection lies in effectively reaching the poorest and most at-risk segments of the population, while supporting the ability of communities in general to secure basic entitlements and develop the capacities required for reducing insecurity over time' (UNDP, 2004. p. 238). In response, the policy recommendations include the strengthening of access to basic public infrastructure, securing adequate energy resources and procedures to implement 'green policies' within relevant government agencies (UNDP, 2004).

The East Timor NHDR addresses urban environmental challenges as threats to environmental security. The report notes an important linkage between environment and health when it states that 'At present there are no effective systems for waste management... [and] this is further polluting the groundwater on which many people rely for drinking water. Environmental degradation ... compromises the health and livelihood systems of future generations' (UNDP, 2002b). Policy recommendations included in the report focus on infrastructural development, health-sector reform and increased expenditure and a robust overhaul of the education sector in an attempt to influence the way in which people think about the environment around them (UNDP, 2002b).

The Lesotho report focuses on measures to improve environmental protection standards, as well as to mainstream environmental considerations into the overall architecture of policy-formulation. The report recommends the strengthening of the National Environment Policy to include provisions for promoting eco-tourism, creating education and employment opportunities through the National Environment Youth Corp. and mandating the undertaking of Environmental Impact Assessments for all development projects (UNDP, 1998a).

Several other reports illustrate the ability of the human security approach and framework to identify creative responses to the major threats to human well-being that are felt and experienced by people in the country concerned, as opposed to following some global blueprint:

- The Macedonian report explores how to combine economic strategies for achieving human development along with human security.
- The Bangladesh report highlights justice and reconciliation as essential components for achieving long run human security.
- The Latvian and Solomon Islands reports devote attention to gender and other human rights as important components of human security and human development, together with steady progress towards the fulfilment of human rights and development goals.
- The Sierra Leone report illustrates the risk of mismanaging natural resources and recommends the creation of pro-poor income-generation strategies when considering environmental protection measures.

- Most reports define the need for a broader approach to monitoring in order to track progress to both human security and human development.

Recognising these broader causes of human insecurity, however, in no way implies the need for *one single solution* to the different causes. Climate change requires a range of actions to tackle climate change, just as urban crime requires a variety of actions to tackle urban crime. Gender violence requires actions, short run and long, to engender new understandings and relationships, as well as to protect women against immediate violations to their situations and rights.

There is, however, an important advantage in assessing and analysing these different problems as important aspects of human security. To do so helps to raise issues of trade-off in decisions about policy alternatives and in the allocation of resources. No longer would one put military spending in a totally separate category, privileging it above other expenditures in assessing how best to meet the various security challenges.

- Doesn't the concept of human security necessarily lead to the encouragement of military responses to whatever security problems are identified?

Judged by the content of the NHDRs on human security, this is a major exaggeration. It is true that the current US Administration led by President Bush has relied heavily on military solutions, internationally and nationally. And this has led many to identify a risk of 'militarisation' of the global development agenda. But such approaches to human security have been strongly rejected by many countries and other parties, both analytically and in terms of policy. Indeed, many close to the UN have argued that the military approaches have been extremely counter-productive and must give way to a broader agenda of non-military actions as outlined in the report of the Secretary General's 2004 High Level Panel on Threats, Challenges and Change (TCC, UNSGCC, 2004), the Secretary General's own report, the Sen-Ogata report entitled *Human Security Now* (Commission on Human Security, 2003) and the foreign policies of Canada and Japan.

The term 'collective comprehensive security', as used in the High Level Panel Report on Threats, Challenges and Change, rather than human security, may encourage a misplaced association with military solutions (TCC, 2004). 'Collective security' has, for many years, been a fundamental concept in (state) Security Studies, stressing the need for co-operation between states to mitigate threats to the collective. Regional security organisations such as NATO owe their existence to this concept. But the High Level Panel used 'comprehensive collective security' in a different and broader sense, broadly in line with ideas of human security. They moved away from a state-based meaning to a people- and community-based understanding. This re-orientation enables collective *comprehensive* security to be understood as the sum of individual and community concerns. Consistent use of the term human security would of course have made the meaning clearer.

It must be noted at this point that within a human security perspective, *non-military* sources of insecurity are more-often-than-not identified as central. One need only consider the vast number of security issues identified by the NHDRs to gauge the applicability of a human security perspective, and its focus on non-military solutions to fostering security. Strategies including especially the need to cope with the differing interests and objectives of the various parties involved, nationally and internationally, are crucial elements of promoting human security. Nonetheless, human security does not rule out concerns with state security, nor with military means as a last resort to ensure this.

468   *R. Jolly and D. Basu Ray*

The following examples from four of the most comprehensive human security NHDRs (Afghanistan, Macedonia, Latvia and Bangladesh) offer in-depth analysis on alternative strategies to military engagement.

The Afghanistan report identifies a number of special problems which can, yet do not necessarily, necessitate a military response to issues which are likely to be present and to affect human security in post-conflict countries: landmines, feelings of mistrust, inadequate and chaotic administration, excessive reliance on expatriates, little attention to capacity building for the longer run, complications of dealing with injustice and inequality among many local groups (with particular focus on warlords in Afghanistan). Several of these have been exacerbated by vast differences in salaries paid to expatriates and those relatively few nationals lucky enough to be associated with the international aid and reconstruction efforts.

The Macedonian report identified personal safety as a focus of popular concern in a survey on human security, which also showed that higher rates of insecurity and victimisation were felt in urban areas by richer parts of the population than by poorer groups (UNDP, 2001). Insecurity was also derived from unsettled ethnic relations—and was especially experienced among the Roma population. The survey revealed that four out of five of the Roma population could not afford to buy sufficient food and nearly two-thirds of the population at large felt insecurity because of their economic position. Not surprisingly, some 40% of the Roma population felt they received less than the required services from the state, more than double the proportion in the Macedonian population as a whole. Nearly three out of five of the Roma population had been asked for bribes by officials—compared to well under one in five of the total Macedonian population(UNDP, 2001).

The Latvian report obtained information on the objective aspects of human security by statistical analysis of such issues as unemployment in the economy, crime and disease. The sense of security and insecurity of people was investigated using surveys, questionnaires, interviews and tests. The report noted that, on the whole, individuals ranked concern about terrorism low in the survey—number 24 or 26 out of some 30 general threats. However, a subsequent poll of students, undertaken a month after the terrorist attack by Chechen militants in Moscow in October 2002, raised the ranking of 'terrorism/war/strained political relations' to become the second most highly rated insecurity factor' (UNDP, 2001).

Human insecurity arising from crime, and the seriously inadequate national institutions of courts and policing to prevent or control it, was the theme of the UNDP report on Human Security in Bangladesh of 2002. The analysis dealt with the legal framework for human security, awareness of rights and legal aid facilities among poor people, the role of the police and the functioning of the court systems, including the village courts and other informal courts. Particular attention was given to violence and repression against women and children.

These brief descriptions make clear that taking action on a human security agenda does not necessarily require military intervention—but nor, in fact, does a state security agenda necessarily require militarisation. The pursuit of human security can be used to generate holistic and cross-cutting initiatives, as these examples have shown.

- Does all this raise excessive hopes of the UN or about its capacity to follow through these ideas into action? Is a human security agenda politically realistic? What do the NHDRs, especially the Afghanistan Report show about the interests involved in adopting—or opposing—a human security approach?

Without doubt, the UN has a highly mixed record of responding to crises and challenges—with the positive responses mostly occurring when the dominant powers wanted to see action and the negative responses occurring when they did not. The UN's own capacity to follow through is independently important but generally not as much as the wishes and support of the major powers. Moreover, the UN's record in matters of economic and social development, including actions in support of health and disease control, has generally been much more positive than in political and military affairs. This pattern is likely to continue with respect to the issues involved in human security.

But one must be clear about what or who one means by the UN. Indeed, we argue that there are 'three UNs'. The first UN is comprised of the member governments as represented in the General Assembly (GA). Then there is what can be described as the second UN, the secretariat, headed by the Secretary General and including the staff members of the many agencies under the UN umbrella, all of whom can exert a considerable influence on decisions and action. Finally, one can refer to the third UN—the NGOs and parts of civil society closely associated with the UN, who have also at times had an important effect on decisions and outcomes, especially by pressing the UN to live up to its commitments and ideals. All three have power and influence, the first formally but the second and third *de facto*. Though not part of the formal organisation or family of organisations, the third UN has grown in strength and influence since 1945 and now forms an identifiable part of an overall system, sharing the UN's objectives (not least as expressed through the Declaration and Conventions on human rights) and in constant interaction with it.

What about the roles of these three UNs for decision making on human security? Human security does not imply centralised decision making—let alone taking all issues to the Security Council. This is a plus. Decision making outside the Security Council and the GA is often better and less contentious. Decisions by regional bodies can sometimes avoid risks and fears of global intervention. Decisions in the WHO, UNDP, UNICEF, UNFPA or WFP are generally more technical and less politicised than in the Security Council or in the GA. There is no reason to think that recognising issues to be part of an agenda for strengthening human security should change these traditions—and they might enhance them.

In the case of Afghanistan, some of the basic difficulties in taking seriously a new approach to human security are well indicated by expenditures. According to the NHDR for Afghanistan, the coalition forces and NATO in 2004 were spending some $13 billion a year on the 'war on terror' and military actions in Afghanistan—on what these parties see as their priorities for achieving security in Afghanistan (and worldwide). Related to this were the still enormous but much lower expenditures on reconstruction and development in Afghanistan, at about $4–5 billion per year, a large part of which goes to expenditures on expatriates and contracts for international companies, largely American based.

One must ask whether all this effort is achieving its stated objectives or even fulfilling what are seen as key national interests in the United States and other main countries of the Coalition or the main allies in the region. The analysis of the Afghanistan NDHR gives many reasons to believe that these objectives are not being fulfilled—that stability is not being achieved, that demobilisation is lagging, that much power remains with the warlords, that the narco-trafficking continues and that very many ordinary people of Afghanistan are frustrated and disillusioned. At what point, does a tipping point occur, for instance, when it becomes clear that some important changes of strategy and approach are required? At that point, we believe that many of the elements of alternative strategy set out in the NDHR on human security might be seen to be in the enlightened interest both of the external coalition and of more democratic elements and groups within Afghanistan itself. Afghanistan could

470   *R. Jolly and D. Basu Ray*

perhaps then become more of a place of stability and less of a threat to global and national human security.

4   CONCLUSIONS

The country level perspective on human security—obtained from analysing some 13 NHDRs—shows the value of human security as an operational approach to people-centred security and demonstrates its ability to identify priorities and important conclusions for national and international policy. The various objections to human security concerns and approaches as elaborated in some recent academic literature hold little water when tested against the approaches and findings of the NHDRs reviewed for this analysis.

The methodology of the Latvian NHDR is of particular relevance for analysing human security in other countries and situations. This approach—surveying a random sample of the population to determine the insecurities which they subjectively felt or objectively experienced as most important, with a ranking and rating of the different insecurities according to intensity—seems applicable in many other countries and situations.

The motivation of governments to implement policies for preventing or mitigating different forms of human insecurity will inevitably vary from country to country. Nonetheless, analyses of human security can still be of great importance and value, even if not directly put into operation. The information obtained and the analysis undertaken of human security needs can still be used to critique the adequacy or neglect of human security issues in current policy or to build coalitions for change and for pressurising policy makers to respond to specific human security needs.

The recent UN agreement to establish a Peacebuilding Commission provides a new challenge and opportunity to apply human security analyses proactively. The work and effectiveness of the Commission will be significantly enhanced if it can (a) rely on country-specific human security analysis to improve its understandings of the context of the problems it will confront, and (b) base its subsequent actions on the objectives and principles of human security. National human security reports (and perhaps also regional and sub-national reports), if prepared objectively by well-informed professionals, can provide a frame of reference to ensure a broad approach to peace-building. This would undoubtedly mark a real advance in international action for peace and security, and as steps to translate national perspectives into global agendas.

5   ACKNOWLEDGEMENTS

The authors are grateful for comments on an earlier draft by Des Gasper and two anonymous reviewers. They have also benefitted from discussions at meetings on human security held under the auspices of Academic Council on the United Nations System (ACUNS), the Von Hugel Institute in Cambridge, the IDS in Sussex and in New York at a meeting convened by the Canadian Government and the UN Intellectual History Project of the Ralph Bunche Center of City University.

REFERENCES

Annan K. 2005. In larger freedom: towards development, security, and human rights for all, United Nations General Assembly, A/59/2005.

Ayoob M. 1997. Defining security: a subaltern realist perspective. In *Critical Security Studies: Cases and Concepts*, Krause K, Williams MC (eds). Borderlines Volume 8, University of Minnesota Press: Minneapolis.

Berman E. 2000. Re-armament in Sierra Leone: one year after the Lomé Peace Agreement. *The Small Arms Survey*, Occasional Paper 1.

Booth K. 1991. Security and emancipation. *Review of International Studies* 17(4).

Busumtwi-Sam J. 2002. Development and human security. *International Journal* 53(2).

Buzan B, Ole Wæver O, Jaap de Wilde J. 1998. *Security: a new framework for analysis*. Lynne Rienner Publishers: London.

Chawla S. 2000. United Nations Mission in Sierra Leone: a search for peace. *Strategic Analysis* 24(9).

Commission on Human Security. 2003. *Human security now*. Communications Development Incorporated: New York.

Dalby S. 1997. Contesting an essential concept. In *Critical Security Studies: Cases and Concepts*, Krause K, Williams MC (eds). Borderlines Volume 8, University of Minnesota Press: Minneapolis.

Deudney D. 2001. Environment and security: muddled thinking. *Bulletin of the Atomic Scientists* 47(3).

Foong-Khong Y. 2001. Human security: a shotgun approach to alleviating human misery? *Global Governance* 7.

Gasper D. 2005. Securing humanity: situating 'human security' as concept and discourse. *Journal of Human Development* 6(2).

Grant JA. 2005. Diamonds, Foreign Aid, and the Uncertain Prospects for Post-Conflict Reconstruction in Sierra Leone. Research Paper No.2005/49, United Nations University.

Hagman L. 2002. Security and Development in Sierra Leone. Working Paper, International Peace Academy.

Homer-Dixon TF. 1991. On the threshold: environmental changes as causes of acute conflict. *International Security* 16(2).

Jolly R, Basu Ray D. 2006. The Human Security Framework and National Human Development Reports: A Review of Experiences and Current Debates. NHDR Occasional Paper 5, Human Development Report Office, UNDP, New York.

Keynes JM. 1964. *The General Theory of Employment, Interest and Money*. Harcourt, Brace Javonovich: New York.

King G, Murray CJL. 2001–2002. Rethinking human security. *Political Science Quarterly* 116(4).

Knudsen OV. 2001. Post-Copenhagen security studies: desecuritizing securitization. *Security Dialogue* 32(3).

MacFarlane SN, Foong-Khong Y. 2006. *Human Security and the UN: A critical history*. Indiana University Press: Bloomington.

Owens H, Arneil B. 1999. The Human Security Paradigm Shift: A New Lens on Canadian Foreign Policy? Report of the University of British Columbia Symposium on Human Security. In Worlds Apart: Human Security and Global Governance, Tehranian M (ed.). I.B. Tauris: London.

Paris R. 2001. Human security: paradigm shift or hot air. *International Security* 26(2).

Stoett P. 1999. *Human and Global Security*. University of Toronto Press: London.

Thomas C. 1999. Introduction. In *Globalisation, Human Security, and the African Experience*, Thomas C, Wilkin P (eds). Colorado, Lynne Rienner: Boulder.

United Nations Development Programme. 1993. Human Development Report 1993—People's Participation. Oxford University Press: New York.

United Nations Development Programme. 1994. Human Development Report 1994—New dimensions of human security. Oxford University Press: New York.

472   *R. Jolly and D. Basu Ray*

United Nations Development Programme. 1998a. Lesotho Human Development Report 1998. Maseru: Lesotho.

United Nations Development Programme. 1998b. Sierra Leone Human Development Report 1998: From Civil Conflict to Human Security. Freetown: Sierra Leone.

United Nations Development Programme. 2001. Macedonia Human Development Report 2001: Social Exclusion and Human Insecurity in FYR Macedonia. FYR Macedonia.

United Nations Development Programme. 2002/2003. Latvia Human Development Report 2002/2003: Human Security. Riga: Latvia.

United Nations Development Programme. 2002a. Bangladesh Human Security Report 2002: In Search of Justice and Dignity. Bangladesh.

United Nations Development Programme. 2002b. East Timor National Human Development Report 2002: The Way Ahead. Dili: East Timor.

United Nations Development Programme. 2002c. Solomon Islands Human Development Report 2002: Building a Nation. University of Queensland: Australia.

United Nations Development Programme. 2004. Afghanistan National Human Development Report 2004: Security with a Human Face; Challenges and Responsibilities. Army Press: Islamabad.

The UN Secretary General's High-level Panel on Threats, Challenges and Change. 2004. *A more secure world: our shared responsibility.* United Nations Press: New York.

Walker RBJ. 1997. The subject of security. In *Critical Security Studies: Cases and Concepts,* Krause K, Williams MC (eds). Borderlines Volume 8, University of Minnesota Press: Minneapolis.

Walt S. 1991. The renaissance of security studies. *International Studies Quarterly* **35**(2): 211–239.

[20]

A Methodologically Pragmatist Approach to Development Ethics

Asunción Lera St Clair

This paper suggests that lessons from the field of environmental ethics and sociological perspectives on knowledge are important tools for rethinking what type of ethical analysis is needed for building up further the field of development ethics and, more generally, for addressing some of the most fundamental ethical problems related to global poverty and development. The paper argues for a methodologically pragmatist approach to development ethics that focuses on the interplay between facts, values, concepts and practices. It views development ethics as a hybrid between a public moral–political philosophy and a public conception of social science. Ethical analyses of poverty and development must lead to fundamental changes in the ways knowledge is produced and justified and must challenge the dominance of global institutions and orthodox economics as the single sources of expert knowledge for development. Two of the main tasks of ethical analysis is to provide tools for the formulation of alternative knowledge for development centred on the equal moral worth of all human beings, and to influence global policy making as well as multilateral institutions' goals and policies. The last section of the paper argues that Amartya Sen's version of the Capability Approach is already methodologically pragmatist and points to some convergence between Sen's work and John Dewey's. Further sociological and methodologically pragmatist analysis of the approach is needed to assess the ways in which it is influencing debates on human development and leading to policy changes, and the possible distortions it suffers when adopted by multilateral agencies and policy makers.

Development ethics is useless unless it can be translated into public action. By public action is meant action taken by public authority, as well as actions taken by private

An earlier version of this paper was presented at the international conference on Ethics and Development at Michigan State University, East Landing (USA) 8–15 April 2005. The section on methodological pragmatism draws from an unpublished paper written with Andrew Light called 'A Pragmatist Methodology for Development Ethics,' presented at the American Philosophical Association (APA) meeting in New York, December 1999. I have updated, transformed and used some parts and insights developed with Light in a way he may not recognize. I thank Andrew Light, David Crocker, Desmond McNeill, and Alf Nilsen, the organizers and the audience at the MSU conference and two reviewers. Special thanks to Des Gasper. My work in completing this paper has been inspired by the writings of Denis Goulet, who passed away at the end of 2006, and by my meetings and interactions with him. Correspondence to: University of Bergen, Norway. Email: asun.st.clair@sos.uib.no

agents by having important consequences for the life of the public community. The
central question is: How can moral guidelines influence decisions of those who hold
power?

The Cruel Choice (Goulet 1971, p. 335)

Introduction

There is an increasing awareness of the ethical aspects of development policy and
practice among scholars, practitioners and development agencies. Development
ethics today is slowly evolving into a wider field of knowledge studied in universities
and research centers and there is an increasing amount of development ethics courses
and seminars.[1] A certain interest in the ethical aspects of development is slowly
making a breakthrough among practitioners, donors and multilateral development
agencies, including the World Bank.[2] The most influential multilateral agency proposing an ethically grounded view on development is the United Nations Development
Programme (UNDP), through its Human Development Report Office and its flagship
publication—the Human Development Reports (HDRs). Amartya Sen's capability
approach provides the intellectual basis of human development (UNDP 1990–2007,
Sen 1999), and there is a fast growing body of work on this approach, its reformulation
in terms of freedom, and the more philosophically grounded version of capabilities
elaborated by Martha Nussbaum.[3] In addition, the revamping of human rights by
most UN agencies and donors has led to important research on the role that rights
may have in redefining development and poverty.[4] Clearly, there is a fast emerging
group of authors working on global justice and global ethics, also touching on
development issues, including this special issue.[5]

  This paper focuses on what type of ethical thinking is needed to address the most
important challenges posed by international development and development aid. As
the opening quote by Goulet rightly argues, development ethics may be useless
unless it has a real impact on those with the power to change the way policies are
elaborated and implemented. Development ethics needs also to reach out to private
actors (including individuals in advanced economies as well as collective private
agents). In other words, development ethics must have a policy impact, to change
practices, and to influence peoples' perception of what is good development for all
and, thus, to lead to alternative courses of action. Even though powerful development
agents are starting to acknowledge some of the roles that values may have in increasing
the effectiveness of development processes, development ethics, as a field of
knowledge, remains marginal among those who have the power and the legitimacy
to frame development problems and to guide global development policy making.
The influence of the capabilities approach and the importance of human development
are increasing, no doubt; but among global institutions, it is too often adopted at a
superficial level and at the expense of engaged critique on the value conflicts and
challenges to neo-liberal policies that the actual implementation of such an alternative
development view may lead to. Human rights are also being adapted and often distorted and instrumentalized to suit the conceptual frameworks of global institutions

responsible for development policy (for example through connecting rights to more widely acknowledged ideas such as 'participation' and 'empowerment')—strategies that have failed to deliver results in other areas, for example gender equality. Ethical thinking and the role of values in development risk is being instrumentalized and narrowed down to justify ongoing development policies, or to justify appeals for charity towards the very poor (McNeill & St. Clair 2006, forthcoming). Ethical analysis then loses its role as providing analytical tools and ethical clarification to formulate alternative knowledge for development centred on the equal moral worth of all human beings, and shifting development from a charity issue to a matter related to questions of global and social justice. Development ethics may miss the opportunity to contribute to the increasingly obvious ethical flaws of neo-liberal ideology and to join forces with a growing body of theories and praxis on global justice, challenging the unfairness of a global system that benefits the powerful and ignores or damages the vulnerable.[6]

The paper argues that one of the main tasks of development ethics is engagement with the knowledge and policies of multilateral institutions—the most powerful actors responsible for framing what is development and what to do to reduce poverty. It suggests that lessons from the field of environmental ethics and sociological perspectives on knowledge are important for achieving such a goal. The paper argues for a methodologically pragmatist approach for development ethics that focuses on the interplay between facts, values, concepts and practices. It views development ethics as a hybrid between a public moral–political philosophy and a public conception of social science. Ethical analyses of poverty and development must lead to fundamental changes in the ways knowledge is produced, legitimized and justified, and to challenge the dominance of global institutions and orthodox economics as the single sources of expert knowledge for development. The last section of the paper argues that Amartya Sen's version of the capability approach is already methodologically pragmatist, that there are interesting similarities between Sen and John Deweys' thought. But it requires more awareness as to the ways in which the approach may be distorted by multilateral agencies and used to justify policies not consistent with the philosophy of the approach.

Third Stage Development Ethics: Addressing the Co-production of Knowledge and Politics

Des Gasper argues that writings on development ethics may be divided into three stages (1997, 2004). The first stage refers to the realization or the experiencing resulting from moral awareness, or an opening and realization that some issues in development may indeed carry ethical consequences, ethical meanings. This first phase, Gasper argues, is more related to experience that raises moral awareness. Second stage development ethics is the phase where researchers or practitioners (who presumably have already experienced stage one) formulate concepts and ideas to capture, reflect upon and theorize on ethical issues in development. The second stage can start with descriptions and clarification of values and value choices in relation to development and development aid. Flowing from this conceptual and theory building phase comes the stage where there is further systematization and assessment of value choices and problems. Third stage development ethics attempts to address opposing ethical views, the need to compromise and negotiate and apply insights from stage two. This is the stage of application, compromise and nego- tiation—the moment of attempting to reach sufficient support in order to influence policy making. Third stage development ethics is the 'ethics of policy planning and professional practice, devising and negotiating and trying to execute value-sensitive action (Gasper 2004, p. xii).'

Gasper acknowledges that all three stages are interconnected, and that his distinction among the stages has merely analytical purposes. The three stages may best be seen as part of an organic process that moves from experiencing the moral dilemmas and ethical questions posed by development, to the conceptualization and theorizing of such ethical issues, and to the negotiation and sorting out of value conflicts and elabor- ation of policies. I wish, however, to push forward Gasper's analysis and argue for the need to concentrate precisely on the intrinsic linkages between the third stage of nego- tiation and policy making for development with both experience, moral awareness and perceptions (stage one) as well as with the elaboration of concepts and theoretical approaches (stage two). This is a more accurate strategy to investigate the way that knowledge and policies are actually produced by global institutions—the most powerful actors in the dominant framing and policy making for development. Rather than at a third stage, value clarification is established in stage one, primarily, due to the overarch- ing importance given to the cognitive values of economics above any other value, includ- ing ethical values.

Organizational cultures and dominant experts in these global institutions tend to be dominated by neo-liberal economics, ill-prepared to deal with the complexities of development processes and their impact on people's lives and the environment; and centred around quantitative analyses built upon a narrow informational basis that tends to discount ethical concerns as relevant knowledge.[7] This blindness towards ethical concerns that characterizes neo-liberal ideas influences not only the choice of concepts, but the ways concepts are elaborated and the specific meanings attached to what are often complex ideas. Explicit value clarification and value choices, if they occur, often mean the seeking of justifications for already decided knowledge systems, where knowledge and action overlaps. These knowledge systems may not necessarily be morally acceptable nor even have any ethical grounding at all. And by the time one reaches the third stage of policy planning and professional practice, alternatives and values have already been sorted out and it is very problematic to have a well- balanced negotiation. Ethically grounded policy proposals may end up being an artificial superimposition of merely rhetorical value claims that may hide the actual value choices made in the early stages. Ethics and development may simply be outright moralizing and patronizing.

I have explored elsewhere some of the processes in which knowledge systems are built within global institutions, in particular, institutions that have taken as their main tasks to produce not only policy but also to perform basic research on poverty and development. Using insights from social studies of science (STS),

Journal of Global Ethics 145

I have argued that ideas in development are best viewed as 'intellectual boundary objects,' and processes of knowledge formulation as boundary work—a combination of strategies and contingencies rather than simply a scientific endeavor (St. Clair 2006a, 2006b). The notion of boundary object, first introduced by Star and Griesemer (1989), refers to objects that serve as interfaces—linkages—between different communities of practice. Boundary objects permit collaboration among diverse partners who view issues from different perspectives, and thus differently, yet permit joint work and collaboration. I have argued that ideas in the multilateral system can be characterized as intellectual boundary objects, as multilateralism is often an arena where ideas ought to serve many users and many purposes, yet provide an interface—a joint space for collaboration. Ideas in the multilateral system are subject to constant negotiation, framing and reframing, as well as to distortions and misuses. Yet, ideas are entangled with political and ideological goals; often political battles are about who names and thus frames social facts. Characterizing ideas as intellectual boundary objects permit us to deepen our look into processes of knowledge production by multilaterals, the ways in which their economic and political power affects the shape of ideas and the policy proposals that flow from specific interpretations of such ideas. The aim would be to investigate what happens inside the global institutions with the power to set the political and intellectual agendas for development along the same lines that Latour and Woolgar investigated on what happens in the every day life of a scientific laboratory. [8]

For example, the World Bank is one of the dominant sources of knowledge for development and poverty reduction. Its research capacities, the influence that the Bank's lending role has in developing countries, and the support it draws from the United States and global financial actors, endow approaches and ideas endorsed by the Bank with a unique power and influence. The Bank may be said to be a major global governance actor as much as a major global knowledge actor—a transnational expertised state-like institution setting the scene for both global politics and global knowledge (St. Clair 2006a). Knowledge produced or supported by the Bank, however, cannot be said to be objective science elaborated independently from politics and disembodied from wider social worlds. Not only is the Bank's knowledge limited by its diverse principals who often pose conflicting demands on the Bank's researchers, but also the legitimacy of such knowledge is drawn through circular processes between the knowledge the Bank produces and the audiences that legitimize that knowledge. Bank researchers tend to address their claims to a particular set of audiences—on the one hand their principals, and on the other, their most powerful peers, mainstream economists. This has enormous consequences for which knowledge counts as legitimate and credible, how ideas are used, transformed and distorted, and for why alternative views tend to be ignored.

It is very common that the justification of, for example, refusing to accept the view that health or education may be best conceptualized as human rights instead of as commodities best supplied by the private sector, is simply because Bank experts address their knowledge claims to a narrow audience of an ideologically-bounded elite of mainstream economists, who are the same audience that then legitimizes such knowledge claims. Accepting health as a human right would challenge the authority of economists because such a definition of health points towards sources of evidence well beyond mainstream economic science and to a broader audience than simply mainstream economists. I argue, thus, that the knowledge-based economic policy dominant in many multilaterals is best seen as straddling an uneven territory between science in the making and politics in the making and not as an objective science or truth speaking to power. It is within this messy interface between knowledge and action, knowledge and politics, institutional cultures and the wider social worlds where we must see the role of ethical values, starting in stage one as defined by Gasper (2004).

Rather than simple social facts waiting to be discovered, poverty and development are complex and ill-structured issues, which cannot be fully captured by the cognitive tools of a single discipline nor subjected to standard methods. Knowledge for development is not reached through objective truths or scientific consensus, rather, it tends to be formed by what can be called 'fact-surrogates', partial accounts of a complex social problem; or as sociologist Stephen Turner puts it, well-structured parts of an ill-structured and complex whole (Turner 2003). The particular shape of these fact-surrogates is decided by the hierarchies of cognitive and moral values entailed by the audiences that legitimize the knowledge claims of these global institutions. These are often the result of a consensus among certain scientists rather than a scientific consensus (St. Clair 2006b). Awareness of the partially constructed character of knowledge is very important, as it is during this messy construction process, where values get chosen and decided upon—some at the expense of others. It is at the very early stages when for example, concerns for human rights, become residual to the values of consumerism and individualism held by mainstream economists. As Alfredo Sfeir Younis, former Senior Adviser to the Managing Directors Office, The World Bank insightfully puts it,

> ... for the time being, the implementation and realization of human rights remain just a residual of another paradigm: i.e., the present paradigm of economic development ... If countries adopt a 'human rights based approach to development', human rights values must permeate each and every aspect of a development strategy, so human rights issues do not come as a residual of economic transactions or other possible leading activities ... What many human rights activists would like to see is that human rights values must cut at the centre of economic values (Sfeir-Younis 2003)

Ideas that challenge mainstream ideology are distorted as a result of the pressures to depoliticize and economize them. And ideas that have ethical content are not excluded from such distorting processes. Value conflicts and trade-offs are commonplace in the battlefield of development agencies, and ethical values that challenge hegemonic ideas and pre-established policy goals tend to be distorted or supplanted by cognitive values. In particular, cognitive values such as measurability, simplicity and efficiency tend to prevail over concerns for global justice or any other ethical principle that challenges the dominance of a market ethic. As politicians also want simple, measurable and quantifiable data, the cognitive values of neo-liberal economics tend to coincide with the cognitive values of policy making and draw still more power from such over-lapping of goals. The widely shared assumption that dominant ideas are value-free enables 'hidden norms' to move freely and shape knowledge and policy for development and poverty in particular ways.

Thus, I emphasize the need for further methodologically pragmatist analysis for development ethics interlinking the experience, theorizing and policy making stages in the processes of constructing knowledge for development. This approach may help to convey that development and global poverty are highly complex social facts, and constructing knowledge about them entails sorting out values—accepting some and rejecting others—from the very early stages of moral awareness and formulating ideas and concepts. From this perspective, the role of a self-conscious methodologi-cally pragmatist development ethics is not only as an interdisciplinary reflection on a public issue, development, but must also evolve into a hybrid between philosophical analysis and social science, addressing the role that not only moral, but also non-moral values have in the formation of knowledge for development and global poverty. Such a truly interdisciplinary endeavour requires not only to address the value conflicts between cognitive and moral values, the processes that construct discourses of fairness, but also to unveil the fairness or unfairness of certain ethical views. Often we tend to disregard the ethical force of what is the dominant global ethic—the ethic of the market. This global ethic, presupposed by mainstream development economics, not only leads to the economization of all social life, but most importantly, it displaces, diffuses and prevents actual ethical reflection (Bauman 2000, 2004; McNeill & St. Clair 2006; Patomaki 2006; St. Clair 2006c).

The characterization I propose for a modified version of Gasper's third stage development ethics flows not only from application of insights from the fields of STS and technology, but also from espousing a philosophically pragmatist methodology that points towards viewing values entangled with empirical accounts of reality; towards the back and forth relations that occur between experiences, perceptions, theories and practices and between knowledge and action. I take such a methodological outlook from the field of environmental ethics, which, I argue, offers us not only important connections between the tasks ahead for addressing jointly environmental sustainability and global justice, but also important methodological lessons for the formulation of a truly interdisciplinary practical ethics that may lead to influence the decisions of those who hold power, which Goulet defined as the overarching goal of development ethics.

A Pragmatist Methodology for Development Ethics

Many in the field of applied ethics have become aware of the need to avoid the mistakes of other fields, where ethical reflection has run parallel and often totally dissociated from the world of action, and from the world of policy. As Gasper (2006) argues, development ethics has always been an interdisciplinary meeting point. This has helped to avoid some of the failures that, for example, led environmental ethics to become disentangled from policy, but the warning against ethical analysis de-linked from practices is now more relevant, as global institutions start adopting normative concepts such as human rights and capabilities; and there is an increasing amount of scholars producing academic work on ethical reflections about global problems. Andrew Light argues that environmental ethics became a haven of extensionism (Light, 1996, 2002). This means that ethical and meta-ethical frameworks, from the history of ethics, have been extended by environmental ethicists to environmental problems. While there is certainly nothing wrong *per se* with extensionism in any applied field—it has after all produced some very interesting work in a variety of subfields—a strong argument can be made that there is something wrong with extensionism if it hinders progress in an applied field, especially where that progress can be measured by the influence of the field in question on the critical problems of the day, central to the interests of the field. Environmental issues, like development, must be understood as a cluster of problems in the world that affect people and that demand an ethical response.

The field of environmental ethics is focused, especially in the United States, on whether nature has value independent from human consideration of that value (often considered as a form of intrinsic value) and then a determination of the duties, obligations or rights that follow from that description of the value of nature Light argues that the resulting philosophical disagreements between non-anthropocentrists (those supporting such a broadly described view) and weak anthropocentrists (those challenging that view on the basis of claims that non-anthropocentric foundations for natural value are incoherent) fail to take into account the moral intuitions of most people with regard to the value of nature. For example, the non-anthropocentric emphasis on determining a value to nature outside human considerations of that value impedes our ability to discuss ways in which anthropogenic impacts on nature can be understood and meliorated through human intuitions about the value of nature. By focusing on whether nature has or does not have intrinsic value, environmental ethics has produced two unfortunate results: first, it excludes from its discussions the many beneficial ways in which environmental protection can be based on human interests, such as founding policies for environmental protection in the common intuitions of obligations to future generations; and second, the focus on abstract concepts of value theory distracts the field from seeking agreement on all those arguments that could morally motivate people to support environmental policies, no matter where those arguments are grounded. Weak anthropocentrists end up spending more of their time debating the value theories of non-anthropocentrists than trying to forge a consensus on the different reasons that can motivate people to protect nature (Light 2002). In short, environmental ethics is not reaching the public nor helping policy makers in their task to articulate policies that make sense for a variety of people and institutions. Environmental ethics today is arguably of interest mainly to other philosophers concerned with abstract debates in value theory.

The pragmatist alternative argues that environmental ethics should break free from these debates and make room for a more public task, at least as part of its mandate. Light's version of this form of pragmatism (which he calls 'methodological environmental pragmatism') is not based on the claim that non-anthropocentric notions of the intrinsic value of nature are necessarily wrong (as the weak anthropocentrist would argue) but instead that there is a task for environmental philosophy beyond simply the search for a foundational theory of the nature of natural value.[9] This is the task of translating the agreed upon objectives of the environmental community, which are reached for a myriad of different reasons and schemes of value, to the wider public. Environmental pragmatists of this school of thought agree that nature is valuable for many reasons and so, when we have an agreed upon end, we wish to translate to the public we do it for as many philosophically valid reasons as is possible to articulate. The advantage of this view is that it does not necessarily require an engagement with and rejection of non-anthropocentrism. Non-anthropocentrists can certainly embrace such a methodologically pragmatist task without giving up their search for the non-instrumental value to nature. They simply need to agree to sometimes set aside their more purely philosophical concerns for this public task in the service of the broader ends of the environmental community.

In the rest of the paper I shall argue that there are important analogies between Light's analysis and debates within development ethics among diverse moral categories, as well as between competing cognitive values, including discussions about the capabilities approach. A methodologically pragmatist development ethics should busy itself in addressing the ways in which debates about human development could be furthered by enrichment and interactions with other global normative discourses such as human rights and human security. A focus on human development is important, because it offers an ethically built view of development already in place among policy makers, with the capacity to make factual changes. In addition, a methodologically pragmatist development ethics would not only address the risks of extensionism proper of philosophical analysis, but also more clearly and explicitly the risks of extending economic theories to a complex and messy world of practices, and challenge the presumption that knowledge and actions are separate. If development ethics is about value conscious ways of thinking about and choosing alternative paths and destinations, as Gasper (2004) rightly argues, then it is the role of the development ethicist to address the processes that decide which paths are taken and which ones are not, and why, from the very early stages of knowledge formation. Being knowledgeable and interacting with practitioners and staff from global institutions is thus part of the role of development ethicists.

But development ethics still displays a tendency to centre on debates about the differences between universalist and particularist views of the essential qualities of a good human life; or on the degree to which it is important to situate views on rights or capabilities within philosophical traditions; or on whether needs, rights or capabilities are the best fundamental concept for development ethics. This tendency may lead to an unfruitful philosophical gridlock with little practical consequences. In my opinion, one way to strengthen human development is to seek synergies between global justice approaches and development ethics (St. Clair 2006c). For example, debates as to whether Thomas Pogge's (2002, 2004, 2007) proposal for viewing severe global poverty as a violation of human rights understood primarily as a violation of liberty rights is philosophically tenable is distracting the attention of many important thinkers at the expense of

150   *A. L. St. Clair*

offering arguments that may lead to influence powerful actors. Pogge's argument is explicitly strategic, aimed to influence the opinions of those who do not view poverty in anyway whatsoever as a question of entitlements and rights, yet who understand the basic language of liberty. At the same time, Pogge's analysis of global poverty draws attention to the unfairness of the institutions that regulate the global economy and situates debates on global poverty and the global institutions responsible for knowledge for development within the macro-framework of globalization. The work of Pogge is also important because he is increasingly centring his work on the unreliability of empirical knowledge about poverty, on the relations between moral and political philosophy and mainstream methodological tendencies in both poverty research and development research. And, although he does not explicitly acknowledge it, his analysis shows the intrinsic relations between the empirical, the political and the normative. For example, Pogge rightly points our attention towards the consequences of the methodological territorialism dominant in poverty research not only on people's moral awareness of poverty but also in leading towards underestimating the actual number of poor people. The assumption that poverty and development are issues bounded by the geographical and political boundaries of the state is one of the leading causes for the blindness people and politicians have towards some of the most fundamental forces producing and perpetuating poverty. In turn, methodological territorialism blinds the citizens of advanced economies from viewing their own entanglement with the poor and, thus, perpetuates the misguided idea that poverty occurs somewhere else and it is those other countries' problems, not their own. It will be important also to see more engagement and linkages on the side of global justice authors, including Pogge, with capabilities perspectives and lessons for reformulating and expanding the idea of human development.

Pogge's global perspective is complementary to the capabilities approach, as it is impossible today to understand development without looking into globalization processes and emerging transnational practices that are affecting the development chances of poor countries. In addition, the emerging consensus on human rights as the leading normative framework for global relations leads towards addressing, to put it broadly, the conflicts raised by the contradictory values of neo-liberal economic globalization and the globalization of human rights and of capabilities including conflicts among various rights and capabilities and various groups. A global perspective leads development ethics to focus its attention not only on the ethical context of human development and capabilities, but often also on contradictory roles of global institutions. For example, the UNDP acts as an institution defending economic globalization, while explicitly defending normative understandings of development as social processes towards the improvement of 'all' people's quality of life. Such contradictory roles affect the chances of the future strengthening of human development, and the UNDP needs to address these conflicts explicitly.

In addition, a methodologically pragmatist development ethics points towards concerns with mainstream economic development doctrines and may add methodological rigor to the analysis I drew earlier from the application of insights from STS.[10] Clearly, mainstream economic thinking, the main builder of knowledge for development, falls into the same types of dogmatism as the meta-ethical debates illustrated by Light (1996, 2004), especially as it works within global institutions. Development economics concentrates often on the application of insights from economic theory to the real world, and presumes a linear relation between the arena of politics and the arena of science. The presumed dichotomy in mainstream and development economics between 'knowledge' and 'action' is one of the main reasons for the persistence of outdated and unhelpful theories. The prevalence of formalized and quantified views may be helpful in providing guidance to policy makers in simple issues, but it is dangerous if used to address highly complex and ill-structured problems, more so if used as a substitution for detailed knowledge of local conditions, as it is often the case amongst experts from global institutions. As Ellerman rightly argues,

> Academic economists and global development bureaucrats have little contact with local realities and thus they tend to be driven by such simplified cartoon models. Exiles who have not participated in the give and take of politics in a country for years if not decades also tend to have cartoon models. It is the combination of power and highly simplified models of complex social realities that is particularly lethal (Ellerman 2005).

A particular example of the disassociation between knowledge and action, between abstract theorizing and the real world of action, is the pervasive view that economic growth reduces poverty almost on a one to one basis. Such 'belief' is more the result of extending economic theory to the real world, while ignoring a messy world of practices and social institutions. As Jan Vandermoortele (2002) reminds us, the combination of an income based definition of poverty together with the uncritical faith in the overarching value of logarithmic regressions leads to the 'dangerous' prediction that poverty lowers at the same pace as economic growth rises. Such thinking commits the fallacy of misplaced concreteness, Vandermoortele rightly argues, as averages are abstractions and not real observations. That is, 'the fact that the income of the poor rises one-for-one with overall per capita income may be statistically correct, but it is not necessarily true (2002, p. 9).'

A pragmatist methodology for development ethics focuses our attention on the ways in which economic science's abstract theorizing plays in practice. It is impossible to claim the same 'certainty of outcomes' in the messy world of practices as it is often claimed in academic theoretical publications. As I have elaborated somewhere else, in practice, there are often massive difficulties in establishing the economic situation of a country (St.Clair 2006b). IMF or Bank missions are messy and complex fact finding exercises, often leading to uncertain and risky guesses that experts are forced to make, due to the lack of data or contradictory statistical reports of different ministries in client countries. Numbers end up often being *interpreted* rather than collected and such interpretations conform more to particular circumstances experts find themselves immersed in or simply those they are able to get because of their social skills rather than the result of an accurate application of economic theory. Development and poverty, in the same way as climate change or environmental sustainability, are highly complex and ill-structured problems, far from mere facts easily defined, measured and planned. Knowledge-based policy recommendations in these arenas are plagued with uncertainties and risks. As Stiglitz vividly argues, uncertainty and risk are defining characteristics of knowledge-based economic policy (2001, 2002).

Most importantly, as I hope to have illustrated earlier, it is at this level of formation of economic knowledge, where values are sorted out, some chosen, some rejected and where the politicization of moral worth occurs. The false belief that economic science provides a true account of reality is perhaps one of the most fundamental reasons for rejecting the role of ethical thinking as valid knowledge for development.[11] Untangling the value problems related to the scientific uncertainties of knowledge for development is, therefore, one of the important tasks for development ethics. This is of particular imoortance for reclaiming the moral worth of all human beings and to prevent intrinsic values from becoming instrumentalized.

There are further lessons to draw from a pragmatist methodology for development ethics. The focus on competing meta-ethical or meta-economic positions can be wrong-headed for other reasons as well. The connection between ethics and public policy does not consist in simply applying a correct moral theory to a specific situation. In fact, we might not want to live in a world where priorities for development policy were thought to reside only in the extension of moral theories. The assumption of an identifiable scheme of moral knowledge would lead to an intractable state of affairs, where no negotiations among competing conceptions of the good or a well-organized society were possible. This would be particularly unfortunate in the case of development because development policy making always takes place within a political framework—one in which the parties are always unequal. The last thing that development aid and co-operation needs is to become part of an inflexible philosophical debate as what has happened, for example, in the case of family planning. The history of the debate about abortion shows the dangers in making the moral dimensions of public policies explicit while leaving untouched the role played by cognitive values and values hidden under the veil of scientism. In this regard, Paul Thompson claims that 'it is at least arguable that the bitterness and inflexibility of the abortion debate today is due to both sides not only having adopted philosophically incompatible positions, but also having buttressed these positions with moral philosophy that demonizes the other side (Thompson 1996).' A similar inflexibility is already the characteristic of globalization debates. Development ethics must aim to cut through it.

The Capabilities Approach and Methodological Pragmatism

I wish to contribute to the debate on the capabilities approach by offering now a brief analysis of the ways in which Sen's capability and freedom approach can be seen as an instance of a methodologically pragmatist development ethic. Development as freedom can be seen as a methodologically pragmatist public philosophy that espouses a theory of valuation but not a theory of value. That some freedoms or capabilities are essential, for Sen, does not entail they follow from a theory of true human nature, nor from a universalist notion of values (neither a universal conception of the validity of all local values nor a general universal conception of value) (Sen 1999, p. 247). Certainly, Sen's approach rests on a universalist presumption about the value of freedom. But this presumption goes hand in hand with the role that bundles of freedoms and capabilities have in leading people to reach fulfilling lives on their own terms. Sen calls these two roles of freedom (i) the evaluative reason, and the (ii) effectiveness reason. Evaluative, because it allows for an assessment of how much progress development has helped in enhancing people's freedoms. Effective, because free agency—the outcome of many interconnected and interdependent freedoms—is a necessary condition for successful development (Sen 1999, p. 4). For example, women who have the freedom to work outside their homes enhance their social standing as well as contribute to the prosperity of their families. Working outside the home usually gives women more visibility, voice and less dependency, as well as enhances their education. This, in turn, strengthens women's agency and usually makes women more informed, able and empowered to influence family decisions.

The bridge Sen builds between the economic, political, social and ethical aspects of development is a public philosophy very much in the sense of the term championed by John Dewey. This is not to say, however, that I am arguing for a form of extensionism with respect to classical American pragmatism, nor that Sen is a pragmatist in the Deweyian sense, but there are nonetheless some interesting similarities between Dewey's and Sen's works. Dewey's social and political philosophy is based on the avoidance of metaphysical and meta-ethical dead ends. Sen and Dewey both try to work out a conception of freedom that does not appeal to ontology or epistemology, and that eventually breaks through the distinction between theory and practice by making both of them part of experience. But how does Dewey situate this form of freedom?

First, Dewey argued that we cannot have *a priori* knowledge of our own nature. As Hilary Putnam (1992) puts it: Dewey's view is that we do not know what our interests and needs are or what we are capable of until we actually engage in politics. A corollary of this view is that there can be no final answer to the question of how we should live, and, therefore, we should always leave it open to further discussion and experimentation. Dewey also warns us about the risks of inverting the relationship between commodities and the good life, and to look for a proper understanding of the role of economics in human life. In his critique of liberalism, Dewey claimed that the new material possibilities resulting from science and technology have brought material security to many, but this abundance is taken as an end in itself and not as a means to a more fulfilling human life. As Dewey claimed:

> The habits of desire and effort that were bred in the age of scarcity do not readily subordinate themselves . . . Even now when there is a vision of an age of abundance and when the vision is supported by hard facts, it is material security as an end that appeals to most rather than the way of living which this security makes possible (vol. 11, p. 44, in Hickman 1998).

Last, at the core of Dewey's thinking, lies a politicized conception of individuality as a social product, which emphasizes the interdependence of politics with socioeconomic factors. Individuality, for Dewey, is the result of an ongoing social development process, a development that occurs because we are involved in many social interdependencies. According to Dewey, 'Individuality, like community, is a process of growth. It is self-realization, the continuous development of one's potentialities (vol. 11, p. 44 in Hickman 1998).' And this social conception of individualism leads Dewey to defend a very particular conception of freedom: 'Freedom conceived as power to act in accord to choice depends upon positive and constructive changes in social arrangements (Dewey 3, pp. 100–101 in Hickman 1998).'

Sen's conception of development as freedom is consistent with the Deweyian tradition as well as similar to Dewey's concern with the relationship between 'our wealth and our ability to live as we would like (Sen 1999, p. 13).' Most importantly, Sen emphasizes a view of participation and public scrutiny in accord with Dewey's experiential philosophy. As the world changes, so do our values, and our opinions of institutions and cultural systems from the past. The task of the pragmatist philosopher is never finished, and it is historical, yet its consequences ought to be thrown into the public arena, in an open-ended process of debate and deliberation.

These similarities make Dewey's and Sen's view of freedom very close—freedom as the ability to choose our own life. Sen, like Dewey, emphasizes the role of politics as well as of ethics in the assessment of the good life, and the need to bring to light the empirical connections among the social, economic, political and ethical. Sen offers a view of development based on both the intrinsic and the consequential value of different freedoms, as well as on the constructive role these freedoms play in the genesis of values and priorities in development decisions. Although Sen accepts that freedom is an end in itself, he cannot defend moral absolutes. Sen would probably agree with Dewey that people cannot really know all their capabilities—least of all how they want to live their lives—before they have full political liberties. But achieving those political liberties, according to Sen, depends on a wide variety of conditions and opportunities. Development as freedom has to leave conceptions of the good life open-ended and exposed to a continuous process of democratic inquiry. After all, Sen, like Dewey and John Rawls, would accept the claim that moral theory may sometimes require revision on the basis of empirically received facts, which help us understand the demands of morality. In order to be consistent, the capabilities approach needs to see lists of capabilities as drafts in progress and place most of its normative emphasis, as Crocker rightly identities, on participatory deliberation (Crocker 2005).

The pragmatist stance of the notion 'capability' has helped in its acceptance as the theoretical basis for human development, as part of the twin boundary object human development-capability (HD-CA), which functions within the UNDP. What seems to have made the difference is the ways in which certain values are imbued in HD-CA. Intellectual boundary objects that have their philosophical underpinnings explicitly elaborated, with embodied ethical principles and which take ethical views as their point of departure have shown to be, at least partly, driving forces towards alternative policy making.[12] This boundary object has demonstrated that an 'idea' is able to force the institution to develop and use it towards more democratic knowledge production.

Journal of Global Ethics 155

Arguably, this represents the substitution of cognitive values by moral values. Indeed, boundary objects with embodied ethical concerns survive better trade-offs with cognitive values and power pressures. They are also more able to lead institutions towards a learning process and to raise support from different stakeholders (thereby, affecting the thresholds of legitimacy and credibility). They may also be able to represent the concerns and needs of non-experts and vulnerable groups who may not be partners in the processes of knowledge production and policy formulation. But the intellectual boundary object HD-CA still lacks a serious assessment of the ways in which development agencies themselves support poverty-producing forces, and are themselves institutional mechanisms preventing the eradication of poverty. As it operates within UNDP, the idea still hides the role of inequalities and compares itself with past policies rather than attempting to create alternative paths of action and change. In particular, HC-CA compares itself to mainstream economics but leaves unanswered perhaps less politically correct questions such as the ways in which over-accumulation (of goods but also perhaps of capabilities) may lead to other people's dispossession, to paraphrase David Harvey (2003). A better intellectual boundary object would compare itself with counterfactuals based on global justice and not only with past or dominant knowledge and policy. Foreseeing the future use of ideas by global institutions, I have proposed, that a well-designed boundary object ought to have *embodied* three main ethical principles: *equity, accountability* and *deliberative participation* (St. Clair 2004). The embodiment of these three principles may act as a conveying device, or as obligatory passing points, to place discussions about global justice at the core of debates about development. In other words, intellectual boundary objects embodied with these three ethical principles can act as *incentives* for better and more stable boundary management and for more salient, legitimate, and credible knowledge. Capability already has some of these norms imbued, clearly the norm of participatory deliberation (Alkire 2002; Crocker 2005, 2006), perhaps less so the equity and accountability norms.

In short, I argue that Sen's capability approach is methodologically pragmatist. Sen's capability and freedom approach reminds us all of something very basic neo-liberals seem to have forgotten: that theoretical freedom is not the same as actual freedom for all. Yet, capability theorists need more engagement with the consequences of such a view as well as with the ways in which it is being used and abused by global institutions. It may be important to investigate the degree to which in its intellectual boundary form, the HD-CA is leading the whole theory towards too much political correctness, by not challenging too frontally the established norms and goals of the UNDP and the development aid bureaucracies, in general. Although I cannot address this issue here, it will be important to follow up on the ways in which there is an increasing tendency to relegate Martha Nussbaum's version of capability to a second place in debates about human development, simply because it lacks that element of correctness that Sen's version captures so well. As much as I favour the deliberation aspect imbued in Sen's version of capabilities, some issues may not be dealt with properly only by open deliberation, as Nussbaum's body of work rightly argues. As Alkire (2002) has illustrated very well, some notion of basic needs is still

156   *A. L. St. Clair*

imbued within capability. Perhaps good boundary predisposing leads to a 'lack of teeth', or too softened version of ideas, or as Gasper names it, they tend to display a 'cautious' boldness.

The capabilities approach, in all its versions, could be improved by making much more explicit the ways in which it differs from neo-liberal economics or other mainstream economic theories. It will be strengthened by clarifying the degree of acceptance of current capitalist globalization; and they ways in which it may be weakened by needing to be 'economics,' albeit with its philosophical underpinnings explicit. Finally, capability may be improved by more self-reflection regarding its position towards other disciplines besides philosophical ethics and mainstream economics. Not only are markets not the best way to allocate resources equitably, they may also be the cause of massive inequalities that prevent people's exercise of their political freedoms and lead to powerlessness.[13] These and other basic insights have had extensive treatment in sociology, anthropology, social psychology and international political economy, and today are being addressed by critical globalization studies.[14]

Concluding Remarks

To conclude, a methodologically pragmatist development ethics may enable philosophers and non-philosophers to ground each other's views, to enrich analysis and critiques of development and to reach forward not only by envisioning better futures and attending to how to generate moral awareness for the poor and vulnerable, but also by engaging in formulating institutional and practical changes that may make a difference in practice. Development ethics is already multidisciplinary but the warning against moralism and against leading debates about the goodness or badness of development and globalization towards unfruitful meta-ethical and meta-theoretical discussions is indeed relevant.

If disembodied from policies and practices, there is a risk that ethics leads to confusing rather than to clarifying policy debates, whether debates centre on competing conceptions of the good, on competing moral categories (e.g. capabilities or rights) or competing economic theories (e.g. social choice or behavioral economics). And given that the empirical, political and normative elements of development debates are entangled, clarifying their moral dimensions may lead disputants to insist on an interpretation of the problems that conforms to their philosophical positions. To avoid falling into moralizing an already polarized debate and, thus, to preclude rather than help political action, development ethics must be necessarily and explicitly both a moral and political philosophy, and a hybrid of philosophy and social science, drawing from practitioners knowledge and practices. Yet, a pragmatic form of this dual strategy would remain agnostic with regard to the possibility of absolute moral and scientific knowledge. A pragmatist methodology would focus attention not only on a plurality of values but also on a plurality of possible epistemologies. It leads our attention towards coping with scientific uncertainty and value conflicts and towards unveiling and avoiding the politization of the moral worth of people, actions and institutions. It is here where the overarching normative value of deep democracy is justified, yet many issues cannot be left to deliberation. The formulation of a methodologically pragmatist approach to development ethics offered here leads our attention towards disentangling false dichotomies, such as, for example, the distinction between altruistic and self-interested behaviour, or the distinction between knowledge and action and between poverty and development research by global institutions as separate realms of global politics. To the question of what comes first: facts, values or practices, I wish to answer, 'all of the above'; as coming to grips with moral conflicts and the sorting of moral responsibilities lies on the interfaces of the three (Busch 2000). In short, a methodologically pragmatist development ethics needs to engage with processes of knowledge formation by global development institutions and to aim at democratizing those by unveiling, pointing and clarifying value choices, conflicts and value laden concepts from the very early stages of knowledge production. Development is a public issue and not a matter to be left only to certain experts. Among all, it is important to retake the meaning of development, to investigate what has happened to it, since the end of World War II, and to divest it from all the negative aspects it has accrued, all the bad habits sewn in by those who have tailored its meaning to goals that may not be the best for the common good.

As Dewey rightly argued, philosophy ought to be a critique of prejudices, a

> . . . kind of intellectual disrobing. We cannot permanently divest ourselves of the intellectual habits we take on and wear when we assimilate the culture of our own time and place. But intelligent furthering of culture demand that we take some of them off, that we inspect them critically to see what they are made of and what wearing them does to us (Dewey 1958, p. 36, quoted in Murphy 1990, p. 70).

Development ethics can contribute to the undressing and redressing of development debates and to attempt to influence those in power to put ethics first rather than prevent ethical debate. As stated at the opening quote, very similar arguments were offered by the pioneer of development ethics, Denis Goulet. In his landmark study, *The Cruel Choice* (1971), he had already warned of the direct relations between moral awareness, technocratic development aid and the forgoing of moral evaluation. Development is, as Goulet rightly and insightfully argued, a 'cruel choice' plagued with value conflicts that deserve 'public' attention, that affect us all, the developed and the developers, the experts and the lay people, the poor and the non-poor. As Gasper insightfully argues, Goulet 'called for methodologically sophisticated ethical investigation and debate that are driven by experience, not primarily based in academic philosophy (2006, p. 2).' A methodologically pragmatist development ethics is an offspring of Goulet's life and work, and a path forward in this interdisciplinary space includes to revisit, update and expand Goulet's insights in a way that it may influence decisions of those who hold power.

Notes

[1] This paper does not aim to present the field of development ethics, nor to outline authors and tasks of global ethics or global justice. The term 'development ethics' emerges in the late 1950s and 1960s and was formulated as field of knowledge by Denis Goulet. See Goulet (1976), and a

158   *A. L. St. Clair*

recent collection of papers written from the 1950s until his death (Goulet 2006). Gasper (2006) offers a summary of the relevance of Goulet's work for current debates on development ethics and development aid. Crocker (1991) and (2006), Gasper (1997a) and (2004) and St. Clair (2006d) offer introductions to the field. For information of course syllabi and activities on development ethics see www.development-ethics.org.

[2] For example, the World Bank has a small department addressing value-related matters, in particular faith-based principles but including also the role of values in development (see Marshall and Keough 2004), and many value-related issues are slowly being taken up by the Bank's key publications, for example the World Development Report 2006 on Equity and Development (World Bank 2006). The Inter-American Development Bank has an Initiative on Social Capital, Ethics and Development (see http://www.iadb.org/etica/ingles/index-i.cfm).

[3] For an updated bibliography on Sen's and Nussbaum work and extensive information on authors, approaches and courses on the capability approach see the Human Development and Capability Association (HDCA) website www.capabilityapproach.com.

[4] See for example OHCHR (2005), Osmani (2005), Sen (2005), Sengupta, Negi, and Basu (2005), Sengupta (2007).

[5] Thomas Pogge (2002, 2007), Barry and Pogge (2005), Follesdal and Pogge (2005), is the most well-known author working on global justice. Among others see also Simon Caney (2006), Barry Gills (2007), this special issue and Commers, Vandekerckhove, and Verlinden (forthcoming 2008). I have addressed the relations between development ethics and global justice in St. Clair (2006c).

[6] See among others Louise Amoore (2005), Atitlio Boron (2006), Jeremy Brecher (2000), Robin Cohen and Shirin Rai (2000), Lawrence Cox and Alf Nilsen (forthcoming), Donatella della Porta (2006), Catherine Eschle and Bice Maiguascha (2005), Susan George (2004), Michael Hardt and Toni Negri (2000 and 2004), Ray Kiely 2005, Marjorie Mayo (2005), David McNally (2002), and Amory Starr (2005).

[7] My critique of economics applies only to neo-liberal economics and to the presumption by many development experts that this is the single most important cognitive tool for framing and formulating development policy. Amartya Sen and many human development economists are aiming precisely to formulate alternative economics (as the subtitle of the *Journal of Human Development* states). There is a very large number of authors addressing very different types of economic science, and the specific shortcomings of neoliberal economics. See for example the *Post-autistic Economics Review* (http://www.paecon.net/). See also for example the work of Paul Ekins, Nicholas Georgescu–Roegen, Peter Söderbaum, C. T. Kurien, Herman Daly, or feminist economists such as Nancy Flobre or Irene Van Stavaren. For a fine and extensive discussion of values and economics see Deirdre N. McCloskey (2006), *The Bourgeois Virtues: Ethics for an Age of Commerce.*

[8] I cannot expand the notion of intellectual boundary objects in this article. I have elaborated it further in St. Clair 2006b, an extensive discussion can be found in St. Clair (2004b), and a working paper currently under peer review. See also McNeill and St. Clair (forthcoming 2008). For a more general analysis of the role of ideas in the multilateral system see Boas and McNeill (2004).

[9] Light distinguishes 'methodological environmental pragmatism' from 'historical environmental pragmatism,' the latter usually indicating a process of extending the work of the traditional pragmatist figures such as Dewey, James, Pierce, etc., to environmental problems (see Light 2004).

[10] Although I do not have space to address this in this paper, I wish to point out that environmental pragmatism may gain much from engaging itself with the ways in which climatologists and environmental scientists in general interpret evidence, the social aspects of such knowledge and the role played by global institutions responsible for formulating scientific knowledge.

[11] The work of Pierre Bourdieu and more recently Mary Douglas are instances of well-known and thorough critiques of the notion that economic science provides a true account of reality.

Journal of Global Ethics 159

[12] See Gasper (2005) for a discussion on the notion of human security using this framework.

[13] If I understand it correctly, this is exactly the main argument of Thomas Pogge in arguing that severe poverty is, *de facto*, a violation of the liberty rights that be traced to an unfair system of global economic relations (past and present).

[14] See for example Applebaum and Robinson (2005) and Gills (2005).

References

Alkire, S. (2002) *Valuing Freedoms: Sen's Capability Approach and Poverty Reduction*, Oxford University Press, Oxford.

Amoore, L. (ed.) (2005) *The Global Resistance Reader*, Routledge, London.

Appelbaum, R. & Robinson, W. (2005) *Critical Globalization Studies*, Routledge, London.

Barry, B. & Pogge, T. (2005) *Global Institutions and Responsibilities: Achieving Global Justice* (Metaphilosophy Series in Philosophy), Blackwell, London.

Bauman, Z. (2000) *Liquid Modernity*, Polity Press, London.

Bauman, Z. (2004) *Wasted lives: Modernity and its outcasts*, Polity Press, London.

Brecher, J. Costello, T. & Smith, B. (2000) *Globalization from Below: The Power of Solidarity*, South End, Boston.

Boron, A. (2005) *Empire and Imperialism: A Critical Reading of Michael Hardt and Antonio Negri*, Zed Books, London.

Busch, L. (2000) *The Eclipse of Morality: Science, State and the Market*, Aldine De Gruyter, New York.

Boas, M. & McNeill, D. (2004) *Global Institutions and Development: Framing the World*. Routledge, London.

Caney, S. (2006) *Justice Beyond Borders: A Global Political Theory*, Oxford University Press, Oxford.

Cohen, R. & Rai, S. (eds.) (2000) *Global Social Movements*, Athlone, London.

Commers, M. R., Andekerckhove, W. & Verlinden, A. (eds.) (forthcoming 2008) *Ethics In An Era Of Globalization*, Ashgate, Aldershot.

Crocker, D. (1991) 'Toward development ethics', *World Development*, vol. 19, no. 5, pp. 457–483.

Crocker, D. (2005) Deliberative Participation: The Capabilities Approach and Deliberative Democracy. Available online at: http://www.iadb.org/etica/sp4321-i/DocHit-i.cfm?DocIndex=1298.

Crocker, D. (2006) 'Development ethics, Globalization, and Stiglitz,' in *Globalization, Development, and Democracy: Philosophical Perspectives*, eds. Krausz, M. & Chatterjee, D. Rowman & Littlefield, Lanham, MD.

Dewey, J. (1958) *Experience and Nature*, Dover Publications, Inc., New York.

Dewey, J. (1998), Later works 11:44. Quoted by John Stuhr in 'Dewey's Social and Political Philosophy' in *Reading Dewey: Interpretations for a Postmodern Generation*, ed. L. Hickman, Indiana University Press, Bloomington, Indiana.

Della Porta, D., Andretta, M., Mosca, L. & Reiter, H. (2006) *Globalisation from Below: Transnational Activists and Protest Networks*, University of Minnesota Press, Minneapolis.

Eschle, C. & Maiguascha, B. (2005) *Critical Theories, International Relations and 'The Anti-Globalisation Movement': The Politics of Global Resistance*, Routledge, London.

Ellerman, D. (2005), 'Can the World bank be Fixed?', *Post Autistic Economics Review* 34 [online] Available at http://www.paecon.net/PAEReview/index.htm

Follesdal, A. & Pogge, T. (2005) *Real World Justice: Grounds, Principles, Human Rights, and Social Institutions* (Studies in Global Justice), Springer Verlag, Berlin, Kluver.

Gasper, D. (1997a), 'Development Ethics – an Emergent Field? A Look at Scope and Structure with Special Reference to the Ethics of Aid', in *Ethics and Development: On Making Moral Choices in Development Cooperation*, ed. C. J., Hammenlink, Kampfen, Netherlands.

Gasper, D. (1997b) 'Sen's Capability Approach and Nussbaum's Capability Ethic', *Journal of International Development*, vol. 9, no. 2, pp. 281–302.

160   A. L. St. Clair

Gasper, D. (2004) *Ethics and Development: From Economism to Human Development*, Edinburgh University Press, Edinburgh.

Gasper, D. (2005) 'Securing Humanity: Situating 'Human Security as a Concept and Discourse', *Journal of Human Development*, vol. 6 no. 2, pp. 221–245.

Gasper, D. (2006) 'Everything for Sale? Ethics of National and International Development', *Special issue of Ethics and Economics / La revue Éthique et Économique*, vol. 4, no. 2. Selected papers from the 7th international conference of the International Development Ethics Association (at Makerere University, July 2006) [Online] Available at http://ethiqueeconomique.neuf.fr/

George, S. (2004) *Another World is possible if...*, Verso, London.

Hardt, M. & Negri, T. (2000) *Empire*, Harvard University Press, Boston.

Hardt, M. (2004) *Multitude*, Penguin, Harmondsworth.

Gills, B. (2005) 'Empire' Versus 'Cosmopolis': The Clash of Globalizations', *Globalizations* Vol. 2, p. 1.

Gills, B. (ed.) (2007), Global *Poverty or Global Justice*, Routledge, London.

Goulet, D. (1971) *The Cruel Choice: A New Concept in the Theory of Development*, Macmillan, New York.

Goulet, D. (2006) *Development Ethics at Work* (Routledge Studies on Development Economics), Routledge, London.

Harvey, D. (2003) *The New Imperialism*, Oxford University Press, Oxford.

Hickman, L. (1998) *Essential Dewey: Pragmatism, Education, Democracy*, Indiana University Press, Bloomington, Indiana.

Kiely, R. (2005) *The Clash of Globalisations: Neo-liberalism, The Third Way, and Anti-Globalisation*, Brill, Amsterdam.

Latour, B. & Woolgar, S. (1986) *Laboratory Life: The Construction of Scientific Facts*, 2nd Edition, Princeton University Press, Princeton.

Light, A. (2002) 'Taking Environmental Ethics Public', in *Environmental Ethics: What Really Matters? What Really Works*, eds. D. Schmidtz & E. Willott, Oxford University Press, Oxford.

Light, A. (2004) 'Methodological Pragmatism, Animal Welfare, and Hunting', in *Animal Pragmatism: Rethinking Human non-Human Relations* ed. A. Light & I. Mckenna, University Press, Bloomington, Indiana.

Light, A. & De-Shalit, A. (eds.) (2003), *Moral and Political Reasoning in Environmental Practice*, MIT Press, Cambridge, Mass achuselts.

Light, A. & Katz, E. (eds.) (1996), *Environmental Pragmatism*, Routledge, London.

Marshall, K. & Keough, L. (2004) *Mind, Heart and Soul in the Fight Against Poverty*, World Bank, Washington DC.

Mayo, M. (2005) *Global Citizens: Social Movements and the Challenge of Globalisation*, Zed Books, London.

McCloskey, D. N. (2006) *The Bourgeois Virtues: Ethics for an Age of Commerce*, University of Chicago Press, Chicago.

McNally, D. (2002) *Another World is Possible: Globalization and Anti-Capitalism*, Arbeiter Ring, Winnipeg.

McNeill, D. & St. Clair, A. L. (2006) 'Development Ethics and Human Rights as the Basis for Poverty Reduction: The Case of the World Bank', in *The World Bank and Governance: A Decade of Reform and Reaction* (Routledge/Warwick Studies in Globalization), eds. D. Stone & C. Wright, Routledge, London.

McNeill, D. & St. Clair, A. L. (forthcoming in 2008) *Ethics Human Rights and Poverty: The Role of Multilateral Organizations*, Routledge, London.

Murphy, J. P. (1990) *Pragmatism: From Pierce to Davidson*, Westview Press, Boulder, Colorado.

Office of the High Commissioner for Human Rights (OHCHR) (2005) *Guidelines for A Human Rights Approach to Poverty Reduction Strategies*. OHCHR, Geneva.

Osmani, S. R. (2005) 'Poverty and Human Rights: Building on the Capability Approach', *Journal of Human Development*, vol. 6, no. 2, pp. 205–219.

Patomaki, H. (2006) 'Global Justice: A Democratic Perspective', *Journal Globalizations*, vol. 3, no. 2, pp. 99–120.

Pogge, T. (2004) 'Assisting the global poor', in *The Ethics of Assistance: Morality and the Distant Needy*, ed. D. Chatterjee, Cambridge University Press, Cambridge, Massachusetls.

Pogge, T. (2002) *World Poverty and human rights: Cosmopolitan Responsibilities and Reforms*, Polity Press, London

Pogge, T. (2004) (ed.) (2007) *Freedom from Poverty as a Human Right: Who Owes What to the Very Poor*, Oxford University Press, Oxford.

Putnam, H. (1992) *Renewing Philosophy*, Harvard University Press, Cambridge.

Sen, A. K. (1999), *Development as Freedom*, Knoff, New York.

Sen, A. K. (2005) 'Human Rights and Capabilities', *Journal of Human Development*, vol. 6, no. 2, pp. 151–166.

Sengupta, A. (2007) 'Poverty Eradication and Human Rights', in *Freedom from Poverty as a Human Right: Who Owes What to the Very Poor*, ed. T. Pogge, Oxford University Press, Oxford.

Sengupta, A., Negi, A. & Basu, M. (2005) *Reflections on the Right to Development*, Sage, New Delhi and London.

Sfeir-Younis, A. (2003), 'Human rights and economic development: Can they be reconciled? A view from the World Bank', in *World bank, IMF and Human Rights* Van Genugten, W., P. Hunt & Mathews, N. S., Wolf Legal Publishers, the Netherlands.

Star, S. L. & Griesemer, J. R. (1989) 'Institutional Ecology, Translations and Boundary Objects: Amateurs and Professionals in Berkeley's Museum of Vertebrate Zoology 1907–39,' *Social Studies of Science*, vol. 19, no. 3, pp. 387–420.

Starr, A. (2005) *Global Revolt: A Guide to the Movements Against Globalization*, Zed Books, London.

St. Clair, A. J. (2004a), 'The Role of Ideas in the United Nations Development Programme', in, *Global institutions and Development: Framing the World*, M. Boas and D. McNeill eds. Routledge, London.

St. Clair, A. L. (2004b), *Poverty Conceptions in the United Nations Development Programme and the World Bank: Knowledge, Politics and Ethics*, Dissertation Thesis, University of Bergen, Norway.

St. Clair, A. L. (2006a), 'The World Bank as a Transnational Expertised Institution', *Journal of Global Governance*, vol. 12, no. 1, pp. 77–95.

St. Clair, A. L. (2006b), 'Global Poverty: The Co-Production of Knowledge and Politics', *Journal of Global Social Policy*, vol. 6, no. 1, pp. 57–78.

St. Clair, A. L. (2006c) 'Global Poverty: The Merging Of Development Ethics and Global Justice', *Journal Globalizations*, vol. 3, no. 2, pp. 139–158.

St. Clair, A. L. (2006d) 'Development Ethics: Open-ended and Inclusive Reflections on Global Development,' in *Poverty, Politics and Development: Interdisciplinary Perspectives*, eds. D. Banik, B. Fagbokforlaget.

Stiglitz, J. (2001) 'Ethics, Economic Advice, and Economic Policy', *Inter American Development Bank Initiative on Ethics, Social Capital and Development*, Electronic Library Online Available at: www.iadb.org/etica/sp4321-i/DocHit-i.cfm?DocIndex=74

Stiglitz, J. (2002), *Globalization and Its Discontents*, W.W. Norton, New York.

Thompson, P. (1996), 'Pragmatism and policy: The case of water', in *Environmental pragmatism*, A. Light, & E. Katz eds. Routledge, London.

Turner, S. (2003) *Liberal Democracy 3.0.*, Sage, London.

United Nations Development Programme (1990–2007), *Human Development Reports*, Oxford University Press, New York.

United Nations Office of the High Commissioner of Human Rights (OHCHR) (2004), *Human Rights and Poverty Reduction: A Conceptual Framework*, United Nations, New York and Geneva.

162   *A. L. St. Clair*

Vandermoortele, J. (2002) 'Are we really reducing global poverty', United Nations Development Programme Bureau of Development Policy, working paper.

World Bank (2006), *World Development Report 2006: Equity and Development*, Oxford University Press, Oxford.

Part V
Ethical Development Policy
and Practice

[21]

Hunger, Capability, and Development

DAVID A. CROCKER[1]

David A. Crocker is a visiting senior research scholar at the Institute for Philosophy and Public Policy and a visiting professor at the School of Public Affairs, University of Maryland-College Park. Crocker has taught philosophy at Colorado State University since 1966 and has twice been a Fulbright scholar at Central American universities. He is a founding member and current president of the International Development Ethics Association (IDEA).

World Hunger and Moral Obligation (WH),[2] the predecessor of the present volume, illustrated and advanced the new philosophical movement called *applied ethics*. The anthology's focus was salutary. The essays addressed the question: "What moral responsibility affluent nations (or those people in them) have to the starving masses?" Among those arguing that nations do have a positive obligation to aid distant and hungry people, there were efforts to explore the nature, foundation, and limits of this obligation. It is now apparent, however, that this initial moral problematic issue needs to be recast and enlarged.

I argue that the philosophical discussion in WH, and innumerable subsequent texts and anthologies in applied ethics, committed what Whitehead called "the fallacy of misplaced concreteness."[3] Philosophers abstracted one part—famine and food aid—from the whole complex of hunger, poverty, and development, and proceeded to consider that part in isolation from other dimensions. We now need to redirect and then broaden our attention with respect to the complex causes, conditions, and cures of hunger. Otherwise, we will have an incomplete and distorted picture of both the facts and the values involved. Instead of philosophical preoccupation with the moral basis for aid from rich countries to famine victims in poor countries, emphasis should be shifted: (1) from moral foundations to interpretative and strategic concepts, (2) from famine to persistent malnutrition, (3) from remedy to prevention, (4) from food availability to food entitlements, (5) from food and food entitlements to capabilities and a capabilities-based model of development. Overall, the progression I favor will take us from an ethics of aid to an ethics for development.

From Moral Foundations to Interpretative and Strategic Concepts

The moral problem of world hunger and the ethics of famine relief were among the first practical issues that philosophers tackled after John Rawls's pivotal 1971 study, *A Theory of Justice*,[4] convinced them that reflection on normative issues was part of the philosopher's task. Although Rawls himself limited ethical analysis to abstract principles of distributive justice, applied philosophical ethicists addressed the ethical and conceptual aspects of a variety of practical problems and policies. In the same year that Rawls's volume appeared, Peter Singer first wrote about famine in East Bengal (now Bangladesh)[5] and, more generally, about "the obligations of the affluent to those in danger of starvation."[6] In his 1974 *New York Times Magazine* article, "Philosophers are Back on the Job,"[7] Singer championed the philosophical turn to applied ethics, employing the ethics of famine relief as a leading example.

Philosophers were back on the job because, as John Dewey had urged 50 years earlier, "philosophy recovers itself when it ceases to be a device for dealing with the problems of philosophers and becomes a method, cultivated by philosophers, for dealing with the problems of men."[8] One of these human problems in the midseventies was whether or not affluent states and their citizens were in any way morally obligated to send food to famine victims in other countries. Is such aid morally required, permissible, or impermissible?

More than two decades later, however, many perceive the problem of "world hunger and moral obligation" differently. When we see pictures—whether in the media or on the cover of WH—of a starving child crouching on infertile soil, the question "Do we have a duty to help?" seems to many beside the point. Of course we should help, provided that such help will do genuine and sustainable good.[9] We should not take seriously those who insist that no action be taken until an argument is found to justify the view that the rich in the North should help the poor in the South. To be sure, there is a place for moral debate with respect to *how much* assistance morality requires us to give distant people, in light of our concomitant obligations to aid our families, friends, and compatriots.[10] And in some contexts—university seminar rooms, for instance—it can be valuable to consider whether we owe the foreign poor anything at all. But usually we see no good reason to doubt that we owe them *something*, if we can be reasonably sure that our help will alleviate their immediate misery and improve their long-term prospects. What challenges aid to distant peoples is not so much skepticism concerning moral foundations as pessimism about practical results.

Unfortunately, preoccupied as they were with the task of justifying aid to distant people, most philosophers evinced scant interest in institutional and practical issues. They seemed to believe that if they could resolve the foundational questions, the rest would be easy; the rational—on its own—would become real. Thus, although WH's editors did challenge their readers to consider, "If one ought to help the hungry, how should one help?" (WH, p.10), the volume's essays almost completely failed to address the best ways to diagnose and remedy the problem of world hunger.

It might be objected that analysis of the causes and cures of world hunger is a purely factual, empirical, or technical matter to which ethicists cannot contribute. Yet I would argue that facts and values cannot be so easily kept separate, for we discern ethically salient features of facts on the basis of our moral values.[11] Ethical reflection, whether the work of philosophers or nonphilosophers, plays not only a critical and guiding role but also an interpretative role in relation to social reality and change. An ethic proposes norms for assessing present social institutions, envisaging future alternatives, and assigning moral obligations. An ethic, finally, provides a basis for deciding how agents should act in particular circumstances. What is equally important and frequently neglected, however, is that a normative vision also informs the ways we discern, describe, explain, and forecast social phenomena. How we "read" the situation, as well as how we describe and classify it, will be a function of our value commitments and even our moral sensitivities.[12] For instance, if we ask, "How is India doing?" we are seeking an empirical analysis of what is going on in that country. Yet alternative ethical perspectives will focus on distinct, though sometimes overlapping, facts: hedonistic utilitarianism attends to pleasures and pains, preference utilitarianism selects preference satisfactions and dissatisfactions (or per capita productivity and consumption), human rights approaches emphasize human rights compliances and violations, and contractarians investigate the distributions of "social primary goods" such as income, wealth, liberties, and opportunities. In each case the ethic structures determine what counts as morally relevant information. One value of dialogue between different ethical perspectives is that we learn to see the world in new and different ways. Moreover, as Sherman says, "how to see becomes as much a matter of inquiry (*zetēsis*) as what to do."[13]

Amartya Sen, Martha Nussbaum, Jean Drèze, and others offer the capabilities ethic as the result of an inquiry about understanding and combating world hunger and other deprivations. Capabilities theorists employ this ethic to appraise social institutions and guide policy-formation and actions.[14] To accomplish this task they defend explicit ethical principles and assign moral responsibilities.[15] The capabilities perspective, however, also yields distinctive ways of perceiving world hunger and understanding its empirical causes and attempted cures. With its emphasis on "the commodity commands [entitlements] and basic capabilities that people enjoy" (HPA, p. 273), the capabilities ethic interprets and supplies a rationale for broadening the investigative focus from food aid for famine victims to the most important (and modifiable) causes, conditions, consequences, and remedies of endemic hunger and other privations.[16] As Drèze and Sen argue, "seeing hunger as entitlement failure points to possible remedies as well as helping us to understand the forces that generate hunger and sustain it" (HPA, p. 24). In this essay I emphasize the interpretative contribution of the capabilities ethic and argue that this normative perspective helps justify a broader approach to world hunger.

In the mid-1990s, philosophical reflection on world hunger remains important. After Ethiopia, Kampuchea, Sudan, Somalia, and Rwanda, however, philosophers are appropriately less concerned with morally justifying aid to the distant hungry and more concerned with the conceptual and ethical dimensions of understanding hunger and with policies for successfully combating it.

From Famine to Persistent Malnutrition

Philosophers, like policymakers and the public, typically pay excessive attention to famine and insufficient attention to persistent malnutrition.[17] Both famine and endemic malnutrition are forms of hunger in the sense of "an inadequacy in dietary intake relative to the kind and quantity of food required for growth, for activity, and for maintenance of good health."[18] Famine and chronic hunger, however, differ in character, causes, consequences, and cures. Famine is dramatic, "involving acute starvation and sharp increase in mortality" (HPA, p. 7). It makes a sensational topic for the evening news or fund-raising rock concerts. Chronic hunger, "involving sustained nutritional deprivation on a persistent basis," has deeper causes than famine and is less visible. Moreover, persistent hunger affects many more people[19] and is harder to eradicate than famine. The consequences of persistent hunger—severe incapacitation, chronic illness and humiliation—may be worse than death. And chronic hunger is itself a killer, since weak or sickly persons are especially prone to deadly diseases. If we are concerned about the misery and mortality caused by famine, we should be even more exercised by the harms caused by persistent malnutrition.

Strategies to combat famine and persistent malnutrition also differ.

> To take one example [of diverse strategies in responding to transitory and endemic hunger], in the context of famine prevention the crucial need for speedy intervention and the scarcity of resources often call for a calculated reliance on existing distributional mechanisms (e.g., the operation of private trade stimulated by cash support to famine victims) to supplement the logistic capability of relief agencies. In the context of combating chronic hunger, on the other hand, there is much greater scope for slower but none the less powerful avenues of action such as institution building, legal reforms, asset redistribution or provisioning in kind (HPA, pp. 7–8).

Famine and chronic malnutrition don't always go together. Nations—for instance, India since independence and Haiti in 1994—can be free of famine and yet beset by endemic malnutrition. A country such as China can achieve a reasonably high level of nutritional well-being and yet be stricken by terrible famines. To be exclusively preoccupied with famine is to ignore food deprivation and misery in countries not prone to famine.

As important as is the distinction between these two types of hunger, we must neither exaggerate the differences nor fail to recognize certain linkages. Not only are famine and chronic malnutrition both forms of hunger, but they have certain causes and remedies in common. Both can be understood as what Drèze and Sen call "entitlement failures" and "capability failures" (of which more presently).

As with many other problems, a nation with the right sort of basic political, economic, and social institutions—for instance, stable families, infrastructure, certain kinds of markets, a democratic government, a free press, and nongovernmental organizations—can prevent and remedy both sorts of hunger, while a society without the right set of interlocking institutions is likely to experience one or the other if not both. Moreover, some of the best short-term and long-term approaches to famine prevention—remunerated public employment and, more generally, sustainable development—build on and often intensify effective efforts to address persistent malnutrition (HPA, p. 158). In contrast, the most common emergency action to combat famine—the herding of people into relief camps in order to dole out free food—jeopardizes long-term solutions by disrupting normal economic activities, upsetting family life, and creating breeding grounds for infectious diseases.

From Remedy to Prevention

Whether concerned with abrupt or chronic hunger, almost all the essays in WH emphasized the moral response to *existing* hunger problems rather than the prevention of *future* ones. Only Onora O'Neill clearly addressed the question of prefamine as well as famine policies (WH, pp. 161–164). On the basis of an expanded conception of the duty not to kill others, O'Neill argued that we have a duty to adopt prefamine policies that ensure that famine is postponed as long as possible and is minimized in severity. Such prefamine policies must include both a population policy and a resources policy, for "a duty to try to postpone the advent and minimize the severity of famine is a duty on the one hand to minimize the number of persons there will be and on the other to maximize the means of subsistence" (WH, p. 163).

O'Neill's approach, however, unfortunately assumes that famines cannot be prevented altogether, only postponed and minimized. This supposition flies in the face of recent historical experience. Drèze and Sen summarize their findings on this point when they observe, "There is no real evidence to doubt that all famines in the modern world are preventable by human action;...many countries—even some very poor ones—manage consistently to prevent them" (HPA, p. 47). Nations that have successfully prevented impending famines (sometimes without outside help) include India (after independence), Cape Verde, Kenya, Zimbabwe, and Botswana (HPA, Chapter 8).

It is also possible to prevent and reduce if not eliminate chronic hunger. We must combat that pessimism—a close cousin of complacency—that assures us that the hungry will always be with us—at least in the same absolute and relative numbers.[20] One of the great achievements of Drèze and Sen is to document, through detailed case studies of successes in fighting hunger, that "there is, in fact, little reason for presuming that the terrible problems of hunger and starvation in the world cannot be changed by human action" (HPA, p. 276). What is needed is a forward-looking perspective for short-term and long-term prevention of both types of hunger.

From Food Availability to Food Entitlements

Moral reflection on the prevention and relief of world hunger must be expanded from food productivity, availability, and distribution to what Sen calls food "entitlements." Popular images of famine relief emphasize policies that, in Garrett Hardin's words, "move food to the people" or "move people to food" (WH, p. 19). In either case, the assumption is that hunger is principally caused by lack of food. Chronic hunger, it is often believed, will be solved by greater agricultural productivity, and famine "relief" consists in getting food and starving people together. Much hunger, however, occurs even when people and ample food—even peak supplies—are in close proximity. For a starving person may have no access to or command over the food that is right next door.

In a country, region, and even village stricken by famine, there is often more than enough food for everyone to be adequately fed. Recent research makes it evident that since 1960 there has been sufficient food to feed all the world's people on a "near-vegetarian diet" and that "we are approaching a second threshold of improved diet sufficiency"[21] in which 10 percent of everyone's diet could consist of animal products. Accordingly, it is often said that the problem is one of distribution. This term, however, is ambiguous. Purely spatial redistribution is insufficient and may not be necessary. Sen reminds us that "people have perished in famines in sight of much food in shops."[22] What good distribution of food should mean is that people have effective access to or can acquire the food (whether presently nearby or far away). Hence, it is better to say that the problem of hunger, whether transitory or persistent, involves an "entitlement failure" in the sense that the hungry person is not able to acquire food or lacks command over food. What is crucial is not the mere food itself, nor the amount of food divided by the number of people in a given area, nor even the food transported to a stricken area. What is decisive is whether particular households and individuals have operative "entitlements" over food. The distinction between households and individuals is important, for households as units may have sufficient food for the nourishment of each family member, yet some members—usually women or female children—may starve because of entitlement failures.

We must be careful here, for Sen's use of the term "entitlement" has caused no little confusion and controversy. Unlike Robert Nozick's normative or prescriptive use of the term, Sen employs "entitlement" in a descriptive way—relatively free of moral endorsement or criticism—to refer to a person's actual or operative command, permitted by law (backed by state power) or custom, over certain commodities.[23] A person's entitlements will be a function of: (1) that person's endowments, for instance, what goods or services he or she has to exchange for food, (2) exchange opportunities, for instance, the going rate of exchange of work for food, (3) legal claims against the state, for instance, rights to work, food stamps, or welfare, and (4) nonlegal but socially approved and operative rules, for instance, the household "social discipline" that mandates that women eat after and less than men.[24]

Generally speaking, an entitlement to food would be the actual ability, whether *morally* justified or not, to acquire food by some legally or socially approved means—whether by producing it, trading for it, buying it, or receiving it in a government feeding program. A Hutu child separated from its family may be morally justified in stealing a meal from a Tutsi food supply center, but has no legal claim or other social basis for effective access to the food. In Sen's sense, then, the child lacks an entitlement to that food.

To view hunger as an entitlement failure does not commit one to the position that hunger is never caused by a lack of food nor that it is always explained by the same set of causes. Rather, the entitlement theory of hunger directs one to examine the various links in a society's "food chain"—production, acquisition, and consumption—any of which can be dysfunctional and thereby result in an entitlement failure. A production failure caused by drought or pests will result in an entitlement failure for those peasants "whose means of survival depend on food that they grow themselves."[25] Even when food is abundant and increasing in an area, landless laborers may starve because they have insufficient money to buy food, no job to get money, nothing of worth to trade for food, or no effective claim on their government or other group.

Conceiving hunger as an entitlement failure also yields ways of preventing impending famines and ways of remedying actual famines. What is needed is not only food but institutions that protect against entitlement failure and restore lost entitlements. Moving food to hungry people may not be necessary, for the food may already be physically present. The problem is that some people cannot gain access to it. Even worse, increasing food availability in a given area may increase the hunger problem. For instance, direct delivery of free food can send market food prices plummeting, thereby causing a disincentive for farmers to grow food. The result is a decline not only in their productivity but also in their own food entitlements. Moreover, even when necessary, food by itself is not sufficient to prevent or cure famine if people never had entitlements to food or lost what they had previously. And it may be that the best way to ensure that people have the ability to command food is not to give them food itself, but rather cash relief or cash for work. Such cash "may provide the ability to command food without directly giving the food."[26] It may also have the effect of increasing food availability, for the cash may "pull" private food traders into the area in order to meet the demand.

One deficiency of the "food availability" approach to hunger is that it is purely aggregative, that is, concerned solely with the amount of food in a given area summed over the number of people. Thus, it has inspired a simplistic and inconclusive debate between "Malthusian optimists," those who think that *the* answer to the "world food problem" is more food, and "Malthusian pessimists," those who think that the answer is fewer people.[27] Another—more deadly—consequence is that data concerning food output and availability often lull government officials and others into a false sense of food security and thereby prevent them from doing what they might to prevent or mitigate famine: "The focus on food per head and Malthusian optimism have literally killed millions."[28] In contrast, Sen's approach is disaggregative with respect to command over food on the part of vulnerable occupation groups, households, and, most important, individuals (see HPA, pp. 30–31). It recognizes that although food is indispensable for famine prevention and remedy, much more than food is needed. According to the capabilities ethic, an approach to hunger that attended exclusively to food and entitlements to food would stop short of the fundamental goal—to reduce human deprivation and contribute to human well-being.

From Food and Food Entitlements to Capabilities and Development

Different moral theories understand human well-being and the good human life in diverse ways. Capabilities theorists choose valuable human "functionings" and capabilities to so function as the basis of their ethical outlook. They argue that these moral categories are superior to other candidates for *fundamental* concepts, such as resources or commodities, utilities, needs, or rights. Although these latter concepts do have a role in a complete moral theory and approach to world hunger, they refer to "moral furniture" that is in some sense secondary. Commodities are at best *means* to the end of valuable functions and abilities to so function. Utilities are only one among several good functionings and may "muffle" and "mute" deprivations. Rights are not free-standing but are best defined in relation to valuable human functions and abilities to so function.[29]

What do capabilities theorists mean by the term *functionings*? A person's functionings consist of his or her physical and mental states ("beings") and activities ("doings"). The most important of these functionings, the failure of which constitutes poverty and the occurrence of which constitutes well-being, "vary from such elementary physical ones as being well-nourished, being adequately clothed and sheltered, avoiding preventable morbidity, and so forth, to more complex social achievements such as taking part in the life of the community, being able to appear in public without shame, and so on."[30] A person's *capabilities* are that set of functionings open to the person, given the person's personal characteristics ("endowment") as well as economic and social opportunities. An alternative formulation is that the general idea of capability refers "to the extent of freedom that people have in pursuing valuable activities or functionings" (HPA, p. 42).

Drèze and Sen give four reasons for expanding the perspective on hunger to include capabilities as well as food and entitlements: (1) individual variability, (2) social variability, (3) diverse means to nourishment, (4) nourishment as a means to other good goals. Let us briefly consider each.

Individual Variability   The capabilities approach recommends itself because it makes sense of and insists on the distinction between food intake and being nourished or capable of being nourished. The focus is not on food in itself nor food as merely ingested, but food as a means to being well-nourished and being able to be well-nourished. Exclusive attention to food, food entitlement, and food intake neglects importantly diverse impacts that the same food can have on different human beings and on the same individual at different times. A particular woman at various stages of her life "requires" different amounts and types of food, depending on her age, her reproductive status, and her state of health. Generally, higher food intake at one time may compensate for lower or no intake at other times without it being true that the person is ever suffering from nutritional distress or malfunctioning.

Instead of identifying hungry people simply by a lack of food intake and mechanically monitoring individuals or dispensing food to them according to nutritional requirements, the focus should be on nutritional functioning and those "nutrition-related capabilities that are crucial to human well-being" (HPA, p. 14). A person's energy level, strength, weight and height (within average parameters that permit exceptions), the ability to be productive, and capacities to avoid morbidity and mortality—all valuable functionings or capabilities to function—should supplement and may be more significant with respect to nutritional well-being than the mere quantity of food or types of nutrients (HPA, p. 41).[31]

Social Variability   In addition to differences in individual or communal biological or physical characteristics, the capabilities approach is sensitive to differences in socially acquired tastes and beliefs with respect to foods. That is, it recognizes that these tastes and beliefs can also block the conversion of food into nutritional functioning. Attempts to relieve hunger sometimes fail because hungry people are unable, for some reason, to eat nutritious food. Hungry people sometimes won't eat because the taste of available grain is too different from that to which they are accustomed. There is evidence that people who receive extra cash for food sometimes fail to improve their nutritional status, apparently because they choose to consume nutritionally deficient foods. If food is to make a difference in people's nutritional and wider well-being, it must be food that the individuals in question are generally willing and able to convert into nutritional functioning.[32] This is not to say that food habits cannot be changed. Rather, it underscores the importance of nutritional education and social criticism of certain food consumption patterns. Even nutritious food to which people are entitled, however, will not by itself protect or restore nutritional well-being.

Diverse Means to Being Well-Nourished   If one goal of public action is to protect, restore, and promote nutritional well-being, we must realize that food is only one means of reaching this goal (HPA, p. 267). A preoccupation with food transfers as the way to address impending or actual hunger ignores the many other means that can serve and may even be necessary to achieve the end of being (able to be) well-nourished. These include "access to health care, medical facilities, elementary education, drinking water, and sanitary facilities" (HPA, p. 13).

To achieve nutritional well-being, a hungry parasite-stricken person needs not only food but also medicine to kill the parasites that cause the malabsorption of consumed food. A disease-enfeebled person who is too weak to eat requires medical care as well as food. A Rwandan youngster separated from its family in a refugee camp may be ignorant of what to eat and what not to eat. Without clean water, basic sanitation, and health education, recipients of nutritious food aid may succumb to malaria, cholera, dysentery, and typhoid before having the chance to be adequately nourished.

In particular situations, the best way to combat famine may not be to dispense food but to supply jobs for those who can work and cash for those who can't (HPA, p. 121). The evidence is impressive

that an increase in the purchasing power of hungry people often
pulls food into a famine area, as private traders find ways of meeting the increased demand (HPA, pp. 88–93). Finally, famine and
chronic hunger are prevented and reduced by long-term development strategies that protect and promote entitlements and valuable
capabilities. In the next section, we will return to the hunger-fight-
ing role of national development strategies and international development. At this juncture, the crucial point is that direct food delivery is only one means, and often not the best means, for fighting
world hunger. The capabilities approach helpfully interprets and
underscores that point when it insists that public action can and
should employ an array of complementary strategies to achieve the
end of nutritional well-being for all.

Food as a Means to Other Components of Well-Being   The capabilities
approach helps widen our vision to see that the food that hungry
people command and consume can accomplish much more than give
them nutritional well-being. Nutritional well-being is only one element in human well-being; the overcoming of transitory or chronic
hunger also enables people and their governments to protect and
promote other ingredients of well-being. Being adequately nourished, for instance, contributes to healthy functioning that is both
good in itself and indispensable to the ability to avoid premature
death and fight off or recover from disease. Having nutritional well-
being and good health, in turn, is crucial to acquiring and exercising other valuable capabilities such as being able to learn, think,
deliberate, and choose as well as be a good pupil, friend, household-
er, parent, worker, or citizen.

Because adequate food and food entitlements can have so many
beneficial consequences in people's lives, creative development programs and projects find ways in which people can link food distrib-
ution/acquirement to other valuable activities. Pregnant and lactating women (and their infants) acquire food supplements in health
clinics, for nutritional deficiencies affect fetal and infant development. Schoolchildren eat free or subsidized lunches at school, for
hungry children don't learn as well and certain nutritional deficiencies result in visual and cognitive impairment.[33]

Nutritional well-being, then, is both constitutive of and a means
to human well-being and personal development. And human development is the ultimate purpose of societal development. Hence, a
more ample perspective on world hunger must include socioeconomic development as part of the cure. Just as the right kind of
development is a large part of the answer to the various problems of
population, so it is crucial to resolving the diverse problems of world
hunger.[34]

In the capabilities approach to international development, the linkage between hunger alleviation and development is spelled out in the language of valuable capabilities and functionings. In this approach, a society's development is conceived as a process of change that protects, restores, strengthens, and expands people's valued and valuable capabilities.[35] Being able to be well nourished and other nutrition-related capabilities are among the most important capabilities. Hence, a society striving to be developed will search for, establish, and maintain institutions and policies that attack and try to eradicate all forms of hunger and the poverty that causes hunger.[36] Even emergency measures to prevent, relieve, or extirpate famine must not undermine and, if possible, should contribute to long-term strategies that "may be used to reduce or eliminate failures of basic capabilities" (HPA, p. 16). Economic, political and other institutions, such as schools and the family, must be modified and development strategies elected in the light of the effect such changes will have on what all persons will be able to do and be.

From the Ethics of Aid to an Ethics for Development

Finally, the ethics of famine relief should be incorporated into an ethics for development. International development ethics evaluates the basic goals and appropriate strategies for morally desirable social change. No longer fixated on the stark options of earlier debates—food aid versus no food aid, aid as duty versus aid as charity—it asks instead what kind of aid is morally defensible and, even more fundamentally, what sort of national and international development aid should foster.

As early as the midfifties, development economists had been examining the developmental impact of different kinds of food aid and trying to design famine relief that would contribute to rather than undermine long-term development goals.[37] Yet in the seventies, philosophers and others, such as Garrett Hardin, failed to refer to the nuanced debate that had been going on for more than 20 years. Furthermore, as one expert on food aid remarks, "many of them did not feel it important to become more than superficially familiar with the technical or institutional aspects of food production, distribution, or policy."[38] As happens all too often, the owl of Minerva—Hegel's image for the philosopher—"spreads its wings only with the falling of dusk" and comes on the scene too late to give "instruction as to what the world ought to be."[39]

Moreover, when philosophers did try to analyze development, they usually emphasized development *aid* that rich countries provided to poor countries, rather than the development *goals* that poor countries set and pursued for themselves. By the mideighties, however, ethicists became increasingly aware that they could not talk about morally justified or unjustified development aid from the outside without first talking about the recipient nation's own development philosophies, goals, strategies, leadership, and will.[40] One marked advantage of the capabilities ethic is that it puts its highest priority on a nation's intellectual and institutional capability for *self*-development without denying the role of international theoretical and practical help (see HPA, p. 273 and "Goods and People").

With respect to morally defensible "development paths," a new discipline—international development ethics—has emerged.[41] Development ethicists ask several related questions. What should count as development? Which should be the most fundamental principles to inform a country's choice of development goals and strategies? What moral issues emerge in development policymaking and practice? How should the burdens and benefits of good development be distributed? What role—if any—should more affluent societies and individuals play in the self-development of those less well off? What are the most serious national and international impediments to good development? Who should decide these questions and by what methods? To what extent, if any, do moral skepticism, political realism, and moral relativism pose a challenge to this boundary-crossing ethical inquiry?

This new discipline is being practiced in ways that sharply distinguish it from the earlier ethics of famine relief. First, development ethics is international in the triple sense that ethicists from diverse societies are trying to forge an international consensus about solutions to global problems. It has become evident that policy analysts and ethicists—whether from "developing" countries or "developed" countries—should not simply accept the operative or professed values implicit in a particular country's established development path. Rather, both cultural insiders and outsiders[42] should engage in an ongoing and critical dialogue that includes explicit ethical analysis, assessment, and construction with respect to universal development ends and generally appropriate means of national, regional, and planetary change. Rather than being predominantly if not exclusively the work of white North American males, as was the case in the initial ethics of famine relief, international development ethics is an inquiry that includes participants from a variety of nations, groups, and moral traditions seeking an international consensus about problems of international scope.[43]

Second, development ethics is interdisciplinary rather than exclusively philosophical. It eschews abstract ethical reflection and relates values to relevant facts in a variety of ways. Development ethicists, as we have seen in Drèze and Sen's work on hunger, evaluate: (1) the normative assumptions of different development models, (2) the empirical categories employed to interpret, explain, and forecast the facts, and (3) development programs, strategies, and institutions.[44]

Finally, development ethics straddles the distinction between theory and practice. Its practitioners include, as well as engage in dialogue with, policymakers and development activists. Instead of conducting a merely academic exercise, development theorists and development practitioners together assess the moral costs and benefits of current development policies, programs, and projects, and articulate alternative development visions.[45]

Famine, food aid, and the ethics of famine relief remain—as they were in the midseventies—pressing personal, national, and international challenges. Philosophers can play a role in meeting these challenges and thereby reducing world hunger. This goal is best achieved, however, when the questions of world hunger and moral obligation are reframed and widened. Since the best long-term cure for hunger is national and international development, we must put emergency food aid in a developmental perspective and incorporate an ethics of famine relief into an international development ethics. To avoid the fallacy of misplaced concreteness is not to eschew abstractions but to place them in their proper relations to each other and to the concrete world of facts and values.

NOTES

1. I owe thanks to my colleagues at the Institute for Philosophy and Public Policy and the School of Public Affairs for illuminating discussions of these issues. Will Alken, Arthur Evenchik, Hugh LaFollette, and James W. Nickel made valuable comments on earlier versions of the essay. I gratefully acknowledge support for this research from the National Endowment for the Humanities (NEH) Grant #RO-22709-94 and from the Global Stewardship Initiative of the Pew Charitable Trusts. The views expressed are mine and not necessarily those of NEH or the Pew Charitable Trusts.

2. William Aiken and Hugh La Follette, eds. *World Hunger and Moral Obligation*, Englewood Cliffs, NJ: Prentice-Hall, 1977. Hereafter I cite this volume as WH.

3. Alfred North Whitehead, *Science and the Modern World*, New York: Macmillan, 1925, p. 200.

4. John Rawls, *A Theory of Justice*, Cambridge, MA: Belknap Press of Harvard University Press, 1971.

5. Peter Singer, "Famine, Affluence, and Morality," *Philosophy and Public Affairs* 1, 1972, pp. 229–243. Singer's initial essay, reproduced with a new "Postscript" in WH, was written in 1971 and first appeared in *Philosophy and Public Affairs* in 1972, the initial year of publication of what was to become the premier philosophical journal in applied ethics.

6. Peter Singer, "Reconsidering the Famine Relief Argument," in Peter G. Brown and Henry Shue, eds., *Food Policy: The Responsibility of the United States in the Life and Death Choices*, New York: Free Press, 1977, p. 36.

7. The *New York Times Magazine*, July 7, 1974, pp. 17–20.

8. "The Need for Recovery of Philosophy" Bernstein, Richard J., ed., *John Dewey: On Experience, Nature and Freedom*, New York: The Liberal Arts Press, 1960, p. 67.

9. A 1995 study by the Program on International Policy Attitudes shows that 80 percent of those polled agreed that "the United States should be willing to share at least a small portion of its wealth with those in the world who are in great need." This belief does not seem to stem solely from a view of national interest. However, 67 percent agreed that "as one of the world's rich nations, the United States has a moral responsibility toward poor nations to help them develop economically and improve their people's lives" and 77 percent rejected the idea that the United States should give aid only when it serves the national interest. Although 87 percent believe that waste and corruption is rife in foreign aid programs, 55 percent said they would be willing to pay more taxes for foreign aid if they knew that "most foreign aid was going to the poor people who really need it rather than to wasteful bureaucracies and corrupt governments." Steven Kull, "Americans and Foreign Aid: A Study of American Public Attitudes," Program on International Policy Attitudes, Center for the Study of Policy attitudes and Center for International and Security Studies at Maryland, School of Public Affairs, University of Maryland, March 1, 1995. pp. 3, 16, 21.

10. See, for example, Catherine W. Wilson, "On Some Alleged Limitations to Moral Endeavor," *Journal of Philosophy* 90 (1993), 275–289. It is beyond the scope of this paper to consider the best way to think about our general duty to assist others and our particular duty to aid the foreign needy.

11. I owe the idea of perceiving or discerning "ethical salience," to Nancy Sherman, *The Fabric of Character: Aristotle's Theory of Virtue*, Oxford: Clarendon Press, 1989, pp. 28–44. See also Martha Nussbaum, *Love's Knowledge: Essays on Philosophy and Literature*, New York, Oxford: Oxford University Press, 1990, especially Chapters 2 and 5.

12. For a discussion of how ethical principles constrain what counts as relevant and irrelevant factual information, see Amartya Sen, "Well-being, Agency, and Freedom: The Dewey Lectures 1984." *Journal of Philosophy* 82 (1985), pp. 169–184. Sherman discusses the way in

which the agent's "reading of the circumstances" may be influenced by his or her moral or immoral character; see *Fabric* p. 29.

13. Sherman, *Fabric* p. 30.

14. See for example, recent volumes in The World Institute for Development Economics Research (WIDER) series *Studies in Development Economics*: Jean Drèze and Amartya Sen, *Hunger and Public Action*, Oxford: Clarendon Press, 1989, hereafter cited in the text as HPA; Jean Drèze and Amartya Sen, eds., *The Political Economy of Hunger. Entitlement and Well-Being*, 3 volumes: Vol. 1, *Entitlement and Well-being*; Vol. 2, *Famine and Prevention*; Vol. 3, *Endemic Hunger*, Oxford: Clarendon Press, 1990; Martha C. Nussbaum and Amartya Sen, eds., *The Quality of Life*, Oxford: Clarendon Press, 1993. See also Keith Griffin and John Knight, eds., *Human Development and the International Development Strategy for the 1990s*, London: Macmillan, 1989. For a bibliography of Sen and Nussbaum's extensive writings and an analysis of the "capabilities ethic" as a feature of the "capabilities approach" to development, see my essays: "Functioning and Capability: The Foundations of Sen's and Nussbaum's Development Ethic," *Political Theory* 20 (November 1992), pp. 584–612; "Functioning and Capability: The Foundations of Sen's and Nussbaum's Development Ethic, Part 2," in Martha C. Nussbaum and Jonathan Glover, eds., *Women, Culture, and Development*, New York: Oxford University Press/Clarendon Press, 1995. For an article that anticipates many of my arguments, but that I did not have an opportunity to read until after the present essay was completed, see George R. Lucas, Jr., "African Famine: New Economic and Ethical Perspecitves," *Journal of Philosophy*, 87 (November 1990): 629–641.

15. See Amartya Sen, "The Right Not to Be Hungry," in G. Floistad, ed., *Contemporary Philosophy: A New Survey*, Vol. II, The Hague: Martinus Nijhoff, 1982, pp. 343–360.

16. Just as one's focus can be too narrow, it can also be so broad as to be disabling. Blaming or praising such large formations as capitalism, socialism, or industrialism commits fallacies of hasty generalization and deters us from examining causes that are both specific and alterable in the short and medium run. I owe this point to James W. Nickel.

17. The editors of WH did distinguish the two types of hunger (WH, p. 1), but they themselves and the anthology's other contributors almost exclusively attended to the plight of famine victims rather than that of the chronically hungry.

18. Sara Millman and Robert W. Kates, "Toward Understanding Hunger," in Lucile F. Newman, ed., *Hunger in History: Food Shortage, Poverty, and Deprivation*, Cambridge, MA: Basil Blackwell, 1990, p. 3.

19. In the fall of 1994, it is estimated that while 800 million people suffer from malnutrition, none suffer from famine. See *Hunger 1995: Causes of Hunger*, Silver Spring, MD: Bread for the World Institute,

1994, p. 10. However, serious potential for famine exists in Rwanda and Afghanistan, and the United States presence in Haiti has averted famine in a country with severe and widespread malnutrition.

20. Studies show that the number of chronically malnourished people in the world decreased from 976 million people in 1975 to 786 million in 1990 and that in the same period, because of a population increase of 1.1 billion, the proportion of hungry people in the developing world declined from 33 percent to 20 percent. See *Hunger 1995: Causes of Hunger*, pp. 10–11.

21. Robert W. Kates and Sara Millman, "On Ending Hunger: The Lessons of History," in *Hunger in History*, p. 404.

22. Amartya Sen, "The Food Problem: Theory and Practice," *Third World Quarterly*, 3 (July 1982); 454.

23. Sen states that "the entitlement of a person stands for the set of different alternative commodity bundles that the person can acquire through the use of the various legal channels of acquirement open to someone in his position" ("Food, Economics and Entitlements," in Drèze and Sen, *The Political Economy of Hunger*, Vol. 1, *Entitlement and Well-Being*, Oxford: Clarendon Press, 1990, p. 36).

24. See HPA, pp. 10–11; Amartya Sen, *Inequality Reexamined*, New York: Russell Sage Foundation; Cambridge: Harvard University Press, 1992, pp. 149–150 and "Goods and People" (in this volume). Charles Gore shows that Sen has gradually expanded his concept of entitlement to include nonlegal—primarily household—rules, but that Sen needs to go further in recognizing the ways in which "socially approved moral rules" may be extra-legal and even antilegal. See Charles Gore, "Entitlement Relations and 'Unruly' Social Practices: A Comment on the Work of Amartya Sen," *Journal of Development Economics* 29 (1993), pp. 429–460.

25. Amartya Sen, "Food Entitlements and Economic Chains," in *Hunger in History*, p. 377.

26. Amartya Sen, "Food, Economics and Entitlements," in *The Political Economy of Hunger*, Vol. 1, *Entitlement and Well-Being*, p. 43.

27. Sen, "The Food Problem," pp. 447–451. Cf. HPA, pp. 24–25 and "Food, Economics, and Entitlements," pp. 35–36.

28. Amartya Sen, "The Food Problem," p. 450. Cf. Amartya Sen, *Poverty and Famines: An Essay on Entitlement and Deprivation*, Oxford: Clarendon Press, 1981, and "Goods and People" (this volume).

29. For a clarification and defense of these claims, see Sen and Nussbaum's writings and my analysis and evaluations of them in the essays referred to in number 14.

30. Sen, *Inequality Reexamined*, p. 110.

31. For a more detailed and technical discussion of these issues by nutritionists who are sympathetic with the capabilities approach, see S.R. Osmani, ed., *Nutrition and Poverty*, Oxford: Clarendon Press, 1992. See also Paul Streeten, *Thinking about Development*, Cambridge: Cambridge University Press, 1995.

32. A new strain of "miracle" rice, which promises enormous productivity gains, will be hybridized with local rice varieties in order to make it acceptable to regional tastes in different parts of the world.

33. Cf. John Osgood Field and Mitchel B. Wallerstein, "Beyond Humanitarianism: A Developmental Perspective on American Food Aid," in *Food Policy*, pp. 234–258.

34. See Amartya Sen, "Population: Delusion and Reality," *New York Review of Books*, 61 (September 22, 1994), pp. 62–71, and "Goods and People" (this volume).

35. See Amartya Sen, "Goods and People" (this volume); "Development: Which Way Now?" in *Resources, Values and Development*, Oxford: Blackwell; Cambridge, MA: Harvard University Press, 1984, pp. 485–508; "The Concept of Development," in Hollis Chenery and T.N. Srinivasan, eds., *Handbook of Development Economics*, vol. 1, Amsterdam: North Holland, 1988, pp. 9–26; "Development as Capability Expansion," in Griffin and Knight, eds., *Human Development and the International Development Strategy for the 1990s*, pp. 41–58; Crocker, "Functioning and Capability," pp. 584–588. See also United Nations Development Programme, *Human Development Report 1994*, New York and Oxford: Oxford University Press, 1994 p. 13: "The purpose of development is to create an environment in which all people can expand their capabilities, and opportunities can be enlarged for both present and future generations.

36. For a detailed examination of intitutions and policies—both national and international—that have proven successful in alleviating hunger and reducing poverty, see HPA and Streeten, *Thinking about Development*.

37. For a good account, with full references, of controversies in the fifties, sixties, and seventies concerning U.S. food aid and development policy, see Anne O. Krueger, Constantine Michalopoulos, and Vernon W. Ruttan, *Aid and Development* Baltimore and London: Johns Hopkins University Press, 1989; Vernon W. Ruttan, ed., *Why Food Aid?* Baltimore and London: Johns Hopkins University Press, 1993, especially pp. 37–129.

38. Ruttan, ed., *Why Food Aid?* p. 66.

39. Georg W.F. Hegel, *Hegel's Philosophy of Right*, trans. T.M. Knox, Oxford: Oxford University Press, 1952, pp. 12–13.

40. See especially, Nigel Dower, *World Poverty: Challenge and Response*, York, UK: Ebor Press, 1983; Onora O'Neill, *Faces of Hunger: An Essay on Poverty, Justice, and Development*, London: Allen & Unwin, 1986; Jerome M. Segal, "What is Development?" Working Paper, DN-1, College Park, MD: Institute for Philosophy and Public Policy, October 1986.

41. For philosophical accounts of development ethics, see David A. Crocker, "Toward Development Ethics," *World Development* 19, no. 5 (1991):457–483, and "Development Ethics and Development Theory-Practice," Discussion Paper CBPE 93-2, College Station:

Center for Biotechnology Policy and Ethics, Texas A&M University, 1993; and Nigel Dower, "What is Development?—A Philosopher's Answer," Centre for Development Studies Occasional Paper Series, 3, Glasgow: University of Glasgow, 1988.

42. David A. Crocker, "Insiders and Outsiders in International Development Ethics," *Ethics and International Affairs* 5 (1991): 149–173.

43. See Godfrey Gunatilleke, Neelen Tiruchelvam, and Radhika Coomaraswamy, eds., *Ethical Dilemmas of Development in Asia*, Lexington, MA: Lexington Books, 1988; Kwame Gyekye, *The Unexamined Life: Philosophy and the African Experience*, Legon: Ghana Universities Press, 1988; Martha Nussbaum, "Aristotelian Social Democracy," in R. Bruce Douglass, Gerald R. Mara, and Henry S. Richardson, eds., *Liberalism and the Good*, New York and London: Routledge, 1990, pp. 203–252; and Luis Camacho, *Ciencia y tecnología en el subdesarrollo*, Cartago: Editorial Tecnológica de Costa Rica, 1993.

44. Since the early sixties, Denis Goulet has been addressing the ethical and value dimensions of development theory and practice. His new book, *Development Ethics: A Guide to Theory and Practice*, New York: Apex Books, 1995, treats development ethics from the perspective of a policy analyst and activist. Economist Paul Streeten, an architect of the basic human needs strategy and currently a consultant with UNDP, has persistently addressed ethical issues in his work; see, for example, *Strategies for Human Development: Global Poverty and Unemployment*, Copenhagen: Handelshjskolens Forlag, 1994.

45. An early anticipation of an integrated approach to world hunger is Peter G. Brown and Henry Shue, eds., *Food Policy: The Responsibility of the United States in the Life and Death Choices*, New York: Free Press, 1977. This anthology, which appeared in the same year as WH, shared WH's deficiencies with respect to minority and international participation. *Food Policy's* contributors, however, included policy analysts and policymakers as well as a variety of academics. Moreover, the volume displayed an excellent balance— as a whole and in several individual essays—of moral, empirical, institutional, political, and policy analysis.

[22]

Democracy and Right to Food

It is widely accepted that the right to food forms one of the basic economic and social rights essential to achieve 'economic democracy' in India. This right is nowhere near realisation in India, where undernutrition levels are among the lowest in the world. The right to food moreover, does not easily translate into well-defined entitlements and responsibilities. Though serious difficulties are involved in making the right to food fully justiciable, new interventions are possible in at least three ways – through legal action, through democratic practice and through changing public perceptions. More importantly, the right to food needs to be linked to other economic and social rights relating to education, work, health and information, which together hold the promise of radical change in public priorities and democratic politics.

JEAN DRÈZE

The right to food can be seen from at least three different perspectives. One is the perspective of the Indian Constitution, especially, the Directive Principles of State Policy. Secondly, we can refer to international declarations and conventions on this matter, starting with the Universal Declaration of Human Rights. Thirdly, it is possible to argue for the right to food as a moral and social right, independently of all these documents. Indeed, it is a basic premise of the human rights movement that all human beings have some fundamental rights, whether or not these rights are already incorporated in national or international law. To illustrate, one can argue that a child has a right to protection from physical punishment at school, whether or not physical punishment is legally permissible.

These three perspectives, of course, are not mutually exclusive. In fact, they complement each other. In this paper, however, I shall concentrate on the first approach, and particularly on the right to food as one of the economic and social rights affirmed in the Directive Principles.[1] There are two reasons for this. One is that this approach appears to me to be particularly coherent and far-reaching. The other reason is that it is important to place the right to food in the larger context of the need to revive the Directive Principles, and their underlying vision of radical social change.

The Directive Principles are chiefly due to B R Ambedkar, and they build on his visionary conception of democracy. This vision, in turn, was intimately related to his notion of the good society as a society based on 'liberty, equality and fraternity'. Democracy, as he saw it, was both the end and the means of this ideal. It was the end because he ultimately considered democracy itself as synonymous with the realisation of liberty, equality and fraternity. At the same time, democracy was also the means through which this ideal was to be attained.

Indeed, in Ambedkar's perspective, democracy was intrinsically geared to social transformation and human progress. In one of the most inspiring definitions of the term, he described democracy as "a form and method of government whereby revolutionary changes in the economic and social life of the people are brought about without bloodshed".[2] For this to happen,

it was essential to link political democracy with economic and social democracy. This was one of the main objectives of the Indian Constitution, and particularly of the Directive Principles. Ambedkar himself put it as follows:

> Our object in framing the Constitution is really two-fold: (i) To lay down the form of political democracy, and (ii) To lay down that our ideal is economic democracy and also to prescribe that every government whatever is in power shall strive to bring about economic democracy. The Directive Principles have a great value, for they lay down that our ideal is economic democracy.[3]

This revolutionary conception of democracy, however, fell into oblivion soon after independence. Indian democracy essentially went the same way as parliamentary democracy in Europe, which Ambedkar considered as 'a name and a farce'.[4] Fifty-five years down the road, economic democracy has been quietly buried as a principle of public policy, and even political democracy is not exactly in the pink of health.

The Nutrition Emergency in India

With this background, let me turn to the question of food. On this, the first point to note is the catastrophic nature of the nutritional situation in India. The second National Family Health Survey (1998-99) provides ample evidence of the problem. To illustrate, according to this survey, 47 per cent of all Indian children are undernourished, 52 per cent of all adult women are anaemic, and 36 per cent have a body mass index (BMI) below the cut-off of 18.5 commonly associated with chronic energy deficiency.[5] These nutritional deficiencies have devastating consequences for the well-being and future of the Indian people. To start with, hunger and undernutrition are intrinsic deprivations and severely diminish the quality of life. Further, undernutrition is associated with reduced learning abilities, greater exposure to disease, and other impairments of individual and social opportunities.

In international perspective, India is one of the most under-nourished countries in the world. According to the latest *Human*

Figure: Average Weight of Indian Children at Different Ages

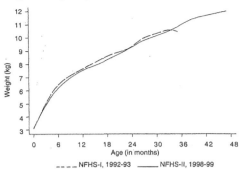

Age (in months)

---- NFHS-I, 1992-93 _____ NFHS-II, 1998-99

Source: Alessandro Tarozzi, unpublished analysis of National Family Health Survey (NFHS) data. The graph relates to boys and girls combined, in rural and urban areas combined.

Development Report, only two countries (Bangladesh and Nepal) have a higher proportion of undernourished children than India, and only two countries (Bangladesh and Ethiopia) have a higher proportion of infants with low birthweight.[6] Even after taking into account various gaps and inaccuracies in the international data, there is another indication here that undernutrition levels in India are extremely high.

The second National Family Health Survey contains a wealth of further evidence on different aspects of the nutrition situation in India. Consumption data, for instance, bring out the frugal nature of food intakes for the majority of the population. Only 55 per cent of adult women in India consume milk or curd at least once a week, only 33 per cent eat fruits at least once a week, and 28 per cent get an egg. The evidence on child morbidity is no less sobering. Among children under the age of three, 30 per cent had fever during the two weeks preceding the survey, 19 per cent had diarrhoea, and another 19 per cent had symptoms of acute respiratory infection.[7] Even after allowing for some overlap between these different groups, this suggests that at least half of all Indian children below three suffer from one of these conditions within any given interval of two weeks.

All the figures cited so far are national averages. It goes without saying that the situation gets worse – far worse – as we consider the poorer states (e g, Jharkhand, Chhattisgarh, Orissa), and the more deprived regions within these poorer states (e g, Palamau in Jharkhand, Sarguja in Chhattisgarh, Kalahandi in Orissa), not to speak of the poorer communities within these deprived regions. Among the sahariyas, musahars, kols, bhuiyas and other marginalised communities, the nutritional situation can only be described as a permanent emergency. To illustrate, in a recent survey of 21 randomly-selected households in a bhuiya hamlet of Palamau district in Jharkhand, 20 reported that they had to 'skip meals regularly'.[8] At the time of the survey, most of the households in this hamlet survived on 'chakora' (a local spinach) and gheti (a wild root), supplemented with some broken rice on lucky days. Some had nothing to eat but chakora.

Another disturbing aspect of the nutrition situation in India is that it shows little sign of major improvement over time. There is evidence of a steady decline of extreme hunger and severe undernutrition.[9] But the general progress of anthropometric

indicators (e g, the heights and weights of Indian children) is very slow. The point is illustrated in figure, which shows the average weight of Indian children at different ages in 1992-93 and 1998-99, based on the first and second rounds of the National Family Health Survey. There is some improvement, but it is not exactly dramatic. Based on the weight-for-age criterion, the proportion of undernourished children declined from 53 per cent in 1992-93 to 47 per cent in 1998-99.[10] If the child undernourishment figures continue to decline at this sluggish rate of 1 percentage point per year, it will take another 40 years before India achieves nutrition levels similar to those of China today.

The comparison between the two surveys also points to the growth of nutritional inequality in the 1990s: anthropometric indicators improved more for urban areas than for rural areas, and more for boys than for girls. For instance, the proportion of undernourished children (based on weight-for-age criteria) declined by 7 percentage points for urban boys between 1992-93 and 1998-99, but only 3 percentage points for rural girls. In other words, the time required for rural Indian girls to 'catch up' with their Chinese counterparts if present rates of improvement continue is not 40 years, but 80 years or so. These patterns are consistent with independent evidence of a sharp increase in economic inequality in the 1990s.[11]

Democracy and Social Rights

Perhaps the most startling aspect of the nutrition situation in India is that there is virtually no discussion of it, outside specialised circles. Chronic hunger rarely figures in public debates and electoral politics. To illustrate, consider the coverage of nutrition issues in the mainstream media. *The Hindu*, one of the finest English-medium dailies, publishes two opinion articles every day on its editorial page. In a recent count of these opinion articles over a period of six months (January to June 2000), it was found that health, nutrition, education, poverty, gender, human rights and related social issues combined accounted for barely 30 out of 300 articles. Among these 300 articles, not one dealt with health or nutrition.[12] As this simple exercise illustrates, the basic needs of the Indian people count for very little in public debates and democratic politics, and nutrition issues are particularly out of focus.

This neglect of social issues in general, and of chronic hunger in particular, is often attributed to 'lack of political will'. This diagnosis is plausible enough, but it does not take us very far since it begs the question as to why there is no political will in the first place. In a democracy, political will is an outcome of democratic politics. Seen in this light, the deafening silence surrounding hunger and nutrition issues in India is an invitation to reflect on the nature and limitations of Indian democracy.

As far as democratic institutions are concerned, India is doing reasonably well in historical and international perspective. To illustrate, in comparison with the US (the self-proclaimed torch-bearer of democracy in the contemporary world), India fares much better in many respects. For instance, India has much higher voter turnout rates (the US are near the rock bottom of the international scale in that respect); it has more extensive provisions for the political representation of socially disadvantaged groups; and it is less vulnerable to the influence of 'big money' in electoral politics. There is also far greater pluralism in Indian than in US politics. Dozens of political parties, from extreme left to extreme right, are represented in India's lower house, in contrast with two parties (with virtually identical political programmes) in the US. Even the quality of the Indian press is much higher, in many respects, than that of its counterpart in the US. The comparison is not entirely to India's advantage (for instance, the US fare better in terms of the freedom of information), and there is, of course, plenty of scope for improving democratic institutions in India. Nevertheless, by contemporary world standards, Indian democracy appears in a reasonably good light as far as its institutional foundations are concerned.

Having said this, Indian democracy has one minor flaw, namely that most people are unable to participate in it due to economic insecurity, lack of education, social discrimination and other forms of disempowerment. Voter turnout rates may be reasonably high (about 60 per cent for parliamentary elections), but informed participation in democratic institutions on a sustained basis is confined to a tiny minority. And even voting is a very limited form of democratic participation when most people are unable to distinguish clearly between the different political parties and their respective programmes.[13]

In short, Indian democracy is trapped in a vicious circle of exclusion and elitism. Because underprivileged sections of the population are excluded from active participation in democratic politics, their aspirations and priorities are not reflected in public policy. The elitist orientation of public policy, in turn, perpetuates the deprivations (poverty, hunger, illiteracy, discrimination, etc) that disempower people and prevent them from participating in democratic politics.

The root of the problem was identified quite clearly by B R Ambedkar in the context of his argument for linking political democracy with economic and social democracy. "On the January 26, 1950," he said, "we are going to enter into a life of contradictions. In politics we will have equality and in social and economic life we will have inequality". The contradiction is still with us today, and in some respects at least, the problem is even intensifying at this time of growing inequality and elitism. India is in some danger of becoming a "business-driven society", to use Noam Chomsky's telling characterisation of US democracy.[14] It is in this context that there is an urgent need to revive the concern with economic and social rights expressed in the Directive Principles of the Constitution, including the right to food. Indeed, as mentioned earlier, the main object of the Directive Principles was precisely to lay the foundations of "economic and social democracy".[15]

Two Illustrations

An example or two may help to convey the potential empowerment value of economic and social rights. One interesting example is the right to education. Until quite recently, the right to education was out of focus in education policy. For instance, the issue was not mentioned in the National Education Policy of 1986. The basic assumption in those days was that large proportions of children were beyond the pale of the schooling system, and that this situation would continue to prevail for many years. Since then, however, there has been a healthy revival of public concern for the right to education. Today, the notion that every child has a fundamental right to elementary education has gained wide acceptance. For instance, if a village does not have a school, the case for providing one immediately does not need to be made – it is taken for granted. And even children belonging to highly disadvantaged families or communities, such as migrant labourers

or (so-called) primitive tribes, are widely considered to have an inalienable right to elementary education. This broad recognition of elementary education as a fundamental right of every child (recently incorporated in the Constitution) has contributed to the relatively rapid expansion of schooling facilities and school participation in the 1990s.[16]

This does not mean that spectacular progress has been made in realising the right to education. Indeed, there are also tendencies on the other side (i e, tendencies inimical to the right to education), such as the crisis of state finances and intense hostility to the 'welfare state' in the corridors of power. Some recent developments, such as the growing reliance on low-quality, 'second-track' schooling facilities to raise enrolment figures, can even be seen as an attack on the fundamental right to education.[17] Nevertheless, it is interesting that the reach of the schooling system has expanded so fast in a period of structural adjustment and general disengagement of the state. The growing recognition of elementary education as a fundamental right of every child has played a part in this achievement. Also, the wide acceptance of elementary education as a fundamental right of every child has given education activists a powerful foothold to resist any attempt to dilute the constitutional commitment to free and compulsory education until the age of 14.

There is an instructive contrast here with the corresponding situation in the field of health care. Unlike elementary education, health care is yet to be widely accepted as a basic right of all Indian citizens.[18] This ambiguity has facilitated the continuation if not intensification of state abdication in this field in the 1990s. Public expenditure on health has declined as a proportion of GDP, from an abysmally low base (about 1 per cent).[19] And the lack of any major initiative in the field of health care during the last 10 years contrasts with wide-ranging innovations in the field of elementary education. Correspondingly, the pattern of accelerated progress in educational achievements in the 1990s does not apply to health indicators. In fact, there have been major setbacks, such as the slowdown of infant mortality decline, and (more recently) the reduction of child vaccination rates in some states.

Another enlightening example is the right to information. Anyone who has worked in rural India is bound to be familiar with the tremendous disempowerment experienced by ordinary citizens due to lack of information and the inaccessibility of public records. Many examples can be given: some people have ration cards, but do not know what they are entitled to buy from the ration shop and at what price; others take bank loans without understanding the conditions of borrowing; TB patients are sent away from public health centres with cough syrups; labourers are unaware of the legal minimum wage; and so on.[20] Another manifestation of the problem is corruption in public life, which thrives on secrecy and the dissimulation of information.

In response to this situation, one could try a 'case by case' approach, in the form of addressing the problem in the specific domain where it occurs. The visionary insight of the 'right to information movement', however, is that the problem can also be tackled across the board, in a lasting manner, by demanding a blanket right of access to all public records at all times for all citizens.[21] This led to a campaign for 'right to information laws', combined with efforts to enable people to use these laws. Going beyond this, the right to information movement can be seen as a step in the larger journey towards public accountability and participatory democracy.

The right to information movement has already led to some concrete results. In Rajasthan, for instance, it has played a crucial role in eradicating the earlier practice of endemic 'fudging' of muster rolls on relief works.[22] This may look like a small victory, but it is actually a significant breakthrough, which paves the way for further action in this field. Ten years ago, the suggestion that corruption in public life can be eradicated, or even substantially reduced, would have seemed very naïve. Today, there is a new sense of possibility in this respect.

The Right to Food

The right to food is, in some ways, a more complex right than the right to education or the right to information. To start with, the entitlements and responsibilities associated with the right to food are far from obvious. In the case of, say, the right to information, some basic entitlements and responsibilities are easy to identify: every citizen has a right of access to public records (subject to specific exceptions, pertaining for instance to 'national security'), and conversely, every civil servant has a duty to part with the relevant records under pre-specified terms. If he or she refuses to do so, action can be taken. To a large extent, the right to information can therefore be translated into legal entitlements and enforced in a court of law. In other words, it is justiciable.

In the case of the right to food, however, matters are more complicated. Broadly speaking, the right to food can be interpreted as a claim of individuals on society (starting but not ending with the state). It is an entitlement to be free from hunger, which derives from the assertion that the society has enough resources, both economic and institutional, to ensure that everyone is adequately nourished. However, difficulties arise as soon as we try to flesh out this broad definition and translate it into specific entitlements and responsibilities.

The term 'freedom from hunger', for instance, lends itself to several interpretations: getting two square meals a day, meeting specific calorie norms, avoiding nutrition-related ailments, and so on. Ideally, the right to food should be seen as a right to 'nutrition', as in Article 47 of the Constitution.[23] However, good nutrition itself depends in complex ways on a wide range of inputs: not just adequate food intake but also clean water, basic health care, good hygiene, and so on. Even if we confine our attention to food intake, the constituents of good nutrition are a matter of debate among nutritionists. For instance, there is some controversy about the importance of various 'micronutrients' for good nutrition. For all these reasons, it is hard to translate the right to food into a specific list of entitlements.

Similar difficulties arise in clarifying the responsibilities associated with the right to food. The primary responsibility is surely with the state, because the state alone commands the resources (economic and institutional) required to protect everyone from hunger, and because the state is generally responsible for safeguarding constitutional rights. However, the right to food is not the responsibility of the state alone. To illustrate, suppose that I come across someone who is dying of starvation on the street. If I am able to do something about it, and if I recognise that every citizen has a right to be free from hunger, it would clearly not be right for me to wash my hands of the situation and say that it is the responsibility of the state. The fact that the state bears the primary responsibility for letting this happen does not absolve me from the duty of intervening, if I am in a position

to do so. In other words, in some circumstances at least, the responsibility for protecting the right to food is a shared responsibility, involving not only the state, but also other institutions or individuals.

To take another example, supposed that a girl is undernourished because she does not get a fair share of food within the family. Clearly, her right to food would be violated. But who is responsible? At some level, state responsibility would be involved, since the state has an overarching duty to eradicate social discrimination. But surely, the girls' parents (or whoever controls the distribution of food within the family) would also bear a substantial part of the responsibility for this situation. Here again, there is a difficulty in apportioning responsibilities for protecting the right to food.

The last example also brings out a related problem, namely, that the right to food is not always 'justiciable', in the sense of being enforceable in a court of law. If a girl is undernourished because of discrimination within the family, I doubt that the best response would be to take her parents to court.[24] Other means of intervention would be required. It is in the light of these and related problems that legal enforcement of the Directive Principles (including the primary duty of the state to raise "the level of nutrition and the standard of living of its people") was explicitly ruled out in the Constitution.

At this point, the reader may wonder whether the right to food has any 'teeth' at all, if it is so difficult to define and so hard to enforce. I would argue that it does have a cutting edge, for at least three reasons.

First, even if the right to food is not always justiciable, some aspects of the right to food (at the very least) are amenable to legal enforcement. This is one crucial lesson of the public interest litigation initiated by the People's Union for Civil Liberties (Rajasthan) in April 2001 with a writ petition to the Supreme Court.[25] The litigation is far from over, but some useful orders have already been passed, such as the interim order of November 28, 2001, directing all state governments to introduce cooked mid-day meals in primary schools. We can plausibly envisage that entitlements of this kind might become part of the law of the land, just as the right of access to public records has found expression in 'right to information laws'.

Indeed, this approach would be highly consistent with the scheme of things initially envisaged by the Constitution. It is often forgotten that while Article 37 explicitly states that the Directive Principles 'shall not be enforced by any court', it goes on to stress (i) that these principles are nevertheless 'fundamental to the governance of the country', and (ii) that "it shall be the duty of the state to apply these principles in making laws". The application of these prescriptions to the right to food is potentially far-reaching. Some good work has been done, for instance, on the possibility of introducing a 'framework law' that would translate a wide range of aspects of the right to food into legal provisions.[26]

I submit that this approach would be more productive than the common proposal that the Directive Principles should somehow be declared "justiciable".[27] For one thing, there are serious difficulties in making the right to food fully justiciable. Much of it ultimately belongs to the domain of democratic politics rather than of legal enforcement. For another, even if the right to food is deemed fully justiciable, it will remain necessary to spell out the constructive interventions through which this right is to be protected. Leaving it to the courts to settle this issue as and when it arises would be both risky and inappropriate. The need would therefore remain for additional legislation, framed through democratic processes, clarifying how the right to food is to be realised. And this is precisely what I am advocating in the first place.

The approach proposed here does not detract from the possibility of claiming the right to food in court as a corollary of the fundamental 'right to life' under Article 21. Indeed, this claim is one aspect of the public interest litigation initiated in April 2001 by the People's Union for Civil Liberties. And the Supreme Court itself has already clarified on various occasions that the right to life implies the right to food.[28] In some circumstances, this recognition can be invoked with good effect. Yet, the persistence of mass hunger in India more than 20 years after the Supreme Court effectively accepted the right to food as a fundamental right clearly indicates that more specific legal provisions are required.

The second reason why the right to food does have a cutting edge, even when it is not enforceable in a court of law, was clearly spelt out by Ambedkar in his defence of the Directive Principles. Essentially, he argued that in a democracy, legal action is not the only means of holding the state accountable to its responsibilities. In cases where rights cannot be enforced through the courts, they can be asserted through other democratic means, based for instance on parliamentary interventions, the electoral process, the media, international solidarity, street action, or even civil disobedience.[29]

This process has worked relatively well with respect to one specific aspect of the right to food – the prevention of famines. As Amartya Sen has noted, in a democratic political system, allowing a famine to develop would be political suicide for the party in office. This is the main reason why every threat of famine in independent India has been boldly dealt with (at least in terms of avoiding excess mortality). The latest example is the drought of 2002-03 in Rajasthan. In the absence of public intervention, drought-affected people would have perished in large numbers. With assembly elections round the corner, however, the government did not take any chances. In late June 2003, close to four million labourers were employed on relief works and related programmes in rural Rajasthan.[30] This was one of the largest public employment programmes ever, in terms of the proportion of the population employed. Famine was averted, not because there is a law against it but because of other democratic safeguards.[31]

Outside the specific context of famine prevention (and other extreme circumstances, such as 'starvation deaths'), democratic practice has delivered rather little, so far, in terms of holding the state accountable to its responsibility for protecting the right to food. However, this situation is not immutable. In fact, I would argue that there are vast possibilities of radical change in this field. These possibilities arise mainly from the growing participation of underprivileged groups in democratic politics, and the fact that food security is one of their main concerns. Another positive development in this context is that the tools of democratic participation are becoming more diverse over time. In his defence of the Directive Principles, Ambedkar focused on the electoral process as the principal means of holding the state accountable outside the courts. Since then, we have learnt not to expect too much from electoral competition in this respect, for reasons discussed earlier. But at the same time, we have good grounds for enhanced confidence about the possibilities of public action outside the traditional arena of electoral politics. These possibilities have already been creatively harnessed for various causes, ranging from gender equality and dalit liberation to war resistance and the defence of civil liberties. There is no reason why these initiatives should not be extended to the assertion of economic and social rights, as is already happening to some extent.

The third argument for asserting the right to food is that, even when they are not enforceable in court, economic and social rights can have a profound influence on public perceptions of who is entitled to what. These perceptions, in turn, can make a concrete difference in diverse ways. For instance, in situations where the effectiveness of food security programmes depend on the vigilance of the public, perceptions of rights can matter a great deal.

To illustrate, consider the public distribution system (PDS). One reason (among others) why the PDS is not in very good shape today is endemic corruption. Now, recent analyses indicate that the extent of corruption in the PDS is much higher in north India than in south India. In north India, about half of the grain meant for distribution to poor households through the PDS seems to end up in the black market, rising to 80 per cent in Bihar and Jharkhand. In south India, the 'leakages' are much smaller, to the extent that they do not show up in secondary data.[32] One reason for this contrast is that people's perceptions of their entitlements under the PDS differ radically between the two regions. In large parts of north India, poor people have very little awareness of their entitlements and how they can be enforced.[33] They are sitting ducks for corrupt PDS dealers, and consider themselves lucky if they get anything at all.[34] In this respect, the situation is very different in the southern region. In Tamil Nadu, for instance, even illiterate dalit women seem to have a sharp awareness of their entitlements, and of the redressal mechanisms that are available in the event where they are cheated.[35] The two factors (awareness of rights and accountability mechanisms) reinforce each other and preserve the integrity of the system. If India's public distribution system is to be revitalised, close attention needs to be paid to the circumstances that shape people's perceptions of their rights as well as their ability to enforce them.

It is in this respect, among others, that the recent division of the rural population between 'BPL' and 'APL' households (below poverty line and above poverty line, respectively), with PDS entitlements being effectively restricted to BPL households, is so pernicious. This division undermines the notion that PDS entitlements are a matter of right, since no-one has a 'right' to a BPL card. It also weakens the ability of BPL households to enforce their rights, by destroying the solidarity between APL and BPL households, and sometimes even pitching one group against the other. The fact that 'vigilance committees', the local watchdogs of the public distribution system, often turn out to consist mainly of APL members, who have no stake in the integrity of the system, does not help either. The need of the hour is to empower disadvantaged households vis-à-vis PDS dealers, but the present targeting system goes in the opposite direction.

Mid-day Meals and Their Wider Significance

These diverse roles of the right to food can be further illustrated with reference to the issue of mid-day meals in primary schools. This is one aspect (perhaps the only aspect) of the right to food that has been significantly consolidated in India in recent years. I believe that this experience is of some significance not only from the point of view of child nutrition but also as a pointer to the scope for further action in this field.

The case for providing cooked mid-day meals in primary schools is very strong. At least three arguments can be invoked in this connection. First, mid-day meals boost school attendance, especially among girls. Second, they protect children from classroom hunger and also enhance child nutrition, if the meal is nutritious. Third, mid-day meals contribute to social equity, in several ways: they teach children to share a common meal irrespective of caste and class, act as a form of income support for poor households, and provide employment opportunities to poor women. The wide-ranging personal and social benefits of mid-day meals have been well demonstrated in states that made an early start down this road, notably Tamil Nadu and Gujarat. More recent experiences in Karnataka, Rajasthan and elsewhere suggest that similar achievements are possible all over the country. In Rajasthan, for instance, girl enrolment in Class 1 jumped by nearly 20 per cent in a single year after mid-day meals were introduced.[36]

On November 28, 2001, the Supreme Court directed all state governments to introduce cooked mid-day meals in primary schools within six months. This interim order came up in the context of the public interest litigation mentioned earlier. Several states (notably Bihar, Jharkhand, Uttar Pradesh and West Bengal) are yet to implement this order. Nevertheless, the coverage of mid-day meal programmes is steadily expanding. Fifty million children are already covered, making this the largest nutrition programme in the world by a long margin. With adequate public pressure, another 50 million children are likely to get on board within a year or so, and the quality of mid-day meal programmes could also be radically enhanced. This would be no small achievement at a time of growing abdication of state responsibility for the well-being of Indian citizens.

With this background, let me clarify how recent experience with mid-day meals illustrates the three possible roles of the right to food discussed earlier. To start with, this experience shows the possibility of bringing some aspects of the right to food within the ambit of legal enforcement. Some commentators are quite unhappy about the Supreme Court 'meddling' with policy issues such as the provision of mid-day meals in primary schools. Having witnessed the court's deliberations at close quarters, I share some of these apprehensions.[37] Yet, the interim order on mid-day meals seems quite reasonable to me, considering that we are dealing here with very basic rights of Indian children (not only the right to food but also the fundamental right to education), and that the effectiveness of mid-day meals in furthering these rights is well established. As things stand, the directive on mid-day meals is only an 'interim order', but there is no reason why mid-day meals should not be given permanent legal status, just as the right to work has found expression in Maharashtra's "employment guarantee act".

Secondly, the mid-day meal story also highlights the importance of campaigning for economic and social rights outside the courts, using all democratic means available. Indeed, had the Supreme Court order on mid-day meals been allowed to take its own course, it is doubtful that it would have been implemented. In this connection, it is worth noting that on the same day (November 28, 2001), the Supreme Court also issued a similar order relating to the Integrated Child Development Services (ICDS), calling inter alia for the provision of functional anganwadis (child care centres) in 'every habitation'. This order, however,

has made no impact so far, and one reason for this is the failure to supplement the court order with active public pressure. Mid-day meals, by contrast, have been the focus of lively campaigns in many states during the last two years. The steady progress of mid-day meals reflects this effective combination of legal action and social action.

Thirdly, mid-day meals provides another useful illustration of the role of economic and social rights in shaping people's perceptions of their entitlements and enhancing their determination to get their due. Here again, the point can be appreciated by looking at contrasts between different states. In Tamil Nadu, where mid-day meals go back to 1925, and were universalised in 1982, the whole arrangement is widely accepted as a basic entitlement of all children and has been internalised by all parties concerned – parents, teachers, cooks, administrators, and children themselves. Mid-day meals are provided on every day of the year, including holidays, and any lapse in this regard would be considered a serious matter. In (say) Chhattisgarh or Madhya Pradesh, by contrast, mid-day meals are still far from being perceived as a basic entitlement of all children. This is one reason why the implementation of mid-day meals remains quite casual in these states, to the extent that the meal often fails to materialise on a particular day, without anyone making a fuss.[38]

Beyond these specific lessons, there is a larger message here about the possibility of bringing democratic politics to bear on issues of hunger and nutrition. The point emerges most sharply in Tamil Nadu, where mid-day meals have been a lively political issue ever since M G Ramachandran (alias 'MGR') threw his weight behind this idea in the early 1980s. In fact, many observers consider this initiative as one of the pillars of MGR's lasting popularity.[39] The prominence of social development issues in Tamil Nadu politics (at least in comparison with other states) is also a major reason for the relatively good quality of nutrition and health services in general, from anganwadis to primary health centres.[40] Elsewhere in India, social issues are nowhere near getting the same attention in state politics, but as argued earlier, this situation is not immutable. There are growing possibilities of public mobilisation on these issues, and the future course of the right to food depends a great deal on the extent to which these opportunities are seized.

Conclusion

The basic argument of this paper is something like this. First, the Indian Constitution and its underlying ideas (chiefly due to Ambedkar) provide a sound framework for thinking about the right to food. In this framework, the right to food is one of the basic economic and social rights that are essential to achieve "economic democracy", without which political democracy is at best incomplete. Indeed, there is an obvious sense in which mass hunger is fundamentally incompatible with democracy in any meaningful sense of the term.

Second, the right to food is nowhere near being realised in India. In fact, undernutrition levels in India are among the highest in the world. Further, the improvement of nutrition indicators over time is very slow. There is also some evidence of increasing disparities in nutritional achievements (between rural and urban areas as well as between boys and girls) in the 1990s. The recent accumulation of nearly 70 million tonnes of grain against a background of widespread hunger is a particularly startling violation of the right to food.

Third, the nutrition situation in India is a sort of 'silent emergency': little attention is paid to it in public debates and democratic politics. This illustrates a more general feature of Indian democracy – its tremendous lack of responsiveness to the needs and aspirations of the underprivileged. Against this background, economic and social rights have a crucial role to play as built-in safeguards against the elitist biases of public policy.

Fifth, the right to food is a somewhat complex right that does not readily translate into well-defined entitlements and responsibilities. The scope for enforcing it through the courts can be significantly enlarged (e g, by consolidating legal provisions for the right to food), but serious difficulties are involved in making it fully justiciable. Nevertheless, the right to food can bring new interventions within the realm of possibility in at least three different ways: through legal action, through democratic practice, and through public perceptions.

Sixth, I have illustrated these different roles of the right to food with reference to the provision of mid-day meals in primary schools. It goes without saying that I am not proposing mid-day meals as an answer to India's massive nutrition problem. Yet, this experience is a helpful illustration of the possibility of effective action in this field. Similar things can be done with respect to many other means of upholding the right to food: employment guarantee acts, the public distribution system, social security arrangements, anganwadi facilities, and land rights, among others.

I end by reiterating that if the right to food is to be achieved, it needs to be linked with other economic and social rights, such as the right to education, the right to work, the right to information and the right to health. These economic and social rights complement and reinforce each other. Taken in isolation, each of them has its limitations, and may not even be realisable within the present structure of property rights. Taken together, however, they hold the promise of radical change in public priorities and democratic politics. This is why it is so important to revive the Directive Principles of the Constitution as well as the visionary conception of democracy that informs them. **EPW**

Address for correspondence:
j_dreze@hotmail.com

Notes

[Adapted from the third C Chandrasekaran Memorial Lecture, delivered at the International Institute for Population Sciences (Mumbai) on November 7, 2003. I am grateful to P Arokiasamy and T K Roy for inviting me to deliver this lecture, and for their overwhelming hospitality.]

1 On the international perspective, see, e g, Raghav Gaiha (2003), Mahendra Dev (2003) and Harsh Mander (2003).

2 Quoted in Bhagwan Das (n d), p 61. Strictly speaking, this was not so much a definition of democracy as a "test" of it. Ambedkar added: "It is perhaps the severest test. But when you are judging the quality of a material you must put it to the severest test." Note also that in other contexts he insisted that democracy was not just a method of government but also a "form of social organisation" and a "way of life".

3 Proceedings of the constituent assembly of India, Friday November 19, 1948; available at http://www.parliamentofindia.nic.in/debates/vol17p9.htm.

4 "The second wrong ideology that has vitiated parliamentary democracy (in western Europe) is the failure to realise that political democracy cannot succeed where there is no social or economic democracy... Democracy is another name for equality. Parliamentary democracy developed a passion for liberty. It never made a nodding acquaintance with equality.

It failed to realise the significance of equality and did not even endeavour to strike a balance between liberty and equality, with the result that liberty swallowed equality and has made democracy a name and a farce", (quoted in Rodriguez, 2002, p 62).

5 International Institute for Population Sciences (2000), pp 246, 250 and 270. The 'child undernutrition' figures are based on weight-for-age data for children under the age of three.

6 United Nations Development Programme (2003), pp 258-261.

7 International Institute for Population Sciences (2000), pp 219 and 244.

8 Bhatia and Drèze (2002).

9 To illustrate: (1) according to the National Sample Survey (unpublished data), the proportion of households that are not getting "two square meals a day throughout the year" declined from 19 per cent in 1983 to 3.3 per cent in 1999-2000; (2) according to the National Nutrition Monitoring Bureau (NNMB), the proportion of "severely undernourished" children (weight-for-age criterion) in eight sample states declined steadily from 17.2 per cent in 1975-80 to 6.4 per cent in 1999-2000, and clinical signs of acute undernutrition such as marasmus and kwashiorkor have virtually disappeared. See National Institute of Nutrition (1997), pp 69-70 and 104, and National Nutrition Monitoring Bureau (2002), p 74. On related matters, see also National Institute of Nutrition (1991, 1997), Sachdev (1997, 2003), Gopalan (2003), among others.

10 International Institute for Population Sciences (1995), p 283, and International Institute for Population Sciences (2000). A similar picture of sluggish nutritional improvement emerges from independent surveys carried out by the National Institute of Nutrition, Hyderabad; see, e g, National Institute of Nutrition (2000, 2002).

11 See, e g, Deaton and Drèze (2002); also Ahluwalia (2000), Kurian (2000), Nagaraj (2000), Banerjee and Piketty (2001), among others.

12 Drèze and Sen (2002), p 302. When I repeated the exercise for the period of January-June 2003, I did find an article dealing with health – it was about the SARS crisis in China!

13 See, e g, Bela Bhatia (2000). The author describes the predicament of dalit women during the 1995 assembly elections in central Bihar as follows: "Most of the women I interviewed had never voted before, nor did they understand the meaning or significance of 'chunav' (elections), vote or parties. While some of them were able to recognise some party symbols, they were often unable to relate the symbol to the party, and none of them could relate it to a particular candidate or programme."

14 See, e g, Chomsky (1998). There are many interesting similarities between Ambedkar and Chomsky's views on democracy, even though Ambedkar was rather less critical of state power. It is perhaps not an accident that both were strongly influenced by John Dewey, an outspoken critic of the concentration of power who viewed politics as "the shadow cast on society by big business" (quoted in Chomsky, 1998, p 87).

15 Whether the Directive Principles went far enough in that respect is another matter. Ambedkar's own blueprint for a 'socialist constitution', sketched in an early memorandum submitted to the constituent assembly (Ambedkar, 1948), included more sweeping changes in economic institutions, especially property rights.

16 On the accelerated progress of literacy and school participation in the nineties, see Drèze and Sen (2002), pp 151-52 and 327-29. On the right to education in India, see Ravi Srivastava (2003), and the literature cited there.

17 See, e g, Anil Sadgopal (2003).

18 There is, however, rapid change in this respect; see, e g, Ravi Duggal (2003) and Abhay Shukla (2003).

19 The ratio picked up again towards the end of the nineties, but mainly because of rapid increases in salaries (based on the recommendations of the Fifth Pay Commission), with little increase – if any – in real inputs.

20 I recently observed an extreme example of such situations in Allahabad district, where some dalit labourers had land titles (received under some "land distribution" scheme) but did not know where their land was. The gram sevak would not show it to them without a hefty bribe, and they were unable to pay. Some of them even suspected that they were working as casual labourers on their own land, encroached by powerful landlords.

21 The right to information movement has been particularly active in Rajasthan during the last 15 years or so, but it has deep roots, going back at least to Jayaprakash Narayan. Another interesting precursor is Jotirao Phule, who was apparently checking muster rolls more than a century before Mazdoor Kisan Shakti Sangathan: "[Phule] enjoyed the company of the labourers and organised them... [He] studied for two or three years how corruption was practised by high officials and engineers.

He knew well how they made up accounts by showing false attendance of labourers and how they divided the profits among themselves" [Keer 1964, p 90].

22 See Drèze and Sen (2002), pp 367-68, and Vivek S (2003). For further discussion of the right to information movement, see particularly Neelabh Mishra (2003).

23 More precisely, one could say that a person's right to food is realised if her life is not impaired or limited by nutritional deficiencies of any kind, or (in a similar vein) that a person's right to food is violated if nutritional deficiencies of any kind prevent her from leading a dignified life. The last definition would make it possible to link the right to food with recent judicial interpretations of the fundamental right to life (Article 21) as a right to 'live with dignity'. I leave it to others to unravel the full implications of this approach, e g, whether a professional weight-lifter has a right to "more food" than an unemployed clerk.

24 This does not mean that it is pointless to make intra-family discrimination illegal. Most of time, laws are enforced by institutions other than the courts. Legal provisions can also have important effects on public perceptions of what is right and wrong. This is one reason, for instance, why compulsory education could make a difference even if the state refrains from enforcing it through the courts, or even from enforcing it at all.

25 Writ Petition (Civil) 196 of 2001. PUCL vs Union of India and others; for further details, see www.righttofood.com.

26 See, e g, Margret Vidar (2003) and Gerald Moore (2003).

27 Variants of this proposal include: (i) converting some Directive Principles into Fundamental Rights (as happened with the right to education), (ii) elastic interpretations of the Fundamental Rights to encompass these Directive Principles (as with the argument that the right to food is implicit in the fundamental "right to life"), and (iii) a constitutional amendment making all Directive Principles justiciable (see, e g, Ravi Duggal, 2003, in the context of the right to health). On related issues, see Mahendra Singh (2003) and the literature cited there.

28 For instance, in Shantistar Builders v Narayan Khimalal Totame (1990) 1 SCC 520, the Supreme Court stated: "The right to life is guaranteed in any civilised society. That would take within its sweep the right to food..." On this and other legal foundations of the claim that the right to life implies the right to food, see Human Rights Law Network (2002).

29 Ambedkar himself focused mainly on electoral politics as the *means* of holding the state accountable to the Directive Principles: "[The party in power] may not have to answer for their breach in a Court of Law. But [it] will certainly have to answer for them before the electorate at election time..." (in Rodriguez, 2002, p 490). The point, however, can be extended to other tools of democratic practice.

30 See http://www.rajasthan.gov.in/relief2002/relief2report_2.pdf.

31 As it turns out, the Congress Party lost the 2003 elections in Rajasthan. But this does not invalidate the argument. It simply shows that preventing famines is not a sufficient condition for winning elections.

32 See Drèze (2002); also Government of India (2002), p 158. These estimates are obtained by "matching" foodgrain offtake from FCI godowns with National Sample Survey data on household purchases from the public distribution system.

33 To illustrate, a recent study of the PDS in Allahabad district found that only 1 per cent of the 1,400 sample households had correct knowledge of their entitlements (Mazumder, 2003, p 21).

34 See, e g, Drèze (2003a). In one village of Sendhwa (Madhya Pradesh), the PDS dealer has apparently struck a deal with the local residents, whereby he keeps all their cards, gives them 20 rupees in cash each month, and takes care of the rest. The most interesting part of the story is that the villagers are apparently satisfied: "20 rupees is better than nothing," they say. This contentment reflects their low expectations of the PDS in ordinary circumstances (Sachin Jain, personal communication).

35 Personal observations based on field work in Dharmapuri district, one of Tamil Nadu's most deprived districts (see also Drèze, 2003b). In one village, dalit women were intrigued by the suggestion that the local dealer might be cheating them. "Where would he go after doing this?," they said. "He lives here, and we will catch him if he cheats us." Their confidence was refreshing, especially in comparison with the disempowerment and helplessness commonly observed among poor households in north India.

36 For further discussion, see Drèze and Goyal (2003), and earlier studies cited there.

37 The proceedings often reminded me of Kropotkin's indictment of the lawyers of his time: "... a race of law-makers legislating without knowing what their laws are about; today voting a law on the sanitation of towns, without the faintest notion of hygiene, tomorrow making regulations for the armament of troops, without so much as understanding a gun; ...legislating at random in all directions, but never forgetting the penalties to be meted out to ragamuffins, the prison and the galleys, which are to be the portion of men a thousand times less immoral than these legislators themselves." (Kropotkin, "Law and Authority", quoted in Bose, 1967, p 266.)

38 Personal observations in Tamil Nadu, Chhattisgarh and Madhya Pradesh. In both Chhattisgarh and Madhya Pradesh, it is not uncommon to find that the mid-day meal has failed to materialise for trivial reasons such as alleged lack of firewood. In one such school, visited at four o'clock in the afternoon, the teachers were least concerned about the fact that the children had not eaten anything since early morning, and even since the previous evening in a few cases. In response to a pointed question about the Supreme Court order, one of them promptly argued that the order required mid-day meals to be served on "200 days in the year only".

39 See, e g, Anita Pratap (2003).

40 For further discussion, see Drèze and Sen (2002), pp 213-18; also Drèze (2003b).

References

Ahluwalia, Montek S (2000): 'Economic Performance of States in Post-Reforms Period', *Economic and Political Weekly*, May 6.

Ambedkar, B R (nd): 'Essential Conditions Precedent for the Successful Working of Democracy', reprinted in Bhagwan Das (nd).

– (1948): 'States and Minorities', memorandum submitted to the Constituent Assembly; reprinted in Government of Maharashtra (1979-98), volume I.

Banerjee, A and T Piketty (2001): 'Are the Rich Growing Richer: Evidence from Indian Tax Data', MIT, Cambridge MA and CEPREMAP, Paris, processed.

Bhagwan Das (ed) (nd): *Thus Spoke Ambedkar*, Vol I, Buddhist Publishing House, Jalandhar.

Bhatia, Bela (2000): 'The Naxalite Movement in Central Bihar', PhD thesis, University of Cambridge.

Bhatia, Bela and Jean, Drèze (2002): 'Still Starving in Jharkhand', *Frontline*, August 16.

Bose, Atindranath (1967): *A History of Anarchism*, World Press, Calcutta.

Chomsky, Noam (1998): *World Orders, Old and New*, Oxford University Press, Delhi.

Deaton, Angus and Jean Drèze (2002): 'Poverty and Inequality in India: A Reexamination', *Economic and Political Weekly*, September 7.

Drèze, Jean (1990): 'Famine Prevention in India' in Drèze, J P and A K Sen (eds) (1990): *The Political Economy of Hunger, Vol 2, Famine Prevention*, Oxford University Press, Oxford.

– (2002): 'Food Security Programmes in Uttar Pradesh', paper presented at a seminar on Labour and Poverty in Uttar Pradesh held at the G B. Pant Social Science Institute, Allahabad, November 22-23, to be published in the proceedings of the seminar.

– (2003a): 'Food Security and the Right to Food' in S Mahendra Dev, K P, Kannan and N Ramachandran (eds) (2003): *Toward a Food Secure India*, Institute for Human Development, New Delhi.

– (2003b): 'Where Welfare Works: Plus Points of the TN Model', *Times of India*, May 21.

Drèze, Jean and Aparajita, Goyal (2003): 'Future of Mid-Day Meals', *Economic and Political Weekly*, November 1.

Drèze, Jean and Amartya, Sen (2002): *India: Development and Participation*, Oxford University Press, New Delhi and Oxford.

Duggal, Ravi (2003): 'Health and Development in India: Moving Towards Right to Healthcare', mimeo, Centre for Enquiry into Health and Allied Themes (CEHAT), Mumbai.

Gaiha, Raghav (2003): 'Does the Right to Food Matter?', *Economic and Political Weekly*, October 4.

Gopalan, C (2003): 'Changing Nutrition Scene in South Asia', paper presented at IX Asian Congress of Nutrition, New Delhi, 23-27 February; available at www.nutritionfoundationofindia.org/archives/apr2003c.htm

Government of India (2002): *Report of the High Level Committee on Long-Term Grain Policy*, Department of Food and Public Distribution, New Delhi.

Government of Maharashtra (1979-98): *Dr Babasaheb Ambedkar: Writings and Speeches*, 16 volumes. Department of Education, Mumbai.

Human Rights Law Network (2002): 'The Right to Food and the Right to Work for Food: Case Law', mimeo, Human Rights Law Network, New Delhi.

International Institute for Population Sciences (1995): *National Family Health Survey 1992-93: India*, IIPS, Mumbai.

– (2000): *National Family Health Survey (NFHS-2) 1998-99: India*, IIPS, Mumbai.

Keer, Dhananjay (1964): *Mahatma Jotirao Phooley: Father of Our Social Revolution*, Popular Prakashan, Bombay.

Kurian, N J (2000): 'Widening Regional Disparities in India: Some Indicators', *Economic and Political Weekly*, February 12.

Mahendra Dev, S (2003): 'Right to Food in India', Working Paper 50, Centre for Economic and Social Studies, Hyderabad.

Mazumder, Bhaskar (2003): 'Public Distribution System in India: A Study of the District of Allahabad, Uttar Pradesh', mimeo, G B Pant Social Science Institute, Allahabad.

Mishra, Neelabh (2003): 'People's Right to Information Movement: Lessons from Rajasthan', Discussion Paper 4, Human Development Resource Centre, UNDP, New Delhi.

Mander, Harsh (2003): 'Social, Economic and Cultural Entitlements and Legal Rights', mimeo, ActionAid, New Delhi.

Mari Bhat, P N (2002): 'Has the Decline in Infant Mortality Rate Slowed Down? A Review of SRS Evidence', paper presented at a national workshop on 'Infant Mortality: Levels, Trends and Interventions' held at New Delhi on April 11-12, 2002.

Moore, Gerald: 'Note on National Framework Legislation', available at http://www.nutrition.uio.no/iprdf/Encounterdocuments/DocO18.html

Nagaraj, R (2000): 'Indian Economy since 1980: Virtuous Growth or Polarisation?', *Economic and Political Weekly*, August 5.

National Institute of Nutrition (1991): *Report of Repeat Surveys (1988-90)*, National Institute of Nutrition, Hyderabad.

– (1997): *25 Years of National Nutrition Monitoring Bureau*, National Institute of Nutrition, Hyderabad.

– (2000): *Annual Report 1999-2000*, NIN, Hyderabad.

– (2002): *Annual Report 2001-02*, NIN, Hyderabad.

– (2000): *Annual Report 1999-2000*, NIN, Hyderabad.

– (2002): *Annual Report 2001-02*, NIN, Hyderabad.

National Nutrition Monitoring Bureau (2002): 'Diet and Nutritional Status of Rural Population', Technical Report 21, NNMB, National Institute of Nutrition, Hyderabad.

Pratap, Anita (2003): 'Strike against Hunger', *Outlook*, August 18.

Rodriguez, Valerian (ed) (2002): *The Essential Writings of Dr Ambekdar*, Oxford University Press, New Delhi.

Sachdev, H P S (1997): 'Nutritional Status of Children and Women in India: Recent Trends', available at www.nutritionfoundationofindia.org/archives/apr2003c.htm/archives/auth-s2v.htm

– (2003): 'Recent Transitions in Anthropometric Profile of Indian Children: Clinical and Public Health Implications', paper presented at IX Asian Congress of Nutrition, New Delhi, February 23-27, available at www.nutritionfoundationofindia.org/archives/apr2003c.htm

Sadgopal, Anil (2003): 'Education for Too Few', *Frontline*, December 5.

Shukla, Abhay (2003): 'The Right to Health Care: Moving from Idea to Reality', mimeo, CEHAT, Mumbai.

Singh, Mahendra P (2003): 'The Statics and the Dynamics of the Fundamental Rights and the Directive Principles: A Human Rights Perspective', mimeo, Law Faculty, Delhi University.

Srivastava, Ravi (2003): 'The Right to Education in India', mimeo, Centre for Development and Human Rights, New Delhi.

United Nations Development Programme (2003): *Human Development Report 2003*, UNDP, New York.

Vaidyanathan, A (2002): 'Food Consumption and Nutrition Status: A Re-Examination Based on Indian Evidence', mimeo, Madras Institute of Development Studies, Chennai.

Vidar, Margret (2003): 'Implementing the Right to Food: Advantages of a Framework Law', paper presented at a seminar convened by FIAN International, held at the Indian Social Institute (New Delhi) on February 24-26.

Vivek, S (2003): 'A Message of Hope', *Humanscape*, December.

Weiner, Myron (1991), *The Child and the State in India*, Princeton University Press, Princeton.

Gopalan, C (2003): 'Changing Nutrition Scene in South Asia', paper presented at IX Asian Congress of Nutrition, New Delhi, 23-27 February; available at www.nutritionfoundationofindia.org/archives/apr2003c.htm

[23]

HOW MUCH DEBT MUST BE CANCELLED?

JOSEPH HANLON*

Development Policy and Practice, The Open University, Milton Keynes, UK

Abstract: Developing country debt now exceeds $2.4 trillion and has become a major international political and economic issue for debtor governments, creditor governments, the IMF and World Bank, and campaigning organizations such as Jubilee 2000. For the poorest countries, debt has become unpayable and debt service an obstacle to development. This paper argues that debt crises and substantial debt cancellation are part of the normal economic cycle, and that an unusual aspect of this cycle has been the unwillingness to cancel debt. Recent historic precedents suggest that at least $1 trillion in debt would need to be cancelled. The paper then uses a 'rights-based approach to development' to estimate that more than $600 billion in debt must be cancelled to release sufficient funds to meet internationally agreed development targets and thus satisfy human rights. Finally, the paper argues that lenders must take responsibility for illegitimate, corrupt and odious loans. Debt cancellation is the norm, not the exception, and the only question is how much.

1 INTRODUCTION

Developing country debt increased tenfold in the 1970s. This was followed by a debt crisis in the early 1980s, in which many countries were unable to meet repayments. In 1982, Mexico and Brazil defaulted. Initially, attempts to resolve the crisis involved rescheduling of debts, normally allowing payments over a longer period. But this proved insufficient.

In the period 1984–91, developing counties paid $209 billion to northern creditors (net — that is, they gave creditors $209 bn more in interest payments and principal repayments than they received in new loans). Yet total debt doubled again in the 1980s, not because of new lending but because old debts were being rolled over. Thus, although there was a net flow of funds from South to North, the total debt increased (see Tables 1 and 2; World Bank, 1991; 1994; 1997; 2000a). For the 38 countries defined by the World Bank as 'severely indebted low income', total debt rose from 5 per cent of GNP in 1970 to 31 per cent of GNP in 1980 to 139 per cent of GNP in 1990, and were at the same level

* Correspondence to: Joseph Hanlon, 7 Ormonde Mansions, 100a Southampton Row, London, WC1B 4BJ, UK. E-mail: j.hanlon@open.ac.uk

878   *J. Hanlon*

in 1999. Many of the poorest countries pay more in debt service than they spend on education or health.

There were two responses to this problem—an increase in new money and a realization that some debt needed to be cancelled. During the early 1980s new lending had fallen, but from 1987 to 1994 lending doubled and in the same period aid more than doubled.

The summit of the Group of Seven (G7) industrialized countries in Toronto in 1988 agreed a new form of rescheduling that in practice included a slight reduction in the debt of the poorest countries. G7 summits in 1991 and 1994 increased the amount of debt of the poorest countries which could be cancelled. Meanwhile, by the mid-1980s banks were beginning to accept that some debt would not be paid, and a secondary market in developing country debt was created; in some cases countries bought back their own debt at a discount (World Bank, 2000a, vol. 1, appendices 2 and 3).

Nevertheless, it was becoming clear that deeper debt cancellation would be needed. At the instigation of the G7 leaders, the World Bank and International Monetary Fund developed the Heavily Indebted Poor Countries Initiative (HIPC) to cancel some debt for up to 41 countries, and this cancellation was extended by the G7 at its 1999 summit in Köln. This affects only a small portion of poor country debt, however (see Table 3). Meanwhile, the international Jubilee 2000 campaign 'to cancel the unpayable debts of the poorest countries' had become, according to World Bank spokesman Anthony Gaeta, 'one of the most effective global lobbying campaigns I have ever seen' (*PR Week*, 16 April 1999).

Although the millennium ended with a new recognition that some debt had to be cancelled, little debt had actually been written off and total poor country debt was still increasing.

This paper opens by arguing that debt crises and cancellation are both normal parts of economic cycles. It then looks at the recent history of the present debt crisis. Next, we look at debt cancellations of the 1930s–60s and their implications, and make a first attempt to see how much debt would need to be cancelled if existing pledges for poverty reduction are to be met. Finally, the paper looks briefly at a set of related moral and political issues, including lender liability, odious debt, and the use of funds released by debt cancellation.

2 CYCLES, LOAN PUSHING AND DEFAULT

Debt and default are not new. The present problem of countries not able to repay debts is very similar to the 1930s — and the 1880s and 1840s.

Table 1. Total debt and debt service, all developing countries

Year	Total debt $ billion	Total debt % of GNP	Annual debt service $ billion	Arrears $ bn
1970	60	5	9	0
1980	610	21	91	5
1990	1480	35	164	111
1999	2554	42	349	139

Note: for 1970 total debt and interest are only for long-term debt.
Source: World Bank 1997, 1998a, and 2000a.

Table 2. Net aid and loan flows to developing countries

Year	Net transfers on debt	Aid grants	Total to South
1984	−22	11	−10
1985	−33	13	−20
1986	−36	14	−22
1987	−34	15	−19
1988	−40	18	−22
1989	−33	19	−14
1990	−10	27	16
1991	−1	35	34
1992	32	31	62
1993	44	28	72
1994	35	33	68
1995	67	33	100
1996	43	28	71
1997	40	26	66
1998	−44	27	−17
1999	−115	26	−88

Notes: Negative means money flowing from poor countries to rich countries.
Net transfers on debt=New loans−capital repayments−interest payments
Aid Grants=grants excluding technical assistance
Source: World Bank 1991, 1999a, 2000a

In the 19th century, the United States was a developing country, and British banks were lending to the new US. 'London saw it as a very unreliable developing country, with a black record of embezzlement, fraudulent prospectuses and default,' wrote Sampson (1981, pp. 29–31, 54–56). But the bankers made loans. In 1842, 11 states including Maryland, Pennsylvania, Mississippi and Louisiana defaulted.

During and after the First World War, the US was relatively wealthy; Europe was poorer and borrowed from the US. In the 1930s Europe defaulted. The United States Treasury (1997) reported that Britain still owes $14.5 bn to the United States for loans during the First World War; only three countries in sub-Saharan Africa have larger debts. France owes $11.8 bn, and the rest of Europe owes another $6.2 bn to the United States. None are repaying this money.[1]

Latin America was a major borrower in the 1920s, mainly paying old loans by taking new ones. But with the 1929 crash, new loans stopped and exports fell dramatically as the industrialized countries became protectionist; by 1934, Latin America had defaulted on 85 per cent of its dollar bonds (Drake, 1989, p. 50). Default was a sensible response to falling commodity prices and unpayable debts; a World Bank study showed that those Latin American countries 'which opted for default recovered more successfully from the ravages of the Great Depression' than those which struggled to pay their debts (Eichengreen and Portes, 1989a).

Debt crises are linked to the business cycle. Economist Charles Kindleberger (1978, pp. 6–23) wrote a book whose title, *Manias, Panics and Crashes*, captures his view of the cycles. He points to the tulip mania of 1634, the South Sea bubble of 1720, the cotton and railway booms of the 1830s, and so on. Kindleberger says that in each cycle, there is a period of growth involving a rise in profits and a rapid expansion of

---

[1] Only three countries repaid their World War I debts to the United States: Cuba, Finland, and Liberia.

880   J. Hanlon

Table 3. Total debt and debt service ratios, 1998

Group	Total debt $ bn	Total debt % GNP	Annual debt services paid $bn
All developing countries	2465	37	296
of which			
93 countries in this study	1700	42	209
of which			
Low income	405	48	25
of which			
Severely indebted low income	211	74	9
Heavily indebted poor country (HIPC)	206	124	7
Sub-Saharan Africa	226	68	15

Source: World Bank 1999a, 2000a
Definitions:

- 'Developing countries' are low and middle income countries, i.e. those with a 1996 GNP per capita, calculated by the *World Bank Atlas* method, less than $9636.
- 'Low income countries' are those below $785 per capita.
- 'Severely indebted' means that either the present value (NPV) of debt exceeds 80 per cent of GNP (NPV/GNP > 80 per cent) or 220 per cent of exports (NPV/XGS > 220 per cent).
- 'Heavily Indebted Poor Countries' (HIPC) are a group of 41 countries which are 'IDA-only' and which have 'unsustainable debt' as defined by the World Bank and IMF.
- 'IDA-only' means countries have the right borrow from the World Bank but are so poor they can only borrow soft loans from the IDA (International Development Association) arm of the Bank. These are countries with a per capita income (GNP) less than $925 (calculated by the *World Bank Atlas* method) and which are not credit-worthy — thus excluding some low income countries such as India, Nigeria and Zimbabwe which are also eligible to borrow from IBRD (International Bank for Reconstruction and Development, the ordinary loan arm of the World Bank).
- 'Unsustainable debt' for an IDA-only country was defined (in 1998; the definition was changed in 1999) as meeting any one of three criteria:
  (a) present value of debt greater than 250 per cent exports (NPV/XGS > 250 per cent) or
  (b) annual debt service greater than 25 per cent of exports (TDS/XGS > 25 per cent) or
  (c) meeting all three of these criteria:
     (i)   present value of debt is greater than 280 per cent of exports (NPV/XGS > 280 per cent), and
     (ii) exports are at least 40 per cent of GDP (XGS/GDP > 40 per cent) and
     (iii) government fiscal revenue is at least 20 per cent of GDP (rev/GDP > 20 per cent)

(Note that in September 1999 the IMF and World Bank at their annual meetings in Washington revised the definition of what debt is 'sustainable': (a) was changed to NPV/XGS > 150 per cent; and (c) was changed to 250 per cent/30 per cent/15 per cent. These changes are not reflected in the table as no data has yet been published for this revised group.) Definitions from World Bank (1999a, 1999b) and IMF (1999).

bank credit. Eventually money growth outstrips production and money goes into speculation. This is often linked to fraud and swindles, as speculators look for ever more profitable investments. This is the period of bubbles or what Kindleberger calls 'manias', and usually involves international lending. Eventually the bubble bursts, prices fall, and investors try to sell or to collect on their loans. This is the period of 'panic' as investors all rush for the exit. The panic feeds on itself, leading to the 'crash'.

Economists point to both long and short cycles, but it may be useful to look at four long cycles (each of which had short cycles within them):[2]

(1) growth 1780–1820, mania 1820s, crisis 1830s & 1840s.
(2) growth 1850s, mania 1860s, crisis 1870s & 1880s.
(3) growth 1893–1913, mania 1920s, crisis 1930s.
(4) growth 1948–1967, mania 1967–1979, crisis since.

---

[2] See, for example, Eichengreen and Lindert (1989, p. 2).

Both the 1870s and the 1930s saw major international depressions. Each mania involved an international lending boom which overlapped with the end of growth in domestic economies of the then developed countries, as lenders were forced to look abroad for higher profits. After each cycle, there have been retrospective complaints of reckless lending and of 'loan pushing' — banks and lending agencies encouraging foreign governments to take loans they do not need, and encouraging borrowers to live beyond their means. Toward the end of the mania, borrowers are encouraged to take new loans simply to repay old ones. With the panic, lending suddenly stops, borrowers cannot repay, and they default.

Francis White, the US Assistant Secretary of State for Latin American Affairs in the early 1930s, commented that 'in the carnival days from 1922 to 1929, when money was easy, many American bankers forsook the dignified, aloof attitude traditional of bankers and became, in reality, high pressure salesmen of money, carrying on a cut-throat competition against their fellow bankers, and once they obtained the business, endeavoured to urge larger loans on the borrowing countries' (Drake, 1989, p. 43).

3 THE 1980S DEBT CRISIS

The 1970s can be seen as the mania phase of the current cycle.[3] It seems likely that the 1979 oil price rise, followed by the 1982 Mexican default, burst the bubble and caused the panic; so far, there has been no depression in the industrialized countries. 'The more recent debt crisis was very much a rerun of that in the 1920s,' noted Derek Aldcroft (1997, p. 121). 'The present wave resembled earlier experiences more closely than most participants realized. The onset of the crisis in 1982 again looked hauntingly familiar to those who have read the history of debt crises. It is the official response to the crisis since 1982 that stands in stark contrast to the past,' wrote Peter Lindert (1989, p. 227).

As we show below, the mania phase was very similar, but in the response to the panic there are two differences between the 1930s and 1980s–1990s that seem important:

- In the 1930s it was the industrialized countries which suffered, while Latin America was hardly harmed — in part because most countries simply defaulted. By contrast, in the 1980s and 1990s, the industrialized and creditor countries have not suffered very much, whereas the crisis in the south has been very serious.
- Governments and creditors have worked in a much more co-ordinated way both to prevent default by individual countries, and to bring collective pressure on debtors.

The 1970s definitely looked like the 1920s, especially in terms of surplus capital and banks 'pushing' loans on developing countries. 'The main explanation' for the sharp rise in lending to developing countries was the 'failure of demand for loans from borrowers in developed countries to keep pace with the expansion of credit availability', noted US Federal Reserve Governor Andrew Brimmer in 1973. This caused 'the Eurocurrency banks (especially in London) ... to push loans to the developing countries with considerable vigor.' Indeed, it has been argued that the Eurodollar market ballooned precisely because there were no regulations and thus riskier loans were possible (Darity and Horn, 1988, p. 8, 9, 15). Kindleberger (1996, p. 183) notes that

---

[3] See, for example, Kindleberger (1996).

882   *J. Hanlon*

in the 1970s, 'Brazil, Mexico, South Korea, Zaire, Peru and others found themselves courted by the Eurocurrency banks, just as in the "good old days" of 1927.'

Brimmer cited a particular form of loan pushing, which involves a drastic softening of terms, and this actually worsened after his warning. Darity and Horn (1988, pp. 11, 15) note that between 1975 and 1979, real interest rates[4] fell and repayment periods increased, and banks became 'aggressive credit promoters ... literally covering the globe to find new borrowers.' According to the World Bank (1990, p. 15), real interest rates fell to a negative 3 per cent in 1975 and stayed negative until 1978. In other words, developing countries were told they could borrow for projects and repay less than they borrowed.

3.1 Changes After 1979

There was a dramatic change in the global economy at the end of the 1970s. It had the effect of transferring resources from the poor countries of the South to the industrialized countries of the North, through higher interest rates and lower commodity prices, in a way that may have helped to avoid a 1930s-style depression.

Real interest rates jumped from -1 per cent in 1978 to $+9$ per cent in 1982 (World Bank, 1990, p. 15). In the 1980s, countries simply borrowed to repay old debts, rather than for new projects. Arrears reached $111 billion by 1990 and total debt had doubled in the decade.

Nevertheless, for the entire nine-year period 1983–91, for all developing countries, debt service (interest plus principal repayments) was greater than new loans; $209 billion was transferred from debtor countries to creditor countries (see Table 1; World Bank, 1991; 1994; 1997). At the same time, commodity prices fell sharply; between 1980 and 1986, terms of trade for sub-Saharan Africa fell by more than 30 per cent. So developing countries were earning less but paying more, and getting deeper in debt.

Higher interest rates and lower commodity prices caused a growing debt crisis, marked by the Mexican default in 1982; between 1983 and 1987, Mexico rescheduled $125 billion in commercial loans. Virtually every developing country had to reschedule its debts.

Eventually aid and new lending began to increase, and in 1991, for the first time in a seven years, aid was larger than the gap between debt service payments and new loans. In other words, for the first time since 1984, there was a net transfer of money from the North to the South.

Why did the developing countries agree to send so much money to the industrialized countries, and not default as they had in the 1930s? 'In the 1980s, creditor-country governments, motivated by the desire to protect their banking systems, have exerted their greatest pressure on the debtor countries, urging full repayment and macroeconomic adjustment,' note Eichengreen and Lindert (1989, p. 7). They have done so largely though their control of the International Monetary Fund, which was only established in 1944 and is, perhaps, the single most important difference between the 1980s and 1930s.

---

[4]London interbank offer rate — LIBOR — minus the US GDP deflator.

Huw Evans (1999), UK Executive Director of the IMF and World Bank 1994–97, wrote recently that the main area of concern in the 1980s was 'the dangers to many of the world's largest banks, and the banking system. Exposure to the debtors by many banks, especially in the United States, but also to a lesser extent in the UK and the rest of Europe, was several times total bank capital. The debt strategy of the 1980s bought time for the banks to rebuild their capital.' In 1989 the US Treasury Secretary Nicholas Brady created the 'Brady bonds' for Latin American countries which were mainly a way of drawing in the US government and IMF and World Bank to bail out US banks. Thus there was a slow but steady run down of debt to banks and its replacement with official debt to international agencies and governments, thus ensuring that the banks were not penalized for unwise lending.

3.2 Official Lenders

An important difference from the 1920s is that today only half of debt is actually private debt — usually bank loans and usually guaranteed by government. Private debt constituted 62 per cent of long term developing country debt in 1980, falling to 49 per cent by 1990 and remaining at that level through the 1990s.

There are three other kinds of debt:

- bilateral non-concessional debt (usually export credits guaranteed by an export credit agency, where they buyer has failed to pay and the debt has been nationalized by the lender country);
- bilateral concessional debt (aid was often given as soft loans in the 1970s, and Germany and Japan continued to do this into the 1990s); and
- multilateral debt (from the IMF, the World Bank, and regional development banks).

The IMF and World Bank, which soon took charge of managing poor country debt repayments, insisted that they be paid preferentially. Bilateral creditors came next, while commercial banks tended to be last in the queue. The Paris Club was set up in 1956 as an informal group of creditor governments, with a permanent secretariat in the French Treasury, and after 1980 debtor governments increasingly were forced to go to the Paris Club to negotiate extensions on their debts.

By the late 1980s, official creditors — governments and the international development banks — realized that simply delaying or reducing payments on commercial loans was not adequate, and that something would have to be done about official loans. The IMF, for example, in 1987 created a new Enhanced Structural Adjustment Facility to give softer loans to poorer countries. But former IMF Executive Director Evans (1999, p. 271) says that 'in reality, the initiative was ... aimed at ensuring that existing IMF loans to these countries — arrears on which were beginning to mount — could be refinanced. ... This initiative confirmed the need for action to reduce debt, but postponed until the mid-1990s the pressure on the IMF to join in effective and comprehensive debt relief.'

Leaders of the Group of Seven (G7) industrialized countries dealt with this issue twice, in Toronto in 1988 and London in 1991, and in each case agreed that the Paris Club of official bilateral creditors would reschedule more debt at concessional interest rates — an admission that full repayment could not be expected.

884   *J. Hanlon*

By the late 1960s, the Paris Club had made all reschedulings conditional on having an agreement with the IMF (Eichengreen and Portes, 1995, pp. 23–24). As Evans (1999, p. 276) notes, the IMF only lent 'modest' amounts of money, but all 'other official flows — aid and export credit and Paris Club rescheduling — were dependent on an IMF programme being in place, which gave these countries big incentives to sign up to IMF programmes.'

IMF programmes always involved cuts in domestic spending and an opening to the global market. They have been widely criticized in the South for being too restrictive and increasing poverty, but they did ensure that poor countries continued to service their debts, at least partly. Thus there was no 1930s style default. Throughout the 1980s and 1990s, the main way of treating the debt crisis has been to lend more money. But simply rolling over loans was creating an impossible problem because of compound interest — interest payments were deferred, but the borrower was charged interest on the unpaid interest.

Debt continued to increase, as countries continued to borrow more money in an effort to repay old debts. This resulted in a huge churning of money. In 1999, for example, all developing countries borrowed $246 billion, but of this $214 billion went back immediately to repay the principal of old loans. Developing countries had to find $135 billion to pay interest on old loans, meaning there was a net transfer to the creditor countries of $103 billion. In the same year, sub-Saharan Africa borrowed $11 billion but repaid $15 billion ($10 billion in principal repayments and $5 billion in interest payments). Thus, nearly half of the $10 billion in aid grants to sub-Saharan that year stayed in the north to help repay old debts (World Bank, 2000a, vol. 1, pp. 238, 250).

4 HISTORIC CANCELLATIONS

Although the emphasis remained on rescheduling and giving new loans to repay old ones, the 1990s saw growing discussion about cancellation. Debt cancellation is not new and is often political.

There was extensive debate on foreign debt in the 1920s, including a discussion of the unpaid 1840s bonds of the US southern states and a suggestion, rejected by the US, that they be swapped for World War I bonds issued by the US. Discussion became more intense after the 1929 crash, and in 1930 the US announced the formal repudiation of the 1840s bonds. This was finally accepted by British bondholders in the 1950s, more than a century after the bonds had been issued (Ugarteche, 2000).

In the early 1940s, creditors were still negotiating with Latin America over the 1930s defaults. In 1945 Peru reached agreement with its US bondholders that unpaid interest between 1931 and 1945 would be cancelled, and the remainder of the debt would be repaid by a maximum of 3.5 per cent of the national budget (Ugarteche, 1999). By 1945 creditors and bond holders had accepted settlements which took the stock of Latin American debt down to one-third of its former value (Díaz Alejandro, 1983, p. 27). During World War II the United States was anxious to gain support from Mexico, and it intervened in the negotiations with the bond-holders. In 1942, it was agreed that 90 per cent of Mexican debt would be written off (Aggarwal, 1989, p. 148).

In 1952 in London a West German team headed by Hermann-Josef Abs negotiated with representatives of 24 creditor governments for nearly a year to try to settle pre- and post-war debts. The context was highly political. The Berlin blockade of 1948–49 had been followed by the creation in 1949 of the Federal Republic of Germany from the territory occupied by the Western allies. The Cold War had begun in earnest and the West was anxious to give West Germany an economic boost in its competition with East Germany. Also, the allies remembered that one cause of World War II was that after World War I Germany had been saddled with heavy debt and reparations payments. Thus the London negotiators for the first time based a debt settlement not on how much the country could be forced to pay, but on how much it could afford to pay if it was allowed to spend for reconstruction and development. Under the London agreement signed 27 February 1953 Germany acknowledged its liability for all pre-war debt, and the allies wrote off most of it. Payments scheduled for 1953 were expected to be 3.5 per cent of exports and 0.4 per cent of GDP, and never rose above this level. The agreement included the unprecedented clause that repayments would only be made out of German trade surpluses — if the allies wanted debt repaid, they had to buy German goods (Hanlon, 1998a; 1999).

The next two major debt settlements were also political. In August 1965 Indonesian President Sukarno withdrew from the World Bank and IMF. The army overthrew Sukarno, put General Suharto in power and massacred up to 750,000 alleged communists. Suharto rejoined the IMF and World Bank. In December 1996 the Paris Club of Western creditors met and rewarded Suharto with a four year moratorium on all debt service payments. Hermann-Josef Abs was sent to negotiate a new debt service agreement. The final deal said that payments would resume in 1970, but were in effect limited to less that 6 per cent of export earnings and 0.7 per cent of GDP (Kuhn Loeb Lehman Brothers, 1979).

In 1991 the United States wrote off $10 billion of Egypt's debt in exchange for Egyptian co-operation in the Gulf War. This was by far the largest single debt cancellation of the 1990s, and accounted for one-third of all developing country debt cancellation in the six years 1990–95.

5 CANCELLATION AND HIPC

In the 1980s, creditors pretended that poor countries would eventually be able to repay because they refused to 'admit to themselves and the world that the debts were no longer worth their face value,' according to Evans (1999, p. 268). Thus they continued to roll over and reschedule loans. The first change came when private lenders, often under pressure from their own country's central banks, began to admit that the chances of collecting some of these loans was small. On their own books they began to write down the value while not actually cancelling that part of the debt; the country was still expected to pay the full amount. That, in turn, led in 1983 to the setting up of a secondary market in Third World debt. Like junk bonds and other risky investments, banks and traders bought and sold Third World debt — at prices that took into account the high probability that the debt would never be repaid (Garrett and Travis, 1999).

886   *J. Hanlon*

The World Bank and the governments of the industrialized countries intervened to bail out the international banks by taking over some of the private debt, usually at a discount, and sometimes even giving countries loans to buy their own debt on the secondary market. The World Bank estimates that between 1989 and the end of 1997, $56 billion in debt had been cancelled—about 10 per cent of developing country commercial loans. Nicaragua and Ethiopia paid as little as 8 per cent of the face value to buy back their own debt, and this ranged up to 91 per cent for Venezuela (World Bank, 1998a, vol. 2, pp. 83–85). But that cancellation must be compared with an increase in total debt over the same period of $972 billion.

The G7 meetings in Naples in 1995 and Lyon in 1997 agreed, for the first time, to the actual (rather than *defacto*) cancellation of a small amount of Paris Club bilateral debt. And in 1996, with the Heavily Indebted Poor Countries (HIPC) Initiative, the World Bank and IMF accepted for the first time that they, too, would have to cancel some debt. The Bank and Fund identified 41 HIPCs, and they used a new concept to define when a debt was 'sustainable'. This was not based on development considerations, as were used in the 1953 German agreement, but rather on how much money could be squeezed out of a poor country. A debt was to be considered sustainable if 'a country is able in all likelihood to meet its current and future external obligations in full without resorting to rescheduling in the future or accumulation of arrears' (World Bank, 1998a, vol. 2, p. 55). All creditors agreed that for these 41 countries, they would cancel debt proportionately to reach the 'sustainable level'.

The World Bank and IMF then decided to assess 'sustainability' in terms of export earnings, rather than the more logical measures of GDP or government budget, and it chose to call debt 'sustainable' at a level that only two year before it had said was 'unsustainable'.[5] A HIPC 'sustainability' criterion defined in 1996 was that annual debt service should be between 20 per cent and 25 per cent of export earnings. The HIPC process proved slow and confusing, and for most countries simply cancelled the debt that was not being serviced, so poor countries which qualified for HIPC gained little. When they met in Köln (Cologne) in 1999, the G7 leaders agreed to lower the 'sustainability' level to, effectively, an annual debt service of 15 per cent of export earnings.[6]

---

[5] The World Bank and IMF use the concept of 'net present value' (NPV) of debt, which is the value which would have to be deposited in an interest bearing account to exactly pay off the debt—thus concessional debt has an NPV less than the face value and commercial debt an NPV more than the face value. In 1994 the World Bank (1994, vol. 1, p. 40) concluded that ratios of NPV debt to export earnings (XGS) in excess of 200 per cent had 'generally proved unsustainable over the medium term'. In 1996, with no public justification, the World Bank and IMF announced that under HIPC debt would be 'sustainable' if the NPV to XGS ratio was between 200 and 250 per cent—a level which just two years before had been said to be 'unsustainable'. For the 41 HIPC countries, debt service due averages 10 per cent of NPV debt, so an NPV to XGS ratio between is equivalent to an annual debt service to export ratio between 20 and 25 per cent, which was the second sustainability criterion set under HIPC.

[6] At Köln the G7 changed one 'sustainability' criterion but not other—the NPV debt to XGS ratio was reduced to 150 per cent, while the annual debt service to export ratio was left between 20 and 25 per cent. But because debt service due for HIPCs is normally 10 per cent of NPV debt, this has the effect of reducing the second criterion to 15 per cent.

After the Köln G7 meeting, it was estimated that about $100 billion[7] in debt of 33 countries would be cancelled by a combination of the Lyon Paris Club agreed terms and the new HIPC terms. The HIPC countries are currently supposed to pay $13 billion per year in debt service, but actually pay about $9 billion; the $100 billion in debt cancellation would cut debt service by about $6 billion per year, but since $4 billion is already not being paid, this would cut debt service of these poor countries from $9 billion to $7 billion per year. In late 1999, the World Bank estimated that eight countries which it defines as 'heavily indebted poor countries' would not have any debt cancelled; other poor and indebted countries, such as Bangladesh and Morocco, remained ineligible even for consideration.

The HIPC debt cancellation process is based entirely on reducing debt to a level to which it can be repaid. It asks no questions about development, poverty, or post-war reconstruction.

6 HOW MUCH DEBT SHOULD BE CANCELLED?

Historic debt settlements tended to be on an individual basis. But it is possible to look back at them and use the HIPC methodology to set alternative cancellation criteria.

HIPC is the first time that export earnings have been formally used as a basis for defining sustainable debt, but it is possible to calculate comparisons. In 1952 the victorious allies originally demanded that Germany pay the equivalent of 10 per cent of export earnings in debt service, and Hermann-Josef Abs said this was intolerable (Hanlon, 1998a). The allies agreed, and Germany only had to pay 3.5 per cent of export earnings. Indonesia was only asked to pay 6 per cent of export earnings. This is compared with 15 per cent of export earnings under the improved HIPC — two-and-a-half times the Indonesia level and more than four times the German level.

Although exports can be seen as one way of measuring a country's income and ability to pay, the level of exports also depends on the size and location of the county. GDP is often considered a better measure. Germany was required to pay 0.4 per cent of GDP and Indonesia 0.7 per cent. In terms of GDP, HIPC country exports are 28.5 per cent of GDP, so debt service of 15 per cent of exports corresponds to debt service of approximately 4.3 per cent of GDP. This is 10 times the level seen as acceptable for Germany in 1953 — 0.4 per cent — and 6 times the level seen as acceptable for Indonesia in 1970 — 0.7 per cent.

Government revenue is an alternative measure, and was the one selected by Peru in 1945. For most countries, government revenue is similar to exports and runs at 15–30 per cent of GDP.

Finally, and most importantly, Germany was expected to pay only when it had a trade surplus — the creditors had to buy German exports if they expected to be repaid.

Using these criteria, we can estimate how much a country can pay in debt service and compare that with the amount that it owes. We look at 93 of the poorest and most indebted countries.[8] In 1998, these 93 countries had a debt of $1700 billion, out of a

---

[7] Face value, not NPV.

[8] We looked at countries with a 1995 GDP at purchasing power parity (PPP) less than $4500, plus those countries defined by the World Bank in 2000 as middle income countries which are severely or moderately indebted. We exclude Europe and the former USSR, Eritrea, and non-reporting countries (Afghanistan, Cuba, DR Korea, Namibia and Iraq).

888   *J. Hanlon*

Table 4. Debt service that could be paid by the 93 countries under various criteria, 1998

	$ bn/year
Debt service due	226
Debt service actually paid	209
Possible debt service under various criteria:	
Peru 1945 criterion	
3.5% of present tax	17
3.5% of reasonable tax*	30
Germany 1953 criterion	
3.5% of exports	33
0.4% of GDP	16
trade surplus	43
Indonesia 1970 criterion	
6% of exports	57
0.7% of GDP	29
HIPC 15% of exports	
applied only to HIPC countries	220
applied to all countries	143
This paper, based on development	156

'Reasonable tax' is 25 per cent of GDP after excluding income before the $1 per day poverty line.

total developing country debt of $2465 billion (see Table 3). In 1998, they owed $226 billion per year in debt service (interest and principal repayments) and actually paid $209 billion of that.

Table 4 sets out the results of applying historic criteria. The implication is that between 75 per cent and 93 per cent of debt would need to be cancelled — which is approximately the proportion of debt which was cancelled after the previous economic cycle. By contrast, HIPC will only cancel 4 per cent of debt.

Looking at export criteria, only 3 of our 93 countries could pay all their debt if the German criterion applied, and only 5 if the Indonesia criterion was used. HIPC only applies to a small group of countries, but if its 15 per cent were extended to all countries in the sample, only 34 would be able to pay all their debts.

7 HUMAN RIGHTS AND DEVELOPMENT GOALS

All of the previous discussion has been about simple fiscal measures of possible debt service payments, based on fixed percentages of GDP, exports or revenue. In this section, we make a first attempt at defining a human rights and development approach to debt cancellation.

'A rights-based approach to development ... has been rising up the agenda', notes Simon Maxwell (1999), director of the Overseas Development Institute. This approach 'sets the achievement of human rights as the objective of development. It uses thinking about human rights as the scaffolding of development policy. It invokes the international apparatus of human rights accountability in support of development action.'

Most importantly, the new 'rights-based approach' strives to put economic and social rights on the same plane as civil and political rights. And it draws directly on the Universal Declaration of Human Rights, adopted by the United Nations more than 50 years ago. Two of these rights are particularly important:

- 'Everyone has the right to a standard of living adequate for the health and well being of himself and his family, including food, clothing, housing and medical care and necessary social services.' (Article 25)
- 'Everyone has the right to education. Education shall be free, at least in the elementary and fundamental stages. Elementary education shall be compulsory.' (Article 26)

'The new rights agenda runs alongside an agenda derived from the international development targets, which focuses on poverty and human development,' Maxwell notes.

7.1 DAC Targets

The most widely cited development targets are the 'DAC targets', adopted in 1996 by the 21 donor countries which are members of the OECD Development Assistance Committee (DAC).[9] These donors committed themselves to a set of six of what they called 'ambitious but realizable goals':

- a reduction by one-half of the proportion of people living in extreme poverty by 2015;
- universal primary education by 2015;
- eliminating gender disparity in education by 2005;
- reduction by two-thirds in infant and child (under 5) mortality and three-fourths in maternal mortality, all by 2015;
- access to reproductive health services for all individuals of appropriate ages by 2015; and
- a end to the loss of environmental resources by 2015.

The DAC targets can be seen as a way of reaching the goals of the Universal Declaration of Human Rights.[10] The international community is now committed to both of these.

Since the late 19th century, it has been recognized that human rights take precedence over debts, however those debts were acquired. Most countries now have bankruptcy laws. If a company goes bankrupt, no one would expect the children of the owners or employees of that company to drop out of school to go to work to pay the company's debts. Similarly, if a man runs up huge debts through drinking or

---

[9] Included in the report 'Shaping the 21st Century: The Contribution of Development Co-operation' adopted at the 34th High Level Meeting of the Development Assistance Committee, 6–7 May 1996 (OECD DAC, 1997).

[10] Note that there is a strong counter-argument that this is inadequate. The DAC targets only call for halving the number of people living in 'extreme poverty', and it is argued that the other half who remain in extreme poverty are having their article 25 right to an adequate standard of living violated. But Maxwell and others argue that a rights-based approach is an advance and involves changing performance standards. Since the DAC targets have been widely accepted, it seems reasonable to use them here.

890   *J. Hanlon*

gambling, no one any longer expects his children to leave school to work to pay the debts.

Yet, these principles are not applied at the level of nations within the global economy. For example, Mozambique is one of the poorest countries in the world, yet even after some debt cancellation it spends as much repaying debts as on health. President Joaquim Chissano has appealed for 100 per cent debt cancellation but this has been rejected by the international community.[11] Tens of thousands of Mozambican children will be denied access to school and to health services because money goes to repay the World Bank and other creditors instead of being spent on poverty reduction.

Simon Maxwell (1999) notes that one aspect of a rights-based approach to development is that 'because rights are universal, the wider international community has at least a moral duty to support rights, including financially, in partnership with states; this moral obligation may extend to non-state actors, particularly international financial institutions, TNCs, and NGOs'.

Thus if a creditor takes money in debt service that is needed by a poor country to fund basic health services, it can be argued that the creditor is violating the human rights of the people of that country—as well as going against the international commitment to the DAC targets. Thus it might be argued that the IMF and World Bank are violating human rights.

Following Maxwell's lead, we use progress toward the DAC targets as a way of measuring satisfaction of human rights. To link this to debt, we estimate how much essential spending is needed to meet the DAC targets, and argue that this must be made before any debt service is paid.

7.2 Defining Essential Spending

In this section, we make a first estimate of how much needs to be spent to meet the DAC targets and how much money is available. Assuming that essential spending takes priority over debt service allows an estimate of how much debt cancellation is required to meet promises the industrialized countries have already made by agreeing the human rights declaration and DAC targets.

There are apparently no published estimates of the cost of meeting the DAC targets for 2015, nor are there any agreed figures as to what is 'essential spending', nor are there agreed estimates of how much tax revenue a country can be expected to raise. Indeed, the latter two issues have been at the heart of the debate of the past two decades.

Lack of data and lack of agreement on tax and spending policies means that we must make a series of often heroic assumptions, and can only make a very rough initial estimate of essential spending.[12] Below, we try to define essential expenditure, set out plausible estimates of income, and then see what is left for debt service. Our 93 countries have 4.2 billion people, of whom 1.2 billion have an income under the

---

[11] For example, Baroness Amos, the British government spokesperson for international development in the House of Lords, on 25 October 1999 in a debate on Mozambique said 'we do not support the call for total debt forgiveness' for Mozambique.

[12] Although these can only be rough estimates, we have been presenting preliminary versions of these calculations over a period of a year, including to a seminar in London on 18 March 1999 attended by representatives of the World Bank and IMF, and they have not been challenged.

international absolute poverty line, $1 per person per day at purchasing power parity (PPP) at 1985 prices.[13]

We first attempt to define Essential Social Spending (ESS). With no published estimates of the cost of meeting the DAC targets, we draw on three different methods:

Cafod extended. The British agency Cafod estimates that a low income country must spend at least $28 per capita per year on health and education (Northover et al., 1998). This, in turn is based on World Bank (1993, p. 66) estimates that low income countries must spend $12 per capita per year on 'public health and minimum essential clinical services', at 1990 prices. To this Cafod adds $12 for education and $4 for inflation and other expenditure, to reach $28. Noting that the World Bank also says that middle income countries must spend $22 per capita on the minimum health package, and we simply extend this to $52 for a Cafod-like package for middle income countries. This gives essential social spending of $136 billion per year.

'20–20': As part of the '20–20 Initiative', the United Nations system (UNDP et al., 1998, p. 20) estimated that an extra $80 billion per year must be spent on the 1.3 billion people living in poverty in order to meet the DAC targets. This is an additional $62 per person per year which must be spent on everyone with an income under the international absolute poverty line, $1 per person per day. We add this to present health and education spending[14] and consider it essential. This gives essential social spending of $309 billion per year.

HDR 96: UNDP's Human Development Report 1996 (p. 113) uses an econometric exercise to estimate that 'a 1 percentage point increase in the average share of GDP invested in health and education is estimated to reduce ... the child mortality rate by 24 percentage points.' One of the DAC targets is cutting infant and child mortality by two-thirds, which would require a transfer of 4 per cent of GDP to health and education. So we add an extra 4 per cent of GDP to present health and education spending and consider this essential. This gives essential social spending of $400 billion per year.

All three of these approaches have methodological problems. But as nothing else is available to allow an estimation of the costs of meeting the DAC targets, and there is no strong reason to choose between them, we simply average the results of these three approaches as at least a rough estimate of essential social spending (ESS).

Social spending is not the only essential spending. The United Nations Conference on Trade and Development (UNCTAD, 1998, p. 130) uses work by Jeffrey Sachs to argue that, in addition to health and education, a government should be spending 2 per cent of GDP on 'public administration', 3 per cent of GDP on 'expenses for police and defence', and 5 per cent on infrastructure such as rural roads which are 'much harder to finance through the market'. UNCTAD and Sachs argue that this is also essential spending which must be made before debt service is paid.

Therefore, we assume that ESS plus 10 per cent of GDP is 'required spending' (RS), which must be made first before any debt service is paid.

---

[13] Note that there are strong reservations about the use of this figure, which is said by some experts to underestimate the level of poverty. See, for example, Michel Chossudovsky, Journal of International Affairs, Fall 1998, 52(1).
[14] From UNDP 1999 and World Bank 2000b, with gaps filled with estimates based on UNDP 1999 averages.

892   *J. Hanlon*

7.3 Available Revenue

The next step is to ask how much tax a country can be expected to raise. Here we follow an estimate first made by Cafod (Northover *et al.*, 1998). All countries have a tax threshold — a level of income below which no tax is paid. Cafod takes the tax threshold at the absolute poverty line, $1 per day, and assumes all income below that is not taxed. The $1 per day poverty threshold is conventionally taken at purchasing power parity (PPP) of 1985 US dollars. For those people earning more than $1/day, we just discount this portion of their earnings. The poorest people who earn below the tax threshold have a share of non-taxable income which is less than the equivalent of $1 per day.[15] By definition, the 'poverty gap' is the amount their earnings fall below $1 a day — in effect, the 'average income shortfall of the poor' (Gordon and Spickler, 1998, p. 103) — and below-poverty-line incomes are taken as $1 per day reduced by this amount, which is then subtracted as non-taxable from GDP.[16]

We assume that above that level, tax can be 25 per cent of income.[17] Clearly, however, this is not just income tax and will include all revenue sources including VAT and sales taxes, duties on alcohol and imports, corporation taxes, etc.

For the poorest countries, aid is a major source of revenue. We assume that technical co-operation, food aid, loans, etc are not available for debt servicing. Thus we only consider what the World Bank in its annual *Global Development Finance* defines as 'grants'. Further, we assume that half of that is allocated by the donors and half is general budget support which can be spent on debt servicing.[18]

Thus we assume that possible government income is possible tax revenue (defined as 25 per cent of income above the poverty line) plus half of grant aid.

7.4 Possible Debt Service

Although much of the debt cancellation literature talks about the volume of debt, what is relevant to a country is the actual debt service (interest plus principal repayments) that it pays. Debt service due[19] is used rather than debt service actually paid, because many of the poorest countries pay only half of what they owe, but the debt remains. The 41 countries defined as Heavily Indebted Poor Countries (HIPC) by the World Bank and International Monetary Fund paid only 71 per cent of

---

[15] From World Bank 2000b. Where data does not exist, we use the averages from UNDP 1998, which are 25.9 per cent for medium human development and 43.8 per cent for low human development.

[16] Accounting for inflation, $1 per day is equivalent to $526 current PPP dollars per year. So the share of GDP excluded from taxation becomes: (526/(GDP per capita at current PPP))×(1−((poverty gap)×(% below $1 per day))). The poverty gap is taken from the World Bank (2000b, Table 2.7, pp. 62–64). Where no data is given, we take 15 per cent as an estimate.

[17] Data on government revenue and spending is available from only a limited number of countries. UNDP (1999, Table 12, p. 184) gives 1997 average tax revenue as 16 per cent of GDP for 'medium human development' countries and 28 per cent for the 'high human development' countries. In 1994, government revenue in sub-Saharan Africa was 21 per cent of GDP (World Bank, 1996, p. 187).

[18] This is hard to estimate because of the complex nature of donor conditions, so this level has been chosen to be generous to donors. OECD DAC (1997, Tables 2 and 27, pp. A4, A46) tables suggest that in 1995 only $7.5 billion was available for debt service — which is less than one-third of grants as given for that year by the World Bank (1997).

[19] Total debt service due is for 1998, the last year for which there is good data. This is taken to be long term debt service due for 1998 (World Bank, 1999a) plus short term debt service actually paid in 1998 (as calculated from World Bank, 2000a).

Table 5. Countries which can pay no debt service and need more aid

Country	Spending ($ million)					Possible government income ($ million)				EDT
	GDP Gross Domestic Product	TDSd Debt service due	ESS Essential social spending	RS Required spending	Non-taxable portion of GDP	MTAX maximum possible tax	AID Grants	INC maximum useable income	INC-RS deficit left after required spending	Total debt—which must be cancelled
Angola	7,470	1,094	654	1,401	34%	1,226	216	1,334	−67	12,173
Bangladesh	42,700	707	3,803	8,073	49%	5,420	657	5,749	−2,324	16,376
Benin	2,310	70	213	444	39%	354	120	414	−30	1,647
Burkina Faso	2,580	66	352	610	44%	361	214	468	−142	1,399
Burundi	885	56	153	242	78%	49	51	74	−168	1,119
Cambodia	2,870	145	274	561	39%	436	170	521	−39	2,210
Chad	1,690	47	203	372	51%	208	83	250	−122	1,091
Congo DR (Kin)	6,940	603	1,076	1,770	56%	766	97	815	−955	12,929
Ethiopia	6,540	612	1,302	1,956	100%	0	418	209	−1,747	10,352
Gambia	420	30	43	85	31%	72	24	84	−1	477
Guinea-Bissau	210	41	30	51	57%	23	48	47	−5	964
India	430,020	10,829	35,182	78,184	30%	75,440	476	75,678	−2,506	98,232
Kenya	11,580	683	1,259	2,417	43%	1,646	197	1,744	−673	7,010
Laos	1,260	34	139	265	38%	196	118	255	−10	2,437
Lesotho	790	65	118	197	26%	147	33	163	−34	692
Liberia	990	93	85	184	58%	103	60	133	−51	2,103
Madagascar	3,750	159	442	817	48%	485	354	662	−155	4,394
Malawi	1,690	103	312	481	69%	130	213	237	−245	2,444
Mali	2,700	133	369	639	52%	326	201	426	−213	3,202
Mongolia	1,040	51	117	221	40%	156	54	183	−38	739
Mozambique	3,890	211	499	888	68%	313	674	650	−239	8,208
Nepal	4,780	93	598	1,076	46%	639	117	698	−378	2,646
Niger	2,050	110	299	504	49%	261	158	340	−163	1,659
Nigeria	41,350	2,803	3,717	7,852	43%	5,875	33	5,892	−1,961	30,315
Pakistan	63,370	4,132	4,517	10,854	33%	10,603	175	10,691	−163	32,229
Rwanda	2,020	41	232	434	78%	114	199	213	−221	1,226
Sierra Leone	647	47	127	192	99%	1	70	36	−156	1,243
Somalia	900	53	195	285	59%	93	68	127	−158	2,635
Tanzania	8,020	302	845	1,647	90%	204	648	528	−1,119	7,603
Togo	1,510	83	161	312	33%	253	63	284	−27	1,448
Uganda	6,780	188	643	1,321	43%	959	433	1,175	−146	3,935
Yemen	4,320	203	451	883	65%	379	125	441	−442	4,138
Zambia	3,350	254	378	713	40%	504	257	633	−81	6,865
Zimbabwe	6,340	756	770	1,404	22%	1,242	153	1,319	−85	4,716
Totals	677,762	24,897	59,561	127,337		108,985	6,977	112,474	−14,863	290,856

All data for 1998, or if not available, most recent year. Number of countries: 34.
Data from: World Bank, *Global Development Finance*, 1998a, 1999, 2000; World Bank, *World Development Report*, 1998b and 1999/2000; World Bank, *World Development Indicators*, 2000; UNDP, *Human Development Report*, 1997, 1998, 1999.
Required spending=Essential Social Spending+10% of GDP
Maximum possible tax=25% of GDP after excluding income below $1/day
Maximum income=maximum possible tax+half of aid grants

894   J. Hanlon

Table 6. Countries which can pay some but not all debt

Country	Spending ($ million 1998)				Possible government income ($ million 1998)					Part of debt which can be paid	EDT Total debt	Debt which cannot be paid
	GDP Gross Domestic Product	TDSd Debt service due	ESS Essential social spending	RS Required spending	Non-taxable portion of GDP	MTAX maximum possible tax	AID Grants	INC maximum useable income	INC-RS income left after required spending —available for debt service			
Algeria	47,350	4,645	3,778	8,513	12%	10,446	107	10,499	1,987	43%	30,665	17,550
Argentina	298,130	25,879	19,535	49,348	5%	70,874	31	70,890	21,541	83%	144,050	24,145
Belize	600	45	59	119	12%	132	31	148	29	64%	338	122
Bolivia	8,590	480	644	1,503	18%	1,756	232	1,872	369	77%	6,078	1,401
Brazil	778,210	47,001	57,370	135,191	8%	178,770	97	178,819	43,628	93%	232,004	16,651
Cameroon	8,700	546	543	1,413	27%	1,593	276	1,731	318	58%	9,829	4,103
Central Afr Rep	1,060	50	128	234	30%	187	102	238	4	8%	921	848
Comoros	200	10	17	37	33%	33	24	45	8	82%	203	37
Congo R (Bras)	1,960	458	160	356	31%	337	53	364	8	2%	5,119	5,031
Côte d'Ivoire	11,000	1,404	762	1,862	29%	1,966	513	2,223	361	26%	14,852	11,037
Djibouti	500	15	37	87	39%	76	48	100	13	90%	288	30
Ecuador	18,360	1,806	1,242	3,078	11%	4,107	66	4,140	1,062	59%	15,140	6,234
Ghana	7,500	511	592	1,342	31%	1,297	239	1,416	75	15%	5,899	5,036
Guinea	3,600	180	251	611	26%	665	172	751	139	77%	3,442	777
Guyana	800	102	75	155	16%	169	105	221	66	65%	1,653	581
Haiti	3,870	42	256	643	39%	593	134	660	17	41%	1,048	614
Honduras	5,370	571	402	939	22%	1,047	163	1,128	190	33%	5,002	3,342
Indonesia	94,160	25,030	4,971	14,387	15%	20,006	255	20,133	5,746	23%	150,875	116,239
Jamaica	6,420	558	548	1,190	15%	1,360	92	1,406	216	39%	3,995	2,448
Jordan	7,390	601	644	1,383	15%	1,569	272	1,705	322	54%	8,485	3,938
Mauritania	990	165	83	182	30%	172	130	237	56	34%	2,589	1,717
Morroco	35,550	3,058	2,487	6,042	16%	7,475	349	7,650	1,608	53%	20,687	9,811
Myanmar	33,000	287	1,402	4,702	42%	4,771	67	4,805	103	36%	5,680	3,635
Nicaragua	2,010	434	176	377	26%	370	345	543	165	38%	5,968	3,692
Panama	9,140	711	813	1,727	7%	2,118	10	2,123	396	56%	6,689	2,968
Papua NG	3,750	303	293	668	19%	759	208	863	195	64%	2,692	962
Philippines	65,110	4,766	4,312	10,823	14%	13,940	184	14,032	3,208	67%	47,817	15,630
SaoTome	41	16	5	10	27%	7	11	13	3	22%	246	193
Senegal	4,680	327	385	853	30%	821	252	947	94	29%	3,861	2,751
Solomon Islands	400	12	34	74	22%	78	10	83	9	78%	152	34
St Vincent	300	23	29	59	12%	66	12	72	13	58%	420	178
Sudan	10,370	381	823	1,860	32%	1,776	188	1,870	9	2%	16,843	16,426
Swaziland	1,300	26	131	261	15%	276	16	284	23	88%	251	29
Syria	17,410	1,401	1,301	3,042	16%	3,675	95	3,723	681	49%	22,435	11,523
Thailand	111,330	11,416	6,913	18,046	8%	25,644	68	25,678	7,632	67%	86,172	28,562
Tunisia	19,960	1,611	1,729	3,725	10%	4,514	61	4,545	820	51%	11,078	5,442
Viet Nam	27,180	1,787	2,048	4,766	31%	4,687	231	4,803	37	2%	22,359	21,893
Totals	1,646,291	136,658	114,976	279,605		368,134	5,249	370,759	91,153	61%	895,825	345,609

All data for 1998, or if not available, most recent year. Number of countries: 37.
Data from: World Bank, *Global Development Finance*, 1998, 1999, 2000; World Bank, *World Development Report*, 1998 and 1999/2000; World Bank, *World Development Indicators*, 2000; UNDP, *Human Development Report*, 1997, 1998, 1999. The unpayable portion of total debt is estimated as being the same as the unpayable portion of debt service.
Required spending=Essential Social Spending+10% of GDP
Maximum possible tax=25% of GDP after excluding income below $1/day
Maximum income=maximum possible tax+half of aid grants

Table 7. Countries which can pay all their debt and still spend for development

Country	GDP Gross Domestic Product	TDSd Debt service due	Spending ($ million 1998)		Non-taxable portion of GDP	Possible government income ($ million 1998)				
			ESS Essential social spending	RS Required spending		MTAX maximum possible tax	AID Grants	INC maximum useable income	INC-RS income left after required spending	EDT Total debt— can be paid
Bhutan	400	6	32	72	33%	67	28	81	9	120
Cape Verde	400	16	35	75	17%	83	62	114	39	244
Chile	78,740	4,088	4,155	12,029	4%	18,872	25	18,884	6,856	36,302
China	959,030	22,640	56,325	152,228	17%	199,779	267	199,913	47,684	154,599
Colombia	102,900	4,794	8,479	18,769	8%	23,745	61	23,776	5,006	33,263
Dominica	200	8	19	39	12%	44	24	56	17	109
Egypt	82,710	1,934	6,793	15,064	17%	17,112	1341	17,782	2,718	31,964
El Salvador	11,870	330	675	1,862	18%	2,440	119	2,499	638	3,633
Eq Guinea	500	12	27	77	28%	90	13	97	19	306
Gabon	5,520	519	214	766	7%	1,288	52	1,314	548	4,425
Guatemala	18,940	444	931	2,825	12%	4,175	152	4,251	1,427	4,565
Lebanon	17,230	546	960	2,683	9%	3,941	107	3,994	1,312	6,725
Malaysia	72,500	4,552	4,476	11,726	6%	16,999	15	17,007	5,281	44,773
Mauritius	4,200	303	242	662	5%	993	12	999	337	2,482
Paraguay	8,610	266	600	1,461	13%	1,873	21	1,883	422	2,305
Peru	62,750	2,233	3,451	9,726	11%	13,939	239	14,059	4,333	32,397
Samoa	200	5	19	39	14%	43	20	53	14	180
Sri Lanka	15,710	464	1,060	2,631	21%	3,098	114	3,155	525	8,526
Turkey	198,840	14,444	10,622	30,506	8%	45,593	62	45,624	15,117	102,074
Uruguay	20,580	1,175	1,042	3,100	6%	4,851	8	4,855	1,755	7,600
Vanuatu	300	3	20	50	15%	64	7	68	18	63
Venezuela	95,020	5,625	6,814	16,316	6%	22,356	22	22,367	6,052	37,003
Totals	1,757,150	64,407	106,988	282,703		381,445	2,771	382,830	100,127	513,658

All data for 1998, or if not available, most recent year. Number of countries: 22
Data from: World Bank, Global Development Finance, 1998, 1999, 2000; World Bank, World Development Report, 1998 and 1999/2000; World Bank, World Development Indicators, 2000; UNDP, Human Development Report, 1997, 1998, 1999.
Required spending=Essential Social Spending+10% of GDP
Maximum possible tax=25% of GDP after excluding income below $1/day
Maximum income=maximum possible tax+half of aid grants

896   *J. Hanlon*

their debt service due in 1998; they owed $13 billion but in fact paid only $9 billion of this.

Essential social spending, required spending, and possible income[20] are calculated as set out above. The results are given in Tables 5–7 which split the 93 countries into three groups.

Table 5 shows countries where the maximum feasible income from taxes and aid is less than the required spending. These 34 countries need an extra $15 billion per year in aid just to meet the DAC targets. In addition, there is no hope of their meeting any of the demands for $25 billion per year in debt service which is owed. They have a total debt of $291 billion, which, under our assumptions, would need to be cancelled.

Table 6 shows 37 countries which have enough potential tax revenue to meet required spending, but not sufficient to pay their debt service. They were expected to pay $137 billion in debt service in 1996 but could only afford to pay $91 billion; $46 billion per year is unpayable. This corresponds to nearly $350 billion in debt which would need to be cancelled.[21] This group includes countries like Argentina and Haiti which could argue that some of the debts are odious (see Section 8, below); the estimation that they have enough money to pay these debts does not remove the moral and political argument that they should not.

Table 7 shows that 22 of these countries can collect enough money to meet domestic spending needs and pay their debts.

These 93 countries owed $226 billion in debt service in 1998, and actually paid $209 billion of it. Based on the assumptions set out above, we estimate that they could only 'afford' to pay $156 billion; the extra $70 billion was money which should have been spent of health, education and development in order to satisfy basic human rights. And, as we argue above, debt relief will not work on its own; in addition, as Table 5 shows, we estimate that $15 billion per year more aid is needed. These estimates suggest that if creditor countries are serious about their commitments to human rights and the DAC targets, they will need to cancel more than $600 billion in debt — compared with the $100 billion agreed by the G7 at Köln.

We estimate that these countries need $85 billion in new aid and reduced debt service, based on consideration of essential social spending. The Economic Commission for Africa (1999, p. 36) estimated that sub-Saharan Africa needed an extra 13.9 per cent of GDP in additional investment resources to reach the growth rate needed to halve the number of people living in absolute poverty by the year 2015. This is $44 billion per year just for Africa, which suggests that our $85 billion for all 93 countries may be an under-estimate.

---

[20] GDP is 1998 GDP (World Bank, 2000b) substituted with 1997 data (UNDP, 1999) in a some cases where the World Bank has no data, and estimated in a few places where neither source has information.

[21] It is not precisely correct to say that the portion of debt needing to be cancelled is the same as the proportion of debt service that cannot be paid, because of the different repayment schedules of different kinds of debt. However data is not available to do a correct detailed calculation, so this method must be used as the only available one to give an estimate. If it is assumed that debt for each country must be cancelled in proportion to the debt service that cannot be paid, Table 6 shows that $346 billion in debt would need to be cancelled — nearly $350 billion.

8 POLITICAL, MORAL AND PRACTICAL ISSUES

So far we have estimated debt cancellation based on ability to pay. But this is based on two assumptions: that the debt should be paid, and that the money will be spent on development to meet the DAC targets. It is beyond the scope of this paper to discuss these assumptions, but a few comments need to be made here.

Even the 'rights-based approach' only considers the amount of debt, and not its history. In this section we cite a 'normative' argument — not that the debt *cannot* be paid, but that some debt *should not* be paid.

Zaire's ruler, Mobutu Sese Seko, was one of the world's most corrupt leaders, and it was for his government that the world 'kleptocracy' was first coined. In 1978 the IMF appointed its own man, Irwin Blumenthal, to a key post in the central bank. He resigned in less than a year saying that 'the corruptive system in Zaire with all its wicked and ugly manifestations' was so serious that there is 'no (repeat: no) prospect for Zaire's creditors to get their money back' (Lissakers, 1992, p. 166).[22] Shortly afterwards, the IMF gave Zaire the largest loan it had ever given to an African country. When Blumenthal wrote his report, Zaire's debt was $5 billion. When Mobutu was overthrown and died in 1998, the debt was over $13 bn, due to huge loans from the IMF, the World Bank and governments.

Philippines dictator Ferdinand Marcos and his wife Imelda are said to have pocketed one-third of the Philippines entire borrowing (Adams, 1991). The most notorious project was the $2.1 billion Bataan nuclear power station which was built on an earthquake fault and never used. Marcos is said to have received $80 million in commissions from builder Westinghouse. Filipinos will continue to pay for this corrupt project until 2018, using 'money that should have gone to basic services like schools and hospitals,' the national treasurer, Leonor Briones, said (*Guardian*, London, 7 September 1999).

Many of the dictators backed by the West during the Cold War are gone, but the creditors demand that the victims must pay the debts of their oppressors. There are two arguments — odious debts and moral hazard — that lenders have no right to demand that the victims repay these debts.

8.1 Odious Debts

In 1898 the United States captured Cuba from Spain, which then demanded that the US pay Cuba's debts. The US refused on the grounds that the debts had been 'imposed on the people of Cuba without their consent and by force of arms'. Furthermore, the US argued that, in such circumstances, 'the creditors, from the beginning, took their chance of the investment'. The concept of 'odious debt' was upheld and formally entered international law in the 1923 judgement of US Chief Justice Taft in the case of *Great Britain vs. Costa Rica* (Adams, 1991).

In 1982, at the height of lending to apartheid South Africa after the United Nations declared apartheid a crime against humanity, two lawyers from the First National Bank of Chicago warned their employers that a majority rule government in South African might not need to repay the loans because 'if the debt of the

---

[22] The bracketed phrase is in the original memo. The publisher of the memo is Karin Lissakers, who has since become US Executive Director of the IMF.

898 *J. Hanlon*

predecessor is deemed to be "odious", i.e. the debt proceeds are used against the interests of the local populace, then the debt may not be chargeable against the successor' (Foorman and Jehle, 1982).

Finally, the International Development Committee (1998, ¶11, 57) of the British House of Commons noted that 'the bulk of Rwanda's external debt was incurred by the genocidal regime which preceded the current administration. ... Some argue that loans were used by the genocidal regime to purchase weapons and that the current administration and, ultimately the people of Rwanda, should not have to repay these odious debts. ... We further recommend that the [UK] government urge all bilateral creditors, in particular France, to cancel debt incurred by the previous regime.'

In another study, I estimated that nearly a quarter of all poor country debt was incurred by dictators. Since this debt had been 'imposed on the people ... without their consent and by force of arms,' it can be argued that successor governments are not liable for those debts (Hanlon, 1998b).

8.2 Moral Hazard

The IMF (1998, p. 8) says that 'moral hazard exists when the provision of insurance against a risk encourages a behaviour that makes that risk more likely to occur. In the case of IMF lending, the concern about moral hazard stems from perceptions that the availability of financial assistance may weaken policy discipline, encourage international investors to take on greater risks in the belief that they will only partially suffer the consequences, or both'.

If generations yet unborn have to pay for Marcos' nuclear power station that never worked, for Mobutu's palaces, and loans to a regime labelled by UN resolutions as committing a 'crime against humanity', then there is a serious problem of 'moral hazard'. Lenders need have no compunction about the morality of the loan, or even if it is a sensible loan; repayment is almost guaranteed.

The IMF and World Bank are in an invidious position and suffer the most risk of moral hazard, because they enforce debt repayments. The Democratic Republic of the Congo will want aid and HIPC debt relief, and that requires them to have IMF and World Bank programmes. That, in turn, gives the IMF and World Bank a heavy weapon to insist that the new government of the DR Congo does not suggest that loans to prop up Mobutu were odious and should not be repaid.

Moral hazard can only be avoided if lending institutions are now forced to accept their responsibility for past bad lending. Cancellation of odious debts can thus be seen as necessary to avoid future moral hazard.

8.3 How the Money is Spent

If debt is to be cancelled because it is odious or because of moral hazard, then creditors have no right to ask how the money released will be used. And in most past debt cancellations, no questions were asked about how the money released was used. The United States does not ask Britain what it does with the money it should be using to pay its World War I debts to the US.

Nevertheless, if we are arguing that debt should be cancelled to release funds for development and to meet the DAC targets, then it may be reasonable to ask the debtor to show the existence of a mechanism to ensure that the funds are used in that way. Although there is a widespread view that there is a need to prevent corruption and prevent elites from wasting the money on their own consumption, there are sharp differences about how this is to be done. Donor agencies and international financial institutions want increased conditionality. Civil society in debtor countries argues that northern imposed conditionality has failed and that there is a need to support democratic and local control of the funds.

Both sides have problematic records. The international financial institutions and creditor countries encouraged corruption by lending to dictators they knew were putting money in Swiss banks, and more recently their record on adjustment and lending has been poor. When the World Bank in engaged in an internal battle over development policy which led to the resignation of two key officials in early 2000, it is hard to argue that the Bank should be allowed to impose conditions.

Democratization is increasing in developing countries and civil society is growing, but institutions are still weak and there remain obvious problems of corruption and inexperience.

Neither North nor South have the moral authority or track record to impose conditions to ensure the wise use of funds released by debt cancellation. So a new and more humble partnership is called for, in which new and more democratic systems evolve.

In this context, it is important to remember that debt cancellation does not release a single block of billions of dollars. Rather, it means that payments need not be made over the term of the loan—often 20 years or more. Thus there is time available to gain experience and strengthen the local democratic structures necessary to ensure the best use of funds released for development.

9 CONCLUSION

As in previous debt cycles, reckless lending has led to unpayable debt. But in previous cycles substantial debt was cancelled; in this cycle this has not happened. This paper has attempted to show a number of different reasons for following the historic pattern, and writing off significant debt.

So far, the international community has proposed to write off about $100 billion of the $2554 billion developing country debt. A 'rights based approach' would require the writing off more than $600 billion in debt owed by 71 countries that cannot afford to pay their full debt service and still meet development and human rights targets to which the international community is already committed. Using historic precedents would require the writing off of $1 trillion or more.

It can also be argued that under international law, up to one-quarter of developing country debt is odious debt, which should not be repaid. Furthermore, lenders must be held responsible for their bad lending.

The debate about debt cancellation continues, but history and present need suggest that much more debt cancellation is likely.

900   *J. Hanlon*

REFERENCES

Adams P. 1991. *Odious Debts*. Earthscan: London.

Aldcroft D. 1997. *Studies in the Interwar European Economy*. Ashgate: Aldershot.

Aggarwal V. 1989. Interpreting the history of Mexico's external debt crisis. In *The International Debt Crisis in Historical Perspective*, Eichengreen and Lindert (eds). MIT Press: Cambridge, MA.

Darity W, Horn B. 1988. *The Loan Pushers*. Ballinger–Harper & Row: Cambridge, MA.

Diaz Alejandro C. 1983. Stories of the 1930s for the 1980s. In *Financial Policies and the World Capital Market*, Armella P, Dornbush R, Obstfeld M (eds). University of Chicago Press: Chicago.

Drake P. 1989. Debt and democracy in Latin America, 1920–1980s. In *Debt and Democracy in Latin America*, Stallings B and Kaufman R (eds). Westview: Boulder, CO.

Economic Commission on Africa. 1999. *Economic Report on Africa 1999*, United Nations Economic and Social Council E/ECA/CM/24/3.

Eichengreen B, Lindert P. 1989. *The International Debt Crisis in Historical Perspective*. MIT Press: Cambridge, MA.

Eichengreen B, Portes R. 1989a. Dealing with Debt: The 1930s and the 1980s. World Bank, Washington, Working Paper WPS 259.

Eichengreen B, Portes R. 1989b. After the deluge: default, negotiation and readjustment during the interwar years. In *The International Debt Crisis in Historical Perspective*, Eichengreen and Lindert (eds). MIT Press: Cambridge, MA.

Eichengreen B, Portes R. 1995. *Crisis? What Crisis? Orderly Workouts for Sovereign Debtors*. Centre for Economic Policy Research: London.

Evans H. 1999. Debt relief for the poorest countries: why did it take so long. *Development Policy Review* 17(3): 267–279.

Foorman J, Jehle M. 1982. *University of Illinois Law Review* **1982**(1).

Garrett J, Travis A. 1999. *Unfinished Business*. Jubilee 2000: London.

Gordon D, Spickler P (eds). 1998. *International Glossary on Poverty*. Zed: London.

Hanlon J. 1998a. We've been here before. Jubilee 2000, London.

Hanlon J. 1998b. Dictators and debt. Jubilee 2000, London.

Hanlon J. 1999. What will it cost to cancel unpayable debt? Jubilee 2000, London.

Hanlon J, Pettifor A. 2000. *Kicking the Habit*. Jubilee 2000: London.

IMF (International Monetary Fund). 1998. *World Economic Outlook 1998*. IMF: Washington DC.

IMF. 1999. *HIPC Initiative Consultation Meeting Background Material*. IMF: Washington DC.

International Development Committee. 1998. *Debt Relief*. House of Commons: London 3rd report.

Kindleberger C. 1978. *Manias, Panics and Crashes*. Basic Books/Macmillan: London.

Kindleberger C. 1996. *Manias, Panics and Crashes*, 3rd edn. John Wiley and Sons: New York.

Kuhn Loeb Lehman Brothers. 1979. The Republic of Indonesia. Kuhn Loeb Lehman Brothers, London.

Lindert P. 1989. Response to debt crisis: what is different about the 1980s? In *The International Debt Crisis in Historical Perspective*, Eichengreen and Lindert (eds). MIT Press: Cambridge, MA.

Lissakers K. 1992. *Banks, Borrowers and the Establishment*. Basic Books: New York.

Maxwell S. 1999. What can we do with a rights-based approach to development? ODI Briefing Paper (3) September, London.

Northover H, Joyner K, Woodward D. 1998. A human development approach to debt relief for the world's poor, Cafod, London.

OECD DAC (Organisation for Economic Co-operation and Development—Development Assistance Committee). 1997. *Development Co-operation Report*. OECD DAC: Paris.

Sampson A. 1981. *The Money Lenders*. Coronet/Hodders and Stoughton: London.

Ugarteche O. 1999. Where there is a will there is a way, paper delivered at Justicia y Paz conference on foreign debt, Barcelona, November.

Ugarteche O. 2000. A fair and transparent arbitration process, paper presented at ILAS, University of London, April.

UNCTAD (United Nations Conference on Trade and Development). 1998. *Trade and Development Report 1998*. UNCTAD: Geneva.

UNDP (United Nations Development Programme). 1996. *Human Development Report 1996*. Oxford University Press: New York.

UNDP. 1997. *Human Development Report 1997*. Oxford University Press: New York.

UNDP. 1998. *Human Development Report 1998*. Oxford University Press: New York.

UNDP. 1999. *Human Development Report 1999*. Oxford University Press: New York.

UNDP, UNESCO, UNFPA, UNICEF, WHO, the World Bank. 1998. *Implementing the 20/20 Initiative*. UNICEF: New York.

United States Treasury. 1997. Indebtedness of foreign governments to the United States arising from World War I as of June 30, 1997, US Treasury, Washington DC, 8 September 1997.

World Bank. 1990. *World Development Report 1990*. Oxford University Press: Oxford.

World Bank. 1991. *World Debt Tables 1991–92*. World Bank: Washington DC.

World Bank. 1993. *World Development Report 1993*. Oxford University Press: New York.

World Bank. 1994. *World Debt Tables 1994–95*. World Bank: Washington DC.

World Bank. 1996. *African Development Indicators 1996*. World Bank: Washington DC.

World Bank. 1997. *Global Development Finance 1997*. World Bank: Washington DC.

World Bank. 1998a. *Global Development Finance 1998*. World Bank: Washington DC.

World Bank. 1998b. *World Development Report 1998/99*. Oxford University Press: New York.

World Bank. 1999a. *Global Development Finance 1999*. World Bank: Washington DC.

World Bank. 1999b. *World Bank Annual Report 1999*. World Bank: Washington DC.

World Bank. 2000a. *Global Development Finance 2000*. World Bank: Washington DC.

World Bank. 2000b. *World Development Indicators 2000*. World Bank: Washington DC.

World Bank. 2000c. *World Development Report 1999/2000*. Oxford University Press: New York.

[24]

Development, displacement and international ethics[1]

Peter Penz

Displacement and international ethics

People displaced by the actions of other people can be deemed, *prima facie* at least, to have been wronged. Development refugees, i.e. those displaced by development projects, policies and processes, have been harmed or coerced by the actions of others. This applies also to those environmental refugees who have been displaced by anthropogenic environmental processes. What is morally owed to the potential and actual victims of such displacement? This question will be addressed first, in order to then move on to focus on a further question: What are the moral obligations of foreign participants in the development process when the displacement of people is a possible or actual result of such development?

This latter question will be addressed within the field of tension between an ethic of state sovereignty and cosmopolitan ethics. The former treats states as morally fundamental and sees international ethics as moral relations between states. Beitz (1979: 63–66) has referred to this perspective as 'the morality of states' and Janna Thompson (1992: 78) as 'just interaction theory'. Cosmopolitan ethics, on the other hand, is based on seeing humanity as part of one global society, and states as institutions that may or may not be conducive to the good governance of this global society. In other words, the ethics of sovereignty treats the state system as the framework for articulating an appropriate international ethic, while cosmopolitanism views international ethics as conceptually prior to the state system and as a basis for evaluating the state system and its propensities. In this chapter, I will argue for the cosmopolitan approach to determining the moral obligations of foreign participants in the development process.

Development refugees, environmental refugees and the Chittagong Hill Tracts case

Before turning to the question of international obligations, it is useful to first briefly clarify ethical obligations within states regarding displacement induced by development and environmental degradation. This task will be contained by limiting it to the obligations of states to their citizens in this policy domain. This will be sufficient for the ensuing discussion about international ethics.

Displacement here refers to forced migration. It occurs in at least two distinguishable forms. Direct displacement consists of evictions. Thus, direct development refugees are people removed for the construction of dams and their reservoirs and other infrastructure projects, such as ports, roads and irrigation canals, by slum clearance and urban redevelopment, and, in forests, for conservation or logging purposes. Indirect displacement by development, on the other hand, is displacement that is mediated by processes not directly under the control of decision makers, such as market processes and environmental degradation resulting from different, interacting development activities. If people move because they have been impoverished by the market-mediated or environmental consequences of development decisions, we can refer to them as indirect development refugees.

Environmental refugees are those displaced by environmental degradation. To the extent that such degradation is the result of one particular economic activity, such as the displacement of river fishers by the pollution of an upstream tannery, it can be taken to be direct displacement. On the other hand, if the displacement occurs as a result of a more interactive pattern of development, the resulting environmental refugees represent indirect displacement. Environmental displacement is thus a form of development-induced displacement that cuts across the distinction between direct and indirect displacement.

An example that illustrates development-induced displacement, including its environmental form, is the region of the Chittagong Hill Tracts in Bangladesh. It is a hilly area in the south-east of the country with thin tropical soil and generally low fertility. It has been inhabited by ethnically distinct hill peoples who have since the introduction of development experienced displacement by a number of different, but interacting, processes. One has been a big hydro-electric dam that displaced about 100,000 hill people. In response to guerrilla activity that this displacement induced, the area was militarised and Bengali settlers, deemed more loyal to the government and in need of land, were moved by the military onto land left fallow in the shifting agriculture that has been practised on this region's hillsides. Apart from the civil war that this set off, it involved a loss of land and livelihood for the hill people. At the same time, intensification of cultivation, including by the hill people, who have experienced substantial natural population growth and have also been left with less land, has led to soil depletion and erosion and some displacement for that reason. The Chakma, Mrong, Marma and other hill peoples have thus experienced a multi-dimensional syndrome of displacement due to a variety of interacting causes (Penz 1993).

Displacement is morally objectionable in the first instance because it involves coercion. This is evident in the case of direct displacement. In the case of indirect displacement, the element of coercion is not always straightforward. If one views forced and voluntary migration as mutually exclusive categories, then it is easy to view much of the migration that is induced by development or environmental degradation as voluntary, since much of the time there is a considerable element of choice as to whether to move or to put up with deteriorating conditions. What is misleading here is to view coercion and choice as mutually exclusive. Even when threatened by death, individuals still have the choice to defy that threat. Thus, members of the Narmada Bachao Andolan, a movement that opposes the construction of the big Narmada dams in India, have announced that they will refuse to move and will accept being drowned when the waters rise. Nevertheless, we would accept that coercion is involved here on the part of those undertaking the dam projects. This can be understood, not as a complete removal of choice, but as a contraction of choice. Thus a person can be deemed to have been coerced when the range of options that are significant to the person are restricted. Choice is not eliminated, but merely restricted.

Displacement is also objectionable to the extent that such forced migration typically makes people worse-off. They are often inadequately compensated for what they lose; they often have to move to areas more poorly endowed; and they often are unfamiliar with the new environment and the skills it requires, and therefore lose in terms of making a living (see McDowell 1996).

Some might respond with the claim that displacement has been ubiquitous in the process of industrialisation and economic growth, that it is unavoidable, that it is better than immobility or that it serves the public interest. Others, on the other hand, treat all displacement as morally unacceptable. The question is whether displacement can, under certain conditions, be justified.

Applied ethics and its methodology

The process of justification, applied as it is to the concrete issue of development and displacement, raises the question of the methodology of applied ethics. Essentially three methodological approaches can be found in applied ethics.

1   The first is the theoretically committed approach of deriving practical judgements and prescriptions from a particular normative theory, to which a foundational commitment has been made. Thus, the theoretical starting point of a utilitarian will be different from that of a Rawlsian social-contract theorist. One difficulty here is that disagreements about normative theories are typically much greater than about practical

judgements and prescriptions emanating from competing theories. Much contestation is thus liable to be devoted to the theoretical foundations, even though the underlying differences may not create much difference at the level of policy evaluation. A second difficulty, at least for applied ethics that is to be useful to non-philosophers and policy makers, is that, outside of philosophical discourse, ethical judgements tend to be made with reference to concrete issues rather than in a theoretical form and non-philosophers therefore tend to be handicapped in assessing theories and tend to be excluded from the discussion.

2   The opposite methodological approach in applied ethics is to respond to practical problems in an entirely *contextual*, or situational, manner without reference to theories, implicitly relying on moral intuitions. These intuitions may be either those of the practical ethicist or they may be those of the culture, sub-culture or community in which the practical problems arise. In the personal version it is not clear how argumentation is to proceed and what are appropriate criteria for resolving disagreements; this approach is always in danger of sliding into arbitrariness or never rising above it. In the communitarian version of this approach, the criterion is conformity with community values. The difficulty here is that there may be no real agreement within communities. This is even more likely when many communities are involved (e.g., not only dam-displaced communities, but potential beneficiaries of rural electrification or irrigation) and when communities are stratified (e.g., by wealth, caste, or gender). Even when there is substantial agreement about community values, there is always the danger that they reflect patterns of domination within the community and the effective silencing of the disadvantaged (or their internalisation of the rationalisation of their underprivileged position, for example, accepting the lesser worth attributed to them). While it is important to bring community values to light, analysis cannot be limited to them. Jamieson (1991: 477–449) has referred to approaches (1) and (2) as, respectively, the 'dominant conception of moral theory' and the approach of the 'anti-theorists'.

3   That brings us to the third methodological approach, a *middle-level analysis*. It focuses on generalisable principles, but does not commit itself to a particular normative theory (Sumner's [1994] 'principlism' – cf. Jamieson 1991: 479–480). Instead of removing value disputes to the level of theory and attempting to resolve them there, as in approach (1), it addresses them within the concrete issues, in this case that of development-induced and environmental displacement. On the other hand, it is important to articulate the general principles at work in the ethical analysis and not to leave them operating at a level which is not explicit and where inconsistencies and controversial implications may remain out of sight, which the strictly contextual approach (2) is prone to do. These features make this middle-level analysis attractive. It can be employed in a dialectical

fashion, by engaging different theoretical perspectives in a 'dialogue' with each other to arrive at a more sophisticated mixed position.

Displacement, the state and moral justification

In accordance with the methodology proposed, the question of the justification of displacement will be explored in terms of three normative perspectives: (1) the public-interest perspective of utilitarianism; (2) the self-determination perspective of libertarianism and the more communal version of it held by some communitarians; and (3) the equal-sharing perspective of egalitarianism. (Finer distinctions within these perspectives will not be pursued here.)

1   The public interest perspective of utilitarianism is readily represented by cost–benefit analysis (see, e.g., Wenz 1988: ch. 10). The question here is simply whether the benefits of development outweigh the costs of its side-effects, including displacement. The distribution of benefits and costs in itself is not a concern in this perspective. Whether those displaced are compensated or not is not part of this particular moral calculus. Nor is whether it is the relatively affluent that benefit and the poor that bear the sacrifices.
2   The self-determination perspective of libertarianism, on the other hand, treats freedom and choice as central. From this perspective displacement is necessarily immoral. This applies also to communal self-determination, since displacement involves the coercive removal or forced migration of whole communities. This certainly seems like a promising antidote to heavy-handed and business-privileging development from the top. However, it completely ignores broader public-interest considerations, such as enhanced productivity resulting from the electricity and irrigation that dams, for example, provide. It is, of course, possible to convert opposition to consent from those required to move by offering them sufficient compensation to move voluntarily, so that they are, ultimately, not displaced (not *forced* to move). However, this creates an incentive for those required to move to try and capture some of the benefits from the project by demanding much higher compensation than is needed merely to not be worse off, and could make the project too costly to finance. This approach also involves a rather restrictive notion of freedom, in that it ignores that choice can be expanded by development. Amartya Sen's (1992: chs 2–4) notion of capacities complicates the issue, but draws attention to both the choice-expanding and choice-restricting aspects of development. Finally, from the next (egalitarian) perspective, this approach does not ensure a just distribution of benefits and can even stand in the way of redistribution, such as land reform, that would serve social justice.

3   The equal-sharing perspective of egalitarianism focuses on the distribu-
     tion of costs and benefits from development as well as on inequalities
     prior to particular development projects or policies. From this perspec-
     tive,   development   should   serve   to   reduce   inequalities.   Thus,
     development-induced displacement could conceivably reduce inequali-
     ties if it primarily benefits the poor and puts the burdens on the
     better-off. Considerations of horizontal equity among the better-off
     would, however, limit or complicate such a process. Even more crucial is
     horizontal equity among the poor in that development can benefit some
     disadvantaged groups (e.g., by electrifying poor villages), while harming
     others (e.g., by displacing them). Compensation is one way of dealing
     with this; having those displaced share in the benefits of development,
     beyond mere compensation, is another. One major concern about the
     egalitarian approach is the maintenance of economic incentives. This
     can be accommodated by qualifying the egalitarian approach by a
     'maximin' distribution approach, i.e., Rawls's difference principle of
     maximising the conditions of the worst-off. This represents a move away
     from the pure version of egalitarianism.

These three perspectives can be brought together by according each of them a
role in a more comprehensive approach to the ethics of development-induced
displacement, including displacement by development-induced environmental
deterioration. Thus, the requirements of self-determination should be recognised as important by providing substantial community control over
environmental decision making and by dealing with the required resettlement
of populations through negotiations and roughly consensual consent, but not
as an unqualified right to veto development projects and policies with
displacement consequences. Refusing such veto power may be justified by
considerations of public interest and distributive justice. In that case, however,
certain conditions would need to be met: compensating those displaced,
minimising displacement in the selection of development options, and giving
priority to poverty alleviation in determining development strategies.

Sovereigntism and international responsibilities

The discussion so far has been of development in a national context.
Development in Third World countries, however, is typically no longer
strictly a national project; it involves foreign actors. It usually did so even
before the current era of globalisation, when development was indeed seen
as essentially a national project. (For this chronological distinction, see
McMichael 1996.) This brings us to the central question of this chapter,
namely what the moral obligations of foreign participants in the development process are, when their participation is in processes that displace
people.

One cluster of positions that provide answers to this question is that of statist ethics. Statist ethics involve two levels or stages of moral consideration. One is that of intra-state ethics, as discussed in the previous section. The other is that of inter-state ethics. Within this perspective, citizens of one country do not stand in a direct moral relationship to citizens of another country. Rather, they have moral rights and obligations in relation to their own state and their state then stands in a moral relationship with the other state, which in turn stands in a moral relationship to its own citizens. The state is the pivotal mediator between foreign actors and the state's citizens. Whatever moral obligations the citizens of one country may have to the citizens of another country arise from the moral relationship between their respective states. For that reason I refer to it as statist ethics.

Within this general orientation to international ethics, the predominant position is that of sovereigntism. By sovereigntism I mean the moral rationale underlying the state system that has prevailed in Europe since the Thirty Years War in the seventeenth century, and that has been globalised through decolonisation in the latter half of the twentieth century. It gives moral primacy in international relations to the principle of state sovereignty. That means respect for the supreme authority of other states within their own territories and thus non-intervention among states. It does not rule out participation by foreign agencies in the economy and development of a particular country. It simply means that such participation has to be under the authority of the host state. In other words, foreign business, governmental aid agencies and non-governmental organisations have to operate within the laws and directives of the host government.

Does this mean that observing the laws and directives of the host state is the only moral obligation of foreign participants? Sovereigntists can answer this question in two quite different ways: (1) One answer is that the home society or polity may impose additional moral requirements regarding dealings with foreigners and that these have to be observed as a result of membership in the home society or polity. For example, if the laws of the host country concerning pollution are lax, there may be legal or moral obligations to observe the home restraints on toxic pollution abroad as much as at home. (2) A second answer may be that to carry domestic restraints from the home country to the host country is an imposition of values from outside the country and thus interferes with state authority or with the politico-cultural autonomy of the host country, whose trade-offs between living standards and environmental standards may be different. I will distinguish between these two positions by treating position (1) as the *national* sovereigntist position, under which actors in a foreign country have obligations to their national home states, beyond their obligation to obey the authority of the host state, while position (2) can be referred to as *territorial* sovereigntism, in that the authority of the home state ends when nationals leave the territory and enter that of another state. National sovereigntism sees sovereignty satisfied when the sovereign state gives its consent to the activities within its territory, while territorial sovereigntism emphasises that consent may be given under conditions of pressure on the host state, such as the withholding of important capital, and treats this as objectionable.

The problem with national sovereigntism is that it does not recognise the weakness of at least some states in the face of the politico-economic power of foreign capital and even of non-governmental organisations, for example in countries such as Bangladesh. The problem with territorial sovereigntism, on the other hand, is that it does not recognise that states do not necessarily act in the interests of their own citizens. In fact, both forms of sovereigntism do not acknowledge adequately the need to apply ethical evaluation to how states treat their own citizens. This suggests the possibility that the kind of ethical perspectives that were employed in the intra-national evaluation of national state policy with regard to development-induced displacement might be applied across borders, which is what the cosmopolitan approach does.

Considerations in favour of cosmopolitanism

The case for the cosmopolitan approach rests not merely on the difficulties of sovereigntism as an ethic, but also on more positive arguments that refer to current and historical developments in the world. These are (1) the increasing economic, social, cultural, and political integration of the world; (2) the nature and history of state boundaries; and (3) the actual behaviour of states.

1   The increasing integration of national societies through various processes is creating what must be considered to be a rapidly emerging world society. Economic globalisation is making families, groups and national and sub-national societies increasingly dependent on economic decisions and developments in other parts of the world. Thus the recent Pacific Asian economic crisis has been greatly affected by the behaviour of foreign capital, including that from the North Atlantic region. The globalisation of communications has made it possible in affluent countries to see what is going on in poor countries and for those in poor countries to see how those in the rich countries live. Extraordinary global mobility brings affluent tourists to poor countries and immigrants and refugees from poor countries to rich countries. Cities such as London, New York and Toronto are becoming extraordinarily cosmopolitan in their ethnic composition. These interdependencies are recognised in the growth of international governance or coordination institutions such as the UN, the World Trade Organization and a multitude of agencies dealing with everything from refugees to postal services and airline regulation. These are all hallmarks of a society, even though

there may be considerable limits to the extent to which people in one part of the world are concerned about what happens to people in other parts. But this also holds, although to a lesser extent, for national societies as well. World society may thus be a thinner society than national societies, but it is a society nevertheless.

2   Even if the identification of people with each other was, in fact, quite weak, the moral significance of state borders is still an issue. State borders have, historically, not been drawn cleanly around ethnic or linguistic groupings, but have emerged from wars that transferred territory, possibly because of the natural resources they contained rather than the people, or because the people provided a work force, a tax base and a source of soldiers, all of which could strengthen the state. Territorial states may have successfully used nationalism to forge national societies, but this often involved the suppression of minority cultures. Territorial states have typically maintained themselves by denying and restricting diversity. This historical element of force in the determination of state borders raises serious questions regarding the moral significance of such borders. The legacy of force is particularly evident in Africa, where colonial borders have been largely maintained into the post-colonial era, and where these borders developed on the basis of contestation and agreement between European powers, with little recognition of ethnic territories. Ethnic wars within territorial states indicate the weakness of national solidarity and of the national scope of moral concern and commitment.

3   The moral rationale for state sovereignty is based, at least in part, on the idea that states protect their respective societies and advance their interests. Yet the actual behaviour of states often reveals a predatory stance towards their citizenry, or one of neglect. Collaboration by foreigners with such states, either through their own states or through non-state agents such as business or non-governmental organisations, may involve complicity in such irresponsible behaviour. This suggests that the consequences of one's actions, which are international in that either the actions take place abroad or the consequences extend across borders, have to be assessed in terms of their impact on individuals and groups, not just countries or states.

These considerations point in the direction of a cosmopolitan approach. While a full case will not be offered here, these points will be taken as sufficient to warrant the application of a cosmopolitan approach to the issue of this chapter, namely that of the international obligations regarding development-induced and environmental displacement. Within a cosmopolitan framework, the obligations of foreign participants in the development process are to the people being affected and to those institutional agents that act on their behalf, but only in that representative capacity.

148	Peter Penz

Cosmopolitanism and international responsibilities

In this framework, the considerations sketched out above under the heading 'Displacement, the state, and moral justification' apply across borders. In other words, moral concern for the citizens of other countries, such as for their well-being, self-determination and equality (among themselves or with citizens elsewhere), is relevant. There is, however, one crucial difference. In the previous situation the relevant state exercises authority; the discussion was thus conducted essentially in terms of the moral responsibility of the state. In the case of foreign individuals or organisations, whether state or non-state, the relevant agents do not exercise such authority. They operate within the authority sphere or sovereignty of another state.

If the host state is a reliable protector and promoter of the interests of its citizens (and other legitimate residents), then the assignment of moral responsibility within a cosmopolitan perspective may not be all that different from the sovereigntist perspective. However, a distinction should at this point be made between two kinds of foreign participants in development, in terms of their functions. One is business organisations whose function is to contribute to economic production, including services, generally on the basis of the pursuit of profits for their investors; the other is non-profit development organisations (NGOs) whose purpose is to protect or advance the interests of people in a development context. (Foreign states can fall on both sides of this distinction: as promoters of their economic interests, such as exports, they fall on the business side; as providers of genuine development assistance, they fall on the non-profit side.)

Given the assumption of moral and competent states, foreign business organisations can reasonably be deemed simply to have the responsibility to obey the laws, regulations and directives of the host state. It is the responsibility of the host state that productive activities and markets operate in a frame where these processes are beneficial and do not harm people in an unjustifiable manner. Thus, when businesses engage in logging, they need not worry about environmental and displacement effects; that is the concern of the state. Business organisations merely observe the constraints imposed on them by the state. There is thus a division of moral labour. It is, of course, possible to adopt a business ethic that goes further in terms of business responsibilities to communities. But this is dependent on the retreat of the state from assuming full responsibility for managing economic processes such that they do not cause unjust harm. It will thus be considered below as part of the limits to the assumption of the fully moral and competent host state.

For non-profit development organisations, on the other hand, the function is to further the interests of people. Since there are limits to what states can do to harness economic processes to promote the general interest and particularly social justice, non-profit organisations have here an important role to pursue action and innovation beyond state policy. This means that, with respect to development-induced and environmental displacement, to some extent they have to make the kind of broad assessment of the causal connections between development processes and their displacement consequences, and of the moral evaluation of the latter that states ought to be making. In other words, their moral responsibilities go considerably beyond observing host-state law.

The assumption of states as fully moral and competent is, however, a particularly artificial one. It is not uncommon for states to fail to ensure that development really does serve the public interest and social justice, that people are appropriately compensated and that policies that minimise displacement are pursued. These failures may be deliberate, as when state policies serve only the interests of an elite, or they may be due to weaknesses of state institutions, such as protection agencies that have insufficient funding, inadequately trained staff, poor management or inadequate authority in relation to state agencies with other mandates (e.g., the development of infrastructure). Much of the time these two causes are intermingled. (This problem applies to some extent to *all* states, but certain developing countries are particularly subject to it.) This phenomenon extends the moral obligations of foreign participants in development, and particularly those of business organisations.

To assess these, it is important to make a distinction between directly and indirectly caused displacement. Where outright evictions are involved, the consequences of the role of foreign business organisations in development are clear. Even though it may be the actions of local business partners that lead to such evictions, the participation of foreign capital definitely makes such foreign participants responsible, because their participation facilitates the displacement. The same applies to displacement due to environmental damage where the cause of such damage can clearly be traced to the activities of the relevant business organisation. On the other hand, where displacement results from more indirect processes, such as market processes or environmental degradation that is due to a variety of sources, then displacement has to be seen as having a range of causal agents. In that case, the causal connection between any particular business and displacement is too diffuse to reasonably assign moral responsibility. Only the local state can effectively assume responsibility for the overall causal process behind the displacement. However, if the whole pattern of development in a country is seriously exploitative and the participation of foreign business simply helps to maintain or extend it, there is a moral obligation to stay out of the development process entirely. Only if there are good grounds to believe that participation by a foreign business would actually undermine such exploitation or the development pattern that makes it possible can it be justified.

Even where that is not the case, there may be a further moral responsibility for foreign business, specifically with respect to environmental displacement. While a particular displacement process may have multiple causal agents, any particular kind of environmental damage may be attributable to a particular business. In that case, that business is responsible for that damage, even though it may not be held responsible for the displacement because that is due to a broader pattern of environmental deterioration. The particular environmental damage rather than the displacement due to multiple causes is the moral reason for abstaining from such business participation in development.

In the case of non-profit development organisations (and the development assistance agencies of states), the broader pattern of moral obligations continues to hold. It is not sufficient to show that no damage is being done; it is necessary to show that good is being done. It is reasonable to expect that such organisations not only avoid directly caused displacement, but also do not further a more complex process that leads to displacement that overall would be unjustifiable. This is not to say that non-profit organisations should never be involved in such processes. Their role may well be to alleviate displacement that is being generated by such processes. As a matter of fact, that consideration may quite properly lead them to participate even in unjust direct displacement, but as agents that alleviate the deleterious consequences of the evictions (e.g., by improving an otherwise deficient resettlement process). But in terms of moral strategy, NGOs also need to be careful here. They could end up being used by state agencies not concerned with justice for those being displaced ('oustees' in India) by performing the function that makes the process sufficiently acceptable to funding organisations (e.g., the World Bank) or the electorate. The basic point here is that, while the function of business organisations is to contribute to economic productivity by engaging in profitable activities so that their moral responsibilities here are confined to the avoidance of harm that can be clearly traced to them, the function of non-profit organisations is to help people benefit from development and they therefore have to assess their contribution to the broader and more complex processes that affect displacement not only directly, but also indirectly.

These considerations, then, also apply to development assistance provided by foreign states. They have the moral responsibility to ensure that such assistance is used beneficially and therefore have to attach conditions to the provision of such assistance. In this case, because inter-state relations are involved, some of the considerations of the sovereigntist perspective remain relevant. This means that, if one state is to respect another as guardian of its own citizens, it cannot establish aid conditions that have very detailed requirements concerning how the public interest and social justice within the country of the host state are to be served. Nevertheless, choices have to be made about which countries to give aid to and for which sectors or projects, and additional broad stipulations can be made concerning the design of projects or programmes. These all provide scope for exercising moral responsibility by the donor state.

Conclusion

The conclusion is that, under a cosmopolitan perspective, the existence of fallible states means that considerable moral responsibility concerning development-induced and environmental displacement, beyond that of observing the laws and decisions of host states, falls on foreign participants in development. This responsibility differs for the different kinds of participants, with business organisations having responsibility only for directly caused displacement, non-profit organisations for a broader pattern of effects, and state development-assistance agencies for some restraint as a part of respect for state sovereignty, even though the latter is not treated as morally fundamental.

Notes

1   This paper was presented at the International Conference on Forced Migration in the South Asian Region: Displacement, Human Rights, and Conflict Resolution, 20–22 April 2000, Centre for Refugee Studies, Jadavpur University, Calcutta, India. A previous version of this chapter (entitled 'Development refugees, environmental refugees, and international obligations: sovereigntist vs. cosmopolitan ethics') was presented at the joint conference of the Society for Applied Philosophy and the International Society for Environmental Ethics on 'Moral and political reasoning in environmental practice', Mansfield College, Oxford University, 27–29 June 1999. The research for the chapter has been supported by two related team-research projects: a project entitled 'International development ethics and population displacement: the nature and limits of Canada's obligations to developing countries', funded by the Social Sciences and Humanities Research Council of Canada; and an Indo-Canadian project entitled 'Economic policy, population displacement, and development ethics', funded by the Shastri Indo-Canadian Institute's Partnership Programme, which was funded in turn by the Canadian International Development Agency. The author of this chapter is principal investigator of both team projects.

References

Beitz, Charles R. (1979) *Political Theory and International Relations*, Princeton: Princeton University Press.

Jamieson, Dale (1991) 'Method and moral theory', in Peter Singer (ed.) *A Companion to Ethics*, Oxford: Blackwell, pp. 476–487.

McDowell, Christopher (ed.) (1996) *Understanding Impoverishment: the Consequences of Development-induced Displacement*, Providence, RI: Berghahn Books.

McMichael, Philip (1996) *Development and Social Change: a Global Perspective*, Thousand Oaks, CA: Pine Forge Press.

Penz, Peter (1993) 'Colonization of tribal lands in Bangladesh and Indonesia: state rationales, rights to land, and environmental justice', in M.C. Howard (ed.) *Asia's Environmental Crisis*, Boulder: Westview Press, pp. 37–72.

Sen, Amartya (1992) *Inequality Reexamined*, Oxford: Clarendon Press.

Sumner, L. Wayne (1994) 'How to do applied ethics', Keynote Address, Annual Conference, Ontario Philosophical Society, York University, 4 November.

152   Peter Penz

Thompson, Janna (1992) *Justice and World Order: a Philosophical Inquiry*, London: Routledge.

Wenz, Peter S. (1988) *Environmental Justice*, Albany, NY: State University of New York Press.

[25]

Global Governance,
Dam Conflicts, and Participation

Denis Goulet*

ABSTRACT

Globalization, as presently conducted, is governed badly. Large dams, long viewed as beneficial and essential to development, have become sites of major social conflict. Participatory decision-making by "affected" populations in macro sectors of development is viewed by many as impossible, notwithstanding its advocacy by the World Commission on Dams on the basis of its "rights and risks" approach. Brazilian initiatives in participatory governance in varied macro sectors, especially in water/dam policy, show that macro participation is feasible. Lessons yielded by dam conflicts in Northeast Brazil suggest how authentic participation can occur in water/dam policy and other arenas of globalization.

I. INTRODUCTION

Three closely linked issues—deficient global governance, worldwide dam policy, and the need for authentic participation in *macro* arenas of policy—are sites of social conflict traceable to opposing normative conceptions of development. In a triangular problematic:

- globalization is denounced as fostering development that is elitist, inequitable, and unsustainable;

---

* *Denis Goulet* is Professor Emeritus, O'Neill Chair in Education for Justice, Department of Economics and Policy Studies, University of Notre Dame, www.nd.edu/~dgoulet.
    The generous assistance of João Paulo Maranhão de Aguiar in arranging site visits, scheduling interviews, and conducting policy debates is gratefully acknowledged. I also thank Maria Lia de Corrêa Araújo and Rosana Garjulli for sharing time, documents, and ideas.

- large dam construction produces social upheaval and exacts excessive human and environmental costs; and

- participation by non-elites is rarely authentic because it is manipulated, unduly circumscribed, or confined to *micro* arenas.

This essay argues that sound global governance[1] can occur only through wider participation of populations affected by large development projects and that participation in macro arenas is feasible.

A. Needed: Better Global Governance

Global circulation systems (of information, economic goods, technology, human resources, and decisional models) are controlled by rich-nation governments, international institutions, and business enterprises that promote patterns of development founded on competitive markets as an organizing principle.[2] Protests at the WTO, World Bank, IMF, and G-7 meetings testify to mass opposition to these institutions and their governance procedures. Thomas Friedman, a staunch champion of globalization, acknowledges that it "is also producing a powerful backlash from those brutalized or left behind by this new system."[3] Friedman later claimed that anti-globalization protesters, "who almost shut Davos down the last two years" were now "nowhere" and that the anti-globalization movement "never did have any real alternative growth strategy."[4] His assessment overlooks the Porto Alegre Forum's decision to protest away from Davos in 2004 and that the work of participant organizations in constructing alternative development strategies continues unabated. Alan Cowell reports

1. Prescriptions to improve global governance abound, *e.g.*, The Handbook of Globalisation (Jonathan Michie ed., 2003); Enhancing Global Governance: Towards a New Diplomacy? (Andrew F. Cooper et al. eds., 2002); Richard Langhorne, The Coming of Globalization: its evolution and contemporary consequences (2001); Jan Aart Scholte, Globalization: A Critical Introduction (2000); The Ends of Globalization: Bringing Society Back In (Don Kalb et al. eds., 2000); Globalization and Global Governance (Raimo Väyrynen ed., 1999); Paul Streeten, Globalisation: Threat or Opportunity? (2001); Debating Development: NGOs and the Future (Deborah Eade & Ernst Ligteringen eds., 2001); A Moral Critique of Development: In Search of Global Responsibilities (Philip Quarles van Ufford & Ananta Kumar Giri eds., 2003); Deepening Democracy: Institutional Innovations in Empowered Participatory Governance (Archon Fung & Erik Olin Wright eds., 2003); NGOs, the UN, & Global Governance (Thomas G. Weiss & Leon Gordenker eds., 1996).
2. *See* Karl Mannheim, Freedom, Power, and Democratic Planning 191 (1950). Mannheim distinguishes between market competition as *organizing principle* and as *social mechanism*. The former cannot produce a just society, he argues; the latter, at least in principle, can.
3. Thomas L. Friedman, The Lexus and the Olive Tree 8 (1999).
4. Thomas L. Friedman, *Elephants Can't Fly*, N.Y. Times, 29 Jan. 2004, at A27.

that at the 2004 Davos World Economic Forum "2,100 participants from 94 lands are mulling developments in a world with no single political focus and no overwhelming economic certainties."[5] Meanwhile, the World Social Forum, held in 2004 in Mumbai before returning to Porto Alegre in 2005, is extending the number and thematic solidity of regional meetings and engaging more civil society agents.

The "antiglobalization movement" favors not the elimination of globalization but "another" globalization; it judges globalization as conducted now to be illegitimate because it is not ethical. The battle is on for what John D. Clark calls "ethical globalization."[6] And in the words of Jan Aart Scholte, global civil society can:

> *promote legitimation*, especially in relation to suprastate governance. Legitimacy exists when people acknowledge that an authority has the right to govern them and that they have a duty to obey its rulings. As a result of such consent, legitimate governance tends to be less violent and more easily executed than illegitimate authority.[7]

1. Conflicts at Dams

Large dams were long viewed as the best means of providing abundant and cheap non-polluting electrical power, water for irrigation and domestic and industrial consumption, and flood and drought control.[8] Twenty years ago, however, the Argentine sociologist Francisco Suarez and his coauthors warned of their harmful effects: coercive displacement of large numbers of poor people, siltation in reservoirs leading to economic inefficiency, salination and waterlogging in irrigated areas, and the creation of health hazards.[9] Even alleged benefits of large dams are now branded as inimical to development,[10] and major conflict attends their construction. Massive population displacement at the Three Gorges Dam in China has aroused

---

5. Alan Cowell, *Economic Talks Draw Elite to Davos, but Have No Salient Issue*, N.Y. Times, 21 Jan. 2004, at A5.
6. John D. Clark, Worlds Apart, Civil Society and the Battle for Ethical Globalization (2003).
7. Jan Aart Scholte, *Global Civil Society, in* The Political Economy of Globalization 173, 192–93 (Ngaire Woods ed., 2000).
8. World Bank Group, *Dam Safety, available at* www4.worldbank.org/legal/legen/legen_dam.html. ICOLD (International Commission on Large Dams) defines a large dam as one with a height of fifteen meters or more from the foundation. Dams between five and fifteen meters in height and having a reservoir volume of more than 3 million cubic meters are also classified as large dams. There are over 45,000 large dams around the world.
9. Francisco Suarez et al., Efectos Sociales de las Grandes Represas en América Latina (1984).
10. *See generally* Patrick McCully, Silenced Rivers: The Ecology and Politics of Large Dams (2001); Paul R. Josephson, Industrialized Nature: Brute Force Technology and the Transformation of the Natural World (2002).

protest worldwide, although dissent within China has been largely silenced. No conflict is more dramatic, however, than that occurring at India's Narmada River when dam elevations were projected. Save the Narmada Movement (Narmada Bachao Andolan) called for work on the dam to be stopped:

> In September 1989, more than 50,000 people gathered in the valley from all over India to pledge to fight "destructive development." . . . [O]ne year later, on 28 September 1990, thousands of villagers made their way on foot and by boat to a little town called Badwani, in Madya Pradesh, to reiterate their pledge to drown rather than agree to move from their homes.[11]

By 1993, sustained protests in India, abetted by international NGO pressure, led the World Bank to withdraw its planned loan of $450 million for Narmada. Seven years later the World Commission on Dams (WCD), created by the World Bank and the World Conservation Union (IUCN), issued a report[12] that brought fresh urgency to debates on whether large dams are good or bad for development, an issue couched by some in terms of "[t]he People vs. Development."[13]

2. Participation in Macro Arenas

Divergent conceptions of development and decision-making are at stake:

> [T]he underlying conflict between the proponents and opponents of dams is not so much about dams *per se* as it is about governance and perceptions of the appropriate way in which societies should make decisions about water and energy projects. At the intellectual heart of this debate is a disagreement about what constitutes desirable "development decision-making." By "development decision-making," I mean the way in which individuals, groups, and institutions decide to adopt and then implement policies, programs, and projects that affect the evolution of either their own and/or other's social and physical environments. The issue of development decision-making is applicable to all societies regardless of their level of development; and it applies to decision-making at the local, national, and international level in both the public and private sectors.[14]

The WCD, comprising major stakeholders (construction firms, international funding agencies, popular movements, and national governments), administered eight detailed case studies of large dams, conducted country reviews, surveyed over 125 dams, held hundreds of consultations world-

---

11. ARUNDHATI ROY, THE COST OF LIVING 37–38 (1999).
12. *See* WORLD COMMISSION ON DAMS, DAMS AND DEVELOPMENT: A NEW FRAMEWORK FOR DECISION-MAKING (2000).
13. Maggie Black, *The Day of Judgement,* NEW INTERNATIONALIST, July 2001, at 9.
14. Daniel Bradlow, *The World Commission on Dams' Contribution to the Broader Debate on Development Decision-Making,* 16 AM. U. INT'L L. REV. 1531, 1533 (2001).

wide, and received over 900 evaluative submissions. Its report was prepared:

> to conduct a rigorous, independent review of the development effectiveness of large dams and assess alternatives for water resources and energy development, and develop internationally acceptable criteria, guidelines and standards for the planning, design, appraisal, construction, operation, monitoring and decommissioning of dams.[15]

The WCD Report has elicited abundant commentaries, many critical of its diagnosis and prescriptions.[16] The Report adopts a "rights and risks" approach to populations affected by dam projects, and recommends participation by them at every stage of decision-making. The WCD Report states that:

> Those whose rights are most affected, or whose entitlements are most threatened, have the greatest stake in the decisions that are taken. The same applies to risk: those groups facing the greatest risk from the development have the greatest stake in the decisions. . . . and, therefore, must have a corresponding place at the negotiating table.[17]

For critics of the Report, substantive participation by non-elites is unrealistic. The general assumption prevailing is that affected populations may have a *vote* on projects, they must not have a *veto*. Many dam engineers and technical experts concur in the view that substantive participation, extending beyond information sharing or consultation, is not feasible.

However, Brazil's experiments in diverse social arenas constitute evidence that macro participation can succeed. Moreover, its initiatives in the wake of dam conflicts suggest that macro participation in the specific sector of water/dam policy is feasible.

II. INITIATIVES IN MACRO PARTICIPATION

In Brazil, polarities surrounding globalization, participation, and dam policy find expression *conceptually* in a growing body of critical writings that advocate alternative globalization and development, and *practically* in

---

15. Biksham Gujja, *Dams and Development—A Call for Follow-up Action, in* THE WORLD COMMISSION ON DAMS, FINAL WCD FORUM: REPORT, RESPONSES, DISCUSSIONS AND OUTCOMES 73, 74 (2001).

16. *See, e.g., Reactions to the Report of the World Commission on Dams,* 16 AM. U. INT'L L. REV. (2001); NAVROZ K. DUBASH ET AL., A WATERSHED IN GLOBAL GOVERNANCE? AN INDEPENDENT ASSESSMENT OF THE WORLD COMMISSION ON DAMS (2001).

17. WORLD COMMISSION ON DAMS, *supra* note 12, at 209.

social experiments in which participatory decision-making occurs in macro arenas.

A. Globalization: A New Model

The late geographer Milton Santos viewed globalization, although unavoidable, as a perverse phenomenon.[18] His work is one of many issuing from Brazil calling for another globalization.[19] The present pattern of globalization is condemned on grounds that it is elitist and secretive in its decision-making procedures, promotes inequitable development, and induces dependency. Secretiveness and elitism, say critics, need to be countered by participation in all sectors of development in which global actors influence planning, implementation, monitoring, and evaluation. The great wealth created by globalization is concentrated inequitably in few hands, destroys livelihoods, and excludes many poor individuals, communities, and countries from access to technological and economic progress. Moreover, by promoting economic growth patterns that are highly destructive of natural capital, globalization renders development unsustainable. Free trade agreements regulated by the World Trade Organization, say critics, apply a double standard: rich exporting nations subsidize trade of their domestically produced goods and impose tariffs on imported counterparts while demanding that developing countries not subsidize their own exporters.[20] Globalization is also blamed because it dilutes sovereignty, restricting the ability of national governments to frame economic policies which favor sound development. Brazilian critics of globalization extend across academic, professional, governmental, and media circles.

Typical alternative advocacy is presented by Helio Jaguaribe, a prestigious political scientist.[21] National security and independence, he argues,

---

18. MILTON SANTOS, POR UMA OUTRA GLOBALIZAÇÃO: DO PENSAMENTO ÚNICO À CONSCIÊNCIA UNIVERSAL (2001).
19. CELSO FURTADO, O CAPITALISMO GLOBAL (1998); CELSO BARROSO LEITE, ANTOLOGIA INFORMAL DA GLOBALIZAÇÃO (2000); CÉSAR BENJAMIN, A OPÇÃO BRASILEIRA (1998); J. MAGALHÃES, BRASIL SÉCULO XXI, UMA ALTERNATIVA AO MODELO NEOLIBERAL (2000); M. TAVARES, DESTRUIÇÃO NÃO CRIADORA (1999); REINALDO GONÇALVES, GLOBALIZAÇÃO E DESNACIONALIZAÇÃO (1999); ELENALDO CELSO TEIXEIRA, O LOCAL E O GLOBAL: LIMITES E DESAFIOS DA PARTICIPAÇÃO CIDADÃ (2001); RUBENS RICUPERO & SÉRGIO FRANÇA DANESE, O PONTO ÓTIMO DA CRISE (1998); LISZT VIEIRA, OS ARGONAUTAS DA CIDADANIA (2001); OCTÁVIO IANNI, TEORIAS DA GLOBALIZAÇÃO (2000); CRISTOVAM BUARQUE, A REVOLUÇÃO NAS PRIORIDADES: DA MODERNIDADE TÉCNICA À MODERNIDADE ÉTICA (2000); ROGÉRIO HAESBAERT, GLOBALIZAÇÃO E FRAGMENTAÇÃO NO MUNDO CONTEMPORÂNEO (2001); ROBERTO LUIS TROSTER, UM NOVO SÉCULO, UM NOVO BRASIL (2001).
20. *See* Tony Smith, *Argentina and Brazil Align to Fight U.S. Trade Policy,* N.Y. TIMES, 21 Oct. 2003, at W1; 3 HÉLIO PEREIRA BICUDO & J.A. GUILHON ALBUQUERQUE, RELAÇÕES INTERNACIONAIS E SUA CONSTRUÇÃO JURÍDICA (1998).
21. HÉLIO JAGUARIBE, BRASIL: ALTERNATIVAS E SAÍDA 88 (2002).

face greater dangers from economic vulnerabilities than from potential military adversaries capable of threatening Brazil's territory. Jaguaribe points to a two-fold financial dependency: (1) 47 percent of the 500 largest firms located in the country are under the control of foreign capital, and (2) the country depends excessively on external sources of financing, a vulnerability reflected in its large current accounts deficits and its high level of debt.[22] Orthodox economists, says Jaguaribe, argue that if the government taking office in January 2003 shows itself to be responsible and competent, it will win the confidence of global financial institutions and foreign investors and can successfully overcome shortfalls in current accounts and manage repayment of debt. In the year 2003 the stock market did register impressive gains. Brazilian shares "rose by an average of 142% in dollar terms," and Lula's government has calmed the fears of foreign investors and creditors. Nevertheless, GDP growth has been negative, at –1.5 percent.[23] The London *Economist* concedes "that most Brazilians are prepared to give Lula time, but that their patience is not endless. Unless the economic pain proves temporary, disenchantment will surely grow."[24]

Jaguaribe condemns orthodox prescriptions as palliatives that fail to deal with Brazil's structural economic vulnerabilities and to confront the generalized social problem facing the country—the existence of large pockets of ignorance and misery affecting the youth in the nations's large-city slums:

> This population is deprived of any hope of acceding to reasonable conditions of life, it channels itself into the drug trade and tends to constitute a reserve army of criminals, which has reached the point of exceeding the police system's ability to cope with it. . . . The orthodox school totally ignores this aspect of the Brazilian crisis and cannot find a solution if it limits its prescription solely to the financial plane, even if in this domain these were to succeed.[25]

Heterodox policy advocates, in Jaguaribe's reading, rely directly on exchange controls and measures to reduce nonessential imports, produce selective import substitution, and lower dependence on foreign capital. Jaguaribe insists that the heterodox approach to solving financial problems needs to embrace a new development model which assures Brazil's autonomy. He argues for

> the vigorous implementation of a new national development project, one which maximizes our capacity to substitute imports in a competitive fashion, which generates a large volume of new exports, which leads to a significant increase

---

22. *Id.* at 89.
23. *Emerging-Market Indicators*, Economist, 10 Jan. 2004, at 90.
24. *The Year of Changing Unexpectedly*, Economist, 3 Jan. 2004, at 23. By midyear 2004 disenchantment was already growing.
25. Jaguaribe, *supra* note 21, at 95.

in investments, which assures a satisfactory level of national control over the country's economy, and which permits the execution of large social projects directed to the eradication of large pockets of ignorance and misery.[26]

Jaguaribe, writing before Lula's ascent to the presidency, considered that Lula "disposes of all the conditions needed to mobilize wide and active popular support for this new national development project."[27] That a new development project is possible is a central article of faith that informs the World Social Forum.

B. World Social Forum

Held in Porto Alegre, Brazil in 2001, 2002, and 2003, in Mumbai, India, in 2004, and once again in Porto Alegre in 2005, the World Social Forum (WSF) met in its three first years on the same dates as the World Economic Forum (WEF), an annual event for over thirty years in Davos, Switzerland. Jagdish Bhagwati correctly labels the Porto Alegre Forum as a "counterpoint to the World Economic Forum."[28] The WSF views participatory democracy as a realistic utopia, an ethical and political model of world governance superior to market-controlled society. In its first year the WSF drew 40,000 participants; by 2003 this had risen to over 100,000, and by 2005 to 150,000. Along with growth in numbers, political visibility achieved by the WSF lends plausibility to the claim that it has become the main arena for the political bargaining of international civil society with elite global institutions. At the origins of WSF are Brazilian social movements, NGOs, labor unions, governmental entities engaged in participatory budgeting, religious organizations, and French media groups opposed to corporate-led globalization. Bernard Cassen, editor of *Le Monde Diplomatique*, considers that

> the mere existence of the FSM [World Social Forum] strips Davos of all legitimacy, which henceforth, in case it endures, will be seen as nothing other than a gathering of corporate interests organized against the aspiration of a world which is more just, displaying greater solidarity, and more concerned with the future of the planet.[29]

After the first WSF, its Organizing Committee and International Council approved a Charter of Principles that highlights the Forum's distinctiveness:

---

26. *Id.* at 99.
27. *Id.* at 103.
28. Jagdish Bhagwati, *Don't Cry for Cancún*, Foreign Affairs, Jan.–Feb. 2004, at 52.
29. Bernard Cassen, *Uma virada politica e cultural, in* Forum Social Mundial, A Construção de um Mundo Melhor 15, 17 (Antonio David Cattani ed., 2001). *Cf.* L. Silveira, Fórum Social Mundial, Impressões (2002).

The World Social Forum is an open meeting place for reflective thinking, democratic debate of ideas, formulation of proposals, free exchange of experiences and linking up for effective action. . . .

The World Social Forum at Porto Alegre was an event localized in time and place. From now on . . . it becomes a permanent process of seeking and building alternatives. . . .

The alternatives proposed . . . are designed to ensure that globalization in solidarity will prevail as a new stage in world history.[30]

The WSF globalizes resistance,[31] and "it is impossible to understand the initiative without linking it to the growing wave of protests in the public forum against globalization in recent years, as in Seattle, Washington, Prague, and Nice."[32] Protest has now moved beyond "expressive politics" into creative thinking about feasible alternatives to elitist, reductionist, and inequality-inducing patterns of globalization. Before the first WSF, Raimo Väyrynen[33] observed that large-scale protest against the World Trade Organization, the IMF, the World Bank, and the Davos Forum stood at a crossroads. Two paths seemed possible: (1) the repetition of purely disruptive demonstrations or (2) dialogue, cooperation, and negotiation founded on hopes that a new globalization was possible. In 2003, Brazil's newly elected President, Lula, was well received at Davos,[34] one day after addressing a crowd of 60,000 at the Porto Alegre Forum. For many it was a sign that WSF had become a potential co-negotiator with elite stewards of globalization. For one commentator:

The end of the decade of massive UN-sponsored global meetings explains in part the growth of the WSF. . . . [T]he self-conscious identity that global civil society gained through those conferences is stronger than ever and is now finding expression in a space created not by a top-down global bureaucracy but by civil society itself.[35]

The WSF process comprises annual formal gatherings as well as multiple local, regional, national, and international actions taken by

---

30. ANOTHER WORLD IS POSSIBLE: POPULAR ALTERNATIVES TO GLOBALIZATION AT THE WORLD SOCIAL FORUM 354–55 (William F. Fisher & Thomas Ponniah eds., 2003).
31. FRANÇOIS HOUTART & FRANÇOIS POLET, O OUTRO DAVOS: MUNDIALIZAÇÃO DE RESISTÊNCIAS E DE LUTAS (2002).
32. C. Grzybowski, *Sim, um outro mundo é possivel, in* FORUM SOCIAL MUNDIAL, A CONSTRUÇÃO DE UM MUNDO MELHOR, *supra* note 29, at 22.
33. Raimo Väyrynen, *Anti-Globalization movements at the Cross-Roads, in* POLICY BRIEF #4, at 1 (The Joan B. Kroc Institute for International Peace Studies/University of Notre Dame ed., 2000), *available at* www.nd.edu/~krocinst/contact.html.
34. C. Leite Neto, *Lula diz não ser mais "militante da oposição,"* FOLHA DE S. PAULO, 28 Jan. 2003, at A7.
35. Frances Korten, *Report from the World Social Forum,* YES!, Spring 2004, *available at* www.yesmagazine.com/article.asp?ID=710.

participants in social movements and organizations in numerous sectors—fair trade, debt relief, resistance to bioengineered crops, transnational financial transfers, women's equality, human rights, peace advocacy, and debates about privatization. In its two "processes" the FSM may be viewed as a dynamic movement leading toward greater participatory global governance. Although elite institutions can choose to ignore alternative problem solvers, their input in global decision-making has nonetheless begun. In millennium year 2000, NGOs influenced International Financial Institutions to change their criteria of debt relief (Jubilee Campaign). The fair trade campaign launched by OXFAM, and assisted by allied "international civil society" groups, expresses the new participatory/policy advocacy role of these groups.[36] And environmental organizations have gained entry into decision-making councils, which set standards of evaluation used by the World Bank and by corporations signing onto the Global Compact.

> Announced by United Nations Secretary-General Kofi Annan at the World Economic Forum in Davos, Switzerland, in January 1999, and formally launched at United Nations Headquarters in July 2000, the Compact calls on companies to embrace nine universal principles in the areas of human rights, labour standards and the environment. It brings companies together with United Nations organizations, international labour, non-governmental organizations (NGOs) and other parties to foster partnerships and to build a more inclusive and equitable global marketplace.[37]

The voice of civil society organizations in the Global Compact Network is weak, inasmuch as the Compact merely *encourages* companies to act in partnership with other actors. Like business codes of conduct worldwide, participation in policy dialogues that the Compact promotes is optional. Macro participation by civil society actors is more substantive in Participatory Budgeting (PB), institutionalized in the Brazilian state of Rio Grande do Sul and Porto Alegre, its capital city.

C. Participatory Budgeting

Introduced a decade earlier in Porto Alegre under the aegis of the PT (Workers' Party), PB was launched statewide in 1999 following the party's electoral victory in the state at large. Porto Alegre was chosen as the site of the WSF because the state of which it is the capital is "the place which has

---

36. Oxfam, Rigged Rules and Double Standards: Trade, Globalization, and the Fight against Poverty 6 (2002).
37. Global Compact, *The Global Compact Corporate Leadership in the World Economy: Kofi Annan, Secretary-General of the United Nations, in* Media Room (15 Mar. 2001), *available at* www.ficci.com/ficci/index.htm.

chosen the possibility of another world."[38] PB is promoted as an enlargement of democracy, the great work of citizenship, and a major instrument
for the fight against poverty.[39] It is an ongoing process of interactive
meetings for purposes of education, consultation, election of delegates, and
direct voting of budget priorities. Porto Alegre's experience has considerably
widened the "tool kit" of participatory instruments and methods.[40]

The history of PB's difficult early period in Porto Alegre is not reviewed
here, nor are its successes and failures assessed. That history has been told
and those assessments made in nuanced critical fashion.[41] Rebecca Abers
tells how disputes between PT militants, who read their 1988 electoral
victory in Porto Alegre as a mandate to install a socialist workers'
government, and other PT officials, who pleaded for "a government for
all,"[42] were resolved by "a government that made alliances for the sake of
governing effectively, included the middle class as a critical electoral ally,
but that gave preference to the poor and to the periphery in policymaking."[43]
Initial obstacles included severe resource constraints, the absence of sound
budgeting data from previous administrations, and the inexperience of PB
pioneers. Major progress occurred in 1990, Abers explains, when administrative, political, and financial changes "transformed the *prefeitura* [munici-
pal administration] over the course of the following years into a highly
popular government that was able to devolve decision-making power to
citizens in areas relevant to their lives."[44]

Institutional arrangements and procedures adopted in Porto Alegre in
the early years have undergone modifications over time. But they have not
been replicated mimetically in other Brazilian cities where past traditions of
community and labor organizing and mobilization by a reformist political
party differ from those present in Porto Alegre. The basic objective of PB
remains the same everywhere, however: to democratize decisions about
public investment projects and services in ways that reduce poverty and
social inequality.

In Porto Alegre early rounds of meetings are open to all, and a list of
works and public services desired by communities is drawn up and an order

---

38.   STATE GOVERNMENT OF RIO GRANDE DO SUL, RIO GRANDE DO SUL, PARTICIPAÇÃO E SOLIDARIEDADE, A
       CONSTRUÇÃO DE UM OUTRO MUNDO (2002).
39.   *Id.* at 3.
40.   MARKUS BROSE & ALESSANDRO VANINI AMARAL, METODOLOGIA PARTICIPATIVA: UMA INTRODUÇÃO A 29
       INSTRUMENTOS (2001).
41.   *See* REBECCA ABERS, INVENTING LOCAL DEMOCRACY: GRASSROOTS POLITICS IN BRAZIL (2000); LUCIANO
       FEDOZZI, O PODER DA ALDEIA, GÊNESE E HISTORIA DO ORÇMENTO PARTICIPATIVO DE PORTO ALEGRE
       (2000).
42.   ABERS, *supra* note 41, at 70.
43.   *Id.* at 71.
44.   *Id.* at 75.

of priorities established. Formal regional and thematic gatherings come later. In regional meetings, elected delegates decide what works will be carried out in their residential locales, and counselors who form the Participatory Budget Council, together with representatives of the municipal government, are elected. Delegates and counselors receive no payment, do not form part of the government, and may have their mandate revoked at any time by the community that elected them.

To assure rotation in popular participation, counselors cannot serve more than two consecutive years. Five thematic sectors receive attention: (1) traffic flows and transportation; (2) economic development and taxation; (3) urban organization and development; (4) health and social assistance; and (5) education, culture, and leisure. The government conducts technical, legal, and financial studies of proposals generated by the popular process, and a budget is prepared, voted, and presented to regional and thematic assemblies. In later stages of the cycle, revisions are made and implementation monitored. An undated government flyer calls PB a practical school of democracy that creates a two-way relationship: the city administration accounts for expenditures, proposes projects and carries them out: the community raises problems, discusses them and decides where public money is to be invested. The sociologist Fedozzi calls PB "an effort to create institutional conditions which favor the emergence of a citizenry, and that this process may be translated by changes in the forms taken by state-society administration."[45]

Processes to empower the hitherto excluded face difficulties because not everyone has the same capacity to participate. Sherry Arnstein, an early theorist of participation, draws up a "ladder of citizen participation" with eight rungs: the bottom two rungs are, in reality, nonparticipation; the middle three signal varying degrees of tokenism; and the top three confer varying degrees of citizen power ("partnership, delegated power, and citizen control").[46] In Arnstein's terms, PB has produced meaningful partnership and citizen control. More importantly, PB provides evidence that citizen participation in macro policy sectors—public investment, banking, agriculture, sanitation, infrastructure, land reform, environment, education, housing, health care, tourism, and culture—is feasible.

---

45. Luciano Fedozzi, Orçamento Participativo, Reflexões sobre a Experiência de Porto Alegre 186 (2001).
46. Sherry R. Arnstein, *A Ladder of Citizen Participation*, 35 J. Am. Institute of Planners 216, 217 (1969).

III. DAM CONFLICTS IN NORTHEAST BRAZIL

Stronger evidence that macro participation is feasible is supplied by institutional innovations following upon dam conflicts in Northeast Brazil. These conflicts have been adequately studied;[47] hence, no detailed account of them is presented here. It is useful to recall the conflict at Itaparica, however, to show how civil society agents, through "uninvited participation," entered arenas previously reserved to technical and political elite decision-makers, and later precipitated formalized non-elite participation in national water and dam policy arenas.

A. Itaparica After Sobradinho

Brazil has long pursued a policy of building large dams. Vast water reserves have led the country to depend on hydropower for over 90 percent of its electricity generation. In addition to monumental dams—Itaipú (12.6 million kilowatts) and Tucuruí (7 million kilowatts)—a network of large dams has been constructed on the São Francisco River. Among these, the Itaparica dam (1.5 actual – 2.5 potential million kilowatts) is important as the site of new patterns of non-elite participation which escalated from *micro* to *macro* arenas of decision-making and proved decisive in resolving conflict.

At Itaparica 49,500 people (20 percent of the total population in eight "municipios") were resettled to make room for a reservoir 100 miles long and twenty-two miles wide. In the wake of grave popular disaffection at Sobradinho in 1979, agricultural workers' unions organized popular resistance at Itaparica. These unions, federated as a sindicate pole (*Polo Sindical*), pressured technical and political agencies, which in the past had monopolized decision-making, to accept poor agricultural workers living on the banks of the river as negotiating partners in deciding resettlement terms. In earlier projects, residents were not informed of flooding schedules and had no voice in negotiating levels of monetary compensation, relocation sites, or terms of economic reactivation. In contrast, displacees at Itaparica, through Polo Sindical as intermediary, negotiated specific details of these disputed issues with governmental and technical agencies.

Polo Sindical's principal interlocutor was CHESF (Companhia Hidro

---

47.   *Cf.* Internal assessments prepared by CHESF and the World Bank; Maria Lia Corrêa de Araújo et al., Sonhos Submersos ou Desenvolvimento? Impactos sociais da Barragem de Itaparica (2000); Henrique O. Monteiro de Barros, Reorganização Espacial e Mudança Social na Área do Reservatório de Itaparica (1985).

Elétrica do São Francisco), a para-statal company created in 1945 and modeled on the Tennessee Valley Authority to serve as the main agent of development and integration into national economic circuits of Brazil's impoverished Northeast region, a scene of recurring catastrophic droughts and violent social upheavals. Since 1948, CHESF has been building dams on the São Francisco River, which courses 2700 kilometers through five states in the region. Planning for the multipurpose Itaparica Dam began in the mid-1970s and was completed in 1988. The World Bank approved a loan of US $232 million for resettlement costs.

At Itaparica CHESF prepared plans to build new cities outside inundated areas for 10,000 urban residents, but initially, made no resettlement plans for 30,000 rural residents, many of whom had no title to the lands they occupied, except to offer them a cash payment. The collective memory of the earlier disaster at Sobradinho,[48] activated by Polo Sindical's organizing efforts, propelled Itaparica residents into refusing to cooperate with surveyors and builders prior to flooding and mounting active resistance to CHESF.

At Sobradinho it had been the Catholic Church, through its Pastoral Land Commission (CPT) and its activist bishop, that mobilized resistance to CHESF's proffered resettlement terms.[49] At Itaparica, in contrast, the main agent of resistance was Polo Sindical, a federation of thirteen rural trade unions and community organizations. Additional support came from the CPT, Brazilian consultant groups, elements of the media, and US-based international NGOs, such as OXFAM and the Environmental Defense Fund (EDF), that engaged in public advocacy directed at the World Bank. The Bank temporarily withheld payment on its resettlement loan and pressed CHESF to formulate detailed resettlement plans for rural displacees. Designated sites were deemed by displacees to be either too distant from the projected new shoreline, of poor soil quality, or otherwise ill-suited for irrigation. In the general popular perception, CHESF withheld information about scheduling of works and ran roughshod over individual complaints regarding compensation terms for expropriated lands, houses, and goods. As this perception mounted, 6,000 people targeted for displacement occupied the reservoir site for six days in December 1986. Coming in the wake of large street demonstrations, challenging letters sent and group remonstrances made to CHESF officials, and repeated sit-ins at construction offices, this major disturbance was widely covered by the national media. It

48.   On the disaster at Sobradinho and its causes, see Anthony Hall, *Grassroots Action for Resettlement Planning: Brazil and Beyond*, 22 WORLD DEVELOPMENT 1795–96 (1994). *Cf.* CHESF, Reservatório de Sobradinho, Reassentamento de Populações, Dados e Informações, (2d ed. Feb. 2004) (on file with author).

49.   SIEGFRIED PATER, O BISPO DOS EXCLUÍDOS: DOM JOSÉ RODRIGUES (1996).

derailed CHESF's project calendar and budget and, together with other government agencies, CHESF found itself obliged to sign an agreement with Polo Sindical acceding to protesters' demands. Issues settled included the provision by CHESF to settlers of information on precise dates for land acquisitions; terms for the transfer of populations, including specifics on housing and irrigation infrastructure and criteria for establishing eligibility for different compensation packages; and the assurance of maintenance payments to settler families until future harvests.

Years later, disputes were still pending over nonfulfillment by CHESF of obligations to construct full irrigation facilities in resettled areas. To these were added budgetary delays, psychological and social problems arising from enforced idleness, alcohol abuse, and, in later years, drug trafficking. Once again, CHESF came to be viewed with hostility, and the earlier climate of the CHESF/Polo Sindical collaboration, won only after severe conflict, crumbled.

CHESF resented making maintenance payments for what seemed to be endless periods and to many individuals who, it suspected, did not apply earlier subsidies to their allotted purposes. For their part, settlers were neither culturally, nor technically, prepared to function in the commercial agriculture dictated by the new conditions. Polo Sindical periodically reissued threats to paralyze CHESF activities at the dam and power station if settlers' demands were not attended to in a timely fashion.

US-based NGOs continued to send protest letters to the World Bank in support of Polo Sindical's demands that the Inspection Panel press CHESF to solve problems. The Inspection Panel, a committee created by the World Bank in 1993, aims at providing an independent forum for citizens who believe that their interests are, or could be, harmed by a project having Bank financing. Dam construction and resettlement efforts produced important benefits, but as Anthony Hall declares: "[D]espite these significant achievements, however, there have been difficulties."[50] The most significant achievement is the fairly smooth transfer of thousands of families to their new homes after floodgates were closed, as Hall notes, "in direct contrast to the traumatic experiences at Sobradinho and in the lower valley a decade earlier." The behavior of Brazilian state agencies at Sobradinho and Itaparica forms part of a larger strategy aimed at altering the power relations of social classes affected by projects and at imposing a certain model of development. "The governmental objective," Corrêa de Araújo writes, "comes to be the *modernization* of agricultural and animal husbandry activities. The new orientations of the economic policy of the government favor the expansion, in rural areas, of the process of 'enterprise formation,'

---

50.   Hall, *supra* note 48.

also defined as the 'industrialization' of Brazilian agriculture and animal husbandry."[51] She calls attention to "perverse effects" and the exclusionary character of the development model favored by military governments and, later, of "compensatory policies" designed to mitigate the harmful impact on the rural population.

> [T]he revision of prior positions, going from markedly authoritarian practices to a phase of greater concern for *social issues* is a reflection of objective changes such as the emergence of new social and political subjects which leads to the dying out of the mediating functions long performed by local chieftains, usually, large landowners.[52]

A popular organization had now won status as an equal negotiating partner with governmental and technical agencies in a large project. This conquest constitutes an upscaling of participation from a micro, to a macro, arena of development. Accordingly, Hall observes, "[I]t is difficult to overstate the importance of the *Polosindical's* influence in guiding developments at Itaparica."[53]

For World Bank officials and consultants, Itaparica is a tragic mistake. A 1997 draft Bank report states that Itaparica:

> serves as a model only of what not to do. At US $185,000 per resettled rural family on the schemes, US $54,000 per hectare, and almost a 1:1 ratio between costs of resettlement and costs of the dam and power plant, the costs of this operation far exceed those for any other involuntary resettlement program . . . *the original proposal for the dam may have been rejected if the full costs of the irrigation resettlement had been accurately assessed. . . . The ten-year delay in installing irrigation infrastructure adds an ugly side to this misadventure. Some said that Sobradinho had offered an opportunity for a broad-based regional development program,* taking imaginative advantage of all the assets created, including the reservoir. *That vision died at Itaparica.* People sit idle in some of the towns and agrovilas and no organized attempt is being made to give them alternative productive employment.[54]

Although CHESF and the World Bank view construction of the dam and the power plant as an excellent and well-managed project, interviews with CHESF engineers, administrators, lawyers, World Bank professionals, NGO representatives, and selected resettled personnel around the reservoir perimeter confirm that, in social aspects, Itaparica was a failed strategy. As

---

51.   Corrêa de Araújo et al., *supra* note 47, at 199. Here, and elsewhere, translated by author.
52.   *Id.*
53.   Hall, *supra* note 48, at 1798.
54.   E.B. Rice/OEDST, Early Experience with Involuntary Settlement: A Follow-Up, Case Study: Brazil—Itaparica 33–34 (5 Dec. 1997) (draft report for CHESF & Eletrobras, on file with author) (italics in original).

the senior policy advisor to the Executive Secretary of the Ministry of Mines and Energy flatly declared, the "great failure of Electrobrás was Itaparica."[55]

Documents issued by CHESF after Itaparica reveal its previously absent commitment to encourage participation. At Sobradinho, CHESF resisted participation by displacees and their Church advocates; at Itaparica, only against its will was it pressured into accepting participation. That it finally did so is due to a change in the federal government's attitude in the 1980s toward "affected" population groups and CHESF's desire not to repeat errors committed at Sobradinho.

By the early 1980s, Corrêa de Araújo explains, "a democratization of the intervention model of the Electricity Sector" had been adopted that "strengthened the discourse of participation, although participation only occurred, in concrete fact, as a result of truly major social pressures."[56] In an interview, Corrêa de Araújo confirms that "the changed national climate in Brazil after 1985, with the end of military dictatorship, meant that new members (more to the left) in ministries and other agencies were more receptive to co-negotiating with the population" and that the "failed experience of CHESF in dealing with population of Sobradinho served as a main reference point for organization and protest, later at Itaparica."[57]

A later interview with CHESF's chief construction engineer at Sobradinho introduced an important qualification to this receptivity, however. He regretted that "participation was conducted in the adversarial, not in the partnership mode."[58] A different CHESF engineer interviewed noted, however, that at Itaparica, for the first time in the annals of dam construction in Brazil, the agency honored irregular land titles, and improvements on lands occupied by displacees were indemnified to those who made them and not to the owners of the land, many of whom are absentee landlords.[59] These measures reflected the "idealistic" identity as something more than a mere engineering firm that CHESF gave itself in its early years.

This same engineer viewed resettlement at Itaparica as a positive achievement. The main practical lesson to be drawn from conflict at Itaparica in his view, is that the financing of dam construction and of resettlement should not be dissociated. Had the two budgets been treated

55. Interview with Paul Nascimento, Asesor da Secretaría Executiva, MME (Advisor, Executive Secretariat, Ministry of Mines and Energy), Brasilia, 11 Feb. 2003.
56. CORRÊA DE ARAÚJO ET AL., *supra* note 47, at 53.
57. Interview with Corrêa de Araújo, Sociologist, FUNDAJ (Joaqim Nabuco Foundation), Recife, 27 July 2001.
58. Interview with João Paulo Maranhão de Aguiar, former Dam Construction Engineer CHESF, presently Advisor to the Presidency, CHESF (São Francisco Hydro-Electric Company), Recife, 31 July 2001.
59. Interview with Wilson Belfort, Engineer, CHESF (São Francisco Hydro-Electric Company), Recife, 15 Jan. 2002.

jointly, much conflict, numerous costly delays, and irreparable loss of trust might have been avoided. Participation, he concludes, although conducted in an adversarial mode, was nonetheless a major factor in making the resettlement process a relative success.

B. Deficient Participation

An earlier examination of Itaparica and other large development projects had led this author to formulate, in 1989, a typology of participation and criteria for judging its quality.[60] Participation is classified and its quality judged according

- to its being valued primarily as end or as means;
- to its scope;
- to its originating agent (the state, the affected populace, some catalyzing third party); and, most importantly,
- to the moment in which it is introduced.

This last criterion is crucial, for the quality of participation differs according to the time when it first occurs

- at initial diagnosis of the problem;
- when response options are identified;
- when one option is selected;
- when organizing to implement action begins;
- when discrete steps in implementing the chosen course are taken;
- when self-correction or evaluation takes place; and
- when further mobilization or organization is debated.

Identifying initial point of entry enables one to determine whether participation is authentic empowerment or mere manipulation. Applying these criteria at Sobradinho, participation never gained entry into decision-making arenas, and at Itaparica, participation came so late that it imposed excessive social and human costs on the total enterprise.

When participation comes late in the sequence of decisions and actions, it signals that technical, political, and managerial elites did not, at

---

60. Denis Goulet, *Participation in Development: New Avenues*, 17 World Development 165, 166–68 (1989).

the outset, intend to include non-elite participatory voices in decisions. In such cases participation by non-elites must be conquered by "forcible entry." Not surprisingly, imposed participation is perceived by elites to operate in the adversarial mode. This perception yields, at best, reluctant collaboration, and at worst, mutual suspicion of willful obstructionism. This is not to say, however, that the acceptance of non-elite participation by traditional elite agents early in the decisional sequence is necessarily better.

When governmental or international agencies, dam construction firms, or expert consultants "invite" the participation of affected groups, the latter readily suspect the former are doing so in order to channel participation in directions consonant with their own elite preferences grounded in technical and political rationality. This is the permanent danger attaching to invited, as opposed to imposed, participation. Nevertheless, at times these twin dangers—adversarial or manipulative participation—can be overcome.

At Itaparica progress was made toward achieving a balance of the three rationalities needed for sound decision-making—technical, political, ethical—each of which is primarily expressed by one category of actors.[61] The encounter of the three rationalities and the three categories of institutional actors embodying them may, over time, undergo a transformation from vertical to circular or horizontal patterns of negotiation.

At one point Polo Sindical engaged the services of an agronomist and economist and, armed with their expert advice, found new grounds for agreement with CHESF. *New patterns of mutuality thus came into play in negotiating arenas and served as a counterweight to initial disparities of bargaining power among elite and non-elite actors.*

Itaparica yields two lessons:

- negotiations are stymied so long as each major actor pursues a single rationality—technical, political, or ethical—in reductionist fashion; and

- conversely, progress appears as interlocutors transcend the bounds of their own narrow rationality and enter into the universe of goals and procedures proper to other rationalities.

After Itaparica, the WCD Report, Narmada, and Three Gorges, a broader lesson is now apparent: National governments, IFIs, dam construction firms, and technical consultants can no longer impose decisions with impunity nor abandon resettled and economically vulnerable populations to their fate after relocation. CHESF, in its post-Itaparica dealings with resident populations, municipal governments, and civil society groups at other São Francisco River dam sites, has incorporated this lesson.

---

61.   Denis Goulet, *Three Rationalities in Development Decision-making*, 14 WORLD DEVELOP-
MENT 301, 301 (1986).

C. Xingó

In its relations with the population surrounding the Xingó dam, the construction of which entailed no significant human displacement, CHESF provides an example of a specialized dam agency giving itself a larger mission through multiple programs to bring social, economic, and cultural development to the region.[62] Xingó Project favors a decentralized model of operation and specific methods that suit the particular needs of communities under consideration.[63] It conducts training activities and demonstration projects, and it provides funding and technical assistance to activities aimed at diversifying economic production in the semi-arid area. Although Xingó officials praise participation, residents and municipal officials in the region, when interviewed, complained that the project remains highly technocratic and does not get close to the people. Nor do intended beneficiaries participate in the planning of broad strategies or specific projects. Many expectations cannot be met because of Xingó Project's insecure funding and heavy dependence for staffing on scholarship recipients seconded from the National Scientific Research Council for relatively short periods. Notwithstanding these difficulties, which Project officials readily acknowledge, results are nonetheless significant.[64]

More important, however, than regional efforts by dam builders to engage in development activities, are innovations in participatory decision-making occurring at the national level. These innovations derive, in large measure, from lessons learned at Itaparica.

IV. WATERSHED COMMITTEES

Law 9433 created watershed committees across all the newly delimited hydrographic regions of the country, defining their mandate to be "the integrated, decentralized, and participatory management of water resources at all territorial levels of administration . . . . [Committees constitute] a new model of management: management shared among the different levels of public power, consumers, and organized civil society."[65]

Brazil's abundant water resources have historically generated a sense of

---

62. Covering twenty-nine municipalities in four states. Population of the area (as of 2001) is 548,000. Programa Xingó, Relatório de Acompanhamento, at 4/9 (31 Mar. 2001) (report on file with author); Programa Xingó, Xingó Informativo, Ano II e III, no. 4, at 1 (Nov. 2000–Apr. 2001) (report on file with author).
63. Programa Xingó, Relatório de Acompanhamento, *supra* note 62, at 4/19.
64. There are a reported 35,000 direct beneficiaries. *See id.* at 17/19. CHESF later extended Xingó Project activities to the Sobradinho Dam region.
65. ANA (Agência Nacional de Águas), Gestão de Bacias no Brazil, Brasília 7 (2002).

complacency that led to a tardy recognition of the need to manage them in order to put an end to "a culture of abusive utilization of rivers and lakes."[66] Regional distribution of water resources within Brazil is highly unequal: 73 percent are concentrated in the Amazon Basin, where only 4 percent of the population resides, while the Southeastern region of the country, which contains 47 percent of the national population, disposes of but 8 percent of water resources.[67] Twenty-three watershed committees composed of federal, state, and municipal government representatives, of organized civil society, and of consumers (*usuários*) have now been constituted, although not all are operating fully.

A wide-ranging interdisciplinary and inter-institutional research program engaging academics and technical specialists, the Watermark (*Marca d'Agua*) Project,[68] was launched in 2001, with an initial life expectancy of five years, possibly extending for ten or more years. Its objective is to evaluate the institutional formation and functioning of fifteen to twenty Brazilian watershed committees for the purpose of capturing the dynamics and performance of this innovation. The Watermark Project highlights two values directly linked to democracy and representation in society: participation and decentralization. It lies beyond the scope of this article to summarize this research enterprise, which is still in relatively early stages. No attempt is made to do so, nor is a detailed portrait of the São Francisco committee, itself in early stages of operation, assayed. It is enlightening, however, to contrast the declared values of the São Francisco Watershed Committee with those which underlay CHESF's decisions at Sobradinho and Itaparica. No less significantly, the new watershed committee's declared values are largely consonant with those recommended by the World Commission on Dams.

A. Values

The São Francisco River Committee[69] endorses the Federal Constitution's declaration that "[a]ll [Brazilians] have the right to an ecologically balanced environment" and formally subscribes to additional values: broad participation in decision-making, the democratic management of water resources,

---

66.   *Id.* at 5.
67.   *Id.* at 4.
68.   For details on the Watermark Project, including design, rationale, objectives, methodology, funding, administrative structure, research personnel, and anticipated results, see Projeto Marca D' Água (the Watermark Project), *available at* www.marcadagua.org.br.
69.   IMAN (Instituto Manoel Novaes), ANA (Agencia Nacional de Aguas), & Ministerio Do Meio Ambiente, Governo Federal, O Comité da Bacia Hidrográfica do Rio São Francisco [hereinafter O Comité] (undated document on file with author).

and the institutional representation of interest groups affected by decisions on power generation, dam construction, and river management.[70] Formal representation in the committee is granted to municipal, state, and federal government agencies, indigenous communities, civil society, and user organizations with specific interests in hydroelectric power, water supply, industry, river transport, navigation, irrigation, fisheries, environment, tourism, and recreation. The overarching goal of the committee, in the words of the Minister of Environment, is "to guarantee the dialogue between the institutions responsible for the management of water resources and the watershed's society at large."[71] Unlike Brazilian rivers that course through a single state, the São Francisco runs through five states and, via tributaries, through a sixth state and the Federal District of Brasilia. The initial composition of sixty elected members was distributed as follows: public entities, 34 percent; user groups, 40 percent; and civil society, 26 percent.

The committee understands "civil society" to mean "organized" groups, ranging from professional associations of fishery workers and agricultural producers to labor unions and social action NGOs. The instrument of coordination of these diverse entities is the Integration Agreement, "a pact signed by ANA (*Agencia Nacional das Aguas* [National Water Agency]), the states, and the committees to establish the integrated management of water resources. Integration consists of the harmonization of criteria and procedures for applying the technical and institutional instruments of management."[72] By granting central importance to the Integration Agreement the committee reflects "the principles of democratization and of ethics."[73] The creation of the São Francisco Watershed Committee is the fruit of a long and complex process of regional and state meetings engaging hundreds of participants in constant negotiation. Regional meetings were preceded by training sessions conducted by ANA and CHESF to initiate state teams to legal, institutional, and methodological elements of water resource planning.[74] These sessions themselves were preceded by efforts to register the full range of user and civil society organizations in each state, followed by publicity and mobilization in preparation of the regional meetings in which indigenous communities were intensely consulted.[75] Electoral procedures had to be crafted and internal regimentation established. The Provisional Directorate, which organized the committee's establishment, regards the state plenaries as "the most significant moment in the process of mobilization."[76]

---

70. *Id.* at 9.
71. *Id.*
72. *Id.* at 18.
73. *Id.*
74. *Id.* at 27.
75. *Id.* at 28.
76. *Id.* at 31.

Watershed values—environmental soundness, participatory decision-making, and representation of all interests—contrast sharply with those invoked by CHESF at Sobradinho and Itaparica. Prior to dam construction, CHESF commissioned an environmental assessment of Sobradinho's impact on the region;[77] and some years after, Itaparica sponsored an environmental study of the region affected by that dam and power plant.[78] In both cases, however, environmental concerns were not centrally important to CHESF. Interviews conducted in 2002 and 2003 in dam regions yielded the frequent complaint, voiced by mayors of affected municipalities, merchants, and agricultural and fishing workers, that dams had destroyed fisheries, dried up tributary streams, and drowned large fertile areas. Consequently, interlocutors placed a high priority on revitalizing the river and its tributaries.[79]

Because Northeast Brazil's semi-arid region is burdened with a violent history of oppressive relationships between political, economic, and technical elites and the population at large, the provisional group designated to constitute the São Francisco Watershed Committee and to establish procedures for the election of its members was acutely sensitive to the need to "guarantee the legitimacy of the process, in terms of participation and representation."[80] Participation in management of water resources had to be authentic. What constitutes "authentic," as distinct from "manipulated," participation has long been disputed. Nevertheless, the government-created watershed committee's stance on participation is evidently a far cry from the attitude displayed by CHESF and other governmental dam agencies in earlier conflictual cases. The lesson has been learned: Participation is desirable, necessary, and must not be resisted.

Watershed committees are enjoined to collaborate with state water resource councils. Together with state councils, committees form part of a national system to assure that water resources are managed as a public good endowed with economic value. The overall system is designed to assure a decentralized, integrated, and participatory form of management. The sociologist Rosana Garjulli explains,

> [A]s mechanisms for assuring participatory management, the [national] legislation on water resources foresees, as part of the institutional structure of the system, the [creation of] watershed committees, and state and national water

---

77.   Robert Goodland, New York Botanical Garden, Sobradinho Hydroelectric Project Environmental Impact Reconnaissance (Sep. 1973) (report on file with author).

78.   Felicio Limeira de França & Margarida Dantas de Oliveira, Usina Hidroeletrica De Itaparica, Aspectos Ambientais De Projetos Cofinanciados Pelo Banco Mundial (1992).

79.   The call for revitalization of the river(s) is a recurring theme of the study produced by an itinerant team making a cultural, environmental, and spiritual evaluation of the river. *Cf.* Luiz Flavio Cappio et al., Rio São Francisco, Uma Caminhada Entre Vita e Morte (2d ed. 2000).

80.   O Comité, *supra* note 69, at 38.

resource councils, which will assume a strategic function as collegial organs of the State [i.e., the national government] and enjoy deliberative power over the management of water resources."[81]

Garjulli contrasts this mandate with values, norms, and behavior of the authoritarian military regime in power between 1964 and 1985, which was characterized by "repression and by the closing off of all democratic channels of participation."[82] For CHESF, the issues at Sobradinho and Itaparica were simple and clear-cut: Electricity was needed to meet industrial and domestic demand, mainly in the Northeast's large coastal cities (secondarily, irrigation waters were needed for export-oriented commercial firms), and decisions about building dams and power plants simply responded to these obvious needs. One important lesson learned at Sobradinho and Itaparica is that *needs* are defined differently by competing interest groups and that the decision to build dams in accord with mere technical exigencies of sound planning is not acceptable.

1. Ceará Learns from Itaparica

One watershed committee has special links to the Itaparica conflict.[83] The Rio Jaguaribe Basin Committee in Ceará, Northeast Brazil's driest state and one with a long history of failed water policy, is related to Itaparica and CHESF in two ways. The first is that dissidents who opposed the construction of Ceará's largest dam, Castanhão, visited Itaparica for the specific purpose of learning how to resist plans prepared by governmental and technical experts and to gain a negotiating voice for affected populations in decision-making. Instead of the large dam proposed by experts, protesters advocated numerous smaller dams judged by them, on the basis of alternative engineering studies, to be technically and economically more efficient, and less destructive of human settlements, local cultural values, and ecological resources. The second link is that, for decades continuing to the present, proposals have been floated to transpose the waters of the São Francisco, for which CHESF is the main responsible agency, to Ceará. Inter-basin water transfer is now a general planning option for all of Brazil's hydrographic regions. Proposals for the possible transfer of waters from the São Francisco River to other basins in semi-arid areas date from the middle of the nineteenth century.

---

81.   Rosana Garjulli, *Construindo a Gestão Participativa, in* O Comité, *supra* note 69, at 42. Translation the author's.
82.   *Id.*
83.   Updated reports on all basin committees can be found on the Watermark Project website, *supra* note 68.

But it was at the start of the '80s decade that the project gained consistency, until it reached the solution to be adopted which is sought nowadays. . . . As more profound studies were made, the present project was formulated, in which the prevailing principle is minimal use of the river's waters, so as to achieve synergy and better utilization of the waters of the receiver basins. . . . The [present] project to transport the waters of the São Francisco River aims, precisely, at replicating in Brazil, with the advantage of hydric synergy, models already proven in the world at large.[84]

The São Francisco transfer scheme, as well as the broad national policy on transfer, are now the subject matter of participatory debate within watershed committees. Although they failed to block the large Castanhão project, during long years of resistance, church organizations, cultural defense groups, and water user organizations gained experience at negotiating with government agencies.[85] One outcome of resistance was the creation of "user committees,"[86] empowered to negotiate the distribution of water allotments for competing uses: local irrigation and electricity for industry or domestic consumption in the distant capital city, Fortaleza. When the Rio Jaguaribe Watershed Committee was created, many members were already experienced in engaging in substantive co-negotiation, not only with state and federal agencies, but also with the World Bank, the Inter-American Development Bank, and international consultants and technical firms, on post-dam construction issues of water adduction, irrigation infrastructure, and statewide water and electricity policy.

V. CONCLUSION

Development theorists and practitioners have long known that participation can succeed in micro arenas: for example, small-scale projects, local cooperatives, and limited issue associations.[87] Many thought, however, that

---

84.   Ministério da Integração Nacional (Ministry of National Integration), Transposição de Águas do São Francisco, Brasilia, at 27–28 (undated document on file with author).

85.   A detailed study of Castanhão is important to trace the growth of participatory institutions in Ceará but lies beyond the scope of this article. Cf. CÁSSIO BORGES, A FACE OCULTA DA BARRAGEM DO CASTANHÃO , EM DEFESA DA ENGENHARIA NACIONAL (THE HIDDEN FACE OF CASTANHÃO DAM, IN DEFENSE OF NATIONAL ENGINEERING) (1999); GOVERNO DO ESTADO DO CEARÁ, RELATÓRIO SÍNTESE DAS ATIVIDADES DESENVOLVIDAS PELO GRUPO DE TRABALHO MULTI-PARTICIPATIVO PARA O ACOMPANHAMENTO DAS OBRAS E AÇÕES DO PROJETO CASTANHÃO, 18.07.1995 A 30.12.2002 (on file with author).

86.   On the organization and methodology of user committees, see Rosana Garjulli, A Participação dos Usuários na Implementação dos Instrumentos de Gestão de Recursos Hídricosos—O caso do Ceará 12 (2001) (unpublished paper presented to IV Diálogo Interamericano de Gerenciamento de Agua "Em Busca De Soluções," 22–26 Apr. 2001).

87.   Cf., GUY GRAN, DEVELOPMENT BY PEOPLE: CITIZEN CONSTRUCTION OF A JUST WORLD (1983); ALBERT O. HIRSCHMAN, GETTING AHEAD COLLECTIVELY: GRASSROOTS EXPERIENCES IN LATIN AMERICA (1984); ACTION

participation is not feasible in macro arenas—national or sectoral policy or large-scale projects. The WCD Report recommends wide-ranging participation of affected groups in large dam projects and national and international water policy. Many responses to the Report, framed by national governments, professional dam associations, international funding agencies, and engineering firms questioned the feasibility, some even the desirability, of participation in macro arenas related to large dams. Brazil's initiatives supply evidence that participatory decision-making in macro arenas is feasible. Of special importance are institutional and procedural innovations in watershed committees, where participation is formally mandated to bring democratic decision-making to water policy.

In developing and developed countries alike, large dams are contested sites where competing views of development are at stake. Disputes revolve around social justice and environmental damage. In the dominant view of development, the priorities are economic growth, technological efficiency, and promoting privatization and market competition as the organizing principle of economic activity. Political and ethical rationality are relegated to second place, behind technical rationality on which it relies decisively. Cost-benefit analysis (CBA), its preferred methodology, is usually employed in a reductionist manner by treating justice and environmental considerations as mere externalities. The alternative view of development correlates highly with the advocacy of non-elite participation in decision-making. Its priorities are poverty eradication, reduced inequality, resistance to privatization, and empowerment of poor populations by granting them effective voices as bearers of ethical rationality in substantive decision-making arenas. Its preferred methodology is non-elite participation in decision-making arenas.

Itaparica played an indispensable role in the creation of legally mandated institutional participation in the very macro arena—dam and water policy—lying at the center of the World Commission on Dams' prescriptions. At large dam sites throughout the world, globalization's major actors increasingly find themselves obliged to share decisions with international NGOs, people's organizations, user groups, and local government representatives. Macro participation by non-elite groups can be feasible, in the right circumstances and when supported; for instance, local NGOs need the assistance of internationally-based NGOs. Brazil's initiatives likewise suggest that theories of participation must undergo drastic reconceptuali-

---

AND KNOWLEDGE: BREAKING THE MONOPOLY WITH PARTICIPATORY ACTION-RESEARCH (Orlando Fals-Borda & Muhammad Anisur Rahman eds., 1991); MATTHIAS STIEFEL & MARSHALL WOLFE, A VOICE FOR THE EXCLUDED: POPULAR PARTICIPATION IN DEVELOPMENT, UTOPIA OR NECESSITY? (1994); ROBERT CHAMBERS, PARTICIPATORY WORKSHOPS: A SOURCEBOOK OF 21 SETS OF IDEAS AND ACTIVITIES (2002); WORLD BANK, THE WORLD BANK PARTICIPATION WORKBOOK (1996).

zation[88] if they are to account adequately for emerging new modes of global governance. When the targets of "uninvited" participation are global institutions at their headquarters or their periodic meetings, governance exercised by NGOs or social movements is indirect—via the cumulative effect of mass demonstrations and sustained advocacy for redress of grievances or rule changes.[89] When, in contrast, the targets are local or national project actors or global institutions engaged in locale-specific actions such as dam construction, governance conducted by NGOs and social movements is direct. Participatory actions in large projects, and engagement therein with global institutions, always occur in the context of a specific national strategy framed under constraints, such as high external indebtedness, excessive economic or financial dependency, mass poverty, or a past history of national policies favoring social inequality. This rooting in a situation-specific total context renders the link of deficient global governance to worldwide dam policy and to the upscaling of participation from micro to macro arenas increasingly evident.

---

88.   For one alternative conceptualization, see DENIS GOULET, INCENTIVES FOR DEVELOPMENT, THE KEY TO EQUITY 159–63 (1989).

89.   On the role of NGOs in reinforcing efforts at reform and rule change, see Andrew Gray, *Development Policy, Development Protest: The World Bank, Indigenous Peoples, and NGOs, in* THE STRUGGLE FOR ACCOUNTABILITY: THE WORLD BANK, NGOs, AND GRASSROOTS MOVEMENTS 267 (Jonathan A. Fox & L. David Brown eds., 1998); Deborah Moore & Leonard Sklar, *Reforming the World Bank's Lending for Water: The Process and Outcome of Developing a Water Resources Management Policy, in* THE STRUGGLE FOR ACCOUNTABILITY, *supra*, at 345; Lori Udall, *The World Bank and Public Accountability: Has Anything Changed, in* THE STRUGGLE FOR ACCOUNTABILITY, *supra*, at 391.

[26]

Ethics, Economic Advice, and Economic Policy
Joseph E. Stiglitz[1]

I wish to use this occasion to discuss the ethical dimensions of a variety of issues in development and international economics that I confronted over the past eight years. Economists have long bought into the importance of self-interest not only in explaining behavior, but also in yielding efficient outcomes. But economists have also long been aware of the limitations of these perspectives. Not only does the self-interest/market paradigm often fail to generate efficient outcomes, but even when it does, these outcomes may not comport with notions of social justice. Still, in the realm of economic policy, governments typically justify foreign aid and other policies aimed at poorer countries in terms of their own self-interest; how such policies increase world incomes, thereby increasing the country's own exports, or contribute to global political stability, from which all benefit. Such arguments deflect attention from the moral justification for these policies.

Ethics in the relationship between developed and less developed countries dictates that the developed countries treat the less developed countries fairly, aware of their disadvantaged economic position, and acknowledging that taking advantage of one's own economic power inevitably will hurt the poor within developing countries. We have seen several instances where, in global economic relationships, this precept has been grossly violated: an international trade agenda set to advance the interests of the more developed countries, at least partially at the expense of the less developed—so much so that on average the world's poorest region was actually worse off at the end of the last round of trade negotiations; and an international environmental agreement that provided that those rich countries who today are polluting more be entitled to continue polluting more into the future.

There are other dimensions to globalization which illustrate the same violation of basic ethical precepts. Consider the argument made for free capital mobility: it increases world efficiency. Never mind the devastation that it might bring to the small poor countries—and the poor within those countries—that are not able to withstand the seemingly irrational vicissitudes of investor sentiments and the consequent reversals of capital flows! But globalization in these factor movements is much like globalization in trade: there we saw how the powerful tell the less developed countries to open their markets to the goods of the more industrial countries, while keeping their own markets closed. The factor which the developed countries export is capital, the factor which the developing countries have in abundance is labor. From an economic perspective, global efficiency can be attained by free mobility of labor every bit as well as it can be attained through free mobility of capital. But the developed countries are not

1   The author is professor of economics at Columbia University. He previously served as senior vice president and chief economist of the World Bank and as Chairman of the U.S. Council of Economic Advisers under President Clinton. Earlier versions of this paper were presented at a meeting in Milan sponsored by the Vatican in connection with the Jubilee, and at a conference at the Interamerican Development Bank in Washington, D.C. in December 2000.

arguing that there should be free mobility of labor; they are not offering to open up their door
to the poor of the world. The reason is obvious: they are aware of the social dislocation—and
the consequent political pressure—that such migration would bring about. But they simply
cannot put themselves in the shoes of the developing countries: they are unsympathetic when
the developing countries raise precisely the same objections to opening up their countries to
the factors and goods which are in abundance in the developed world.

I shall conduct my discussion at the level of pragmatic ethics, that is, I shall not try to *derive*
the ethical principles from first order considerations. Rather, I shall explore the implications
of certain widely held ethical precepts for the conduct of international economic relations.
By the same token, I shall *evaluate* certain actions, ascertaining which can be viewed as
principled actions. I shall not undertake the far more ambitious goal of defining a set of
principles for action, though to be sure, what I shall say will be thought of as a prelude to that
task. I will use this occasion to raise questions as much as provide answers.[2]

There are five concepts, in particular, on which I will focus: honesty, fairness, social justice
(including a concern for the poor), externalities, and responsibility. While the meaning of
most of these terms should be self-evident, let me comment briefly on each. Honesty goes
beyond outright lying; it comes closer to the dictum of telling the truth, the whole truth, and
nothing but the truth. Misrepresentation—asserting that there is evidence for some proposition
when there is none—violates the principle of honesty.[3] Fairness includes what economists
call horizontal equity—either treating everyone the same (e.g. not discriminating on the basis
of race or gender), or, to the extent that it is desirable to treat those in different circumstances
differently (e.g. the aged and the handicapped may need special treatment) treating those in
similar positions similarly. The hard question, of course, is what are meaningful differences,
differences that could justify differences in treatment? Favoritism—including giving special
treatment to special interests—is thus a violation of the ethical norm of fairness. Social justice
includes helping those in need, and doing so in ways that enhance their sense of dignity
and the ability to assume individual responsibility for themselves. "Externalities" entail that
individuals should not impose costs on others. Littering is, in this view, "wrong," a violation of
an ethical norm. Responsibility is the ethical norm that individuals should take responsibility
for their own actions and for the consequences of those actions.

---

2   Much of what I have to say could be justified in terms of more general principles, e.g. Kant's
categorical imperative, or the Rawlsian analysis of social justice. The latter may be particularly useful in
approaching the issues of equity discussed below: what kind of international social and economic order
would one want *behind the veil of ignorance*, not knowing whether one would be born in a developed
or developing country. Towards the end of this paper, I shall try to put some of the ethical precepts into
a broader context: the rules and norms that facilitate cooperative social interactions.

3   Honesty is a precept that can be taken as a value on its own, or as *instrumental*: actions taken
on the basis of distorted information may lead to adverse results. Presumably, one of the reasons for
dishonesty is to induce others to take actions which, were they to know the truth, they would not. Thus
not disclosing fully the risks of capital market liberalization—and purporting that there are gains from
such liberalization when there is little evidence that there are such gains—may induce countries to
liberalize when, were they provided with more accurate information, they would not; even if the country
would have, in any case, liberalize its capital markets, the distorted information may lead it not to
provide the safety net that it would have provided, were it fully aware of the risks.

Ethical issues arise in every aspect of economics and economic policy making. We recognize, for instance, the ethical problems posed by *conflicts of interest;* and the multitude of positions that individuals have also makes such conflicts of interest inevitable. Today, modern ethical *norms* require *disclosure* of significant conflicts of interest, reflecting the precept of honesty. It is commonly not viewed to be immoral to take actions, in the role of a fiduciary, or to provide advice from which one might oneself benefit; but it is immoral not to disclose the conflict of interest, so that those affected can take appropriate precautions. The modern theory of agency recognizes that agents do not in general *adopt* the interests of those (the principal) who they are supposed to be serving as their own; it is the responsibility of the principal to design incentive structures which align those interests, as much as possible. But it is wrong for the agent, for instance, to steal, to accept kickbacks from clients, or to engage in a host of other corrupt practices.

Advisors face ethical issues. Government bureaucrats and elected officials face ethical issues, such as those associated with corruption. Governments face ethical issues in the design of programs; and international institutions face ethical issues. I begin this paper by subjecting the role of economic advisor to ethical analysis: what does it mean to be an *ethical* economic advisor? The question is an important one, because the international financial institutions are actively involved in providing economic advice. In doing so, do they behave ethically? I will then examine specific issues: ethics in the treatment of developing countries by developed countries, e.g. ethics in the area of trade, global environmental policies, debt forgiveness, growth strategies, crisis management, and finally, ethical issues in population policy.

The Ethics of the Economic Advisor

Most professions have clear ethical principles. In medicine, these are embedded in the Hippocratic Oath. These include "do no harm." In a sense, the ethical norms seek to mitigate the adverse consequences of the unbridled pursuit of self-interest, in particular those that arise whenever there are agency problems (where, because of lack of information, one party can take advantage of another.) Violating these ethical principles harms the entire profession (there is, in this sense, an externality). It destroys *trust.* It is, for instance, unethical for a doctor to prescribe a medicine because he receives a kickback from the manufacturer. The patient, not knowing the reason a doctor prescribes a particular medicine over another, assumes the doctor is prescribing the medicine in the best interest of the patient, not because the doctor is receiving a kickback. Thus, actions which could lead to a conflict of interest between the professional and the person for whom he or she is providing a service are unethical. Since a central part of the service being provided by most professions is information, honesty is a critical virtue.

There is a large economic cost to the destruction of trust. In simplistic models, individual self-interest leads to efficient outcomes; individuals act, and are expected to act, in their self-interest. But in modern theories in which information imperfections and incomplete markets play an important role, self-interested behavior in general does not yield efficient outcomes. Equilibria based on trust can yield better outcomes than those in which trust is absent. The patient, for instance, will be induced to get second and third opinions, because he will be suspicious of the disinterested nature of the advice of the doctor, if he believes that the doctor has a large financial stake in the advice. There is thus an *instrumental* argument for ethical behavior.

Some principles governing the behavior of economic advisors are straightforward. Clearly there is an ethical mandate not to take advantage of inside information obtained as an advise for profit, or to *directly* use connections generated in his advisory role for profit.[4] Furthermore there are ethical (and often legal) norms for disclosure. Transparency mitigates, but does no totally eliminate, the danger that advice would be driven by self-interest. A consultant to firm that had a short position in the stock of the firm would have an incentive to provide advice that would lead to the decrease in the market value of the firm. Few firms would allow the consultant to maintain such a position *were they to know about it.* Similarly, a consultant to a firm hired to advise a firm on the choice of a supplier should not have a financial interest in one of the suppliers, and if he does, he should disclose it; not to do so would be unethical

But there are less straightforward implications as well, and it is to these to which I want to call attention. First, *honesty* requires full disclosure of the *limits* of knowledge. Indeed, this has become explicitly part of the norms of good science. In the hard sciences one always presents the range of estimates, the confidence intervals with which certain results are held The recognition of these uncertainties is even more important in the social sciences. Different propositions are held with different degrees of confidence. For instance, economists can claim with considerable certainty that if a government spends well beyond its revenues for an extended period of time, problems are likely to be encountered, or that hyperinflation has adverse effects on the economy. We can claim with some confidence that capital market liberalization is associated with greater risks, particularly for small, open, developing economies. On the other hand, *honesty* would dictate that an adviser recommending capital market liberalization reveals that empirical evidence proving that capital market liberalization leads to faster growth is absent, and that economic theories supporting capital market liberalization are disputed. H would qualify any argument saying that capital account liberalization is helpful in inducing foreign direct investment by pointing out, however, that the developing country that has been most successful in recruiting foreign direct investment, China, has not liberalized its capital account.

Secondly, *honesty* requires revealing that there is more than one Pareto efficient policy There are tradeoffs, with different policies affecting different groups differently, imposing different risks on different segments of society. Economic advice should focus on ensuring the *efficiency* of policies (to put it technically, to ensure that the economy is on the Pareto frontier) but it is the responsibility of political processes to choose the points on the Pareto frontier When an economist recommends a particular point on the frontier, he is using the cover of his supposed economic expertise to advance a political position. This is a misrepresentation It becomes a particularly serious misrepresentation when he, or interests with which he is affiliated, might be expected to benefit disproportionately from the particular policies being pursued. For instance, if there are a range of policies, some of which are more advantageous to those in the financial market, it would be unethical for an advisor representing financial interests not to disclose the fact that the particular policy he advocates would be particula

---

4   The most famous instance in recent years of an alleged violation of this ethical norm was in Russia, where two of the American advisers were accused of using their inside connections to obtain licenses for friends to establish funds.

advantageous to those groups. In the public sphere today, there is a problem of "revolving doors." Individuals have what might be viewed as a *contingent* interest. Those who serve special interests well while in public service often get rewarded with lucrative positions after public service. Many governments are aware of the conflict of interest to which that gives rise, and to mitigate the ethical issues which inevitably arise, insist that those who leave government service do not enter into the employ of those where there might be a conflict of interest for a period of time, or restrict the kinds of activities in which they can be engaged. Certainly without such rules (but even with them) it would be unethical to give such advice which favors those interests, without disclosing both the consequences for those groups and what might be viewed as the contingent interest of the advisor. (To be sure, the firms hiring these "devoted" public services claim that they do so not as a reward for past services but on the basis of demonstrated acumen while in public service. It should be obvious that it is virtually impossible to draw the line between the two.)

Thirdly, concern for social justice should make an economic advisor particularly attentive to the consequences of policies for the poor. Information does affect action, and while the economist has a moral responsibility not to impose his values, he also has a moral responsibility to ensure the information is available on the basis of which *moral policy decisions*—for instance, decisions that reflect the principles of social justice—can be made.[5] If a policy imposes risks on the economy and if those risks are likely to be borne to a significant degree by the poor, then the adviser should point that out, especially if the risks are borne disproportionately by the poor. To the extent possible, there is a moral responsibility to think creatively about what kinds of policies might enhance the opportunities for the poor, allowing them to take more responsibility for their own well being. Similarly, since there is a moral imperative to be concerned with future generations, the economist should be attentive to the consequences to the environment, and should provide information that can lead to better environmental policies.[6]

These are general precepts which apply to all policy advisors. I have argued that one of the advantages of the institutional structure of the Council of Economic Advisers in the United States is that it reduces the scope for conflicts of interests.[7] The members are appointed for a short term and return to academia. Thus their incentive is to provide relatively accurate information, advice which will stand up to the scrutiny of their *academic* peers. The norms of the economics profession require making most of the distinctions I have alluded to, including distinguishing between special interests and general interests, efficiency effects and distribution effects. (Furthermore, U.S. government regulations require that they dispense

---

5   I realize that there is a fine line that I am treading: I argued earlier that the economist should, in effect, distinguish the economist's role in defining opportunity sets from the political task of choosing among the points in the opportunity set. But the information supplied about the points in the opportunity set—e.g. their impact on the poor—can affect the choices made. Someone not sharing the *values,* not concerned for the poor, might argue not only that providing that information is irrelevant, but distorts the political process of decision making.

6   We should thus view "green accounting" not just as a matter of providing a *good* accounting framework, but as a *moral* issue.

7   See Joseph Stiglitz, "Looking out for the National Interest: the Principles of the Council of Economic Advisers," *American Economic Review*, 87 (2), May 1997, pp. 109–113.

of all financial interests or put them into blind trusts; and in any case, few have substantial financial interests.

One of the main activities of the international financial institutions is giving advice. In assessing the way that international financial institutions dispense advice, I feel that all too often they fall short on all counts described above. They push a particular set of policies, a loan conditionalities, rather than outline the range of policies and trade-offs and encourage the countries themselves to take responsibility for choosing among alternative policies. They fail to clarify the uncertainties associated with the policies they promote, making assertions about the policies' efficacy that cannot be supported by evidence. Most importantly, at least in the past, not only have they failed to pay due concern to the possible adverse effects of the policies on the poor, they have not even disclosed the likely risks. They have continually pushed policies entailing "pain," seemingly almost oblivious to who within the country has to bear that pain. Many of their policies seem to disproportionately benefit financial interests and they fail both to point this out, and to disclose what I have viewed as the *contingent* interests of their staff—evidenced by the fact that many staff members leave the IMF (or World Bank) to work for private financial institutions.[8]

Facing Moral Dilemmas as an Economic Advisor

This brings me to perhaps the hardest moral question facing the policy adviser. What should he or she do when confronted with a policy that he believes is, in some sense, "immoral"? Should he speak out, but thereby risk possibly losing influence? Is silence a form of complicity? There are no easy answers, but a couple of examples may help illustrate the nature of the dilemma. When President Johnson's economic advisers tried to forecast where the economy was going (and therefore what kinds of macro-policies would be required to sustain non-inflationary full employment), they were confronted with the following problem: The government was spending more on the Vietnam War than it would admit to. On the one hand, the advisers could pretend that the official numbers were correct, thereby recommending a clearly misguided fiscal policy. On the other hand, they could choose not to use the official numbers and instead to use more accurate numbers, but this would violate the "confidences" of government. But maintaining this confidence was in itself morally questionable: in democratic societies, one might argue there is a moral imperative for openness and transparency; after all, a public official is the "servant" of the people and the people have a right to know what the government is doing. A few years later, President Reagan's economic adviser, Marty Feldstein, faced a similar problem: he had long argued for the importance of high national savings; yet Reagan had pushed a tax cut which resulted in huge deficits, potentially undermining the future prosperity of the country. A few economists predicted that, contrary to all the evidence, the tax cut would generate enough growth so that there would not be a deficit. Intellectual honesty would require discussing the absence of evidence for that conclusion, and the risks associated with the high deficits. In this instance, Feldstein took a strong public stand, pointing out the potential adverse consequences of the policy; but in doing so, he undermined the effectiveness of the Council of Economic Advisers within the Reagan Administration.

---

8   The number one person in the IMF recently moved directly from the IMF to take the vice chairmanship of Citibank Group.

I faced a similar dilemma as Chief economist at the World Bank. I believed the policies pursued by the IMF in the wake of the East Asia financial crisis would lead to deeper, longer recessions and depressions than necessary. I believed that the financial interests of the foreign creditors were placed above the concerns for the poor and small businesses. The policies pushed by the IMF, I believed, would almost surely wreck havoc on their lives and livelihoods. I tried quietly within the institutional processes to change the policies, or at least promote open discussion of the policies (given my belief that the errors were so obvious that any open discussion would quickly bring about a reversal of course). But with the great institutional rigidities (and the powerful special interests and their ideologies), I not only could not reverse policies, I could not even engender open discourse. It seemed to me that there was a basic moral issue: how could I remain silent? I felt a strong moral obligation to speak out. At the very least, to point out the risks of these policies?

What should one say about the moral stance of those who worked hard to quash public discussions? They argued that open discussion could undermine confidence in the policies, and the lack of confidence would impede the desired effects. Thus, speaking out was, in their mind, *wrong*, because without the confidence, capital would continue to flow out of the country, and this capital outflow would further weaken the economy, hurting the poor. They were arguing, in effect, not only for a lack of openness and transparency, but for a kind of dishonesty: asserting that the policies were likely to be more effective than the evidence warranted. The dangers of this stance should be obvious: in almost every arena, government could argue that dishonesty, partial truths, are "means" that justify the ends. To be sure, the Treasury or IMF may believe in their case. But the Department of Defense may argue the same thing about every aspect of its activities (from the toxicity of Agent Orange to the true magnitude of the threat of an enemy.) Such positions are not only dangerous and undermine democracy, but are ultimately self-defeating. Repeated assertions of this kind undermine the credibility of government. In the economic arena, they are particularly problematic, because inevitably the predictions will frequently be proven wrong, and the expost excuses always seem absurd; and indeed, that lack of credibility based on its overconfident forecasts itself contributes to the lack of efficacy of the IMF's policies. In the end, this lack of credibility made my decision easier: whether I spoke out or not would have little effect on the confidence in the policy; but speaking out might have some effect on the policy chosen, thereby averting, or at least reducing, the recessionary consequences.

In general, there is no easy answer to these moral dilemmas facing the policy advisor. Each situation is different. A critical judgment is what actions he can undertake that will most likely bring about the actions which he believes are morally right. In some cases, resignation may be the most effective answer; but even when that is contemplated, there is an important issue of timing. A well timed resignation can sometimes bring about change more effectively than any amount of argumentation. The resignation is often seen as a costly move, and as such, the fact that a public official—who has often worked hard to obtain the prominent position—is willing to undertake such a measure provides an effective signal concerning the depth of feeling on the issue.

Ethics and International Economic Policy

I have argued that, while we expect individuals to act by and large in their self interest, there are circumstances in which we say such behavior is *unethical*. So too for countries. We expect countries, by and large, to pursue policies which are in the interests of their citizens. But there are limits, behaviors which are unethical, or border on the unethical. To some, for a rich and powerful country to abrogate its word is simply *real politick:* what can anyone do in retaliation? Some would go further, and say for government officials not to do so would be abrogating their responsibilities to their citizens, whose welfare they are supposed to be maximizing. If they can do so by lying, cheating, or stealing, so be it. Again, one can argue against such behavior on instrumental grounds; in today's world even a powerful country needs the cooperation of others, and if it develops a reputation for mistreating others, for dishonesty, for breaking its words, it will find it more difficult eliciting that cooperation. The lack of trust has even more important consequences in the international arena than in the arena of economics; in economics, legal enforcement mechanisms can provide a partial substitute for trust. In the international arena, that is not the case.

In the following subsections, I want to review several recent issues in international economic policy through the lens of practical ethics. Each of these issues can be approached in other ways, and I do not intend to provide a comprehensive treatment of any of them. I do believe, however, that approaching these issues from the ethical perspective provides new insights—including insights into why it is that some of these issues have taken on such moral overtones.

Debt Forgiveness

Debt forgiveness has become the subject of enormous public discussion. There seems something peculiar about very poor countries transferring money to richer countries year after year. Many countries have to spend a huge fraction of their export earnings to service their debt, leaving little remaining to spend on improving the plight of the poor. The debt overhang impedes growth and poverty reduction. Without debt forgiveness, prospects for these countries are bleak.

Here, I do not want to address the economic issues, but rather the moral issues and dilemmas. There are four, in particular, which have not received sufficient attention. The first concerns *fairness* among developing countries. The amount of resources transferred from the rich to the poor will, in any case, be limited. The question is who will receive these funds? The funds used for debt forgiveness could have been used to aid other needy countries, in particular countries that are equally poor, but had repaid their debt. Is it fair that those who have lived up to the terms of the loan contract should be worse off than those, no better off in a fundamental sense, who do not?

The second issue revolves around the moral responsibility of the lenders. Consider loans made to Mobutu in his hey day. The lenders knew of his corruption. They knew that the money would not go to the people in the country. At best, it was Cold War lending, pure and simple; at worst, it was lending to ensure that Western companies could continue to exploit the rich natural resources. Why should the people of the Congo—who had no say in the choice of Mobutu as their leader—have to pay for the money that was given to and squandered by

Mobutu. Doesn't the moral responsibility lie with the lender? (Such debts have come to be called *otiose* debts, with many critics of the lending policies suggesting that there is no *moral* obligation on the part of the debtor to repay the debt, and that there is a moral obligation on the part of the creditor to forgive the debt.)

This seems like an easy case, where the moral responsibility of the lenders cannot be avoided. But there are cases that might seem slightly more problematic. Consider the 1998 IMF loan to Russia. There, there was an elected government, though one for which there was considerable evidence of corruption. It was perfectly clear at the time that Russia's exchange rate was overvalued; the overvalued exchange rate was having an adverse effect on their economy; the IMF imposed contractionary policies (part of the conditionalities imposed for assistance) caused a deep plunge in their economy leading to enormous increases in poverty (from 2% under the previous regime, to almost 50% by 1998); and the policies of privatization and free capital outflows which the Fund also had pushed led to a few oligarchs accumulating huge amounts of wealth. Should the IMF have lent billions of dollars to the country; knowing full well that there was a high likelihood that the funds would simply enable a few oligarchs to take more money out of the country; knowing that it would saddle the country with increased indebtedness; knowing that the poor taxpayers would eventually have to pay back; knowing that in any case it was unlikely to facilitate the resumption of growth (and indeed, by sustaining the exchange rate at an overvalued level, actually had an adverse effect on growth)? And if the IMF did lend the country money, and if the money then was, in effect, used to enable oligarchs to take more of their wealth out of the country at more favorable terms, and if the economic polices failed, what is the moral obligation of the citizens of the country to repay the loan, or of the Fund to forgive the loan? What is the moral responsibility for their misguided advice, for their complicity in providing funds where there was such a high likelihood of abuse?

The third issue concerns the nature of the debt contract, and the advice given to the countries. In well functioning capital markets, the risk associated with any contract is divided among the parties, with the party most able to bear the risk bearing the risk disproportionately. But capital markets do not work as well in practice as they do in theory. It is the developing countries that bear the brunt of the risks associated with exchange rate and interest rate changes, and it is large changes in exchange rates and interest rates that have led many of the countries to their current predicament. The international financial institutions, of course, have the opportunity—I might say the obligation—to design contracts which reflect an appropriate sharing the risk burden; but they have failed to do so. And they have failed, in many cases, to advice the country of the risks associated with the borrowing policies which they recommended. For instance, prior to the Russian 1998 crisis the IMF advised Russia to borrow in dollars, seemingly because the interest rate was lower. But the IMF, of all institutions, believes in well functioning markets and should have also pointed out that if markets were working well, then the differences in interest rates (between the dollar and ruble rates) reflected the risk of exchange rate change, and that if Russia did borrow more in dollars, the consequences in the event of a devaluation (which at the time seemed highly likely) would be very severe. The *moral* weight for debt forgiveness seems greater because of these poorly designed contracts and the incomplete, and in some cases, misguided advice.

The fourth relates to the issue of conflicts of interest that I raised earlier in this essay. One of the functions of the large bail-out loans has been to provide funds with which Western banks can be repaid. There are potential conflicts of interest (at the individual[9] and organizational level[10]): much of the benefits to these loans are workers, and others remaining within the country. *Ethical* advice and lending practice would require that this be pointed out. When there has not been adequate disclosure, what is the *moral* obligation of the borrower to repay? Of the lender to forgive?

Ethical issues associated with repaying debts, and debt enforcement, are longstanding, and complicated. Over time, there has clearly been a change in ethical views. Debtor prisons were employed in the nineteenth century in Britain. Most people today would view such treatment as cruel punishment, *unethical*, no matter how strong the incentives for repayment it provides. Similarly, bonded labor, sometimes used as a debt enforcement mechanism in developing countries, is not only illegal in most countries, it is also unethical, a step away from slavery. For a country to march into another to enforce a debt contract too would today be viewed as unethical, though it occurred several times in the nineteenth century. At the individual level, usurious interest rates and the imposition of other "conditions" associated with loan sharking are viewed as unethical. The extensive conditionalities imposed by the IMF in the context of the loans to countries in desperate need for funds raise similar questions: when do such conditionalities represent an abuse of power, and in that sense are unethical? These are questions I will briefly touch upon later.

Providing Loans

In approaching the problem of whether to give a country a loan, a simple question needs to be posed: will the country, as a whole, be better off with the loan than without it, taking into account that it will be more indebted? If there is a reasonable chance that the country will be worse off, the *moral* case (as well as the economic case) is questionable. The incentives of the *lending institution and its staff* and the incentives of the borrowing *government* may differ markedly from these *moral* dictates. The government may feel that the money may give it a chance to survive; if the money fails to work, it will be someone else's problem. To return to the IMF loan to Russia, one of the arguments for giving the money was that it would enhance the survival of Yeltsin, viewed as a friend of the IMF and the US; more to the point, the downfall of Yeltsin would be seen as a failure of IMF and U.S. Treasury policy. The incentives of the IMF and the US Treasury did not necessarily, in this sense, coincide with the interests of Russia, though to be sure, the IMF and U.S. Treasury might have thought that they were in a better position to make the appropriate political judgments than were the voters in Russia. (The discrepancy between individual and organizational incentives has been emphasized in the organizational literature; for instance, the theory of escalating commitment points out that the cost to an individual of abandoning a strategy that he has advocated may be greater than the cost to the organization.)

---

9   That is, many of those responsible for making the loans have, and will have, connections with the financial institutions being bailed out.

10   That is, finance ministries (U.S. Treasury) and central banks, with close ties to the financial community, in the advanced industrial countries—the lenders—are responsible for the lending decisions.

To provide another example: in the recent Argentina debacle, at the time of the August 2001 loan, even IMF Board members were skeptical that the money was going to make any difference. The country would be left more in debt, but the likelihood that it would enable the country to survive for more than a few months without a major default or devaluation was slim. It could conceivably be viewed, however, in the interests of the Deputy managing director, who was about to depart. Not lending would have precipitated a crisis then and there, and it would have made apparent, that the policies he had pushed had been a dramatic failure. If there was even a small chance that the program might work, his policies might be vindicated. If they failed, he did not bear the costs: it was the people in the country that bore the increased indebtedness. So cynical had some of the Board members become at this juncture that they talked about the $8 billion as a going away present for the departing deputy managing director; the money was likely to hold things together until he left the Fund, sparing him the immediate embarrassment, but not much longer.

In short, there are reasons to believe that the interests of the borrowing government and lending institution (IMF) may differ markedly from those of the people in the country. The IMF and its staff would like to persuade others that they are unlike other public and private institutions; while they recognize the role of rent seeking and distorted incentives especially in governmental institutions, they themselves believe that they are immune from such distortions. There is little in the way of theory or evidence to support such a view. When money was lent to a country for reasons other than promoting the development of the country (e.g. to maintain friendship with the ruling government in the Cold War) the ethical case for debt forgiveness is enhanced; the moral obligation for repayment is reduced.

So far, I have emphasized the consequence that there are numerous instances in which loans have been given when they arguably should not have been, raising ethical issues about repayment. There are similar issues, circumstances in which one might argue that loans should be given, but the money is withheld, or conditions are imposed, taking advantage of the weakened position of the borrower. Ecuador provides a possible example. Providing money at a critical stage to a country facing a liquidity crisis because of a series of adverse shocks, including low oil prices, a weak agricultural position because of el niño, and a disease affecting shrimp, one of its major export crops (because of its oil reserves, its long term financial position was more positive) would have made economic sense and would have been the *ethical* thing to do. It might have enabled the survival of a democratically elected government. But the IMF had been extensively criticized for large bail outs; there was pressure for a policy of "bail-ins"—private sector participation. It was too risky to try this new strategy on rich and powerful countries like Brazil and Russia; weak countries like Romania and Ecuador were chosen for the experiment, with adverse consequences for both.

Developed Countries' Trade Policy

The riots in Seattle brought home the extent of dissatisfaction with the way that international trade negotiations have been conducted, and are likely to be conducted in the future. The agenda had been set by the rich and powerful countries, to reflect vested interests in their countries. And the outcomes had reflected their economic power. Indeed, by one calculation, Sub Saharan Africa was actually worse off after the Uruguay round of trade negotiations (which was completed in 1994) than before. The United States pushed for liberalization of financial services and information technology and for more extensive protection of intellectual property. It was less concerned about other services, such as marine and construction, or even the potential adverse effects of the rigid enforcement of intellectual property on those in the developing countries whose lives depended on the availability of cheap drugs. In trade negotiations with Korea (and other countries), it pushed for rapid financial and capital market liberalization, knowing full well the risks which those policies imposed on the country.[11] The welfare of the US financial community was put above the welfare of the developing countries' workers. In dragging its feet in negotiations leading up to the admission of China to the WTO, the United States went so far as to argue that China was not a developing country—though the World Bank (and every other international agency) classifies it as such.

At one level, it is natural for a country to pursue its own interests. But, as I asked earlier, at what point does this pursuit of a country's own interest (or, as is more frequently the case, special interests within one's country) at the expense of the poor, become a *moral* issue?

There is one aspect of these discussions that particularly troubles me *as an economic adviser*: when the arguments used for the US position border on hypocrisy and dishonesty. For instance, while the US (and the IMF) lectured developing countries on the evils of subsidies and the virtues of free trade, Western governments maintained huge subsides and trade barriers in agriculture, the areas of comparative advantage for many developing countries. The US and Europe accused others of dumping—and under that ruse created new trade barriers— even though few economists would characterize what the countries were doing as dumping. Would it not have been better to have been more honest and forthright, to admit that political pressures at home forced us to have policies which were hard to justify?

Global Externalities: The Global Environment

We teach our children early on that it is *wrong* to litter. This is an example of an *externality*, an action by one individual that affects others and for which they do not bear the costs. Government policies are designed to limit the extent of externalities, but they are imperfect: social control mechanisms—a sense of what is right and wrong, *ethical* presuppositions—are more effective. The actions of those in one country similarly have effects on others, and given the absence or weaknesses of international law, there is a need for reliance on ethical norms. For instance, it is wrong for a country to locate a garbage dump on its boundary so that the downward wind pollutes the air of its neighbor.

The realization that we all share the same planet, that its resources are limited, and that bad policies can squander those resources, leaving future generations at risk, has come about only slowly. There is now general recognition of the *dangers* of global warming, and the Rio and Kyoto conventions are testimony to this global concern. But there is a deeply troubling aspect of the framework of these conventions. It is based on cutbacks in current emission levels. It is hard to detect an underlying principle of equity: the developed countries seem to have the right to pollute more than the less developed countries (on a per capita basis) simply because

---

11 This policy was pushed by the US Treasury, even though the Council of Economic Advisers not only warned about the risks imposed by the policy and the dubious benefits to the country, but also argued that there were few benefits to the US as a whole; the policy was another example of special interests having sway.

they have polluted more in the past. Is there any moral justification for such a policy? There are alternative frameworks, involving for instance agreements to undertake common policies (e.g. universal taxes on carbon emissions) that would seem to have a stronger ethical basis.

The ethical stance of the United States, the largest emitter of greenhouse gases, both on a per capita basis and absolutely) is even harder to comprehend. It claims that it need not do anything because the developing countries have not bound themselves to doing anything, even though the build-up of greenhouse gases is largely due to the advanced industrial countries, and even though, were they to make a commitment not to emit at levels that exceed that of the United States on a per capita basis, it will be decades before that constraint will be binding.

Intergenerational Equity, the Environment, Population Policy

There are moral dimensions not only of how we treat others who are alive today, but also how we treat future generations. By using up natural resources, without leaving compensating endowments of physical capital, we leave future generations more impoverished. This violates principles of intergenerational *equity* or *social justice*. Many developing countries today are exploiting their limited natural resources, without adequate provisions for the future. There are accounting frameworks (green accounting) that are designed to encourage better intergenerational equity. Governments should be encouraged not only to use such accounting frameworks, but to set aside funds or to invest in physical and human capital.

Perhaps the most important determinant of environmental degradation (including that related to carbon emissions) is population growth. Population growth imposes a wide variety of externalities (a point recognized long ago by Edgeworth [1888][12]). Countries with high rates of population growth have a hard time increasing incomes (per capita), and thus face a greater prospect of increasing poverty. Indeed, in the last decade of the last century, in the race between improving standards of living and population growth, the latter won: while the percentage of the population in poverty fell, the absolute number of people living in absolute poverty increased. Those with large families not only have a hard time feeding their children (and childhood malnutrition has lifelong effects), but they cannot afford to educate them, thereby condemning another generation to poverty and suffering. We now have the means of controlling population. I would argue that there is a *moral* obligation for governments to pursue such policies.

Crises

Earlier, I briefly alluded to the moral dilemmas I saw when confronting the global financial crisis. I do not want to address here the problem of parsing out "blame" for the crisis and the failed management of the crisis. I want to focus on the *ethics* of international advice and assistance. To be sure, policies within the affected countries did contribute to the crisis: corruption and inadequate financial regulation played their part. But that is not the issue. The issue is how to intervene in the crisis in ways that minimize the damage, particularly to the

---

12 See Edgeworth, "Mathematical Theory of Banking", Journal of Royal Statistical Society, 1888.

poor, providing at the same time the foundations for correcting the underlying problems. The IMF failed to do this.[13]

The interests of foreign creditors were put ahead of the concerns for the workers and small businesses, with devastating effects, from soaring unemployment to plummeting wages. These parties were innocent bystanders; it was not their borrowing that had led to the crisis. Food subsidies for the poor were cut, just when they were most needed. The political and social unrest—with many people dying—was predictable, and predicted. What is the moral responsibility for those who push for the policies that had such disastrous consequences? Especially when their prior advice, encouraging, even demanding rapid capital market liberalization was probably the single most important factor contributing to the occurrence of the crisis in the first place? And, even more so, when the policies put forward fail to have the predicted outcomes, the IMF and the U.S. Treasury shifted blame to the country—and in doing so contributed further to investor flight. As Jeffrey Sachs pointed out, it was like crying fire in a crowded theater. Doing so not only is bad economic policy, and an abuse of the trust and confidence placed in the institutions. It is arguably a fundamentally *immoral* act, just as crying fire in a crowded theatre—and knowing that doing so might generate a riot and needless death—would be an immoral act. These are questions that all too seldom have been raised within the international institutions or the governments which dominate their policies. But they are the questions which are increasingly being asked by ordinary citizens both in the Third World and in the more advanced industrial countries.

The governments in power, which acquiesced in those policies, bear some responsibility, but they often view themselves as having no choice—and were told that they did not in effect have any choice. The outside advisers did have a choice in the advice they prescribed. Indeed, there was controversy about the appropriateness of different policies. Thus, the issue is not whether the affected countries themselves and their governments bear some responsibility; they do. Rather, my concern here is the moral culpability of the IMF, which it has yet to recognize.

I want to briefly refer to several of the ethical dimensions of the IMF's behavior. First, in providing its advice, the advisers did not act *honestly* in conveying the risks and uncertainties and in presenting the range of alternatives. Secondly, there is the issue of the trade-off between devaluations and interest rate increases, and moral issues concerning *responsibility.* The IMF held that only by increasing interest rates could they forestall further declines in the exchange rate. In fact, the high interest rate policies were ineffective in forestalling the decline in the

---

13 The IMF has claimed that the quick recovery of several of the countries affected by the global crisis is proof that its medicine works. A closer look at the pattern of recoveries does not support this conclusion, as I argue elsewhere. The country that has been the most assiduous follower of the IMF prescriptions, Thailand, still has a GDP below the pre-crisis level, and almost 40% of loans are non-performing. Malaysia had a quick recovery, but never had an IMF program. Indonesia is still in a deep recession, partly attributable to the riots that were inspired by the failed IMF policies, partly attributable to the fact that those policies led to massive bankruptcies, from which the country has yet to recover, and partly due to the strategy of restructuring the financial system led to runs which undermined the entire private banking system. Korea's recovery in part was due to the fact that it did not listen to the IMF at key points: had it followed their advice in disposing of the so-called excess capital in the chip industry, it would have missed out on the global turnaround in that market that fueled the recovery. The growth in Russia and Brazil was because of the devaluations, which the IMF policies only delayed.

exchange rate, and may have actually contributed to it; by helping deepen the recession/ depression, capital was induced to flee, rather than attracted into the country. But this mistake in economic judgment[14] should not be confused with the deeper moral issue. At the root of the crisis in several of the countries was excessive borrowing abroad. Those borrowing could have, and most economists would say, should have obtained "cover" (effectively insurance) against a change in the exchange rate. No government guarantees its exchange rate; and there is no such thing as fixed exchange rates. Exchange rates change; the only difference in regimes concerns the frequency, magnitude, and more generally the rules that govern those changes. The market was, in effect, telling borrowers that there was a risk of devaluation (in equilibrium, the difference in interest rates at home and abroad is equal to the expected rate of change of the exchange rate, plus a risk premium). The stance of the IMF, once the crisis occurred, was to bail-out those who had gambled on the exchange rate not changing (who had not bought cover), at the expense of the innocent bystanders. In a sense, those who *caused* the crisis, by borrowing excessively abroad short term, were let off the hook (at least partially), at the expense of those who were only engaged in normal business borrowing. Put this way, the bail-out raises disturbing moral issues, beside the broader *moral hazard* issues that have been extensively discussed (the pattern of IMF inspired bail-outs reduce the incentive of those borrowing abroad to obtain cover.)

Growth and Poverty Reduction Strategies

Today, everyone pays obeisance to the importance of reducing poverty. The IMF changed the name of its program for developing countries from ESAF to incorporate the words "poverty and growth." Trickle down economics—whereby one justifies programs that make the rich still richer but arguing that the benefits eventually trickle down to the poor—is no longer in fashion. But putting rhetoric aside, there is an active debate concerning economic policies. The position of the US Treasury and the IMF can be characterized as "trickle down plus": growth is necessary and almost sufficient for reducing poverty, and subsequently the best strategy for helping the poor is to adopt growth maximizing reforms—the same neoliberal agenda, with its emphasis on privatization and liberalization, that prevailed over the past two decades, augmented by education and health. The modifications in the traditional formula represent important steps in the right direction. But the underlying prescription is faulty in several respects. The fact of the matter is that the countries that have been most successful

---

14 There were other mistakes in economic judgment: the IMF concluded (without deep empirical work) that allowing the exchange rate to fall would harm the economy more than letting interest rates rise. In fact, in several countries, this was almost surely not the case. For instance in Thailand, those who borrowed abroad were the real estate firms (and those who had lent to them), who were already dead, in the wake of the collapse of the real estate bubble, and for whom a further fall in the exchange rate would have had little effect (though it may adversely affect the amount that foreign creditors could obtain); and exporters, who would gain as much in earnings as they would lose on their balance sheet. Perhaps the reason that they did not go into a close empirical evaluation of the effects was that that was not really their concern; they were more focused on the impact of the countries' ability to repay the loans to their creditors. But this change in mandate from the purposes for which the institution was created—to help sustain a country in the face of a threatened downturn—and this obfuscation of the true objective of the policy (if correct) is itself deeply troubling, and raises moral issues.

in development over the past half a century—the countries of East Asia-- have not followed the Washington consensus policies. And many of the countries that have followed the Washington consensus policies have not done particularly well (though the "doctor" claims that the prescriptions were not followed sufficiently closely). *Honesty* should have dictated full disclosure: the evidence in favor of the Washington consensus policies is at best mixed; and failing to provide such honesty *raises* moral issues.[15]

But perhaps more important, *concern for the poor* should have dictated greater attention to the consequences of the policies for poor, and an awareness that the countries that have done the best job of reduce illustrate what I have in mind:

- The countries that have done best in improving the plight of the poor have had an explicitly pro-poor growth strategy that goes beyond simply paying lip service to education and health.
- Unless the poor are given assets—as in land reform—they are likely to remain mired in poverty. But land reform may challenge vested interests. It is curious that while those who currently own large amounts of wealth in many of the poor countries acquired this wealth in ways that have little legitimacy (e.g. through the exercise of brute force by colonial masters), taking wealth away from these individuals is viewed as an abrogation of basic values of "property rights."
- The disparity between the ownership of resources (like land) and labor results in institutions, like sharecropping, which lead to attenuated incentives and reduced output. Under sharecropping, tenant farmers face in effect a tax rate of 50% (or more). While the IMF speaks out strongly against high tax rates, and their enervating effects on effort, it has not spoken out as strongly in favor of a land reform which reduces these agency problems, and increases economic efficiency at the same time that it increases equity.
- Some of the economic reforms advocated by the IMF and the US Treasury have dubious effects on growth, but increase the country's vulnerability to shocks. (Capital market liberalization represents the most obvious example.) It is the poor who inevitably bear the brunt of the downturns, regardless of the lip-service paid to the importance of creating safety nets. Honesty would require observing that even in the most developed countries, safety nets for farmers and the self-employed are inadequate.
- But even the benefits of trade liberalization become more questionable, unless accompanied by measures that enable the creation of new enterprises and jobs; but IMF packages often have accompanied trade liberalization measures by high interest rates that would make job creation a virtual impossibility, even in a well functioning market economy. The point is a simple one: trade liberalization often leads to a loss of jobs. The free market ideology argues that this enables a flow of resources from less efficient uses to more efficient uses. Were that the case! The problem is that in many less developed countries markets do not work well (that is part and parcel of being less developed). Unemployment rates are high. Job creation is difficult. Moving

---

15 Interestingly, in the 1996 World Development Report: "From Plan to Market" on transition, the most successful transition—that of China—is given short shrift, being relegated largely to "boxes." Was this because its success—including its success in reducing poverty—ran so counter to the prevailing orthodoxy?

labor from low productivity jobs to unemployment decreases a country's GDP and increases poverty. But often, that is precisely the effect of IMF packages combining liberalization with high interest rates.

- And even if the country is successful in creating new jobs, the poor may be adversely affected, because greater openness can lead to greater sensitivity to shocks from the outside world, the brunt of which is borne by the poor. Insecurity is one of the major problems facing the poor, and policies that increase that sense of insecurity adversely affect the plight of the poor.
- Privatization programs have often had adverse effects, particularly on the poor. The rapid privatization programs have led to privatization of monopolies, without regulatory oversight; and these monopolies, while they may or may not have proven more efficient in production, have sometimes proven more efficient in exploiting consumers. Privatization has proven an important vehicle for both corruption and increasing inequality, a point brought out forcefully by the experiences in Russia. Indeed, one of the incentives for rapid privatization there was that those that received state assets at below market value then made a contribution (not just in terms of finance, but also in terms of the even more valuable organizational support and media coverage) to support Yeltsin's reelection. The silence in the face of the corrupt loans-for-share deal spoke loudly: the means justifies the end!
- The IMF has taken a particularly narrow (and peculiar) definition of good budgetary policy, in which foreign aid is not included, or discounted, as a revenue source. The alleged reason for this is that foreign aid is volatile, and therefore cannot be counted upon. The World Bank analyzed this allegation, and showed that tax revenues were even more volatile. Hence, according to Fund logic, tax revenues should not be included in revenues either, in which case no country is in budgetary balance! More to the point, the appropriate response to volatile income flows is flexible expenditures. Countries build new schools and health clinics as they receive the money; when the aid stops, so does the construction. In long discussions with the Fund, I have never seen an adequate justification for the Fund's stance. But the consequences should be clear. It means that an increase in foreign aid may not result in more schools or health clinics, only more money going to the country's reserves.

The economics of these policies has long been debated, both within the economics profession and within civil society. My point in raising these issues is not to rehearse that debate, but to emphasize the moral dimension. The budgetary stance of the Fund means that fewer schools and clinics are built, to the detriment of the poor. This and the other policies described above increase the risks faced by the poor. In some cases, such as capital market liberalization, these policies seem of questionable benefit to the country as a whole, though they might bring benefit to the financial communities both within the country or, more likely, abroad. But there have been sins of omission as well as commission: land reform would have arguably increased both equity and efficiency.

In retrospect, as we look back at the colonial policies, at the unfair trade treaties foisted on Japan, at the Opium Wars, we shudder at their seeming lack of moral justification. We look with derision at writings describing the White Man's Burden, especially in light of the legacy that was left in Africa and in so many other places in the colonial world. We no longer use military power to open markets, but the advanced industrial countries do use their economic power. They use their economic power to forge international agreements where a disproportionate part of the benefits accrue to the developed countries, and in which in some cases, the less developed countries are even worse off. In this section, I have asked whether the same objections raised to colonialism could, in fact, be applied to the economic policies foisted on these countries. Even when they help the poor, are there alternative policies which might have helped them even more, or which would have imposed less risk on them? Have the international institutions that have pushed these policies been honest in portraying these risks? Have they been dishonest in exaggerating the evidence concerning their economic benefits? (Certainly, the benefits promised from economic reform in Russia have far exceeded what has been delivered. Poverty rates have increased, in a short span of 10 years, from 2% to almost 50%!) Perhaps we should ask, will our children's children look at current economic relationships with the same shock—the same sense of moral outrage with which we look at the colonial experience. The experiences in Seattle and Washington, and extensive conversations with young people around the world, suggest that we may not have to wait for these reactions: the youth of today are questioning the moral legitimacy of these policies. The defenders of these policies claim there is no alternative; there is a single recipe for success. In this they are wrong, and if there was a single *best* recipe, the countries which have succeeded in simultaneously growing and reducing poverty would have given credence to the view that it is not the one that the international institutions have prescribed, with their inadequate attention to democratic, equitable, and sustainable development.

A General Perspective

Ethics has to do with an individual's relationship with other individuals, with the community and with society more broadly. Ethics involves the recognized moral rules required to live together in wellfunctioning communities. It is *wrong* to murder or assault or otherwise cause harm to another. But in modern societies harm to others can be done in a variety of ways— when an individual litters, he harms the environment, and hence injures the well being of anyone who values the environment. Simple maxims such as "do unto others as you would have them do unto you" or "don't do unto others as you would not have them do unto you" and touchstones such as Kant's categorical imperative provide widely accepted guidelines, though to be sure, the world is complex enough that the application in particular circumstances may not be obvious, or even unambiguous. Earlier, we observed that from today's vantage point, we look upon slavery with abhorrence, and colonialism—and the colonial mentality—too is viewed as a violation of basic ethical norms. But is one man's—or one country's—imposition of his will on another, by force of economic power more acceptable than an imposition by force of military power? In the nineteenth century, the two were often intertwined, with military power being used to enforce economic obligations. Today, matters are, perhaps, more subtle, but does this make them any more acceptable? In ordinary life, it would be viewed as a breach of ethical norms to take advantage of an individual's temporary misfortune, but at the international level, this is sometimes seen as simply the natural state of affairs. Should the imposition of conditions on the countries that needed finance in the last global crisis— conditions that were unrelated to the crisis, or to the repayment of the loan—be considered a breach of ethical norms? Even if it is (at least from the perspective of the party imposing the conditions) for the own good of the other party?

Many ethical precepts are concerned with actions that undermine "community." The development process, no matter how well it is carried on, typically undermines some traditional values, some aspects of traditional culture. But if carried on in the wrong way, it can have a devastating effect. The way that the transition from Communism to a market economy was carried on in Russia has been a disaster, by any account, with poverty soaring (as we have noted, to the point where close to half of the population is in poverty) and output falling, while a few people have garnered huge riches. No wonder that there has been a complete erosion in the sense of community, in basic norms of behavior, matched by the growth of "mafia" activity. Economists have begun to talk about these ideas in terms of the concept of social capital. One of the reasons for the difference between China's successful transition and Russia's failure is the relative preservation of social capital in the former, and its destruction in the latter.[16] But we also know that economic policies play a critical role: transitions accomplished through Bolshevik means, or with Bolshevik speed, or with the Bolshevik lack of concern for building social consensus, are more likely to lead to an erosion of social capital. In the case of Russia, the rapid privatizations helped erode what little social capital was left over from the Communist reign: they resulted in a few individuals seizing control of vast assets formerly owned by the State, with free capital mobility almost inviting them to take their illbegotten gains abroad, while the State claimed it did not have enough resources even to pay pensions.

We often talk about the "social contract." The social contract is never formally written down, but that does not mean that it can nonetheless still be broken, or be perceived to be broken. Hyperinflation is widely criticized because it undermines the social contract. What happened in Russia has been widely viewed within as a violation of the social contract. While the IMF argued during the midst of the global financial crisis that not repaying creditors was a violation of the sanctity of contracts, even though bankruptcy is a central institution in capitalism, they seemed to pay little attention to the violation of an even more important contract, the social contract; and one can view the disastrous consequences in Indonesia as partially a reflection of this breach of contract.

If, as a result of the erosion of the social contract, there is a weakening of social cohesion, in ways which lead to more violence, more corruption, more crime, what is the culpability of those who have contributed to this evisceration of social capital? To what extent should they be held *morally* responsible for the consequences, especially when these consequences are the predictable—if not inevitable, at least highly likely—result of their actions?

I am raising here some fundamental issues: earlier, I argued that economic policies are often pursued, with too little attention to their effect on the poor, to the sense of security. This, I suggest is a violation of basic ethical precepts. But economic policies are even less concerned with their impact on the community, on traditional social safety nets and traditional relationships. "Flexible labor markets" mean that employers should feel free to discharge workers as soon as they are not needed; there is no moral obligation to see workers through

---

16 See Hussein, Stern, and Stiglitz, "Chinese Reforms from a Comparative Perspective," *Incentives, Organization, and Public Economics: Papers in Honour of Sir James Mirrlees*, Peter J. Hammond and Gareth D. Myles (eds.), Oxford University Press, 2000, pp. 243–277.

the hard times. Any policy that undermines the sense of community, social norms, a country's culture and pride, can, from this perspective, be viewed as a violation of ethical principles.

Individual and Institutional Responsibility

The thesis that I have advanced so far is that policies towards and within developing countries can be looked at from an ethical perspective, in terms of how they comport with basic precepts of moral behavior; and so too can the behavior of those who are called upon to provide advice to developing countries. In these terms, we have seen that many of the actions undertaken by governments and recommended by outsiders, including the IMF, do not fare well. There have been large—and some might argue, unnecessarily large—adverse consequences for the poor. I have not spoken here of the full toll which, for instance, the way the Asia crisis was handled by the IMF has had. It was not only that poverty increased, but the cutbacks in social and health expenditures, say, in Thailand exacerbated the economic downturn, led to an increase in AIDS, and the poverty itself led to an increase in childhood prostitution.

In American jurisprudence, in many states, there is the principle of contributory negligence. All parties that had a role in the adverse outcome are held, in part, responsible. Similar issues arise in the realm of ethics. To be sure, the governments made the final decision about what policies were to be pursued. But the governments were often pushed to undertake the policies by the IMF, and felt that they had little room for maneuver. Here, we do not have to parse the "blame." What we can say unambiguously is that the IMF and others who supported and especially those like the US Treasury who pushed those policies, bear considerable moral culpability for the outcomes.

In the Holocaust, the world also came to an understanding that those who stand idly by when they see others commit (what they view as potentially) heinous acts also bear a certain moral responsibility. The institutions in our society that are the guardians of our morals have an especial responsibility for taking up these issues. This is particularly important given the inadequacies in our system of global governance, where the voices of the poor and the voices of poor countries are barely heard, even in matters that affect their lives and livelihoods, where democratic principles are systematically ignored. The good news is that throughout the world today, there is a growing recognition of the importance of these issues. It is an opportune time for those with moral authority to raise their voices and join the chorus of the concerned.

Concluding Remarks

The past half-century has shown that with growth, development is possible, but far from inevitable. It has shown too that growth with poverty reduction is possible, but it is far from easy. There are a host of ongoing policy debates about the best way to pursue poverty reduction and growth. My concern in this paper has not been to rehearse that debate—though inevitably I have had to touch on some of the more controversial issues—but to suggest that there are dimensions of that debate which can usefully be looked at from a *moral* dimensions, from precepts concerning such values as honesty, fairness, and a concern for the poor. Some might argue that such language speaks to the heart, and not just the head. But I would argue that decisions about public policies inevitably need to speak both to the heart and the head, that it is important to think deep and hard about the moral dimensions of our economic decisions, and that one can, and indeed one should, combine this kind of moral analysis with a hard headed analysis of the consequences and risks associated with alternative policies. Indeed, the lack of a moral demand to do so has all too often allowed ideology to have sway—an ideology that dishonestly claims more favorable and more certain benefits than the evidence would support, an ideology that suppresses meaningful democratic discussions of alternative courses of action, and that ignores, or at least puts insufficient weight, on the adverse consequences to the poor. Thus, I see the new humanism as a complement to hard economic reasoning, not antithetical to it; and I see the two working together as holding the greatest promise for a future international economic order based on social justice.

[27]

Autonomy-Respecting Assistance: Toward An Alternative Theory of Development Assistance

David Ellerman
University of California at Riverside
david@ellerman.org

Abstract   The purpose of this paper is outline an alternative theory of development assistance by analyzing the old strategies for technical cooperation, capacity-building and, in broader terms, development assistance in a way that will point to new strategies. The perspective is the very old idea that the best form of assistance is to *help people help themselves*. The problem is how can the helpers supply help that actually furthers rather than overrides or undercuts the goal of the doers helping themselves? This problem of supplying help to self-help, "assisted self-reliance" or assisted autonomy, is the *fundamental conundrum* of development assistance. The forms of help that override or undercut people's capacity to help themselves will be called "unhelpful help." These two overriding and undercutting forms of unhelpful help are analyzed and strategies for autonomy-respecting help are presented. Moreover the volitional and cognitive sides of development assistance are given separate but parallel treatment.

Keywords: development assistance, unhelpful help, social engineering, benevolent help, autonomy-respecting assistance, volitional and cognitive aspects

INTRODUCTION AND OVERVIEW

Development Assistance As Helping People Help Themselves

The purpose of this paper is to analyze the old strategies for technical cooperation, capacity-building and, in broader terms, development assistance in a way that will point to new strategies. There is an emerging consensus that the old strategies have failed in general—and nowhere is the failure more acute than in Africa. It is time to rethink development assistance from the ground up.

The perspective developed is the very old idea that the best form of assistance is to *help people help themselves* (see Ellerman forthcoming). We are all familiar with the ancient Chinese saying that if you give people fish, you feed them for a day, but if you teach them how to fish—or rather, if you help them learn how to fish—they can feed themselves for a lifetime.

The Helper – Doer Relationship

Development assistance is analyzed as a relationship between those offering assistance in some form, the helper or helpers, and those receiving the assistance, the doer or doers.[1] The helpers could be individuals, NGOs, or official bilateral or multilateral development agencies, and the doers could be individuals, organizations or various levels of government in the developing countries. The relationship is the helper-doer relationship.

The Fundamental Conundrum of Development Assistance

The assumed goal is transformation towards autonomous development on the part of the doers, with the doers helping themselves. The problem is how can the helpers supply help that actually furthers rather than overrides or undercuts the goal of the doers helping themselves? This is actually a conundrum. This paradox of supplying help to self-help, "assisted self-reliance"[2] or assisted autonomy, is the *fundamental conundrum* of development assistance. Over the years, the debates about aid, assistance and capacity-building keep circling around and around this basic conundrum.

Unhelpful Help: Social Engineering and Benevolent Aid

There are many strategies for development assistance that may supply help in some form but actually do not help people help themselves. The forms of help that override or undercut people's capacity to help themselves will be called "unhelpful help."

There are essentially two ways that the helper's will can supplant the doer's will to thwart autonomy and self-help:

---

1 Doing includes thinking; "doer" is not juxtaposed to "thinker." Instead, doers actively undertaking tasks are juxtaposed to the passive recipients of aid, teaching or technical assistance.

2 The phrase is from Uphoff (1998: 19). David Korten terms it the "central paradox of social development: the need to exert influence over people for the purpose of building their capacity to control their own lives" (1983: 220). See also Chapter 8 of Fisher (1993) on the "central paradox of social development."

AUTONOMY-RESPECTING ASSISTANCE

(1) The helper, by social engineering, deliberately tries to impose his will on the doer; or

(2) The helper, by benevolent aid, replaces the doer's will with her will through a dependency relationship, perhaps inadvertently.

"Override" or "undercut" are shorthand terms for these two conceptually distinct yin-and-yang forms of unhelpful help (which may be combined, as when benevolence hides the desire to control).[3]

The Volitional and Cognitive Dimensions of Help

All human action has both a cognitive side and a motivational (or volitional) side.[4] It is useful to parse the analysis of assistance (helpful or unhelpful) into the cognitive and volitional dimensions. Since there seem to be two forms of unhelpful help plus a positive notion of autonomy-respecting help each of which has the two dimensions of help, we have a 3×2 table to map out the forms of help.

The following six sections explain the six boxes in this 3×2 table.

THE VOLITIONAL DIMENSION OF SOCIAL ENGINEERING

The "overriding" form of unhelpful help is a type of social engineering. If we use the metaphor of the doers as trying to work their way through a maze, then the helpers as social engineers perceive themselves as helicoptering over the maze, seeing the path to the goal, and supplying instructions (knowledge) along with carrots and sticks (incentives) to override the doers' own motivation and push the doers in the right direction. The helpers supply a set of blueprint instructions about what the doers should be doing, and they offer motivation to follow this blueprint through various forms of aid to override the doers' own motivations. In the end, this strategy of assistance fails because both the motivation and the knowledge are external to the doers and attempt to override the autonomy of the doers.

---

3 In Albert Memmi's work on dependence (1984), he found essentially the same two forms of an unhelpful helper-doer relationship. In the social engineering case, the "helper" is the dominator or colonizer while the "doer" is the subjugated one or the colonized. In the case of "oppressive benevolence" (to use John Dewey's phrase), the "helper" is the provider and the "doer" is the dependent.

4 In cognition, the idea is to get one's representation of the world to correspond with the world, while in volitional action, the idea is to get the actual state of affairs to correspond to some intended or desired state. As Marx noted, there is both "describing the world" and "changing the world." In biology, organisms have sensory (afferent) and motor (efferent) systems.

Table 1: Three modes of help X Two dimensions of help

Help	Volitional dimension	Cognitive dimension
Unhelpful help #1: social engineering	Helper providing "motivation" for doer to do the "right thing" (aid and conditionalities as "carrots and sticks")	Helper as authority teaching "answers" to passive doer (learner) like "pouring water into a pitcher."
Unhelpful help #2: benevolent aid	Helper provides aid to doer to "solve problem" by relieving symptoms until next time.	Helper giving "answers" to doer to save doer the trouble of learning and appropriating knowledge.
Autonomy-respecting help	Enabling-helper searches for where "virtue is afoot on its own" in the small and catalyzes social and economic linkages to spread successes.	Socratic-Helper does not give answers but facilitates doers' own-learning (e.g., experiments) and then peer-to-peer learning between doers.

On the volitional or motivational side, if actions are undertaken by the doers simply to receive aid (external incentives), then the actions will be poorly implemented (e.g., gamed to just get the aid) and most likely will not be sustained when the incentives are removed. But these problems are only the symptoms of an inherent flaw in aid-seeking reforms.

The inherent failure of the attempt to "buy" genuine reforms can be explained with a simple scheme: Action = behavior (observable) + motivation (largely unobservable). There is the old idea that "You can't buy love." If it's love, then you didn't buy it, and if you did buy it, then it isn't love—only some love-like behavior. It's the same with genuine reforms. If the "reforms" are undertaken in order to obey the conditionalities and get aid, then the "reforms" are only aid-seeking and not genuine. And if the reforms are genuine (e.g., growing out of the doers' own endogenous motivation to change), then external aid cannot be in the motivational "driver's seat"—although aid may have a secondary role as a means to the doers' own-motivated ends.[5] If the aid "made all the

---

5 In the popular "self-help" literature, this is Stephen Covey's principle (1990) that there is no outside-in road to inside-out change.

difference" as helpers usually want, then it defeated its purpose. It is only when the aid did not "make a difference" in motivating the reform that it could be effective.

> Paradoxically, therefore, program aid is fully effective only when it does not achieve anything—when, that is, no quid pro quo (in the sense of a policy that would not have been undertaken in the absence of aid) is exacted as the price of aid.
>
> (Hirschman 1971: 204)

This paradox has totally flummoxed the international finance institutions. A direct motivation-supplying approach is self-defeating. Like shining a light to get a better look at "darkness," the approach dispels the goal.[6] Reform-buying help will generate reform-selling activities (which are "reform behavior + aid-seeking motivation") instead of genuine reforms (which are "reform behavior + own-motivation"). The overriding carrots and sticks will tend to crowd-out and eventually atrophy any own-motivation for reforms.

THE VOLITIONAL DIMENSION OF BENEVOLENT AID

The second form of unhelpful help occurs when the helper undercuts self-help by inadvertently supplying the motivation for the doer to be in or remain in a condition to receive help. One prominent example of this is long-term charitable relief. The world is awash with disasters that call for various forms of short-term charitable relief. The point is not to oppose these operations but to point out how charitable relief operates in the longer term to erode the doers' incentives to help themselves—and thus creates a dependency relationship. In this sense, charitable relief in the longer term is an undercutting form of unhelpful help.[7]

---

6 To illustrate the self-defeating nature of using objective or outside-in approaches to subjective or inside-out change, the mid-nineteenth century Danish philosopher, Søren Kierkegaard, used stories of putting a cap on a certain type of elf (1989: 12, 468) or putting special armor on the god Mars (1992: 174) to see how they looked when, in each case, the act made them invisible. In his terms, an objective approach could not lead to a subjective result.

7 This is analogous to the case where an injured wild animal is nursed back to health in captivity, but then, having been in captivity so long, is no longer able to function in the wild. Another similar situation is where, through the use of drugs or being kept in an artificially sterile environment, a person does not build up a natural resistance to certain germs in the normal environment so that the person has become dependent on staying on the drugs or staying in the sterile environment. For related notions, see Gronemeyer (1992) on "help [that] does not help," the late Ivan Illich's notion of "counterproductivity" (1978) and the "Disabling Professions" (2000), and John McKnight's notion of "disabling help" (1995).

Sometimes aid is sought by a country because of a self-perceived lack of efficacy. Aid granted out of benevolence, even without carrots and sticks, has the adverse effect of reinforcing the lack of self-confidence and doubts about one's own efficacy. Charitable aid to relieve the symptoms of poverty may create a situation of "moral hazard" (see below) that weakens reform incentives and attenuates efforts for positive change to eliminate poverty.[8]

What are the roots of own-motivation for reform? Leaving aside any helpers, the doers' own motivation for reform may be provided by the negative consequences of not doing it or to obtain certain positive consequences. Benevolent aid undercuts this own-motivation for reform by providing aid to directly relieve the negative consequences or to bring about the positive consequences—all without having to undertake the reform itself. Since this aid undercuts the own-motivation for reform, it may well be combined with "replacement" motivation in the form of carrots and sticks externally supplied in a social engineering mode. This soft-hard combination, in fact, is the *modus operandi* of "adjustment lending" (as well as many other welfare programs). The loan goes directly into the country's budget to benevolently relieve the endogenous pressures to make reforms, but then conditionalities are imposed as the externally-supplied replacement motivation to make the reforms. The resulting marionette-like "reform behavior" is ineffective and then the hamster-wheel of conventional assistance can take another turn a few years later with "tougher conditionalities" and "strengthened monitoring."

All aid to adults based on the simple condition of needing aid risks this displacement of motivation. The working assumption is that the condition of needing aid was externally imposed (e.g., a natural disaster); the aid recipient shares no responsibility. But over the course of time, such aid tends to undermine this assumption as the aid slowly becomes a reward for staying in the state of needing aid,[9] all of which creates dependency and learned helplessness. Thus relief becomes the unhelpful help that undermines self-help.

"Moral hazard" refers to the phenomenon where excessive insurance relieves the insured from taking normal precautions so risky behaviour might be increased. The phrase is applied generally to opportunistic actions undertaken because some arrangement has relieved the doers from bearing

---

8 See Maren (1997) or the game theory model of the Samaritan's Dilemma in Buchanan (1977) and in Ostrom et al. (2001).

9 See Murray (1984) or Ellwood (1988) on the "helping conundrums".

the full responsibility for their actions. Benevolent help undercuts the incentives for people to help themselves.

In the insurance example, the limit case of no insurance (which means complete self-insurance) certainly solves the problem of moral hazard since the individual then has a full incentive to take precautions to prevent accidents. Yet the no-insurance option foregoes the benefits of insurance. There is no first-best solution of complete insurance without moral hazard, but there are partial solutions in the form of co-payments and deductibles so that the insured party retains some risk (negative consequences) and thus some incentive to take normal precautions.

In a similar manner, the conservative approach of no assistance could be seen as the "tough love" limit case. It certainly solves the problem of softened incentives for self-help, but it foregoes forms of positive assistance that might be autonomy-respecting. The idea of co-payments and deductibles carries over to the idea of substantial matching funds from the doers. Thus the doers will have solved the problem of substantially funding the positive consequences in question; the benefits will not just be "purchased" with the benevolent aid.

This problem suggests the possibility that the post-World War II development assistance effort from the developed countries to the developing world has created a massive generalized moral hazard problem. Among development economists, the late Peter Bauer (1976) developed these arguments about aid with particular force. William Easterly (2001) has summarized the empirical results that, on the whole, document the lack of success in the last half century of development assistance based on various combinations of social engineering and benevolent aid and Nicholas van de Walle (2001) has focused on the results in Africa.

Surely one bright spot was the Marshall Plan, which, in many ways, provided a model for later development efforts. Yet it also contained the seeds of moral hazard. Robert Marjolin, the French architect of the Marshall Plan, noted in a 1952 memo that American aid continuing over a longer term could have precisely that effect:

> Although American aid has been a necessary remedy over a period, and will continue to be for a time, one is bound to acknowledge that in the long run it has had dangerous psychological and political effects.... It is making more difficult the task of the governments of Western Europe trying to bring about a thorough economic and financial rehabilitation. The idea that it is always possible to call on American aid, that here is the ever-present cure for external payments deficits, is a factor destructive of willpower. It is difficult to hope that, while this recourse continues to exist, the nations of Western Europe will apply, for a sufficient length

of time, the courageous economic and financial policy that will enable them to meet their needs from their own resources without the contribution of external aid.

(quoted in Marjolin, 1989: 241)

However, the demands of the Korean War and the lack of a permanent aid bureaucracy resulted in the winding down of American aid. If the industrial countries of Western Europe faced moral hazard problems in the short-lived Marshall Plan, one can only begin to fathom the extent of the moral hazard problem today in developing countries that face well-established professional aid-providers in the developed countries who must constantly reinvent ways to move the money.

Money is a mixed blessing—to the extent that it is a blessing at all in development assistance. As long as money continues to be the leading edge of development assistance, then the problems of moral hazard will only be compounded.

THE COGNITIVE DIMENSION OF SOCIAL ENGINEERING

If we return to the metaphor of the social engineering helpers as helicoptering over the maze, then they not only supply motivation to the doers in the maze, they supply "knowledge" in the form of a blueprint or roadmap about how to get out of the maze. This "knowledge" often fails for a number of practical reasons. One problem is the difference between general and local knowledge; instructions supplied by a central helping agency would not be adapted to local circumstances. Secondly, there is the distinction between codified explicit knowledge and more tacit know-how knowledge. Only codified knowledge can be transmitted from a helping agency; tacit know-how needs to be soaked-up by working with those who have already carried out the reforms or by one's own experimentation and learning by doing. Thirdly there is the *Rashomon* effect where different people or groups may draw rather different lessons from the same story of success or failure (see Schön 1971: 210). Consider, for example, the different "readings" of the East Asian success stories or the failure of the Russian reforms. Some mis-readings are very much theory-based on the part of helpers—helpers who are so "scientific" that they "would rather have people die by the right therapy than be cured by the wrong." (Lewis 1925: 124) And last but hardly least, there may be strong ideological pressures on the helping agencies to broadcast certain messages and not others—regardless of the messages emerging from the success/failure stories.

These problems with externally-supplied knowledge are symptoms of a more inherent failure. A belief or judgment can be parsed according to a simple scheme: Belief = proposition + grounds for belief. Any proposition that is accepted solely on the grounds of an external authority is only a borrowed opinion, not knowledge. The doer needs to be engaged in an active search for knowledge, and that search begins with knowing that one does not know. This point goes back to Socrates.

> That real education aims at imparting knowledge rather than opinion, that knowledge cannot be handed over ready-made but has to be appropriated by the knower, that appropriation is possible only through one's own search, and that to make him aware of his ignorance is to start a man on the search for knowledge—these are the considerations that govern and determine the Socratic method of teaching.
>
> (Versényi 1963: 117)

The cognitive form of social engineering aims for the mentality wherein the doers will accept beliefs based essentially on an external "expert" authority— or, in a negative form, to reject a belief just because it is espoused by some demonized anti-authority. But in modern times, this is not done crudely. The engineering-oriented helping agency transmits or disseminates answers to the doers by wrapping its "authority" up in one-sided arguments and biased statistics all delivered in an avalanche of publications and in public-relations-style reform campaigns.

THE COGNITIVE DIMENSION OF BENEVOLENT AID

The cognitive dimension has to do with the grounds for judgment and belief, not with the motivation for learning (the latter being part of the volitional or motivational dimension). The social engineering approach tries to establish an external authority as the sufficient grounds for belief so that the authority substitutes for or replaces the doer's own grounds for judgment based on experience and reasoning. The benevolent form of unhelpful cognitive "help" operates in a different manner by giving the answers to save the doer or doers the "trouble" of learning through their own experience and reasoning.

A simple everyday example is that of a parent who "helps" a child with homework by giving the answers in such a way that the child does not learn how to find the answers himself or herself. The training wings of the major development agencies are full of people who would not think of just giving their children the answers to homework problems but spend their day-jobs designing training programs to disseminate "the answers" to developing countries.

In development assistance, unhelpful cognitive help takes the form of teaching and training courses given by development agencies and their consultants to transmit "development knowledge" to developing countries.

157

Even when the knowledge is genuine, this form of help spares the doers the job of capacity-building to find the answers themselves. This builds dependency more than capacity. This form of unhelpful help is often supported at both the agency and country levels. Indeed, there is a self-reinforcing lock-in between developing countries that *want* "The Answer" and development agencies that *have* "The Answer."

> [Policy-makers] will be supplied with a great many ideas, suggestions, plans, and ideologies, frequently of foreign origin or based on foreign experience . . . . Genuine learning about the problem will sometimes be prevented not only by the local policy-makers' eagerness to jump to a ready-made solution, but also by the insistent offer of help and advice on the part of powerful outsiders(. [S]uch practices [will] tend to cut short that "long confrontation between man and a situation" (Camus) so fruitful for the achievement of genuine progress in problem-solving.
>
> (Hirschman 1973: 239–240)[10]

This form of unhelpful help is also evident in the agencies that keep performing economic and sector analysis work for a country which leads to little building of capacity or even recognition of existing capacity in the country.

> Why is it that so many of these countries are still being treated as if they had learned very little in these years of tutelage and guidance? Surely this isn't true. If it isn't true, then why do the technical staffs of aiding agencies, national and multinational, and outside experts, so often continue to conduct exhaustive and repetitive reviews and to pass judgments on these countries with the same particularity exercised a decade before? A school in which pupils never seem to be eligible for promotion to a higher grade would not seem to be a very good school.
>
> (Lilienthal 1967: 55)

A similar problem arises even in the normal consulting business. Under the pressure of events, management brings in an expert consultant to solve a problem rather than undertake the time-consuming job of building internal capacity. From the consultant's viewpoint, the idea is to solve the short-term problem in a way that will not build internal capacity but will foster a "long-term relationship" with the client.[11]

This concludes the analysis of the two forms of unhelpful help (social engineering and benevolent aid) in both their motivational and cognitive dimensions. The benevolent impulse to give charitable relief and the

---

10 To "cut short" the process of learning and problem-solving by giving answers is the cognitive version of the undercutting form of unhelpful help.

11 See the analysis of "shifting the burden" as the "generic dynamics of addiction" in Senge (1990: 104–113).

enlightened impulse to do social engineering are the Scylla and Charybdis of development assistance.

Again and again, one finds social engineering blueprints to "do action X" or to "believe proposition P" being defended on the grounds that the doers should indeed do X or that P is indeed true. But there seems to be little or no real recognition that if the doers do X only to satisfy conditionalities and thus receive aid, then the motive will falsify the action, the reforms will not be well implemented, and the policy changes will not be sustained. Or if P is asserted only the basis of authority, then leaders will not be able to defend P to skeptics and will not be able to mobilize difficult changes based on such borrowed knowledge.

And again and again, one finds benevolent aid being defended as "doing good" in the sense of delivering resources or knowledge to the poor without any real recognition as to how this undercuts the incentives for developing volitional and cognitive self-reliance. All the arguments about the relief being "help" miss the point. Yes, it is "help", an unhelpful form of "help" that in the longer term undercuts capacity-building and autonomous development.

I noted at the outset that the idea of "helping people help themselves" presents the fundamental conundrum of development assistance. The unhelpful forms of help fail to resolve the conundrum by supplying help in ways that sacrifice people helping themselves.

THE COGNITIVE DIMENSION OF AUTONOMY-RESPECTING HELP

How can help actually be helpful in the sense of the old slogan about "helping people help themselves"? Let us start with the cognitive dimension. The helping approaches of engineering and benevolence fail because they either override or undercut the autonomy of the doers. There is no way to directly or heteronomously assist autonomy. Own-motivation and own-judgment cannot be based on externally supplied motivation or authority.[12]

> How in logic can the teacher dragoon his pupil into thinking for himself, impose initiative upon him, drive him into self-motion, conscript him into volunteering, enforce originality upon him, or make him operate spontaneously? The answer is

---

12 There is no "outside in" way to deliver "inside out" change (see Covey 1990). Some major agencies show their failure to understand this point by labeling their education programs as "Learning Delivery Programs." An agency can deliver training or teaching—and learning may or may not take place, but an agency cannot "deliver learning".

> that he cannot—and the reason why we half felt that we must do so was that we were unwittingly enslaved by the crude, semi-hydraulic idea that in essence to teach is to pump propositions, like "Waterloo, 1815," into the pupils' ears, until they regurgitate them automatically.
>
> (Ryle 1967: 118)

Autonomy-respecting assistance must be indirect.[13] The role of the autonomy-respecting cognitive helper is not to teach or disseminate knowledge but is the Socratic role of being a midwife or facilitator of a learning process on the part of the doers. The teacher may try to transmit "knowledge" but the student can only receive a borrowed opinion.[14] Gaining knowledge requires a more active process of appropriation on the part of the learner-doer, and the key to this more indirect approach is for the cognitive helper to facilitate the doer in taking that active role. In a slogan: "Stop the teaching so that the learning can begin!" In the Chinese proverb, the idea is not to "teach people how to fish," but to "help people learn how to fish." As George Bernard Shaw put it: "If you teach a man anything he will never learn it" (1961: 11). Or as management theorist Douglas McGregor said: "Fundamentally the staff man…must create a situation in which members of [line] management can learn, rather than one in which they are taught…" (1966: 161). José Ortega y Gasset suggested: "He who wants to teach a truth should place us in the position to discover it ourselves" (1961: 67). Or as Myles Horton, founder of the Highlander Folk School, maintained: "You don't just tell people something; you find a way to use situations to educate them so that they can learn to figure things out themselves" (1998:122).

Once "the wheel" has been invented, it is not necessary for each doer to "reinvent the wheel"—particularly within a country or region where solutions might have some similarity. But there are nevertheless better and worse ways

---

13 "The best kind of help to others, whenever possible, is indirect, and consists in such modifications of the conditions of life, of the general level of subsistence, as enables them independently to help themselves." (Dewey and Tufts 1908: 390).

14 " [The teacher] does not give knowledge. Knowledge cannot be given. If you ask me a question all I can do in my reply is to try to put into words a part of my experience. But you get only the words, not the experience. To make meaning out of my words, you must use your own experience…. But to the extent that you do share some of my experience, then by talking about my experience, by throwing a light on part of it, I may reveal to you something in your experience that you had not seen before, or help you to see it in a new way, to make, in David Hawkins's words, 'transitions and consolidations.' "(Holt 1976: 85) The referenced passage by Hawkins is: "The teacher offers the learner some kind of loan of himself or herself, some kind of auxiliary equipment which will enable the learner to make transitions and consolidations he could not otherwise have made. And if this equipment is of the kind to be itself internalized, the learner not only learns, but begins, in the process, to be his own teacher—and that is how the loan is repaid…." (quoted in Holt 1976: 60; from Hawkins 1973 and reprinted in Hawkins 2000: 44).

of disseminating and diffusing knowledge and innovation. In the standard hub and spokes model of diffusion (e.g., Rogers 1983), the central hub acts as the authority that learns and then disseminates innovations to the doers in the periphery.

> [The standard approach] treats government as center, the rest of society as periphery. Central has responsibility for the formation of new policy and for its imposition on localities at the periphery. Central attempts to 'train' agencies at the periphery. In spite of the language of experimentation, government-initiated learning tends to be confined to efforts to induce localities to behave in conformity with central policy. Localities learn to beat the system. Government tends to bury failure or learn from it only in the sense of veering away from it. Evaluation, then, tends to be limited to the role of establishing and monitoring the extent of peripheral conformity with central policy.
>
> (Schön 1971: 177)

This model of hub and spokes social learning and diffusion is rather unsuitable in an area such as development knowledge where Donald Schön (1971) noted that novel complexity, genuine uncertainty, conflict of values, unique circumstances, and structural instabilities take us "beyond the stable state."

What is the alternative? The alternative is a decentralized social learning model. Experimentation and self-directed learning are encouraged in the periphery. The center tries to recognize successes and then to foster horizontal doer-to-doer learning within the periphery. Instead of using resources to "buy" implementation of centrally determined policies, the center uses resources to help those who are trying to solve a certain problem to learn from others who seem to have attacked the problem successfully.

> Government cannot play the role of 'experimenter for the nation', seeking first to identify the correct solution, then to train society at large in its adaptation. The opportunity for learning is primarily in discovered systems at the periphery, not in the nexus of official policies at the center. Central's role is to detect significant shifts at the periphery, to pay explicit attention to the emergence of ideas in good currency, and to derive themes of policy by induction. The movement of learning is as much from periphery to periphery, or periphery to center, as from center to periphery. Central comes to function as facilitator of society's learning, rather than as society's trainer.
>
> (Schön 1971: 177–178)

In this model of decentralized social learning, the role of the center or helper is that of a broker fostering horizontal learning in the form of visits, secondments, twinning arrangements, or consulting contracts between successful doers and would-be doers. This is "peer-to-peer" or "South-to-South" technical assistance that is at best only facilitated by the helper. Thus we arrive at two ways than an autonomy-respecting helping agency can enable learning: Socratic help to self-learning and the brokering of doer-to-doer learning—both of which are juxtaposed to the "dissemination" model (see Figure 1).

There is a necessary caveat. This does not mean that the alternative approach will never work. There will always be a few cases where some externally supplied "fix" of technical knowledge will make "all the difference" to the doers even though the knowledge was not the result of any real learning process and thus was not "owned" by the doers. Examples might include learning to set certain tax or tariff rates, resolve technical problems with infrastructure, develop new improved seeds that can be readily used, or find a drug or medical procedure that can be readily implemented to save lives. Those inclined to social engineering will flood their minds with such "vaccinating children" cases as if they were the typical case of "technical assistance" rather than a limited special case.

THE VOLITIONAL DIMENSION OF AUTONOMY-RESPECTING HELP

Returning to the maze analogy, the social engineer helicoptering over the maze not only tried to disseminate the knowledge of how to get out of the maze but also tried to provide the motivation to use the supplied roadmap. On the knowledge side, I argued against the vertical dissemination of answers in

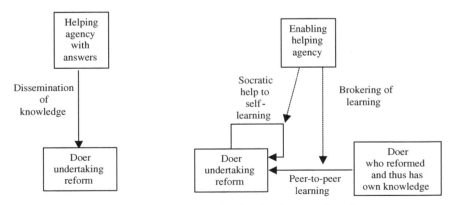

Figure 1: Unhelpful and helpful strategies for development learning

favor of encouraging decentralized experimentation, self-directed learning, and then the brokering of horizontal learning between doers.

I will make the analogous argument on the motivational side. The best linkage between the helping agency at the macro level and the doers at the micro level is not for the agency (as "principal" in a principal-agent relationship) to try to "vertically" supply exogenous motivation for the doers (as "agents"), e.g., carrots and sticks contained in loan or aid conditionalities. The alternative to "supplying" motivation is to *find* it. Helpers need to find where positive change is underway on its own to address pressing problems—perhaps only on a small scale. And embedded in any society are linkages and pressures that could be thought of as the endogenous transmitters of motives for action. The best role for the helping agency is to try to catalyze those endogenous linkages that will amplify and spread any discovered developmental successes. The idea is to foster transformation not by imposing motivations from the outside but by catalyzing the motivational mechanisms already endogenous in a society.

This treatment of autonomy-respecting help is a rendition of Albert Hirschman's notion of "unbalanced growth" (1961) which he juxtaposed to the social engineering vision of integrated big-push "balanced growth" programs. The helper starts by searching for the successes, perhaps hidden successes, which can then spawn more transformation.

> I began to look for elements and processes...that *did* work, perhaps in roundabout and unappreciated fashion. [T]his search for possible *hidden rationalities* was to give an underlying unity to my work. ...[T]he hidden rationalities I was after were precisely and principally *processes of growth and change already under way* in the societies I studied, processes that were often unnoticed by the actors immediately involved, as well as by foreign experts and advisors.
>
> (Hirschman, 1984: 91–93)

Hirschman at one point refers to the principle of unbalanced growth as "the idea of maximizing induced decisionmaking" (1994: 278). The problem-solving pressures induced by *"change already under way"* will call forth otherwise unused resources and enlist otherwise untapped energies. As reform efforts move from one bottleneck and crisis to another (in comparison with the smooth planned allocation of resources in a project), then "resources and abilities that are hidden, scattered, or badly utilized" (1961: 5) will be mobilized. Reform programs need to awaken and enlist local energies and knowledge for trial-and-error problem solving. But each problem solved brings to the foreground other problems and opportunities using forward and backward linkages. Change unfolds because "one thing leads to another" endogenously—not because a rational plan is being motivated and implemented.

As these social processes develop largely on the basis of their own released energies, new demands will be made on the center or government to reform institutions, to provide infrastructure, and to clear away impediments, and that in turn will spur further progress on the ground. These induced demands for reforms are quite different from the externally imposed conditionalities that stipulate certain reforms. In psychological terms, the domestic induced demands for reforms supplies the government with a more "intrinsic" or "own" motivation for reform in contrast to the "tough performance-based" carrots and sticks imposed by external development agencies and donors. Thus the external helping agency, instead of trying to buy reforms with conditional aid, should find where virtue is afoot on its own to address "pressing problems"—that pressure not being eliminated by benevolent aid—and use resources to catalyze and grow that virtue, using the linkages to induce larger demands for reforms on the government (see Figure 2).

There is again a necessary caveat. This does not mean that the alternative approach will never work. There may always be the cases where the helper can supply external motivation for a "stroke of the pen" reform that requires little or no institutional development.[15] Helping agencies might "dream" of such

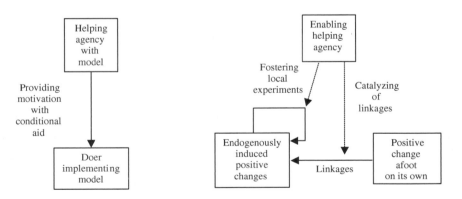

Figure 2: Unhelpful and helpful strategies for motivating change

15 "The more workable and more popular commitments are precisely those that are highly visible, verifiable, measurable and, at their best, irreversible. One thinks of a revision of the customs tariff, of the imposition of credit restrictions in order to curb inflation, or, most typically perhaps, of a devaluation." (Hirschman 1971: 206)

propitious interventions being ubiquitous but unfortunately they are rare special cases.

I have now completed the six sections expanding on the two forms of unhelpful help in their volitional and cognitive dimensions and on the cognitive and volitional dimensions of autonomy-respecting help. I conclude by underscoring the common theme.

CONCLUSION: THE COMMON THEME OF AUTONOMY-RESPECTING ASSISTANCE

In the cognitive case, the juxtaposition between the two strategies is based on whether the knowledge comes to the doers from the expert-helpers or arises out of the doers' own learning processes including interactions with other similar doers. Where the doers do not have the relevant knowledge, then the Socratic-helper would encourage the doers to search, experiment, and study other doers (and would refrain from disseminating what the helper took to be the answers). Once working answers were found by some doers, the helper would promote peer-to-peer learning to spread, to adapt, and to scale up the knowledge to other doers. The knowledge thus arises out the doers' own learning processes (experimentation and adapted cross-learning) so it is owned knowledge.

In contrast, the engineering-oriented helping agency has answers from whatever source (e.g., globe-scanning researchers) and transmits or disseminates them to the doers based on its "authority" and one-sided arguments delivered in public-relations-style reform campaigns. Since the helping agency has, in the fullness of its knowledge and expertise, already decided on the answers, there is no need to overload, distract, or confuse the doers with the arguments for the alternatives. Soliciting alternative viewpoints is discouraged in order to maintain "consistency in the policy dialogue" between the helper and doers. Thus the doers are saved the "trouble" of going through "that 'long confrontation between man and a situation' (Camus) so fruitful for the achievement of genuine progress in problem-solving." (Hirschman 1973: 240) The knowledge, however, is then only the borrowed opinion of experts, may be ill-adapted to the doers' circumstances, would be devoid of the tacit know-how components of knowledge, and may be heavily laden with theory or ideology or both.

This assistance of the helping agency does not respect the cognitive autonomy of the doers; the doers are being "fed" knowledge by the helpers. In contrast, the Socratic-helper provides assistance in a way that is enabling rather than controlling—that respects rather than overrides or undercuts the cognitive autonomy of the doers.

Development Ethics

The same themes play out regarding motivation. In the engineering model, where the helper is "controlling," the helper provides the motivation externally in the form of conditions on loans or aid. Since the motivation of the doers, by assumption in the principal-agent relationship, is to get the aid-bait rather than to undertake the reform as an own-motivated effort to solve pressing problems, the situation is ripe for all sorts of games—as is clear to anyone who has observed the "aid business" during the last half century (e.g., Dichter 2003).

The alternative to the helper supplying motivation is where the helper finds virtue afoot on its own. "In these situations, the donor would set himself the task of rewarding virtue (or rather, what he considers as such) where virtue appears of its own accord" (Hirschman 1971: 204). The helper would try to catalyze linkages, maximize demonstration effects, and in other ways to amplify the found small beginnings of positive change. Since the initial efforts and the transmitting linkages are endogenous to the system, these reforms might be catalyzed and strengthen by the helper but are not dependent on the helpers for the continuance of the reforms. Moreover, the reforms are more likely to be genuine rather than "aid-seeking" due to the internal motivation. Since the helpers are trying to strengthen or amplify the doers' actions taken on the basis of own motivation to solve pressing problems—rather than override those motives with "tough output-based conditionalities" or undercut the motives with benevolent aid—the helpers are providing autonomy-respecting assistance.

REFERENCES

Bauer, P. T. (1976) *Dissent on Development*, Cambridge: Harvard University Press.

Buchanan, J. (1977) "The Samaritan's Dilemma," in J. Buchanan (ed.) *Freedom in Constitutional Contract*, College Station: Texas A&M University Press.

Covey, S. (1990) *The Seven Habits of Highly Effective People*, New York: Simon & Schuster.

Dewey, J. and Tufts, J. (1908) *Ethics*, New York: Henry Holt.

Dichter, T. (2003) *Despite Good Intentions: Why Development Assistance to the Third World has Failed*, Amherst MA: University of Massachusetts Press.

Easterly, W. (2001) *The Elusive Quest for Growth: Economists' Adventures and Misadventures in the Tropics*, Cambridge MA: MIT Press.

Ellerman, D. (forthcoming) *Helping People Help Themselves*, Ann Arbor: University of Michigan Press. Précis available at: www.ellerman.org.

Ellwood, D. (1988) *Poor Support: Poverty in the American Family*, New York: Basic Books.

Fisher, J. (1993) *The Road From Rio: Sustainable Development and the Nongovernmental Movement in the Third World*, Westport CN: Praeger.

Gronemeyer, M. (1992) "Helping," in W. Sachs (ed.) *The Development Dictionary: A Guide to Knowledge as Power*, London: Zed Books: 51 – 69.

Hawkins, D. (1973) "What It Means To Teach," *Teachers' College Record* 75(1): 7 – 16.

Hawkins, D. (2000) *The Roots of Literacy*, Boulder: University Press of Colorado.

Hirschman, A. O. (1961) *The Strategy of Economic Development*, New Haven: Yale University Press.

Hirschman, A. O. (1971) *A Bias for Hope: Essays on Development and Latin America*, New Haven: Yale University Press.

Hirschman, A. O. (1973) *Journeys Toward Progress*, New York: Norton.

Hirschman, A. O. (1984) "A Dissenter's Confession: 'The Strategy of Economic Development' Revisited," in G. Meier and D. Seers (eds) *Pioneers in Development*, New York: Oxford University Press: 87 – 111.

Hirschman, A. O. (1994) "A Propensity to Self-Subversion," in L. Rodwin and D. Schön (eds) *Rethinking the Development Experience: Essays Provoked by the Work of Albert O. Hirschman*, Washington: Brookings Institution: 277 – 283.

Holt, J. (1976) *Instead of Education: Ways to Help People Do Things Better*, New York: Delta.

Horton, M., with, Kohl, J. and Kohl, H. (1998) *The Long Haul: An Autobiography*, New York: Teachers College Press.

Illich, I. (1978) *Toward a History of Needs*, New York: Pantheon Books.

Illich, I., Zola, I., McKnight, J., Caplan, J. and Shaiken, H. (2000) *Disabling Professions*, New York: Marion Boyars.

Kierkegaard, S. (1989) *The Concept of Irony with Continual Reference to Socrates*, Princeton: Princeton University Press.

Kierkegaard, S. (1992) *Concluding Unscientific Postscript to Philosophical Fragments*, Princeton: Princeton University Press.

Korten, D. C. (1983) "Social Development: putting people first," in D. Korten and F. Alfonso (eds) *Bureaucracy and the Poor: Closing the Gap*, West Hartford CN: Kumarian Press: 201 – 221.

Lewis, S. (1925) *Arrowsmith*, New York: P.F. Collier & Son.

Lilienthal, D. (1967) *Management: a humanist art*, New York: Columbia University Press.

Maren, M. (1997) *The Road to Hell: The Ravaging Effects of Foreign Aid and International Charity*, New York: Free Press.

Marjolin, R. (1989) *Architect of European Unity: Memoirs 1911 – 1986*, trans W. Hall, London: Weidenfeld and Nicolson.

McGregor, D. (1966) *Leadership and Motivation*, Cambridge: MIT Press.

McKnight, J. (1995) *The Careless Society: Community and Its Counterfeits*, New York: Basic Books.

Memmi, A. (1984) *Dependence: A Sketch for a Portrait of the Dependent*, trans P. A. Facey, Boston: Beacon Press.

Murray, C. (1984) *Losing Ground: American Social Policy 1959 – 1980*, New York: Basic Books.

Ortega y Gasset, J. (1961) *Meditations on Quixote*, New York: Norton.

167

Ostrom, E., Gibson, C., Shivakumar, S. and Andersson, K. (2001) *Aid, Incentives, and Sustainability: An Institutional Analysis of Development Cooperation*, Bloomington, IN: Workshop in Political Theory and Policy Analysis for the Swedish International Development Agency (Sida).

Rogers, E. (1983) *Diffusion of Innovations*, third edn, New York: Free Press.

Ryle, G. (1967) "Teaching and Training," in R. S. Peters (ed.) *The Concept of Education*, London: Routledge & Kegan Paul: 105–119.

Schön, D. A. (1971) *Beyond the Stable State*, New York: Norton.

Senge, P. (1990) *The Fifth Discipline: The Art and Practice of the Learning Organization*, New York: Currency Doubleday.

Shaw, G. B. (1961) *Back to Methuselah*, Baltimore: Penguin.

Uphoff, N., Esman, M. and Krishna, A. (1998) *Reasons for Success: Learning from Instructive Experiences in Rural Development*, West Hartford CN: Kumarian Press.

Van de Walle, N. (2001) *African Economies and the Politics of Permanent Crisis, 1979–1999*, New York: Cambridge University Press.

Versényi, L. (1963) *Socratic Humanism*, New Haven: Yale University Press.

[28]

Responsible Well-Being — A Personal Agenda for Development

ROBERT CHAMBERS*

Institute of Development Studies, Brighton, U.K.

Summary. — If development means good change, questions arise about what is good, and what sorts of change matter. Answers can be personally defined and redefined. The changing words, meanings and concepts of development discourse both reflect and influence what is done. The realities of the powerful tend to dominate. Drawing on experience with participatory approaches and methods which enable poor and marginalized people to express their realities, responsible well-being is proposed as a central concept for a development agenda. This links with capabilities and livelihoods, and is based on equity and sustainability as principles. The primacy of personal actions and non-actions in development points to the need for a pedagogy for the non-oppressed. This includes self-critical awareness, thinking through the effects of actions, and enabling those with power and wealth to experience being better off with less. Others are invited and encouraged to reflect, improve on this analysis, and write their own agenda.

Key words — development vocabulary, ethics, methods, participation, poverty, well-being

It is not that we should simply seek new and better ways for managing society, the economy and the world. The point is that we should fundamentally change how we behave (Havel, 1992).

What we need is an impassioned, intellectually honest, and, above all, open-ended debate about how each person should best conduct his or her life (Forsyth, 1991, p. 269).

includes trying to understand ourselves and changing what we do. Doubt, self-awareness and embracing error are virtues. This means that while thinking and acting we also question how we think, what we think, and the rightness of what we do. It is in that tentative and self-doubting spirit that this editorial is written.

1. INTRODUCTION

To write about a development agenda is rash and perhaps arrogant. There are multiple realities — ecological, economic, social, political, and personal. Change accelerates and uncontrolled global forces make prediction ever harder. Any development agenda is value-laden, and some academics abhor anything that smacks of moralizing. Yet not to ask questions about values is value-laden by default, and not to consider good things to do is a tacit surrender to professional conditioning, personal reflexes, and fatalism. Perhaps the right course is for each of us to reflect, articulate and share our own ideas about values, problems, potentials and priorities, accepting these as provisional and fallible. Paraphrasing Heraclitus, we can then recognize that concerning what we think and what we should do, nothing will be permanent but change. Right behavior then

2. WHAT IS DEVELOPMENT?

The eternal challenge of development is to do better. Usually this is tackled by identifying policies, programs and projects. Both the *Human Development Report 1997* (UNDP, 1997) and the *World Development Report 1997* (World Bank, 1997) follow in a long tradition by listing policies and actions to make the world a better place, especially for the poor. The argument of this editorial is that this does not go far enough. There is a crucial missing link. We need to add the personal dimension. This implies stepping back and engaging in critical self-examination. To do better, we have to examine not just the normally defined agenda of development "out there," but ourselves, how our

*I am grateful to Geoff Barnard, Jenny Chambers and Janet Craswell for helpful comments on a draft of this editorial.

ideas are formed, how we think, how we change, and what we do and do not do.

Words are a starting point. Fritjof Capra (1996, p. 282) has put it that:

> The uniqueness of being human lies in our ability to continually weave the linguistic network in which we are embedded. To be human is to exist in language. In language we coordinate our behaviour, and together in language we bring forth our world.

For professionals committed to development, the world we wish to bring forth is linked to what we mean by development.

On the cover of *The Development Dictionary* (Sachs, 1992), a sentence by Wolfgang Sachs proclaims, "The idea of Development stands today like a ruin in the intellectual landscape. Its shadow obscures our vision." In an editorial in the Forest Trees and People Newsletter (1995, pp. 26–27) Daphne Thuvesson has written "As the existing system crumbles around us, new and exciting alternatives are sprouting up in the rubble."

Sachs's pessimism and Thuvesson's optimism are both needed.[1] The record of "development" is mixed. Those who damn the errors, failures and deficits tend to ignore the counterfactual, how much worse things could have been if nothing had been done. Those who laud achievements and successes tend to overlook how much better things might have been even than they were. A balanced view has to recognise renewals and continuities in the landscape as well as ruins and rubble, and older trees as well as new sprouts.

To explore the terrain, let us start, as *The Development Dictionary* does, by examining words and concepts that are common currency in contemporary development discourse and with which we seek to "bring forth our world."

Development has been taken to mean different things at different times, in different places, and by different people in different professions and organizations. The dominant meanings have been those attributed by economists and used in economics.

Development has thus often been equated with economic development, and economic development in turn with economic growth, often abbreviated simply to growth. But the meanings given to development have also evolved,[2] not least through the concept of human development in the *Human Development Reports* of UNDP. In all cases, though, however clinical the analysis or disparate the definitions, the word seems to have had two aspects: it has been normative; and it has involved change. So the underlying meaning of development has been good change. That is the sense in which it is used here. Views have differed, and perhaps always should and will differ, about what is good and what sorts of change are significant.

Change is continuous in what changes and how it changes, and in what we see as good. All this is reflected in words and meanings. These are both formative and adaptive: they both influence and express conditions, ideologies, perceptions, practices and priorities. That vocabularies and meanings evolve is then itself necessary and good, and both cause and effect of other changes.

3. A CHANGING VOCABULARY

So it has been that new words have been continuously introduced and spread. Additions to the common lexicon of development in the past two decades have been prolific. New words have been added faster than old have fallen into disuse. Some such as integrated, coordinated, planning and socialism have peaked and passed into decline. Others in the eclectic and perhaps ephemeral language of post-modernism, such as deconstruction, narrative and meta-narrative, text and subtext, have largely languished in academic and literary backwaters. Others, such as equity and poverty, have been robust and resilient. Yet others, some old, some new, which have come close to the mainstream of much development discourse during the past two decades include:

> accountability, capabilities, civil society, consumer, decentralisation, democracy, deprivation, diversity, empowerment, entitlement, environment, gender, globalization, governance, human rights, livelihood, market, ownership, participation, partnership, pluralism, process, stakeholder, sustainability, transparency, vulnerability, well-being.

Of these only three — environment, market and participation — receive chapters in *The Development Dictionary*.

4. THE POWER OF LANGUAGE

The power of vocabulary to change how we think and what we do is easy to underestimate. It influences the course of development in many ways: through changing the agenda; through modifying mindsets; through legitimating new actions; and through stimulating and focusing research and learning.

New language is easily dismissed as rhetoric or jargon. Seasoned skeptics can see changes in words and meanings as transient, superficial, and insignificant. Those impelled by authority or prudence to use new words signal their cynicism by dubbing them "buzz words," "flavour of the month," and "politically correct." So consultants, bureaucrats, and those seeking contracts, support, security or promotion, tap out and parrot[3] the latest vocabulary.

Language is, however, about much more than rhetoric and opportunism. It shapes and interacts with the ways we think and behave. An obvious case is gender syntax. Reversing "he or she" to "she or he," or using "she" as the pronoun for "the African farmer," have not come easily to many, but their capacity to challenge and shock, and their gradual acceptance, have been a small but significant bridgehead into male-biased thinking and patriarchy. So in our development context, we can see that language has helped to bring forth and change the world of development professionals. This has happened in three ways: introducing, stressing and defining words; combining them in new ways; and listing and disaggregating.

(a) *Introducing, stressing and defining words*

How the thinking and actions of development professionals may have been affected over the past two decades can be assessed by reflecting on the contexts of the words listed above. Table 1 shows how they can be separated.

A personal impression is that 20 years ago none of these, except equity and poverty, was as prominent as today. Increasingly, these words are embedded in the mindsets of development professionals, and increasingly used by them unreflectively, that is to say, without forcing, and without feeling insecure or self-conscious or a need to justify or explain their use. In this process they change how development realities are constructed and seen. An example is the new and specialized meanings of capabilities and of entitlements as progressively elaborated by Amartya Sen (1981, 1985). New words can also confront old. Livelihood has been put forward as a challenge to the reductionism and specificity of employment. Deprivation has been put forward as a challenge to the narrowness of poverty.

(b) *Combining words*

Combinations of words have been influential in three ways.

First, they have been used to focus and present radical concepts in a technical guise. *Primary stakeholders* as proposed in the World Bank,[4] is a technical phrase which implies a priority for poor people affected positively or negatively by a policy, project or program. The term was widely welcomed and applauded but reportedly had to be put in cold storage by the Bank because of political pressures from governments in the South. But by then it had escaped and had a life of its own. *Social development* was not much used 20 years ago, but now there are many social development advisers, and the Social Development Summit was held in Copenhagen in 1995.

Second, combining words can expand disciplinary views and provide bridges between disciplines. Put negatively "Like blinkers, the terms we adopt to express ourselves limit the range of our view" (Capra, 1996, p. 268). Put positively, we can expand and alter our view and what we do by combining terms. This can be illustrated by the shift in priorities and thinking has been taking place from things and infrastructure to people and capabilities. As the importance of people has risen in the development agenda, the practical question has been how to help the professions, notably engineering and economics, that have dominated donor agencies especially the World Bank, to accommodate the new priorities. The transition has been eased linguistically by applying to people the familiar language and concepts of things and numbers. So we have learned to speak of *human capital, human infrastructure, human resource development, social infrastructure, social investment*, and now *social capital*. On the negative side, these may standardize, depersonalize, and miss much that matters to people, and may purport to measure what cannot meaningfully be measured. On the positive side, they make it easier for economists to incorporate people and social institutions in their mental and mathematical models.

Third, combinations of words can be formative, starting largely undefined and presenting a challenge and opportunity to provide a meaning, as this editorial does below with *responsible well-being*. *Sustainable livelihoods* was embodied in the title of a conference (Conroy and Litvinoff, 1988), caught on as a phrase, and then was progressively explored and elaborated for meanings of sustainable, of livelihood,

Table 1. *Development vocabulary*

The human condition	capabilities, deprivation, entitlement, livelihood, poverty, vulnerability, well-being
Organization, power, and relationships	accountability, consumer, decentralisation, empowerment, ownership, participation, partnership, process, stakeholder, transparency
Domains, dimensions	civil society, environment, globalization, governance, market
Values	democracy, diversity, equity, gender, human rights, pluralism, sustainability

and of the two words taken together (e.g., Chambers and Conway, 1992; Bernstein *et al.*, 1992). *Social exclusion* opens up a new perspective on deprivation. Most recently, *state capability* (World Bank, 1997, *passim*) draws attention to what a state can and should do in relation to its ability to act.

(c) *Listing and disaggregating*

Listing and disaggregating are means of qualifying the reductionism of much development thinking. Listing adds diversity and complexity. Disaggregating unpacks concepts. Thus the reductionism of poverty defined for professional convenience by a single measure of income or consumption has been qualified in three ways: by listing and examining other dimensions of deprivation, such as vulnerability, physical weakness, powerlessness, discrimination, humiliation and social exclusion; by separating out aspects of poverty itself, and using the terms income-poverty (as in UNDP, 1997, *passim*) or consumption-poverty for that subset which is normally measured and used for comparisons; and by enabling poor people themselves to use their own words and concepts to express, list and analyze their realities, local, complex, diverse, dynamic and uncontrollable as they so often are (Chambers, 1997, Chapter 8).

5. WHOSE LANGUAGE COUNTS?

If vocabulary can make so much difference, we must ask: who changes the words we use? Whose language brings forth our world and guides our actions? Who defines what words mean?

The world brought forth is usually constructed by the powerful in central places or by those well placed to influence them. The words and concepts of development both express and form the mindsets, and values of dominant linguistic groups, disciplines and professions, and organizations. Among linguistic groups, the English language is, irreversibly it seems, the most influential. Other transnational languages such as Arabic, Chinese, French, Portuguese, Russian, and Spanish — can dominate national and other vernaculars. Among disciplines and professions, the words and concepts of engineering preoccupied with things, and applied economics preoccupied with quantification, still set the agenda and vocabulary of much development discourse. The procedures which fit and reinforce their paradigms, such as the logical framework and social cost-benefit analysis, are authoritatively taught and required. Among organizations, those clustered in the Eastern United States are pervasively influential, including the World Bank and the International Monetary Fund

(IMF), with the greatest concentration of development professionals, power and intellectual capability in the world; UNDP increasingly through the *Human Development Report*; and the US government. These are major sources of new vocabulary and ideas which gain currency. The President of the World Bank, in particular, exercises enormous power over development thinking and action through the words he,[5] or his speech-writers, choose to use. Robert McNamara's 1973 Nairobi speech on poverty is an example, followed now by James Wolfensohn's promotion of participation.

6. PERSONAL VALUES AND CONCEPTS

All, though, need not be determined by the powerful, from the central cores and from above. Richard Forsyth (1991) has presented a challenge for each person to devise her or his own religion. Similarly, development professionals, in a spirit of self-doubting pluralism, can help one another by drawing up and sharing personal lists and patterns of values and concepts, and seeing where and how these differ and cohere. There is space here for reflection on how one's personal realities and values have been formed, and to choose, change and give meaning to a personal list of words and concepts. There is scope here too to give priority to the values and preferences of the weak.

For all development professionals, there are many sources of values, vision and concepts. The great religions will always be sources of inspiration to explore for values and vision. For analytical concepts and insights there are now numerous new sources. The theories of chaos, edge of chaos and complexity (Gleick, 1988; Resnick, 1994; Waldrop, 1994) contribute insights and analogies: how complex self-organizing systems can be based on few rules, with parallels in decentralized, democratic and diverse human organization; how small actions at certain times can have huge effects later, pointing to the power of individual choice and responsibility; and how there can be zones of stability in turbulence, suggesting reassertions of continuities even in chaotic conditions. The new ecology contributes understandings of local heterogeneity, networks, dynamism, sequences, transitions and synergies, with continuous change and adaptation: in Capra's (1996, p. 295) words some of the basic principles are "interdependence, recycling, partnership, flexibility, diversity and, as a consequence of all those, sustainability." Other sources include soft systems theory (Checkland, 1981) and management theory and practice (e.g. Peters, 1989; Senge, 1990; Handy, 1990). Sources such as these present vocabularies, concepts and ways of thinking to be tapped and more can be expected.

Another source is the experience with PRA (participatory rural appraisal). This has influenced my own view. Others will judge for themselves whether for them too it may help. PRA[6] is a family of continuously evolving approaches, methods, values and behaviors which has turned much that is conventional on its head. It seeks to enable local and marginalized people to share, enhance and analyze their knowledge of life and conditions, and to plan, act, monitor and evaluate. In its philosophy, practice and vocabulary it has come to stress

— the question "whose reality counts?" raising issues of equity and empowerment, and of enabling women, poor people and others who are marginalized to express their realities and make them count

— the primacy of the personal, especially behavior and attitudes, and exercising personal judgement and responsibility.

Let us examine these in turn.

7. WHOSE REALITY COUNTS?

In our world of global communication, those who are connected electronically are a new exclusive elite. Those who are not connected to Internet, e-mail and fax are a new group of the excluded. At the same time, the realities of professionals and of poor people are notoriously disparate. Again and again the realities of those who are poor and marginalized are ignored or misread. The challenge is how to give voice to those who are left out and to make their reality count.

Participatory methodologies, perhaps most notably PRA, have shown both power and popularity in enabling those who are subordinate to express their realities. Participatory poverty assessments (PPAs) using PRA approaches and methods have been pioneered in Ghana (Norton *et al.*, 1995; Dogbe, forthcoming), Zambia (Norton *et al.*, 1994; Norton and Owen 1996), South Africa (Attwood, 1996; May, 1996; Murphy, 1995; Teixeira and Chambers, 1995), and most recently in Bangladesh (UNDP, 1996), using a variety of processes (for reviews see Norton and Stephens, 1995; Robb, forthcoming; Chambers and Blackburn, 1996; Holland with Blackburn, forthcoming; Norton, forthcoming).

Insights and priorities have included, for example, the importance of all-weather roads for access to medical treatment and markets during the rains, the need to reschedule the timing of school fees away from the most difficult time of year, and training health staff to be friendly and respectful to poor people seeking treatment. In Bangladesh, where the focus of analysis by poor people was on "doables," differences in priorities between women and men, and between urban and rural, were highlighted (UNDP, 1996). The first doable priority of urban women was drinking water, and the second private places for washing. A widespread desire of poor people was enforcement of the anti-dowry laws. Elsewhere, a better understanding of sectoral priorities, for example between health and education, has also resulted.

Thematic investigations using PRA approaches and methods have also illuminated local realities in a range of contexts, for example:

— area stigma — how living in an area with a bad reputation for violence makes it difficult to get jobs (from Jamaica — Moser and Holland, 1995; Levy, 1996);

— how a quarter of girls of school age were "invisible" to the official system (from The Gambia — Kane *et al.*, 1996);

— how the problems and priorities of women differ not only from those of men but also between women depending on their access to basic services and infrastructures, and their social background (from Morocco — Shah and Bourarach, 1995);

— how an official belief that indigenous tenure systems no longer existed was wrong, and how diverse and crucial they were (from Guinea — Freudenberger, forthcoming);

— the ability of local people to define sustainable management and conservation practices for themselves (from India and Pakistan — Gujja *et al.*, forthcoming)

Strikingly, through PRA processes local people have again and again presented values and preferences which differ from those of outsiders or those supposed for local people by outsiders. When asked to card sort households in what was originally wealth ranking (Grandin, 1988) local people have so consistently sorted not by wealth but by some composite concept close to well-being, that the process has been renamed well-being ranking. In well-being, income has often had a surprisingly low priority compared with health, family life, respect and social values.[7] Empirically, well-being and its close equivalents seem to express a widespread human value open to diverse local and individual definitions.

PPAs and PRA approaches and methods are not panaceas. They do, though, present new opportunities for policy influence on behalf of those normally excluded. They can bring poor people and policy-makers together in new ways. They can present realities in visual diagrams with a new credibility. To the question "Whose Voice Counts?" they have shown that the answer can be, more than before, the voices of those previously unheard.

8. PERSONAL BEHAVIOR AND ATTITUDES

The experience of PRA has been expressed in, or leads to, words and concepts which have not been prominent in mainstream development thinking. Some of these are:

commitment, disempowerment, doubt, fulfillment, fun,[8] generosity,[9] responsibility, self-critical awareness, sharing, and trust

These have had little place in the headlines of the literature of development. None features as a chapter heading in the *Development Dictionary* (Sachs, 1992).[10]

In addition, PRA has adopted and evolved a number of injunctions

— ask them
— be nice to people
— don't rush
— embrace error
— facilitate
— hand over the stick
— have fun
— relax
— they can do it (i.e. have confidence that people are capable)

Strikingly, these words, phrases and injunctions point to personal behavior and attitudes. The three original pillars of PRA (Mascarenhas *et al.*, 1991) were:

— methods (many involving visualizations through diagramming, mapping, scoring and so on)
— sharing
— behavior and attitudes

There is a growing consensus that of these by far the most important is behavior and attitudes (see, e.g., Absalom *et al.*, 1995; Kumar, 1996; Blackburn with Holland, forthcoming). Yet these have been absent from most professional training and from most agendas of development. Taken together with the one sentence manual "Use your own best judgement at all times," the experience and ethics of PRA stress not just personal behavior and attitudes, but personal responsibility.

9. RESPONSIBLE WELL-BEING

The two themes generated by the PRA experience — locally defined concepts of well-being, and personal responsibility — can be combined as responsible well-being, a two-word concept to explore. The challenge is to see what this might mean for all people, in their relations with themselves, with others, and with the environment. Two basic principles on which there is wide agreement are equity and sustainability. Two elements which are both ends and means in development thinking are

livelihood and capabilities.[11] These can be linked with each other as in Figure 1.

The overarching end is well-being, supported by capabilities and livelihood. Equity and sustainability as principles qualify livelihood to become livelihood *security*, and well-being to become *responsible* well-being.

Each word can be presented in a statement:

— *The objective of development is well-being for all.* Well-being can be described as the experience of good quality of life. Well-being and its opposite, ill-being, differ from wealth and poverty. Well-being and ill-being are words with equivalents in many languages. Unlike wealth, well-being is open to the whole range of human experience, social, psychological and spiritual as well as material. It has many elements. Each person can define it for herself or himself. Perhaps most people would agree to including living standards, access to basic services, security and freedom from fear, health, good relations with others, friendship, love, peace of mind, choice, creativity, fulfillment and fun. Extreme poverty and ill-being go together, but the link between wealth and well-being is weak or even negative: reducing poverty usually diminishes ill-being; amassing wealth does not assure well-being and may diminish it.

— *Livelihood security is basic to well-being.* Livelihood can be defined as adequate stocks and flows of food and cash to meet basic needs and to support well-being. Security refers to secure rights, physical safety and reliable access to resources, food and income, and basic services. It includes tangible and intangible assets to offset risk, ease shocks and meet contingencies.[12] Sustainable livelihoods maintain or enhance resource productivity on a long-term basis and equitable livelihoods maintain or enhance the livelihoods and well-being of others.

— *Capabilities are means to livelihood and well-being.* Capabilities refers to what people are capable of doing and being. They are means to livelihood and fulfilment; and their enlargement through learning, practice, training and education are means to better living and to well-being.

— *Equity: the poor, weak, vulnerable and exploited should come first.* Equity qualifies all initiatives in development. Equity includes human rights, intergenerational and gender equity, and the reversals of putting the last first and the first last, to be considered in all contexts. The reversals are not absolute, but to balance and level.

— *Sustainability: to be good, conditions and change must be sustainable — economically, socially, institutionally, and environmentally.* Sustainability means that long-term perspectives should apply to all policies and actions, with

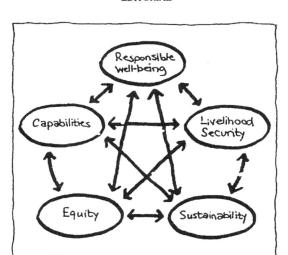

Note: The overarching end is well-being, with capabilities and livelihood as means. Equity and sustainability are principles which qualify livelihood to become livelihood security, and well-being to become *responsible* well-being.

Figure 1. *The web of responsible well-being.*

sustainable well-being and sustainable livelihoods as objectives for present and future generations.

When well-being is qualified by equity and sustainability it becomes *responsible* well-being, as the overarching end, to which all else is means. Well-being is then not at the cost of equity and sustainability, but is enhanced when it contributes to them. Responsible well-being recognizes obligations to others, both those alive and future generations, and to their quality of life. In general, the word "responsible" has moral force in proportion to wealth and power: the wealthier and more powerful people are, the greater the actual or potential impact of their actions or inactions, and so the greater the scope and need for their well-being to be responsible. Responsible well-being refers thus to doing as well as being; it is "by" as well as "for". The objective of development then becomes *responsible well-being by all and for all.*

10. THE PRIMACY OF THE PERSONAL

Because the *responsible* of responsible well-being applies to all human beings, it points to the personal dimension.

The neglect of the personal dimension in development at first sight seems bizarre. It is self-evident to the point of embarrassment that most of what happens is the result of what sort of people we are, how we perceive realities, and what we

do and do not do. Whether change is good or bad is largely determined by personal actions, whether by political leaders, officials, professionals or local people, by international currency speculators, executives of transnational corporations, non-government organization (NGO) workers, or researchers, by mothers, fathers or children, or by soldiers, secret agents, journalists, lawyers, police, or protesters. Especially, what happens depends on those who are powerful and wealthy. One might have supposed then that trying to understand and change their perceptions, motivations and behaviors would have been at the center of development and development studies, and a major concern for the IMF, the World Bank, other donor agencies, governments and NGOs. Yet there have been few studies of individual officials as leaders.[13] Studies of greed and generosity are few.[14] There are quite a number of institutes devoted to development studies but there is, to my knowledge, no institute devoted to the study of greed or power.

Part of the neglect stems from academic culture with its anathema of evangelism, its value of objectivity, and its search for general rather than individual explanations. More potently, perhaps, the neglect is a defence. It can disturb profoundly to reflect on what one does and does not do. It embarrasses to be confronted by poverty and suffering compared with one's own condition. When a poor farmer in India asked me my income I could not reply. To put the personal to the fore in this editorial is to expose my own hypocrisy, and to make it difficult to continue. But hypocrisy is no excuse for silence.

The enormity of this missing link is illustrated by the most recent *Human Development* and *World Development Reports* (UNDP, 1997; World Bank, 1997). The *Human Development Report 1997* is concerned with poverty. It recommends six essential actions — empowering individuals, households and communities; strengthening gender equality; accelerating pro-poor growth; improving the management of globalization; ensuring an active state; and taking special actions for special situations. All of these require action by those who are powerful and relatively wealthy. For its part, the *World Development Report 1997* is devoted to The State in a Changing World. It presents many recommendations for action. In recognizing the importance of leadership and vision (e.g., pp. 14, 123, 154–155, 166), noting political constraints and vested interests, and lamenting the "unbridled pursuit of riches or power" (p. 159) it gets closer to the personal. But it does not go the whole way. It does not come to terms with the need for personal change. Where the moving force is to come from is not clear. Incentives are recommended, but the question remains who determines and pushes through the incentives. Neither report confronts the personal dimension.

In contrast, the concept of responsible well-being puts the personal in the center. Responsible well-being is an individual condition. The major issue is how to encourage and enable the powerful and wealthy accept this ideal, or something close to it, and to define it for themselves in ways which make things better for those who are weak and poor.

11. A PEDAGOGY FOR THE NON-OPPRESSED[15]

For responsible well-being, it is then especially individuals who are powerful and wealthy who have to change. This entails confronting and transforming abuses of power and wealth. For this, one need is for a pedagogy for the non-oppressed (including ourselves, the sort of people who read *World Development*), to enable us to think and act differently. There are many disparate domains for analysis and action, among them: how we treat and bring up children; how to achieve reconciliation after conflict; how donor agency staff behave on mission (as noted by Taylor, 1997, pp. 151–152 in an earlier editorial); how to rehabilitate those who have suffered a PhD. Besides these and others, and relating directly to responsible well-being, three areas stand out for methodological innovation and application:

(a) *How to facilitate personal change and self-critical epistemological awareness*

Methodologies exist, and more are needed, to facilitate personal awareness, including epistemological awareness, meaning being self-critically aware of how we learn and mislearn and how we construct our realities. It is difficult to exaggerate the central importance of this subject. The degree to which economists have been found to disagree (see, e.g., Frey *et al.*, 1984, pp. 986–989) is, to a non-economist, alarming when they exercise so much power. It is also striking how dramatically their dominant views change, as illustrated in Hans Singer's (Singer, 1997) earlier editorial on "The Golden Age of the Keynesian Consensus — The Pendulum Swings Back." Part of the way to resolve differences between economists, and to enable them to be more in touch and less wrong, is through self-aware introspection; it is through reflection to understand how their views, like those of others, have been formed, and to be open to doubt and embracing error.

Similarly, reflection and awareness of interpersonal behavior and power relations is critical. On the behavior and perceptions of donor staff on mission and of host government staff who deal with them, depends the well-being of millions of poor people. Because of their power, such missions are vulnerable to being misled. Yet to my knowledge they have never been studied or documented beyond the level of personal anecdote.

The implication is programs for self-critical awareness, and attitude and behavior change, which in turn have implications for bureaucratic recruitment, procedures, incentives and cultures. The World Bank under the leadership of James Wolfensohn, is attempting to grasp this nettle. Senior staff are not only to receive exposure to management practices in institutions such as Harvard, but are also to have a week of immersion in a village or slum. This may seem a small innovation. It is, though, a major departure from past practice, and if it lasts and spreads, may prove a defining watershed of change.

(b) *How to enable those with power and wealth to think through and recognize the effects of their actions and non-actions*

The truism of "out of sight, out of mind" has awesome implications for those with power to make a difference. A little reflection on causal chains will suggest that a decision in a meeting in Washington to hold a poor African country to debt repayments will kill children; but those who make the decision will never see this, and never be called to account. Indeed, they deserve sympathy and understanding for the responsibility they shoulder, though those they harm deserve an altogether different level of compassion.

A mechanism is needed for such meetings, and for individual decisions and actions, for thinking through the implications. Lessons could be learned from therapeutic jurisprudence where attempts are made to identify the effects of proposed laws. With development decisions two advocates could be appointed to argue, one on behalf of women, children, the poor and the excluded, and one on behalf of future generations, in each case analyzing and presenting likely effects of alternatives. The causal and linkage diagramming which has proved effective in PRA could be part of the analysis.

Many of the key decisions that affect the poor are made by those who work for transnational corporations. Nothing said here should weaken the normal means of trying to influence them, through ethical investments and consumption, through organized pressure and through governments. But in addition, they too can be invited to define responsible well-being for themselves; they too are human and capable of good actions. At the launch of the *Human Development Report 1997*, the Nobel Peace Prize laureate Oscar Arias asked whether aerospace executives who sold arms to countries with bad human rights records would read the diaries of those in prison. Perhaps those executives should be invited and encouraged, again and again, to read those diaries, and to analyze, in a participatory way, the causal links between their arms sales and the repression and imprisonment of others. Perhaps all of us could and should do the same for our actions and inactions, using visual diagramming as a tool. Perhaps companies should be shamed who do not include advocates of the poor and of future generations in their deliberations. If some would show leadership in these directions, others might follow.

(c) *How to enable those with more wealth and power to welcome having less*

For well-being to be responsible, in a sustainable global eco-social system, those with more have to accept having less. This applies to both wealth and power. The biggest challenge for development as good change in the long term, is to find more ways in which those with more wealth and power will not just accept having less, but will welcome it as a means to well-being, to a better quality of life.

Much normal thinking about wealth and power is zero-sum. In this thinking, for those with less to gain, those with more must have less, and so lose. If all are assumed to be selfish, zero-sum conflict can appear

inevitable. But as Norman Uphoff (1992) has argued, there is scope for positive sum thinking and action. In conflict resolution there are often gains for all. Generosity brings its own non-material rewards. Empowering others can be deeply satisfying. The PRA experience of changing dominating behavior, sitting down, handing over the stick, and enabling others to conduct their own analysis and explore their own realities, has often been a source of excitement, fun, fulfillment and learning for all those concerned. The needs and opportunities here have barely begun to be recognised. The methodological challenge is to find more ways for reversing the normal view: for those with wealth and power to find and feel themselves better off with less; for having less in material terms to be experienced as a gain; and for disempowering oneself to empower others to be experienced as positive.

12. CONCLUSION

In a context of accelerating change, words and concepts will continue to succeed one another. The question is whether in the volatile and transient vocabulary of development, some stable continuity of core concepts, continuously redefined, can or should be sought. An analogy from chaos theory is a strange attractor, a pattern continuously reaffirmed in turbulence, like the Red Spot on Jupiter. The same words or concepts might then be used, in the same relations with each other, as in the web of responsible well-being, while being constantly reexamined and redefined both collectively and individually.

Responsible well-being, interlinked with capabilities and livelihood, and with foundations in principles of equity and sustainability, is simply one set of concepts inviting exploration. Whether it can serve a common purpose others can judge. Whether concepts such as these can go further and be drivers for good change is for trial. In the spirit of the one sentence manual adopted in PRA — "Use your own best judgement at all times" — each development professional can critically reflect, and draw up and use a personal list of ends and means. Perhaps what we should seek, then, is not consensus but pluralism, not a conclusion but a process, and not permanence but change in evolving concepts. For that we need an ethic of action, self-critical reflection, search and sharing.

In that spirit, let me conclude by inviting and encouraging others to reflect, to think out their own concepts and definitions, and to write and share their own editorials, improving on what has been presented here.

NOTES

1. For a classical and entertaining discussion of the need for the interaction of both poles of a range of development dichotomies, see Streeten (1983).

2. See e.g., *Forty Years in Development: The Search for Social Justice* (1997), *Development* **40**(1) for a useful overview

3. Or, to change the zoological metaphor

> Consultants with contracts to win
> use language they know to be in
> Chameleons, they
> fake a fashion display
> camouflaging for cash is no sin

4. The term "primary stakeholders," defined as "those expected to benefit from or be adversely affected by Bank-supported operations, particularly the poor and marginalized" had a checkered history. It was included in early drafts of The World Bank and Participation: Report to the Learning Group on Participatory Development, and applauded by many Bank-watchers. But it was dropped from the final version (World Bank, 1994), reportedly because some Bank Directors from countries of the South objected that it constituted interference with internal political affairs.

5. All Presidents of the World Bank so far have been men.

6. For introductory sources see Mascarenhas *et al.* (1991); and Chambers (1997). For recent sources and concerns see RRA Notes (1988–present) (now *PLA Notes*), Absalom *et al.* (1995), Mallik *et al.* (1996), and Kumar (1996).

7. For fuller presentations of the evidence about wealth and well-being as criteria see *RRA Notes*, No. 15 and Chambers (1997), pp. 176–179

8. In this list, fun is an apple among oranges. The other words are serious and moral. Fun looks frivolous. That fun is out of reach for so many — the desperately sick, suffering and poor, those who are abused, trapped, victims of violence, those fleeing in terror from war — may make it seem obscene in a development vocabulary. But it is as important as the others. With play and fun come creativity, laughter, the breakdown of barriers, the expression of realities, new insights, and the weakening of defences and

of structures of power. That it is out of reach for so many is an outrage.

9. In an earlier draft I used altruism. But altruism is an austere, unsmiling word with overtones of "do-gooding." I am grateful to Normal Uphoff (1992, p. 341) for pointing out that altruism and generosity can be used interchangeably. His chapter 12 is exciting and essential reading on this.

10. There is, however, a chapter by Marianne Gronemeyer on "Helping" which is close to altruism or generosity. But the chapter has a negative orientation. Gronemeyer analyzes the modernizing of the idea of help. Help, she argues, has evolved from spontaneous response to a cry of need to an instrument for the sophisticated exercise of power, in which neediness is determined not by the cry of the afflicted but by the diagnosis of the development establishment.

11. Parts of the text of this section are derived from Chambers (1997, Chapter 1), with minor modifications.

12. For further discussion of livelihoods, including sustainable livelihoods, see Chambers (1987), Conroy and Litvinoff (1988), Bernstein *et al.* (1992), Chambers and Conway (1992), and Davies (1996).

13. David Leonard's (Leonard, 1991) study *African Successes: Four Public Managers in Kenyan Rural Development* is a notable exception.

14. One study (Frank *et al.*, 1993) found alarmingly that economists were more likely than non-economists to act in a non-trusting, non-cooperative, self-interested manner. The median gift to big charities by economists among 1245 randomly selected college professors was substantially lower than for non-economists; and about 9% of economists gave nothing, as against a range of 1 to 4% for other disciplines. In a prisoners' dilemma game economics students defected 60% of the time compared with 39% for non-economists.

15. A sharper antithesis to *Pedagogy of the Oppressed* (Freire, 1970) would be "pedagogy for the oppressors," but this would unnecessarily alienate some, and not apply to others who might also benefit from a pedagogy for the non-oppressed.

REFERENCES

Absalom, E. *et al.* (1995) Participatory methods and approaches: Sharing our concerns and looking to the future. *PLA Notes* **22**, 5–10.

Attwood, H. (1996) South African participatory poverty assessment process: Were the voices of the poor heard? Paper for the PRA and Policy Workshop, IDS, Sussex, May 13–14.

Bernstein, H., Crow, B., and Johnson, H., eds. (1992) *Rural Livelihoods: Crises and Responses.* Oxford University Press in association with the Open University, Oxford, UK.

Blackburn, J. with Holland, J. eds. (forthcoming) *Who Changes? Institutionalising Participation in Development.* Intermediate Technology Publications, London.

Capra, F. (1996) *The Web of Being: A New Synthesis of Mind and Matter.* Harper Collins, London.

Chambers, R. (1987) Sustainable livelihoods, environment and development: Putting poor people first. *Discussion Paper* 240, IDS, University of Sussex, Brighton, UK.

Chambers, R. (1997) *Whose Reality Counts? Putting the First Last.* Intermediate Technology Publications, London.

Chambers, R. and Conway, G. (1992) Sustainable rural livelihoods: practical concepts for the 21st century. *IDS Discussion Paper* 296, IDS, University of Sussex, Brighton, UK.

Chambers, R. and Blackburn J. (1996) *The Power of Participation: PRA and Policy.* Briefing Paper, IDS, University of Sussex, Brighton, UK.

Checkland, P. (1981) *Systems Thinking, Systems Practice.* John Wiley and Sons, Chichester, UK.

Conroy, C. and Litvinoff, M. eds. (1988) *The Greening of Aid: Sustainable Livelihoods in Practice.* Earthscan Publications, London.

Davies, S. (1996) *Adaptable Livelihoods: Coping with Food Insecurity in the Malian Sahel.* Macmillan, London.

Dogbe, T. (forthcoming) The one who rides the donkey does not know the ground is hot: CEDEP's involvement in the Ghana PPA. In *Whose Voice? Participatory Research and Policy Change*, ed. J. Holland with J. Blackburn. Intermediate Technology Publications, London.

Forsyth, R. S. (1991) Towards a grounded morality. *Changes* 9(4), 264–278.

Frank, R., Gilovich, T. and Regan, D. (1993) Does studying economics inhibit cooperation? *Journal of Economic Perspectives*, Spring.

Freire, P. (1970) *Pedagogy of the Oppressed.* The Seabury Press, New York.

Freudenberger, K. S. (forthcoming) The use of RRA to inform policy: Tenure issues in Madagascar and Guinea. In *Whose Voice? Participatory Research and Policy Change*, ed. J. Holland with J. Blackburn. Intermediate Technology Publications, London.

Frey, B., Pommerehne, W. W., Schneider, F. and Gilbert, G. (1984) Consensus and dissension among economists: An empircal enquiry. *American Economic Review* 74(5), 986–994.

Gleick, J. (1988) *Chaos: Making a New Science.* Sphere Books, London.

Grandin, B. (1988) *Wealth Ranking in Smallholder Communities: A Field Manual.* Intermediate Technology Publications, London.

Gujja, B., Pimbert, M. and Shah, M. (forthcoming) Village Voices Challenging Wetland Management Policies: PRA Experiences from Pakistan and India. In *Whose Voice? Participatory Research and Policy Change*, ed. J. Holland with J. Blackburn. Intermediate Technology Publications, London.

Handy, C. (1990) *The Age of Unreason.* Arrow Books, London.

Havel, V. (1992) Condensation of a speech to the Davos Development Conference. Report in *New York Times*, March 1.

Holland, J. with Blackburn, J. eds. (forthcoming) *Whose Voice? Participatory Research and Policy Change.* Intermediate Technology Publications, London.

Kane, E., Bruce, L., Sey, H. and O'Reilly de Brun, M. (1996) Girls' education in the Gambia. Paper for the PRA and Policy Workshop March 13–14, IDS, University of Sussex, Brighton, UK.

Kumar, S., ed. (1996) *ABC of PRA: Attitude Behaviour Change.* South-South Workshop on PRA: Attitudes and Behaviour, July 1–10, organized by ActionAid India and SPEECH, ActionAid, Bangalore.

Leonard, D. K. (1991) *African Successes: Four Public Managers in Kenyan Rural Development.* University of California Press, Berkeley.

Levy, H., ed. (1996) *The Cry 'Respect': Urban Violence and Poverty in Jamaica.* Centre for Population, Community and Social Change, University of the West Indies, Mona, Kingston, Jamaica.

Mallik, A. H. *et al.* (1996) Sharing our experiences: An appeal to donors and governments. *PLA Notes* 27(74–76), October.

Mascarenhas, J., *et al.* (1991) Proceedings of the February 1991 Bangalore PRA Workshop. *RRA Notes*, 13 (August).

May, J. (1996), Kicking down doors and lighting fires: Participating in policy — The SA-PPA experience. Paper for the PRA and Policy Workshop, May 13–14, IDS Sussex, Brighton, UK.

Moser, C., and Holland, J. (1995) *A Participatory Study of Urban Poverty and Violence in Jamaica: Analysis of Research Results.* Urban Development Division, World Bank, Washington, DC, December.

Murphy, C. (1995) *Implications of Poverty for Black Rural Women in Kwazulu/Natal.* Report for the South African Participatory Poverty Assessment, Institute of Natural Resources, Scottsville, South Africa.

Norton, A. (forthcoming) Some reflections on the PPA processes and lessons learned. In *Whose Voice? Participatory Research and Policy Change*, ed. J. Holland with J. Blackburn. Intermediate Technology Publications, London.

Norton, A. and Owen, D. (1996) The Zambia Participatory Poverty Assessment: Notes on the process and lessons learned. Paper for the PRA and Policy Workshop, IDS Sussex, Brighton, UK.

Norton, A. and Stephens, T. (1995) *Participation in Poverty Assessments.* Environment Department Papers, Participation Series, Social Policy and Resettlement Division, The World Bank, Washington, DC, June.

Norton, A., Owen, D., and Milimo, J. (1994) *Zambia Participatory Poverty Assessment: Volume 5: Participatory Poverty Assessment.* Report 12985-ZA, Southern Africa Department, The World Bank, Washington, DC, November 30.

Norton, A., Kroboe, D., Bortei-Dorku, E., and Dogbe, D. K. T. (1995) *Ghana Participatory Poverty Assessment: Consolidated Report on Poverty Assessment in Ghana Using Qualitative and Participatory Research Methods: Draft Report.* AFTHR, The World Bank, Washington, DC.

Peters, T. (1989) *Thriving on Chaos: Handbook for a Management Revolution.* Pan Books, London.

RRA Notes/PLA Notes (1988–present), published by the International Insitute for Environment and Development, London.

Resnick, M. (1994) *Turtles, Termites and Traffic Jams: Explorations in Massively Parallel Microworlds.* MIT Press, Cambridge, MA.

Robb, C. (forthcoming) World Bank PPA methodology, and the World Bank PPA impact analysis, Annexes 1 and 2. In *Whose Voice? Participatory Research and Policy Change,* ed. J. Holland with J. Blackburn. Intermediate Technology Publications, London.

Sen, A. (1981) *Poverty and Famines: An Essay on Entitlement and Deprivation.* Clarendon Press, Oxford.

Sen, A. (1985) *Commodities and Capabilities.* North Holland, Amsterdam.

Sachs, W., ed. (1992) *The Development Dictionary: A Guide to Knowledge as Power.* Zed Books, London.

Senge, P. (1990) *The Fifth Discipline: The Art and Practice of the Learning Organization.* Doubleday, New York.

Shah, M. K. and Bourarach, K. (1995) *Participatory Assessment of Women's Problems and Concerns in Morocco,* Report submitted to the World Bank, Washington, DC.

Singer, H. (1997) Editorial: The golden age of the Keynesian consensus — the pendulum swings back. *World Development* 25(3), 293–295.

Streeten, P. (1983) Development dichotomies. *World Development* 11(10), 875–889.

Taylor, L. (1997) Editorial: The revival of the liberal creed — The IMF and the World Bank in a globalized economy. *World Development* 25(2), 145–152.

Teixeira, L. and Chambers, F. (1995) *Child Support in Small Towns in the Eastern Cape.* Black Sash Advice Office, Port Elizabeth.

UNDP (1997) *Human Development Report.* Oxford University Press, New York.

UNDP (1996) *UNDP's 1996 Report on Human Development in Bangladesh: A Pro-Poor Agenda, Volume 3: Poor People's Perspectives.* UNDP, Dhaka, Bangladesh.

Uphoff, N. (1992) *Learning from Gal Oya: Possibilities for Participatory Development and Post-Newtonian Social Science.* Cornell University Press, Ithaca.

Waldrop, M. M. (1994) *Complexity: the Emerging Science at the Edge of Order and Chaos.* Penguin Books, London.

World Bank (1994) *The World Bank and Participation.* Operations Policy Department, World Bank. Washington, DC, September.

World Bank (1997) *World Development Report 1997: The State in a Changing World.* Oxford University Press, New York.

Name Index